FINANCE FOR EXECUTIVES
Managing for Value Creation

FINANCE FOR EXECUTIVES
Managing for Value Creation

GABRIEL HAWAWINI
INSEAD
CLAUDE VIALLET
INSEAD

 South-Western College Publishing
an International Thomson Publishing company I(T)P®

Cincinnati • Albany • Boston • Detroit • Johannesburg • London • Madrid • Melbourne • Mexico City
New York • Pacific Grove • San Francisco • Scottsdale • Singapore • Tokyo • Toronto

Publisher/Team Director: Jack W. Calhoun
Acquisitions Editor: Michael B. Mercier
Developmental Editor: Dennis Hanseman
Production Editor: Sharon L. Smith
Marketing Manager: Lisa L. Lysne
Production House: Carlisle Publishers Services
Cover Design: Ann Small
Cover Photo: © Artville
Internal Design: Cynthia Crampton

Copyright © 1999
by South-Western College Publishing
Cincinnati, Ohio

Hawawini, Gabriel.
    Finance for executives: managing for value creation/Gabriel
Hawawini, Claude Viallet.
        p.   cm.
    Includes bibliographical references and index.
    ISBN 0-538-85395-6
    1. Corporations—Finance.   2. Business enterprises—Finance.
3. Managerial accounting.   I. Viallet, Claude.   II. Title.
HG4011.H374   1998
658.15—dc21   98-24204
                                                 CIP

    4 5 6 7 8 D1 4 3 2 1 0 9

Printed in the United States of America

I(T)P®
International Thomson Publishing
South-Western College Publishing is an ITP Company.
The ITP trademark is used under license.

To our spouses and children, with love and gratitude,

GH
CV

TABLE OF CONTENTS

PART IV

MAKING VALUE-CREATING FINANCING DECISIONS

PART V

MAKING VALUE-CREATING BUSINESS DECISIONS

PREFACE

Finance is an essential and exciting area of management that many executives want to discover or explore in more depth. Most finance textbooks, however, are either too advanced or too simplistic for many non-financial managers. Our challenge was to write an introductory text that is specifically addressed to executives, and that is both practical and rigorous.

The target audience is executives directly and indirectly involved with financial matters and financial management—that is, just about every executive. The text will also work well in executives development programs, including executive MBA programs. Over the past four years, most of the material in this book has been used by over 2,000 managers from around the world. Business students, both undergraduates and graduates, have found it either a good substitute for, or a helpful complement to, their main textbook.

Finance for Executives has a number of important features:

- **It is based on the principle that firms should be managed to increase the wealth of their shareholders**

Managers must make decisions that are expected to increase the wealth of shareholders. This fundamental principle underlies our approach to management. The book was designed to improve your ability to make decisions that create shareholder value, including decisions to restructure existing operations, launch a new product, buy a new asset, acquire another company, and finance the firm's investments.

- **It fills the gap between introductory accounting and finance manuals for non-financial managers and advanced texts in corporate finance**

Finance for Executives is based on modern finance principles. It emphasizes rigorous analysis but avoids complicated formulas that have no direct application to decision making. Whenever a formula is used in the text, we explain the intuition behind it and provide detailed applications. The mathematical derivation of the formulas is given in the appendices that follow the chapter where they first appear. Recognizing that executives often approach financial problems from a financial accounting perspective, we begin with a solid review of the financial accounting system.

We then show how this framework can be extended and used to make sound financial decisions that enhance the firm's value.

- **Most chapters are self-contained**

Most chapters can be read without prior reading of the others. Where knowledge of a previous chapter would enhance comprehension of a specific section, we direct the reader back to that previously developed material. Further advice on this score is provided below in the section entitled "How to Read This Book."

- **It can be read in its entirety or used as a reference tool**

The book can be used as a quick reference whenever there is a need to brush up on a specific topic or close a gap in your financial management knowledge. A comprehensive glossary and the index at the end of the book will help you determine which chapters deal with the desired issue or topic. Most financial terms are explained when first introduced in the text; they appear in **boldface** type and are defined in the glossary.

- **Data from the same companies are used throughout the book to illustrate diagnostic techniques and valuation methods**

We focus on the same set of firms to illustrate most of the topics covered in this book. This approach provides a common thread that reinforces understanding.

- **Each chapter is followed by review problems**

The review problems that appear at the end of each chapter allow you to test your knowledge of the subject. *Most of the questions require use of a financial calculator.* Detailed, step-by-step solutions can be found at the end of the book.

THE STRUCTURE OF THE TEXT

Although the book consists of self-contained chapters, those chapters do follow a logical sequence built around the idea of value creation. The overall structure of the book is summarized in the following diagram, which shows the *value-based business model.* Managers must raise cash (the right-hand side) in order to finance investments (the left-hand side) that are expected to increase the firm's value and augment the wealth of shareholders.

Part I begins with a chapter that surveys the principles and tools executives need to know in order to manage for value creation. Chapter 2 then explains and illustrates how balance sheets and income statements are constructed and interpreted.

Part II reviews the techniques executives use to assess a firm's financial health, evaluate and plan its future development, and make decisions that enhance its chances of survival and success. The chapters in this part examine in detail a number of financial diagnostics and managerial tools

WHAT'S IN THIS BOOK?

PART I: INTRODUCTION

Chapter 1:
What does managing for value creation mean?

Chapter 2:
How are balance sheets and income statements constructed?

PART II: FINANCIAL DIAGNOSIS AND MANAGEMENT

Chapters 3 to 5:
How do financial structure and operational efficiency affect a firm's liquidity (Chapter 3), its ability to generate cash (Chapter 4) and its profitability, risk, and capacity to grow (Chapter 5)

PART IV: FINANCING DECISIONS

Chapter 9:
How do firms raise the funds needed to finance their investments?

Chapter 10:
What is the cost of these funds?

Chapter 11:
What is the best mix of shareholders' funds and borrowed funds?

PART III: INVESTMENT DECISIONS

Chapter 6 to 8:
How should firms evaluate investment proposals and select value-creating projects?

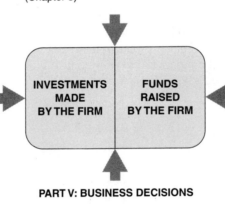

INVESTMENTS MADE BY THE FIRM | FUNDS RAISED BY THE FIRM

PART V: BUSINESS DECISIONS

Chapter 12:
How is a business valued?

Chapter 13:
How do international activities affect business decisions?

Chapter 14:
Is the firm using its resources to create shareholder value?

that were introduced in Chapter 1. Chapter 3 shows how to evaluate a firm's liquidity position and operational efficiency. Chapter 4 shows how to assess the firm's ability to generate and control its cash flow. Chapter 5 identifies the factors that drive a firm's profitability, analyzes the extent of its exposure to business and financial risks, and evaluates its capacity to finance its activities and achieve sustainable growth.

Part III demonstrates how managers should make investment decisions that maximize the firm's value. Chapter 6 examines the net present value (NPV) rule in detail and shows how to apply this rule to make value-creating investment decisions. Chapter 7 reviews a number of alternative approaches to the NPV rule, including the internal rate of return (IRR) and the payback period rules, and compares them to the NPV rule. Chapter 8 shows how to identify and estimate the cash flows generated by an investment proposal and how to assess the proposal's capacity to create value.

Part IV explains how managers should make financing decisions that maximize value. Chapter 9 looks at the function of financial markets as a source of cash and examines the role markets play in the process of value creation. Chapter 10 shows how to estimate the cost of capital for a project and for the entire firm. Chapter 11 explains how a firm can make value-creating financing decisions by designing a capital structure (the mix of owners' funds and borrowed funds) that maximizes its market value and minimizes its cost of capital.

Part V concludes with three chapters on making value-creating business decisions. Chapter 12 reviews various models and techniques used to value firms, particularly in the context of an acquisition. Chapter 13 looks at financial management and value creation in an international environment where currency and country risks must be taken into account. Chapter 14 summarizes the analytical framework underlying the process of value creation and examines some of the related empirical evidence.

HOW TO READ THIS BOOK

Depending on your background and your needs, you may want to use this book in different ways. Here are a few guidelines.

- If you are unfamiliar with financial management and financial accounting, you may want to begin by reading Chapter 1. It provides an overview of these subjects and will help you understand the fundamental objective of modern corporate finance and the logical relationships among the various issues and topics that make up that field. Although reading the first chapter will facilitate the understanding of those that follow it, *it is not necessary to read it in order to comprehend the rest of the book—the chapters are self-contained.*
- If you are not familiar with financial statements, it would be helpful, but not essential, to read Chapter 2 before you go through Part II. Chapter 2 explains balance sheets and income statements.

- If you are not familiar with the techniques of discounted cash flows, you should read Chapter 6 before going through Part III. Chapter 6 reviews the foundations of discounted cash flow techniques.
- If you are unfamiliar with the functioning of financial markets, your should read Chapter 9 before going through Part IV. Chapter 9 provides an overview of the structure, organization, and role of financial markets.
- Lastly, if you have a basic knowledge of accounting and finance, you can go directly to the chapter dealing with the issue you wish to explore. Since the chapters are self-contained, you will not have to review the preceding chapters to fully understand your chosen chapter.

ABOUT THE AUTHORS

Gabriel Hawawini (Ph.D., New York University) is Henry Grunfeld Chaired Professor of Investment Banking at INSEAD—the European Institute of Business Administration. He has also taught finance at New York University, Columbia University, and the Wharton School of the University of Pennsylvania where he won the Helen Kardon Moss Anvil Award for Excellence in Teaching.

Professor Hawawini is the author of ten books and over 60 research papers. Besides serving as Vice President of the French Finance Association, he has organized, directed, and taught in management development programs at INSEAD and around the world.

Claude Viallet (Ph.D., Northwestern University) is Professor of Finance at INSEAD and Visiting Professor of Finance at Northwestern University. Before joining INSEAD, he worked as a project manager at a major oil company and as chief financial officer of a service company in Paris.

Professor Viallet has been President of the European Finance Association and has published widely in leading academic and professional journals. He too has organized, directed, and taught in management development programs in Europe, the United States, Asia, and Latin America.

ACKNOWLEDGEMENTS

A number of colleagues and friends have been most generous with the time they spent reading the manuscript for this book and providing specific comments. We thank John Boquist (Indiana University), Roger Mesznik (Baruch College of the City University of New York), Pierre Michel (University of Liège), Steve Mott, Ian Reed, Aris Stouraitis (Imperial College, London), Lucie Teplá (INSEAD), Jean B. Viallet, and especially Barbara Sheridan, our copyeditor, who did a terrific job converting our final manuscript into a polished product. We are also indebted to Alex Nikolaev of Saint Louis University, who checked the solutions to all of the end-of-chapter problems.

Other colleagues and friends provided detailed comments on selected chapters. They include Paolo Fulghieri, Herwig Langohr, Lee Remmers, David Young, Charlotte Butler, and David Champion, all at INSEAD, as well as Soren Bjerre-Nielsen (Danisco A/S), Dwight Grant (University of New Mexico), Laurent Jacque (Tufts University), Art Raviv (Northwestern University), Maria Vassalou (Columbia University), and Ingo Walter (New York University). We have also received many useful comments from participants in public and company-specific seminars we run at INSEAD and on companies' premises. Remaining errors are, of course, ours.

Gabriel Hawawini
Claude Viallet
Fontainebleau
May 1998

1 FINANCIAL MANAGEMENT AND VALUE CREATION: AN OVERVIEW

An executive cannot be an effective manager without a clear understanding of the principles and practices of modern finance. The good news is that these principles and practices can be communicated simply without sacrificing thoroughness or rigor. Indeed, you will discover that most of the concepts and methods underlying modern corporate finance are based on business common sense. But, translating business common sense into an effective management system can be a real challenge. It requires, in addition to a solid understanding of fundamental principles, the determination and the discipline to manage a business according to the precepts of modern finance. Consider, for example, one of financial management's most useful guiding principles:

Managers should manage their firm's resources with the objective of increasing the firm's market value.

This may seem to be an obvious statement. But, you probably know a number of companies that are *not* managed to their full potential value. You may even know well-intentioned managers who are value destroyers. Their misguided actions, or lack of actions, actually reduce the value of their firm.

How do you manage for value creation? This book should help you find the answer. Our main objective is to present and explain the methods and tools that will help you determine whether the firm's current investments are creating value and, if they are not, what remedial actions should be taken to improve operations. We also show you how to determine whether a business proposal—such as the decision to buy a piece of equipment, launch a new product, acquire another firm, or restructure existing operations—has the potential to raise the firm's value. Finally, we show you that managing with the goal of raising the firm's value provides the basis for an integrated financial management system that not only helps you evaluate actual business performance and make sound business decisions but also helps you design effective management compensation packages—compensation packages that align the interests of the firm's managers with those of the firm's owners.

This introductory chapter reviews some of the most challenging issues and questions raised by modern corporate finance and gives a general but comprehensive overview. Although the topics of this chapter are examined in detail in later chapters, many of the important terms and concepts are introduced and defined here. After reading this chapter, you should understand:

- The meaning of managing a business for value creation.
- How to measure the value that may be created by a business proposal, such as an investment project, a change in the firm's financial structure, a business acquisition, or the decision to invest in a foreign country.
- The significance of the firm's cost of capital and how it is measured.
- The function of financial markets as a source of corporate funds and the role they play in the value-creation process.
- A firm's business cycle and how it determines the firm's capacity to grow.
- The basic structure and the logic behind a firm's balance sheet and income statement and how data from both statements can be combined to evaluate the firm's profitability and its ability to generate cash.
- Risk, how to measure it and how it affects the firm's cost of capital.
- The terms "market value added" and "economic value added" and how they relate to the goal of managing for value creation.

THE KEY QUESTION: WILL YOUR DECISION CREATE VALUE?

Suppose you have identified a need in the marketplace for a new product. You believe you can manufacture that product cheaply and rapidly. You are even confident you can sell it for a tidy profit. Should you go ahead? You should not make this decision until after you check the project's long-term financial viability. How will your firm finance the project? Where will the money come from? Will the project be sufficiently profitable to cover the cost of the funds required to support it? More to the point, will the firm be more valuable *with* the project or *without* it? We believe that you should answer these questions before making a final decision.

In most cases, the proposed venture will not be financed with your money. It will be financed by the firm's owners, its **shareholders** (you may be one of them), and by those who lend money to the firm, the **debtholders**. Cash contributed by shareholders is called **equity capital**; cash contributed by lenders is **debt capital**. As with any other resource, capital is not free. It has a cost. Your venture will attract outside capital only if it is sufficiently profitable to cover the cost of that capital. But this will probably not be enough to convince the firm's owners to let you go ahead with the project. The firm's owners want to *increase* the firm's value, and in order to do this, a project's expected return must *exceed* its financing cost. In other words, before deciding to go ahead with a business proposal, you should ask yourself the Key Question:

Will the proposal raise the firm's market value?

If, in light of existing information and proper analysis, you can confidently answer yes, then go ahead. Otherwise, you should abandon the project.

The Key Question applies not only to a business proposal but also to current operations. If some existing investments are destroying rather than creating value, you should take immediate corrective actions. If these actions fail to improve performance, you should seriously consider selling those investments.

THE IMPORTANCE OF MANAGING FOR VALUE CREATION

We realize, of course, that the Key Question is much easier asked than answered. The next section describes how to apply the **fundamental finance principle** to help you answer the question. Before introducing that principle, we want to explain why the paramount objective of management should be the creation of value for the firm's owners. This objective makes business common sense if you think about a firm that fails to create value for its owners: it will be unable to attract the equity capital it needs to fund its activities. And without equity capital, no firm can survive.

You may rightly ask whether we are forgetting the contributions of employees, customers, and suppliers. No firm can succeed without them. Great companies do not only have satisfied shareholders; they also have loyal customers, motivated employees, and reliable suppliers. The point, of course, is not to neglect customers, squeeze suppliers, or ignore the interest of employees for the benefit of owners: More value for shareholders does not mean less value for employees, customers, or suppliers. On the contrary, firms managed with a focus on creating value for their shareholders are among those that have built durable and valuable relationships with their customers, employees, and suppliers. They know that dealing successfully with employees, customers, and suppliers is an important element in achieving their ultimate objective of creating value for their shareholders.

Indeed, there is evidence that firms that take care of their customers and employees also deliver value to their shareholders. Consider the results of a survey that asked more than 10,000 executives, outside directors, and financial analysts to rate the ten largest U.S. companies in their industry according to the following eight criteria: (1) quality of management; (2) quality of products or services; (3) ability to attract, develop, and keep talented people; (4) company's value as a long-term investment; (5) use of corporate assets; (6) financial soundness; (7) capacity to innovate; and (8) community and environmental responsibilities.[1] The ten companies with the highest scores produced an average compound annual

---

[1]*Fortune* (March 4, 1996).

return of 22 percent for their shareholders during the period 1985 to 1995 while the Standard & Poor's market index (an average of 500 companies) produced a return of 15 percent. What was the stock market performance of the ten companies with the lowest scores? They were value destroyers. They delivered a *negative* average compound annual return of 3 percent to their shareholders .

An analysis based on only the three criteria that relate to the way companies treat their customers (the second criterion), their employees (the third criterion), and their community (the last criterion) showed similar results. The companies with the highest scores in these three areas achieved an average compound annual return of 19 percent while those with the lowest scores produced a *negative* annual return of 5 percent.

The above results clearly indicate that the ability of firms to create value for their shareholders is related to the way they treat their customers, employees, and community. But you should not conclude that the guaranteed recipe for value creation consists in delighting customers, establishing durable relations with suppliers, and motivating employees. There are firms that deal successfully with their customers, employees, and suppliers but that are unable to translate this goodwill into a higher firm value. What should the firm's managers do in this case? They must revise the firm's current business strategy. Shareholders will eventually question the relevance of a strategy that does not allow the firm to produce a satisfactory return on the equity capital they have invested in it. Dissatisfied shareholders, particularly those holding a significant portion of the firm's equity capital, may try to force the firm's management to change course or may try to oust the existing management team. Or, they may simply withdraw their support by selling their holdings to others who might force changes.

Whether shareholders will be successful in getting management to change its strategy, or even be replaced, depends on a number of factors, including the institutional and legal frameworks that govern the relationship between management and shareholders and the structure and organization of the country's equity markets in which the firm's shares are listed and traded. We simply suggest that no firm can afford to have delighted customers, motivated employees, and devoted suppliers for too long if it does not also have satisfied shareholders.

When asked in whose interest corporations are run, Mr. Jack Welch, the CEO of General Electric, replied: "A proper balance between shareholders, employees, and communities is what we all try to achieve. But it is a tough balancing act because, in the end, if you don't satisfy shareholders, you don't have the flexibility to do the things you have to do to take care of employees or communities. In our society, whether we like it or not, we have to satisfy shareholders."[2] And how do you satisfy shareholders? Mr. Roberto Goizueta, the former Chairman and CEO of the Coca-Cola Company and an ardent believer in the maximization of shareholders' wealth, once said: "Management doesn't get paid to make shareholders comfortable. We get paid to make the shareholders rich."[3]

---

[2]*Fortune* (May 29, 1995): 75.

[3]A. Shapiro, *Modern Corporate Finance* (The Macmillan Publishing Company, 1990), 333.

THE SATURN STORY

In the mid-eighties, General Motors, the world's largest vehicle manufacturer, faced strong competition from foreign producers of small, efficient, reliable, and inexpensive cars. In response to this challenge, GM set up a separate company to build an entirely new car, the Saturn. The car was designed, produced, and sold according to the best practices available at the time. Workers were highly motivated, car dealers could not keep up with demand, and customers were extremely satisfied with their cars. According to these criteria, Saturn was an undeniable success story.

However, at the time of this writing, the project had not delivered the rise in value of GM's shares that management had hoped would occur. Why? The Saturn project has not created value because most observers think that it is unlikely ever to become profitable. From the project's inception until the mid-nineties, GM invested more than $6 billion to develop, manufacture, and launch the Saturn. According to knowledgeable consultants, this amount is so large that, in order for GM to earn an acceptable return for its shareholders, "it would have to operate existing facilities at full capacity forever, earn more than double standard profit margins, and keep 40 percent of the dealers' sticker price as net cash flow."[4] How long should a firm fund a project that delights its customers, pleases its distributors, and satisfies its employees but fails to deliver value to its shareholders?

THE FUNDAMENTAL FINANCE PRINCIPLE

Recall the Key Question you should ask before making a business decision: Will the decision create value for the firm's owners? The question can be answered with the help of the fundamental finance principle:

> **A business proposal—such as a new investment, the acquisition of another company, or a restructuring plan—will raise the firm's value only if the present value of the future stream of net cash benefits the proposal is expected to generate exceeds the initial cash outlay required to carry out the proposal.**

The **present value** of the future stream of expected net cash benefits is the amount of dollars that makes the firm's owners *indifferent* between receiving that sum today or getting the expected future cash-flow stream. For example, if the firm's owners are indifferent between receiving a cash dividend of $100,000 today or getting an expected cash dividend of $114,000 next year, then $100,000 is the present value of $114,000 expected next year.

---

[4]J.M. McTaggart, P.W. Kontes, and M.C. Mankins, *The Value Imperative* (The Free Press, 1994), 16.

MEASURING VALUE CREATION WITH NET PRESENT VALUE

The difference between a proposal's present value and the initial cash outlay required to implement the proposal is the proposal's **net present value** or **NPV**:

Net present value = −Initial cash outlay + Present value of future net cash benefits

We can use the net present value concept to restate the fundamental finance principle more succinctly:

> **A business proposal creates value if its net present value is positive and destroys value if its net present value is negative.**

To follow up on our numerical example, suppose the proposal requires the firm to invest $95,000 today in order to generate the expected $114,000 in dividends next year. The proposal's net present value is the difference between $100,000 (the present value of the expected $114,000) and the $95,000 initial cash outlay required to obtain the expected $114,000 in one year:

$$\text{Net present value of proposal} = -\$95,000 + \text{Present value of } \$114,000$$
$$= -\$95,000 + \$100,000$$
$$= \$5,000$$

Because the net present value is positive, we would say that the proposal, if adopted, could create $5,000 of value.

The proposal's net present value is its value *today,* and the $5,000 goes to the investors who *own* the project, in other words to the shareholders of the firm that undertakes the project. This means that the shareholders should be able to sell their equity stake in the company, *including* the project, for $5,000 more than what they could sell it for if the project did not exist, even though the project is only a proposal. It has not yet been undertaken. The firm's ability to identify the project and the market expectation that the firm will carry out the project successfully create *today's* increase in the firm's value and in the wealth of its shareholders.

Suppose the firm has 100,000 shares of common stock. If these shares are listed and traded on a stock exchange, their price should rise by 5 cents ($5,000 of value created divided by 100,000 shares) on the day the project is announced, assuming the announcement is unanticipated and the market agrees with the firm's analysis of the project's profitability. We return to this point later in the chapter when we examine the role played by financial markets in the process of value creation.

ONLY CASH MATTERS

The fundamental finance principle requires that the initial investment needed to undertake a proposal, as well as the stream of net future benefits it is expected to generate, be measured in cash. They should not be measured with the accounting numbers associated with the proposal, such as the project's expected revenues, expenses, and profits that will be recorded in the firm's financial statements, because these accounting numbers are usually different from their cash equivalents.

Exhibit 1.1 illustrates why only cash figures are used to measure a proposal's net present value. The investors who are financing the proposal—the firm's shareholders and debtholders—have invested *cash* in the firm and are thus only interested in *cash* returns. They are not interested in accounting measures of costs and benefits.

Chapter 4 discusses cash flows and how they should be measured; Chapter 8 shows how to estimate the cash flows that are relevant to an investment decision.

DISCOUNT RATES

The proposal in our example is expected to generate $114,000 in one year. The present value of that future cash flow is $100,000. Recall that this present value is the amount of cash that makes the firm's owners indifferent between receiving this cash today or receiving the expected $114,000 in one year. This is the same as saying that the firm's owners expect to receive a return of 14 percent from the project because $100,000 invested at 14 percent will yield $114,000 in one year. The 14 percent is called the **discount rate**: it is the rate at which the future cash flow must be *discounted* in order to find its present value.

If we want to estimate the net present value of a proposal, we must first discount its future cash-flow stream to find its present value and then deduct from that present value the initial cash outlay required to carry out the proposal. The case of our numerical example is shown in Exhibit 1.2. Chapter 6 examines the discounting mechanism in detail and explains how to calculate present values and how to estimate a project's net present value when the project has an expected cash-flow stream that is longer than one year.

In our example, we know the discount rate because we already know the expected future cash flow and its present value. However, this is not usually the case. In general, a proposal's future cash flow must be estimated and the discount rate must be determined. But, what discount rate should be used? *A proposal's appropriate discount rate is the cost of financing the proposal.*

EXHIBIT 1.1   Only Cash Matters to Investors.

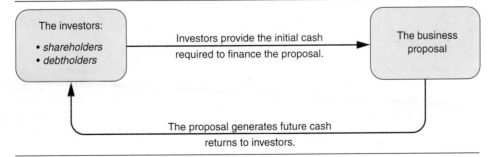

EXHIBIT 1.2   Using the Discount Rate to Estimate the NPV.

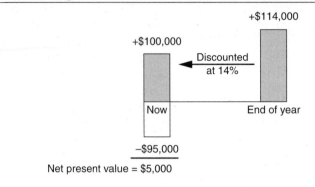

Net present value = $5,000

In the example, the return expected from the project must be at least 14 percent in order to induce shareholders to invest in the project. In other words, because 14 percent is the rate of return required by shareholders to fund the project, it is also the project's cost of equity capital. It represents the cost of using shareholders' cash to finance the investment proposal.

A PROPOSAL'S COST OF CAPITAL

Firms typically finance their investment proposals with a combination of equity capital and debt capital, and both shareholders and debtholders require a return from their contribution to the financing of the proposal. When a project is funded with both equity and debt capital, the cost of capital is no longer equal to just the cost of equity. It is the weighted average of the project's cost of equity and its aftertax cost of debt, where the weights are the proportions of equity and debt financing in the total capital employed to fund the project.

To illustrate, suppose a project will be financed 50 percent with equity and 50 percent with debt. Also, assume the project has an estimated cost of equity of 16 percent and an aftertax cost of debt of 6 percent. Then, the project's **weighted average cost of capital** or **WACC** is equal to 11 percent:

$$\text{Project cost of capital (WACC)} = [6\% \times 50\%] + [16\% \times 50\%]$$
$$= 3\% + 8\%$$
$$= 11\%$$

In other words, the contribution of debt financing to the project's cost of capital is 3 percent (50 percent of 6 percent) and that of equity financing is 8 percent (50 percent of 16 percent), as shown in Exhibit 1.3.

The cost of debt is taken *after tax* because firms can deduct from their pretax profits the interest they pay on the money they borrow (interest payments are a

EXHIBIT 1.3   The Cost of Financing a Business Proposal Is Its Weighted Average Cost of Capital.

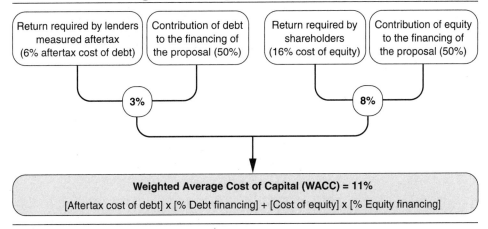

tax-deductible expense). Suppose the firm can borrow at 10 percent to finance 50 percent of the project. With a 40 percent corporate tax rate, the *aftertax* cost of debt is only 6 percent (10 percent minus 40 percent of 10 percent) because every dollar of interest expense will reduce the firm's *pretax* profits by one dollar and save the firm the 40 cents of taxes *it would have paid* if interest expenses were not tax-deductible.

If the proportions of equity and debt financing are modified, the weighted average cost of capital will be affected, not only because the financing proportions have changed but also because the cost of debt and the cost of equity also change when the financing proportions are altered. Chapter 10 shows how to estimate a project's cost of debt, its cost of equity, and its weighted average cost of capital. Chapter 11 demonstrates how the weighted average cost of capital is affected when the financing proportions change.

APPLYING THE FUNDAMENTAL FINANCE PRINCIPLE

The fundamental finance principle has widespread applications in major areas of corporate decision making. In this book, we address the capital budgeting decision (whether an investment project should be accepted or rejected); the capital structure decision (how much of the firm's assets should be financed with debt and how much with equity); the business acquisition decision (how much should be paid to acquire another company); and the foreign investment decision (how to account for multiple-currency cash flows and for the extra risk of operating in a foreign country). The capital budgeting decision is covered in Chapters 6 through 8, the capital structure decision in Chapter 11, the acquisition decision in Chapter 12, and the management of cross-border operations in Chapter 13. This section provides an overview of these corporate decisions.

THE CAPITAL BUDGETING DECISION

The **capital budgeting decision,** also called the **capital expenditure decision,** concerns the acquisition of fixed assets, such as plants and equipment. This is a major corporate decision because it typically affects the firm's business performance for a long period of time. The decision criteria used in capital budgeting, such as the **net present value rule** and the **internal rate of return rule,** are direct applications of the fundamental finance principle.

The net present value (NPV) rule

According to the net present value rule, an investment project with a positive NPV should be undertaken and one with a negative NPV should be rejected:

> **A project should be undertaken if its net present value is positive and should be rejected if its net present value is negative.**

The NPV rule is a direct application of the fundamental finance principle because it states that a project should be undertaken only if it creates value. If the project has a positive NPV, it creates value because the present value of its expected future cash benefits is *greater* than the initial cash outlay required to launch the project. If the proposal has a negative NPV, it destroys value because the present value of its expected future cash benefits is *less* than the initial cash outlay required to launch the project. If a business proposal has a zero NPV, the firm breaks even in the sense that the proposal neither creates nor destroys value: the present value of its expected future cash benefits is equal to the initial cash outlay required to undertake the project.

The internal rate of return (IRR) rule

One of the most commonly used alternatives to the NPV rule, especially in the analysis of capital expenditures, is the internal rate of return rule. A project's **internal rate of return** or **IRR** is the rate for which the proposal's NPV is zero. To illustrate, suppose a project that requires an initial investment of $100,000 is expected to generate a net cash flow of $115,000 in a year. At 15 percent, the project has a zero NPV because the present value of $115,000 at 15 percent is equal to $100,000, the project's initial cash outlay. Because 15 percent is the rate for which the project's NPV is zero, it is the project's IRR. Chapter 7 shows how to calculate the IRR of multiple-year projects.

To use the IRR rule to determine whether a project creates value, we must compare the project's IRR to its weighted average cost of capital. Suppose the project that has an IRR of 15 percent has an estimated WACC of 12 percent. In this case, the project creates value because its profitability, measured by its IRR, *exceeds* the cost of financing the project, measured by its estimated WACC. If the project's IRR is *lower* than its WACC, the project cannot be financed profitably and should be rejected. In general:

A project should be undertaken if its internal rate of return is higher than its cost of capital and should be rejected if its internal rate of return is lower than its cost of capital.

Chapter 7 examines the properties of the IRR rule and other capital budgeting rules, compares them to the NPV criterion, and shows why the NPV rule is the most reliable method for making capital budgeting decisions.

Sources of value creation in a business proposal

We have seen that firms with positive net present value proposals are expected to generate excess cash profits, cash profits above the level required to remunerate the firm's shareholders. However, there is nothing more powerful than excess cash profits to attract a horde of eager competitors into a market. Clearly, the challenge for firms with recurrent positive NPV businesses is to keep competitors at bay and prevent them from entering their markets. They must erect **entry barriers** that are costly enough to discourage potential competitors. How costly? The entry barriers must be costly enough to make the NPV of their competitors' proposals to enter the market negative, but not so costly as to wipe out their own positive NPV.

What are these entry barriers? Some of the most effective barriers are patents or trademarks on products that competitors are legally prevented from copying or imitating. For example, in the early nineties, Glaxo, a British pharmaceutical company, owned the patent for the world's best selling ulcer drug (sold under the name of Zantac). This drug had annual sales of $3 billion and a significantly positive NPV. As a result, Glaxo created considerable value for its shareholders during that period of time. Coca-Cola uses superior marketing and advertising expertise to build product recognition. Because Coca-Cola's trademarked image cannot be copied, product recognition leads to increased sales and value creation.

Effective barriers also include licenses purchased from governments to, for example, exploit a natural resource, operate a telecommunication network, or run a casino. A license can also be bought from a company to distribute its products abroad. For example, before Nissan—Japan's second largest vehicle manufacturer—took over the distribution of its cars in the UK, the private distributor of Nissan cars in that country became one of Britain's richest men, thanks to his exclusive right to sell Nissans in the UK.

Entry barriers can also be erected by creating a unique distribution channel. For example, Dell Computers has thrived by selling directly to customers, over the phone and via the internet, computers that are practically manufactured to order and delivered by mail.

In addition, some firms have raised entry barriers around markets for standard products that, in principle, could be reproduced easily and legally. They have simply managed to become their market's lowest cost producer or service deliverer. Their market is protected because no one else is capable of producing the goods or services as cheaply as they can.

The point we want to make is that positive NPV businesses are not easily created, discovered, or protected. Firms that have developed or found positive NPV businesses have to prevent competitors from entering their markets and reducing their excess profit to zero.

THE CAPITAL STRUCTURE DECISION

Why would a firm want to modify its capital structure? As shown in Chapter 11, a firm's capital structure usually affects its value. And, there is a particular capital structure for which the firm's value is the highest. The fundamental finance principle can help you determine the optimal capital structure, the one that maximizes the firm's value.

Contrary to an investment decision, the decision to change the firm's capital structure is not accompanied by an initial cash outlay. For example, if a firm decides to replace $10 million of equity with $10 million of debt, the net effect on the firm's cash position will be zero (we ignore the transaction costs required to carry out this capital restructuring). Thus, to apply the fundamental finance principle to the capital structure decision, we simply need to find out if the present value of the future cash flows that the firm's assets are expected to generate will increase or decrease as a result of the decision to change the structure of the capital employed to finance these assets.

As illustrated in Exhibit 1.4, debtholders have fixed claims on the cash flows generated by the firm's assets (interest payments plus the repayment of the amount borrowed). Hence, if a change in the firm's capital structure results in an increase in the present value of the cash flows from assets, then this increase will go entirely to shareholders' claims. Thus, *the firm's optimal capital structure is the one that provides the greatest increase in the present value of the cash flows from assets.*

To illustrate, suppose $10 million is borrowed at 10 percent and the corporate tax rate is 40 percent. Interest expenses are $1 million (10 percent of $10 million) and the firm's taxable profits are reduced by that amount because interest expenses are tax-deductible. The $1 million reduction in taxable profits will save the firm's owners $400,000 in taxes *every year* (40 percent of $1 million). This savings occurs because the firm can deduct interest expenses from taxable profits. Conclusion: Everything else the same, the new capital structure creates $400,000 of value to the firm's owners every year. Unfortunately for shareholders, other things usually do not remain the same.

As the firm replaces increasing amounts of equity with borrowed funds, the *risk* that it may be unable to **service its debt** (pay interest and repay the loan in

EXHIBIT 1.4   The Optimal Capital Structure Is the One that Provides the Greatest Increase in the Cash Flows from Assets.

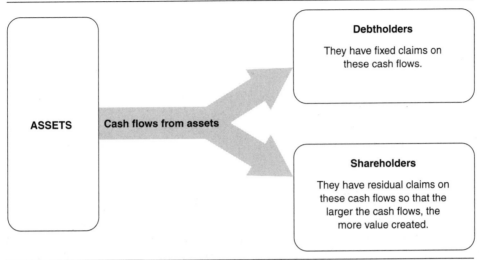

full and on time) will rise. This risk, called **financial distress risk,** generates costs that reduce the cash flows from the firm's assets and decrease the firm's value, thus offsetting the value created by the tax benefits of debt financing. Examples of these costs include the loss of sales due to customers' reluctance to buy products from a firm that may soon experience financial difficulties and the inability to obtain supplies from companies that are reluctant to provide goods and services to a firm that may be unable to pay for them. As long as the present value of the tax savings from debt financing is higher than the present value of the expected costs of financial distress, additional borrowing will increase the firm's value. When the present value of the tax advantage of debt financing is exactly offset by the present value of the expected costs of financial distress, the firm has reached its optimal capital structure. This **trade-off theory of capital structure** is examined in detail in Chapter 11, along with a review of a number of other factors managers must consider when they establish their firm's capital structure.

THE BUSINESS ACQUISITION DECISION

The acquisition of a company is just another type of investment, albeit a large one. It will create value for the shareholders of the acquiring firm only if the present value of the future net cash flows that the assets of the target firm are expected to generate after the acquisition *exceeds* the price paid to acquire the target company's assets (which is the same as the initial cash outlay). Applying the fundamental finance principle, we can write:

$$\text{NPV(acquisition)} = -\text{ Price paid to acquire the target company's assets}$$
$$+ \text{ Present value of the post-acquisition net cash flows}$$
$$\text{from the target's assets}$$

If this net present value is positive, the acquisition is a value-creating investment. If it is negative, the acquisition is a value-destroying investment. Chapter 12 shows how the post-acquisition cash flows can be estimated, depending on the type of acquisition envisioned. For a **pure conglomerate merger,** one in which the business to be acquired is unrelated to the business of the acquiring firm, the relevant cash flows are those generated by the assets of the target company "standing alone" or "as is."

Sometimes, an acquisition is expected to generate **synergies** that will raise sales or reduce costs *beyond the sum of the two companies' pre-acquisition sales and costs.* In this case, we have to estimate the amounts by which the cash flows of the target company's assets are expected to increase when the acquisition is achieved, taking into account any synergistic effects. (If the cash flows generated by the *acquiring* company's assets are also affected by the acquisition, this effect must be taken into account, too.) The discount rate that should be used to estimate the present value of these cash flows and the various steps required to determine whether an acquisition proposal will create value are the subjects of Chapter 12.

THE FOREIGN INVESTMENT DECISION

As for any other type of investment, investing abroad requires spending cash now with the expectation that the present value of the future net cash flows generated by the investment will be higher than the amount poured into the investment. Again, the fundamental finance principle is applicable. However, the implementation of the principle is somewhat more complicated than for a domestic investment because the cash flows from a cross-border investment are usually denominated in a different currency than the home currency and are exposed to additional risks, such as **currency risk** and **political** (or **country) risk.**

Currency risk refers to the risk associated with *unanticipated changes* in the value of the currency in which the investment cash flows are denominated; country risk refers to the risk associated with *unexpected events,* such as expropriation and exchange controls, that may adversely affect the project's future cash-flow stream. Chapter 13 examines these risks in detail and shows how they should be taken into account in the analysis of a cross-border investment project. For example, Chapter 13 explains why you should not add a "fudge" factor to the cost of capital to reflect the added risks of a cross-border project, while leaving the project's expected cash flows unchanged from what their value would be if the project were a domestic one. Instead, we suggest you investigate the nature of the particular country risk and adjust the project's future cash flows accordingly, without modifying the cost of capital.

After an investment project is undertaken, currency and political risks must be managed on a day-to-day basis. Chapter 13 describes how managers can reduce their firm's exposure to these risks. In particular, it explains how managers can use foreign exchange instruments, such as forward, futures, and options contracts, as well as currency swaps, to reduce the impact of currency movements on the cash flows generated by a foreign project.

THE ROLE OF FINANCIAL MARKETS

Financial markets play a key role in the process of business growth and value creation by performing two fundamental functions (see Exhibit 1.5). As **primary markets,** they provide the financing required to fund new business ventures and sustain business growth. They perform this function by acting as intermediaries between individuals and companies that have a cash surplus they wish to invest and companies that have a cash deficit they wish to eliminate by raising new capital through the issuance of **securities** (certificates that recognize the rights of the holder). As **secondary markets,** they provide an efficient mechanism for trading **outstanding** (already issued) securities and translating the value-creating (or value-destroying) decisions of firms into increases (or decreases) in shareholders' wealth via higher (or lower) security prices.

These two functions are not independent of one another. The price of securities in the secondary markets is determined by the buying and selling carried out

EXHIBIT 1.5   The Dual Functions of Financial Markets.

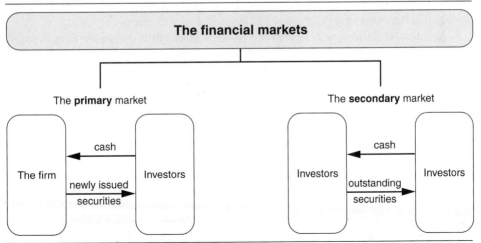

by traders in these markets. The price observed in the secondary market is then used by **investment** (or **merchant**) **bankers** as a benchmark against which they can set the price of newly issued securities in the primary market. (Investment bankers are intermediaries that help companies issue securities to raise funds in financial markets.) Thus, a well-functioning secondary market facilitates the pricing of new securities issued in the primary market. As a consequence, the two markets are closely related. The structure and organization of financial markets, the role played by investment bankers, and the determination of the price of the securities traded in these markets are examined in detail in Chapter 9. This section provides an overview of the role of financial markets in value creation and as a source of capital.

THE EQUITY MARKET

In an **efficient equity market,** the share prices of firms adjust instantly to new and relevant information as soon as it becomes available to market participants. Relevant information is any piece of news that is expected to affect a firm's future cash-flow stream. In an efficient equity market, stock prices should rise instantly on favorable news and drop instantly on unfavorable news (assuming, of course, that the piece of news was unanticipated). You can see why efficient equity markets play a key role in the process of value creation. As soon as a company announces a business decision that market participants interpret as having a positive net present value, the company's market value should rise by an amount equal to the market's estimation of that decision's positive net present value. Shareholders who wish to cash in do not have to wait for the firm to actually carry out its business decision. All they have to do is sell their shares to immediately receive their part of the value created by the firm's positive announcement. The opposite is also true. If market participants believe the decision has a negative net present value, the company's aggregate market value should fall by an amount equal to the market's estimation of that decision's negative net present value and shareholders will suffer an immediate loss.

Are equity markets efficient processors of information? And do they actually provide an efficient mechanism to determine reliable stock prices? The evidence indicates that *on average* most well-developed stock markets around the world can be described as sufficiently efficient to be relied on to provide unbiased estimates of share prices. The story that follows provides an illustration of how the stock markets react to firms' announcements that could affect their future cash-flow stream.

WHAT IS BAD FOR GENERAL MOTORS IS GOOD FOR VOLKSWAGEN . . . AND VICE VERSA

This is the story of Mr. Lopez and the New York and Frankfurt stock markets. Mr. Lopez was a powerful executive in charge of worldwide purchasing for General Motors (GM), a key position considering GM's bloated cost structure and substandard profit margin. According to press reports, Mr. Lopez and his team were able to shave close to $1 billion off GM's annual costs. This feat made him one of GM's most valuable employees. But valuable employees attract competitors' attention. In early 1993, Mr. Lopez was approached by Volkswagen (another car manufacturer with a bloated cost structure and a substandard profit margin) to join that company and apply his valuable cost-cutting talent to its operations. But GM could not afford to lose Mr. Lopez's invaluable services. It offered him a big raise and promoted him to group vice-president. This seemed to settle the matter: Mr. Lopez was to stay with GM.

But on Thursday, March 11, 1993, a rumor began to spread around Detroit and Wall Street: Mr. Lopez was about to leave GM and join Volkswagen. On Friday, March 12, 1993, VW confirmed that Mr. Lopez would join the company. How did GM and VW share prices react to the news? On the New York Stock Exchange, the price of GM's shares dropped 4.4 percent between Wednesday's close and Friday's close while the market (the Dow Jones Industrial Index) dropped only 1.4 percent over the same two-day period. At that time, a 1 percent drop in the stock price of GM corresponded to $280 million of value destruction. If we remove the 1.4 percent drop in the market from the 4.4 percent drop in the stock price of GM, the remaining 3 percent corresponds to $840 million of value destruction in 48 hours (3 times $280 million), the equivalent of almost one year's cost-cutting efforts.

On the Frankfurt Stock Exchange, the price of VW's shares rose 1.8 percent while the market (the DAX Index) *fell* 0.2 percent. Adjusted for market movement, the rise in price of VW's shares was 2 percent and corresponded at the time to approximately $90 million of value creation.

Obviously, Mr. Lopez's decision to move from GM to VW was a negative net present value proposition for GM and a positive one for VW. The prevailing consensus among financial analysts was that Mr. Lopez and his team, which was expected to follow him to VW, were not easily replaceable. Costs would no longer be under tight control at GM without the presence of Mr. Lopez and his team, and costs at VW would be significantly tightened up when they moved to VW. Note, however, that Mr. Lopez's transfer from GM to VW resulted in a net value destruction of $750 million (GM's loss of $840 million net of VW's gain of $90 million). Given the size of GM, Mr. Lopez and his team were clearly more valuable to GM's shareholders than they were to VW's owners.

Then, over the weekend, GM made Mr. Lopez an offer he could not refuse: a promotion to executive vice-president responsible for all of GM's North American auto operations. Mr. Lopez was staying with GM after all. On Monday, March 15, the stock price of GM rose 1.3 percent on the news while the U.S. market was up 0.3 percent and the stock price of VW fell 2.5 percent while the German market dropped 0.3 percent. GM recovered a third of its lost value while VW lost all of its previous gains. The markets were not convinced that Mr. Lopez would stay with GM but also thought that he would most likely not join VW.

But hold on, the story is not finished yet. On Tuesday, March 16, VW announced that Mr. Lopez had definitely joined the company as the head of worldwide production and a member of its managing board. GM confirmed that Mr. Lopez had officially resigned and was leaving the company. Guess what? The share price of GM fell 1.3 percent on a flat U.S. market and that of VW rose 1.8 percent while the German market dropped 0.3 percent. VW recovered its previous 2 percent rise (after adjusting for the market movement) despite the fact that the same day the company announced a dramatic reduction in both its profits and dividends for 1992 in comparison to 1991.

Mr. Lopez's story clearly illustrates the role played by the U.S. and German stock markets as instantaneous processors of news and as translators of relevant information about companies into value creation when the news is favorable and value destruction when it is unfavorable.[5]

EXTERNAL VERSUS INTERNAL FINANCING

We now consider how financial markets function as primary markets. In this role, they act as a source of external financing to companies. Firms can raise equity capital by issuing shares of common stock in the equity market, or they can borrow by issuing debt securities in the debt markets. As mentioned earlier, to carry out this fund raising task, they employ the services of investment bankers (as opposed to **commercial bankers** who extend loans). Short-term funds can be raised by issuing **commercial paper** in the **money market,** and long-term funds can be raised by issuing **bonds** in the **corporate bond market.** These markets, and the securities that are traded in them, are described in Chapter 9.

Debt financing is necessarily external. It is either borrowed from financial institutions, such as banks and insurance companies, or raised in the debt markets by issuing commercial paper or corporate bonds. Equity financing, however, can be either external (in the form of a new equity issue) or internal. **Internal equity financing** refers to **retained earnings,** the part of a firm's profit that the firm's owners decide to invest back into their company instead of to withdraw in the form of a **cash dividend.** The percentage of profit retained within the firm is called the **profit retention rate.** The percentage paid out in the form of a cash dividend is known as the **dividend payout ratio.**

Companies retain part (and sometimes all) of their profit because, for most firms, *regular* access to external equity financing is often unavailable and, when it is available, is relatively expensive. For example, fees must be paid to investment bankers and numerous costs are incurred to comply with the rules and regulations that govern external equity funding. Hence, calling on existing and new shareholders to raise external equity through a new share issue is usually an infrequent event in the life of a company. Most firms rely primarily on internal equity financing, through profit retention, to build up their equity capital. Profit retention

---

[5]Mr. Lopez's story had a follow-up. Immediately after he joined VW, GM alleged that he stole confidential documents and engaged in a legal battle with VW for financial damages. The dispute ended in January 1997 with an out-of-court settlement. The controversy had depressed VW share price, but, when the settlement was announced, VW share price went up 4 percent.

is the fuel of sustainable business expansion. No business can travel the road of long-term growth without retaining some of its profit on a continual basis.

HOW FAST CAN A FIRM GROW?

In the remainder of this chapter, we use a fictitious firm—Hologram Lighting Company (HLC)—to present a preliminary analysis of various financial management topics. These topics are considered in detail in later chapters. Our goal here is to provide an overview of the financial analysis required to identify value-creating firms and value-destroying firms.

The relationship between profit-retention and business growth is illustrated in Exhibit 1.6 for Hologram Lighting Company. Start with the top box and move clockwise. Assume that HLC has an initial capital of $1,000 million (in most of the remainder of this chapter, we drop the reference to millions for the sake of simplicity). One half of HLC's capital ($500) is borrowed and the other half consists of shareholders' funds (owners' equity). In other words, HLC's **debt-to-equity ratio** is equal to one.

Before we examine the remaining figures and ratios in Exhibit 1.6, we need to look at the overall picture. The following dialogue explains the system that ties together the various drivers of business growth and value creation.

"Why does HLC need capital?"

"It has to acquire assets. Without the financing made available by equity and debt capital, HLC would not be able to buy assets."

"Of course, but why does HLC need assets?"

"It has to generate sales. Without productive assets, such as equipment and machinery, HLC would not be able to manufacture goods for sale."

"Surely, but then why does HLC need sales?"

"It has to make profits. Without sales revenues, how could HLC generate any profits?"

"True, but then why does HLC need profits?"

"It must reward its owners (the shareholders) in the form of dividend payments and must build up its capital base. By retaining part of its profits, HLC will be able to increase its equity capital which, in turn, will allow it to increase the amount of cash it can borrow from creditors. With a debt-to-equity ratio equal to one, HLC needs one dollar of additional equity to be able to borrow one extra dollar."

"I understand. One last question. Why does HLC need more capital?"

"To acquire more assets, to generate more sales, to produce higher profits, to pay dividends, to increase retained earnings, to build up equity capital, to raise new debt, and to grow the business."

EXHIBIT 1.6 HLC's Business Cycle.

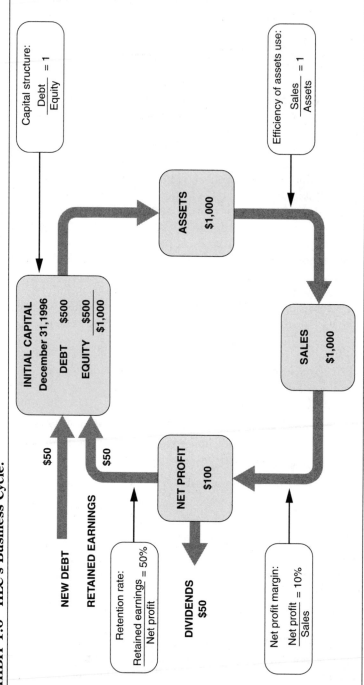

Capital structure:

$$\frac{Debt}{Equity} = 1$$

Efficiency of assets use:

$$\frac{Sales}{Assets} = 1$$

ASSETS
$1,000

INITIAL CAPITAL
December 31, 1996

DEBT $500
EQUITY $500
            $1,000

SALES
$1,000

$50

NEW DEBT

RETAINED EARNINGS

$50

NET PROFIT
$100

Retention rate:

$$\frac{Retained\ earnings}{Net\ profit} = 50\%$$

DIVIDENDS
$50

Net profit margin:

$$\frac{Net\ profit}{Sales} = 10\%$$

20

This sequence of events is called the firm's **business cycle.** With an initial capital of $1,000, HLC can finance an equal amount of assets. This $1,000 of assets is used by HLC to generate sales. The amount of sales depends on the efficiency with which HLC manages its assets. Usually, this efficiency is measured by the **sales-to-asset ratio** (also known as the firm's **asset turns, asset rotation,** or **asset turnover**). For simplicity, we assume in Exhibit 1.6 that this ratio is equal to one for HLC, meaning that its $1,000 of assets will generate $1,000 of sales.

HLC can increase its asset turns either by generating *more* than one dollar of sales per dollar of assets or by generating one dollar of sales with *less* than one dollar of assets. Whether HLC can increase its sales will depend on the structure and conditions of the market in which it operates and on its competitive position in its industry. Whether HLC can reduce the amount of assets needed to generate one dollar of sales will depend on the ability of HLC's operations managers to manage assets, such as inventories and fixed assets, at their optimal level of efficiency.

If we assume a **net profit margin (net profit-to-sales ratio)** of 10 percent, the $1,000 of sales will generate a net profit of $100 (10 percent of $1,000). What will HLC do with the $100 profit? Assuming a retention rate of 50 percent, $50 will be reinvested in the business in the form of retained earnings and $50 will be distributed to shareholders in the form of dividends. With $50 of additional equity capital, HLC will be able to borrow $50 (recall that HLC has a debt-to-equity ratio of one). These transactions will raise HLC's total capital to $1,100: $550 of equity capital (initial equity of $500 plus $50 of retained earnings) and $550 of debt capital (initial debt of $500 plus $50 of additional borrowing). HLC will start a new cycle with $1,100 of capital which will finance $1,100 of assets from which $1,100 of sales will be generated (assuming that the sales-to-assets ratio remains equal to one). And with a net profit margin of 10 percent, the $1,100 of sales will, in turn, generate $110 profit. If the profit retention rate remains at 50 percent, $55 will be added to HLC's equity capital and $55 will be distributed as dividends.

When HLC began the new business cycle, equity capital had increased by 10 percent (from an initial amount of $500 to $550). So did the borrowed funds (from $500 to $550), total capital (from $1,000 to $1,100), and total assets (from $1,000 to $1,100). As a consequence, sales will also increase by 10 percent (from $1,000 to $1,100), as will profit (from $100 to $110), retained earnings (from $50 to $55), and dividend payments (from $50 to $55). They will all be growing at 10 percent. This rate is called the **self-sustainable growth rate (SGR).** It is the fastest growth rate in sales that HLC can achieve by retaining 50 percent of its profit and keeping both its operating and financing policies unchanged (a sales-to-assets ratio of one, a net profit margin of 10 percent, a retention rate of 50 percent, and a debt-to-equity ratio of one).

The self-sustainable growth rate is an important indicator of business performance and an important component of a firm's financial strategy. Chapter 5 shows how a firm can raise its self-sustainable growth rate, and Chapter 14 shows how the self-sustainable-growth-rate concept can be used to formulate an optimal financial strategy.

HLC'S FINANCIAL STATEMENTS

Financial statements, better known as **balance sheets** and **income statements,** are the end-products of the financial accounting process. This process, shown in Exhibit 1.7, records the financial transactions between the firm and the rest of the world.

The balance sheet is a statement that shows what a firm's shareholders own, called **assets** (such as cash, inventories, plants, and equipment), and what they owe, called **liabilities** (such as money owed to banks and suppliers), at a specific date (usually at the end of a year or a quarter). The difference between a firm's assets and its liabilities is an accounting estimate of the equity shareholders have invested in their firm; owners' equity is also called the **book value of equity.** The book value of equity depends on the accounting conventions used in estimating

EXHIBIT 1.7　A Simplified View of the Financial Accounting Process.

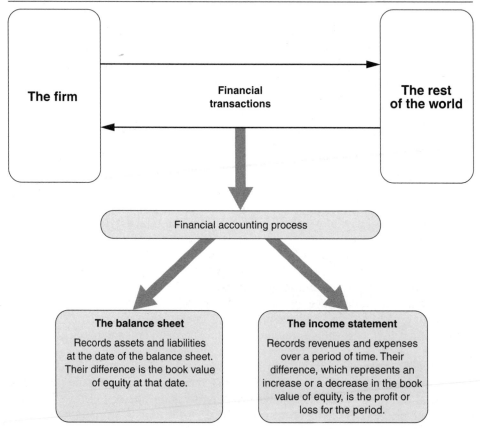

the firm's assets and liabilities. Thus, the book value of the same company may be different if it is estimated according to French accounting rules rather than American accounting conventions because French and American accounting standards are not the same.

The purpose of the income statement, also called the **profit and loss statement,** is to provide an estimate of the *change* in the book value of equity over a period of time (usually a year or a quarter). This change, called **net profit** when it is positive and **net loss** when it is negative, is the difference between the firm's **revenues** and its **expenses.** A revenue is any transaction occurring during the accounting period that increases the book value of equity; an expense is any transaction that decreases the book value of equity. As in the case of the balance sheet, the income statement is drawn according to accounting conventions that may differ from one country to another.

A detailed analysis of a firm's financial statements is presented in Chapter 2. In this section, we present a simplified version of HLC's financial statements and use them to show how they can provide valuable information about a firm's financial performance.

HLC'S BALANCE SHEETS

The upper part of Exhibit 1.8 illustrates simplified versions of HLC's standard balance sheets for the periods ending December 31, 1996, and December 31, 1997. The left side lists the firm's assets with their corresponding accounting values at the date of the balance sheet. The right side lists the firm's liabilities and shareholders' equity with their corresponding accounting values at the same date. The data are in millions of dollars.

The assets recorded at the end of 1996 include $100 of **cash,** $150 of **accounts receivable** (also called **trade receivables** or **trade debtors,** these accounts represent cash owed to HLC by its customers for sales made on credit), $250 of **inventories** (raw materials, work in process, and finished goods not yet sold), and $600 of **net fixed assets** (long-term assets, such as equipment, machinery, and buildings). When estimating the net value of fixed assets, an accountant deducts from the purchase price of the assets the accumulated **depreciation expenses** to account for the loss in value due to the wear and tear of the assets.

How were these assets financed? According to the right side of the balance sheets, they were financed with $200 of short-term borrowing from banks, $100 of **accounts payable** (also called **trade payables** or **trade creditors,** these accounts represent cash owed by HLC to its suppliers of raw material for purchases made on credit and not yet paid), $300 of long-term debt, and $500 of equity capital. Recall that HLC's business cycle in Exhibit 1.6 shows $1,000 of assets financed with $500 of equity capital and $500 of debt. But, the asset side of the firm's balance sheet shows the amount of assets recorded at that date as $1,100. Why the difference?

EXHIBIT 1.8   **HLC's Balance Sheets on December 31, 1996, and December 31, 1997.**

Figures in millions of dollars

FROM HLC'S STANDARD BALANCE SHEETS:						
ASSETS			LIABILITIES AND OWNERS' EQUITY			
	DECEMBER 31 1996	DECEMBER 31 1997			DECEMBER 31 1996	DECEMBER 31 1997
Cash	$100	$110	Short-term borrowing		$200	$220
Accounts receivable	150	165	Accounts payable		100	110
Inventories	250	275	Long-term debt		300	330
Net fixed assets	600	660	Owners' equity		500	550
TOTAL	$1,100	$1,210		TOTAL	$1,100	$1,210

TO HLC'S MANAGERIAL BALANCE SHEETS:						
INVESTED CAPITAL OR NET ASSETS			CAPITAL EMPLOYED			
	DECEMBER 31 1996	DECEMBER 31 1997			DECEMBER 31 1996	DECEMBER 31 1997
Cash	$100	$110	Short-term borrowing		$200	$220
Working capital requirement (WCR)[1]	300	330	Long-term debt		300	330
Net fixed assets	600	660	Owners' equity		500	550
TOTAL	$1,000	$1,100		TOTAL	$1,000	$1,100

[1]Working capital requirement (WCR) = Accounts receivable + Inventories − Accounts payable

The net investment required to operate HLC's fixed assets

HLC must hold both trade receivables and inventories because sales are not paid immediately by customers and goods must be manufactured and stored before they can be sold. Without inventories and receivables, HLC would be unable to produce goods and sell them. However, these accounts represent required investments that HLC must finance. This financing is partly provided by trade payables because HLC does not have to pay its suppliers immediately. As a result, the *net* investment that HLC must make in order to support its production and sales activities is equal to the sum of its trade receivables and inventories less its trade payables. This net investment in operations, which is required to generate sales and profits from the firm's fixed assets, is called **working capital requirement (WCR).**

HLC's WCR on December 31, 1996, was equal to $300 ($150 of receivables plus $250 of inventories less $100 of payables). The optimal management of a firm's working capital requirement, which is one of the most effective ways to create value through improved efficiency, is a major topic of Chapter 3.

HLC's managerial balance sheet

The lower part of Exhibit 1.8 shows a variant of HLC's balance sheet, called the **managerial balance sheet.** The left side of the managerial balance sheet lists the firm's **invested capital** or **net assets:** cash ($100), working capital requirement ($300), and net fixed assets ($600). It is this $1,000 of net assets, not the $1,100 of assets in the standard balance sheet, that must be financed by debt and equity capital. To finance these net assets, HLC employed the $1,000 of capital listed on the right side of the managerial balance sheet: $200 of short-term debt, $300 of long-term debt, and $500 of equity capital.

The managerial balance sheet gives a clearer picture of the structure of the firm's investments and the capital it employs to finance them than a standard balance sheet does. Capital invested in cash, operations, and fixed assets is reported under the heading "invested capital" or "net assets." And the sources of capital used to fund these net assets are reported under the heading "capital employed." Chapter 3 shows why the managerial balance sheet is a better starting point for analyzing, interpreting, and evaluating the firm's investing, operating, and financing strategies.

Is HLC's capital structure optimal? We indicated earlier that a debt-to-equity ratio of one is the preferred (or optimal) capital structure for HLC. How a firm should establish an optimal capital structure is the topic of Chapter 11. Given that half of HLC's capital is in the form of debt, the next question is: How much debt should be short term and how much long term? Of HLC's total debt, 40 percent is short term ($200 out of $500 of total debt) and 60 percent is long term. Is that debt structure appropriate and, more generally, what should be the optimal term structure of a firm's debt? These questions are addressed in Chapter 3.

HLC's balance sheet at the end of 1997

How does HLC's balance sheet look a year later? Because HLC is growing at 10 percent per year, we made the simplifying assumptions that all the entries in both its standard and managerial balance sheets have grown by 10 percent. How much new investment in fixed assets did HLC make in 1997? Be careful, the answer is *not* $60 (the difference between $660 of net fixed assets at the end of 1997 and the initial $600 of net fixed assets) because fixed assets are reported in the balance sheet after depreciation expenses are deducted. If we assume that the initial fixed assets are depreciated $60 a year and that HLC had made $120 in new investments by the end of 1997, then net fixed assets at the end of that year must be equal to $660 (the initial net fixed assets of $600 less $60 of depreciation expenses plus the $120 of new investments at the end of the year).

HLC'S INCOME STATEMENT

A simplified version of HLC's income statement for 1997 is shown in Exhibit 1.9. HLC had sales revenues of $1,000 and total expenses (including taxes) of $900, producing a reported net profit or **earnings after tax (EAT)** of $100. What is the structure of HLC's expenses? HLC had operating expenses of $760 (including $60 of depreciation expenses), interest expenses of $40 (based on an 8 percent average cost of debt on total debt of $500), and tax liability of $100 (corresponding to a 50 percent corporate tax rate on a pretax profit of $200).

The difference between sales and operating expenses is called **earnings before interest and tax** or **EBIT** (also called **pretax operating profit** or **trading profit**). In 1997, HLC's EBIT was $240 ($1,000 of sales less $760 of operating expenses). Of the $240 of EBIT, $40 went to banks as interest payments on the $500 of funds they lent HLC, leaving $200 as **earnings before tax** or **EBT.** A further and final $100 went to the government as tax, leaving $100 of earnings after tax. As already mentioned, this $100 belongs to HLC's shareholders. According to the information in Exhibit 1.9, $50 is reinvested in the business as retained earnings and $50 is paid to shareholders as dividend payments.

Think of earnings before interest and tax as profit from HLC's operations that will be shared by three categories of claimants in accordance with a legally established order. Debtholders are the first claimants. They are entitled to $40 of interest payment. They are followed by the tax authorities that have a claim to $100, which represents the tax HLC owes the government. Finally, the owners or shareholders are entitled to whatever is left. They, in effect, have a *residual ownership* of the firm's pretax operating profit. This entitlement order for the firm's earnings makes the remuneration of the suppliers of debt capital (interest payment) a tax-deductible

EXHIBIT 1.9   HLC's Simplified 1997 Income Statement.

Figures in millions of dollars.

Sales	**$1,000**
Less operating expenses (including $60 of depreciation expenses)	($760)
Earnings before interest and tax (EBIT)	**$240**
Less interest expenses (8% × $500)	(40)
Earnings before tax (EBT)	**$200**
Less tax expenses (50% × $200)	(100)
Earnings after tax (EAT)	**$100**
Retained earnings = $50	
Dividend payment = $50	

expense. This is why the firm's cost of debt should be measured net of the corporation tax the firm has saved. This is not the case for the firm's owners. They are remunerated on an aftertax basis because their share of the firm's operating profit is the firm's earnings after tax.

HOW PROFITABLE IS HLC?

Information provided in the firm's balance sheets and income statement can be combined to evaluate its financial performance, in particular the profitability of its equity capital and the profitability of its invested capital.

THE PROFITABILITY OF HLC'S EQUITY CAPITAL

How profitable was HLC to its owners in 1997? Owners had $500 of equity capital invested in HLC at the beginning of the year. That investment generated a year-end profit of $100. Half of this profit, which belongs entirely to the firm's owners, was reinvested in the firm and the other half was paid out as cash dividends. The owners' return on investment is equal to 20 percent ($100 of net profit divided by $500 of initial equity investment). This return, which is a measure of HLC's profitability to its shareholders, is called **return on equity (ROE):**

$$\text{ROE} = \frac{\text{Earnings after tax (EAT)}}{\text{Owners' equity}} = \frac{\$100}{\$500} = 20\%$$

THE PROFITABILITY OF HLC'S INVESTED CAPITAL

To measure the aftertax profitability of HLC's invested capital, we must use the aftertax profits generated by that investment. This is the firm's *aftertax operating profit,* which is equal to EBIT $(1-\text{tax rate})$. The tax rate is applied *before* interest expenses are deducted from earnings because we want to measure the profitability of the firm's *total* capital which is provided by both shareholders and debtholders. Dividing the aftertax operating profit by the amount of capital that was used to generate the profit gives a measure of the firm's **return on invested capital (ROIC).** For HLC:

$$\text{Return on invested capital (ROIC)} = \frac{\text{Aftertax operating profit}}{\text{Invested capital}}$$

$$= \frac{\$240(1-50\%)}{\$1,000} = 12\%$$

Return on invested capital (ROIC) is the same as **return on net assets (RONA)** or **return on capital employed (ROCE)** because invested capital is the same as net assets and both are equal to capital employed, as indicated in the managerial balance sheet shown in Exhibit 1.8. Chapter 5 examines the relationship between a firm's return on equity and its return on invested capital and analyzes in detail how managerial decisions can improve these two measures of profitability.

HOW MUCH CASH HAS HLC GENERATED?

The cash flows expected from a business proposal are a key factor in deciding whether the proposal will create or destroy value. Measuring the cash flows generated by the firm's activities on a continuous basis is thus essential to verify that these activities indeed create value. How can a firm's balance sheets and income statements be used to estimate how much cash its activities generate? Chapter 4 answers this question in detail and examines the managerial implications of running a business with a focus on generating cash and creating value. In this section, we just want to provide some insights on the issue of estimating cash flows from financial statements.

In 1997, HLC generated a pretax operating profit, or earnings before interest and tax (EBIT), of $240 and a net profit, or earnings after tax (EAT), of $100, as indicated in its income statement in Exhibit 1.9. However, these accounting figures do not represent cash. To illustrate this point, note that an increase in sales will increase both EBIT and EAT, but will not generate cash until HLC's customers pay for what they bought. We want to know how much *cash* HLC generated in 1997, that is, how much cash there is behind EBIT and EAT.

One answer is provided by HLC's balance sheets in Exhibit 1.8. At the beginning of 1997 (the end of 1996), HLC had $100 in cash. At the end of the year, it had $110 in cash. The $10 increase in cash is the *total net cash flow* generated by HLC in 1997. In other words, the net outcome of *all* cash transactions (all cash payments and all cash receipts) made by HLC in 1997 was $10 (actually $10 million, because the data in the financial statements are in millions).

SOURCES OF CASH

A firm can get cash from three sources: (1) It can borrow it or issue new shares (a financing decision); (2) It can sell some of its assets (an investment, or, more precisely, a divestment or asset disposal, decision); (3) It can generate it from its operations. We know that HLC generated a total net cash flow of $10 in 1997. We want to find out the respective contributions of operating, investing, and financing activities to that total net cash flow. In particular, we want to find out whether operations, the heart of the business, is generating any cash. A firm that does not generate sufficient cash from its operations over a period of time may destroy value and be headed for trouble. It can buy time by borrowing or by selling assets, but these sources of cash will eventually dry up.

CASH FLOW GENERATED BY OPERATING ACTIVITIES

We can use HLC's balance sheets and income statement to find out how much cash HLC has generated from operations, net of taxes, in 1997. The income statement in Exhibit 1.9 shows that the firm sold $1,000 worth of goods and incurred $760 of operating expenses, leaving $240 as earnings before interest and tax. Deducting the $100 tax expenses leaves $140. However, the $760 of operating expenses includes $60 of depreciation, and depreciation is not a cash expense (more on this in Chapter 4). Thus, depreciation expenses must be excluded from the operating expenses because we are looking for cash and not profits. Adding $60 to the $140, we get $200. Now, note that HLC invested extra dollars to finance the growth of its inventories and trade receivables, net of the funding provided by its trade payables; that is, HLC had to finance the growth of its working capital requirement in 1997. The balance sheets in Exhibit 1.8 show that the growth of working capital requirement was equal to $30, the difference between a WCR of $330 at the end of 1997 and a WCR of $300 at the end of 1996. Thus, HLC's aftertax cash flow from operating activities, or net operating cash flow, is $170 ($200 less $30).

CASH FLOWS FROM INVESTING AND FINANCING ACTIVITIES

Recall that HLC made an additional investment in fixed assets (usually referred to as a **capital expenditure**) of $120 at the end of 1997. This expenditure resulted in a net cash outflow of $120 that is related to HLC's investing activities.

What are the cash movements related to HLC's financing activities? First, HLC had to remunerate its suppliers of capital. The income statement in Exhibit 1.9 shows HLC paid $40 in interest to its bank on the $500 borrowings and paid $50 in dividends to its shareholders, representing a total cash outflow of $90 for the year. Did HLC borrow new funds during the year? The answer is yes, as shown in the balance sheets in Exhibit 1.8. Short-term debt rose by $20 and long-term debt by $30. Thus, HLC borrowed $50 in 1997, representing a net cash inflow of $50 for the year. No new (external) equity was issued during the year, so there were no cash movements related to equity in 1997. Thus, the total net cash flow related to financing activities in 1997 amounted to a $40 cash outflow (outflows of $40 in interest payments and $50 in dividend payments less an inflow of $50 from new borrowings).

PUTTING IT TOGETHER: HLC'S CASH FLOW STATEMENT

We can now summarize all of HLC's 1997 cash movements by drawing a cash flow statement, as shown in Exhibit 1.10. Operating activities added $170 in cash, after tax payments. New investments consumed $120 in cash and financing activities absorbed an additional $40. The total cash flow resulting from all these transactions is a net cash inflow of $10 ($170 from operations less $120 from investment less $40 from

EXHIBIT 1.10   HLC's 1997 Cash Flow Statement.

Figures in millions of dollars

CASH FLOW FROM OPERATING ACTIVITIES		
Sales	$1,000	
Less operating expenses (which include depreciation expenses)	(760)	
Less tax expenses	(100)	
Plus depreciation expenses	60	
Less cash used to finance the growth of WCR	(30)	
A. NET OPERATING CASH FLOW		**$170**
CASH FLOW FROM INVESTING ACTIVITIES		
Capital expenditures	(120)	
B. NET CASH FLOW FROM INVESTING ACTIVITIES		**(120)**
CASH FLOWS FROM FINANCING ACTIVITIES		
New borrowing	50	
Interest payments	(40)	
Dividend payments	(50)	
C. NET CASH FLOW FROM FINANCING ACTIVITIES		**(40)**
D. TOTAL NET CASH FLOW (A + B + C)		**10**
E. CASH HELD AT THE BEGINNING OF THE YEAR		**$100**
F. CASH HELD AT THE END OF THE YEAR (E + D)		**$110**

financing). HLC began the year with $100, so its cash holding at the end of the year is $110 ($100 at the beginning of the year plus the $10 generated during the year).

Note that we knew that HLC's net change in cash holding during the year was $10 *before we drew the cash flow statement.* All we had to do was to examine HLC's opening and closing balance sheets in Exhibit 1.8. The cash flow statement is useful because it provides a breakdown of HLC's cash flow into the three main corporate activities: operations, investment, and financing. Chapter 4 shows alternative ways of presenting a firm's cash flows and analyzes the relationship between managerial decisions and cash flows.

HOW RISKY IS HLC?

A firm does not know for certain whether its projected sales figures will actually be achieved. The firm may sell more or less than what it expected to sell. This is risk. It originates from uncertain sales figures and works itself through the firm's income statement until it finally hits the **bottom line,** that is, the firm's **net profit.**

EXHIBIT 1.11   HLC Income Statement: Impact on EBIT, EBT, and EAT of a 10% Drop or Rise in Sales.

Figures in millions of dollars

	EXPECTED[1]	SALES DOWN 10%		SALES UP 10%	
Sales	$1,000	$900	–10%	$1,100	+10%
Less variable operating expenses[2]	(380)	(342)	–10%	(418)	+10%
Less fixed operating expenses[3]	(380)	(380)	same	(380)	same
EBIT (earnings before interest & tax)	$240	$178	–26%	$302	+26%
Less fixed interest expenses	(40)	(40)	same	(40)	same
EBT (earnings before tax)	$200	$138	–31%	$262	+31%
Less variable tax expenses (50%)	(100)	(69)	–31%	(131)	+31%
EAT (earnings after tax)	$100	$69	–31%	$131	+31%

[1]The expected income statement is the same as the one shown in Exhibit 1.9.

[2]One half of total operating expenses of $760 in Exhibit 1.9.

[3]One half of total operating expenses of $760 in Exhibit 1.9. Note that the $60 of depreciation expenses are fixed and, hence, included in the $380 of fixed operating expenses.

We can examine this transmission mechanism using HLC's 1997 income statement. At the beginning of the year, HLC does not know with certainty whether it will achieve its $1,000 target sales. The first column of Exhibit 1.11 reports *expected* sales of $1,000, which may or may not be achieved. Suppose that half of HLC's total expenses are fixed ($380) and the other half are variable ($380). Deducting these expenses from the $1,000 of expected sales provides an *expected* earnings before interest and tax (EBIT) of $240. From this figure, $40 of *fixed* interest expenses and $100 of *variable* tax expenses are deducted to yield an *expected* net profit of $100.

Now suppose that sales, which are volatile, either fall short of their expected value by 10 percent (go down to $900 as shown in the second column in Exhibit 1.11) or exceed their expected value by 10 percent (go up to $1,100 as reported in the fourth column in Exhibit 1.11). How will this 10 percent variation in sales affect HLC's pretax operating profit (EBIT)? A 10 percent change in sales induces a 10 percent change in *variable* costs but leaves *fixed* costs unaffected (by definition, if costs are fixed, their level does not change when sales vary). As a result, EBIT rises by 26 percent if sales go up by 10 percent and drops by 26 percent if sales go down by 10 percent, as indicated in Exhibit 1.11. EBIT fluctuates more widely than sales. In other words, *operating profits are more risky than sales*. This occurs because some of the firm's operating expenses are fixed. If they were all variable, then EBIT would fluctuate by 10 percent, exactly like sales, and sales and EBIT would incur the same risk (same degree of fluctuation). Notice that the presence of *fixed* interest expenses increases risk further. Indeed, net profits (EAT) fluctuate by 31 percent in response to the 10 percent fluctuation in sales.

The above example illustrates an important phenomenon: *The higher the proportion of fixed expenses (both operational and financial) relative to total expenses, the riskier the firm's net profits in comparison to the risk of its sales.* The transmission of risk from sales to profits is illustrated in Exhibit 1.12. First, sales fluctuate because of the uncertain economic, political, social, and competitive environments in which firms operate. This is **economic risk.** This initial risk is then magnified by the presence of fixed operating expenses that create **operational risk.** The cumulative effect of economic risk and operational risk is called **business risk.** Finally, business risk is further magnified by the presence of fixed interest expenses that create **financial risk.** The cumulative effect of business risk and financial risk is transmitted to net profits, whose resulting fluctuations reflect the **total risk.**

Total risk is borne by the firm's owners. Owners have a claim on the firm's residual gains (the firm's net profits) but they must bear any residual losses. While the remuneration of HLC's lenders is fixed, the remuneration of HLC's owners is the firm's uncertain profits. Thus, equity capital, the owners' investment, is riskier than debt capital, the lenders' investment. For this reason, HLC's owners require a higher rate of return on their equity investment than the return required by HLC's lenders. HLC's cost of equity might be 16 percent while the firm's cost of debt is only 8 percent (see Exhibit 1.9). Most shareholders dislike risk—they are **risk averse**—and they require a higher rate of return to compensate them for the higher level of risk attached to equity capital. The impact of risk on the firm's profitability is examined in detail in Chapter 5. The relationship between risk and the rate of return required by the suppliers of capital is explored in Chapters 10 and 11.

IS HLC CREATING VALUE?

The ultimate success of a firm is not measured only by its capacity to grow its sales, produce profits, or generate cash from its operations. In the final analysis, what really matters is whether the firm's activities are creating value for its owners. How can we find out whether a firm is creating value?

We can answer that question by applying the fundamental finance principle to *all* the firm's invested capital, instead of to just a single project as we did earlier. According to the fundamental finance principle, a firm is creating value if the net present value of *all* its investments is positive. We can measure this net present value by deducting the total amount of capital employed to finance the firm's investments from the market value of the firm's capital (the market value of its equity and debt capital):

NPV(entire firm) = Market value of the firm's capital − Total capital employed

This net present value is usually referred to as the firm's **market value added** or **MVA.** If MVA is positive, the firm is creating value because the market value of its capital exceeds the amount of capital invested in it. If MVA is negative, the firm is destroying value.

EXHIBIT 1.12 Sources of Risk that Increase Profit Volatility.

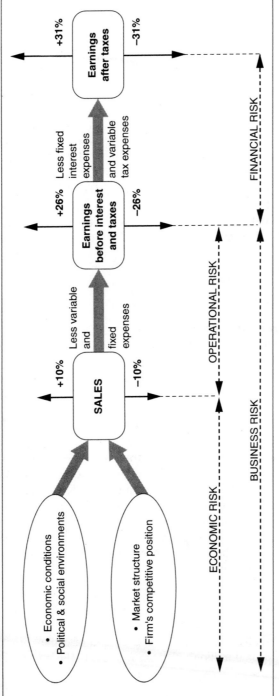

Let's estimate HLC's MVA on December 31, 1997. Its total capital employed on that date is $1,100 million, as shown on the right side of HLC's managerial balance sheet in Exhibit 1.8. This is a measure of the total amount of capital that shareholders and debtholders have invested in the firm as of December 31, 1997. What is the market value of that capital on December 31, 1997? It is the sum of the market value of its equity (its **market capitalization**) and the market value of its debt on December 31, 1997. To estimate these values, we need market data for HLC's equity and debt capital on that date. Suppose HLC has 10 million shares outstanding whose price on December 31, 1997, was $90 per share. The market value of HLC's equity capital was thus $900 million ($90 multiplied by 10 million shares) on that date. Assume further that the total market value of HLC's debt on December 31, 1997, was $550 million, the same as its book value reported in Exhibit 1.8. Thus, the total market value of HLC's invested capital on December 31, 1997, was $1,450 million ($900 million of equity plus $550 million of debt). We can now find HLC's MVA— the difference between the market value of its capital and the amount of capital employed to create that value:

$$\text{MVA}_{12/31/1997} = \text{Market value of capital}_{12/31/1997} - \text{Capital employed}_{12/31/1997}$$
$$= \$1,450 \text{ million} - \$1,100 \text{ million}$$
$$\text{MVA}_{12/31/1997} = +\$350 \text{ million}$$

HLC was a value creator on December 31, 1997. Its management created $350 million of wealth to its shareholders because the $1,100 million of capital invested in the firm was worth $1,450 million on that date.

What drives value creation and MVA? A firm's MVA is positive if the market expects the firm to generate positive **economic value added,** or **EVA,** in the future. What is EVA and how is it measured? A firm's EVA is equal to the *aftertax operating profit* generated by the firm's net assets less the dollar cost of the capital employed to finance these assets.

Let's go back to HLC for an illustration. In 1997, HLC's net assets generated pretax operating profit of $240 million, as reported in its income statement in Exhibit 1.9. With a 50 percent corporate tax rate, aftertax operating profit was $120 million. To generate that profit in 1997, HLC used $1,000 million of capital, as shown in the managerial balance sheet for December 31, 1996 (Exhibit 1.8). One half of that capital was in the form of equity whose cost, we assume, is 16 percent. The other half was in the form of debt with an aftertax cost of 4 percent (the pretax cost of debt is 8 percent and the tax rate is 50 percent). HLC's weighted average cost of capital is:

$$\text{WACC} = [4\% \times 50\%] + [16\% \times 50\%] = 2\% + 8\% = 10\%$$

Therefore, the dollar cost of the $1,000 million of capital employed is $100 million (10 percent of $1,000 million). We can now find HLC's economic value added during 1997:

$$\text{EVA}_{1997} = \text{Aftertax operating profit} - \text{Dollar cost of capital employed}$$

$$EVA_{1997} = \text{Aftertax operating profit} - (\text{Capital employed} \times WACC)$$
$$= \$120 \text{ million} - (\$1{,}000 \text{ million} \times 10\%)$$
$$= \$120 \text{ million} - \$100 \text{ million}$$
$$= \$20 \text{ million}$$

HLC generated \$120 million of aftertax operating profit (sometimes referred to as **NOPAT** or **net operating profit after tax**) but "consumed" \$100 million of capital in the process. Therefore, HLC generated a positive EVA of \$20 million in 1997. As long as HLC keeps generating positive EVAs, it will create value, a phenomenon discussed in Chapter 14.

Note that if we factor out the term "capital employed" we can rewrite the equation for finding economic value added:

$$EVA = \text{Aftertax operating profit} - (\text{Capital employed} \times WACC)$$

$$EVA = \left[\frac{\text{Aftertax operating profit}}{\text{Capital employed}} - WACC\right] \times \text{Capital employed}$$

Capital employed is equal to invested capital, as shown in the managerial balance sheets in Exhibit 1.8. Thus, the ratio in the brackets is the firm's aftertax return on invested capital (ROIC), and EVA can be restated as:

$$EVA = (ROIC - WACC) \times \textbf{Invested capital}$$

HLC's ROIC in 1997 is 12 percent (\$120 of aftertax operating profit divided by \$1,000 of invested capital), so we have:

$$EVA_{1997} = [12\% - 10\%] \times \$1{,}000 \text{ million} = 2\% \times \$1{,}000 \text{ million} = \$20 \text{ million}$$

This alternative way of expressing economic value added says that EVA will be positive (negative) if the firm's return on invested capital is higher (lower) than the cost of that capital, measured by the firm's WACC. Chapter 14 examines in detail the concepts of market value added and economic value added as measures of value creation and tools for effective capital management.

SUMMARY

The ultimate objective of financial management is value creation. This simply means that before making a business decision, managers should always ask themselves the Key Question: *Will the decision raise the market value of their firm?* If, in light of existing information and proper analysis, they can confidently answer yes, then they should go ahead.

The Key Question can be answered with the help of the fundamental finance principle. This principle states that a business proposal, such as a new investment, the acquisition of another company, or a restructuring plan, will create value only if the present value of its expected future cash benefits exceeds the initial cash outlay required to undertake the proposal. In other words, a business proposal creates value only if its net present value is positive.

The fundamental finance principle can be applied to major corporate decisions, such as whether or not to invest in a new project, to modify the firm's capital structure, to acquire another company, or to invest abroad. The implementation of the principle requires the estimation of (1) the future cash-flow stream the decision is expected to generate and (2) the cost of financing the proposal. In general, both inputs are not easy to determine. Several chapters in this book are devoted to the issue of how these two inputs can be estimated because they lie at the heart of all sound financial management systems.

Financial markets are not only a source of capital to finance corporate growth but also a processor of information and an indicator of value creation. Firms, however, do not go to the financial markets to raise fresh equity every time they need additional equity capital to finance their growth. They can retain a portion of their profits and use it to meet their funding needs. Profit retention is necessary for a firm to sustain long-term growth.

Despite the fact that a firm's financial statements are prepared according to accounting conventions that generally do not reflect market values, these statements are often a useful source of information when evaluating a firm's financial performance. The example of Hologram Lighting Company (HLC) provides preliminary answers to the following six questions:

1. How fast can a firm grow without raising new equity? Look at the self-sustainable growth rate.
2. How profitable is the firm? Look at return on equity and return on invested capital.
3. How much cash is the firm generating? Look at net operating cash flow.
4. How risky is the firm? Look at business and financial risks.
5. What is the firm's cost of capital? Look at the weighted average cost of capital.
6. Is the firm creating value? Look at market value added and economic value added.

The last chapter in this book shows that these various measures of performance together with the fundamental finance principle, form the basis of a comprehensive **value-based management system.**

REFERENCES AND FURTHER READING

1. Brealey, Richard, and Stewart Myers. *Principles of Corporate Finance*. 5th ed. McGraw-Hill, 1996. See chapters 1 and 2.
2. McTaggart, James, Peter Kontes, and Micheal Mankins. *The Value Imperative*. The Free Press, 1994. See chapters 2, 3, and 4.

3. Rappaport, Alfred. *Creating Shareholder Value.* The Free Press, 1998. See chapter 1.
4. Ross, Stephen, Randolph Westerfield, and Jeffrey Jaffe. *Corporate Finance.* 4th ed. Irwin, 1996. See chapters 1 to 3.
5. Stuart, Bennett. *The Quest for Value.* HarperCollins, 1991. See chapters 1, 2, and 3.

REVIEW PROBLEMS

1.1. The fundamental finance principle.

The Pioneering Manufacturing Company (PMC) is considering the three one-year projects whose estimated net cash flows are reported below. The firm can borrow at 10 percent and is subject to a corporate tax rate of 25 percent. Its estimated cost of equity capital is 15 percent and its optimal capital structure is reached when its debt-to-equity ratio is 2/3.

PROJECT	INITIAL CASH OUTLAY	YEAR-END NET CASH BENEFITS
A	$90,000	$112,000
B	$160,000	$168,000
C	$250,000	$280,000

a. Why is PMC's cost of equity higher than its cost of debt?
b. What is PMC's weighted average cost of capital?
c. Apply the net present rule to the three projects. Which have the potential to create value if undertaken?
d. PMC's current share price is $10 and the firm has 100,000 shares outstanding. If the company announces that it has decided to undertake all three projects, how would PMC's share price react? What are the key assumptions regarding the market and the company behavior that will trigger this expected price reaction?
e. What are the three projects' estimated internal rates of return? What do these rates indicate and what can you conclude?
f. Suppose PMC decides to issue debt and use the proceeds of the sale to repurchase some of its shares in the market. Is this action expected to create or destroy value? Explain why.
g. Suppose PMC decides to issue new shares and use the proceeds of the sale to repay part of its debt. Is this action expected to create or destroy value? Explain why and contrast your answer with that of the previous question.

1.2. Cash flow and profitability analysis; capacity to grow and create value.
The balance sheets of the General Electronics Company (GEC) on December 31, 1996, and December 31, 1997, and its 1997 income statement are given below.

BALANCE SHEETS (IN MILLIONS)					
	12/31/1996	12/31/1997		12/31/1996	12/31/1997
Cash	$60	$75	Short-term debt	$70	$100
Trade debtors	180	210	Trade creditors	140	160
Inventories	120	145	Long-term debt	195	185
Net fixed assets	450	460[1]	Owners' equity	405	445[2]
Total assets	**$810**	**$890**	**Total liabilities & equity**	**$810**	**$890**

NOTES

1. New assets worth $40 million were acquired during 1997, and depreciation was $30 million. Thus, net fixed assets at year-end 1997 is $460 million, that is, ($450 + $40 − $30) million.
2. No new equity was issued in 1997. The increase in owners' equity is due to $40 million of retained earnings.

INCOME STATEMENT (IN MILLIONS)	
	YEAR 1997
Sales	**$1,600**
Operating expenses other than depreciation	(1,400)
Depreciation expenses	(30)
Earnings before interest and tax (EBIT)	**170**
Interest expenses	(30)
Earnings before tax (EBT)	**140**
Tax expenses (at 40% tax rate)	(56)
Earnings after tax (EAT) or net profit	**$84**
Retained earnings	$40
Dividend payment	$44

GEC can borrow at 10 percent and its estimated cost of equity is 16 percent. Its share price at year-end 1997 was $20 and the company had 30 million shares outstanding.

a. Restate GEC balance sheets in their managerial form. What does working capital requirement represent?

b. How much cash has been generated by operating activities during 1997? What is the cash flow from investment activities in 1997? From financing activities? Draw a cash flow statement for the year 1997.

c. What is the company's profitability from the perspective of its shareholders? Provide a profitability ratio based on each of the following: (1) beginning (1996) owners' equity; (2) average (1996 and 1997) owners' equity; and (3) ending (1997) owners' equity. Compare the three ratios.

d. What is the company's aftertax operating profitability measured by its return on invested capital? Use beginning (1996) invested capital.

e. What are the four key ratios driving GEC's business cycle?

f. If GEC does not modify its operating and financing policies, what is the maximum growth rate it can sustain?

g. How should GEC modify its operating policy if it wants to grow its sales at a faster rate than its maximum sustainable rate found in part f?

h. How should GEC modify its financing policy if it wants to grow its sales at a faster rate than its maximum sustainable rate found in part f?

i. Assuming that the market value of GEC's debt capital is the same as that of its reported book value, what is the company's estimated weighted average cost of capital on December 1997 based on (1) its market value and (2) its book value? Is there a significant difference between the two estimated WACCs? Why?

j. Has GEC created value to its shareholders as of December 1997? Explain your answer.

2 UNDERSTANDING BALANCE SHEETS AND INCOME STATEMENTS

Firms are required by regulatory authorities and the stock markets in which their shares are traded—if they are listed on a stock exchange—to provide financial information about their business transactions. The purpose of financial accounting is to systematically collect, organize, and present financial information according to standard rules known as *accounting principles* or *accounting standards*. The formal outputs of the financial accounting process are the financial statements.

This chapter presents an overview of the two most important financial statements: the balance sheet and the income statement (also called the profit and loss statement or P&L account). The approach is that of the user of the financial data, not that of the supplier. The words and expressions that are commonly employed in financial accounting are defined and the logic of and the relationship between the firm's balance sheet and its income statement are explained. After reading this chapter, you should understand:

- The terminology generally used in financial accounting.
- How balance sheets and income statements are prepared and how they are interrelated.
- The most important accounting principles used to prepare financial statements.
- How business and financial decisions affect the balance sheet and income statement.

FINANCIAL ACCOUNTING STATEMENTS

Financial statements are formal documents issued by firms to provide financial information about their business and financial transactions. Firms must regularly issue at least two primary statements: a **balance sheet** and an **income statement.** In some cases, regulatory authorities also require the firm to produce a **statement of cash flows** that provides information about the cash transactions between the firm and the outside world. This chapter examines the primary statements, leaving the analysis of cash flows to Chapter 4.

The fundamental objective of the balance sheet is to determine the value of the net investment made by the firm's owners (the **shareholders**) in their firm at a specific date. The objective of the income statement is to measure the net profit (or loss) generated by the firm's activities during a period of time referred to as the **accounting period** (usually a year). Net profit (or loss) is a measure of the *change* in the value of the owners' investment in their firm during that period of time. In other words, a profit increases the value of the owners' investment while a loss reduces it.

The balance sheet has information about what shareholders collectively own and what they owe at the date of the statement. The income statement has information about the firm's activities that resulted in increases and decreases in the value of the owners' investment during a period of time. In addition, notes are usually added to the financial statements. They provide additional information about the statements' accounts, such as their nature and the way they have been valued.

Financial statements are prepared according to **accounting standards** or **accounting principles.** These standards may differ from one country to another.[1] Furthermore, accountants have some leeway in implementing them, mostly in the valuation of some items in the balance sheet and income statement. Thus, to make meaningful comparisons between financial statements over time and across firms, it is necessary to check that the standards used and their implementation are identical from one period to another and from one firm to another. If they are not, adjustments need to be made.

Usually, firms prepare two sets of statements, one for financial reporting purposes and one for tax purposes. Only the first set of statements is public. It can be found in the **annual report** that firms publish every year and is the one examined in this chapter.[2]

To illustrate how business transactions are recorded in balance sheets and income statements and to facilitate the understanding of the logic behind these statements, we use the fictitious firm Office Supplies Distributors (OS Distributors), a nationwide distributor of office equipment and supplies. Exhibit 2.1 presents OS Distributors' balance sheets at the end of years 1995, 1996, and 1997. Notes on the balance sheets provide detailed information about some of the statements' accounts. Exhibit 2.2 shows the company's income statements for the years 1995, 1996, and 1997. Each income statement spans a full year, in this case, from

---

[1]In the United States, these standards are collectively known as Generally Accepted Accounting Principles (GAAP).

[2]In the United States, publicly held companies are required to provide another report, called the 10K, to all shareholders who request it. The 10K is a detailed version of the statements appearing in the annual report.

EXHIBIT 2.1　OS Distributors' Balance Sheets.

Figures in millions of dollars

ASSETS	DECEMBER 31, 1995		DECEMBER 31, 1996		DECEMBER 31, 1997	
• **CURRENT ASSETS**		$104.0		$119.0		$137.0
Cash[1]	$6.0		$12.0		$8.0	
Accounts receivable	44.0		48.0		56.0	
Inventories	52.0		57.0		72.0	
Prepaid expenses[2]	2.0		2.0		1.0	
• **NONCURRENT ASSETS**		56.0		51.0		53.0
Financial assets and intangibles	0.0		0.0		0.0	
Property, plant, and equipment (net)		56.0		51.0		53.0
Gross value[3]	$90.0		$90.0		$93.0	
Accumulated depreciation	(34.0)		(39.0)		(40.0)	
TOTAL ASSETS		$160.0		$170.0		$190.0
LIABILITIES AND OWNERS' EQUITY						
• **CURRENT LIABILITIES**		$54.0		$66.0		$75.0
Short-term debt						
Owed to banks	$7.0		$14.0		$15.0	
Current portion of long-term debt	8.0		8.0		8.0	
Accounts payable	37.0		40.0		48.0	
Accrued expenses[4]	2.0		4.0		4.0	
• **NONCURRENT LIABILITIES**		42.0		34.0		38.0
Long-term debt[5]	42.0		34.0		38.0	
• **Owners' equity[6]**	64.0	64.0	70.0	70.0	77.0	77.0
TOTAL LIABILITIES AND OWNERS' EQUITY		$160.0		$170.0		$190.0

Notes

1. Consists of cash in hand and checking accounts held to facilitate operating activities.
2. Prepaid expenses is rent paid in advance (when recognized in the income statement, rent is included in selling, general, and administrative expenses).
3. In 1996, there was no disposal of existing fixed assets or acquisition of new fixed assets. However, during 1997, a warehouse was enlarged at a cost of $12 million and existing fixed assets, bought for $9 million in the past, were sold at their net book value of $2 million.
4. Accrued expenses consist of wages and taxes payable.
5. Long-term debt is repaid at the rate of $8 million per year. No new long-term debt was incurred during 1996, but during 1997 a mortgage loan was obtained from the bank to finance the extension of a warehouse (see Note 3).
6. During the three years, no new shares were issued and none were repurchased.

43

EXHIBIT 2.2 OS Distributors' Income Statements.

Figures in millions of dollars

	1995	% of Sales	1996	% of Sales	1997	% of Sales
• Net sales	$390.0		$420.0		$480.0	
Cost of goods sold	($328.0)		($353.0)		($400.0)	
• Gross profit	62.0	15.9%	67.0	15.9%	80.0	16.7%
Selling, general, and administrative expenses	(39.8)		(43.7)		(48.0)	
Depreciation expenses	(5.0)		(5.0)		(8.0)	
• Operating profit	17.2	4.4%	18.3	4.4%	24.0	5.0%
Extraordinary items	0		0		0	
• Earnings before interest and tax (EBIT)	17.2	4.4%	18.3	4.4%	24.0	5.0%
Net interest expenses[1]	(5.5)		(5.0)		(7.0)	
• Earnings before tax (EBT)	11.7	3.0%	13.3	3.2%	17.0	3.5%
Income tax expense	(4.7)		(5.3)		(6.8)	
• Earnings after tax (EAT)	$7.0	1.8%	$8.0	1.9%	$10.2	2.1%
Dividends	$2.0		$2.0		$3.2	
• Retained earnings	$5.0		$6.0		$7.0	

Notes
1. There is no interest income, so net interest expenses are equal to interest expenses.

January 1 to December 31. Two balance sheets flank an income statement: an *opening*, or *beginning*, balance sheet on December 31 of the *previous* year and a *closing*, or *ending*, balance sheet on December 31 of the *same* year.[3] We have a complete set of statements for OS Distributors only for the years 1996 and 1997.

THE BALANCE SHEET

The main purpose of the balance sheet is to provide an estimate of the cumulative investment made by shareholders in their firm at a given point in time, generally at the end of the accounting period. This investment is known as **owners' equity**; it is the difference, at a particular date, between what a firm's shareholders collectively own, called **assets** (such as cash, inventories, equipment, and buildings), and what they owe, called **liabilities** (such as debts owed to banks and suppliers):

$$\text{Owners' equity} = \text{Assets} - \text{Liabilities} \tag{2.1}$$

Many other terms are used to refer to owners' equity, including **shareholders' equity, shareholders' funds, book value of equity, net worth,** and **net asset value.**

OS Distributors' balance sheet in Exhibit 2.1 is not in the format shown by equation 2.1. In the exhibit, assets are listed in one section and liabilities and owners' equity are in a different section. However, the dollar value of assets is equal to the sum of the dollar value of liabilities and owner's equity because equation 2.1 can be written as:

$$\text{Assets} = \text{Liabilities} + \text{Owners' equity} \tag{2.2}$$

According to equation 2.2, a firm's total assets must have the same value as the sum of its liabilities and owners' equity. In general, balance sheets follow the format of Exhibit 2.1 and equation 2.2.

According to accounting conventions, assets are classified in *decreasing* order of **liquidity,** where liquidity is a measure of the speed with which assets can be converted into cash. Cash, the most liquid of all assets,[4] is listed first, and land, the least liquid of all assets, is shown last. Assets are divided into two categories: **current assets** and **fixed** (or **noncurrent**) **assets.** Current assets are those assets that are expected to be turned into cash within one year while fixed assets have a life that is longer than one year.

Liabilities are listed in *increasing* order of **maturity,** where maturity is a measure of the time before the liability is due. **Short-term liabilities** are listed first and **long-term liabilities** are shown last. Liabilities are followed by owners' equity

---

[3]Note that the closing balance sheet of a given year is the same as the opening balance sheet of the following year.

[4]As the most liquid of all assets, cash is also the medium of exchange for assets and liabilities. It serves as a basis for measuring the value of all assets and liabilities.

(which does not have to be repaid because it represents the owners' investment in their firm). Liabilities are also divided into two categories: **current liabilities,** which are obligations that must be paid within one year, and **noncurrent liabilities,** which are not due until after one year.

Assets and liabilities are usually recorded according to the **conservatism principle.** According to this principle, when in doubt, assets and liabilities should be reported at a value that would be *least* likely to overstate assets or to understate liabilities.

OS Distributors' owners' equity was $64 million, $70 million, and $77 million at the end of 1995, 1996, and 1997, respectively. At each of these points in time, owners' equity was equal to the difference between the firm's total assets and its total liabilities. For example, on December 31, 1996, owners' equity was equal to the difference between total assets of $170 million and total liabilities of $100 million ($66 million of current liabilities plus $34 million of long-term debt). Note that owners' equity is a **residual value.** It is equal to whatever dollar amounts are left after deducting all the firm's liabilities from its total amount of assets. If total liabilities *exceed* total assets, owners' equity is *negative* and the firm is technically bankrupt. The following sections present a detailed analysis of the balance sheet structure.

CURRENT, OR SHORT-TERM, ASSETS

Current assets include cash and cash equivalents, accounts receivable, inventories, and prepaid expenses.

Cash and cash equivalents

Cash and cash equivalents includes cash in hand and on deposit with banks and short-term investments with a maturity not exceeding one year. These short-term investments are usually referred to as **marketable securities.** They carry little risk and are highly liquid, meaning that they can be easily sold (converted into cash) with minimal change in value, that is, with relatively small capital gain or loss. Examples of marketable securities are **certificates of deposit** issued by banks, shares in **money market funds,** short-term **government bills,** and **commercial papers** issued by corporations with good credit ratings. These securities are described in Chapter 9.

OS Distributors held $6 million in cash at the end of 1995. This amount rose to $12 million at the end of 1996 and then fell to $8 million at the end of 1997 (see Exhibit 2.1). Chapter 4 examines in detail why OS Distributors experienced these particular movements in its cash holdings. Note that OS Distributors did not hold any marketable securities at the dates of the balance sheets.

Accounts receivable

Most firms do not receive immediate cash payments for their goods or services. They usually let their customers pay their invoices at a later date. The invoices that have not yet been paid by customers at the date of the balance sheet are recorded as **accounts receivable,** also called **trade receivables** or, simply, **receivables.** Accounts receivable are debts owed to the firm by its customers and, for this reason, are also known as **trade debtors.** These assets will be converted into cash when customers pay their bills. The amount is usually reported *net* of advances from customers and of **allowances for doubtful accounts.** Doubtful accounts arise when it is expected that some customers will not meet their payment obligations.

OS Distributors' receivables have grown steadily during the three-year period, rising from $44 million at the end of 1995 to $56 million at the end of 1997 (see Exhibit 2.1). Chapter 3 examines whether this phenomenon should be a cause of concern or whether it is justified by the firm's activity.

Inventories

Inventories are goods held by the firm for future sales (finished goods) or for use in the manufacturing of goods to be sold at a later date (raw materials and work in process). Thus, a manufacturing firm normally has three inventory accounts: one for raw materials, one for work in process, and a third for finished goods. Inventories are reported in the balance sheet at cost unless their market value has fallen below their cost. If, for example, some inventories have become obsolete and have an estimated liquidation value lower than their cost, then the firm should report these inventories at their (lower) estimated value. This method, called the **lower-of-cost-or-market,** is an example of the conservatism principle mentioned earlier.

The cost assigned to materials that have not yet entered the production process at the date of the balance sheet is reported as **raw materials inventory.** In addition, some of the units in production may not yet have been completed. The cost of the raw materials that were used in the production of these units plus the labor and other costs applicable to these unfinished units make up the **work in process inventory.** Finally, the cost of completed units not yet sold at the date of the balance sheet constitutes the **finished goods inventory.**

Inventories for OS Distributors consist of goods purchased from manufacturers and stored in its warehouses until sold to retail stores. Like receivables, inventories have grown during the period 1995 to 1997; they rose from $52 million at the end of 1995 to $72 million at the end of 1997. Again, Chapter 3 examines whether this growth should be worrisome or whether it is justified by the firm's operations.

The growth in inventories could be due to an increase in the price of the items purchased by OS Distributors from its suppliers for resale to its customers. Suppose it paid $100 for an item purchased two weeks ago, $101 for the same item purchased last week, and $102 for the same item purchased this week. OS Distributors holds three identical items in its inventory but paid a different price for each of them. When it sells one of these items to a customer, a question arises: Which one has it sold? The first ($100), the second ($101), or the third ($102)?

If OS Distributors uses the **first-in, first-out** (or **FIFO**) **method** to measure the cost of its inventories, it will assume that it sold the first item it acquired ($100). If it uses the **last-in, first-out** (or **LIFO**) **method,** it will assume it sold the last item it acquired ($102). Alternatively, OS Distributors could use the **average cost method.** In this case, it will assume it sold an item at the average of the three prices ($101). The implication is clear: The firm's financial statements will be different depending on which of the three valuation methods is adopted. After the sale of one item, there are two left in inventories. With FIFO, the reported value of the remaining two items is $203 ($101 plus $102); with LIFO, the value is $201 ($100 plus $101); and with averaging, the value is $202 ($101 plus $101). Furthermore, if we assume that the item was sold to a customer for $110, the reported gross profit will be $10 with FIFO ($110 less $100), $8 with LIFO ($110 less $102), and $9 with the average cost method ($110 less $101). Compared to LIFO, FIFO *overstates* both the value of inventories ($203 instead of $201) and reported gross profits ($10 instead of $8).

Prepaid expenses

Prepaid expenses recorded on a balance sheet are payments made by the firm for goods or services it will receive *after* the date of the balance sheet. A typical example is the payment for an insurance policy that will provide protection for a period of time that extends beyond the date of the balance sheet. It is recorded as a prepaid expense because the payment is made before the firm can benefit from the insurance coverage. Other common prepaid expenses include prepaid rent and leases. OS Distributors' balance sheets in Exhibit 2.1 indicate that the firm had $2 million of prepaid expenses at the end of 1995 and 1996 and $1 million at the end of 1997.

The way prepaid expenses are accounted for illustrates a key accounting principle, known as the **matching principle.** This principle states that expenses are recognized (in the income statement) not when they are paid but during the period when they effectively contribute to the firm's revenues. Expenses *prepaid* by the firm must be carried in its balance sheet as an asset until they become a recognized expense in its (future) income statement.

Suppose, for example, that on January 1, 1992, OS Distributors paid rent for three years, including rent for 1992. The rent for the first year (1992) would be recorded as an expense in the 1992 income statement. The remaining two thirds of the total rent paid on January 1, 1992, and not "consumed" on that date, would be reported as prepaid expenses in the balance sheet at the end of 1992. In the balance sheet at the end of 1993, prepaid rent would represent only one third of the total rent payment. On December 31, 1994, the total rent payment would be completely "consumed" and no prepaid rent would appear in the balance sheet on that date.

NONCURRENT, OR FIXED, ASSETS

Noncurrent assets, also called fixed or **capital assets,** are assets that are expected to produce economic benefits for more than one year. These assets are of two types: tangible and intangible. **Tangible assets** include items such as land, buildings, machines, and furniture, collectively called **property, plant, and equipment.** They also include long-term financial assets, such as shares in other companies and loans extended to other firms. **Intangible assets** include items such as patents, trademarks, copyrights, and goodwill.

Tangible assets

Nonfinancial tangible assets are generally reported at their **historical cost,** which is, the price the firm paid for them. As time passes, the value of these assets is expected to decrease. In order to account for this loss of value, their purchase price, reported in the balance sheet as the **gross value** of fixed assets, is systematically reduced (or written down) over their expected useful life.[5] This periodic and systematic value-reduction process is called **depreciation.** If depreciation is done on a yearly basis, the dollar amount by which the gross value of fixed assets is reduced is called annual **depreciation charges** or **expenses.** This dollar amount is determined by the length of the period over which the asset is depreciated and the speed with which depreciation takes place.

Several methods are used to determine the annual depreciation charge. The most commonly used is the **straight-line depreciation method.** When this method is used, the firm's assets are depreciated by an equal amount each year. According to the less frequently used **accelerated depreciation method,** the depreciation charge is higher in the early years of the asset's life and lower in the later years. The *total* amount that is depreciated is the same regardless of the depreciation method used; it is equal to the acquisition cost of the asset, assuming that the asset will be worthless at the end of the period over which it is depreciated.

To illustrate the effect of different depreciation methods, consider a firm that paid $300,000 at the beginning of the year for a machine that will be fully depreciated over a period of three years. Although the $300,000 was paid during the year the asset was bought, this amount is not recognized as an expense for that year. If a straight-line depreciation schedule is applied, one third of the equipment cost is depreciated every year and the annual depreciation charge is equal to one third of $300,000, that is, $100,000. An accelerated depreciation schedule would call for half the cost of the equipment to be depreciated the first year, one third the second year, and one sixth the third year. The annual depreciation charges would then be $150,000 the first year (one half of $300,000), $100,000 the second year (one third of $300,000) and $50,000 the third year (one sixth of $300,000).

The value at which a fixed asset is reported in the balance sheet is its **net book value.** If the firm applies the **historical** or **acquisition cost principle** to value its fixed assets, then the net book value of a fixed asset is equal to its acquisition price less the accumulated depreciation since that asset was bought. In the

---

[5]Note that plant and equipment are systematically depreciated but not land. It is assumed that the value of land does not decline with the passage of time.

EXHIBIT 2.3   Computation of Net Book Value for Two Depreciation Methods.

Figures in thousands of dollars

	Straight-line method			Accelerated method		
	Year 1	Year 2	Year 3	Year 1	Year 2	Year 3
Gross value (acquisition cost)	$300	$300	$300	$300	$300	$300
Annual depreciation charge	($100)	($100)	($100)	($150)	($100)	($50)
Accumulated depreciation	(100)	(200)	(300)	(150)	(250)	(300)
Net book value	$200	$100	$0	$150	$50	$0

above example, the net book value of the equipment at the end of each year after the asset was bought is computed as shown in Exhibit 2.3 for the two depreciation methods.

In some countries, for example the Netherlands, companies listed on the stock exchange can choose to value their assets at their **replacement cost** instead of their historical cost. According to the **replacement cost principle,** the net book value of an asset is equal to the price the firm *would have to pay* at the date of the balance sheet to replace that asset less the amount of accumulated depreciation. The depreciation *method* is the same as the one used when the historical cost principle is applied. The depreciation *expenses,* however, are different because the value of the assets to be depreciated is no longer the same.

Consider the machine in the above example. Under the acquisition cost principle and the three-year straight-line depreciation schedule, its net book value was $200,000 at the end of the first year (acquisition price of $300,000 less accumulated depreciation of $100,000). Assume that it would have cost $330,000 to replace it at that date. Under the replacement cost principle, the base price on which the straight-line depreciation schedule must be applied is no longer the price at which the machine was bought ($300,000) but its replacement value of $330,000. Accordingly, the annual depreciation charge is now $110,000 (one third of $330,000) and not $100,000 (one third of $300,000). As a result, the net book value of the asset would be $220,000 (base price of $330,000 less accumulated depreciation of $110,000) instead of $200,000.

The above examples clearly illustrate that fixed asset values reported in the balance sheet can differ considerably, depending on the valuation principle used and the depreciation method applied. It is therefore important to check both before comparing the financial performance of different firms on the basis of their financial statements.

Intangible assets

Intangible assets include patents, copyrights, property rights, franchises, licenses, and goodwill. When one firm acquires the assets of another for a price higher than the net book value in the acquired firm's balance sheet, this difference is **goodwill.** For example, suppose Firm A pays $10 million for the assets of Firm B, and the net book value of those assets is $7 million. This transaction creates $3 million of goodwill on the balance sheet of Firm A.

Intangible assets are recorded at cost. As in the case of tangible assets, their value is usually gradually reduced as time passes. This cost reduction process, called **amortization,** follows the same principles as depreciation for tangible assets.

OS Distributors' noncurrent assets

We can now examine the structure of OS Distributors' fixed assets, as reported in Exhibit 2.1. They include only property, plant, and equipment. Their net book value was $56 million at the end of 1995, $51 million at the end of 1996, and $53 million at the end of 1997. Annual depreciation charges, recorded as expenses in OS Distributors' income statements in Exhibit 2.2, were $5 million, $5 million, and $8 million, respectively.

At the end of 1995, the book value of OS Distributors' fixed assets before depreciation (their gross value) was $90 million. This was the price paid when these assets were acquired. Accumulated depreciation was $34 million, so the net book value of the firm's fixed assets was $56 million, the difference between their gross value ($90 million) and accumulated depreciation ($34 million).

During 1996, there were no changes in fixed assets, so their gross value remained at $90 million. (See Note 3 in Exhibit 2.1.) Net fixed assets, however, dropped to $51 million because accumulated depreciation increased to $39 million, the sum of accumulated depreciation at the end of 1995 ($34 million) and the additional depreciation charges in 1996 ($5 million).

During 1997, OS Distributors enlarged its warehouse at a cost of $12 million. That same year the firm sold a piece of equipment no longer needed at its net book value of $2 million. (The equipment was bought some time ago for $9 million and had been depreciated by $7 million.) What was the effect of these two transactions on the value of net fixed assets at the end of 1997? The gross value of the fixed assets increased by $12 million when the warehouse was enlarged and decreased by $9 million when the equipment no longer needed was sold. Together, these two transactions increased the gross value of the fixed assets from $90 million at the end of 1996 to $93 million at the end of 1997 ($90 million plus $12 million less $9 million), as shown in Exhibit 2.1. At the same time, accumulated depreciation increased by $8 million (the 1997 depreciation charge) and decreased by $7 million (the recorded accumulated depreciation of the piece of equipment that was sold the same year). Thus, accumulated depreciation increased to $40 million ($39 million of initial accumulated depreciation plus $8 million less $7 million). Consequently, the net book value of OS Distributors' fixed assets at the end of 1997 was equal to $53 million ($93 million less $40 million).

We could have obtained the same net book value of $53 million in a different way: Start with the $51 million of net fixed assets at the end of 1996, add the $12 million cost of the warehouse extension, and subtract both the net book value of the piece of equipment that was sold ($2 million) and the 1997 depreciation charge of $8 million ($51 million plus $12 million less $2 million less $8 million equals $53 million). More generally:

Net fixed assets at the end of a period =
Net fixed assets at the beginning of the period
+ Gross value of fixed assets acquired during the period
− Net book value of fixed assets sold during the period
− Depreciation charges for the period   (2.3)

CURRENT, OR SHORT-TERM, LIABILITIES

Current liabilities include short-term debt, accounts payable, and accrued expenses.

Short-term debt

Short-term debt, also called **notes payable,** include bank **overdrafts, drawings** on **lines of credit,** and short-term **promissory notes.** The portion of any long-term debt due within a year is also a short-term obligation and is recorded in the balance sheet as short-term borrowings.

OS Distributors' short-term borrowings consist of debt owed to banks and the portion of long-term debt repaid by the firm at the rate of $8 million per year from 1995 to 1997. In total, short-term borrowing grew from $15 million at the end of 1995 to $23 million at the end of 1997.

Accounts payable

Accounts payable, also called **trade payables** or, simply, **payables,** are liabilities to the firm's suppliers of goods and services. Payables arise because the firm does not usually pay its suppliers immediately for the goods and services received from them. As a result, there is a time lag between the receipt of goods or services and payment for them. Until payment is made, the firm must recognize in its balance sheet the credit extended by its suppliers (for this reason, payables are also known as **trade creditors**). Accounts payable are equal to the dollar value of the invoices the firm has received from its suppliers but has not yet paid at the date of the balance sheet.

The balance sheets in Exhibit 2.1 show that OS Distributors' payables have increased from $37 million at the end of 1995 to $48 million at the end of 1997. Is that increase justified? This question is examined in the next chapter.

Accrued expenses

Accrued expenses are liabilities other than short-term debt and accounts payable that are associated with the firm's operations. They arise from the lag between the date at which these expenses have been incurred and the date at which they are paid. Examples are taxes, wages, and Social Security contributions that are due but have not yet been paid on the date of the balance sheet. Note that the allocation of expenses to the accrued expenses account in the balance sheet is another application of the matching principle.

OS Distributors' accrued expenses were $2 million at year-end 1995 and $4 million at the end of years 1996 and 1997. They consist of wages and taxes payable. **Wages payable** represents compensation for vacation days owed to OS Distributors' employees that had not yet been taken at the date of the balance sheets. OS Distributors must recognize its "debt" to its employees as wages payable in its balance sheet. Similarly, **taxes payable** are the amount of taxes owed at the date of the balance sheets. They are a debt to the tax collection agency and are recognized as taxes payable in the balance sheet until the firm pays its tax bill.

NONCURRENT LIABILITIES

Long-term liabilities reported on the balance sheet are liabilities with a maturity longer than one year at the date of the balance sheet. Examples of long-term liabilities include **long-term debt** owed to lenders, **pension liabilities** owed to employees (to be paid to them when they retire), and **deferred taxes** owed to the government's tax collection agency.

Deferred taxes originate from the difference between the amount of tax due on the firm's reported pretax profit and the amount of tax claimed by the tax authorities. These two measures of tax due may differ because firms usually depreciate their fixed assets on a straight-line basis in their financial statements but the tax authorities usually apply accelerated depreciation schedules to the same assets in order to determine the amount of taxes the firm must pay. Depreciation is a tax-deductible expense, so the two approaches can produce different taxable income and, thus, different tax expenses.

Consider a firm with $1,000,000 of revenues and $700,000 of expenses *before* depreciation charges are deducted. If depreciation charges are $100,000 on the basis of a straight-line depreciation schedule and $150,000 on the basis of an accelerated depreciation schedule, then profit before tax is $200,000 in the first case ($1,000,000 less $700,000 less $100,000) and $150,000 in the second ($1,000,000 less $700,000 less $150,000). If the tax rate is 40 percent, then the amount of tax is $80,000 (40 percent of $200,000) when straight-line depreciation is used and is $60,000 (40 percent of $150,000) when accelerated depreciation is used. In other words, the firm reports a tax expense of $80,000 in its income statement but actually owes only $60,000 in taxes. The difference of $20,000 between the two tax estimates represents a *postponement* not an *elimination* of the tax owed to the collecting agency. The amount that is depreciated (the asset acquisition price) and the total amount that is deductible are the same in both cases; hence, the $20,000 must be recognized as a liability in the firm's balance sheet.[6]

OS Distributors had an outstanding (not yet repaid) long-term debt of $50 million at the end of 1995. However, the firm repays $8 million of this debt every year and this amount is recorded as a short-term borrowing (current portion of long-term debt). As a result, the long-term debt in the 1995 balance sheet was equal to only $42 million ($50 million less $8 million). At the end of 1996, the firm had repaid $8 million of its outstanding debt, but it still owed $42 million, $8 million of which was due in 1997. Consequently, its long-term debt at that date was $34 million ($42 million less $8 million) and the current portion of its long-term debt was $8 million.

In 1997, the firm borrowed $12 million to finance the extension of its warehouse. As a consequence, long-term debt increased by $12 million in 1997 while still decreasing by the annual repayment of $8 million. Therefore, the long-term debt at the end of 1997 was equal to $38 million (the initial $34 million less $8 million to be repaid during the year plus $12 million of new debt). In general:

Long-term debt at the end of a period =
Long-term debt at the beginning of the period
− Portion of long-term debt repaid during the period
+ New long-term debt issued during the period   (2.4)

OWNERS' EQUITY

As shown in equation 2.1, owners' equity at the date of the balance sheet is simply the difference between the book value of the firm's assets and liabilities at that same date. The book value of the investment made in the firm by OS Distributors' owners is reported at the bottom of the balance sheets in Exhibit 2.1. Owners' equity has grown from $64 million at the end of 1995 to $77 million at the end of 1997.

In most balance sheets, the owners' equity account shows several components, each representing a source of equity. Because one of these sources is the firm's profit, we postpone the presentation of the components of owners' equity (and the reason for the growth of OS Distributors' equity) until after the firm's income statement is discussed.

---

[6]Compared to the straight-line depreciation method, accelerated depreciation schedules overestimate depreciation expenses (underestimate profit before tax) during the beginning of the life of an asset, and likewise underestimate depreciation expenses (overestimate profit before tax) towards the end of the asset's life. Accordingly, the firm pays less taxes during the early years and more taxes towards the last years of the asset's life.

THE INCOME STATEMENT

The purpose of the income statement, also called the **profit and loss** or **P&L statement,** is to present a summary of the operating and financial transactions that have contributed to the change in the firm's owners' equity during the accounting period. The accounting period is usually one year, but limited versions of the income statement can be produced more frequently, as often as quarterly.

We define **revenues** as the transactions that increase owners' equity and **expenses** as the transactions that decrease it during the accounting period.[7] It follows that the net change in owners' equity during that period, known as **net income, net profit,** or, as shown in Exhibit 2.2, **earnings after tax (EAT),** is simply:

$$\text{Earnings after tax} = \text{Revenues} - \text{Expenses} \qquad (2.5)$$

This relationship is the model used to construct a firm's income statement. The firm's revenues are recorded first. They originate from many sources, including the sales of goods and services and the collection of fees and rental income. Then the firm's expenses are listed. They include material costs, depreciation charges, salaries, wages, administrative and marketing expenses, and interest and tax expenses. Expenses are deducted from revenues in a multiple-step procedure in order to measure the contribution of different activities to the firm's earnings after tax (see Exhibit 2.2). The revenues and expenses related to the firm's operating activities are shown first, and then those related to nonoperating activities, such as financing. Finally, the tax expenses are reported. A detailed explanation of the structure of a firm's income statement is given in the following sections.

Among the many accounting principles used to construct financial statements, two are of particular importance in understanding the income statement. First is the **realization principle,** which says that a revenue is recognized during the period when the transaction generating the revenue takes place, *not when the cash from the transaction is received.* In other words, the firm's revenues increase when a product it sells or a service it renders is invoiced or sent to the customer, not when the cash payment takes place. Revenues are unaffected when payment is made for the product or service. When the payment is received, the firm adjusts its balance sheet accordingly: Cash rises by the amount received and accounts receivable decreases by the same amount.

The second principle is the matching principle, which was explained in the discussion of the valuation of prepaid expenses. According to this principle, expenses associated with a product or service are recognized when the product is sold or the service rendered, *not when the expense is actually paid.* For example, consider a distribution company that purchases an item from a wholesaler, stocks it, and then

---

[7]There is one exception to these definitions. The issuance of new shares increases owners' equity and the repurchase of outstanding shares decreases it. These transactions, however, are not recorded in the firm's income statement as revenue or expense.

sells it. Expenses will increase during the period when the item is sold, not when it was purchased and not when the company paid for it.

The realization and matching principles form the basis of what is known as **accrual accounting.** A consequence of accrual accounting is that a firm's earnings after tax is *not* equal to the difference between the firm's cash inflows and outflows that occurred during the accounting period (the firm's **net cash flow**). For example, the fact that OS Distributors realized a net profit of $10.2 million in 1997 does not mean that the firm has generated $10.2 million of cash during that year. A detailed analysis of the relationship between a firm's profits and its cash flows is presented in Chapter 4.

NET SALES

For most firms, sales are the main source of revenues. The revenues of the accounting period, net of any discounts and allowances for defective merchandise, make up the **net sales** account. OS Distributors' sales grew 7.7 percent during 1996, from $390 million in 1995 to $420 million in 1996. Sales rose to $480 million in 1997. Thus, the growth rate in 1997 was 14.3 percent, almost double the 1996 growth rate. The next chapter examines the consequences of this acceleration in the growth rate in sales on the firm's income statement and balance sheet.

Cost of goods sold

The **cost of goods sold (COGS),** sometimes called **cost of sales,** represents the cost of the goods the firm has sold during the accounting period. For a distribution company, such as OS Distributors, the cost of goods sold is the acquisition price of the items sold from inventory plus any direct costs related to these items. In a manufacturing firm, goods incur various costs in the process of transformation from raw material to finished product, such as labor costs and manufacturing overhead. These costs make up the value of the finished goods inventory. They become cost of goods sold when the goods are released from inventory for sale. Depreciation expenses on plant and equipment are often included in the cost of goods sold, although some firms report depreciation as a separate account in their income statement.

OS Distributors' cost of goods sold consists of goods purchased from manufacturers for resale to retailers. (Depreciation expenses on the firm's warehouses are shown separately.) Cost of goods sold rose from $328 million in 1995 to $400 million in 1997.

GROSS PROFIT

Gross profit is the first and broadest measure of the firm's profit shown in its income statement. It is the difference between the firm's net sales and its cost of goods sold. OS Distributors' gross profit was $62 million in 1995, $67 million in 1996, and $80 million in 1997. Gross profit rose from 15.9 percent of sales in 1995 to 16.7 percent of sales in 1997 because the firm's cost of goods sold grew at a slower rate than sales.

Selling, general, and administrative expenses

Selling, general, and administrative expenses (SG&A's), sometimes referred to as **overhead expenses** or simply **overhead,** are the expenses incurred by the firm that relate to the sale of its products and the running of its operations during the accounting period. Expenses related to the training of salespeople are an example of overhead. For OS Distributors, selling, general, and administrative expenses amounted to $39.8 million in 1995, $43.7 million in 1996, and $48 million in 1997.

Depreciation expenses

Depreciation expenses are the depreciation charges defined in the discussion of the balance sheet. They represent the portion of the cost of fixed assets that is allocated to the accounting period. When a fixed asset is purchased, the firm incurs a *cost* equal to the purchase price. This cost is recorded in the balance sheet as the gross value of the fixed asset. It is then charged or "expensed" (according to a depreciation schedule) over the years during which the asset is expected to generate some benefits. The amount expensed during each accounting period is recorded in the income statement in the depreciation expenses account.

If the firm expensed the full cost of a fixed asset the same year it acquired it, the matching principle would be violated. A fixed asset, by definition, generates benefits beyond the year in which it was purchased. Thus, allocating its full cost to the purchase year would cause a mismatch between expenses and revenues for a number of years.

OPERATING PROFIT

Operating profit is a measure of the firm's profit from operations that takes into account all of the firm's recorded expenses related to its operating activities: its cost of goods sold, its SG&A's, and its depreciation expenses. It is the difference between the firm's gross profit and the sum of the SG&A's and depreciation expenses. It measures the profit generated by the firm's normal and recurrent business activities before interest expenses and taxes. OS Distributors generated an operating profit of $17.2 million in 1995, $18.3 million in 1996, and $24 million in 1997. Operating profit, measured as a percentage of sales, has risen from 4.4 percent of sales in 1995 to 5 percent of sales in 1997.

Extraordinary items

This account represents the balance of the gains and losses that result from infrequent business transactions not directly related to the firm's recurrent activities during the accounting period. For example, extraordinary items include the profit or loss made from selling land or properties and the destruction of assets resulting from a fire or other calamity.

EARNINGS BEFORE INTEREST AND TAX (EBIT)

Earnings before interest and tax, or **EBIT,** is the firm's operating profit less any extraordinary losses plus any extraordinary gains reported in its income statement. It is a measure of a firm's profits before taking into account the interest expenses it has incurred on its borrowings and the taxes it owes. Hence, it is not affected by either the firm's decision to borrow or the incidence of taxation on its profits. Chapter 5 shows that earnings before interest and tax plays an important role in the analysis of a firm's profitability because it enables the comparison of profitability for firms with different debt policies and tax obligations.

Earnings before interest and tax is shared among three claimants according to a legally established order. Lenders are the first claimants; they are entitled to receive interest income on the loans they extended to the firm. Then, the tax authority collects the tax the firm owes. Finally, the firm's owners are entitled to whatever is left. Because there are no extraordinary items reported in OS Distributors' income statements, its earnings before interest and tax is the same as its operating profit.

Net interest expenses

Net interest expenses is the difference between the interest expenses incurred by the firm on its borrowings and any income it received from its financial investments during the accounting period. OS Distributors has no interest income; hence, the firm's net interest expenses are equal to its total interest expenses.

EARNINGS BEFORE TAX (EBT)

Earnings before tax, or **EBT,** is the difference between the firm's earnings before interest and tax (EBIT) and its net interest expenses. It is a measure of a firm's profits before taking taxation into account. OS Distributors' earnings before taxes were $11.7 million in 1995, $13.3 million in 1996, and $17 million in 1997. Expressed as a percentage of sales, EBT grew from 3 percent of sales in 1995 to 3.5 percent of sales in 1997. This improvement in the firm's pretax profits in comparison to its sales is analyzed in detail in Chapter 5.

Income tax expense

The **income tax expense** account is a tax provision computed in accordance with the firm's accounting rules. As mentioned earlier, this tax provision frequently differs from the actual income tax that the firm must pay. The difference is accounted for in the deferred tax account in the balance sheet. OS Distributors has no deferred taxes. Tax expenses are thus equal to 40 percent of the firm's pretax profits.

EARNINGS AFTER TAX (EAT)

Earnings after tax, or **EAT,** is obtained by deducting the firm's income tax expense from its reported pretax profits, or earnings before tax (EBT). It is the firm's net profit or net income, often referred to as the firm's **bottom line.** When earnings after tax is positive, the firm has generated a profit and is said to be **in the black.** When its earnings after tax is negative, the firm has generated a loss and is said to be **in the red.** More precisely, earnings after tax is a measure of the net change in owners' equity resulting from the transactions recorded in the income statement during the accounting period.

OS Distributors' earnings after tax was $7 million in 1995, $8 million in 1996, and $10.2 million in 1997. As a percentage of sales, it has grown from 1.8 percent in 1995 to 2.1 percent in 1997. Are the levels and growth rates of OS Distributors' earnings after tax adequate? The answer to this important question is the topic of Chapter 5.

RECONCILING BALANCE SHEETS AND INCOME STATEMENTS

Transactions other than those recorded in the income statement affect owners' equity. When a firm declares a **cash dividend** be paid to its owners, the book value of owners' equity in the firm's balance sheet decreases by the amount of the declared dividend. Thus, the *net* increase in owners' equity is the difference between earnings after tax and dividends. This difference is called **retained earnings.** When a firm sells (issues) new shares during the accounting period, the amount raised, less issuance costs, increases the firm's owners' equity. Conversely, when a firm repurchases some of its own shares, the amount paid to the shareholders who tender their shares, less transaction costs, decreases the firm's owners' equity. In general:

Net change in owners' equity = Earnings after tax − Dividends
$$+ \textbf{ Amount raised by new share issuance}$$
$$- \textbf{ Amount paid for share repurchase}$$

(2.6)

OS Distributors did not issue or repurchase shares during the three-year period from 1995 to 1997. (See Note 6 in Exhibit 2.1.) As a result, each year's change in owners' equity was exactly equal to the retained earnings from that year. Retained earnings are reported at the bottom of Exhibit 2.2. OS Distributors retained $5 million of its net earnings at the end of 1995, $6 million at the end of 1996, and $7 million at the end of 1997. Therefore, owners' equity at the end of 1996 was equal to $70 million, the sum of owners' equity at the end of 1995 ($64 million) and earnings retained in 1996 ($6 million). At the end of 1997, owners' equity had grown to $77 million, the sum of owners' equity at the end of 1996 ($70 million) and earnings retained in 1997 ($7 million).

The link between a firm's balance sheets and its income statements is illustrated in Exhibit 2.4 for OS Distributors. On the left side of this exhibit is OS Distributors' balance sheet drawn up on December 31, 1996, and on the right side is its balance sheet drawn up on December 31, 1997. Between the two balance sheets is the income statement for the year 1997. The balance sheet identity, expressed in equation 2.2, is illustrated by showing the book value of the firm's assets on the left side and the sum of its liabilities and owners' equity on the other side. The income statement identity, expressed in equation 2.5, is illustrated by showing the firm's revenues on the left side and the sum of its expenses and its reported profits on the other side.

OS Distributors generated sales of $480 million during 1997, using for that purpose an initial amount of assets equal to $170 million (as indicated on the balance sheet at the end of 1996). After deducting $469.8 million of total expenses from its sales, OS Distributors reported a year-end net profit of $10.2 million in 1997. It retained $7 million of that profit and declared a dividend of $3.2 million. Because it had not raised new equity in 1997, the firm's owners' equity increased at the end of 1997 to $77 million, the sum of its original owners' equity of $70 million and the retained profit of $7 million.

THE STRUCTURE OF THE OWNERS' EQUITY ACCOUNT

Our analysis of owners' equity has shown that the *changes* in owners' equity come from earnings that are retained, net of any new issues of equity or any share repurchases that occurred during the accounting period. The owners' equity account in the balance sheet represents the accumulated contribution of these changes over many accounting periods, from the date at which the firm was created until the date of the balance sheet. To help clarify the origin of its equity, most firms provide a breakdown of their owners' equity into separate accounts that identify the different sources of equity. The most common items making up the owners' equity account are shown in Exhibit 2.5, which presents a detailed account of OS Distributors' owners' equity at year-end 1997.

The first source of equity shown is **common stock.** The dollar amount is the number of shares the firm has issued since its creation multiplied by the **par value,** or **stated value,** of the shares. The par value of a common stock is an *arbitrary* fixed

EXHIBIT 2.4 OS Distributors: The Link Between the Balance Sheets and the Income Statement.

Figures in millions of dollars and data from Exhibit 2.1 and Exhibit 2.2

Balance Sheet
December 31, 1996

| Assets $170 | Liabilities $100 |
| | Owners' equity $70 |

Income Statement
Year 1997

| Revenues $480 | Expenses $469.8 |
| | Net Profit $10.2 |

Dividends $3.2

Balance Sheet
December 31, 1997

| Assets $190 | Liabilities $113 |
| | Owners' equity $77 |

Retained earnings $7

EXHIBIT 2.5   OS Distributors Owners' Equity on December 31, 1997.

Figures in millions of dollars

	DECEMBER 31, 1997
Owners' equity	**$77**
Common stock	$10
10,000,000 shares at par value of $1	
Paid-in capital in excess of par	20
Accumulated retained earnings	47
(Treasury stocks)	(0)

value attached to each share of stock. Unrelated to the market price of a share of common stock, par value is the amount that was set by those who created the firm and is stated in the firm's charter. It represents the maximum liability of the owner of the share in the event of the firm's dissolution. OS Distributors had 10 million shares outstanding at the end of 1997, and each of the firm's shares has a par value of $1. Thus, the firm's common stock was recorded at $10 million at the end of 1997.

The second source of equity shown is **paid-in capital in excess of par.** This is the difference between the cumulative amount of cash that the firm received from shares issued up to the date of the balance sheet and the cash it would have received if those shares had been issued at par value. The paid-in capital of OS Distributors was $20 million at the end of 1997, indicating the firm issued shares in the past that were sold at prices higher than $1. Suppose, for example, that one million shares were sold five years ago for $5 each. That year, OS Distributors' paid-in capital in excess of par increased by $4 million, one million shares multiplied by the difference between $5 and a par value of $1.

The third source of equity, **accumulated retained earnings** or **reserves,** is the total amount of retained earnings since the creation of the firm. For OS Distributors, this "earned" capital amounted to $47 million at the end of 1997.

The last account, **treasury stock,** is subtracted from the previous ones. It represents the amount the firm spent to repurchase its own shares up to the date of the balance sheet. OS Distributors has not repurchased any of its shares, so this account remains equal to zero.

SUMMARY

This chapter explains how a firm's balance sheet and income statement are prepared, what type of information they provide, and how they are related to each other. The next three chapters show how this information is used to assess the business and financial performance of firms.

The usefulness of financial statements, however, is often limited by the relative quality of the information they contain. Financial statements are prepared according to principles and rules that are not necessarily applied in the same fashion and with the same rigor by all firms. Furthermore, accounting rules differ from country to country and even from industry to industry within the same country, making intercountry and interindustry comparisons often quite challenging. Thus, to make meaningful comparisons between financial statements over time and across firms, it is necessary to check that the standards used and their implementations are identical from one period to another and from one firm to another. If they are not, adjustments need to be made.

For these reasons, a firm's financial statements should be interpreted with a critical eye. You should never take a firm's reported profit figures or asset values at face value. Always ask yourself how they were generated and which rules were used to estimate them. This point is clearly illustrated in Exhibit 2.6 with the case of the Singer Company.

EXHIBIT 2.6   How to Spot the Seams at Singer*

Investors love a good story, and Singer Co. has all the makings of a best-seller: a strong brand name, operating in exploding consumer markets such as China and India and plenty of fans on Wall Street. Singer, which is synonymous with sewing machines, also uses its name to sell televisions, refrigerators and washing machines in more than 100 countries.

Analysts rave about the company's consistent earnings, which have risen for 23 consecutive quarters. James G. Ting, 44, the Chinese-Canadian businessman who took over Singer in 1989, wants people to consider the stock as much a blue-chip as Du Pont Co. or Coca-Cola Co.

Singer, however, is not the real thing. Without doing anything illegal, and with the blessing of auditors at Ernst & Young, the company employs a myriad of tactics to brighten its profit picture. Nearly one-fifth of the $98.5 million that the company earned last year came from sources other than basic operations: asset sales, one-time investment gains and interest income and fees from affiliated companies.

Singer's story provides clear examples of reasons that investors need to look at more than just the bottom line to determine the quality of a company's earnings.

The basic lessons:

• **Profits can be too predictable.** Wall Street hates to be surprised, and Singer has a history of meeting analysts' earnings-per-share expectations quarter after quarter almost to the penny.

Only the devaluation of the Mexican peso caused the company to miss the mark by 9 cents when it reported fourth-quarter 1994 results—the first time Singer's earnings had significantly trailed expectations since it went public in 1991.

Whenever a company's profit projections are so completely on target, however, investors should wonder how it is pulling off the feat—especially when it is subject to wildly fluctuating currencies.

EXHIBIT 2.6   (Continued)

• **Family ties can be too close.**
Investors should also look out when
much of a company's business involves
dealings with related businesses.
Singer has close ties to a Canadian
holding company, Semi-Tech Corp.,
and Mr. Ting is chairman of both
companies.

Semi-Tech (Global) Ltd., a Hong
Kong-based company also headed by
Mr. Ting, bought Singer in 1989 from a
group including Paul A. Bilzerian, the
former Singer chairman who was
convicted that year of securities fraud
and sentenced to four years in prison.
Semi-Tech later sold a majority of
Singer's shares to the public. Almost
half of Singer's stock is still owned by
Semi-Tech, however; and only two of
its eight directors are not linked to
Semi-Tech. "It's very incestuous", said
Howard Schilit, who heads the Center
for Financial Research and Analysis in
Rockville, Maryland.

Singer seems to use these
relationships to particular advantage.
For instance, Semi-Tech Global, a
company in which Semi-Tech Corp. has
a big stake, owns a group of lackluster
businesses that used to be owned by
Singer. If the businesses turn around,
Singer has the right to buy them at low
prices—indeed, it has already bought
back 7 of the original 12.

• **The best profits are the year-in,
year-out kind.**
Of the $98.5 million profit that Singer
reported for last year, a high 18

percent came from one-time gains: a
$4.7 million profit on investments,
foreign-exchange gains of $600,000,
asset sales totaling $4.8 million, $5.3
million in interest income and $2
million in consulting fees.

• **Cash is more important than
earnings.**
At healthy companies, cash flow—
which excludes noncash items such as
depreciation—roughly approximates
net income over time.

In Singer's annual report, Mr.
Ting says that its cash flow "remained
strong" as $46 million more cash
flowed into the company's coffers
than flowed out last year.

That claim would be beyond
question if all the incoming cash
came from operations. But at least
$132 million came from a rise in
borrowings. Looking just at
operations, Singer's cash flow has
significantly trailed its reported
earnings.

• **Cash beats credit any day.**
Whenever a company allows
consumers to buy its wares on
generous terms, investors should
look for signs that customers are not
paying their bills.

In Singer's case, half of its sales
come from Asia and Latin America,
and much of its success results from
making it easy for people of limited
means to buy items such as
refrigerators on credit.

*This article was written by Reed Abelson. It appeared in the *International Herald Tribune* dated
May 15, 1995. © The New York Times.

REFERENCES AND FURTHER READING

1. Kieso, Donald, and Jerry Weygandt. *Intermediate Accounting.* 8th ed. John Wiley, 1995. See chapters 1 to 4, 5 (section 1), 7 to 16, 19, and 20.

REVIEW PROBLEMS

2.1. Constructing income statements and balance sheets.
Based on the information provided below, prepare the following financial statements for CompuStores, a company that assembles and distributes personal computers:

a. An income statement for the calendar year 1997.

b. A balance sheet on December 31, 1996.

c. A balance sheet on December 31, 1997.

1. Accounts receivable increased by $6,400,000 in 1997.
2. Profits in 1997 were taxed at 40 percent.
3. At the end of 1997, inventories equaled 10 percent of the year's sales.
4. The net book value of fixed assets at the end of 1996 was $76 million.
5. Cost of goods sold, other than the direct labor expenses related to the assembling of computers, equaled 70 percent of sales in 1997.
6. The average interest rate on short- and long-term borrowing in 1997 was 10 percent of the amount of funds borrowed at the *beginning* of the year.
7. Accounts receivable at the end of 1997 equaled 12 percent of sales.
8. Accounts payable at the end of 1996 equaled $30 million.
9. Depreciation expenses were $9 million in 1997.
10. The company owed its employees $4 million at the end of 1996; a year later it owed them $1,810,000.
11. Material purchased in 1997 amounted to $228 million.
12. Selling, general, and administrative expenses for 1997 were $18 million.
13. Fees related to a technical license amount to $4 million per year.
14. Taxes payable in 1996 equaled $6 million and the company paid in advance the same amount on December 15, 1996.
15. The balance of long-term debt was $27 million at the end of 1996, of which $4 million was due at year-end.
16. There was no issuance of shares of common stocks or repurchase of outstanding shares in 1997.
17. Direct labor expenses equaled 11.25 percent of sales.
18. Repayment of long-term debt is $4 million per year in 1997.
19. Inventories rose from $28 million at the end of 1996 to $32 million at the end of 1997.

20. In 1997, one of the company's warehouses was enlarged at a cost of $14 million, which was partly financed with a $6 million long-term loan.
21. 1997 dividend payments were $9,360,000.
22. Accounts payable at the end of 1997 equaled 1.85 of a month of purchases.
23. Equity capital at the end of 1996 was $81 million.
24. At the end of 1996, the company had enough cash that it could have immediately paid 1/4 of its accounts payable; at the end of 1997, it could have paid only 1/10.
25. The company paid in advance $9,600,000 of taxes on December 15, 1997.
26. The company's line of credit was $3 million at the end of 1996. A year later it increased by 2/3.
27. In 1997, the company had a $2 million nonrecurrent loss related to the discontinuation of an old product line.
28. The company prepaid $1,500,000 on rent and insurance in 1996, and $2,085,000 a year later.

2.2. Forecasting income statements and balance sheets.

Having prepared CompuStores' financial statements for the year 1997, the company's financial manager now wishes to *forecast* next year's income statement and balance sheet (called projected or **pro forma statements**). Prepare these projected statements using the following assumptions and the 1997 statements in the previous problem.

1. Sales are expected to grow by 10 percent.
2. Gross profit and the components of the cost of goods sold, expressed as a percentage of sales, should be the same as in 1997.
3. Selling, general, and administrative expenses will rise by $4,280,000.
4. The licensing fee, depreciation expenses, interest payments, and corporate tax rate are not expected to change next year.
5. Collection of receivables, payment of payables, and inventory management should be at the same level of efficiency as the previous year. Thus, accounts receivable should be collected at the same speed as in 1997 and will remain at 12 percent of the year's sales. Accounts payable should still be 1.85 of a month of purchases, and inventories should stay at 10 percent of sales.
6. Prepaid and accrued expenses are not expected to change.
7. The company should upgrade one of its assembly lines at a cost equal to the year's depreciation.
8. There will not be any new borrowing or issuance of new shares of common stocks.
9. The company wishes to hold as much cash in 1998 as it did in 1997 and will pay a dividend that will allow it to achieve this objective.

3 ASSESSING LIQUIDITY AND OPERATIONAL EFFICIENCY

A firm that can no longer pay its creditors—its bankers and suppliers—is illiquid and technically bankrupt, a situation that no manager wishes to face. Managers must make decisions that do not endanger their firm's liquidity—a term that refers to the firm's ability to meet its *recurrent* cash obligations towards various creditors. A firm's liquidity is driven by the structure of its balance sheet, namely, by the nature and composition of its assets and the way they are financed.

It is easier to understand and measure a firm's liquidity if its standard balance sheet is restructured to emphasize the concerns of its operating and financial managers rather than those of its accountant and auditors. In this restructured balance sheet, called the *managerial balance sheet,* the firm's investments are classified into three categories: (1) cash and cash-equivalent assets; (2) assets required to support the firm's *operating* activities, such as inventories and trade receivables, less the firm's operating liabilities, such as trade payables; and (3) fixed assets, such as plant and equipment.

To finance these investments, the firm uses a combination of short-term and long-term sources of funds. One way a firm can manage its balance sheet and enhance its liquidity is by using the *matching strategy*. This strategy requires that long-term investments be financed with long-term funds and short-term investments with short-term funds. The matching principle helps explain how a firm's liquidity should be measured and how liquidity is affected by managerial decisions.

This chapter explains the managerial balance sheet and the matching strategy and discusses how liquidity can be measured. New concepts and terms, such as *working capital requirement, net short-term financing,* and *net long-term financing,* are introduced, and then we show how they can be combined to construct a reliable measure of a firm's liquidity. Other, more traditional indicators of liquidity, such as the *current ratio* and the *acid test ratio,* are also presented and compared with our suggested measure. To illustrate these concepts, we use OS Distributors, the company whose balance sheets and income statements for the years 1995 to 1997 are described in Chapter 2. After reading this chapter, you should understand:

- How to restructure a standard balance sheet into a managerial balance sheet.
- The meaning of working capital requirement, net long-term financing, net short-term financing, net working capital, current ratio, acid test ratio, and other ratios used to measure, analyze, and manage liquidity.
- How to measure a firm's investment in its operating activities using information drawn from its balance sheet.
- The meaning of interest-rate risk and funding risk.
- How a firm's operating decisions affect the firm's liquidity.
- How to improve a firm's liquidity through better management of the firm's operating cycle.

THE MANAGERIAL BALANCE SHEET

Recall that the purpose of the firm's standard balance sheet is to determine the investment made by the firm's owners—its shareholders—in their firm at a specific date. The investment, called owners' equity, is the difference between the firm's assets and liabilities, where assets are items owned by shareholders and liabilities are debts owed to creditors, suppliers, employees, and other entities. This type of balance sheet, shown in Exhibit 3.1 for OS Distributors, emphasizes the accounting view in determining the owners' investment in the firm.

For managers of a firm's operating activities, the standard balance sheet may not be the most appropriate tool for assessing their contribution to the firm's financial performance. To illustrate this point, consider trade payables. They are correctly recorded in the balance sheet as a liability because they represent cash owed to suppliers. Most operating managers, however, would consider trade payables an account under their full responsibility, much like trade receivables (cash owed by customers) and inventories, both of which are recorded on the asset side of the balance sheet. It makes more managerial sense to associate trade payables with trade receivables and inventories rather than to combine them with other liabilities—such as short-term borrowings and long-term debt—that are primarily the responsibility of the financial manager.

In the following sections, we show how to restructure the standard balance sheet into the **managerial balance sheet,** a variation that we believe provides a more appropriate tool to identify the links between managerial decisions and financial performance. The managerial balance sheet is shown and contrasted with the standard one in Exhibit 3.2. On the left side of the managerial balance sheet, three

EXHIBIT 3.1 OS Distributors' Balance Sheets.

Figures in millions of dollars

ASSETS		December 31, 1995		December 31, 1996		December 31, 1997	
• CURRENT ASSETS			$104.0		$119.0		$137.0
Cash[1]		$6.0		$12.0		$8.0	
Accounts receivable		44.0		48.0		56.0	
Inventories		52.0		57.0		72.0	
Prepaid expenses[2]		2.0		2.0		1.0	
• NONCURRENT ASSETS			56.0		51.0		53.0
Financial assets and intangibles		0.0		0.0		0.0	
Property, plant, and equipment (net)		56.0		51.0		53.0	
Gross value[3]	$90.0			$90.0		$93.0	
Accumulated depreciation	(34.0)			(39.0)		(40.0)	
TOTAL ASSETS			$160.0		$170.0		$190.0

LIABILITIES AND OWNERS' EQUITY

		December 31, 1995		December 31, 1996		December 31, 1997	
• CURRENT LIABILITIES			$54.0		$66.0		$75.0
Short-term debt		$15.0		$22.0		$23.0	
Owed to banks	$7.0			$14.0		$15.0	
Current portion of long-term debt	8.0			8.0		8.0	
Accounts payable		37.0		40.0		48.0	
Accrued expenses[4]		2.0		4.0		4.0	
• NONCURRENT LIABILITIES			42.0		34.0		38.0
Long-term debt[5]		42.0		34.0		38.0	
• Owners' equity[6]		64.0	64.0	70.0	70.0	77.0	77.0
TOTAL LIABILITIES AND OWNERS' EQUITY			$160.0		$170.0		$190.0

Notes

1. Consists of cash in hand and checking accounts held to facilitate operating activities.
2. Prepaid expenses is rent paid in advance (when recognized in the income statement, rent is included in selling, general, and administrative expenses).
3. In 1996, there was no disposal of existing fixed assets or acquisition of new fixed assets. However, during 1997, a warehouse was enlarged at a cost of $12 million and existing fixed assets, bought for $9 million in the past, were sold at their net book value of $2 million.
4. Accrued expenses consist of wages and taxes payable.
5. Long-term debt is repaid at the rate of $8 million per year. No new long-term debt was incurred during 1996, but during 1997 a mortgage loan was obtained from the bank to finance the extension of a warehouse (see Note 3).
6. During the three years, no new shares were issued and none were repurchased.

EXHIBIT 3.2 The Managerial Balance Sheet Versus the Standard Balance Sheet.

THE MANAGERIAL BALANCE SHEET

INVESTED CAPITAL OR NET ASSETS	CAPITAL EMPLOYED
Cash	Short-term debt
Working capital requirement (WCR) *Operating assets* *less* *Operating liabilities*	**Long-term financing** *Long-term debt* *plus* *Owners' equity*
Net fixed assets	

THE STANDARD BALANCE SHEET

TOTAL ASSETS	LIABILITIES AND OWNER'S EQUITY
Cash	Short-term debt
Operating assets *Accounts receivable* *plus* *Inventories* *plus* *Prepaid expenses*	**Operating liabilities** *Accounts payable* *plus* *Accrued expenses*
Net fixed assets	**Long-term financing** *Long-term debt* *plus* *Owners' equity*

items are grouped under the heading **invested capital,** which is also referred to as **net assets.** These are cash and cash-equivalent holdings, **working capital requirement** (the difference between the firm's **operating assets** and its **operating liabilities**), and net fixed assets:

Invested capital = Net assets   (3.1)
                = Cash + Working capital requirement + Net fixed assets

On the right side of the managerial balance sheet, two items are grouped under the heading **capital employed.** These are short-term debt and long-term financing, the latter consisting of long-term debt and equity capital (as in previous chapters, we use the terms *financing, funding,* and *capital* interchangeably):

Capital employed = Short-term debt + Long-term debt + Equity capital (3.2)

The managerial balance sheet provides a snapshot of the total capital the firm has available at a point in time (the capital employed shown on the right side) and the way that capital is invested in the firm's net assets (the invested capital shown on the left side). The following sections examine the structure of the managerial balance sheet and its relevance to the measurement of the firm's liquidity.

THE THREE COMPONENTS OF A FIRM'S INVESTED CAPITAL

A firm's capital is used to finance investments in (1) cash and cash-equivalent assets; (2) working capital requirement, the difference between operating assets and operating liabilities; and (3) fixed assets, such as property, plant, and equipment. We begin with a brief review of cash and fixed assets and then analyze working capital requirement in more detail.

Cash and cash-equivalent assets

Firms hold cash and cash-equivalent assets (also called **liquid assets**) for at least two reasons: (1) as a precautionary measure to allow the firm to pay its bills promptly and meet unexpected expenses, if any; and (2) to acquire potentially valuable assets on short notice. Also, firms sometimes hold cash because banks require their corporate clients to maintain some **compensating balances** for services they provide to the firm. We use the generic word *cash* to refer not only to cash in hand but also to any cash-equivalent assets.

As shown in Exhibit 3.1, OS Distributors does not hold any cash-equivalent assets, such as marketable securities (securities that can be sold rapidly without a significant loss of value). The firm held $6 million in cash at the end of 1995, $12 million at the end of 1996, and $8 million at the end of 1997. Note 1 explains that this cash was mostly used to facilitate its operating activities. The changes in the firm's cash position between 1995 and 1997 are explained in the next chapter.

Investment in fixed assets

Investments in fixed assets include items such as property, plant, and equipment. Their book value is recorded in the balance sheet as net fixed assets, which is their purchase price less accumulated depreciation. Exhibit 3.1 indicates that the book value of OS Distributors' fixed assets was $56 million in 1995, $51 million in 1996, and $53 million in 1997. Decisions regarding the acquisition and disposal of long-term assets are part of the firm's strategic activities, which are analyzed in detail in Chapters 6 through 8. The focus of this and the following two chapters is the firm's operating activities.

Working capital requirement

Fixed assets alone cannot generate sales and profits. The managerial activities required to operate these assets in order to generate sales and profit are referred to as the firm's **operating activities.** These activities require investments in the form of inventories and trade receivables that are generated by the firm's **operating cycle,** described in Exhibit 3.3 for a manufacturing company.

The cycle starts on the right side with *procurement,* the act of acquiring raw materials. It is followed by *production,* during which the raw materials are transformed into finished goods. The cycle continues with the *sales* of these goods, ending when *cash* is collected from customers. The cycle repeats itself as long as the firm's production activity continues.

Each stage in the operating cycle affects the firm's balance sheet. Exhibit 3.3 shows the balance sheet accounts that change at each stage of the cycle. For example, when the firm buys raw materials (procurement), both inventories and accounts payable increase by the same amount—the former to reflect the purchase of the raw materials and the latter to acknowledge a debt to the firm's suppliers.

An alternative way of describing the operating cycle is shown in Exhibit 3.4. Note that the firm pays its suppliers *before* receiving cash from its customers because it must hold inventories (of raw materials, work in process, and final goods) and accounts receivable over a period of time that is *longer* than its payment period. The period between the date the firm pays its suppliers and the date it collects its invoices is called the **cash-to-cash period** (or **cycle**) or the **cash conversion period** (or **cycle**).

What is the *net* investment (at the date of the balance sheet) that the firm must make to support its operating cycle? It is simply the sum of its inventories and accounts receivable less its accounts payable. If prepaid expenses are included in the firm's operating assets and accrued expenses are included in its operating liabilities, then the firm's net investment in its operating cycle is measured (at the date of the balance sheet) by the difference between its operating assets and operating liabilities. This difference is called the firm's working capital requirement or **WCR:**

$$\text{Working capital requirement (WCR)} =$$
$$[\textbf{Accounts receivable} + \textbf{Inventories} + \textbf{Prepaid expenses}]$$
$$- [\textbf{Accounts payable} + \textbf{Accrued expenses}] \qquad (3.3)$$

EXHIBIT 3.3   The Firm's Operating Cycle and Its Impact on the Firm's Balance Sheet.

Δ = change in the balance sheet account

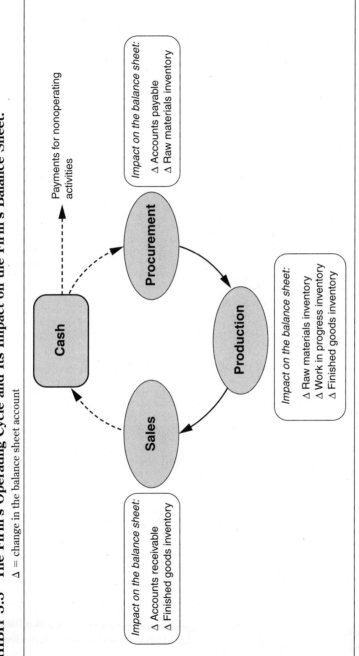

Impact on the balance sheet:
Δ Accounts payable
Δ Raw materials inventory

Impact on the balance sheet:
Δ Raw materials inventory
Δ Work in progress inventory
Δ Finished goods inventory

Impact on the balance sheet:
Δ Accounts receivable
Δ Finished goods inventory

Payments for nonoperating activities

Cash

Procurement

Production

Sales

EXHIBIT 3.4   The Firm's Operating Cycle, Showing Cash-to-Cash Period.

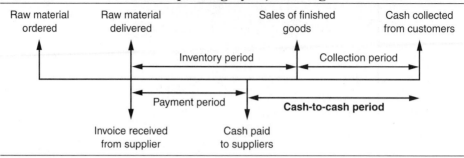

Working capital requirement does not include the firm's cash holdings because the cash account in a balance sheet represents the amount of cash left when *all* the investments made by the firm, including working capital requirement, have been paid for. Cash is affected by the way a firm runs its operating cycle but, strictly speaking, is not part of it. Also, working capital requirement does not include the firm's short-term debt. Short-term debt is used to *finance* the firm's investments, including its working capital requirement. It may contribute to the financing of the firm's operating cycle, but it is not a component of it.

For most firms, operating assets exceed operating liabilities and working capital requirement is *positive*. When the opposite occurs, working capital requirement is *negative* and the firm's operating cycle becomes a *source of cash* rather than a use of funds. Firms with a negative working capital requirement are found in the retail and service sectors of the economy. Such firms collect cash from their customers before they pay their suppliers and carry small inventories relative to their sales. Large supermarkets are a typical example. They sell mostly for cash and, thus, have few receivables. And, because their inventories move rapidly, they are usually low relative to the sales they generate. The amount of money they owe their suppliers, however, can be very large because big supermarket chains often manage to extract very generous credit terms from their suppliers. Few receivables, low inventories, and large amounts of payables is the perfect recipe for turning the firm's operating cycle into a source of cash.

For example, consider Carrefour, one of Europe's biggest chains of very large supermarkets. Exhibit 3.5 shows some figures taken from the company's 1994 and 1995 balance sheets and income statements. The amounts are converted into U.S. dollars at the rate of five French francs to the dollar. The firm has almost no prepaid or accrued expenses, so its working capital requirement is equal to the sum of the company's receivables and inventories less its payables. Note the negative sign and the magnitude of WCR. At the end of 1995, WCR was worth $3.2 billion. This negative working capital requirement is a major *source of cash* to the company and explains why the company's cash and cash-equivalent investments are roughly of the same magnitude as its working capital requirement. Other firms with a negative working capital requirement are in industries

EXHIBIT 3.5   **Extracts from Carrefour's Balance Sheets and Income Statements.**

Figures in millions of dollars

YEAR	RECEIVABLES	INVENTORIES	PAYABLES	WCR[1]	CASH[2]	SALES
1994	$68	$1,939	$5,296	−$3,289	$3,123	$27,260
1995	84	2,172	5,484	−3,228	3,281	28,922

Source: Company's Annual Report.
[1]WCR = Working capital requirement = Receivables + Inventories − Payables
[2]Includes cash lent to other companies.

such as publishing (you pay for your subscription before you receive your magazine) and air transportation (you pay for your trip before your departure).

With the information in the balance sheets in Exhibit 3.1, we can calculate OS Distributors' working capital requirement on December 31, 1995, 1996, and 1997, using equation 3.3:

$$WCR_{12/31/95} = \$44 \text{ million} + \$52 \text{ million} + \$2 \text{ million}$$
$$- \$37 \text{ million} - \$2 \text{ million} = \$59 \text{ million}$$

$$WCR_{12/31/96} = \$48 \text{ million} + \$57 \text{ million} + \$2 \text{ million}$$
$$- \$40 \text{ million} - \$4 \text{ million} = \$63 \text{ million}$$

$$WCR_{12/31/97} = \$56 \text{ million} + \$72 \text{ million} + \$1 \text{ million}$$
$$- \$48 \text{ million} - \$4 \text{ million} = \$77 \text{ million}$$

These are the figures reported in OS Distributors' managerial balance sheets shown in Exhibit 3.6. OS Distributors' WCR has risen from $59 million in 1995 to $77 million in 1997. How can we explain this growth? We examine this issue later in the chapter.

THE COMPONENTS OF CAPITAL EMPLOYED

How should the firm's net assets be financed? There are two primary sources of capital available to firms: the equity capital provided by owners and the debt capital provided by debtholders. Debt can be *short term* (due to be repaid within one year) or *long term* (due to be repaid after one year.)[1] Thus, a firm's total capital employed can be classified either as equity and debt capital or as **long-term financing** (equity plus long-term debt) and **short-term financing** (short-term debt). The

---

[1]This distinction is somewhat arbitrary, but it is the one used in standard accounting models. In practice, there is a "gray area" of medium-term debt, due to be repaid after one year but less than, say, three years.

EXHIBIT 3.6   OS Distributors' Managerial Balance Sheets.

All data from the balance sheets in Exhibit 3.1; figures in millions of dollars

		DECEMBER 31, 1995			DECEMBER 31, 1996			DECEMBER 31, 1997	
INVESTED CAPITAL OR NET ASSETS									
• Cash		$ 6.0	5%		$ 12.0	10%		$ 8.0	6%
• Working capital requirement (WCR)[1]		59.0	49%		63.0	50%		77.0	56%
• Net fixed assets		56.0	46%		51.0	40%		53.0	38%
TOTAL INVESTED CAPITAL OR NET ASSETS		**$121.0**	**100%**		**$126.0**	**100%**		**$138.0**	**100%**
CAPITAL EMPLOYED									
• Short-term debt		$15.0	12%		$22.0	17%		$23.0	17%
• Long-term financing		106.0	88%		104.0	83%		115.0	83%
Long-term debt	$42.0			$34.0			$38.0		
Owners' equity	64.0			70.0			77.0		
TOTAL CAPITAL EMPLOYED		**$121.0**	**100%**		**$126.0**	**100%**		**$138.0**	**100%**

[1]WCR = (Accounts receivable + Inventories + Prepaid expenses) − (Accounts payable + Accrued expenses). These amounts are given in Exhibit 3.1.

first approach distinguishes the *nature* of the firm's capital employed while the second distinguishes its *duration*.

Given these alternative sources of capital, the firm's managers must answer two questions in deciding what strategy should be adopted to fund the firm's net assets:

1. What is the best combination of equity capital and debt capital?
2. What proportion of borrowed funds should be in the form of long-term debt and what proportion in the form of short-term debt?

The answer to the first question affects the firm's profitability and financial risk. It is examined in detail in Chapters 5 and 11. The answer to the second question affects primarily the firm's liquidity.[2] It is examined later in this chapter.

THE STRUCTURE OF THE MANAGERIAL BALANCE SHEET

Exhibit 3.2 compares the structure of the standard balance sheet to that of the managerial balance sheet. The two statements differ in the way operating assets and operating liabilities are handled. In the standard balance sheet, operating liabilities are part of the firm's total liabilities. In the managerial balance sheet, operating liabilities are deducted from operating assets in order to determine the net investment required to support the firm's operations, in other words, its working capital requirement. Adding the cash and net fixed assets accounts to working capital requirement gives the firm's net assets or invested capital. What remains on the liability side of the balance sheet after the operating liabilities are removed are the sources of funds needed to finance net assets: short-term debt, long-term debt, and owners' equity. The sum of these sources of funds is the total capital employed.

Now consider Exhibit 3.6, which shows OS Distributors' managerial balance sheets. At the end of 1997, the firm's net assets or invested capital of $138 million were funded with $23 million of short-term borrowings and $115 million of long-term financing ($38 million of long-term debt plus $77 million of owners' equity). The managerial balance sheets show that the proportion of cash held by the firm fluctuated between 5 and 10 percent of total invested capital. The proportion of working capital requirement fluctuated between 49 and 56 percent and that of net fixed assets between 38 and 46 percent. The relatively large amount of working capital requirement is not surprising given that OS Distributors is a wholesale distribution company. Compared with typical manufacturing companies, firms in the wholesale distribution business have a significant amount of capital invested in their

---

[2]A distinction needs to be made between liquidity and **solvency.** Liquidity refers to the firm's ability to meet its cash obligations in the short term while solvency refers to the same concept but from a long-term perspective. In the case of solvency, the issue is whether the firm can raise the funds required to sustain its long-term growth, service its long-term debt, and distribute a regular stream of dividends to its shareholders. The issue of solvency is dealt with in Chapter 5 in conjunction with the analysis of profitability.

operating cycle. Turning to the structure of capital employed, notice that 83 to 88 percent of OS Distributors' investments were financed with long-term funds compared with 12 to 17 percent with short-term debt.

THE MATCHING STRATEGY

In deciding how much of the firm's investments should be financed with long-term funds and how much with short-term debt, most firms try to apply the **matching strategy.** According to this strategy, long-term investments should be financed with long-term funds and short-term investments should be financed with short-term funds. By matching the life of an asset and the duration of its financing source, a firm can minimize the risk of *not* being able to finance the asset over its entire useful life.

Consider a piece of equipment with a useful life of five years. Its purchase price can be financed either with a five-year loan (a matched financing strategy) or with a one-year renewable loan (a mismatched financing strategy), both at the same interest rate. Which of the two strategies is riskier?

The mismatched strategy is riskier for two reasons. First, the interest rate, and thus the cost of financing the equipment, may change during the following four years. Second, the lender may be unwilling to renew the one-year loan, thus forcing the firm to repay its loan after one year. This situation may require the sale of the equipment and the early termination of the investment. These two types of risk, called **interest-rate risk** and **funding risk,** respectively, are much lower under the matching strategy.

However, matching the maturity structure of the firm's sources of financing with the maturity of its assets is not necessarily the *optimal* financing strategy for every firm at all times. Some firms, at times, may be willing to carry some interest-rate and funding risks if they expect short-term interest rates to go down.[3] On the other hand, firms that are more risk-averse may choose to carry more long-term funds than necessary under the matching strategy. Appendix 3.1 provides an illustration of matched and mismatched financing strategies for firms with growing and seasonal sales.

We can use the managerial balance sheets in Exhibit 3.6 to find out whether OS Distributors has been applying the matching strategy during the period 1995 to 1997. We examine each of the three investments and their financing. Cash, a short-term asset, has been fully funded with short-term debt at the end of each year and was thus matched. Similarly, net fixed assets, which are long-term investments, have been fully funded with long-term financing and were thus also matched. The matching strategy applied in both cases. Does it also apply to working capital requirement?

Before we can answer this question, we need to know if working capital requirement is a short-term or a long-term investment. At first glance, it may seem

---

[3]If the short-term interest rate is expected to go down, then a short-term loan that is renewable over the life of the asset would be cheaper than a long-term loan that matches the life of the asset.

EXHIBIT 3.7 **The Behavior of Working Capital Requirement (WCR) over Time for a Firm with Seasonal Sales.**

WCR is assumed to be set at 25 percent of sales

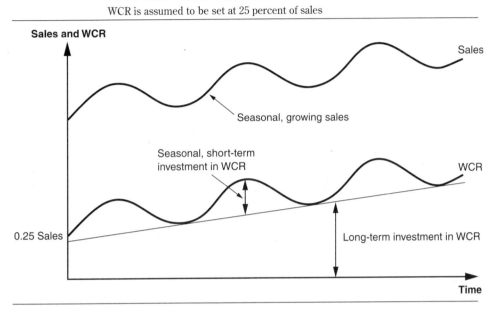

that WCR is a short-term investment because it is made up of current assets, which will become cash within a year, and current liabilities, which will decrease the firm's cash holdings within a year. But, the answer is not that simple. Although these assets and liabilities are classified as current, or short-term, they will be replaced by *new* current assets and *new* current liabilities as the operating cycle repeats. So, as long as the firm stays in business, working capital requirement will remain in its (managerial) balance sheet and, hence, is more *permanent* than transient in nature. In other words, working capital requirement is essentially a long-term investment. Under a matching strategy, it should be financed with long-term funds. Exhibit 3.6 indicates that a small proportion of OS Distributors' working capital requirement was financed with short-term funds, implying that the firm did not adhere strictly to the matching strategy.[4]

There is one type of firm that can adhere to the matching strategy but not entirely finance working capital requirement with long-term funds. Consider a firm that has growing but *seasonal* sales. If the firm maintains a constant ratio of working capital requirement to sales over time, then its working capital requirement will also display a seasonal growth behavior. Exhibit 3.7 illustrates this situation for WCR equal to 25 percent of sales. In this case, working capital requirement has a

---

[4]The firm had more short-term debt than cash in 1995, 1996, and 1997. The difference went to finance part of its investment in working capital.

long-term growth component and a *short-term seasonal component.* According to the matching strategy, the long-term growth component should be financed with long-term funds and the seasonal component with short-term funds. Applying this funding strategy should minimize both interest-rate and funding risks.

A MEASURE OF LIQUIDITY BASED ON THE FUNDING STRUCTURE OF WORKING CAPITAL REQUIREMENT

For most firms that adopt it, the matching strategy is an objective rather than a day-to-day reality. The goal of management is for long-term funds to match the firm's long-term investments (net fixed assets and most of the working capital requirement) and for short-term funds to match the firm's short-term investments (cash and marketable securities) *over time.* This objective may not be easily achieved in practice and, at times, the firm may find itself in a mismatched situation where a *significant* portion of its working capital is funded with short-term debt. This situation can create a liquidity problem. This section presents a measure of liquidity that managers can use to monitor their firm's liquidity position. This measure is based on the funding structure of working capital requirement—more precisely, on the portion of WCR that is funded with long-term financing.

How much long-term financing is available to fund the firm's working capital requirement? Because net fixed assets are funded with long-term financing, any long-term financing in *excess* of net fixed assets can be used to fund working capital requirement. These excess long-term funds are called **net long-term financing or NLF:**

Net long-term financing (NLF) = Long-term financing – Net fixed assets   (3.4)

Net long-term financing is the portion of the firm's long-term financing available to finance the firm's other two fundamental investments, its working capital requirement and cash. Exhibit 3.8 shows that OS Distributors' NLF at the end of 1997 was $62 million. It is equal to the firm's $115 million of long-term financing ($38 million of long-term debt plus $77 million of equity) less the $53 million of net fixed assets.

How much short-term financing is used to fund the firm's working capital requirement? It is simply the amount of short-term debt that is not used to finance the firm's remaining assets, that is, cash. The amount of short-term debt in excess of cash is called **net short-term financing or NSF:**

Net short-term financing (NSF) = Short-term debt – Cash   (3.5)

As shown in Exhibit 3.8, OS Distributors' working capital requirement of $77 million at the end of 1997 was financed with $62 million of long-term funds (NLF = $62 million) and $15 million of short-term funds (NSF = $15 million). Thus, in 1997, 80.5 percent of WCR was funded with long-term financing and 19.5 percent

EXHIBIT 3.8 OS Distributors' Net Investment in Its Operating Cycle and Its Financing.

All data from the balance sheets in Exhibit 3.1; figures in millions of dollars

	DECEMBER 31, 1995	DECEMBER 31, 1996	DECEMBER 31, 1997
NET INVESTMENT IN THE OPERATING CYCLE OR WORKING CAPITAL REQUIREMENT (WCR)			
WCR = [Accounts receivable + Inventories + Prepaid expenses] − [Accounts payable + Accrued expenses]	[$44 + $52 + $2] − [$37 + $2] = $59	[$48 + $57 + $2] − [$40 + $4] = $63	[$56 + $72 + $1] − [$48 + $4] = $77
THE FINANCING OF THE OPERATING CYCLE			
Net long-term financing (NLF) = Long-term debt + Owners' equity − Net fixed assets	$42 + $64 − $56 = $50	$34 + $70 − $51 = $53	$38 + $77 − $53 = $62
Net short-term financing (NSF) = Short-term debt − Cash	$15 − $6 = $9	$22 − $12 = $10	$23 − $8 = $15
NLF/WCR = percentage of working capital requirement financed long term	$50/$59 = 84.7%	$53/$63 = 84.1%	$62/$77 = 80.5%
NSF/WCR = percentage of working capital requirement financed short term	$9/$59 = 15.3% 100.0%	$10/$63 = 15.9% 100.0%	$15/$77 = 19.5% 100.0%
WORKING CAPITAL REQUIREMENT AND ITS FINANCING	WCR $59 NSF $9 15.3% / NLF $50 84.7%	WCR $63 NSF $10 15.9% / NLF $53 84.1%	WCR $77 NSF $15 19.5% / NLF $62 80.5%

81

was funded with short-term debt, as illustrated at the bottom of Exhibit 3.8. The ratio of net long-term financing to WCR is the firm's **liquidity ratio:**

$$\textbf{Liquidity ratio} = \frac{\textbf{Long-term financing} - \textbf{Net fixed assets}}{\textbf{Working capital requirement}} \qquad (3.6)$$

$$= \frac{\textbf{Net long-term financing}}{\textbf{WCR}} = \frac{\textbf{NLF}}{\textbf{WCR}}$$

OS Distributors' liquidity ratio dropped from 84.7 percent in 1995 to 80.5 percent in 1997, indicating a slight deterioration in the firm's liquidity position. In general, all else the same, the higher the proportion of working capital requirement financed with long-term funds, the more liquid is the firm. This is the case because working capital is essentially a long-term investment; financing it with higher proportions of short-term funds creates a mismatch between investment and funding durations that could lead to a liquidity problem. In other words, the higher the liquidity ratio, the more liquid is the firm.

If we deduct net long-term financing from working capital requirement, we get the portion of WCR that is financed with short-term funds, in other words, net short-term financing:

$$\textbf{Working capital requirement} - \textbf{Net long-term financing}$$
$$= \textbf{Net short-term financing}$$

This equation clearly shows that the amount of *net* short-term financing depends on the relative amounts of working capital and *net* long-term financing. As the amount of long-term funds used to finance working capital requirement (net long-term financing) increases, the firm's liquidity ratio rises (see equation 3.6). Simultaneously, the amount of short-term funds used to finance working capital requirement (net short-term financing) decreases. In other words, when the firm increases its liquidity ratio, it is also reducing its net short-term financing.

IMPROVING LIQUIDITY THROUGH BETTER MANAGEMENT OF THE OPERATING CYCLE

What drives a firm's liquidity? The answer to this question is given by the liquidity ratio in equation 3.6: A firm's liquidity is the consequence of decisions that affect its net long-term financing (the numerator of the liquidity ratio) and its working capital requirement (the denominator of the liquidity ratio). A firm's liquidity position will improve if its liquidity ratio rises. According to equation 3.6, this will happen if:

1. Long-term financing increases, and/or
2. Net fixed assets decrease, and/or
3. Working capital requirement decreases.

Decisions related to the management of long-term financing and net fixed assets are *strategic* in nature. Long-term financing will increase if the firm (1) issues long-term debt, (2) raises new equity capital (issues new shares), or (3) increases retained earnings (reduces dividend payments). Net fixed assets will decrease if the firm sells property and other fixed assets. Generally, both these decisions are infrequent and involve large amounts of cash. They are also prepared well in advance so that the firm's financial manager, who actively participates in this decision-making process, can easily forecast their impact on the firm's liquidity.

Decisions affecting the firm's working capital requirement are related to the management of the firm's *operating* cycle. They determine the amount of receivables, inventories, prepaid expenses, payables, and accrued expenses in the firm's balance sheet. Contrary to strategic decisions, operating decisions are made frequently (a company receives payments from its customers many times a day), they involve relatively small amounts of cash, and, often, they do *not* directly involve the firm's financial manager. They affect the firm's liquidity continuously and are difficult to forecast in the aggregate. It is through them that a firm's *operating* managers influence the firm's liquidity. The lower the firm's investment in its operating cycle, the lower its working capital requirement and the higher the firm's liquidity. Furthermore, the lower the frequency of unexpected changes in the firm's working capital requirement, the less volatile the firm's liquidity position and the easier it is to manage. Clearly, *the control of the amount and fluctuations of a firm's working capital requirement is the key to the sound management of the firm's liquidity.*

Controlling working capital requirement requires identifying and understanding the factors that affect its size. Five items make up a firm's working capital requirement: receivables, inventories, prepaid expenses, payables, and accrued expenses. The size of these five items depends on the following three basic factors:

1. The nature of the *economic sector* in which the firm operates
2. The *degree of efficiency* with which the firm manages its operating cycle
3. The *level and growth of sales.*

THE IMPACT OF THE FIRM'S SECTOR ON ITS WORKING CAPITAL REQUIREMENT

The nature of a business, the technology it uses, and the economic sector in which it operates affect the amount of working capital requirement it needs to support a given level of sales. For example, an equipment manufacturer needs more working capital than a chain of grocery stores does to support the *same* level of sales. The business system underlying a chain of grocery stores allows it to operate with significantly lower amounts of receivables and inventories than those of a manufacturing company with the same amount of sales. As mentioned earlier, some firms, such as large supermarket chains, have a negative working capital requirement; in this case, the firm's operating cycle is a source of cash rather than a use of capital.

The sectoral effect on working capital requirement can be measured by computing the ratio of WCR to sales for a sample of firms in the same sector. Exhibit 3.9 reports this ratio for a number of U.S. industries. Firms in sectors with higher ratios require larger investments in their operating cycles to generate a dollar of sales. This indicates a longer operating cycle for firms in those industries. For example, in 1996, a typical firm in the electronic components sector needed, on average, to invest in its operating cycle an amount of capital equal to 24 percent of its sales. A grocery store had, on average, *no* net investment in its operating cycle because the average WCR-to-sales ratio for the sector was zero in 1996. This difference simply reflects the fact that the operating cycle of a typical company in the electronic components industry is significantly longer than that of a typical grocery store. Note the stability over time of the sectors' WCR-to-sales ratios. During the five-year period from 1992 to 1996, the spread between the highest and lowest ratio for a sector rarely exceeded three percentage points. This means that the ratios in Exhibit 3.9 are fairly reliable sectoral benchmarks.

Exhibit 3.10 shows that OS Distributors' ratio of WCR to sales rose from 15 percent in 1995 to 16 percent in 1997, indicating a slight deterioration in the management of its operating cycle during that period. Also, OS Distributors' WCR-to-sales ratio is significantly higher than its sector average of 10 percent reported in Exhibit 3.9 (wholesale durables), indicating a less efficient use of working capital than the average U.S. wholesaler.

THE IMPACT OF MANAGERIAL EFFICIENCY ON WORKING CAPITAL REQUIREMENT

Firms in the same sector do not necessarily have the same ratio of WCR to sales. Even though they face similar constraints, some are able to manage their working capital better than others. For example, if a firm does not control its inventories and receivables as well as its sector's average, its WCR-to-sales ratio will be higher than that of its sector.

Several ratios can be used to estimate the efficiency with which a firm manages the components of its working capital requirement. They have the advantages of being simple and of requiring data readily available in balance sheets and income statements. These ratios, discussed in the following sections, provide managers and analysts with good signals regarding both changes in a firms' managerial efficiency over time and differences across firms in the same sector.

Inventory turnover

A firm's **inventory turnover,** or **inventory turn,** is generally defined as the ratio of its cost of goods sold to its end-of-period inventories:

$$\text{Inventory turnover} = \frac{\textbf{Cost of goods sold}}{\textbf{Ending inventories}} \qquad (3.7)$$

EXHIBIT 3.9   Some Benchmark Ratios of Working Capital Requirement to Sales for a Sample of U.S. Sectors[1].

SECTOR	WORKING CAPITAL REQUIREMENT AS PERCENTAGE OF SALES		
	1996	HIGHEST: 1992-96	LOWEST: 1992-96
Electronic components	24%	25%	22%
Aircraft	22%	22%	19%
Measurement instruments	21%	22%	21%
Steel works	20%	20%	18%
Motor vehicles	20%	20%	19%
Machinery & equipment	19%	21%	18%
Textiles	17%	20%	17%
Chemicals	17%	17%	14%
Wood products & buildings	16%	16%	14%
Apparel products	15%	17%	15%
Department stores	15%	19%	13%
Plastic products	14%	15%	14%
Computing equipment	14%	17%	14%
Retail: Nongrocery stores	12%	15%	12%
Paper	11%	12%	10%
AVERAGE: ALL SECTORS	**10%**	**11%**	**10%**
Drugs	10%	13%	10%
Wholesale: Durables	10%	10%	7%
Soaps & perfumes	8%	8%	7%
Food	7%	7%	5%
Wholesale: Nondurables	5%	6%	5%
Telephone	3%	3%	−2%
Oil & natural gas	2%	3%	2%
Publishing	2%	2%	1%
Beverages	1%	1%	0%
Electric services	0%	2%	0%
Grocery stores	0%	1%	0%
Natural gas: Distribution	−1%	2%	−1%
Services[2]	−1%	−1%	−5%
Air transportation[3]	−13%	−11%	−13%

[1]Source: Calculated by the authors using *Compustat* data.
[2]The services sector covers a varieties of industries, including advertising, cleaning, data processing, research and development, and management consultancy.
[3]The air transportation sector covers scheduled and nonscheduled air transportation as well as air courier services and airports and terminal services.

EXHIBIT 3.10 OS Distributors' Management of Its Operating Cycle.

All data from the balance sheets in Exhibit 3.1 and the income statements in Exhibit 2.2; figures in millions of dollars

RATIO	OBJECTIVE	DECEMBER 31, 1995	DECEMBER 31, 1996	DECEMBER 31, 1997
Working capital requirement (WCR)[1] / **Sales**	To evaluate the overall efficiency with which the firm's operating cycle is managed	$\dfrac{\$59}{\$390} = 15\%$	$\dfrac{\$63}{\$420} = 15\%$	$\dfrac{\$77}{\$420} = 16\%$
Cost of goods sold (COGS) / **Inventories**	To evaluate the efficiency with which inventories are managed	$\dfrac{\$328}{\$52} = 6.3 \text{ times}$	$\dfrac{\$353}{\$57} = 6.2 \text{ times}$	$\dfrac{\$400}{\$72} = 5.6 \text{ times}$
Accounts receivable / **Average daily sales[2]**	To evaluate the efficiency with which accounts receivable are managed	$\dfrac{\$44}{\$390/365} = 41 \text{ days}$	$\dfrac{\$48}{\$420/365} = 42 \text{ days}$	$\dfrac{\$56}{\$480/365} = 43 \text{ days}$
Accounts payable / **Average daily purchases[2,3]**	To evaluate the efficiency with which accounts payable are managed	$\dfrac{\$37}{\$332/365} = 41 \text{ days}$	$\dfrac{\$40}{\$358/365} = 41 \text{ days}$	$\dfrac{\$48}{\$415/365} = 42 \text{ days}$

[1]WCR is found in Exhibit 3.6.

[2]We assume the year has 365 days.

[3]Purchases are equal to COGS plus the *change* in inventories (see equation 3.11). In 1994, inventories were $48, thus purchases (1995) = $328 + ($52 − $48) = $332. Purchases (1996) = $353 + ($57 − $52) = $358; and purchases (1997) = $400 + ($72 − $57) = $415.

For a distribution company, an inventory turnover of, say, six means that, on average, items in inventory turn over six times per year. Or, to put it another way, an item stays on the firm's shelves for two months, on average. The *higher* the inventory turnover, the *lower* the firm's investment in inventories and the *higher* the efficiency with which the firm manages its inventories.

When cost of goods sold is not available, the level of sales is often used as a substitute in computing inventory turnover. Sometimes, inventories at the end of the period are replaced by average inventories during the period. Strictly speaking, the definition of inventory turnover given in equation 3.7 applies only to finished goods. To obtain the turnover for raw material inventory, the cost of goods sold in equation 3.7 is replaced by the amount of purchases.

The ratios reported in Exhibit 3.10 indicate that OS Distributors' inventory turnover deteriorated slightly, dropping from 6.3 times at the end of 1995 to 5.6 times at the end of 1997.

Average collection period

Also called the **average age of accounts receivable,** or **days of sales outstanding (DSO),** the **average collection period,** expressed in days, is defined as accounts receivable at the end of the period divided by the average daily sales during that period:

$$\text{Average collection period} = \frac{\text{Receivables}_{\text{end}}}{\text{Average daily sales}} \quad (3.8)$$

The average collection period is the number of days' worth of sales that have not yet been collected at the date of the balance sheet. It is an estimate of the *average* numbers of days the firm must wait from the time it ships its goods or delivers its service until its customers pay their bills. The faster the bills are collected, the *lower* the firm's receivables, the *higher* the efficiency with which the firm manages its receivables, and the *lower* its working capital requirement.

This ratio is just an average; it does not represent the actual number of days a firm must wait between when a sale is made and when payment for it is collected. Not all customers settle their invoices after the same number of days. Some pay earlier than the average collection period and others pay later. If there is a group of customers that is often late in paying its bills, the firm should monitor that group separately.

OS Distributors' average collection periods, reported in Exhibit 3.10, indicate a slight lengthening of its collection period from 41 days at the end of 1995 to 43 days at the end of 1997.

Average payment period

The **average payment period** is to purchases what the average collection period is to sales. It is defined as the ratio of accounts payable at the end of the period to the average daily purchases during that period:

$$\textbf{Average payment period} = \frac{\textbf{Payables}_{end}}{\textbf{Average daily purchases}} \qquad (3.9)$$

The average payment period is the number of days' worth of purchases that have not yet been paid at the date of the balance sheet. The *longer* the average payment period, the *higher* the firm's payables and the *lower* its working capital requirement.

To compute the average daily purchases, you need to know the amount of purchases made during the accounting period ending at the date of the balance sheet. Although this information is not directly reported in the firm's financial statements, purchases made during the accounting period can be obtained indirectly from data provided in balance sheets and income statements.

First, we consider a manufacturing firm. The cost of the goods manufactured during the accounting period equals the cost of purchases plus the cost of production. We add this sum to the beginning of the period's inventories account (raw material, work in process, and finished goods inventories). As the firm sells its finished goods, inventories decrease by the cost of goods sold (COGS). The net effect of these transactions is the ending inventories:

Beginning inventories + purchases + production costs − COGS = Ending inventories

We can rearrange the terms in the above equation to calculate the firm's purchases during the accounting period as a function of COGS, production costs, and the change in inventories:

$$\text{Purchases} = \text{COGS} + \text{Change in inventories} - \text{Production costs} \qquad (3.10)$$

where the change in inventories equals the firm's ending inventories less its beginning inventories during the accounting period.

For a trading firm with no production costs, such as OS Distributors, equation 3.10 simplifies to:

$$\text{Purchases} = \text{COGS} + \text{Change in inventories} \qquad (3.11)$$

Equation 3.11 could have been obtained directly because, for a distributor, if the amount of goods purchased during the accounting period exceeds the amount of goods sold during that period, the inventories account will increase by the difference. If a distributor sells more goods than it buys during the accounting period, the inventories account will decrease by the difference.

EXHIBIT 3.11   Raiding a Company's Hidden Cash*

Reducing working capital yields two powerful benefits. First, every dollar freed from inventories or receivables rings up a one-time $1 contribution to cash flow. Second, the quest for zero working capital permanently raises earnings. Like all capital, working capital costs money, so reducing it yields savings. In addition, cutting working capital forces companies to produce and deliver faster than the competition, enabling them to win new business and charge premium prices for filling rush orders. As inventories evaporate, warehouses disappear. Companies no longer need forklift drivers or schedulers to plan production months in advance.

Over the 12 months that ended May 1996, Campbell Soup pared working capital by $80 million. It used the cash to develop new products and buy companies in Britain, Australia, and other countries. But Campbell also expects to harvest an *extra* $50 million in profits over the next few years by lowering overtime, storage costs, and other expenses—savings that will persist year after year.

The most important discipline that zero working capital necessitates is speed. Many companies today produce elaborate long-term forecasts of orders. They then manufacture their product weeks or months in advance, creating big inventories; eventually they fill orders from the bulging stocks.

Minimizing working capital forces organizations to demolish that system. Scrapping forecasts, companies manufacture goods as they are ordered. The best companies start producing an auto braking system or cereal flavor after receiving an order and yet still manage to deliver just when the customer needs it.

The system, known as demand flow or demand-based management, builds on the familiar idea of just-in-time inventories but is far broader. Most companies achieve just-in-time in one or two areas. They demand daily shipments from suppliers, for example, or dispatch finished products the hour the customer wants them. But just-in-time deliveries don't guarantee efficiency. To meet the rapid schedule, many companies simply ship from huge inventories. They still manufacture weeks or months in advance.

Achieving zero working capital requires that every order and part move at maximum pace, never stopping. Orders streak from the processing department to the plant. Flexible factories manufacture each product every day. Finished goods flow from the assembly line onto waiting trucks. Manufacturers press suppliers to cut inventories as well, since minimal stocks translate into lower raw materials prices to the manufacturer. Instead of cluttering plants or warehouses, parts and products hurtle through the pipeline. As velocity rises, inventory—working capital—dwindles. That's why working capital levels are such a useful yardstick for efficiency and why, in the 1990s, manufacturers with the least working capital per dollar of sales will reign as the world's best-run companies.

* Extracted from an article by Shawn Tally in *Fortune,* August 22, 1996.

The purchases of OS Distributors reported in Exhibit 3.10 are computed according to equation 3.11. These purchases are divided by 365 to obtain the average daily purchases for each year. Notice that the average payment period rose slightly from 41 to 42 days of purchases.

THE IMPACT OF SALES GROWTH ON WORKING CAPITAL REQUIREMENT

Suppose a firm's sales are expected to grow by 10 percent next year. How would the firm's working capital requirement be affected if there is *no change in the efficiency* with which its operating cycle is managed (same inventory turnover and same collection and payment periods)? Even though efficiency remains the same, higher sales will require additional investments in the firm's operating cycle because the firm will need more receivables, more inventories, and more payables to support its additional sales. As a consequence, the firm's working capital requirement will increase. As a first approximation, you can expect WCR to grow at the same rate as sales, that is, at 10 percent.

Consider the case of OS Distributors. At the end of 1997, its WCR was equal to $77 million. If sales are expected to grow by 10 percent in 1998 and the WCR-to-sales ratio is expected to remain the same as in 1997, then we can expect OS Distributors' working capital requirement also to grow by 10 percent, or $7.7 million, in 1998. Thus, OS Distributors will need $7.7 million of cash to finance the anticipated growth of its WCR. If OS Distributors does not have or cannot obtain $7.7 million of cash, it may face a liquidity problem.

As this example illustrates, an unplanned or unexpected growth in sales may create liquidity problems. These problems can be alleviated if management maintains a tight control over the firm's operating cycle and anticipates the funding needs that will result from future changes in the firm's working capital requirement. How far can managers try to squeeze working capital requirement to release the cash tied up by the firm's operating cycle? An increasing number of *manufacturing firms* have set themselves the ambitious goal of operating with close to *zero* WCR. The article reproduced in Exhibit 3.11 explains how this can be achieved.

Inflation also puts pressure on the firm's working capital requirement. When the price level rises, the nominal value of the firm's sales will rise even though the number of units sold may not change. Inflated sales figures require higher levels of receivables; thus the firm's investment in its operating cycle will increase unless management becomes more efficient.

TRADITIONAL MEASURES OF LIQUIDITY

Some of the traditional measures of a firm's liquidity are reviewed in this section. We also explain why these measures are often *not* reliable indicators of the firm's liquidity.

NET WORKING CAPITAL

The traditional definition of a firm's **net working capital (NWC)** is the difference between its current assets and its current liabilities. The rationale for this definition is that the higher the firm's net working capital, the easier it would be in the case of default to meet the firm's current liabilities by selling its current assets. However, we are interested in estimating a company's ability to meet its cash obligation on a *continual* basis as opposed to its ability to meet the same obligations only in the case of default. Thus, this definition of NWC is of limited value.

There is an alternative, and in our opinion superior, way to interpret net working capital. We write the balance sheet identity as follows:

Current assets + Net fixed assets = Current liabilities + Long-term financing

Rearranging the terms in this equation, we get:

Current assets − Current liabilities = Long-term financing − Net fixed assets

which, using the definition of net working capital, can be written as:

$$\text{Net working capital} = \text{Long-term financing} - \text{Net fixed assets} \qquad (3.12)$$

Now compare equation 3.12 with equation 3.4, which measures the net long-term funds available to finance working capital requirement. *Net working capital* given by equation 3.12 and *net long-term financing* given by equation 3.4 are the same. In other words, net working capital can be interpreted in the same way as net long-term financing. The definition of net working capital as long-term financing less net fixed assets has a clear economic meaning. It says that net working capital is the net result of the firm's long-term strategic decisions, whereas the traditional definition of net working capital has no particular managerial meaning. Furthermore, using the traditional definition of net working capital may lead to the conclusion that net working capital is determined by the firm's short-term, operating decisions, which we know is not the case.

Exhibit 3.12 reports OS Distributors' net working capital at the end of 1995, 1996, and 1997, using the two definitions presented above. Net working capital grew from $50 million at the end of 1995 to $62 million at the end of 1997.

THE CURRENT RATIO

The **current ratio** is obtained by dividing the firm's current assets by its current liabilities:

$$\textbf{Current ratio} = \frac{\textbf{Current assets}}{\textbf{Current liabilities}} \qquad (3.13)$$

EXHIBIT 3.12 OS Distributors' Net Working Capital (NWC) and Current and Quick Ratios.

All data from the balance sheets in Exhibit 3.1; figures in millions of dollars

	DECEMBER 31, 1995	DECEMBER 31, 1996	DECEMBER 31, 1997
• NWC = [Current assets − Current liabilities][1]	$104 − $54 = **$50**	$119 − $66 = **53**	$137 − $75 = **$62**
• NWC = [Long-term financing[2] − Net fixed assets][3]	($42 + $64) − $56 = **$50**	($34 + $70) − $51 = **$53**	($38 + $77) − $53 = **$62**
• Current ratio = $\dfrac{\text{Current assets}}{\text{Current liabilities}}$	$\dfrac{\$104}{\$54} = \mathbf{1.93}$	$\dfrac{\$119}{\$66} = \mathbf{1.80}$	$\dfrac{\$137}{\$75} = \mathbf{1.83}$
• Quick ratio = $\dfrac{\text{Cash + Accounts receivable}}{\text{Current liabilities}}$	$\dfrac{\$6 + \$44}{\$54} = \mathbf{0.93}$	$\dfrac{\$12 + \$48}{\$66} = \mathbf{0.91}$	$\dfrac{\$8 + \$56}{\$75} = \mathbf{0.85}$

[1]This is the traditional definition of net working capital.
[2]Long-term financing = Long-term debt + Owners' equity.
[3]According to this definition, net working capital is the same as net long-term financing (see equation 3.4).

It is often said that the larger the current ratio, the more liquid the firm and that the ratio should be at least greater than one and preferably close to two. This reasoning, similar to that used for the traditional definition of net working capital, is based on the notion that the higher the current ratio, the easier it would be for the firm to repay its short-term liabilities with the cash raised from the sale of its short-term assets. For this to be possible, the firm's current assets should be at least equal to its current liabilities. In other words, its current ratio should be at least equal to one.

But if liquidity increases when the current ratio increases, why not have clients pay as late as possible in order to increase the firm's accounts receivable, why not keep as many goods as possible in stock, and why not pay the firm's suppliers as soon as possible? The first two decisions will significantly increase the firm's current assets and the third decision will substantially reduce its current liabilities. As a result, the firm's current ratio will go sky-high. But, has the firm's liquidity increased? Certainly not. The current ratio is definitely not a reliable measure of the firm's liquidity.

The value of OS Distributors' current ratio at the end of 1995, 1996, and 1997 is given in Exhibit 3.12. It varied from a low of 1.80 in 1996 to a high of 1.93 in 1995.

THE ACID TEST OR QUICK RATIO

Sometimes, analysts modify the current ratio by eliminating the relatively illiquid inventories and prepaid expenses from the firm's current assets. What remains is simply the sum of cash and receivables, the two most liquid current assets, also called **quick assets.** The result is called the **acid test** or **quick ratio:**

$$\textbf{Acid test or quick ratio} = \frac{\textbf{Cash + Accounts receivable}}{\textbf{Current liabilities}} \qquad (3.14)$$

The quick ratio is an improvement over the current ratio, but it still emphasizes a *liquidation view* of the firm as opposed to a *going-concern approach* to liquidity analysis. Furthermore, a firm's inventories are not always less liquid than its accounts receivable.

The value of OS Distributors' quick ratio is reported in Exhibit 3.12. It varied from a low of 0.85 in 1997 to a high of 0.93 in 1995. Creditors usually prefer a ratio close to one for most manufacturing firms.

SUMMARY

A firm's liquidity is driven by the structure of its balance sheet, that is, by the nature and composition of its assets and the way they are financed. Liquidity is easier to analyze if the standard balance sheet is restructured into the managerial balance sheet. This alternative presentation identifies the three components of the firm's invested capital: (1) cash, (2) working capital requirement, and (3) net fixed assets; and it identifies the three sources of capital employed to finance them: (1) short-term debt, (2) long-term debt, and (3) equity capital. Working capital requirement, which measures the firm's investment in its operating cycle, is equal to the difference between operating assets (accounts receivable, inventories and prepaid expenses) and operating liabilities (accounts payable and accrued expenses).

A firm's liquidity, which refers to its ability to meet its recurrent cash obligations, should be measured with the ratio of its net long-term financing to working capital requirement, where net long-term financing is the sum of equity capital and long-term debt minus net fixed assets. The higher that ratio, the higher the proportion of working capital that is financed with long-term funds and the higher the firm's liquidity.

The relatively smaller portion of working capital that is not financed with long-term funds is obviously financed with short-term debt. These short-term borrowings in *excess* of cash are called net short-term financing. In order to minimize the effect of both interest-rate risk (unexpected changes in short-term interest rates) and funding risk (unexpected cuts in the availability of short-term debt), most firms should limit the short-term financing of their working capital to its seasonal short-term component while financing the permanent long-term component with long-term funds. This approach to funding is known as the matching strategy.

The key to good liquidity management is good management of the firm's working capital cycle; a liquidity crisis is often the symptom of a mismanaged working capital cycle. If a firm's working capital requirement grows out of control and is not properly financed, liquidity problems appear immediately. Broadly speaking, good management of the working capital cycle means two things. First, accounts receivable and inventories, the two major components of working capital, must be held at their *minimum* levels relative to sales. This will allow the firm to save the cash it would have needed to fund a larger amount of receivables and inventories. Second, because working capital requirement is essentially a long-term investment, a firm's liquidity will rise as higher proportions of its working capital are financed with long-term funds.

Finally, the ratio of net long-term financing to working capital requirement is a superior indicator of a firm's liquidity position than the traditional benchmarks of net working capital, current ratio, or quick ratio. These last two ratios may be good indicators of a firm's ability to rapidly repay its current liabilities with the cash raised from the sale of its current assets, but they are not reliable measures of its capacity to meet its cash obligations on a *recurrent* basis.

3.1 FINANCING STRATEGIES

Firms may choose different financial strategies regarding the maturity structure of the funds used to finance their invested capital (cash, working capital requirement, and net fixed assets). The matching strategy, examined in this chapter, is the most common strategy and calls for matching the duration of the sources of funds with that of the investments. Some firms, however, may adopt other financing strategies, depending on the level of risk they are willing to take. They can adopt a **conservative strategy** if they want less risk or an **aggressive strategy** if they are prepared to accept more risk. This appendix examines the three strategies for a firm with seasonal and growing sales. The three strategies are illustrated in Exhibits A3.1, A3.2, and A3.3.

EXHIBIT A3.1   Financing Investments Using a Matching Strategy.

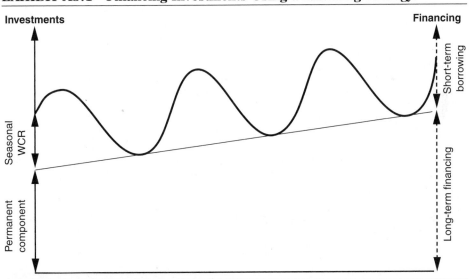

EXHIBIT A3.2   Financing Investments Using a Conservative Strategy.

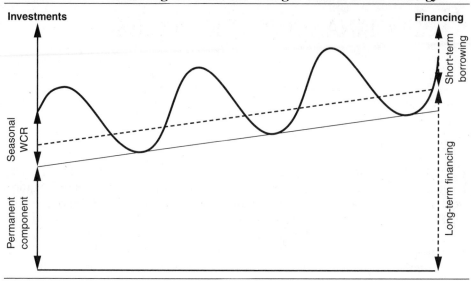

EXHIBIT A3.3   Financing Investments Using an Aggressive Strategy.

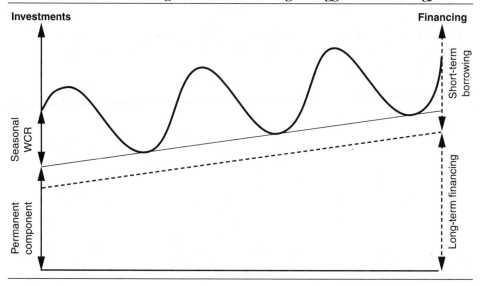

A firm with seasonal sales experiences changes in its working capital requirement during the seasonal cycle. Working capital requirement increases as sales increase and decreases as sales decrease. This is shown in Exhibit 3.7, where the behavior of working capital requirement is structured into a long-term, nonseasonal growth component and a short-term seasonal component. This short-term component of WCR is usually the only component of the firm's three fundamental investments that is directly linked to changes in sales during the seasonal cycle. The sum of net fixed assets, cash, and the long-term component of WCR makes up the firm's *permanent* nonseasonal investments. These investments are not significantly affected by seasonality in sales. Seasonal and permanent components of the firm's investments are shown on the left side of Exhibits A3.1 to A3.3. The right side shows the two components of the financing policy: long-term financing (owners' equity plus long-term debt) and short-term borrowing.

Exhibit A3.1 illustrates the matching strategy. Permanent investment is financed with long-term funds and seasonal investment with short-term funds. The objective of this strategy is to minimize (but not completely eliminate) the risk resulting from having a mismatched balance sheet.

Exhibit A3.2 shows the effect of adopting a conservative strategy. Permanent needs and some seasonal needs are financed with long-term funds. In this case, short-term borrowing covers only a portion of the firm's seasonal needs. At times, near the cyclical trough, the firm would have some excess cash (negative short-term financing). This "margin of safety" can be used to meet unforeseen cash needs that would have to be financed by an increase in short-term borrowing under the matching strategy.

The aggressive strategy, illustrated in Exhibit A3.3, implies that the firm uses short-term funds to finance a portion of the permanent component of its investments. This strategy is riskier than either of the other two strategies because the firm would bear more interest-rate risk and more funding risk. The interest-rate risk originates from possible variations in the level of interest rates during the useful life of the investments; the funding risk refers to the possibility that the firm may not be able to renew the short-term loans needed to finance a portion of the permanent component of the firm's investments. A firm may choose to bear more interest-rate and funding risks if it expects the short-term interest rate to decrease and, on average, to be lower than the current long-term rate over the useful life of the investment. In some instances, a firm may be forced to adopt an aggressive strategy. This situation happens when firms have limited access to long-term financial markets and must rely heavily on short-term financing.

REFERENCES AND FURTHER READING

1. Brealey, Richard, and Stewart Myers. *Principles of Corporate Finance.* 5th ed. McGraw-Hill, 1996. See chapters 29 to 31.
2. Hill, Ned, and William Sartoris. *Short-term Financial Management.* 2d ed. Macmillan, 1992. See chapters 1, 7, 9, 10, and Part V.
3. Ross, Stephen, Randolph Westerfield, and Jeffrey Jaffe. *Corporate Finance.* 4th ed. Irwin, 1996. See chapters 26 to 28.

REVIEW PROBLEMS

3.1. Evaluating managerial performance.

Allied & Consolidated Clothier (ACC), a manufacturer of coats and other garments, launched an aggressive marketing program aimed at raising the growth rate in sales in 1997 by at least 50 percent compared to the growth rate achieved in 1996. The company's financial statements from 1995 to 1997 are shown below. The income statements span a calendar year and balance sheets are dated December 31. All figures are in millions of dollars.

BALANCE SHEETS (IN MILLIONS)							
	1995	**1996**	**1997**		**1995**	**1996**	**1997**
Cash	$100	$90	$50	Short-term debt	$80	$90	$135
Trade receivables	200	230	290	Trade payables	170	180	220
Inventories	160	170	300	Accrued expenses	40	45	50
Prepaid expenses	30	30	35	Long-term debt	140	120	100
Net fixed assets	390	390	365	Owners' equity	450	475	535
Total assets	**$880**	**$910**	**$1,040**	**Liabilities & owners' equity**	**$880**	**$910**	**$1,040**

INCOME STATEMENTS (IN MILLIONS)			
	1995	**1996**	**1997**
Net sales	**$1,200**	**$1,350**	**$1,600**
Cost of goods sold	860	970	1,160
Selling, general, and administrative expenses	150	165	200
Depreciation expenses	40	50	55
Earnings before interest and tax (EBIT)	**150**	**165**	**185**
Net interest expenses	20	20	25
Earnings before tax (EBT)	**130**	**145**	**160**
Income tax expenses	40	45	50
Earnings after tax (EAT) or net profit	**$90**	**$100**	**$110**
Dividends	$75	$75	$50
Retained earnings	$15	$25	$60

a. Has ACC achieved its marketing objective?

b. Restate ACC's balance sheets in their managerial form. What does working capital requirement measure? Is it a long-term or a short-term investment?

c. Examine the structures of invested capital and capital employed in the managerial balance sheets prepared in part b (state each component as a percentage of the total). What do you observe?

d. Compare the 1995 balance sheet to the 1997 balance sheet. Are these balance sheets matched or unmatched?

e. Analyze ACC's operational efficiency from 1995 to 1997. Calculate and compare the following efficiency ratios for the three-year period. What can you conclude?

   1. Working capital requirement-to-sales ratio
   2. Average collection period
   3. Inventory turnover
   4. Average payment period (use cost of goods sold)

f. Analyze ACC's liquidity position from 1995 to 1997. Calculate and compare the following liquidity ratios for the three-year period. What can you conclude?

   1. The liquidity ratio (net long term financing to working capital requirement)
   2. The current ratio
   3. The quick ratio

g. What general conclusion can you draw from your analysis?

3.2. Working capital management for a retailer.

The consolidated financial statements of Carrefour, the French retailer, for year-end 1996 and 1997 are shown below.

BALANCE SHEETS (in millions of French Francs)					
	1995	**1996**		**1995**	**1996**
Current assets			**Liabilities**		
Cash and securities	FRF4,068	FRF2,960	Trade payables	FRF27,418	FRF29,836
Trade receivables	418	540	Other current liabilities[2]	9,715	10,725
Inventories	10,860	12,310	Long-term borrowings	4,764	7,840
Other current assets[1]	12,387	15,034	Other long-term liabilities	3,180	3,604
Capital assets			**Stockholders' equity**	**19,566**	**24,342**
Fixed assets	26,978	33,671			
Intangible assets	5,761	6,754			
Financial assets	4,171	5,078			
			Liabilities and owners' equity		
Total assets	**FRF64,643**	**FRF76,347**		FRF64,643	FRF76,347

Notes:

1. Mostly loans to other companies, including loans to nonconsolidated affiliated companies and deferred and recoverable taxes.

2. Short-term debts and accruals.

INCOME STATEMENTS (IN MILLIONS OF FRENCH FRANCS)	YEAR 1995	YEAR 1996
Net sales	FRF144,612	FRF154,905
Cost of sales	(118,212)	(125,072)
Gross margin from operations	26,400	29,833
Selling, general, and administrative expenses	(20,229)	(22,184)
Depreciation, amortization and provisions	(3,598)	(4,020)
Financial income, net of expenses	1,692	1,609
Income before taxes	4,265	5,238
Income taxes	(1,382)	(1,637)
Income adjustments (due to consolidation of accounts)	(193)	(362)
Net income	FRF2,690	FRF3,289

a. Calculate working capital requirement at year-end 1995 and 1996. Interpret your results.

b. Calculate the ratio of working capital to sales. What is the impact of faster growth on Carrefour's liquidity position?

c. What were Carrefour's average collection periods, inventory turnover, and average payment periods (based on cost of sales) in 1995 and 1996? What can you conclude regarding the impact of these parameters on the magnitude of Carrefour's working capital requirement?

d. Calculate Carrefour's current ratios and quick ratios. What can you conclude as to the reliability of these liquidity ratios for the case of retailers such as Carrefour?

CHAPTER

4 MEASURING CASH FLOWS

If a firm keeps spending more cash than it generates, it will eventually run into trouble. Thus, the ability of managers to make decisions that generate cash over time is essential to a firm's long-term survival. Making profits will help, but only if those profits can be quickly converted into cash. The firm's suppliers, its bankers, and the tax authorities require payment in cash, not profits. The road to business success is cluttered with bankrupt firms that were actually showing a profit in their last published income statement. Statistics for most developed countries indicate that almost four out of five firms that went bankrupt were actually profitable; they died from a lack of cash, not from meager profits.

There are two categories of cash flow: cash inflows, which are the number of dollars that come into the firm, and cash outflows, which are the number of dollars that go out of the firm. A successful value-creating manager must have a clear understanding of how these cash flows are measured, what their sources are, and how they should be managed.

This chapter presents a general framework for analyzing cash flows and their relation to business decisions. We first construct a preliminary cash flow statement based on the firm's three fundamental activities: operating, investing, and financing activities. Next, we show how to use the firm's balance sheets and income statements to measure the cash flows generated by each of these activities during the accounting period. We then put all the information together in a detailed cash flow statement. Finally, we present alternative methods for calculating cash flows that are often used by firms in presenting their cash flow statements. As in Chapter 3, OS Distributors' financial statements for the years 1995, 1996, and 1997 are used to illustrate the analysis. After reading this chapter, you should understand:

- The relationship between cash and cash flows.
- The relationship between profit and cash flows.
- How business decisions affect cash flows.

- How to use a firm's balance sheets and income statements to calculate the cash flows generated by the firm's operating, investing, and financing activities.
- How to prepare and interpret a cash flow statement.

CASH FLOWS AND THEIR SOURCES

The amount of cash held by a firm at a particular time is found on the asset side of its balance sheet. OS Distributors' balance sheets in Exhibit 4.1 show that the firm had $6 million in cash at the end of 1995, $12 million at the end of 1996, and $8 million at the end of 1997. If **total net cash flow** is the difference between the total amount of dollars received (cash inflows) and the total amount of dollars paid out (cash outflows) over a period of time, we can easily find OS Distributors' total net cash flow in 1996 and 1997. Each time OS Distributors received a dollar, its cash account increased by a dollar; each time it spent a dollar, its cash account decreased by a dollar. The amount of cash held by OS Distributors increased from $6 million to $12 million between December 31, 1995, and December 31, 1996. Therefore, during 1996, its activities must have generated a *positive* total net cash flow of $6 million, the difference between $12 million and $6 million. During 1997, the firm generated a *negative* total net cash flow of $4 million because cash decreased from $12 million to $8 million during that year. Thus, a firm's total net cash flow is equal to the *change* in the firm's cash position during a period of time.

Total net cash flow, which accounts for *all* the transactions the firm undertakes during a period of time, is, unfortunately, too broad a measure of a firm's net cash flow to be a useful indicator of the firm's ability to generate a surplus of cash over time. We want to know the *particular* activities that have contributed to an improvement and the *particular* activities that have contributed to a deterioration in the firm's cash position during a given period of time. For example, we want to identify activities associated with the following transactions: the firm receives cash from a customer (a cash *inflow* resulting from an operating activity); the firm purchases some new equipment (a cash *outflow* resulting from an investment decision); or the firm borrows from its bank (a cash *inflow* resulting from a financing decision). Each of these transactions will cause a change in the firm's cash position.

In general, a firm's cash position will change as a result of decisions related to three separate types of activities: (1) operating activities, (2) investment activities, and (3) financing activities. These activities are usually both a source of cash inflows and a source of cash outflows. Exhibit 4.2 shows typical transactions associated with each of these activities. The upper part of the exhibit presents the sources of cash inflow and the lower part presents the sources of cash outflow from these transactions. Each type of activity generates a net cash flow. The net cash flow for operating activities is called **net operating cash flow (NOCF);** for investing activities, **net cash flow from investing activities;** and for financing activities, **net cash flow from financing activities.** Each type of activity is related to a specific section of the firm's managerial balance sheet

EXHIBIT 4.1 OS Distributors' Balance Sheets.

Figures in millions of dollars

	DECEMBER 31, 1995		DECEMBER 31, 1996		DECEMBER 31, 1997	
ASSETS						
• *CURRENT ASSETS*		$104.0		$119.0		$137.0
Cash[1]		$6.0		$12.0		$8.0
Accounts receivable		44.0		48.0		56.0
Inventories		52.0		57.0		72.0
Prepaid expenses[2]		2.0		2.0		1.0
• *NONCURRENT ASSETS*		56.0		51.0		53.0
Financial assets and intangibles		0.0		0.0		0.0
Property, plant, and equipment (net)		56.0		51.0		53.0
Gross value[3]	$90.0		$90.0		$93.0	
Accumulated depreciation	(34.0)		(39.0)		(40.0)	
TOTAL ASSETS		$160.0		$170.0		$190.0
LIABILITIES AND OWNERS' EQUITY						
• *CURRENT LIABILITIES*		$54.0		$66.0		$75.0
Short-term debt		$15.0		$22.0		$23.0
Owed to banks	$7.0		$14.0		$15.0	
Current portion of long-term debt	8.0		8.0		8.0	
Accounts payable		37.0		40.0		48.0
Accrued expenses[4]		2.0		4.0		4.0
• *NONCURRENT LIABILITIES*		42.0		34.0		38.0
Long-term debt[5]		42.0		34.0		38.0
• *Owners' equity[6]*		64.0		70.0		77.0
TOTAL LIABILITIES AND OWNERS' EQUITY		$160.0		$170.0		$190.0

Notes

1. Consists of cash in hand and checking accounts held to facilitate operating activities.
2. Prepaid expenses is rent paid in advance (when recognized in the income statement, rent is included in selling, general, and administrative expenses).
3. In 1996, there was no disposal of existing fixed assets or acquisition of new fixed assets. However, during 1997, a warehouse was enlarged at a cost of $12 million and existing fixed assets, bought for $9 million in the past, were sold at their net book value of $2 million.
4. Accrued expenses consist of wages and taxes payable.
5. Long-term debt is repaid at the rate of $8 million per year. No new long-term debt was incurred during 1996, but during 1997 a mortgage loan was obtained from the bank to finance the extension of a warehouse (see Note 3).
6. During the three years, no new shares were issued and none were repurchased.

103

EXHIBIT 4.2 **Sources of Cash Inflow and Cash Outflow.**

Amounts are OS Distributors' cash flows in millions of dollars in 1997

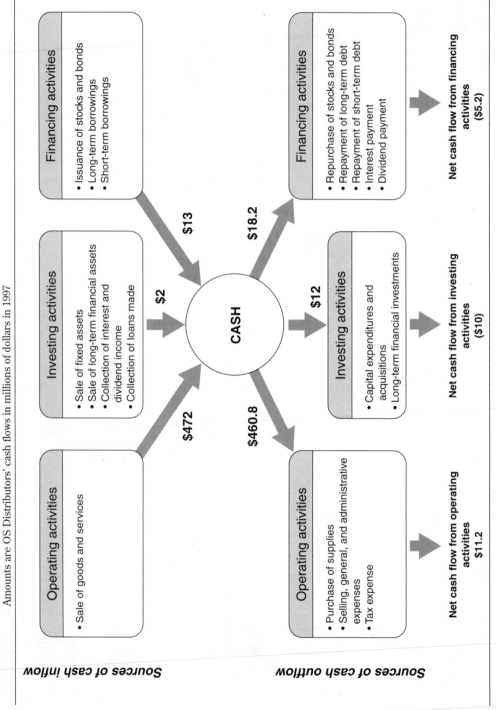

EXHIBIT 4.3   OS Distributors' Preliminary Cash Flow Statement for 1997.

Figures in millions of dollars

• CASH ON JANUARY 1, 1997[1]		**$12**
Net operating cash flow (NOCF)	$11.2	
+ Net cash flow from investment decisions	($10.0)	
+ Net cash flow from financing decisions	($5.2)	
Total net cash flow for year 1997		($4)
CASH ON DECEMBER 31, 1997		**$8**

[1]Cash on January 1, 1997, is the same as cash on December 31, 1996. See balance sheets in Exhibit 4.1.

which was introduced in Chapter 3. Operating activities, and thus NOCF, are associated with the firm's working capital requirement, which is the difference between its operating assets (its receivables, inventories and prepaid expenses) and its operating liabilities (its payables and accrued expenses). Investment activities are associated with net fixed assets.[1] Financing decisions are associated with the entire funding side of the managerial balance sheet, called capital employed. We explain how to calculate the cash flow amounts shown in Exhibit 4.2 in the next sections.

Exhibit 4.3 shows a preliminary cash flow statement for OS Distributors for 1997, using the information in Exhibit 4.2. The statement breaks down the change in the firm's cash position according to its operating, investing, and financing activities. The firm began the year with $12 million in cash (see Exhibit 4.1). As shown in Exhibit 4.2, its operations generated a cash inflow of $472 million and a cash outflow of $460.8 million. Hence, net cash flow from operating activities, that is, net operating cash flow, is equal to $11.2 million ($472 million less $460.8 million). Investment activities absorbed $10 million of cash and financing activities absorbed $5.2 million, leaving OS Distributors with a cash deficit of $4 million for the year ($11.2 million less $10 million less $5.2 million). This deficit was financed by taking $4 million from OS Distributors' cash account, leaving the firm with $8 million in cash at the end of 1997 (see Exhibit 4.1).

Notice that there is no obvious relationship between total net cash flow and net profit (earnings after tax) of the same year. In 1997, OS Distributors "lost" $4 million cash but generated $10.2 million in net profit (see OS Distributors' income statements in Exhibit 4.4).

[1]Net fixed assets include long-term financial assets that are considered a part of the firm's "investing activities." Cash inflows occur when long-term financial assets are sold, interest and dividend income are collected, and long-term loans, which were extended by the firm to outsiders, are repaid. Cash outflows occur when long-term financial assets are purchased and long-term loans are made to outsiders.

EXHIBIT 4.4 OS Distributors' Income Statements.

Figures in millions of dollars

	1995	% of Sales	1996	% of Sales	1997	% of Sales
• Net sales	$390.0		$420.0		$480.0	
Cost of goods sold	($328.0)		($353.0)		($400.0)	
• Gross profit	62.0	15.9%	67.0	15.9%	80.0	16.7%
Selling, general, and administrative expenses	(39.8)		(43.7)		(48.0)	
Depreciation expenses	(5.0)		(5.0)		(8.0)	
• Operating profit	17.2	4.4%	18.3	4.4%	24.0	5.0%
Extraordinary items	0		0		0	
• Earnings before interest and tax (EBIT)	17.2	4.4%	18.3	4.4%	24.0	5.0%
Net interest expenses[1]	(5.5)		(5.0)		(7.0)	
• Earnings before tax (EBT)	11.7	3.0%	13.3	3.2%	17.0	3.5%
Income tax expense	(4.7)		(5.3)		(6.8)	
• Earnings after tax (EAT)	$7.0	1.8%	$8.0	1.9%	$10.2	2.1%
Dividends	$2.0		$2.0		$3.2	
• Retained earnings	$5.0		$6.0		$7.0	

Notes
1. There is no interest income, so net interest expenses are equal to interest expenses.

PREPARING A DETAILED CASH FLOW STATEMENT

Detailed cash flow statements for OS Distributors for the two years ending on December 31, 1996 and December 31, 1997 are shown in Exhibit 4.5. The sources of cash inflow and outflow are those identified in Exhibit 4.2 and the amounts are derived from the firm's balance sheets at year-end 1995, 1996, and 1997 and its income statements for the years 1996 and 1997. The next sections explain how these cash flows are calculated.

In order to prepare a cash flow statement for a given year, we need an income statement for that year and two balance sheets, one at the beginning of the year (the same as the one at the end of the previous year) and the other at the end of

EXHIBIT 4.5   OS Distributors' Cash Flow Statements.

Figures in millions of dollars

	1996	**1997**
• CASH FLOWS FROM OPERATING ACTIVITIES		
(+) Net sales	$420.0	$480.0
(−) Cost of goods sold	(353.0)	(400.0)
(−) Selling, general, and administrative expenses[1]	(43.7)	(48.0)
(−) Tax expenses	(5.3)	(6.8)
(−) Change in working capital requirement	(4.0)	(14.0)
A. NET OPERATING CASH FLOW (NOCF)	**$14.0**	**$11.2**
• CASH FLOWS FROM INVESTING ACTIVITIES		
(+) Sale of fixed assets	0	2.0
(−) Capital expenditures and acquisitions	0	(12.0)
B. NET CASH FLOW FROM INVESTING ACTIVITIES	**$0**	**($10.0)**
• CASH FLOWS FROM FINANCING ACTIVITIES		
(+) Increase in long-term borrowings	0	12.0
(+) Increase in short-term borrowings	7.0	1.0
(−) Long-term debt repaid	(8.0)	(8.0)
(−) Interest payment	(5.0)	(7.0)
(−) Dividend payment	(2.0)	(3.2)
C. NET CASH FLOW FROM FINANCING ACTIVITIES	**($8.0)**	**($5.2)**
D. TOTAL NET CASH FLOW (A+B+C)	**$6.0**	**$(4.0)**
E. OPENING CASH	**$6.0**	**$12.0**
F. CLOSING CASH (E+D)	**$12.0**	**$8.0**

[1]Excluding depreciation expenses

the year. The balance sheet at the beginning of 1995 is not available, so a cash flow statement for OS Distributors for 1995 cannot be prepared.

NET CASH FLOW FROM OPERATING ACTIVITIES

Net cash flow from operating activities, or net operating cash flow (NOCF), is simply the net cash flow originating from the firm's operating activities during the period under consideration:

$$\text{Net operating cash flow (NOCF)} = \text{Cash inflow from operations}$$
$$- \text{Cash outflow from operations}$$

The sources of operating cash flows are the operating revenues and expenses in the income statement (see Exhibit 4.4). Operating revenues are net sales, and operating expenses are the sum of cost of goods sold, selling, general, and administrative expenses, and depreciation and tax expenses. However, not all these revenues or expenses generate or consume cash. A typical example is depreciation. There is no one to whom the firm pays depreciation.[2] Consequently, depreciation is excluded from the calculation of net operating cash flow. Furthermore, even though revenues and expenses eventually end up as cash inflows or outflows, they are not recorded as such in the income statement. As discussed in Chapter 2, revenues are shown in the income statement only when recognized, that is, when customers are invoiced, not when cash changes hands. Thus, an increase in revenues does not necessarily imply a corresponding cash inflow. Expenses are recorded only when they generate a corresponding revenue, not when they are paid. Thus, an increase in expenses does not necessarily imply a corresponding cash outflow. How then can we measure the cash flows from operating revenues and operating expenses?

We first consider the cash inflows from operations, the cash flows that originate from the sale of goods and services. Each time a customer is invoiced, the firm's accountant records the sale by increasing both the firm's net sales account and its accounts receivable by the amount of the sale. Cash comes in later when the customer pays. At that time, the accountant records the transaction by increasing the firm's cash account and decreasing its accounts receivable by the amount paid. Therefore, by following what happens to receivables over a period of time, we can estimate the cash inflow from sales during that period. Starting at the beginning of the period, receivables increase each time a sale is made and decrease each time a bill is paid. We can write:

$$\text{Accounts receivable}_{end} = \text{Accounts receivable}_{beginning} + \text{Sales}$$
$$- \text{Cash inflow from sales}$$

---

[2]When a fixed asset is acquired there is a cash outflow equal to the acquisition price of the asset. When that asset is subsequently depreciated over a period of time, the firm no longer experiences any cash movements related to the purchase of the asset.

Rearranging the terms of the above equation gives:

$$\text{Cash inflow from sales} = \text{Sales} - [\text{Accounts receivable}_{end} - \text{Accounts receivable}_{beginning}]$$

This equation can be written as:

$$\text{Cash inflow from sales} = \text{Sales} - \Delta\text{Accounts receivable}$$

where ΔAccounts receivable is the change in receivables during the estimation period.

When accounts receivable *increase* during a period of time (ΔAccounts receivable *positive*), the cash inflow from sales is *less* than the sales revenue during that period of time. When they *decrease* (ΔAccounts receivable *negative*), the corresponding cash inflow from sales is *more* than the sales revenue during that period of time. Hence, *given a target level of sales, the key to higher cash inflow from sales is a faster collection of accounts receivable.*

The procedure for estimating the cash inflow from sales can be applied to all the operating expenses that involve cash transactions. As shown in Appendix 4.1, the related cash outflow is obtained by adjusting the dollar amount of an income statement account with the change in the corresponding balance sheet account during the period. But the balance sheet accounts used for the adjustments are exclusively those related to the firm's operating cycle, which, by definition, are the accounts that make up its working capital requirement. The result, as shown in the appendix, is a very simple formula for obtaining the net operating cash flow from balance sheet and income statement accounts:

NOCF = Sales − COGS − SG&A expenses − Tax expenses − ΔWCR (4.1)

where NOCF is net operating cash flow; COGS is cost of goods sold; SG&A expenses is selling, general, and administrative expenses; and ΔWCR is the change in working capital requirement.

Let's consider an intuitive interpretation of equation 4.1. The firm's operations generate revenues and expenses that are recorded in the income statement and captured by the first four terms on the right side of the equation. These activities require an investment in the firm's operating cycle that is recorded in the balance sheet and that is measured by the change in working capital requirement during the period. Working capital requirement changes with the change in the amount of cash due to the firm by its customers, the change in the amount of cash paid for inventories, and the change in the amount of cash owed by the firm to its suppliers and other creditors. That is, the increase in working capital requirement (ΔWCR) represents the amount of cash the firm has used to finance the growth of its investment in operations. Because this cash is unavailable to the firm, it reduces its operating cash flow.

Using the data in Exhibit 4.6, which reproduce the managerial balance sheets of OS Distributors presented in Chapter 3, we can compute the change in OS Distributors' working capital requirement in 1996 and 1997 as follows:

$$\Delta WCR_{1996} = WCR_{12/31/96} - WCR_{12/31/95} = \$63 \text{ million} - \$59 \text{ million}$$
$$= \$4 \text{ million}$$

$$\Delta WCR_{1997} = WCR_{12/31/97} - WCR_{12/31/96} = \$77 \text{ million} - \$63 \text{ million}$$
$$= \$14 \text{ million}$$

Using equation 4.1 and the data in the income statements in Exhibit 4.4, we can now calculate the firm's net operating cash flow in 1996 and 1997:

$$NOCF_{1996} = \$420 \text{ million} - \$353 \text{ million} - \$43.7 \text{ million} - \$5.3 \text{ million}$$
$$- \$4 \text{ million} = \$14.0 \text{ million}$$

$$NOCF_{1997} = \$480 \text{ million} - \$400 \text{ million} - \$48 \text{ million} - \$6.8 \text{ million}$$
$$- \$14 \text{ million} = \$11.2 \text{ million}$$

The upper part of Exhibit 4.5 presents OS Distributors' net operating cash flow for 1996 and 1997, calculated using equation 4.1. Note the contribution of the change in working capital requirement to net operating cash flow in the two years. In 1996, the \$4 million increase in WCR represented less than 30 percent of NOCF; in 1997, it represented more than 120 percent of NOCF. In other words, the decrease in net operating cash flow that OS Distributors experienced in 1997 as compared to 1996 is mostly due to the growth of its investment in operations that was required to support growing sales.

Net operating cash flow can also be computed using a different approach. Because earnings before interest and tax (EBIT) is equal to sales less the sum of cost of goods sold (COGS), selling, general, and administrative expenses (SG&A), and depreciation expenses (see Exhibit 4.4), we can write:

$$\text{EBIT} + \text{Depreciation expenses} = \text{Sales} - \text{COGS} - \text{SG\&A expenses} \quad (4.2)$$

Replacing the "Sales − COGS − SG&A expenses" in equation 4.1 with "EBIT plus depreciation expenses," we get:

NOCF = EBIT + Depreciation expenses − Tax expenses − ΔWCR   **(4.3)**

For OS Distributors, we have:

$$NOCF_{1996} = \$18.3 \text{ million} + \$5 \text{ million} - \$5.3 \text{ million} - \$4 \text{ million} = \$14.0 \text{ million}$$

$$NOCF_{1997} = \$24 \text{ million} + \$8 \text{ million} - \$6.8 \text{ million} - \$14 \text{ million} = \$11.2 \text{ million}$$

A compact version of equation 4.3 can be obtained by noting that "EBIT plus depreciation" in equation 4.2 is equal to earnings before interest, tax, *depreciation,*

EXHIBIT 4.6 OS Distributors' Managerial Balance Sheets.

All data from the balance sheets in Exhibit 4.1; figures in millions of dollars

	DECEMBER 31, 1995		DECEMBER 31, 1996		DECEMBER 31, 1997	
INVESTED CAPITAL OR NET ASSETS						
• Cash	$ 6.0	5%	$ 12.0	10%	$ 8.0	6%
• Working capital requirement (WCR)[1]	59.0	49%	63.0	50%	77.0	56%
• Net fixed assets	56.0	46%	51.0	40%	53.0	38%
TOTAL INVESTED CAPITAL OR NET ASSETS	$121.0	100%	$126.0	100%	$138.0	100%
CAPITAL EMPLOYED						
• Short-term debt	$15.0	12%	$22.0	17%	$23.0	17%
• Long-term financing	106.0	88%	104.0	83%	115.0	83%
Long-term debt	$42.0		$34.0		$38.0	
Owners' equity	64.0		70.0		77.0	
TOTAL CAPITAL EMPLOYED	$121.0	100%	$126.0	100%	$138.0	100%

[1]WCR = (Accounts receivable + Inventories + Prepaid expenses) − (Accounts payable + Accrued expenses). These amounts are given in Exhibit 4.1.

and *amortization,* known as EBITDA.[3] Replacing EBIT plus depreciation by EBITDA in equation 4.3 we get:

$$\textbf{NOCF} = \textbf{EBITDA} - \textbf{Tax expenses} - \Delta\textbf{WCR}$$

For OS Distributors, EBITDA is equal to $23.3 million in 1996 ($18.3 million plus $5 million) and $32 million in 1997 ($24 million plus $8 million).

NET CASH FLOW FROM INVESTING ACTIVITIES

The firm's investments during the accounting period are not directly reported in its balance sheet or income statement. The balance sheet only reports the net book value of all the firm's fixed assets, and the income statement only reports the depreciation expenses for the accounting period. Fortunately, firms usually provide supplementary information in the form of notes to their financial statements from which it is possible to estimate the cash flows related to the firm's investing activities during the accounting period.

For example, Note 3 at the bottom of OS Distributor's balance sheets in Exhibit 4.1 explains that the firm did not sell or acquire fixed assets during 1996. However, during 1997, a warehouse was enlarged at a cost of $12 million and existing assets were sold at their book value of $2 million. Because OS Distributors does not hold any long-term financial assets, the cash flows from its investing activities are related only to the acquisition and disposal of fixed assets. They are shown in the second part of the cash flow statement in Exhibit 4.5. The net effect of the firm's investment decisions is a net cash flow of zero in 1996 and $10 million in 1997.

We can check that the net fixed assets accounts in the balance sheets are consistent with this information. Note that over a period of time these accounts increase when the firm acquires fixed assets and decrease when the firm deducts depreciation expenses and sells fixed assets. Thus:

$$\text{Net fixed assets}_{\text{end}} = \text{Net fixed assets}_{\text{beginning}} + \text{Fixed assets acquisitions}$$
$$- \text{Depreciation expenses} - \text{Fixed assets disposals} \qquad (4.5)$$

OS Distributors had no fixed assets acquisitions or disposals during 1996. The 1996 income statement shows depreciation expenses of $5 million, and the 1995 balance sheet indicates net fixed assets at the end of 1995 as $56 million. As a result:

$$\text{Net fixed assets}_{12/31/96} = \$56 \text{ million} + \$0 - \$5 \text{ million} - \$0 = \$51 \text{ million}$$

This is the same amount of net fixed assets reported in the balance sheet at the end of 1996. In 1997, OS Distributors acquired $12 million of new assets, sold $2 million

---

[3]An alternative expression for EBITDA is **earnings before depreciation, interest, and tax** or **EBDIT**.

of old assets, and had depreciation expenses of $8 million. Given that net fixed assets at the end of 1996 were $51 million, we have:

$$\text{Net fixed assets}_{12/31/97} = \$51 \text{ million} + \$12 \text{ million} - \$8 \text{ million} - \$2 \text{ million} = \$53 \text{ million}^4$$

Net Cash Flow from Assets

The sum of the net cash flows from operating and investment activities is a measure of the net cash flow generated by the firm's invested capital or net assets. These are the assets reported on the upper part of the managerial balance sheet shown in Exhibit 4.6. Exhibit 4.5 indicates that OS Distributors' net cash flow from assets was $14 million in 1996 ($14 million plus zero) and $1.2 million in 1997 ($11.2 million minus $10 million). This measure of cash flow is often called free cash flow; but, free cash flow has several alternative definitions, so we prefer to refer to the sum of net cash flows from operating and investing activities as net cash flow from assets.

Net cash flow from assets is the cash flow generated by the firm's invested capital. The remaining portion of a firm's total net cash flow is the cash flow from its financing activities. This cash flow corresponds to the capital employed shown in the managerial balance sheet.

NET CASH FLOW FROM FINANCING ACTIVITIES

A firm can carry out a large number of financing transactions. Some will add cash to the firm while others will absorb cash. The most frequently reported transactions are presented in Exhibit 4.2. They are reported for OS Distributors in the third part of the detailed cash flow statement shown in Exhibit 4.5. We can use the data from OS Distributors' balance sheets in Exhibit 4.1 and the data from its income statements in Exhibit 4.4 to identify and calculate the cash flows related to its financing decisions in 1996 and 1997.

In 1996, the firm increased its short-term borrowings by $7 million, as shown by the increase in its short-term bank debt from $7 million to $14 million during that year. During the same period, it repaid $8 million of its long-term debt (Note 5). The 1996 income statement shows that the firm paid $5 million in interest and $2 million in dividends. In 1997, short-term borrowings increased by $1 million, from $14 million to $15 million. The firm's long-term debt increased by the $12 million borrowed to finance the extension of its warehouse (Note 5), and the firm

---

[4]The value of disposed assets in equation 4.5 is the net book value of the assets. If the sale price is different, the difference is either an extraordinary gain (the sale price is higher than the net book value) or an extraordinary loss (the asset is sold at a lower price than the net book value). These gains or losses are accounted for in the income statement and affect the firm's earnings after tax.

continued to repay $8 million of its existing long-term debt (Note 5). Interest payments were $7 million and dividend payments amounted to $3.2 million.[5] In total, net cash flow from financing activities was a negative $8 million in 1996 and a negative $5.2 million in 1997, as shown in Exhibit 4.5.

THE CASH FLOW STATEMENT

The firm's total net cash flow is the balance of the firm's cash flows related to its operating, investing, and financing activities during a period of time. Recall that this net cash flow must be equal to the firm's change in its cash position during the period. We can now reconcile the cash flows from OS Distributors' activities in 1996 and 1997 with the changes in its cash position during these two years.

The firm's cash position at the beginning of 1996 was $6 million, as shown in line E of the cash flow statement in Exhibit 4.5. This is the amount of cash shown in the firm's balance sheet at year-end 1995 in Exhibit 4.1. During 1996, operations generated a net operating cash flow of $14 million (line A). The firm made no investments in 1996 (line B), and its financing activities absorbed $8 million of cash (line C). Hence, its total net cash flow was $6 million, the difference between $14 million and $8 million (line D). Its cash position was $6 million at the beginning of the year, so its cash position at the end of 1996 was $12 million, the sum of the initial $6 million and the additional $6 million generated during the year (line F). This is the amount shown in the firm's balance sheet at the same date.

During 1997, there was a total net cash outflow of $4 million (operations generated $11.2 million, investing activities absorbed $10 million, and financing activities absorbed $5.2 million). OS Distributors began the year with $12 million in cash, so it ended the year with $8 million, the initial $12 million less the $4 million consumed during the year.

Note that OS Distributors' cash flow statements are not needed to learn that the firm generated $6 million in cash in 1996 and consumed $4 million in 1997. This information is already available in the balance sheets given in Exhibit 4.1. OS Distributors' cash position was $6 million at the end of 1995, $12 million at the end of 1996, and $8 million at the end of 1997. Hence, total net cash flow is $6 million in 1996 ($12 million less $6 million) and a negative $4 million in 1997 ($8 million less $12 million). If this is the case, what is the usefulness of a cash flow statement?

The cash flow statement tells how and why the firm's cash position has changed during a particular period of time. It tells which of the firm's decisions have generated cash and which have absorbed cash. A sequence of historical cash flow statements indicates whether and how a firm's cash flow is improving or deteriorating and, thus, whether the firm is in a sound financial position or heading toward troubled times.

---

[5]Interest and dividend payments are equal to the figures shown in the income statements because OS Distributors does not have any accrued interest payable or accrued dividend payable. At the end of both years (1996 and 1997), the firm paid its interest expenses and its dividends for the year.

TWO VARIATIONS OF THE CASH FLOW STATEMENT

For internal purposes, some firms prefer to classify the cash flows from investing and financing activities reported in Exhibit 4.5 as cash flows they cannot control and cash flows they can control. Further, firms are required by regulatory authorities to provide a **statement of cash flows** that classifies the firm's cash flows as still different groupings. These two variations of the cash flow statement are analyzed in this section.

NONDISCRETIONARY VERSUS DISCRETIONARY CASH FLOWS

Consider a firm that wishes to finance the acquisition of a new asset only with internally generated cash. In other words, the firm does not want to raise any outside funds (borrow or issue equity funds) or sell existing assets or reduce its cash holdings. How then can the firm finance the acquisition? Can the firm's aftertax cash flow generated by operations, its net operating cash flow, be used to finance the acquisition? Not entirely. The firm has some financial obligations to meet; it must pay interest on its existing debt and may have a contractual obligation to repay some of its outstanding debt. The cash outflows that the firm is legally obliged to meet are called **nondiscretionary cash flows.** Hence, cash flow available to finance the acquisition is the firm's net operating cash flow less its nondiscretionary cash flow. This cash flow is called **discretionary cash flow.** It is the cash flow available for strategic investment decisions (capital expenditure or acquisitions, for example) and strategic financing decisions (paying dividends or buying back some of its outstanding stocks and bonds, for example) after all the firm's financial obligations are met.

Exhibit 4.7 presents a cash flow statement for OS Distributors that separates nondiscretionary and discretionary cash flows. Consider OS Distributors' position in 1997 when it needed to enlarge its warehouse at a cost of $12 million. Net operating cash flow is $11.2 million and the firm's contractual financial obligations are $7 million of interest payment and $8 million of loan repayment. There is no interest received or loan repaid to the firm. Thus, the cash available to finance the enlargement of its warehouse was a negative $3.8 million ($11.2 million less $7 million less $8 million). Consequently, OS Distributors could not finance this investment without raising new funds, selling some of its existing assets, or drawing down its cash balance.

What did OS Distributors actually do? It borrowed $13 million ($12 million long-term and $1 million short-term) and sold $2 million worth of existing assets, thus, raising a total of $15 million in cash. It used $12 million to finance the extension of the warehouse (capital expenditure) and $3.2 million to pay dividends, leaving OS Distributors with a total net cash outflow of $4 million, the same as the one shown in the cash flow statement in Exhibit 4.5. This cash deficit was financed by a $4 million decrease in the firm's cash position.

EXHIBIT 4.7   OS Distributors' Cash Flow Statements: Nondiscretionary Versus Discretionary Cash Flows.

Figures in millions of dollars

	1996	1997
• CASH FLOWS FROM OPERATING ACTIVITIES		
(+) Net sales	$420.0	$480.0
(−) Cost of goods sold	(353.0)	(400.0)
(−) Selling, general, and administrative expenses[1]	(43.7)	(48.0)
(−) Tax expenses	(5.3)	(6.8)
(−) Change in working capital requirement	(4.0)	(14.0)
A. NET OPERATING CASH FLOW (NOCF)	**$14.0**	**$11.2**
• NONDISCRETIONARY CASH FLOWS		
(−) Long-term debt repaid	(8.0)	(8.0)
(−) Interest payment	(5.0)	(7.0)
B. NONDISCRETIONARY NET CASH FLOW	**($13.0)**	**($15.0)**
C. CASH FLOW AVAILABLE FOR STRATEGIC DECISIONS (A+B)	**$1.0**	**($3.8)**
• DISCRETIONARY CASH FLOWS		
(+) Increase in long-term borrowings	0	12.0
(+) Increase in short-term borrowings	7.0	1.0
(+) Sale of fixed assets	0	2.0
(−) Capital expenditures and acquisitions	0	(12.0)
(−) Dividend payment	(2.0)	(3.2)
D. DISCRETIONARY NET CASH FLOW	**$5.0**	**($0.2)**
E. TOTAL NET CASH FLOW (C+D)	**$6.0**	**($4.0)**
E. OPENING CASH	**$6.0**	**$12.0**
F. CLOSING CASH (E+F)	**$12.0**	**$8.0**

[1]Excluding depreciation expenses

THE STATEMENT OF CASH FLOWS

The Financial Accounting Standards Board (FASB), one of the major U.S. organizations in charge of developing accounting standards, issued *Standard No. 95* in November 1987 entitled "statement of cash flows." Like the cash flow statement presented in the previous section, the statement of cash flows provides information on cash flows related to operating, investing, and financing activities, in that order.

**EXHIBIT 4.8 OS Distributors' Statements of Cash Flow:
Financial Accounting Standards Board (FASB) 95.**

Figures in million of dollars

	1996	1997
• CASH FLOWS FROM OPERATING ACTIVITIES		
(+) Earnings after tax	$8.0	10.2
(+) Depreciation expenses	5.0	8.0
(−) Change in working capital requirement	(4.0)	(14.0)
A. NET CASH PROVIDED BY OPERATING ACTIVITIES	**$9.0**	**$4.2**
• CASH FLOWS FROM INVESTING ACTIVITIES		
(+) Sale of fixed assets	0	2.0
(−) Capital expenditures and acquisitions	0	(12.0)
B. NET CASH FLOW FROM INVESTING ACTIVITIES	**$0**	**($10.0)**
• CASH FLOWS FROM FINANCING ACTIVITIES		
(+) Increase in long-term borrowings	0	12.0
(+) Increase in short-term borrowings	7.0	1.0
(−) Long-term debt repaid	(8.0)	(8.0)
(−) Dividend payment	(2.0)	(3.2)
C. NET CASH FLOW FROM FINANCING ACTIVITIES	**($3.0)**	**$1.8**
D. TOTAL NET CASH FLOW (A+B+C)	**$6.0**	**($4.0)**
E. OPENING POSITION	**$6.0**	**$12.0**
F. CLOSING POSITION (E+D)	**$12.0**	**$8.0**

However, the way these cash flows are calculated and the allocation of cash flows to these three activities are somewhat different, as can be seen by comparing Exhibit 4.8, which presents OS Distributors' statement of cash flows, with the cash flow statements in Exhibit 4.5.

Cash flows from operating activities

The net cash flow provided by operating activities in the statement of cash flows differs from the net operating cash flow (NOCF) in Exhibit 4.5 in two ways. First, it is estimated according to the **indirect method.** This method starts with earnings after tax and adjusts them for noncash items and transactions that are not related to the firm's operating activities. Second, the firm's operating activities include interest expenses which, in our approach, are part of the firm's financing activities.[6]

For OS Distributors in 1997, earnings after tax were $10.2 million (see Exhibit 4.4); depreciation expenses of $8 million are added because these expenses are not cash-related items. The balance of $18.2 million is then adjusted by the $14 million change in the firm's working capital requirement, as shown in Exhibit 4.5. The net cash flow from operating activities is thus $4.2 million ($18.2 million less $14 million). The difference between this amount and the net operating cash flow in Exhibit 4.5 is $7 million ($11.2 million less $4.2 million), which is, not surprisingly, the firm's net interest expenses for 1997.

Cash flows from investing and financing activities

The cash flows related to investing and financing activities are reported in the statement of cash flows the same way they are presented in our cash flow statement, except (1) interest payments are not shown as a financing activity, and (2) interest and dividends received from financial investments are not recorded as an investment activity. Because these items are already taken into account in the earnings after tax they are already included in the operating activities section of the statement. The differences between the two variations of the cash flow statement can be seen by comparing the statements in Exhibits 4.8, 4.7, and 4.5.

BANKERS' CASH FLOW VERSUS NET OPERATING CASH FLOW

A popular measure of a firm's cash flow is **bankers' cash flow** or **cash earnings.** It is usually defined as the sum of earnings after tax (EAT) and depreciation expenses (other noncash items are also added if there are any):

Bankers' cash flow = Earnings after tax (EAT) + Depreciation expenses (4.6)

Bankers' cash flow is derived exclusively from income statement accounts. It ignores any balance sheet adjustments. Because income statement accounts are usually not cash-related accounts, bankers' cash flow is not really a measure of cash flow. How does bankers' cash flow compare to net operating cash flow?

From Exhibit 4.4:

Earnings after tax (EAT) = Sales − Cost of goods sold − Selling, general, and administrative expenses − Depreciation expenses − Net interest expenses − Tax expenses

---

[6]Under the alternative or **direct method,** which was used in the cash flow statements in Exhibits 4.5 and 4.7, cash receipts and cash disbursements related to operating activities are reported directly and separately.

Substituting for EAT in equation 4.6 cancels the depreciation expenses. We now have:

Bankers' cash flow = Sales − Cost of goods sold
　　　　　　　　　 − Selling, general, and administrative expenses
　　　　　　　　　 − Net interest expenses − Tax expenses　　　　(4.7)

Comparing equation 4.7 and equation 4.1 leads to the following:

Net operating cash flow = Bankers' cash flow
　　　　　　　　　　　 + Net interest expenses − ΔWCR　　　(4.8)

where ΔWCR is the change in the firm's working capital requirement.

Thus, bankers' cash flow and net operating cash flow are equivalent only when (1) there is no variation in the firm's working capital requirement (ΔWCR = 0), and (2) net interest expenses are zero. This situation is unlikely.

Consider OS Distributors. Its net operating cash flow was $14 million in 1996 and $11.2 million in 1997 (see Exhibit 4.5). What was its bankers' cash flow? Applying equation 4.6 to the data from OS Distributors' income statement (see Exhibit 4.4), we get:

Bankers' cash flow$_{1996}$ = $8 million + $5 million = $13 million

Bankers' cash flow$_{1997}$ = $10.2 million + $8 million = $18.2 million.

While net operating cash flow *declined* by 20 percent between 1996 and 1997 (decreasing from $14 million to $11.2 million), bankers' cash flow *rose* by 40 percent during the same period. Net operating cash flow, a true measure of cash flow, takes into account the fact that in 1997 the firm had to invest an additional $14 million in its operations (ΔWCR = $14 million). Bankers' cash flow, which ignores changes in the firm's working capital requirement, behaves like a profit measure.

When a firm experiences a period of rapid growth, its profits usually rise. Consequently, the firm's bankers' cash flow increases according to equation 4.6. But because sales also increase during a period of rapid growth, so does working capital requirement. As a result, the firm's cash holding decreases. This explains why a firm can show a hefty bankers' cash flow and, simultaneously, find itself in a difficult cash position. Managers need to be wary of the traditional bankers' cash flow as a measure of a firm's change in cash position. Under the same circumstances—a period of rapid growth—net operating cash flow, which is negatively related to changes in working capital requirement (see equation 4.1), would decrease, providing the right signal: Sales growth has produced a corresponding growth in working capital requirement which, in turn, is putting pressure on the firm's net operating cash flow.

Finally, note that equation 4.8 provides another method for estimating a firm's net operating cash flow: Start with bankers' cash flow, add the firm's net interest expenses, and deduct the change in working capital requirement during the year. For OS Distributors in 1997, bankers' cash flow is $18.2 million. Interest expenses were $7 million and the change in working capital requirement was

$14 million. Hence, net operating cash flow was equal to $11.2 million ($18.2 million plus $7 million less $14 million).

MANAGERIAL IMPLICATIONS

Net operating cash flow, as defined in equation 4.1, can be written as a margin component less an investment component:

Net operating cash flow = Margin component − Investment component (4.9)

The margin component is defined as sales less the sum of cost of goods sold (COGS), selling, general, and administrative (SG&A) expenses, and tax expenses. The investment component is the change in the firm's working capital requirement.

Exhibit 4.9 shows the two components of OS Distributors' net operating cash flow in 1996 and 1997. Sales grew by 14.3 percent between 1996 and 1997 and the margin component increased by 40 percent. If the performance of OS Distributors' managers is measured only in terms of their contribution to profits, their 1997 performance was remarkable. However, in order to generate this higher margin in 1997, managers had to increase investment in the firm's operating cycle (working capital requirement) from $4 million to $14 million, a year-to-year growth of 250 percent! The net result is not flattering for OS Distributors' operating cash flow. Because the investment component of net operating cash flow grew much faster than its margin component, the firm's net operating cash flow actually *declined* by 20 percent. The implication is clear: *If margin decisions are made without consider-*

EXHIBIT 4.9   **Margin and Investment Components for OS Distributors' Net Operating Cash Flow.**

Figures in millions of dollars

	1996	**1997**	**PERCENTAGE CHANGE**
Sales	$420.0	$480.0	14.3%
less COGS	(353.0)	(400.0)	
less SG&A expenses	(43.7)	(48.0)	
less tax expenses	(5.3)	(6.8)	
= margin component	**$18.0**	**$25.2**	**40%**
Working capital requirement at the beginning of the year	$59.0	$63.0	
less working capital requirement at the end of the year	63.0	77.0	
= investment component	**($4.0)**	**($14.0)**	**250%**
NOCF = Margin − Investment	**$14.0**	**$11.2**	**−20%**

ing their effects on the firm's investment in its operating cycle, the result may be disastrous for operating cash flow.

Equation 4.9 indicates that firms should run and monitor their operating activities on the basis of net operating cash flow rather than margin. Monitoring the performance of operating managers on the basis of their contribution to the growth of net operating cash flow will encourage them to widen the firm's margin without letting investment in operations (working capital requirement) grow too fast and offset the contribution of wider margin to the firm's operating cash flow. The net effect will be a higher operating cash flow for the firm.

SUMMARY

A firm can be viewed as a "cash machine." It has to make strategic investment and funding decisions in order to generate more cash than it consumes. Strategic investment decisions include the building of plants, the purchase of equipment, and the acquisition of other businesses. Strategic funding decisions include long-term borrowing and the issuance of shares. The various cash flow statements presented in this chapter provide useful information about these decisions by showing how much money the firm has spent and how much money it has earned as a consequence of these decisions.

However, even though *strategic* decisions are the keys to the firm's long-term ability to create value, they do not guarantee that the "machine" will permanently produce excess cash. Only good *operating* decisions, that is, efficient day-to-day management of the firm's operating cycle (the machine's "engine") can, over time, help generate more cash than is consumed.

The relevant measure of the cash flow generated by operations is net operating cash flow. It is the net cash flow generated by *running* the business, not by selling some of its assets or borrowing from banks.

There are alternative approaches to calculating a firm's net operating cash flow. One approach is given by equation 4.1. In this formula, net operating cash flow equals sales less operating expenses (excluding depreciation expenses, a noncash item), tax expenses, and the change in the firm's working capital requirement. Another approach is given by equation 4.3. In this case, net operating cash flow equals earnings before interest and tax plus depreciation expenses less tax expenses and the change in the firm's working capital requirement. For a firm with a rising (and positive) working capital requirement, the change in working capital requirement represents the cash used to finance the growth in the firm's net investment in its operating cycle. The more cash that goes to fund operations (to support additional inventories and receivables for example), the weaker the firm's net operating cash flow. Thus, net operating cash flow is a better indicator of the ability of a firm to generate cash than the popular bankers' cash flow because bankers' cash flow ignores changes in working capital requirement and defines cash flow as the sum of net profit and depreciation expenses.

Net operating cash flow can be defined as the difference between a margin component and an investment component. The margin component is the firm's operating margin (its sales less its operating expenses, excluding depreciation expenses); the investment component is the change in the firm's working capital requirement.

Three types of cash flow statements are used interchangeably by firms. One distinguishes between cash flows generated from the firm's operating activities (its net operating cash flow), its investing activities, and its financing activities. Another distinguishes nondiscretionary cash flows from cash flows for which management has full discretion. The last one is the statement of cash flows recommended by the Financial Accounting Standards Board.

4.1 OBTAINING THE NET OPERATING CASH FLOW FROM BALANCE SHEET AND INCOME STATEMENT ACCOUNTS

Net operating cash flow (NOCF) is defined as the difference between the cash inflow and the cash outflow from the firm's operating activities. This appendix shows how these cash flows can be estimated from the balance sheets and income statement, using the estimation of OS Distributors' net operating cash flow in 1997 as an illustration.

MEASURING CASH INFLOW FROM OPERATIONS

As shown in Chapter 4, cash inflow from sales can be measured by tracing what happens to accounts receivable during the estimation period. This cash inflow is equal to sales adjusted by the change in receivables during the period:

$$\text{Cash inflow from sales} = \text{Sales} - \Delta\text{Accounts receivable} \qquad (A4.1)$$

where ΔAccounts receivable is the change in accounts receivable during the period.

Thus, the cash inflow from sales is calculated using information from the period's income statement and from the opening and closing balance sheets that surround the income statement. For example, what is the cash inflow from sales for OS Distributors in 1997? The balance sheets in Exhibit 4.1 show that accounts receivable at the end of 1996 and 1997 are equal to $48 million and $56 million, respectively. Therefore:

$$\Delta\text{Accounts receivable}_{1997} = \$56 \text{ million} - \$48 \text{ million} = \$8 \text{ million}$$

The 1997 sales are equal to $480 million, as shown in the 1997 income statement in Exhibit 4.4. From equation A4.1:

$$\text{Cash inflow from sales}_{1997} = \$480 \text{ million} - \$8 \text{ million} = \$472 \text{ million}$$

which is the amount reported in Exhibit 4.2.

MEASURING CASH OUTFLOW FROM OPERATIONS

Cash outflow from operations includes payments to suppliers for purchased goods; cash expenses related to selling, general, and administrative (SG&A) expenses, *excluding* depreciation, which is not a cash item; and tax payments. We can write:

$$\text{Cash outflow from operations} = \text{Cash outflow from purchases} \\ + \text{Cash outflow from SG\&A and taxes}$$

Cash outflow from purchases

To determine cash payments to suppliers, we use the same approach as the one used to calculate cash receipts from customers. Instead of tracing what happens to receivables during the estimation period, we trace what happens to payables. Each time the firm receives an invoice from one of its suppliers, accounts payable increase by the amount of the invoice and each time the firm pays an invoice, accounts payable decrease by the amount paid. Thus:

$$\text{Accounts payable}_{end} = \text{Accounts payable}_{beginning} + \text{Purchases} \\ - \text{Cash outflow from purchases}$$

Rearranging the terms of the equation, we get:

$$\text{Cash outflow from purchases} = \text{Purchases} - [\text{Accounts payable}_{end} \\ - \text{Accounts payable}_{beginning}]$$

This equation can be written as:

$$\text{Cash outflow from purchases} = \text{Purchases} - \Delta\text{Accounts payable} \qquad \text{(A4.2)}$$

where ΔAccounts payable is the change in payables during the estimation period.

However, unlike sales, purchases are not shown in the income statement. They must be computed indirectly from the data provided by the income statement and the balance sheets. For a distributor, inventories at the beginning of the period increase by the cost of purchases made during the period. When the firm sells the goods, these costs are released to the cost of goods sold (COGS) account. Thus, we can write:

$$\text{Inventories}_{beginning} + \text{Purchases} - \text{COGS} = \text{Inventories}_{end}$$

Rearranging the terms of the equation, we get:

$$\text{Purchases} = \text{COGS} + \Delta\text{Inventories} \qquad \text{(A4.3)}$$

where ΔInventories is the change in inventories during the period.

Equation A4.3 could have been obtained directly because, for a distributor, if the amount of goods purchased during the accounting period exceeds the amount of goods sold during that period, the inventories account will increase by the difference. If a distributor sells more goods than it buys during the accounting period, the inventories account will decrease by the difference.

Substituting the value of purchases given by equation A4.3 into equation A4.2 yields the following value for the firm's cash outflows from purchases:

$$\begin{aligned}
\text{Cash outflow from purchases} = \text{COGS} &+ \Delta\text{Inventories} \\
&- \Delta\text{Accounts payable} \qquad \text{(A4.4)}
\end{aligned}$$

Using the data in OS Distributors' 1997 income statement and in the balance sheets at the end of 1996 and 1997, the cash outflow from the firm's operations in 1997 is:

$$\begin{aligned}
\text{Cash outflow from purchases}_{1997} = \$400 \text{ million} &+ [\$72 \text{ million} - \$57 \text{ million}] \\
&- [\$48 \text{ million} - \$40 \text{ million}] \\
= \$407 \text{ million}
\end{aligned}$$

The first term on the right side of the equation is the cost of goods sold in 1997. The second term is the change in the inventories account in 1997. This is the difference between the inventories at year-end 1997 ($72 million) and year-end 1996 ($57 million). The third term is the change in accounts payable between year-end 1997 ($48 million) and year-end 1996 ($40 million).

Cash outflow from SG&A and tax expenses

To determine the amount of cash paid for selling, general, and administrative (SG&A) expenses and tax expenses during the estimation period, we must adjust them for any change in prepaid expenses and accrued expenses. This approach is similar to adjusting purchases for changes in accounts payable in order to determine the cash payments to suppliers. For example, when OS Distributors' prepaid expenses decreased by $1 million in 1997 (Exhibit 4.1), cash paid for operating expenses (in this case, rent payments as indicated in Note 2 to the balance sheet) was $1 million less than the expense reported in the income statement for 1997. To convert operating expenses into cash payments, the decrease of $1 million must be deducted from the expenses. If the prepaid expenses had increased, the increase would have been added to the expenses. In 1996, OS Distributors' accrued expenses increased by $2 million. This means that cash paid for operating expenses (in this case, payments for wages and tax, as indicated in Note 4 to the balance sheet) was $2 million lower than the expenses recorded in the 1996 income statement. As a result, the $2 million must be subtracted from operating expenses to arrive at the cash payment. If the accrued expenses had decreased, the decrease would have been added to the expenses. Therefore, if ΔAccrued expenses and ΔPrepaid expenses represent the change in the accrued and pre-paid expenses accounts, respectively, we can write:

$$\text{Cash outflow from SG\&A and tax expenses} = \text{SG\&A expenses}$$
$$+ \text{ Tax expenses} + \Delta\text{Prepaid expenses} - \Delta\text{Accrued expenses} \quad \text{(A4.5)}$$

Applying equation A4.5 to OS Distributors in 1997, we get:

$$\text{Cash outflow from SG\&A and tax expenses}_{1997} = \$48 \text{ million} + \$6.8 \text{ million}$$
$$+ [\$1 \text{ million} - \$2 \text{ million}] - [\$4 \text{ million} - \$4 \text{ million}] = \$53.8 \text{ million}$$

The terms in the first set of brackets are the selling, general, and administrative expenses and tax expenses from the 1997 income statement in Exhibit 4.4. The terms in the second and third set of brackets are the changes in prepaid expenses and accrued expenses taken from the balance sheets at year-end 1996 and 1997 in Exhibit 4.1.

NET OPERATING CASH FLOW

We can now derive a general formula for a firm's net operating cash flow. Adding the cash outflow from purchases in equation A4.4 to the cash outflow from selling, general, and administrative expenses and tax expenses in equation A4.4, we get the total cash outflow from operations:

$$\text{Cash outflow from operations} = \text{COGS} + \Delta\text{Inventories} - \Delta\text{Accounts payable}$$
$$+ \text{SG\&A and tax expenses} + \Delta\text{Prepaid expenses}$$
$$- \Delta\text{Accrued expenses}$$

Rearranging the terms of the equation, we get:

$$\text{Cash outflow from operations} = \text{COGS} + \text{SG\&A and tax expenses}$$
$$+ \Delta\text{Inventories} + \Delta\text{Prepaid expenses}$$
$$- \Delta\text{Accounts payable} - \Delta\text{Accrued expenses} \quad \text{(A4.6)}$$

For OS Distributors, using data from the income statements and balance sheets in Exhibit 4.1 and 4.5, we have:

$$\text{Cash outflow from operations}_{1997} = [\$400 \text{ million} + \$48 \text{ million} + \$6.8 \text{ million}]$$
$$+ [\$72 \text{ million} - \$57 \text{ million}]$$
$$+ [\$1 \text{ million} - \$2 \text{ million}]$$
$$- [\$48 \text{ million} - \$40 \text{ million}]$$
$$- [\$4 \text{ million} - \$4 \text{ million}]$$
$$= \$460.8 \text{ million}$$

which is the amount shown in Exhibit 4.2.

We can now estimate net operating cash flow by finding the difference between cash inflow from operations, equation A4.1, and cash outflow from operations, equation A4.6:

$$\text{NOCF} = [\text{Sales} - \Delta\text{Accounts receivable}] - [\text{COGS} + \text{SG\&A expenses}$$
$$+ \text{Tax expenses} + \Delta\text{Inventories} + \Delta\text{Prepaid expenses}$$
$$- \Delta\text{Accrued expenses} - \Delta\text{Accounts payable}]$$

The terms in this equation can be rearranged to yield:

$$\text{NOCF} = [\text{Sales} - \text{COGS} - \text{SG\&A expenses} - \text{Tax expenses}]$$
$$- [\Delta\text{Accounts Receivables} + \Delta\text{Inventories} + \Delta\text{Prepaid expenses}$$
$$- \Delta\text{Accounts payable} - \Delta\text{Accrued expenses}]$$

The first three items in the second set of brackets measure the *changes* in the firm's operating assets and the last two terms measure the *changes* in its operating liabilities. Recall that the difference between the firm's operating assets and its operating liabilities represents the accounting estimate of the firm's net investment in its operating cycle and is called working capital requirement (WCR). Therefore, the expression in the second set of brackets represents the *change* in the firm's working capital requirement, or ΔWCR. Thus:

$$\text{NOCF} = \text{Sales} - \text{COGS} - \text{SG\&A expenses} - \text{Tax expenses} - \Delta\text{WCR}$$

which is equation 4.1.

REFERENCES AND FURTHER READING

1. Kieso, Donald, and Jerry Weygandt. *Intermediate Accounting.* 8th ed. John Wiley, 1995. See chapters 5 (section 2) and 24.

REVIEW PROBLEMS

4.1. Constructing and interpreting cash flow statements.
The financial statements of Allied & Consolidated Clothier (ACC), a manufacturer of coats and other garments, are shown below. ACC's operational efficiency and liquidity position were analyzed in Chapter 3. The income statements span a calendar year and balance sheets are dated December 31. All figures are in millions of dollars.

BALANCE SHEETS (IN MILLIONS)							
	1995	**1996**	**1997**		**1995**	**1996**	**1997**
Cash	$100	$90	$50	Short-term debt	$80	$90	$135
Trade receivables	200	230	290	Trade payables	170	180	220
Inventories	160	170	300	Accrued expenses	40	45	50
Prepaid expenses	30	30	35	Long-term debt	140	120	100
Net fixed assets	390	390	365	Owners' equity	450	475	535
Total assets	**$880**	**$910**	**$1,040**	**Liabilities & owners' equity**	**$880**	**$910**	**$1,040**

INCOME STATEMENTS (IN MILLIONS)			
	YEAR 1995	**YEAR 1996**	**YEAR 1997**
Net sales	**$1,200**	**$1,350**	**$1,600**
Cost of goods sold	860	970	1,160
Selling, general, & administrative expenses	150	165	200
Depreciation expenses	40	50	55
Earnings before interest and tax (EBIT)	**150**	**165**	**185**
Net interest expenses	20	20	25
Earnings before tax (EBT)	**130**	**145**	**160**
Income tax expenses	40	45	50
Earnings after tax (EAT) or net profit	**$90**	**$100**	**$110**
Retained earnings	$15	$25	$60
Dividends	$75	$75	$50

a. Prepare a standard cash flow statement for the years 1996 and 1997. Interpret your results.

b. Calculate net operating cash flow in 1996 and 1997, using earnings before interest and tax (EBIT). What is the difference between this approach and the one in the cash flow statement in part a?

c. Calculate net operating cash flow in 1996 and 1997, using earnings before interest, tax, depreciation, and amortization (EBITDA). What is the difference between this approach and the ones in parts a and b?

d. Calculate net operating cash flow as the difference between cash inflows from operations and cash outflows from operations (refer to Appendix 4.1 to measure the latter).

e. What are cash flows from assets in 1996 and 1997? What do they measure?

f. What are bankers' cash flows, or cash earnings, in 1996 and 1997? How do they compare to net operating cash flows? What is the major weakness of this cash flow measure?

g. Separate the margin component from the investment component in the net operating cash flows in 1996 and 1997. What can you conclude?

h. Prepare a cash flow statement based on discretionary and nondiscretionary cash flows for 1996 and 1997. What is the advantage of such statements compared to the standard statements prepared in part a?

i. Prepare a statement of cash flows for 1996 and 1997. What is the difference between this type of statement and the one prepared in part a?

4.2. Examining the operating cash flow of a retailer.

Return to the 1995 and 1996 financial statements for Carrefour, the French retailer whose operational efficiency and liquidity positions were examined in problem 3.2 of Chapter 3.

a. What is the cash flow that Carrefour has generated from its operating activities in 1996?

b. Separate the margin component from the investment component in the net operating cash flow in 1996. What can you conclude regarding Carrefour's growth strategy?

5 DIAGNOSING PROFITABILITY, RISK, AND GROWTH

What impact do managerial decisions have on the firm's profitability? At first glance, this may seem to be an easy question. To find the answer, all you need to do is compare this year's net profit to last year's figure. If there is an increase, you can conclude managers improved profitability. If there is a decrease, you can assume managers did not run the firm profitably. Unfortunately, this straightforward comparison may not tell the whole story.

Suppose, for example, that higher profits came from an increase in sales that was achieved by giving customers significantly more time than usual to pay their bills and by simultaneously letting the firm's inventories rise to unusual levels in order to meet every customer's request promptly. In this case, looking just at profits in the firm's income statement does not provide the full picture. The rises in sales and profits have been achieved by increasing the size of the firm's balance sheet through higher accounts receivable and inventories. And, a larger balance sheet means that more capital is used to finance the firm's activities. Because capital is costly, a larger balance sheet may be detrimental to the firm. You need to know, instead, whether *profits per dollar of asset employed* has increased.

Alternatively, suppose a drop in profits came from a rise in interest expenses due to additional borrowing. This does not mean that financial managers made borrowing decisions that impaired profitability. Borrowing can be advantageous under certain conditions. If this were not the case, then firms wishing to achieve higher levels of profitability would never borrow. Our point is that an increase or a decrease in profits, in and of itself, is not a good indicator of a firm's financial performance.

The integrated approach to profitability analysis presented in this chapter takes into account the effects of managerial decisions not only on the firm's income statement but also on its balance sheet. For example, the approach is able to differentiate between an increase in profits that is accompanied by a rise in accounts receivable (a balance sheet item) from one that is accompanied by no change in receivables. We also show that an increase in borrowing does not necessarily reduce the firm's profitability. Alternative measures of profitability are discussed and we explain how they are related to one another. We also show how financial leverage, a measure of the impact of borrowing on a firm's profitability, affects the firm's riskiness. Finally, we review the concept of self-sustainable growth and its application to the management of the firm's growth strategy. As in previous chapters, the financial statements of OS Distributors are used to illustrate our analysis. After reading this chapter, you should understand:

- How to measure a firm's profitability.
- The key drivers of profitability.
- How to analyze the structure of a firm's overall profitability.
- How business risk and the use of debt financing affect profitability.
- How to assess a firm's capacity to finance its expected growth in sales.

MEASURES OF PROFITABILITY

Every manager has a favorite measure of profitability. It is usually a ratio calculated by dividing the firm's earnings after tax (net profit) by (1) sales to get **return on sales (ROS),** or (2) total assets to get **return on assets (ROA),**[1] or (3) owners' equity to get **return on equity (ROE).** Return on sales, or profit per dollar of sales, is traditionally used to measure the ability of managers to generate profits from the firm's sales; return on assets, or profit per dollar of assets, measures their ability to generate profits from the firm's assets. Return on equity, or profit per dollar of equity, is the standard measure of the profitability of the firm's equity capital, or owners' funds.

The measure of profitability that is adopted depends on the manager's area of responsibility. A sales manager would look at return on sales; the manager of an operating unit, with responsibility for that unit's assets, would choose return on assets. The chief executive, concerned with the firm's profitability to the shareholders who invested equity capital in the firm, would pay attention primarily to return on equity.

The three measures of profitability raise a number of questions. How are they related to one another? Which one is the most *comprehensive* indicator of profitability? How do managerial decisions affect profitability? How does risk affect profitability? These questions are answered in this chapter.

---

[1] A variation of ROA is **return on investment (ROI),** where the term *investment* refers to either the firm's total assets or a subset of its assets.

RETURN ON EQUITY

Return on equity (ROE) is the most comprehensive indicator of profitability because it is the final outcome of *all* the firm's activities and decisions made during the year. It considers the operating and investing decisions as well as the financing and tax-related decisions. The following sections show how to calculate ROE and then explain why it is the most comprehensive measure of profitability.

MEASURING RETURN ON EQUITY

Return on equity measures the firm's profitability from the perspective of the owners, those who invested equity capital in the firm. Their reward is the firm's net profit. The return on their investment is the ratio of earnings after tax (EAT) to owners' equity:

$$\text{Return on equity (ROE)} = \frac{\textbf{Earnings after tax (EAT)}}{\textbf{Owners' equity}} \qquad (5.1)$$

The amount of investment in the denominator of a profitability ratio, owners' equity in this case, can be measured at the beginning or the end of the period during which EAT was generated. In general, taking the average of the beginning and ending figures is usually the best alternative. The examples in this chapter use the *year-end* figures in all the profitability ratios because we want to compare the *three* years of data reported in OS Distributors' financial statements.

Based on the earnings and equity figures in Exhibits 5.1 and 5.2, OS Distributors' return on equity rose from 10.9 percent in 1995 (EAT of $7 million divided by $64 million of equity) to 13.2 percent in 1997 (EAT of $10.2 million divided by $77 million of equity). What are the firm's activities and decisions that produced this rise in ROE? To be able to answer this question, we must first find out how the firm's operating and financing activities affect its return on equity.

THE IMPACT OF OPERATING DECISIONS
ON RETURN ON EQUITY

Operating decisions, broadly defined, involve the acquisition and disposal of fixed assets and the management of the firm's operating assets (such as inventories and trade receivables) and operating liabilities (mostly trade payables). ROS (*net profit* per dollar of sales) and ROA (*net profit* per dollar of total assets) are not appropriate measures of the profitability generated by the firm's operating activities because they are calculated with *net profit* (earnings after tax). Net profit is obtained after deducting *interest expenses*—the outcome of a *financing* decision—from the firm's pretax operating profit. ROS and ROA are thus affected by financing

EXHIBIT 5.1 OS Distributors' Balance Sheets.

Figures in millions of dollars

ASSETS	DECEMBER 31, 1995		DECEMBER 31, 1996		DECEMBER 31, 1997	
• **CURRENT ASSETS**		$104.0		$119.0		$137.0
Cash[1]		$6.0		$12.0		$8.0
Accounts receivable		44.0		48.0		56.0
Inventories		52.0		57.0		72.0
Prepaid expenses[2]		2.0		2.0		1.0
• **NONCURRENT ASSETS**		56.0		51.0		53.0
Financial assets and intangibles		0.0		0.0		0.0
Property, plant, and equipment (net)		56.0		51.0		53.0
Gross value[3]	$90.0		$90.0		$93.0	
Accumulated depreciation	(34.0)		(39.0)		(40.0)	
TOTAL ASSETS		$160.0		$170.0		$190.0
LIABILITIES AND OWNERS' EQUITY						
• **CURRENT LIABILITIES**		$54.0		$66.0		$75.0
Short-term debt		$15.0		$22.0		$23.0
Owed to banks	$7.0		$14.0		$15.0	
Current portion of long-term debt	8.0		8.0		8.0	
Accounts payable		37.0		40.0		48.0
Accrued expenses[4]		2.0		4.0		4.0
• **NONCURRENT LIABILITIES**		42.0		34.0		38.0
Long-term debt[5]		42.0		34.0		38.0
• **Owners' equity[6]**		64.0		70.0		77.0
		64.0		70.0		77.0
TOTAL LIABILITIES AND OWNERS' EQUITY		$160.0		$170.0		$190.0

Notes
1. Consists of cash in hand and checking accounts held to facilitate operating activities.
2. Prepaid expenses is rent paid in advance (when recognized in the income statement, rent is included in selling, general, and administrative expenses).
3. In 1996, there was no disposal of existing fixed assets or acquisition of new fixed assets. However, during 1997, a warehouse was enlarged at a cost of $12 million and existing fixed assets, bought for $9 million in the past, were sold at their net book value of $2 million.
4. Accrued expenses consist of wages and taxes payable.
5. Long-term debt is repaid at the rate of $8 million per year. No new long-term debt was incurred during 1996, but during 1997 a mortgage loan was obtained from the bank to finance the extension of a warehouse (see Note 3).
6. During the three years, no new shares were issued and none were repurchased.

134

EXHIBIT 5.2 OS Distributors' Income Statements.

Figures in millions of dollars

	1995	% of Sales	1996	% of Sales	1997	% of Sales
• Net sales	$390.0		$420.0		$480.0	
Cost of goods sold	($328.0)		($353.0)		($400.0)	
• Gross profit	62.0	15.9%	67.0	15.9%	80.0	16.7%
Selling, general, and administrative expenses	(39.8)		(43.7)		(48.0)	
Depreciation expenses	(5.0)		(5.0)		(8.0)	
• Operating profit	17.2	4.4%	18.3	4.4%	24.0	5.0%
Extraordinary items	0		0		0	
• Earnings before interest and tax (EBIT)	17.2	4.4%	18.3	4.4%	24.0	5.0%
Net interest expenses[1]	(5.5)		(5.0)		(7.0)	
• Earnings before tax (EBT)	11.7	3.0%	13.3	3.2%	17.0	3.5%
Income tax expense	(4.7)		(5.3)		(6.8)	
• Earnings after tax (EAT)	$7.0	1.8%	$8.0	1.9%	$10.2	2.1%
Dividends	$2.0		$2.0		$3.2	
• Retained earnings	$5.0		$6.0		$7.0	

Notes

1. There is no interest income, so net interest expenses are equal to interest expenses.

135

decisions and do not reflect *only* operating decisions. The following sections present three ratios that are commonly used as substitutes for ROS and ROA when evaluating the specific contribution of operating decisions to the firm's overall profitability.

Return on invested capital (ROIC)

A relevant measure of operating profitability should have in its numerator the firm's pretax *operating* profit, or earnings before interest and tax (EBIT), and should have in its denominator the investments that were used to generate EBIT. EBIT is shown in the firm's income statement (see Exhibit 5.2), and the appropriate investments are shown in its restructured or managerial balance sheet, which was introduced in Chapter 3 (see Exhibit 5.3). The investments are listed on the upper section of the managerial balance sheet and are referred to as either *invested capital* or *net assets*. We have:

Invested capital = Net assets
$$= \textbf{Cash} + \textbf{Working capital requirement} + \textbf{Net fixed assets} \quad (5.2)$$

Cash and net fixed assets are the same as those in the standard balance sheets in Exhibit 5.1. Working capital requirement, a measure of the firm's *net* investment in its operating cycle, is the difference between operating assets (receivables, inventories and prepaid expenses) and operating liabilities (payables and accrued expenses).

Thus, a firm's operating profitability can be measured by the ratio of its EBIT to its invested capital. This ratio is known as the firm's **return on invested capital** or **ROIC:**

$$\textbf{Return on invested capital (ROIC)} = \frac{\textbf{Earnings before interest and tax (EBIT)}}{\textbf{Invested capital}}$$

$$(5.3)$$

There are several noteworthy observations to make regarding this definition of operating profitability. First, return on invested capital can be measured *before* tax, as shown above, or *after* tax. To get the aftertax ROIC, EBIT in equation (5.3) must be reduced by the amount of tax it generates. Thus, the numerator of equation 5.3 becomes EBIT less (EBIT × tax rate), that is, EBIT (1 − tax rate).

Second, the ratio in equation 5.3 can be interpreted in several ways. Invested capital is the same as net assets, so operating profitability can be also called **return on net assets** or **RONA.** Furthermore, according to the managerial balance sheet (see Exhibit 5.3), total invested capital (or total net assets) is equal to total capital employed, the sum of all the sources of capital used to finance net assets (both debt and equity capital). Thus, ROIC and RONA are also equal to **return on capital employed** or **ROCE.**

Third, cash is included in the definition of invested capital and net assets (see Exhibit 5.3). Therefore, any interest *income* earned on cash balances should be *included* in EBIT.

EXHIBIT 5.3   OS Distributors' Managerial Balance Sheets.

All data from the balance sheets in Exhibit 5.1; figures in millions of dollars

	DECEMBER 31, 1995		DECEMBER 31, 1996		DECEMBER 31, 1997	
INVESTED CAPITAL OR NET ASSETS						
• Cash	$6.0	5%	$12.0	10%	$8.0	6%
• Working capital requirement (WCR)[1]	59.0	49%	63.0	50%	77.0	56%
• Net fixed assets	56.0	46%	51.0	40%	53.0	38%
TOTAL INVESTED CAPITAL OR NET ASSETS	**$121.0**	**100%**	**$126.0**	**100%**	**$138.0**	**100%**
CAPITAL EMPLOYED						
• Short-term debt	$15.0	12%	$22.0	17%	$23.0	17%
• Long-term financing	106.0	88%	104.0	83%	115.0	83%
Long-term debt	$42.0		$34.0		$38.0	
Owners' equity	64.0		70.0		77.0	
TOTAL CAPITAL EMPLOYED	**$121.0**	**100%**	**$126.0**	**100%**	**$138.0**	**100%**

[1]WCR = (Accounts receivable + Inventories + Prepaid expenses) − (Accounts payable + Accrued expenses). These amounts are given in Exhibit 5.1.

Fourth, to evaluate the performance of a business unit that has no control over its cash, a variation of ROIC can be constructed. This ratio would *exclude* cash from invested capital and *exclude* interest income from EBIT. This measure of operating profitability can be called **return on business assets** or **ROBA.**

Another measure of operating profitability is **return on total assets** or **ROTA,** the ratio of EBIT to the firm's *total* assets as reported in its standard balance sheet. Note the distinction we make between ROTA and ROA (return on assets). The former is the ratio of EBIT to total assets whereas the latter is the ratio of EAT to total assets.

In this and the remaining chapters, we measure operating profitability with return on invested capital. But keep in mind that, according to our definition of invested capital, ROIC is the same as return on net assets (RONA) and the same as return on capital employed (ROCE). Finally, note that ROBA or ROTA can be substituted in the following analysis without any loss of generality.

OS Distributors' pretax ROIC is given in the last column of Exhibit 5.4. It rose from 14.2 percent in 1995 to 17.4 percent in 1997. To understand why this improvement occurred, we need to know what drives operating profitability.

EXHIBIT 5.4   **The Structure of OS Distributors' Return on Invested Capital.**

All data from the income statements in Exhibit 5.2 and the balance sheets in Exhibit 5.3; figures in millions of dollars

YEAR	OPERATING PROFIT MARGIN		CAPITAL TURNOVER[1]		RETURN ON INVESTED CAPITAL[3]
	$\dfrac{\text{EBIT}}{\text{SALES}}$	$\times$	$\dfrac{\text{SALES}}{\text{INVESTED CAPITAL}^2}$	$=$	$\dfrac{\text{EBIT}}{\text{INVESTED CAPITAL}}$
	$\dfrac{\$17.2}{\$390}$	$\times$	$\dfrac{\$390}{\$121}$	$=$	$\dfrac{\$17.2}{\$121}$
1995	**4.4%**	$\times$	**3.2**	$=$	**14.2%**
	$\dfrac{\$18.3}{\$420}$	$\times$	$\dfrac{\$420}{\$126}$	$=$	$\dfrac{\$18.3}{\$126}$
1996	**4.4%**	$\times$	**3.3**	$=$	**14.5%**
	$\dfrac{\$24}{\$480}$	$\times$	$\dfrac{\$480}{\$138}$	$=$	$\dfrac{\$24}{\$138}$
1997	**5.0%**	$\times$	**3.5**	$=$	**17.4%**

[1]Capital turnover is the same as net asset turnover (see Note 2 below).
[2]Invested capital (same as net assets) = Cash + Working capital requirement + Net fixed assets.
[3]Return on invested capital (ROIC) = Return on net assets (RONA).

The drivers of operating profitability

Return on invested capital is the ratio of pretax operating profit to invested capital, so any improvement in ROIC must be the outcome of (1) an increase in EBIT for the same level of invested capital, that is, an improvement in **operating profit margin** and/or (2) a reduction of invested capital for the same level of EBIT, that is, an improvement in **capital turnover** (also called **net asset turnover**), a measure of the efficiency with which invested capital, or net assets, is used to generate sales.

To find out how these two drivers of operating profitability affect return on invested capital, we write equation 5.3 as follows:

$$\text{ROIC} = \frac{\text{EBIT}}{\text{Invested capital}} = \frac{\text{EBIT}}{\text{Sales}} \times \frac{\text{Sales}}{\text{Invested capital}} \qquad (5.4)$$

The first ratio on the right side of equation 5.4 is the firm's operating profit margin (EBIT/sales) and the second is its capital turnover. Thus, a firm's ROIC is simply the product of its operating profit margin and its capital turnover:

Return on invested capital = Operating profit margin × Capital turnover

For example, Exhibit 5.4 shows that OS Distributors had an operating profit margin of 4.4 percent in 1995, meaning that it generated that year, on average, $4.4 of pretax operating profit per $100 of sales. Its capital turnover was 3.2, indicating that the company needed, on average, $100 of invested capital to generate $320 of sales.

Obviously, the higher a firm's operating profit margin and capital turnover, the higher its operating profitability. A higher operating profit margin is achieved by (1) increasing sales through higher prices and/or higher volume at a higher rate than operating expenses and/or (2) reducing operating expenses at a higher rate than sales. A higher capital turnover is achieved through a better use of the assets required to support the firm's sales activities, for example, through a faster inventory turn, a shorter collection period for the firm's receivables, or fewer fixed assets per dollar of sales.

As shown in Exhibit 5.4, OS Distributors' operating profitability rose slightly from 14.2 percent in 1995 to 14.5 percent in 1996 due to a small rise in capital turnover from 3.2 to 3.3. In 1997, operating profitability increased to 17.4 percent as a result of a rise in operating profit margin from 4.4 percent to 5.0 percent accompanied by an increase in capital turnover from 3.3 to 3.5.

If the key to higher operating profitability is a combination of higher operating profit margin and faster capital turnover, what are the underlying factors that would allow a firm to achieve this? Appendix 5.1 presents a summary of a study that analyzed the factors that affect the pretax operating profitability of a large sample of businesses across many countries. Beyond the specific characteristics of the market in which a business competes (the degree of innovation and technical change, the relative power of customers and suppliers, and the market's rate of growth), three factors emerge from the study: (1) the firm's competitive position as measured by its *market share* relative to that of its competitors, (2) the relative *quality of its products and services,* and (3) the firm's *cost and assets structures,* namely, the composition and concentration of its assets, the structure of its costs, and its degrees of vertical integration and capacity utilization.

The results of the study indicate that *high market share and superior product quality, on average, boost operating profitability, and high investments and high fixed costs, on average, depress it.* In the sample, those businesses with the highest market shares and superior products and services had an average pretax operating profitability of 39 percent; those with inferior products and services had an average pretax operating profitability of only 9 percent. Businesses with low capital turnover—those with relatively higher fixed assets and fixed costs per dollar of sales—were, on average, unable to offset their lower capital turnover with higher operating profit margin and hence had, in general, lower pretax operating profitability than businesses with high capital turnover. Businesses with a capital turnover below 1.5 had an average pretax operating profitability of 8 percent whereas those with a turnover above 3.3 had an average pretax operating profitability of 38 percent. For a more detailed examination and interpretation of these results, see Appendix 5.1.

The link between return on equity and operating profitability

To understand the link between return on equity (ROE) and operating profitability, as measured by return on invested capital (ROIC), consider the case of a firm that has not borrowed a single dollar; its net assets are entirely financed with equity capital. What is the relationship between this firm's *pretax* ROE and its *pretax* ROIC? If the firm has not borrowed a single dollar, it has no interest expenses. Thus, its pretax profit, or earnings before tax (EBT), must be equal to its earnings before interest and tax (EBIT). And, if the firm's assets are entirely equity financed, then the firm's invested capital must be equal to its owners' equity. In other words, *if a firm does not borrow, its pretax return on invested capital is equal to its pretax return on equity.*[2]

THE IMPACT OF FINANCING DECISIONS ON RETURN ON EQUITY

If return on invested capital and return on equity are the same when a firm does not borrow, then any difference between them must be due to the use of debt to finance the firm's net assets. What are the effects of the firm's financing decisions on its return on equity?

Let's consider what happens when a firm replaces some of its equity capital with an equal amount of debt. The higher proportion of debt financing resulting

---

[2]We show later that the statement is also correct if returns are measured *after* taxes.

from this **recapitalization**[3] increases the firm's **financial leverage** or **gearing.** A firm without borrowed funds is said to be **unlevered;** the higher the amount of debt relative to equity, the higher the firm's financial leverage. A higher leverage affects the firm's ROE in two ways. First, the firm's interest expenses increase and its earnings after tax (EAT) decrease. This will reduce ROE because EAT is the numerator of ROE. Second, owners' equity decreases because debt has replaced equity. This will increase ROE because owners' equity is the denominator of ROE. Conclusion: You cannot predict how financial leverage affects the firm's ROE. There is a **financial cost effect** that *reduces* ROE (more interest expenses) and a simultaneous **financial structure effect** that *increases* ROE (less equity capital). The net effect depends on the strength of the former relative to the latter. If the financial cost effect is weaker than the financial structure effect, higher financial leverage will increase the firm's ROE. If it is stronger, higher financial leverage will decrease the firm's ROE. The ratios that measure these two effects are discussed in the following sections.

The financial cost ratio

The financial cost effect is captured in the firm's income statement. It is measured with the **financial cost ratio,** which is defined as the firm's earnings before tax (EBT) divided by its earnings before interest and tax (EBIT):

$$\text{Financial cost ratio} = \frac{\textbf{Earnings before tax (EBT)}}{\textbf{Earnings before interest and tax (EBIT)}} \quad (5.5)$$

As the amount of debt financing *increases,* (1) EBT relative to EBIT *decreases,* (2) the financial cost ratio *decreases,* and (3) the firm's return on equity *decreases,* all else the same. If the firm is entirely equity financed, then the ratio is equal to one because EBT and EBIT are equal in this case. This is the maximum value of the ratio. If the firm borrows, its financial cost ratio will be smaller than one.

OS Distributors' financial cost ratios are given in the fourth column of Exhibit 5.5. The ratio was 0.68 in 1995, 0.73 in 1996, and 0.71 in 1997. The ratios indicate that OS Distributors had interest expenses during the three years (the three ratios are smaller than one) and that interest expenses relative to pretax operating profit (EBIT) were highest in 1995 (the ratio is lowest that year).

A popular ratio, similar to the financial cost ratio, is the **times-interest-earned ratio** or **interest coverage ratio.** It is defined as earnings before interest and tax divided by interest expenses:

$$\text{Times interest earned} = \frac{\textbf{Earnings before interest and tax (EBIT)}}{\textbf{Interest expenses}} \quad (5.6)$$

---

[3]The substitution of debt for equity, leaving assets unchanged, is called a recapitalization. It can be carried out by using the proceeds from borrowing to buy back common stocks from shareholders. The repurchased shares reduce the firm's equity by the same amount.

EXHIBIT 5.5 The Structure of OS Distributors' Return on Equity.

All data from the balance sheets in Exhibits 5.1 and 5.3 and the income statements in Exhibit 5.2; figures in millions of dollars

ROE	=	OPERATING PROFITABILITY	×	FINANCIAL LEVERAGE MULTIPLIER	×	TAX EFFECT

$$\text{ROE} = \frac{\text{EAT}}{\text{Owners' equity}} = \left[\frac{\text{Operating profit margin}}{} \times \frac{\text{Capital turnover}}{}\right] \times \left[\frac{\text{Financial cost ratio}}{} \times \frac{\text{Financial structure ratio}}{}\right] \times \left[\frac{\text{Tax-effect ratio}}{}\right]$$

$$\frac{\text{EAT}}{\text{Owners' equity}} = \frac{\text{EBIT}}{\text{Sales}} \times \frac{\text{Sales}}{\text{Invested capital}} \times \frac{\text{EBT}}{\text{EBIT}} \times \frac{\text{Invested capital}}{\text{Owners' equity}} \times \frac{\text{EAT}}{\text{EBT}}$$

Return on invested capital (ROIC) ⟵ Operating Profitability

Financial leverage multiplier ⟵ Financial Leverage Multiplier

1995

$$\frac{\$7}{\$64} = \frac{\$17.2}{\$390} \times \frac{\$390}{\$121} \times \frac{\$11.7}{\$17.2} \times \frac{\$121}{\$64} \times \frac{\$7}{\$11.7}$$

$$10.9\% = 4.4\% \times 3.2 \times 0.68 \times 1.89 \times 0.60$$

ROIC = 14.2%   Financial leverage multiplier = 1.29

1996

$$\frac{\$8}{\$70} = \frac{\$18.3}{\$420} \times \frac{\$420}{\$126} \times \frac{\$13.3}{\$18.3} \times \frac{\$126}{\$70} \times \frac{\$8}{\$13.3}$$

$$11.4\% = 4.4\% \times 3.3 \times 0.73 \times 1.80 \times 0.60$$

ROIC = 14.5%   Financial leverage multiplier = 1.31

1997

$$\frac{\$10.2}{\$77} = \frac{\$24}{\$480} \times \frac{\$480}{\$138} \times \frac{\$17}{\$24} \times \frac{\$138}{\$77} \times \frac{\$10.2}{\$17}$$

$$13.2\% = 5.0\% \times 3.5 \times 0.71 \times 1.79 \times 0.60$$

ROIC = 17.4%   Financial leverage multiplier = 1.27

This ratio indicates how many times the firm's pretax operating profit (EBIT) covers its interest expenses. For example, OS Distributors' 1997 income statement in Exhibit 5.2 shows that the firm's EBIT of $24 million covered its $7 million of interest expenses 3.4 times ($24 million divided by $7 million). The higher the ratio, the higher the firm's ability to meet its interest payments.

The financial structure ratio

The financial structure effect is captured in the firm's balance sheet. It is measured with the **financial structure ratio,** also known as the **equity multiplier.** This ratio is invested capital, or net assets, divided by owners' equity:

$$\text{Financial structure ratio} = \frac{\textbf{Invested capital or net assets}}{\textbf{Owners' equity}} \tag{5.7}$$

For a given amount of invested capital, as the amount of debt financing *increases,* (1) owners' equity *decreases,* (2) the financial structure ratio *increases,* and (3) the firm's return on equity *increases,* all else the same. If the firm's invested capital is entirely financed with equity, then invested capital is equal to owners' equity and the financial structure ratio is equal to one, its minimum value. It can reach, theoretically, very large values as more debt is used to finance the firm's net assets.

OS Distributors' financial structure ratios are given in the fifth column of Exhibit 5.5. The ratio went from 1.89 in 1995 to 1.79 in 1997, indicating that the *proportion* of OS Distributors' net assets that were financed with debt decreased during that period.

Other measures of financial leverage

The financial structure ratio is one of several debt ratios used to measure the firm's borrowing relative to its equity financing. Other popular ratios include the **debt-to-equity ratio,** or simply the **debt ratio,** (debt divided by owners' equity) and the **debt-to-invested capital ratio** (debt divided by the sum of debt and equity). Our financial structure ratio is related to these two ratios as follows:

$$\text{Financial structure ratio} = \frac{\text{Invested capital}}{\text{Owners' equity}} = \frac{\text{Owners' equity} + \text{Debt}}{\text{Owners' equity}} \tag{5.8}$$

$$= 1 + \frac{\text{Debt}}{\text{Equity}}$$

$$\text{Financial structure ratio} = \frac{\text{Invested capital}}{\text{Owners' equity}} = \frac{\text{Invested capital}}{\text{Invested capital} - \text{Debt}}$$

$$= \frac{1}{1 - \dfrac{\text{Debt}}{\text{Invested capital}}}$$

For example, if a firm is financed with an equal amount of debt and equity then its financial structure ratio is 2 (invested capital is twice owners' equity), its debt-to-equity ratio is 1, and its debt-to-invested capital ratio is 0.5. Note that when the firm increases its borrowing, the three debt ratios increase.

THE INCIDENCE OF TAXATION ON RETURN ON EQUITY

The third determinant of a firm's ROE is the incidence of corporate taxation. The higher the tax rate applied to a firm's earnings before tax (EBT), the lower its ROE. The incidence of tax is measured by the **tax effect ratio:**

$$\text{Tax effect ratio} = \frac{\textbf{Earnings after tax (EAT)}}{\textbf{Earnings before tax (EBT)}}$$

EAT is equal to EBT(1 − effective tax rate), so the tax-effect ratio is equal to one less the effective corporate tax rate:

$$\text{Tax effect ratio} = \frac{\text{EAT}}{\text{EBT}} = \frac{\text{EBT(1 − effective tax rate)}}{\text{EBT}}$$

$$= 1 - \text{effective tax rate} \qquad (5.9)$$

As the effective corporate tax rate increases, the tax-effect ratio decreases and the firm keeps a smaller percentage of its pretax earnings. Other things being equal, the firm's ROE decreases. Consider OS Distributors. Its pretax earnings (EBT) are taxed at the rate of 40 percent; hence, its tax-effect ratio is 60 percent, as shown in the last column of Exhibit 5.5.

The relevant corporate tax rate is the **effective tax rate** the firm pays, not the **statutory tax rate.** The effective tax rate can be significantly lower than the maximum statutory tax rate imposed by the tax authority if some of the firm's earnings are exempt from taxes. For example, the statutory corporate tax rate in the United States was equal to 34 percent in 1990. But, data from DEC's and IBM's annual reports for that year (Exhibit 5.6) reveal a significant difference between their effective tax rates. DEC's annual report stated that the company's lower effective tax rate of 24.5 percent was due mostly to manufacturing operations located in

EXHIBIT 5.6   Comparison of Effective Tax Rates in 1990.

Figures in thousands of dollars

FIRM	EBT	EAT	EQUITY	PRETAX ROE	TAX-EFFECT RATIO	AFTERTAX ROE	EFFECTIVE TAX RATE
DEC	$1,421	$1,073	$8,036	17.7%	75.5%	13.4%	24.5%
IBM	$10,203	$6,020	$42,832	23.8%	59.0%	14.0%	41.0%

Source: Companies' Annual Reports.

countries that offer tax breaks to attract foreign companies. IBM's annual report stated that the company's higher effective tax rate of 41 percent was due to higher taxes on earnings of non-U.S. operations. Taxes on foreign earnings reduced DEC's tax rate but raised that of IBM.

Notice the incidence on the two companies' profitability of the difference in their effective tax rates. IBM's pretax ROE of 23.8 percent is significantly higher than DEC's pretax ROE of 17.7 percent but their aftertax ROE's are almost the same (14.0 percent and 13.4 percent, respectively). IBM's superior pretax profitability that year was significantly diminished by the incidence of corporate taxes, but DEC managed to soften the impact of taxation on profitability by making earlier, tax-reducing decisions.

Our point is that a firm should plan to minimize its tax liabilities as early as possible. For example, when evaluating an investment proposal, it should consider locating in countries or regions that offer significant tax breaks. By reducing its effective tax rate to its lowest possible level, the firm will raise its ROE.

PUTTING IT ALL TOGETHER: THE STRUCTURE OF A FIRM'S PROFITABILITY

The previous sections identify five ratios that affect a firm's return on equity: (1) the operating profit margin (EBIT/sales), (2) the capital or net asset turnover (sales/invested capital), (3) the financial cost ratio (EBT/EBIT), (4) the financial structure ratio (invested capital/equity), and (5) the tax effect ratio (EAT/EBT). The relationship that ties these ratios to the firm's return on equity is straightforward. *ROE is simply equal to the product of these five ratios:*

$$
\text{ROE} = \frac{\text{EAT}}{\text{Owners' equity}} \tag{5.10}
$$

$$
= \frac{\text{EBIT}}{\text{Sales}} \times \frac{\text{Sales}}{\text{Invested capital}} \times \frac{\text{EBT}}{\text{EBIT}} \times \frac{\text{Invested capital}}{\text{Owners' equity}} \times \frac{\text{EAT}}{\text{EBT}}
$$

The product of the five ratios on the right side of equation 5.10 is equal to EAT divided by owners' equity. You can check this by simply canceling EBIT, sales, invested capital, and EBT because they appear in both a numerator and a denominator. The only items left are EAT in the numerator and owners' equity in the denominator.

The first two ratios capture the impact of the firm's investing and operating decisions on its overall profitability. Their product is equal to the firm's pretax operating profitability measured by the return on invested capital (ROIC in equation 5.4). The third and fourth ratios capture the impact of the firm's financial policy on its overall profitability. We call their product the firm's **financial leverage multiplier:**

$$
\textbf{Financial leverage multiplier =}
$$
$$
\textbf{Financial cost ratio} \times \textbf{Financial structure ratio} \tag{5.11}
$$

The last ratio captures the effect of corporate taxation on return on equity and, as shown earlier, is equal to (1 − effective tax rate). Thus, equation 5.10 can be written as:

ROE = ROIC × Financial leverage multiplier × (1 − effective tax rate)   (5.12)

If we ignore the incidence of taxes on profitability and focus on *pretax* ROE, equation 5.12 can be written as:

$$\text{pretax ROE} = \text{ROIC} \times \text{Financial leverage multiplier}$$

Obviously, if the financial leverage multiplier is greater than one, pretax ROE exceeds ROIC. If it is less than one, pretax ROE is lower than ROIC. Exhibit 5.7 provides a pictorial representation of the five ratios behind ROE and the way they are related.

We can now examine the structure of OS Distributors' profitability, shown in Exhibit 5.5. Compare ROE in 1995 to ROE in 1997: It increased from 10.9 percent in 1995 to 13.2 percent in 1997. Is this small improvement the outcome of improved operating performance, a higher financial leverage multiplier, or a reduction in OS Distributors' effective tax rate? The exhibit indicates that the improvement in ROE is due to a better operating margin coupled with a higher capital turnover.[4] These pushed operating profitability from 14.2 percent to 17.4 percent. The financial leverage multiplier declined slightly, from 1.29 to 1.27, and the tax effect was unchanged.

THE STRUCTURE OF RETURN ON EQUITY ACROSS INDUSTRIES

The *structure* of a firm's return on equity depends to a large extent on the nature of the industry in which it operates and the competitive advantages it has been able to achieve over time. Exhibit 5.8 reports the ROE structure of five U.S. companies for 1995. The companies include a bank, a car manufacturer, a pharmaceutical company, a chain of retail stores, and a beverage company with a strong brand name. All are leaders in their respective sectors. Given the reported ROE structures, try to determine which company belongs to which structure before reading the next paragraphs.

Firm 1 is Coca-Cola, the beverage company. Its strong brand name and superior marketing skills allow it to achieve the highest operating profitability (ROIC is 44 percent). ROIC is driven by the second highest operating profit margin (26 percent) and capital turnover (1.70 times). Its pretax ROE of 80 percent is also the highest, thanks to its ability to magnify its strong operating profitability with a high financial leverage multiplier of 1.82.

---

[4]A firm's capital turnover can increase as a result of the depreciation of fixed assets, which reduces net fixed assets. When this is the case, the improvement in turnover cannot be attributed to better management of the firm's invested capital.

EXHIBIT 5.7 The Drivers of Return on Equity.

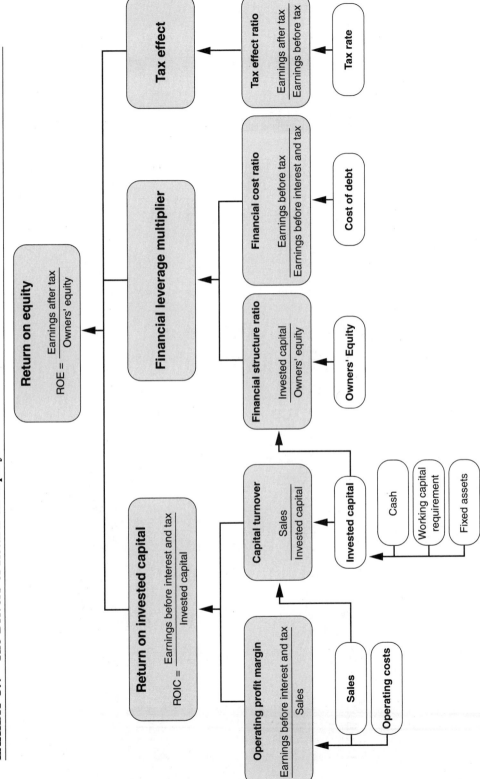

EXHIBIT 5.8 The Structure of Return on Equity for Five Firms in Different Sectors (December 1995).[1]

Company[2]	Operating Profit Margin[3] (1)	Capital Turnover[4] (2)	Return on Invested Capital[5] (3) = (1)×(2)	Financial Leverage Multiplier[6] (4)	Pretax Return on Equity[7] (5) = (3)×(4)	Tax Effect[8] (6)	Return on Equity[9] (7) = (5)×(6)
1	26%	1.70	44%	1.82	80%	0.69	55%
2	30%	0.90	27%	1.26	34%	0.70	24%
3	5.6%	3.24	18%	1.67	30%	0.63	19%
4	12%	0.65	7.8%	3.08	24%	0.62	15%
5	24%	0.34	8.2%	2.80	23%	0.66	15%

[1]Compiled by the authors with accounting data from *Compustat*.
[2]See text for names of companies.
[3]Operating profit margin = Earnings before interest and tax/Sales.
[4]Capital turnover = Sales/Invested capital, where invested capital = Cash + Working capital requirement + Net fixed assets.
[5]Return on invested capital = Earnings before interest and tax/Invested capital.
[6]Financial leverage multiplier = Pretax return on equity/Return on invested capital.
[7]Pretax return on equity = Earnings before tax/Owners' equity.
[8]Tax effect = Earnings after tax/Earnings before tax = (1 − effective tax rate).
[9]Return on equity = Earnings after tax/Owners' equity.

Firm 2 is Merck, the pharmaceutical company. It has the highest operating profit margin (30 percent), presumably because it can sell its unique products at a premium. But it is more capital intensive than Coca-Cola; hence, its capital turnover is much lower (0.90 times). And because it faces a significantly higher business risk than Coca-Cola (much of its R&D investment may never yield a successful drug), it has a more conservative financial leverage multiplier of 1.26. The result is a pretax ROE of 34 percent, less than half that of Coca-Cola's.

Firm 3 is Wal-Mart Stores, the retail chain. Because it competes on prices, it has the lowest operating profit margin (5.6 percent). But this low margin is compensated by a high capital turnover; half of its assets are inventories of goods that turn over fast. The resulting 18 percent operating profitability, the third highest in the exhibit, is magnified to a pretax ROE of 30 percent by a financial leverage multiplier of 1.67.

Firm 4 is Ford Motor Company. It has a relatively low operating profit margin (12 percent) due to price competition and a slow capital turnover of 0.65 (it is a very capital intensive business). The result is the lowest operating profitability (7.8 percent) in the exhibit. This low operating profitability is then levered up to a pretax ROE of 24 percent through the highest financial leverage multiplier (3.08) reported in the exhibit. In other words, Ford is able to compensate for its low operating profitability by funding its assets with relatively more debt than the average industrial company.

Firm 5 is Banc One. Its operating margin is relatively strong for a bank, but its capital turnover is low because banks typically use a relatively larger amount of invested capital (mostly loans made to customers) to generate the same revenues as a typical industrial company. The combination produces an operating profitability of only 8.2 percent. This operating profitability is magnified to a pretax ROE of 23 percent, thanks to a financial leverage multiplier of 2.80 built on the funds deposited with the bank.

OTHER MEASURES OF PROFITABILITY

The measures of profitability discussed so far are based on the accounting data shown on a firm's income statement and balance sheet. A number of other popular profitability-related ratios combine financial *accounting* data with financial *market* data. These ratios include the firm's **earnings per share,** its **price-to-earnings ratio,** and its **market-to-book ratio.**

EARNINGS PER SHARE (EPS)

Earnings per share, or EPS, is simply the firm's earnings after tax divided by its total number of shares outstanding:

$$\textbf{Earnings per share (EPS)} = \frac{\textbf{Earnings after tax}}{\textbf{Number of shares outstanding}} \quad (5.13)$$

EPS, a favorite of financial analysts, is no more than a "normalized" measure of the firm's earnings after tax. OS Distributors has 10 million shares outstanding (see Exhibit 2.5 in Chapter 2) and has generated earnings after tax of $10.2 million in 1997. Thus, its EPS in 1997 is equal to $1.02 ($10.2 million divided by 10 million shares).

THE PRICE-TO-EARNINGS RATIO (P/E)

The price-to-earnings ratio, also known as the firm's **earnings multiple,** P/E, or PER, is another favorite of financial analysts. It is defined as:

$$\text{Price-to-earnings ratio (P/E)} = \frac{\textbf{Share price}}{\textbf{Earnings per share}} \qquad (5.14)$$

Suppose OS distributors had shares listed on a stock market. If the quoted price per share was $14, then OS Distributors' P/E would be 13.7 ($14 divided by $1.02). In other words, OS Distributors would be trading at 13.7 times its current earnings (this is why a firm's P/E is also known as its earnings multiple). Higher price-to-earnings ratios mean that investors in the market are assigning higher values to each dollar of current earnings per share generated by the firm. Chapter 12 examines the determinants of firms' P/E and explains why price-to-earnings ratios vary across firms.

THE MARKET-TO-BOOK RATIO

The third ratio, the market-to-book ratio, is defined as:

$$\text{Market-to-book ratio} = \frac{\textbf{Share price}}{\textbf{Book value per share}} \qquad (5.15)$$

where book value per share is equal to the firm's owners' equity, as recorded in its balance sheet, divided by the number of shares outstanding.

For OS Distributors, book value per share is $7.7 at the end of 1997 ($77 million book value of equity divided by 10 million shares). Given a share price of $14, the market-to-book ratio is 1.8 (a share price of $14 divided by a book value per share of $7.7). In other words, OS Distributors' shares are traded in the market at a premium over book value—1.8 times their book value. The fact that OS Distributors' shares trade at a premium means the firm is creating value for its shareholders.

FINANCIAL LEVERAGE AND RISK

A firm's financial structure affects its return on equity through the financial leverage multiplier. How exactly does financial leverage work? Consider two firms with identical net assets that are funded with $100 million of capital. The only difference between the two firms is their financing strategy. One firm finances its net assets *exclusively* with equity (the unlevered firm); the other firm finances half of its net assets with $50 million of equity and the balance with $50 million of borrowed funds at a cost of debt of 10 percent (the levered firm). For the sake of simplicity, assume that the firms pay no corporate taxes (this assumption does not affect the conclusion).

Let's now introduce risk into the analysis. At the beginning of the year, when the two firms established their capital structure, they did not know what their year-end pretax operating profit (EBIT) would be. Thus, suppose they forecasted three equally likely levels of EBIT, each based on different expectations regarding the economic environment during the coming year. If the economic environment was favorable, EBIT would be $14 million. If it was average, EBIT would be $10 million. And if it was unfavorable, EBIT would be only $8 million. Which of these three possible levels of EBIT the firm achieved would not be known until the end of the year. This situation is what we call **business risk.** *A firm faces business risk because of its inability to know for certain the outcome of its current investing and operating decisions.* The best a firm can do is determine alternative outcomes for EBIT and their likelihood of occurrence.

The two firms have invested the same amount of capital and face the same probability distribution of EBIT, so they have the same business risk. How will the difference in their financing strategies affect their profitability? Exhibit 5.9 shows each firm's profitability ratios—return on invested capital (ROIC) and return on equity (ROE)—for each of the three possible levels of EBIT. Consider first the case of the unlevered firm. The firm's operating profitability (ROIC) varies from a high of 14 percent (EBIT of $14 million divided by $100 million of invested capital) to a low of 8 percent. Its ROE is equal to its ROIC because it has no debt and pays no taxes (both its financial leverage multiplier and its tax-effect ratio are equal to one).

What is the profitability of the levered firm? Its ROIC is the same as that of the unlevered firm because both firms have identical net assets and operating profit. The firm pays no taxes, its interest expenses are equal to $5 million (10 percent of $50 million of debt), and it has $50 million of equity capital. Its ROE is thus:

$$\text{ROE} = \frac{\text{EBIT} - \text{Interest expenses}}{\text{Owners' equity}} = \frac{\text{EBIT} - \$5 \text{ million}}{\$50 \text{ million}}$$

EXHIBIT 5.9   Effect of Financing on Profitability for Different Levels of EBIT.

ALTERNATIVE LEVELS OF PRETAX OPERATING PROFIT	PROFITABILITY OF THE FIRM WITH 100% EQUITY FINANCING		PROFITABILITY OF THE FIRM WITH 50% EQUITY FINANCING	
EBIT	ROIC	ROE	ROIC	ROE
$14 million	14%	14%	14%	18%
$10 million	10%	10%	10%	10%
$8 million	8%	8%	8%	6%

When EBIT is $14 million, ROE is 18 percent ($14 million minus $5 million divided by $50 million). In this case, the levered firm's ROE is *higher* than that of the unlevered firm (18 percent versus 14 percent). Although the $5 million of interest expenses for the levered firm reduced owners' profit to $9 million ($14 million of EBIT less the $5 million of interest expenses), *profit per dollar of invested equity* (ROE) rose to 18 percent because the equity base is smaller for the levered firm than for the unlevered firm ($50 million instead of $100 million). In this case, financial leverage is *favorable* to the owners of the levered firm because a positive financial structure effect has more than offset a negative financial cost effect.

When EBIT is equal to $10 million, the levered firm's ROE is 10 percent. In this case, financial leverage is neutral because the levered firm's ROE is equal to that of the unlevered firm. Finally, when EBIT is equal to $8 million, the levered firm's ROE is 6 percent. In this case, financial leverage is *unfavorable* to the firm's owners because the levered firm's ROE is lower than that of the unlevered firm (6 percent versus 8 percent). Notice how financial leverage (borrowing at a fixed rate of interest) affects return on equity. The unlevered firm's ROE varies from a high of 14 percent to a low of 8 percent in response to changes in EBIT, whereas the levered firm's ROE varies from a high of 18 percent to a low of 6 percent in response to the same changes in EBIT. The two firms face the same business risk—the changes in EBIT are the same for both. However, the levered firm's ROE varies more widely than the ROE of the unlevered firm. In other words, *financial leverage (borrowing) magnifies a firm's business risk.* Borrowing at a fixed interest rate adds **financial risk** to the firm's existing business risk. The owners of the levered firm face *both* business risk and financial risk, whereas the owners of the unlevered firm face only business risk. The levered firm is riskier than the unlevered one and its risk increases with rising levels of borrowing.

HOW DOES FINANCIAL LEVERAGE WORK?

Why is financial leverage favorable to the firm's owners when EBIT is $14 million (they get a *higher* ROE than the firm that has not borrowed), neutral when EBIT is $10 million (they get the *same* ROE as the firm that has not borrowed), and unfavorable when EBIT is $8 million (they get a *lower* ROE than the firm that has not borrowed)? The answer is straightforward. In the first case, the firm's owners borrow at 10 percent to finance assets that generate a return of 14 percent (ROIC is equal to 14 percent in the first case). You do not have to be a financial wizard to realize that borrowing at 10 percent to achieve a return on investment of 14 percent is a profitable proposition. Financial leverage enhances the firm's overall profitability (its ROE). In the second case, the firm borrows at 10 percent to achieve a ROIC of 10 percent. Financial leverage is neutral and ROE is the same as if there were no borrowing. In the third case, the firm borrows at 10 percent to achieve a ROIC of only 8 percent. This is clearly a losing proposition. Borrowing, in this case, turns out to be a poor decision.

Appendix 5.2 shows how to derive the relationship that links a firm's ROE to its ROIC *for a given cost of debt* and *a given debt-to-equity ratio*. The appendix shows that a firm's ROE can be written as follows:

$$\textbf{ROE} = \textbf{ROIC}(1 - t) + [\textbf{ROIC} - \textbf{Cost of debt}](1 - t) \times \frac{\textbf{Debt}}{\textbf{Owners' equity}}$$

$$(5.16)$$

where "t" is the effective corporate tax rate. For any given debt-to-equity ratio, ROE will be higher than ROIC if ROIC is higher than the cost of debt. When ROIC is equal to the cost of debt, ROE is equal to ROIC. And when ROIC is smaller than the cost of debt, ROE is smaller than ROIC. To illustrate this relationship, we return to our earlier example. The 50 percent equity-financed firm has a debt-to-equity ratio of one ($50 million of debt divided by $50 million of equity). The cost of debt is 10 percent and the firm does not pay any tax (t = 0). There are three possible cases:

1. When ROIC = **14%,** ROE = 14% + [14% − 10%] × 1 = 14% + 4% = **18%**
2. When ROIC = **10%,** ROE = 10% + [10% − 10%] × 1 = 10% + 0% = **10%**
3. When ROIC = **8%,** ROE = 8% + [8% − 10%] × 1 = 8% − 2% = **6%**

Although we can compute a firm's ROE for any combination of ROIC and debt-to-equity ratio, the formula will *never* provide the *optimal* or best level of debt for the firm. We return to this issue in Chapter 11 when we examine how a firm should determine its capital structure.

TWO RELATED CAVEATS: RISK AND THE ABILITY TO CREATE VALUE

One obvious conclusion from the previous discussion is that a firm seeking to enhance its ROE should borrow as long as its ROIC exceeds its cost of debt and should refrain from borrowing whenever its ROIC is lower than its cost of debt. There are, however, two important and related caveats to this conclusion.

The first is that managers do not know their firm's *future* ROIC at the time they borrow to fund the firm's assets. Hence, they can only compare the cost of debt to an *expected* (risky) ROIC that may or may not be the one the firm will eventually achieve. Risk cannot be ignored when applying the ROE formula. Higher levels of *expected* ROIC will produce higher levels of *expected* ROE. However, the *expectation* of achieving a higher ROE must be weighed against the risk of not achieving it.

The second caveat, which is related to the first, is that a high *expected* ROE does not necessarily mean that the firm is creating value for its owners. Consider again the firm with a debt-to-equity ratio of one that can borrow at 10 percent. Suppose the firm can acquire assets that are expected to generate a return on invested capital of 14 percent. As shown above, financial leverage will have a positive impact on the firm's return on equity, which will reach 18 percent. But this does not mean that the firm should acquire the assets. What if the firm's owners expect a return of, say, 25 percent to compensate them for the business and financial risks attached to the equity they have invested in the firm? If this is the case, then the acquisition's expected return on equity of 18 percent is not sufficient to remunerate the firm's owners. The acquisition should not be undertaken because it is not a value-creating proposition.

SELF-SUSTAINABLE GROWTH

Without a sustainable level of profit, a firm will be constrained in its ability to finance its future growth. Consider OS Distributors. Sales in 1997 grew by 14.3 percent, from $420 million to $480 million. Suppose OS Distributors expects sales to grow by, say, 15 percent next year. As sales increase, more receivables will be generated, more inventories will be needed, and eventually more fixed assets will be required to support the higher levels of sales. This growth in assets will have to be financed with debt, equity, or a combination of these two sources of funds. How can OS Distributors' management anticipate the financing implications of the expected growth in sales?

There are two ways firms can finance their anticipated growth: internally, through the retention of profits (retained earnings), or externally, through the issuance of shares and through borrowing. Because external equity financing is more costly than internal equity financing,[5] firms often try to finance their expected growth with internally generated equity (retained earnings). For this reason, managers need to have an indicator of the *maximum* growth their firm can achieve *without raising external equity.* The firm's **self-sustainable growth rate** is this indicator. It is *the maximum rate of growth in sales a firm can achieve without issuing new shares or changing either its operating policy (same operating profit margin and capital turnover) or its financing policy (same debt-to-equity ratio and dividend payout ratio).*

How is the self-sustainable growth rate determined? Let's begin by estimating the rate for OS Distributors at the end of 1997. From the firm's financial data in Exhibits 5.2 and 5.3, we know the firm's $70 million equity at the beginning of 1997 (the same as end of 1996) generated $10.2 million in earnings after tax. The firm retained $7 million and distributed the balance of $3.2 million to owners in the form of dividends. As a result, owners' equity increased by 10 percent, from $70 million to $77 million. If the firm expects its equity to increase by the same percentage next year and if it wants to maintain its current debt-to-equity ratio, then its debt must also increase by 10 percent. If both owners' equity and debt increase by 10 percent, their sum, which is equal to the firm's invested capital, will also increase by 10 percent. Further, if the firm's capital turnover (sales divided by invested capital) does not change, sales will also increase by 10 percent. *This 10 percent growth in sales is OS Distributors' self-sustainable growth rate.* It is equal to the 10 percent growth in the firm's equity, and is the fastest growth rate in sales the firm can achieve without

---

[5]Raising equity through the issuance of shares involves transaction costs that can add several percentage points to the cost of equity.

changing its capital structure and operating policy and without raising new equity through a share issue.

From this example, we can now derive a general formula to compute the self-sustainable growth rate of any firm. We define a firm's equity retention rate as the ratio of its retained earnings to its earnings after tax:

$$\textbf{Equity retention rate} = \frac{\textbf{Retained earnings}}{\textbf{Earnings after tax}} \qquad (5.17)$$

Then, the self-sustainable growth rate, which is equal to the rate of increase in owners' equity, can be written as:

$$\text{Self-sustainable growth rate} = \frac{\text{Retained earnings}}{\text{Owners' equity}}$$

$$= \frac{\text{Retention rate} \times \text{EAT}}{\text{Owners' equity}}$$

$$= \text{Retention rate} \times \frac{\text{EAT}}{\text{Owners' equity}}$$

$$\textbf{Self-sustainable growth rate} = \textbf{Retention rate} \times \textbf{Return on equity} \qquad (5.18)$$

where return on equity is calculated by dividing the year's net profit or earnings after tax (EAT) by the book value of the firm's equity at the *beginning* of the year.

Return on equity can be written as the product of operating profit margin, capital turnover, financial leverage, and the tax-effect ratio (see equations 5.10 and 5.11). Thus, the firm's self-sustainable growth rate can be written as:

$$\begin{aligned}
\textbf{Self-sustainable growth rate} = \ &\textbf{Retention rate} \times \textbf{Operating margin} \\
&\times \textbf{Capital turnover} \\
&\times \textbf{Financial leverage multiplier} \\
&\times \textbf{(1 − effective tax rate)}
\end{aligned}$$

This equation clearly identifies the five factors that determine the firm's capacity to grow *without* raising new equity. The second and third factors reflect the firm's operating policy (its operating profit margin and capital turnover), the first and fourth reflect its financing policy (its profit retention rate and financial leverage multiplier), and the fifth reflects the effective rate at which its pretax profit is taxed. The point to remember is: *If these five factors stay fixed, a firm cannot grow its sales faster than its self-sustainable growth rate unless it issues new shares.*

Let's return to OS Distributors. Exhibit 5.10 shows the firm's self-sustainable growth rate in 1996 and 1997, computed according to equation 5.18, and the growth in sales experienced by the firm during these two years. OS Distributors' self-sustainable growth rate was 10 percent in 1997, slightly higher than its value of 9.4 percent a year earlier. Its sales, however, grew by 14.3 percent during 1997, a rate almost twice that achieved the previous year (7.7 percent). How did OS Distributors grow its sales by 14.3 percent in 1997 with roughly the same self-sustainable

EXHIBIT 5.10   OS Distributors' Self-Sustainable Growth Rate Compared to Growth in Sales.

YEAR	RETENTION RATE	RETURN ON EQUITY	SELF-SUSTAINABLE GROWTH RATE	GROWTH IN SALES
1997	$\dfrac{7.0}{10.2} = 0.69$	$\dfrac{10.2}{70.0} = 14.6\%$	$0.69 \times 14.6\% = \mathbf{10\%}$	**14.3%**
1996	$\dfrac{6.0}{8.0} = 0.75$	$\dfrac{8.0}{64.0} = 12.5\%$	$0.75 \times 12.5\% = \mathbf{9.4\%}$	**7.7%**

growth rate as in 1996 without issuing new shares? In other words, where did the firm get the additional capital required to grow sales beyond the self-sustainable growth rate of 10 percent? The answer is found in OS Distributors' managerial balance sheet in Exhibit 5.3. Cash decreased from $12 million at the beginning of 1997 to $8 million at the end of that year, a one-year drop of 33 percent. Thus, OS Distributors used its cash holdings to finance the gap between its self-sustainable growth rate and its growth in sales.

This example illustrates an important point: *Firms with sales growing faster than their self-sustainable growth rate will eventually experience a cash deficit; firms with sales growing slower than their self-sustainable growth rate will eventually generate a cash surplus.* This phenomenon is illustrated in Exhibit 5.11. Firms positioned on the line that bisects the plane are in **financial balance.** Their self-sustainable growth rate is equal to their growth in sales. Firms with sales growth exceeding their self-sustainable growth rate are located above the line, and firms with sales growth slower than their self-sustainable growth rate are located below the line. Cash deficit firms face a *funding problem;* firms with a cash surplus have an *investment problem*—they generate more cash than they can invest.

How can management respond to unsustainable levels of growth in sales, that is, to growth rates that exceed the firm's self-sustainable growth rate? For example, suppose OS Distributors expects its sales to grow by 15 percent next year. This growth rate is clearly unsustainable if OS Distributors maintains its self-sustainable growth rate at its current level of 10 percent (see the initial position of OS Distributors at point A in Exhibit 5.11). If raising new equity is not an option, then OS Distributors' management will have to make operating and/or financing decisions that will boost the firm's self-sustainable growth rate to 15 percent (see the desired final position of OS Distributors at point B in Exhibit 5.11). Otherwise, OS Distributors will experience a continued loss of cash next year that may eventually initiate a funding and liquidity crisis.

Let's examine some of the options available to OS Distributors. If we assume that next year's return on equity will be the same as this year's (14.6 percent), then one possible option is to retain 100 percent of the firm's profit. With a retention rate of one, the firm's self-sustainable growth rate will be equal to its return on equity. Thus, this option, which implies an elimination of dividend payments,

EXHIBIT 5.11   Sales Growth and Cash Condition.

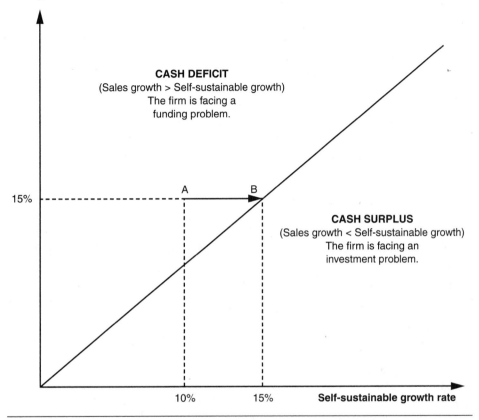

Sales growth

CASH DEFICIT
(Sales growth > Self-sustainable growth)
The firm is facing a
funding problem.

CASH SURPLUS
(Sales growth < Self-sustainable growth)
The firm is facing an
investment problem.

15%

A   B

10%   15%   **Self-sustainable growth rate**

would raise the firm's self-sustainable growth rate to 14.6 percent, a figure close to the firm's 15 percent expected growth in sales. But, it is unlikely the firm's owners will find this option acceptable. They will probably impose some financial constraints on the firm's management. Let's assume (1) they are unwilling to cut dividends below 20 percent of profits and (2) their estimation of the firm's optimal debt-to-equity ratio is one (implying a financial structure ratio of two, as indicated by equation 5.8). *After management has met these financial constraints, the firm's self-sustainable growth rate can only be increased through an improvement in the firm's operating profitability.*

How much does OS Distributors' operating profitability, measured by its return on invested capital, need to increase to bring its self-sustainable growth rate up to its target rate of 15 percent? To answer this question, we first look at return on equity. A firm's self-sustainable growth rate is equal to its retention rate multiplied by its return on equity. To achieve a self-sustainable growth rate of 15 percent with a retention rate of 0.80 (which corresponds to a dividend payout ratio of 20 percent), the firm's return on equity must be equal to:

$$\text{ROE} = \frac{\text{Self-sustainable growth rate}}{\text{Retention rate}} = \frac{15\%}{0.80} = 18.7\%$$

To achieve a target self-sustainable growth rate of 15 percent with a retention rate of 80 percent, OS Distributors' ROE must rise to 18.7 percent. What combination of financial leverage and return on invested capital (ROIC) will provide an ROE of 18.7 percent? Rearranging the terms in equation 5.12, we have:

$$\text{ROIC} = \frac{\text{ROE}}{\text{Financial leverage multiplier} \times (1 - \text{effective tax rate})}$$

Recall that the financial leverage multiplier is the product of the financial *structure* ratio and the financial *cost* ratio. Given a target debt-to-equity ratio of one, the financial *structure* ratio is two. If we assume the financial *cost* ratio will remain at 0.71 as in 1997, then the financial leverage multiplier will be equal to two multiplied by 0.71. With a desired return on equity of 18.7 percent and a tax rate of 60 percent, the implied return on invested capital (ROIC) is:

$$\text{ROIC} = \frac{18.7\%}{2.0 \times 0.71 \times 0.60} = \frac{18.7\%}{0.85} = 22\%$$

Thus, OS Distributors' operating profitability must increase to 22 percent to bring its self-sustainable growth rate up to 15 percent. So, how can the firm's operations achieve a return on invested capital of 22 percent next year? Return on invested capital can only rise through a combination of higher operating profit margin and faster capital turnover. Suppose in a previous meeting of OS Distributors' managers, the marketing manager said that operating profit margin is expected to rise to 5.5 percent next year. How high must capital turnover rise to achieve a return on invested capital of 22 percent given that operating profit margin is expected to be 5.5 percent? Return on invested capital is the product of capital turnover and operating profit margin, so:

$$\text{Capital turnover} = \frac{\text{Return on invested capital}}{\text{Operating profit margin}} = \frac{22\%}{5.5\%} = 4.0$$

We now know that OS Distributors must raise its capital turnover to 4.0 next year in order to raise its self-sustainable growth rate to 15 percent. How can this objective be achieved? The operations manager will have to focus first on the firm's working capital requirement; receivables will have to be collected faster and inventories will have to turn over as quickly as possible. However, there is less of an opportunity to rapidly improve the firm's fixed asset turnover ratio (fixed assets divided by sales) because OS Distributors, being in the distribution business, uses a relatively small amount of fixed assets. But, this challenge may have to be addressed eventually if OS Distributors is to raise its self-sustainable growth rate to 15 percent without raising new equity.

The conclusion is inescapable: Given OS Distributors' financial constraints, if the firm's management cannot achieve the targeted improvements in the firm's operations, then the firm's owners will have to either inject new equity into the business or issue new shares.

SUMMARY

A firm's profitability, risk, and growth are related to one another and must be managed in a way that allows the firm to grow smoothly without impairing its ability to create wealth for its owners. A firm's return on equity (ROE) measures the firm's overall profitability and is affected by the firm's operating, investing, and financing activities and taxation.

The impact of operating and investing activities on ROE is captured by return on invested capital (ROIC), which is obtained by dividing the firm's earnings before interest and tax (EBIT) by its invested capital (the sum of cash, working capital requirement, and net fixed assets). Because invested capital is also called net assets, a firm's ROIC is the same as its return on net assets (RONA). Also, ROIC can be written as equal to the firm's operating profit margin (EBIT/sales) multiplied by its capital turnover (sales/invested capital), the latter being the same as net asset turnover. Empirical evidence indicates that a firm's operating profitability is essentially driven by its competitive position (the size of its market share), the relative quality of its products and services, and the structure of its costs and assets.

A firm's financing strategy also has an impact on ROE. A firm's pretax ROE is equal to its operating profitability multiplied by the financial leverage multiplier, a measure of the effect of borrowing on the firm's profitability. When operating profitability *exceeds* the cost of debt, the financial leverage multiplier is *higher* than one and financial leverage is *favorable* to the firm's owners. When operating profitability is *lower* than the cost of debt, the firm's financial leverage multiplier is *lower* than one and financial leverage is *unfavorable* to the firm's owners. However, a firm cannot easily take advantage of favorable financial leverage due to business risk, the unpredictable fluctuations in the firm's EBIT and operating profitability. The firm will generally be unable to predict its operating profitability at the time it borrows to finance its investments. Financial leverage adds another layer of risk to the firm's business risk, and this additional risk, called financial risk, affects the firm's performance.

Finally, taxation affects ROE. Firms should try to minimize the negative impact of corporate taxes on their profitability by taking advantage, whenever possible, of tax holidays and tax subsidies that are offered, for example, by countries or regions that want to attract investments.

Other measures of profitability, besides ROE, include the firm's earnings per share (earnings after tax divided by the number of shares outstanding), its price-to-earnings ratio (share price divided by earnings per share), and its market-to-book ratio (share price divided by book value per share).

The ability of a firm to finance its growth is determined by its self-sustainable growth rate. This rate is equal to the fraction of profits retained by the firm (its retention rate) multiplied by its return on equity. A firm's self-sustainable growth rate indicates whether the firm can finance its anticipated growth in sales without raising new equity or changing either its operating policy (same operating profit margin and capital turnover) or its financing policy (same debt-to-equity and dividend-payout ratios). A firm that grows its sales faster than its self-sustainable growth rate will eventually experience a cash deficit. If it is unable to raise its self-sustainable growth rate through a higher profit retention rate and/or a higher return on equity, then its only option for eliminating its cash deficit is to issue new equity. A firm that is unable to grow its sales as fast as its self-sustainable growth rate will eventually experience a cash surplus. A firm facing this situation must then decide how to spend its cash surplus to create value for its owners. If it is unable to find value-creating investment opportunities it should simply return the excess cash to its shareholders through a dividend payment or a share repurchase program.

5.1 FACTORS AFFECTING A FIRM'S OPERATING PROFITABILITY

The relative importance of the factors that affect return on invested capital (ROIC) can only be determined empirically by examining the historical relationships between these factors and the pretax operating profitability of a large sample of firms. A study of this type was conducted on a sample that included more than 3,000 businesses that were drawn from some 500 corporations (mostly North American and European) and covered a wide range of industries.[6] The pretax operating profitability of a business was measured by its four-year average ROIC with data from 1973 to 1990. The businesses in the sample had an average ROIC of 22 percent and the distribution of their ROIC is shown in Exhibit A5.1. Even though the average ROIC for the entire sample of businesses was 22 percent, there is a wide variation in the ROIC: 16 percent of the businesses had a negative ROIC while 12 percent generated a ROIC in excess of 50 percent.

A statistical study of the sample identified 30 factors that collectively explain 80 percent of the variation in ROIC. Three factors, however, stand out. These are the percentage of the total market served by a business (its market share), the quality of the products or services it offers its customers, and the structure of its assets

EXHIBIT A5.1 Distribution of ROIC for 3,000 Businesses in Study.

Percentage of businesses that fall in ROIC range

ROIC	Negative	0% to 10%	10% to 20%	20% to 30%	30% to 40%	40% to 50%	Above 50%
Percent	16%	16%	21%	17%	11%	7%	12%

[6]The unit of analysis was not an entire company but a business division within a corporation selling a distinct product or service to an identifiable group of customers. The data was collected by the Profit Impact of Market Strategy (PIMS) Program. For further information, refer to the article by K. Jagiello and G. Mandry "Structural Determinants of Performance: Insight from the PIMS Data Base" in *The Handbook of Management,* edited by D. F. Channon (Blackwell: 1996).

and costs. *High market share and superior product quality, on average, boost ROIC while high investments and fixed costs, on average, depress ROIC.* These general findings are examined more closely in the following paragraphs.

MARKET SHARE

A business's market share is measured by the ratio of its sales to the total sales in the served market. The relationship between the market share of the businesses in the sample and their four-year average ROIC is shown in Exhibit A5.2. These findings raise an immediate question. Why are businesses with higher market share generally more profitable? Size and the control of a larger share of the served market allow these businesses, on average, to enjoy relatively higher profit margins via lower cost per unit of output and stable output prices. That is, these businesses can spread their fixed costs over a larger volume, purchase inputs in bulk at a discount, and prevent market forces from putting excessive downward pressure on their product prices.

The positive relationship between profitability and market share held *on average* for the businesses in the sample. Higher market share did not necessarily yield higher profitability. More than 20 percent of the businesses in the sample that had a market share above 40 percent had a ROIC of less than 22 percent (the average ROIC for the sample).

PERCEIVED PRODUCT QUALITY

Product or service quality is measured relative to the competition and from the perspective of the customer. It is calculated by taking the difference between the percentage of a business's sales volume from products or services that are judged superior to those available from leading competitors and the percentage of those judged inferior.[7] The relationship between the four-year average ROIC for a business in the sample and the relative perceived quality of its products and services is shown in Exhibit A5.3. Businesses were assigned to five categories, depending on the value of their index of relative perceived quality.

EXHIBIT A5.2   Relationship between Market Share and ROIC for Businesses in Study.

MARKET SHARE	Up to 8%	8% to 15%	15% to 24%	24% to 38%	Above 38%
ROIC	10%	17%	21%	26%	38%

---

[7]For example, if 50% of the sales volume of a business is from products considered superior and 20% from products considered inferior, then the relative product quality index is 30% (50% − 20%).

Businesses whose products or services were perceived to be of superior quality were, on average, more profitable than businesses whose products or services were perceived to be of inferior quality. On average, the profitability of a business in the superior category was double the profitability of a business in the inferior category. Higher profitability is achieved via relatively higher margins, probably because businesses with superior products or services are able to avoid price competition. This allows them to protect their margin from being squeezed by competitive downward pricing.

The favorable effects of high market share and perceived product quality on a business's profitability were cumulative in this study. Businesses in the sample with the highest market shares and superior products or services had an average ROIC of 39 percent while those with the lowest market shares and inferior products or services had an average ROIC of only 9 percent.

ASSET AND COST STRUCTURES

The third factor that had a significant influence on the profitability of a business was its capital turnover. As shown in Exhibit A5.4, average ROIC rose as capital turnover increased. This relationship is not surprising. ROIC is equal to operating profit margin multiplied by capital turnover, so ROIC should rise when capital turnover increases. However, the empirical evidence also indicated that businesses with low capital turnover (businesses that require intensive investment in assets to produce sales) did not generate, on average, a high enough margin from their operating activities to compensate them for their lower capital turnover. This phenomenon manifests itself clearly in the data shown in Exhibit A5.4. Businesses with a capital turnover lower than 1.5 had the smallest average operating profit margin.

EXHIBIT A5.3 Relationship between Product Quality and ROIC for Businesses in Study.

| | INFERIOR | | | | SUPERIOR |
RELATIVE PERCEIVED QUALITY	BOTTOM FIFTH	2ND FIFTH	3RD FIFTH	4TH FIFTH	TOP FIFTH
ROIC	15%	18%	22%	25%	32%

EXHIBIT A5.4 Relationship between Capital Turnover and Both ROIC and Operating Profit Margin for Businesses in Study.

CAPITAL TURNOVER	Below 1.5	1.5 to 2.0	2.0 to 2.5	2.5 to 3.3	Above 3.3
ROIC	8%	15%	22%	28%	38%
Operating profit margin	6.4%	8.2%	9.8%	9.8%	8.6%

Why are businesses with low capital turnover usually unable to generate higher profit margins? One explanation is that investment intensive businesses with low capital turnover usually have relatively high fixed costs and are usually prone to price and marketing wars that weaken their margin. When economic conditions become unfavorable, there is a tendency for these businesses to cut prices in order to maintain high rates of capacity utilization. Furthermore, because these businesses have relatively high amounts of capital tied up in their operations, they cannot easily exit the business (they have high **exit barriers**). They usually try to ride the unfavorable market conditions in the hope of better future days. This behavior is typical in such sectors as airlines, refining, commodity pulp and paper, shipbuilding, and base chemicals.

5.2 THE RELATIONSHIP BETWEEN A FIRM'S ROE AND ITS AFTERTAX ROIC

The following abbreviations and relationships are used in this appendix:

EBIT = Earnings before interest and tax

EAT = Earnings after tax

t = Effective tax rate

Debt = Total borrowings

Invested capital = Owners' equity + Debt

COD = Average cost of debt

Interest expenses = COD × Debt

$$\text{ROE} = \text{Return on equity} = \frac{\text{EAT}}{\text{Owners' equity}}$$

$$\text{ROIC} = \text{Return on invested capital} = \frac{\text{EBIT}}{\text{Invested capital}}$$

To derive the relationship between a firm's ROE and its aftertax ROIC, we begin with the following equation:

$$\text{EAT} = (\text{EBIT} - \text{interest expenses}) \times (1 - t)$$

We then perform a series of substitutions and recombine terms:

$$
\begin{aligned}
\text{EAT} &= \text{EBIT}(1 - t) - \text{COD} \times \text{Debt}(1 - t) \\
&= \text{ROIC}(1 - t) \times \text{Invested capital} - \text{COD} \times \text{Debt}(1 - t) \\
&= \text{ROIC}(1 - t) \times (\text{Owners' equity} + \text{Debt}) - \text{COD} \times \text{Debt}(1 - t) \\
&= \text{ROIC}(1 - t) \times \text{Owners' equity} + \text{ROIC}(1 - t) \times \text{Debt} - \text{COD} \times \text{Debt}(1 - t) \\
&= \text{ROIC}(1 - t) \times \text{Owners' equity} + [\text{ROIC} - \text{COD}](1 - t) \times \text{Debt}
\end{aligned}
$$

Dividing both sides of the last equation by owners' equity, we get:

$$\frac{\text{EAT}}{\text{Owners' equity}} = \text{ROE}$$

$$= \text{ROIC}(1 - t) + [\text{ROIC} - \text{COD}](1 - t) \times \frac{\text{Debt}}{\text{Owners' equity}}$$

or

$$\text{ROE} = \text{ROIC}(1 - t) + [\text{ROIC} - \text{Cost of debt}](1 - t) \times \frac{\text{Debt}}{\text{Owners' equity}}$$

which is equation 5.16.

REFERENCES AND FURTHER READING

1. Brealey, Richard, and Stewart Myers. *Principles of Corporate Finance.* 5th ed. McGraw-Hill, 1996. See chapter 27.
2. Clark, John, Thomas Hindelang, and Robert Pritchard. *Capital Budgeting: Planning and Control of Capital Expenditures.* 3d ed. Prentice-Hall, 1989. See chapter 24.
3. Jagiello, K., and G. Mandry. "Structural Determinants of Performance: Insight from the PIMS Data Base." *The Handbook of Management.* Edited by D. F. Channon. Blackwell, 1996.
4. Rappaport, Alfred. *Creating Shareholder Value.* The Free Press, 1998. See chapter 2.

REVIEW PROBLEMS

5.1 Profitability analysis.

The financial statements of Allied & Consolidated Clothier (ACC), a manufacturer of coats and other garments, are shown below. ACC's operational efficiency, liquidity position, and cash flow statements were analyzed in Chapters 3 and 4. The income statements span a calendar year and balance sheets are dated December 31. All figures are in millions of dollars.

BALANCE SHEETS (IN MILLIONS)						
	1995	**1996**	**1997**		**1995**	**1996**	**1997**
Cash	$100	$90	$50	Short-term debt	$80	$90	$135
Trade receivables	200	230	290	Trade payables	170	180	220
Prepaid expenses	160	170	300	Accrued expenses	40	45	50
Inventories	30	30	35	Long-term debt	140	120	100
Net fixed assets	390	390	365	Owners' equity	450	475	535
Total assets	**$880**	**$910**	**$1,040**	**Total liabilities & equity**	**$880**	**$910**	**$1,040**

INCOME STATEMENTS (IN MILLIONS)			
	YEAR 1995	YEAR 1996	YEAR 1997
Net sales	$1,200	$1,350	$1,600
Cost of Goods Sold	860	970	1,160
Selling, general & administrative expenses	150	165	200
Depreciation expenses	40	50	55
Earnings before interest and tax (EBIT)	150	165	185
Net interest expenses	20	20	25
Earnings before tax (EBT)	130	145	160
Income tax expenses	40	45	50
Earnings after tax (EAT) or net profit	$90	$100	$110
Retained earnings	$15	$25	$60
Dividend	$75	$75	$50

a. Restructure ACC's balance sheets in their managerial form.

b. Calculate ACC's return on equity (ROE) in 1995, 1996, and 1997, both before and after tax (use year-end owners' equity).

c. Calculate ACC's pretax operating profitability in 1995, 1996, and 1997, using year-end data and the three measures of operating profitability presented in the chapter: Return on invested capital (ROIC), return on total assets (ROTA), and return on business assets (ROBA). Explain how these measures are different. Why do these measures of profitability differ from return on assets (ROA), which we defined as net profit over total assets?

d. What are return on net assets (RONA) and return on capital employed (ROCE)?

e. What are the drivers of return on invested capital? Provide a measure of these drivers in 1995, 1996, and 1997. What can you conclude when you compare ACC's operating profitability in 1997 to its 1995 performance?

f. Why is pretax return on equity (see part b) higher than pretax return on invested capital (see part c)?

g. Given your answer to part f, is it correct to claim that as long as ACC borrows to finance its investments, its shareholders are better off because they will have a higher ROE?

h. Provide measures of the extent of ACC's borrowing in 1995, 1996, and 1997, using the ratios that follow. Briefly compare the information provided by these financial ratios.

   1. Financial cost ratio

   2. Times interest earned

   3. Financial structure ratio

   4. Debt-to-equity ratio

   5. Debt-to-invested capital ratio

    i. Break down ROE into its five fundamental components in 1995, 1996, and 1997. What can you conclude about the structure of ACC's profitability?

    j. Given that ACC has 50 million shares outstanding that were worth $20 at the end of 1995, $24 at the end of 1996, and $30 at the end of 1997, what were ACC's earnings per share, price-to-earnings ratio, and market-to-book ratio on those dates? What information do these measures of profitability provide?

5.2 ROE structure across industries.

Balance sheet and profitability structures for three companies are shown below. The information was drawn from their 1996 annual reports. The companies are Microsoft, the software developer; Boeing, the aircraft manufacturer; and Singapore Airlines, the Asian airline company. Identify each company and explain your choice.

BALANCE SHEET STRUCTURE (IN PERCENTAGE)	COMPANY A	COMPANY B	COMPANY C
Cash and securities	14.3	9.3	68.8
Accounts receivable	5.4	8.6	6.3
Inventories	44.9	0.9	0.1
Other current assets	2.4	0.0	2.6
Fixed assets	33.0	81.2	22.2
Total assets	*100.0%*	*100.0%*	*100.0%*
Short-term debt	0.1	0.3	0.0
Accounts payable	9.7	12.7	8.0
Accruals and others	39.7[1]	6.1	16.0
Long-term debt	10.8	3.4	0.0
Other long-term liabilities	10.0	3.2	0.0
Owners' equity	29.7	74.3	76.0
Total liabilities & equity	*100.0%*	*100.0%*	*100.0%*

[1]29% represents advance payments by clients.

PROFITABILITY STRUCTURE	COMPANY A	COMPANY B	COMPANY C
ROTA = EBIT/Total assets	**3.7%**	**8.4%**	**30.5%**
Margin = EBIT/Sales	6.0%	15.7%	35.5%
Total asset turnover = Sales/Total assets	0.62	0.53	0.86
Leverage effect = pretax ROE/ROTA	3.38	1.32	1.60
Pretax ROE = EBT/Owners' equity	**12.7%**	**11.0%**	**48.9%**
Tax effect = EAT/EBT = (1 − effective tax rate)	0.80	0.95	0.65
Aftertax ROE = EAT/Owners' equity	**10.0%**	**10.5%**	**31.8%**

5.3 Sustainable growth analysis.

Return to Allied & Consolidated Clothier whose financial statements are reported in problem 5.1.

a. Compare the company's growth rate in sales in 1997 to its sustainable growth rate that same year. What can you conclude?

b. Suppose that ACC expects its sales to grow by 25 percent in 1998.

   1. How much equity capital will it need to finance that growth if it does not modify its financing policy and operational efficiency? How will ACC get this equity capital?

   2. What will be the consequence of the 25 percent growth in sales on the firm's debt-to-equity ratio if ACC does not issue new equity, modify its dividend policy, or change its operational efficiency?

   3. What will be the consequence of the 25 percent growth in sales on the firm's retention policy if ACC does not issue new equity, modify its debt-to-equity ratio, or change its operational efficiency?

   4. How should ACC modify its operational efficiency if it wishes to grow its sales by 25 percent without issuing new equity or modifying its financing policy?

c. Suppose that ACC expects its sales to grow by 10 percent in 1998.

   1. What will be the consequence of the 10 percent growth in sales on the firm's cash position if ACC does not modify its financing policy or change its operational efficiency?

   2. What can ACC do with the extra cash? What should it do?

CHAPTER

6 USING THE NET PRESENT VALUE RULE TO MAKE VALUE-CREATING INVESTMENT DECISIONS

One of the most important decisions a manager can make is the capital investment decision. This key decision requires spending cash now in order to acquire long-lived assets that will be a source of cash flows in the future. A successful capital investment program will contribute positively to the firm's financial performance for many years. The firm's managers will be commended for their skills in identifying potentially successful projects and carrying them to fruition (we use the terms *project, investment,* and *proposal* interchangeably). However, if the capital investment program fails, the firm's performance may be affected negatively for years. Moreover, the firm's suppliers of funds—the shareholders and creditors—could lose confidence in the ability of the firm's managers to make good investment decisions and may become reluctant to provide additional funds in the future.

What is a good investment decision? From a financial management perspective, *a good investment decision is a decision that raises the current market value of the firm's equity, thereby creating value for the firm's owners.* An investment decision can have other objectives, but managers who ignore the value-creation objective may jeopardize both the future of their firm and their employment prospects. The value-creating investment decision must raise *market* value, not *book* value or accounting profit. Shareholders cash in on their investment by selling their shares for cash, not for accounting profits.

Capital budgeting involves comparing the amount of cash spent today on an investment with the cash inflows expected from it in the future. However, future cash flows are spread over time and cannot be compared directly because a dollar received earlier is worth more than a dollar received later. One reason for this is that the firm can earn interest on earlier cash inflows. This preference for "early cash" is called the *time value of money.*

Discounting is the mechanism used to convert *future* cash flows into today's equivalent value, which is known as present value or discounted value. In other words, discounting adjusts future cash flows for the time value of money. For example, a riskless cash inflow of $1,100 available one year from now is worth $1,000 today if the firm can earn 10 percent on cash deposited now in a riskfree savings account. The $1,000 is the *present value,* or *discounted value,* of the $1,100 of future cash inflow at a discount rate of 10 percent. This chapter shows how to calculate the discounted value of a stream of cash flows occurring at any date in the future.

Apart from the timing issue, there is also the issue of the risk associated with future cash flows. Future cash flows are risky because there is always some probability that the cash flows realized in the future may not be the expected ones.

Decision models that consider both the time value of money and the risk of an investment's cash flows are called *discounted cash flow (DCF) models.* This chapter presents the net present value (NPV) model and briefly examines a useful variation, the profitability index (PI). The next chapter presents and compares other DCF and non-DCF models and concludes that the NPV approach to investment appraisal is superior to alternative methods.

There are two critical elements in a DCF valuation. One is the identification and measurement of the project's expected cash flows and the other is the estimation of the appropriate discount rate required to calculate the project's present value. Chapter 8 is devoted entirely to the first issue and Chapter 10 deals with the second. In this chapter, we assume both the investment's expected cash-flow stream and its appropriate discount rate are known and show how to calculate the investment's NPV. We also explain what NPV measures, how it is derived, and how it should be interpreted.

The valuation of a project is a critical element in the capital investment process but it is not the only one. Thus, we review the major steps involved in a capital investment decision before we explain how to perform an NPV analysis. After reading this chapter, you should understand:

- The major steps involved in a capital budgeting decision.
- How to calculate the present value of a stream of future cash flows.
- The net present value (NPV) rule and how to apply it to investment decisions.
- Why a project's NPV is a measure of the value it creates.
- How to use the NPV rule to choose between projects with different sizes or different useful lives.
- How the flexibility of a project can be described with the help of managerial options.

THE CAPITAL INVESTMENT PROCESS

The **capital investment decision,** also called the **capital budgeting decision** or **capital expenditure decision,** involves several steps, as summarized in Exhibit 6.1. The process is initiated when the firm *identifies* business opportunities that can be translated into potentially valuable investment proposals. This is arguably the

EXHIBIT 6.1   The Capital Investment Process

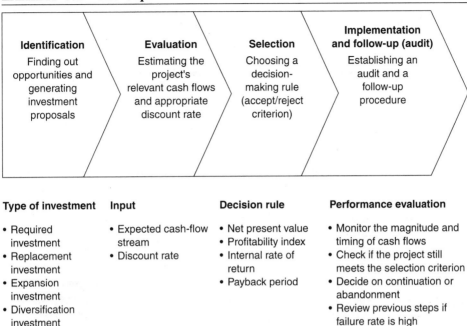

Identification	Evaluation	Selection	Implementation and follow-up (audit)
Finding out opportunities and generating investment proposals	Estimating the project's relevant cash flows and appropriate discount rate	Choosing a decision-making rule (accept/reject criterion)	Establishing an audit and a follow-up procedure

Type of investment	Input	Decision rule	Performance evaluation
• Required investment • Replacement investment • Expansion investment • Diversification investment	• Expected cash-flow stream • Discount rate	• Net present value • Profitability index • Internal rate of return • Payback period	• Monitor the magnitude and timing of cash flows • Check if the project still meets the selection criterion • Decide on continuation or abandonment • Review previous steps if failure rate is high

most important step in the process. Management must foster a climate within the firm that is conducive to the generation of ideas and the uncovering of opportunities that could lead to successful long-term investments.

Identified investment proposals must then be *evaluated* financially. The inputs required for financial evaluation of a project include the estimation of its useful life, the cash flows the project is expected to generate over that period, and the appropriate discount rate required to calculate the present value of the project's expected cash-flow stream. This is the second most challenging step in the capital expenditure decision. Estimating the parameters required for financial analysis of a proposed investment is not an easy task, as Chapters 8 and 10 explain.

Proposals are usually classified by how difficult it is to estimate the key parameters needed for financial evaluation. **Required investments** are those the firm must make to comply with safety, health, and environmental regulations. Firms want to know if the present value of the cash expenses needed to comply with the regulations is greater than the cost of closing down. Estimating such expenses should not be too complicated because, in most cases, they are already specified by the regulatory authorities. **Replacement investments** are essentially cost-saving projects that do not generate extra cash inflows. Their future cash benefits (basically cash savings) consist of reductions in anticipated costs that managers can identify with relative ease. Financial evaluation for **expansion investments** is more challenging because these projects require the firm to estimate the additional sales revenues, margins, and working capital that the expansion is expected to generate. Finally, financial evaluation for **diversification investments** is usually the most difficult. The cash flows these proposals are expected to generate are probably the hardest to forecast because the firm will enter an industry it does not know as well as its own.

After the proposal's financial parameters have been estimated, an investment criterion should be applied to *decide* whether the proposal will be accepted or rejected. This chapter examines the **net present value rule** in detail and the profitability index briefly. The next chapter looks at other popular selection criteria, such as the internal rate of return and the payback period, and discusses the profitability index in detail.

Finally, accepted proposals must be *implemented.* But the capital investment process does not end at this point. Projects should be audited regularly throughout their lives. As projects are being carried out, the magnitude and the timing of their cash flows must be monitored to ascertain that they are in line with budgeted figures. If future cash flows fall short of expectation, the projects will obviously not be as profitable as anticipated. If the audit indicates that the expected remaining benefits of an existing investment are lower than the costs of terminating the investment, the firm must abandon it. The firm's owners will be better off without it than with it. Furthermore, the firm should learn from the mistakes uncovered by the regular audits. This information can help improve the firm's capital budgeting process by preventing it from repeating the same mistakes on future projects.

We now analyze a simple investment decision to illustrate how an investment's net present value is calculated and how it is used to decide whether to accept or reject an investment proposal.

WOULD YOU BUY THIS PARCEL OF LAND?

Suppose a parcel of land near where you live is on sale for $10,000. If the parcel is not sold today, it will be taken off the market. The parcel would be an ideal location for a residential home. Unfortunately, the local authorities have so far refused to allow any construction on it. But, you have just learned that they will reverse their decision in the coming year. If you purchase the parcel of land now, you expect to be able to sell it for $11,000 next year when a building permit will be available. The sequence of the two cash flows is shown in Exhibit 6.2, where the cash *outflow* is represented by a descending arrow and the cash *inflow* by an ascending arrow. Given the pattern of cash flows in Exhibit 6.2, you can easily calculate your expected return on investment. It is 10 percent, an expected gain of $1,000 on an investment of $10,000.

Suppose today is your lucky day and you have just received notification that you have inherited exactly $10,000, available immediately. Should you purchase the parcel of land? You should not make this decision without additional information.

EXHIBIT 6.2   Cash-Flow Time Line for Parcel of Land.

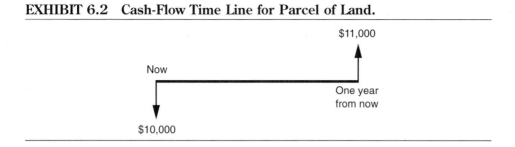

One valuable piece of information is the highest return you can earn on a *comparable* investment. If you can earn *more* than 10 percent on a truly comparable or **alternative investment,** you should not buy the land.

THE ALTERNATIVE INVESTMENT

The alternative investment and the one under consideration must be compared to see if they share the same attributes. The most important attribute is *risk*. The parcel of land is a risky investment because you do not know for certain that it will sell for $11,000 next year. There is some probability that it will sell for more or less than its expected future price. The higher the probability that actual cash flows will deviate from their expected values, the higher the risk of the expected cash-flow stream. The alternative investment must have the same risk characteristics as the parcel of land. In financial terminology, they should both belong to the same **risk class.**

Another relevant investment characteristic is the *tax treatment* of the investment's expected gains. It must be the same for the two investments because investors are only interested in their *aftertax* return on investment. For the time being, and for the sake of simplicity, we assume that you live in a country that does not tax investment income. Thus, the alternative investment has the same tax treatment as the land.

The *liquidity* of the investment, that is, the ability to trade it at its current market price, is still another investment attribute that might be considered when identifying investments that are similar to the parcel of land. Risk and taxes, however, are the most important characteristics the two investments must share.

THE OPPORTUNITY COST OF CAPITAL

In order to estimate the rate of return on an alternative investment in the same risk class as the parcel of land, we look at the return on comparable parcels of land in the market. To further simplify the analysis at this stage, we assume that the proposed investment is *riskless* to you. If you sell the land next year for less than

$11,000, we will pay you the difference; if you sell it for more than $11,000, you will give us the difference. This deal assures you that you will get $11,000 regardless of the market price of the parcel of land next year. Because the project is now riskless, the alternative investment is the deposit of the inherited $10,000 in a savings account that is government-insured, which is currently offering a 6 percent return. This is the expected return from any project that is riskless. This is also the return that you will give up if you buy the land, so it is called the **project's opportunity cost of capital,** or simply, the **project's cost of capital.** Now, should you purchase the parcel of land? In this situation, you should buy the land because you will earn a 10 percent return on the land and will earn only 6 percent on the savings account.

Comparing a project's return with the return offered by an alternative investment is a very simple and straightforward approach to investment analysis. Although this approach works well for one-period projects (like the parcel of land), it may sometimes fail when the project has cash flows spread over several periods. In this case, there exist particular patterns of cash flows (to be examined in the next chapter) for which we cannot compute a unique and unambiguous rate of return. However, another approach to evaluating projects can deal with any pattern of cash flows. This approach uses net present value.

THE NET PRESENT VALUE RULE

The approach to investment analysis in the previous section compares the rates of return for two investments—the parcel of land and the savings account. Instead, the $10,000 payable *now* to acquire the land can be compared with the dollar amount that would have to be invested *now* in the savings account in order to have $11,000 one year from now. This comparison is the foundation of the net present value rule and is explained first for a one-period investment.[1]

A ONE-PERIOD INVESTMENT

How much should you invest now in a savings account with a 6 percent interest rate if you want to receive $11,000 in one year? The answer is $10,377. Because if you invest $10,377 at 6 percent now, in one year you will have $11,000, the sum of your initial deposit ($10,377) and the interest earned on it in one year ($623):

$$\$10,377 + \$10,377 \times 6\% = \$10,377 + \$623 = \$11,000$$

This equation can be written as:

$$\$10,377 + \$10,377 \times 6\% = \$10,377 \times (1 + 0.06) = \$11,000$$

---

[1]The period could be of any duration. In this instance, we assume a period of one year.

The **compounded value,** or **future value,** of $10,377 at 6 percent for one year is $11,000. The term $(1 + 0.06)$ is called the one-year **compound factor** at 6 percent. It is equal to 1.06 (one plus the 6 percent interest rate).

How did we find the $10,377 in the first place? We simply divided the future cash flow of $11,000 by $(1 + 0.06)$, the one-year compound factor:

$$\frac{\$11,000}{(1 + 0.06)} = \$10,377$$

This equation can be written as:

$$\$11,000 \times \frac{1}{1 + 0.06} = \$11,000 \times 0.9434 = \$10,377$$

The **discounted value,** or **present value,** of $11,000 at 6 percent for one year is $10,377. The term $\dfrac{1}{(1 + 0.06)}$ is called the one-year **discount factor (DF)** at 6 percent. It is equal to 0.9434, the present value, at a 6-percent discount rate, of one dollar to be received in one year. That is, one dollar in one year is worth approximately 94 cents today if the discount rate is 6 percent. Discounting has "shrunk" the dollar by roughly 6 percent.

The discount factor is the *inverse* of the compound factor and discounting is the *reverse* of compounding. Compounding provides the future cash flow ($11,000) given the present one ($10,377) while discounting provides the present cash flow ($10,377) given the future one ($11,000). *In other words, at 6 percent you should be indifferent between $10,377 now or $11,000 in one year. At that rate, the two cash flows are equivalent.*

Let's return to the comparison between the parcel of land and the savings account. The parcel of land costs $10,000 and generates $11,000 in one year. The savings account requires a deposit of $10,377 to generate $11,000 in one year. Which one do you prefer? Obviously, you would prefer the parcel of land because both investments generate the same cash inflows in one year but the parcel of land requires a smaller initial investment.

The difference between $10,377 (the present value at 6 percent of the $11,000 future cash flow the land will generate in one year) and the initial cash outlay of $10,000 (the cost of the land) is called the **net present value (NPV)** of the parcel of land. It is usually presented as follows:

NPV(Land) = −[Initial cash outlay] + [Present value of future cash
             flow at the cost of capital]

NPV(Land at 6%) = −[$10,000] + [$10,377] = +$377

The NPV is positive so you should purchase the parcel of land. The present value of its future cash inflow is higher than its present cost. If the NPV had been negative, you would have invested in the savings account. In general, *an investment should be*

EXHIBIT 6.3   **Time Line for One-Period Project.**

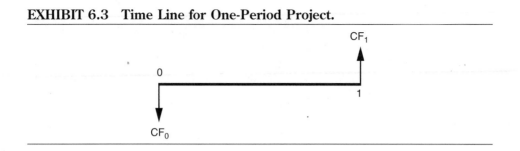

accepted if its NPV is positive and should be rejected if its NPV is negative. This is the present value rule. If the NPV had been zero, you would be indifferent between buying the parcel of land and depositing your money in the savings account.

    In Exhibit 6.3, CF_0 designates the initial cash outlay (the cash flow at time 0) and CF_1 designates the cash flow at the end of a one-period project (the cash flow at time 1). If k is the opportunity cost of capital, then the NPV of a one-period investment can be written as:

$$\text{NPV(Investment)} = -CF_0 + CF_1 \times \frac{1}{(1 + k)^1} = -CF_0 + CF_1 \times DF_1$$

where $DF_1 = \dfrac{1}{(1 + k)^1}$ is the one-year discount factor at cost of capital k. For the land project, we have:

$$\begin{aligned}
\text{NPV(Land at 6\%)} &= -\$10{,}000 + \$11{,}000 \times DF_1 \\
&= -\$10{,}000 + \$11{,}000 \times \frac{1}{(1 + 0.06)^1} \\
&= -\$10{,}000 + \$11{,}000 \times 0.9434 \\
&= -\$10{,}000 + \$10{,}377 = +\$377
\end{aligned}$$

A TWO-PERIOD INVESTMENT WITHOUT INTERMEDIATE CASH FLOWS

Suppose you will receive the future cash flow of $11,000 for the parcel of land not in one year but in two years, all else unchanged. The sequence of cash flows now looks like the one in Exhibit 6.4. Should you still buy the parcel of land? Before you decide, you need to consider the **time value of money:** $11,000 in two years is not as valuable as $11,000 in one year. How much would you have to invest now in the 6 percent savings account to receive $11,000 two years from now? In other words, what is the present value of a parcel of land that will yield $11,000 in two years if your opportunity cost of capital is 6 percent? It is $9,790 because $9,790 invested at

EXHIBIT 6.4   Time Line for Two-Period Investment, No Intermediate Cash Flows.

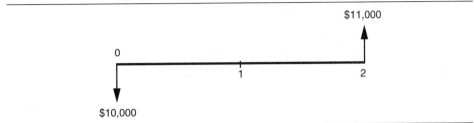

6 percent per year will produce $11,000 in two years. In one year, the $9,790 will grow to $9,790 × (1 + 0.06). This amount will in turn grow by (1 + 0.06) during the second year. We can write:

$$[\$9,790 \times (1 + 0.06)] \times (1 + 0.06) = \$9,790 \times (1 + 0.06)^2$$
$$= \$9,790 \times 1.1236 = \$11,000$$

where $(1 + 0.06)^2$, which is equal to 1.1236, is the two-year compound factor at 6 percent. The $9,790 present value is found by simply discounting the future value of $11,000 twice at 6 percent, that is:

$$\text{PV}(\$11,000 \text{ at } 6\%) = \$11,000 \times \frac{1}{(1 + 0.06)(1 + 0.06)}$$
$$= \$11,000 \times \frac{1}{(1 + 0.06)^2}$$
$$= \$11,000 \times 0.8900 = \$9,790$$

where 0.8900 is the two-year discount factor at 6 percent, that is:

$$\text{DF}_2 = \frac{1}{(1 + 0.06)^2} = 0.8900.$$

You have to invest only $9,790 in the savings account now to receive $11,000 in two years, whereas you have to invest $10,000 in the parcel of land to receive the same amount at the same date. The savings account is clearly the better investment because it requires a smaller initial cash outlay to generate the same payoff in two years.

Now, consider the net present value of the land for this case. We have:

$$\text{NPV}(\text{Land at } 6\%) = -\text{Initial cash outlay} + \text{Present value of } \$11,000 \text{ at } 6\%$$
$$= -\$10,000 + \$9,790 = -\$210$$

The NPV is negative, so the previous net present value rule is still valid: Accept a project if its net present value is positive and reject it if its net present value is negative.

EXHIBIT 6.5   Time Line for Two-Period Investment with Intermediate Cash Flow.

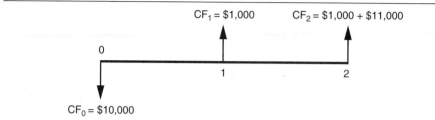

A TWO-PERIOD INVESTMENT WITH AN INTERMEDIATE CASH FLOW

Given the two-year land investment in the previous section, suppose you could rent the parcel of land during the two years. The land is fertile and you should be able to rent it to a vegetable gardener or farmer for, say, $1,000 per year, payable at the end of each year. The cash-flow profile of the investment in the parcel of land now looks like the one in Exhibit 6.5. The investment requires an initial cash outlay (CF_0) of $10,000, yields a first-year cash flow (CF_1) of $1,000, and a terminal cash flow (CF_2) of $12,000, the sum of the second-year $1,000 rent and the $11,000 resale value of the land. Should you purchase the parcel of land in this case? The present value (PV) of the land's future cash-flow stream ($CF_1 = \$1,000$ and $CF_2 = \$12,000$) at a cost of capital of 6 percent is:

$$\begin{aligned} PV(CF_1, CF_2 \text{ at } 6\%) &= CF_1 \times DF_1 + CF_2 \times DF_2 \\ &= \$1,000 \times 0.9434 + \$12,000 \times 0.8900 \\ &= \$943 + \$10,680 = \$11,623 \end{aligned}$$

where $DF_1 = 0.9434$ is the one-year discount factor at 6 percent and $DF_2 = 0.8900$ is the two-year discount factor at 6 percent. The present value of the land's future cash-flow stream ($11,623) is greater than its cost ($10,000), so you should purchase the land. The net present value of the parcel of land is the difference between $11,623 and $10,000:

$$NPV(\text{Land}) = -\$10,000 + \$11,623 = +\$1,623$$

It is positive, indicating that the investment should be accepted. The net present value rule continues to hold: Accept a project when its NPV is positive and reject it when it is negative.

MULTIPLE-PERIOD INVESTMENTS

The analysis of the two-period investment case can be extended easily to a multiple-period investment with any number of intermediate cash flows. The longer the duration of the expected cash-flow stream, the longer the calculation, but the NPV approach still works. A business investment project can always be reduced to a

EXHIBIT 6.6 Time Line for Multiple-Period Investments— The General Case.

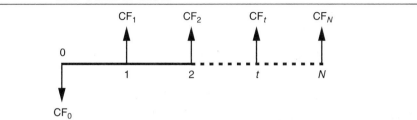

stream of expected periodic cash flows, so the NPV rule can be applied directly to the analysis of a capital expenditure.

Let's call CF_t the expected cash flow at the end of year t from an investment project that requires an initial cash outlay CF_0. Assume that the investment will generate a stream of cash flows for a duration of N years. The cash-flow profile of the investment would now look like the one in Exhibit 6.6. As before, the net present value of the investment is the difference between the present value of its expected cash-flow stream and the investment's initial cash outlay. The present value, $PV(CF_t)$, of a cash flow occurring at time t, at cost of capital k, is:

$$PV(CF_t) = CF_t \times \frac{1}{(1 + k)^t} = CF_t \times DF_t$$

where $DF_t = \dfrac{1}{(1 + k)^t}$ is the t-period discount factor at cost of capital k. DF_t is the present value at cost of capital k of *one* dollar of cash flow occurring at time t. It follows that the present value of CF_t dollars of cash flow must be equal to CF_t multiplied by DF_t.

We can express the net present value of an investment with a cash-flow stream lasting for N years and cost of capital k as follows:

$$NPV(k,N) = -CF_0 + CF_1 \times DF_1 + CF_2 \times DF_2$$
$$+ \ldots + CF_t \times DF_t + \ldots + CF_N \times DF_N$$

The previous decision rule still holds: *An investment should be undertaken if its net present value is positive and should be rejected if its net present value is negative.* If the NPV is zero, you should be indifferent between accepting or rejecting the investment.

Replacing DF_1 with $\dfrac{1}{(1 + k)^1}$, DF_2 with $\dfrac{1}{(1 + k)^2}$, DF_t with $\dfrac{1}{(1 + k)^t}$, and DF_N with $\dfrac{1}{(1 + k)^N}$ in the above equation, we have another familiar expression for net present value:

$$\mathbf{NPV}(k,N) = -\mathbf{CF_0} + \frac{\mathbf{CF_1}}{(1 + k)^1} + \frac{\mathbf{CF_2}}{(1 + k)^2}$$
$$+ \ldots + \frac{\mathbf{CF_t}}{(1 + k)^t} + \ldots + \frac{\mathbf{CF_N}}{(1 + k)^N}$$

This equation can be written as:

$$NPV(k, N) = -CF_0 + \sum_{t=1}^{N} \frac{CF_t}{(1 + k)^t}$$

where $\sum_{t=1}^{N} \frac{CF_t}{(1 + k)^t}$ is the sum of the terms $\frac{CF_t}{(1 + k)^t}$ from t equals 1 to t equals N.

APPLYING THE NET PRESENT VALUE RULE TO A CAPITAL INVESTMENT DECISION

Applying the net present value rule to a capital expenditure decision is a straightforward exercise *assuming that all the relevant inputs have been estimated*. These inputs are the stream of cash flows that the project is expected to generate over its anticipated useful life and the cost of capital applicable to the investment under consideration. After these inputs are estimated, the present value of the project's stream of expected cash flows is calculated by discounting the cash flows at the project's cost of capital. Then, the project's initial cash outlay is subtracted from this present value to find the project's net present value. If the net present value is positive, the project is accepted; if the net present value is negative, the project is rejected. We use an example to explain the procedure.

Sunlight Manufacturing Company (SMC) has been successfully producing and selling various types of electrical equipment for the last 20 years and is currently considering adding a new product to its existing product line. The firm would have to spend $2,360,000 now to launch the designer desk lamp, which is expected to be obsolete after five years. The investment is expected to generate an annual net cash flow of $832,000 at the end of its first year, $822,000 at the end of its second year, $692,000 at the end of its third year, and $554,000 at the end of its fourth year and a terminal net cash flow of $466,000 at the end of its fifth year. The terminal cash flow includes the estimated resale value of any equipment used to manufacture the product, net of any liquidation cost. The project's estimated cost of capital is 10 percent. Should SMC launch the new product? To answer this question, we find the project's net present value. First, the present value of each expected cash flow is calculated by multiplying it by its corresponding discount factor at the cost of capital of 10 percent (see Exhibit 6.7). Then, the initial cash outlay of $2,360,000 is subtracted from the total present value of the project's expected cash-flow stream to obtain the project's net present value:

NPV(New product at 10%) = -$2,360,000 + $2,623,293 = $263,293

The project's net present value is positive, so SMC should launch the designer desk lamp.

As you may have already noticed, the computation of net present values for multiple-period projects can be tedious. Fortunately, most electronic financial calculators

EXHIBIT 6.7   Calculation of Present Value for SMC Designer Desk Lamp.

Present value of CF_1 = \$832,000 $\times \dfrac{1}{(1 + 0.10)^1}$ = \$832,000 $\times$ 0.9091 = \$756,371

Present value of CF_2 = \$822,000 $\times \dfrac{1}{(1 + 0.10)^2}$ = \$822,000 $\times$ 0.8264 = \$679,301

Present value of CF_3 = \$692,000 $\times \dfrac{1}{(1 + 0.10)^3}$ = \$692,000 $\times$ 0.7513 = \$519,900

Present value of CF_4 = \$554,000 $\times \dfrac{1}{(1 + 0.10)^4}$ = \$554,000 $\times$ 0.6830 = \$378,382

Present value of CF_5 = \$466,000 $\times \dfrac{1}{(1 + 0.10)^5}$ = \$466,000 $\times$ 0.6209 = \$289,339

Total present value at 10%	$2,623,293

have several financial functions, including an NPV function. To use this function, simply enter the cash flow values starting with the initial cash outlay and ending with the fifth year's cash flow. Then, enter the investment's cost of capital and press the NPV key. The calculator will compute the present values of the expected cash-flow stream and provide the project's NPV.[2] The procedure is similar for a spreadsheet application on a computer. A far more complex and challenging task is the estimation of the inputs required to perform this calculation, namely, the project's expected cash-flow stream and its corresponding cost of capital. These issues are addressed in Chapters 8 and 10, respectively.

WHY THE NPV RULE IS A GOOD INVESTMENT RULE

The net present value rule is a desirable investment decision rule because, as discussed in this section, it has the following properties:

1. It is a measure of value creation: When the project's net present value is positive, the project creates value, and when it is negative, the project destroys value.
2. It adjusts for the timing of the project's expected cash flows.
3. It adjusts for the risk of the project's expected cash flows.
4. It is additive.

[2]A calculator will not indicate an NPV of exactly \$263,293 because that number has been computed with discount factors that have been rounded to the fourth decimal point. The NPV provided by a calculator is more accurate.

The first three properties are essential for any selection criterion used to decide whether to accept or reject a capital investment. In Chapter 7, the comparisons of the NPV rule to alternative selection criteria are based on these important properties. The additive property of the net present value rule simply means that if one project has an NPV of $100,000 and another an NPV of $50,000, then the two projects, taken together, have a combined NPV of $150,000, assuming that the two projects are independent. This property has several useful implications.

A MEASURE OF VALUE CREATION

At the beginning of the chapter, we defined a good investment decision as one that increases the market value of the firm's equity. Would a positive NPV project be one?

Consider again the one-period real estate investment example. Recall that the initial cash outlay is $10,000 and that the present value of its expected cash inflow of $11,000 is $10,377 at 6 percent. Suppose you make the investment and, as soon as you have done so, an interested investor wants to purchase the parcel of land from you.

What *minimum* price should you quote? You should not accept any price less than $10,377. If you sell it for less, say $10,200, the best alternative investment available is to put the $10,200 in a savings account. After a year, you will have $10,812 ($10,200 plus 6 percent of $10,200 or $612). This is less than the $11,000 you will receive in a year from your parcel of land. Clearly, you would not want to sell the land for less than $10,377.

What is the *maximum* price the interested investor would be willing to pay for the parcel of land? The maximum price for the investor is also $10,377. This is the amount the investor would have to spend now on the alternative investment (the savings account) to have an amount in a year equal to the return on the land. At a higher purchase price, the investor will be "poorer" than if the money was put in the alternative investment.

If there is a price that both you and the interested investor can agree on, it is $10,377. This would also be the price at which your new property would be sold to any other buyer in an active real estate market. Thus, $10,377 is the *market value* of the parcel of land. In other words, its present value is also its market value. By extension, this is also true for any capital investment. In fact, *the present value of a project's expected cash-flow stream at its cost of capital is actually an estimate of how much the project would sell for if a market existed for it.* In other words, the market value of any investment is determined by the present value of the cash flows that it is expected to generate in the future.

The parcel of land you bought for only $10,000 has a market value of $10,377. Thus, your wealth has increased by $377 ($10,377 less $10,000). This is exactly the same as the net present value of the investment. By extension, *the net present value of an investment project represents the immediate change in the wealth of the firm's owners if the project is accepted.* If positive, the project creates value for the firm's owners; if negative, it destroys value. From the perspective of owners, a decision to invest in a positive net present value project is clearly a good investment decision. It increases their current wealth.

While a project with a positive NPV is expected to create value if the project is undertaken, NPV does not provide any indication about the source of value creation. Firms can generate positive NPV projects and create value for their shareholders for many reasons. The firm may have creative managers supported by a superior work force. It may hold a strong position in a product or service market that makes it difficult for new entrants to compete on an equal footing. More importantly, some projects cannot be easily replicated by competitors either because they require expertise that is specific to the firm or because they are protected by patents. For these reasons, a firm may be able to generate cash flows from some of its investments that have present values higher than the cost of investing in these projects.

ADJUSTMENT FOR THE TIMING OF THE PROJECT'S CASH FLOWS

A good investment decision must take into consideration the timing of the investment's expected cash flows. Does the net present value rule do this? A project's NPV is the difference between the present value of its expected cash flows and its current cost. The present values of these cash flows are obtained by discounting each of them at the project's opportunity cost of capital. The more distant the cash flows, the lower their contribution to the investment's present value because the discount factor, $\dfrac{1}{(1 + k)^t}$, by which the cash flows are multiplied in the net present value formula becomes smaller as t increases. Thus, the net present value rule adjusts for the timing of a project's expected cash flows.

To illustrate, consider two five-year investments, A and B. Both require an initial cash outlay of $1 million and have a cost of capital of 10 percent. The cash flows expected from the two investments are shown in Exhibit 6.8.

Assume that the investments are **mutually exclusive,** meaning that if one is chosen the other must be turned down. (An example is the choice between building

EXHIBIT 6.8 Cash Flows for Two Investments with $CF_0 = \$1$ Million and $k = 0.10$.

END OF YEAR	INVESTMENT A	INVESTMENT B
1	$CF_1 = \$800,000$	$CF_1 = \$100,000$
2	$CF_2 = \ 600,000$	$CF_2 = \ 200,000$
3	$CF_3 = \ 400,000$	$CF_3 = \ 400,000$
4	$CF_4 = \ 200,000$	$CF_4 = \ 600,000$
5	$CF_5 = \ 100,000$	$CF_5 = \ 800,000$
Total Cash Flows	**$2,100,000**	**$2,100,000**

either a bridge or a tunnel to allow traffic to cross a river.) A firm confronted with this choice should prefer to invest in project A because it would receive cash faster than if it invests in B. Does the net present value rule lead to the same selection? To find out, we first compute the present values of the two investments' expected cash flows, as shown in Exhibit 6.9. The initial cash outflow is $1 million in both cases. Thus:

$$NPV \text{ (A at 10\%)} = -\$1,000,000 + \$1,722,361 = \$722,361$$

$$NPV \text{ (B at 10\%)} = -\$1,000,000 + \$1,463,269 = \$463,269$$

Both investments are worth undertaking because both have a positive NPV. However, the NPV of investment A is larger than the NPV of investment B. In other words, the NPV rule favors the investment with the faster cash return.

EXHIBIT 6.9   **Present Values of Cash Flows for Two Investments.**
Figures from Exhibit 6.8

END OF YEAR	INVESTMENT A OPPORTUNITY COST OF CAPITAL = 10%
1	PV($800,000) = $800,000 × 0.9091 = $727,273
2	PV($600,000) = 600,000 × 0.8264 = 495,868
3	PV($400,000) = 400,000 × 0.7513 = 300,526
4	PV($200,000) = 200,000 × 0.6830 = 136,602
5	PV($100,000) = 100,000 × 0.6209 = 62,092
	Total present values **$1,722,361**

END OF YEAR	INVESTMENT B OPPORTUNITY COST OF CAPITAL = 10%
1	PV($100,000) = $100,000 × 0.9091 = $ 90,909
2	PV($200,000) = 200,000 × 0.8264 = 165,289
3	PV($400,000) = 400,000 × 0.7513 = 300,526
4	PV($600,000) = 600,000 × 0.6830 = 409,808
5	PV($800,000) = 800,000 × 0.6209 = 496,737
	Total present values **$1,463,269**

ADJUSTMENT FOR THE RISK OF THE PROJECT'S CASH FLOWS

Does the net present value rule consider the risk of a project? It certainly does. *The risk adjustment is made through the project's discount rate.* As the risk of the stream of future cash flows expected from the investment increases, the discount rate (the opportunity cost of capital) used to calculate the present value of the expected cash-flow stream should also increase. The reason is that investors are **risk averse.** They buy shares of firms with riskier projects only if they expect to earn a higher return to compensate them for the higher risk they have to bear.[3] By discounting the future stream of expected cash flows at a rate that increases with risk, the net present value rule adjusts not only for the time value of money but also for the project's risk.

To illustrate, consider two five-year investments, C and D, both requiring the same initial cash outlay of $1 million. Investment D is riskier than investment C. As a result, it has an opportunity cost of capital of 15 percent while C has an opportunity cost of capital of only 12 percent. The two investments have the identical expected cash-flow streams shown in Exhibit 6.10.

Assume again that the investments are mutually exclusive; the firm can only choose one of the two. A firm making investment decisions on behalf of risk-averse investors should prefer investment C. Its expected cash flows are identical to those of investment D but they are *less risky.* Does the net present value rule favor the same investment? To find out, we again compute the present values of the investments' expected cash flows, as shown in Exhibit 6.11. The initial cash outflow is $1 million in both cases. Thus:

$$NPV(C \text{ at } 12\%) = -\$1,000,000 + \$1,081,432 = \$81,432$$

$$NPV(D \text{ at } 15\%) = -\$1,000,000 + \$1,005,646 = \$5,646$$

EXHIBIT 6.10 **Cash Flows for Two Investments with $CF_0 = \$1$ Million, $k = 0.12$ for Investment C, and $k = 0.15$ for Investment D.**

END OF YEAR	INVESTMENT C	INVESTMENT D
1	$CF_1 = \$300,000$	$CF_1 = \$300,000$
2	$CF_2 = 300,000$	$CF_2 = 300,000$
3	$CF_3 = 300,000$	$CF_3 = 300,000$
4	$CF_4 = 300,000$	$CF_4 = 300,000$
5	$CF_5 = 300,000$	$CF_5 = 300,000$
Total cash flows	**$1,500,000**	**$1,500,000**

[3]The relationship between the returns investors will require and the risk they are willing to bear is discussed in Chapter 10.

EXHIBIT 6.11　Present Values of Cash Flows for Two Investments.

Figures from Exhibit 6.10

END OF YEAR	INVESTMENT C OPPORTUNITY COST OF CAPITAL = 12%
1	PV($300,000) = $300,000 × 0.8929 = $267,857
2	PV($300,000) = 300,000 × 0.7972 = 239,158
3	PV($300,000) = 300,000 × 0.7118 = 213,534
4	PV($300,000) = 300,000 × 0.6355 = 190,655
5	PV($300,000) = 300,000 × 0.5674 = 170,228
	Total present values　　　$1,081,432

END OF YEAR	INVESTMENT D OPPORTUNITY COST OF CAPITAL = 15%
1	PV($300,000) = $300,000 × 0.8696 = $260,869
2	PV($300,000) = 300,000 × 0.7561 = 226,843
3	PV($300,000) = 300,000 × 0.6575 = 197,255
4	PV($300,000) = 300,000 × 0.5718 = 171,526
5	PV($300,000) = 300,000 × 0.4972 = 149,153
	Total present values　　　$1,005,646

The investment with the lower risk (investment C) has the larger NPV. In other words, the net present value rule favors the same investment as the one the firm would select. The higher the risk attached to a project's stream of expected cash flows, the higher the opportunity cost of capital required to discount those cash flows, and the lower the project's NPV. In other words, the net present value method adjusts for the risk of a project by raising the project's cost of capital to reflect the higher risk of the project's expected cash flows. The effect of this adjustment is to reduce the project's NPV, thus making it less attractive to the firm.

ADDITIVE PROPERTY

The additive property of the net present value rule has practical implications for the capital expenditure decision. Consider again investments A and B presented earlier and assume now that they are no longer mutually exclusive, the firm can choose to invest in both projects. Because the net present value rule is additive, the value created by the two investments taken together is equal to the sum of their net present values:[4]

$$NPV(A + B) = NPV(A) + NPV(B)$$

$$NPV(A + B) = \$722,361 + \$463,269 = \$1,185,630$$

Thus, to find the NPV of investing in both projects, there is no need to calculate the sum of their combined cash flows, discount them at their cost of capital of 10 percent, and deduct the $2 million initial cash outlay required to launch the two projects. The sum of their net present values produces the same result. Together, the two projects should raise the market value of the firm's equity by an estimated $1,185,630.

The additive property has other useful implications. Suppose that the analysis of investment B overlooked a relevant and recurrent cost that would have reduced each annual cash flow by an estimated $50,000. To determine the investment's NPV with the corrected cash flows, simply calculate the present value of the future stream of "overlooked" cash outflows ($50,000 per year) and add it to the NPV of the original investment. Our calculator[5] indicates that:

$$NPV(-\$50,000 \text{ for 5 years at } 10\%) = -\$189,539$$

The corrected NPV is thus:

$$NPV(\text{Corrected}) = NPV(\text{Original}) + NPV(-\$50,000 \text{ series})$$
$$= \$463,269 - \$189,539 = \$273,730$$

The NPV is still positive. The project remains attractive but the magnitude of its NPV has been reduced by almost 41 percent.

The additive property can also help the firm's managers determine the *change* in the value created by an investment if the risk of its expected cash-flow stream is suddenly revised upward or if the magnitude of its expected cash flows is revised downward. Suppose the risk of investment C, discussed earlier, is revised upward. The appropriate discount rate, which reflects the investment's higher risk, is no longer 12 percent but, say, 15 percent. The firm should expect the upward revision of the risk of investment C to reduce the market value of the firm's equity by $75,786, an amount equal to the net present value of the additional risk:

$$NPV(\text{Additional risk}) = NPV(C \text{ at } 15\%) - NPV(C \text{ at } 12\%)$$
$$= \$5,646 - \$81,432 = -\$75,786$$

How much can the value of investment C be reduced due to overlooked future costs, initial cost overrun, or higher than expected levels of risk and *still earn its*

---

[4]The implicit assumption is that the projects' expected cash-flow streams are independent of one another. Investing in one project will have no effect on the cash-flow stream of the other.
[5]If you have not yet bought a financial calculator, it is time you did. Trust us, it is a positive NPV proposition.

cost of capital? For investment C to still earn its 12 percent cost of capital, its value can be reduced no more than $81,432, the NPV of the original investment. The upward revision of the project's risk (which resulted in an increase in the cost of capital to 15 percent) has already reduced the project's initial NPV by $75,786. If the present value of, say, additional overlooked costs exceeds $5,646 ($81,432 less $75,786), the project's NPV will become negative and will no longer earn its *new* opportunity cost of capital of 15 percent. In other words, an investment's positive NPV is a measure of value creation to the firm's owners *only if the project proceeds according to the budgeted figures.* From the firm's managers' perspective, a project's positive NPV is the maximum present value that they can afford to "lose" on the project (due to downward revision of the project's cash flows and/or upward revision of the project's risk) and still earn the project's cost of capital. Further "losses" will change the project's NPV to a negative value, and the investment will become a value-destroying proposition.

SPECIAL CASES OF CAPITAL BUDGETING

We have examined how the timing and the risk of expected cash flows affect the net present values of investments with equal sizes and equal lives. However, projects usually have different sizes or different life spans. For example, a firm's investment budget may not be large enough to allow the firm to fund all its investment proposals that have a positive NPV. When these proposals vary greatly in size (measured by their initial cash outlay), managers have to decide which positive NPV project to accept and which to reject, a process called budgeting under **capital rationing.** Managers may also have several choices for replacing an aging machine, with each possibility having a different expected useful life. The following sections show how to use the net present value method to select investments with different sizes or different life spans.

COMPARING PROJECTS OF UNEQUAL SIZE

Suppose that a firm is considering three investments, as described in Exhibit 6.12. According to the net present value rule, all three investments should be undertaken because they all have a positive NPV and, hence, all three create value. However, the firm can invest in all three projects only if (1) the projects are mutually exclusive, and (2) the firm can raise the $2 million it needs to launch the three projects (the sum of their initial cash outlays).

What if the firm can only raise $1 million? In this case, the choice narrows down to either investing only in E or investing in both F and G. Investments F and G are clearly the superior choice because they have a value-creating potential of $272,727 (the sum of their net present values) compared to only $140,496 for investment E. Thus, *if there is a limit on the total capital available for investment, the firm*

EXHIBIT 6.12   Cash Flows, Present Values, and Net Present Values for Three Investments of Unequal Size with $k = 0.10$.

	INVESTMENT E	INVESTMENT F	INVESTMENT G
(1) Initial cash outlay (CF_0)	$1,000,000	$500,000	$500,000
Year-one cash flow (CF_1)	800,000	200,000	100,000
Year-two cash flow (CF_2)	500,000	510,000	700,000
(2) Present value of CF_1 and CF_2 at 10%	$1,140,496	$603,306	$669,421
Net present value = (2) minus (1)	**$140,496**	**$103,306**	**$169,421**

cannot simply select the project with the highest NPV.[6] It must first find out the combination of investments with the highest present value of future cash flows *per dollar of initial cash outlay.* This can be done by using the project's **profitability index.** An investment's profitability index is defined as the ratio of the present value of the investment's expected cash-flow stream to the investment's initial cash outlay. The profitability indexes of investments E, F, and G are shown in Exhibit 6.13.

An investment's profitability index is equivalent to a benefit-to-cost ratio. If the investment has a positive NPV, then its benefit (line 2 of Exhibit 6.13) must exceed its cost (line 1 of the exhibit) and its profitability index is greater than one. If it has a negative NPV, then its cost must exceed its benefit and its profitability index is less than one. Investments E, F, and G all have a positive NPV, so their profitability

EXHIBIT 6.13   Profitability Indexes for Three Investments of Unequal Size.

Figures from Exhibit 6.12

	INVESTMENT E	INVESTMENT F	INVESTMENT G
(1) Initial cash outlay	$1,000,000	$500,000	$500,000
(2) Present value of future cash-flow stream	$1,140,496	$603,306	$669,421
(3) **Profitability index** $= \dfrac{(2)}{(1)}$	$\dfrac{\$1,140,496}{\$1,000,000} = 1.14$	$\dfrac{\$603,306}{\$500,000} = 1.21$	$\dfrac{\$669,421}{\$500,000} = 1.34$

[6]This problem arises only because the three projects do not have the same initial size. If they did, then the projects should be ranked by decreasing order of their NPV and the projects with the largest NPV should be selected.

indexes are all greater than one. Project E yields 14 cents of present value per dollar of initial investment, project F yields 21 cents, and project G yields 34 cents.

If the firm has limited funds available for investment, it should first rank the three projects in decreasing order of their profitability indexes (first G, then F, and finally E). Then, *it should select projects with the highest profitability indexes until it has allocated the total amount of funds at its disposal.* In our case, this allocation rule will select project G and then project F for a total investment of $1 million.

Allocating limited capital to a set of projects on the basis of their profitability indexes does not, unfortunately, resolve the size problem entirely because this method deals with a situation where the limit on capital expenditures is imposed during the year the projects are under review. In our case, the $1 million limit applies to the initial year. What will happen next year?

Suppose that the $1 million limit on capital applies again the following year and that project H, costing $1.8 million and having an NPV of $400,000, becomes available. Will the firm be able to finance project H? The firm will have a *maximum* of $1.3 million of funds to invest: The $1 million capital budget plus the $300,000 of cash flow generated by projects F and G at the end of year one. (Recall that the firm selected projects F and G last year and that their combined first-year cash flows are equal to $300,000, as indicated in Exhibit 6.12). Project H costs $1.8 million, so $1.3 million is not enough to fund it. It will have to be turned down. Conclusion: Because the firm invested in projects F and G last year, it must now turn down a project with a $400,000 NPV.

If the firm had selected investment E last year, it would be able to fund investment H. Investment E would have generated $800,000 at the end of year one, which, added to the $1 million capital budget, would provide the funds required to invest in H. Investments E and H have a combined NPV of $540,496 ($140,496 plus $400,000), a higher value than the combination of F and G ($103,306 plus $169,421), even after adjusting the NPV of project H to account for the fact that it occurs a year later.[7]

Thus, *a firm operating under capital constraints should not make today's investment decisions without considering investments that may be available tomorrow.* However, this may be difficult in practice because information about tomorrow's investments may not be readily available today. If the firm does not know enough about future potential projects, then using the profitability index to make optimal decisions on the basis of currently available information may be the *second best* solution. The next chapter discusses the profitability index in more detail and reexamines its reliability as a rule to select alternative investments.

COMPARING PROJECTS WITH UNEQUAL LIFE SPANS

We now consider a firm that must make a choice between two investments with unequal life spans. Suppose a firm must decide whether to purchase machine A or

---

[7]The $400,000 NPV of project H is only worth $363,636 a year earlier if discounted at the firm's cost of capital of 10 percent.

machine B. Machine A costs $80,000, has a useful life of two years, and has annual maintenance costs of $4,000. It is assumed to be worthless after two years of operation. Machine B costs $120,000, has a useful life of four years, and has annual maintenance costs of $3,000. It will be worthless in four years. Machine B is 50 percent more expensive than A but its useful life is twice as long and its annual maintenance costs are lower. The two machines are expected to generate the same annual cash flows. The firm's managers want to find out which machine the firm should buy.

If the two machines generate identical future annual cash inflows, the one with the lower present value of overall costs should be preferred because its *net present value* would be higher. The problem is that the two machines have unequal life spans; machine A will last for two years and machine B will last for four years. We cannot make a meaningful comparison unless both machines operate over the same period of time. Thus, we assume that at the end of the second year the firm will purchase a new machine A that will last for two years. With this approach, we can compare a sequence of *two* machine A's lasting four years to *one* machine B, also lasting four years.

Let's assume that the appropriate cost of capital applicable to this type of cost analysis is 10 percent. The relevant streams of cash outflows for two machine A's and one machine B and their present values at 10 percent are shown in Exhibit 6.14. The present value of the total cost of a sequence of two machine A's ($158,795) is higher than the present value of the total cost of a single machine B ($129,509) over the same span of useful life. The firm should buy machine B even though it is more expensive. The present value of the total cost of a *single* machine A bought today is only equal to $86,924 (not shown in the exhibit). If the firm compares that cost with the cost of machine B ($129,509), it will find machine A cheaper and will incorrectly purchase it.

In the case we have just examined, a sequence of two machines A's is equivalent to one machine B. If, for example, machine B had a five-year useful life and machine A had only a three-year life, we would have compared a sequence of *five* Machine A's against a sequence of *three* Machine B's in order to have two sequences with *equal lives* of 15 years. Fortunately, a shortcut exists that avoids these tedious calculations. We convert each machine's total stream of cash outflows into an equivalent stream of *equal* annual cash flows with the same present value as the total cash-outflow stream (called the **constant annual-equivalent cash flow** or *annuity-equivalent cash flow*). Then, we simply compare the size of the annuities. A firm should select the machine with the lowest annuity-equivalent cash flow. Appendix 6.1 shows how to calculate these constant annual-equivalent cash flows. These cash flows for the original case are shown in Exhibit 6.15.

The total stream of cash outflows generated by machine A has a two-year annuity-equivalent cash outflow of $50,096, and the total stream of cash outflows generated by machine B has a four-year annuity-equivalent cash outflow of $40,855. Because $40,855 is less than $50,096, machine B should be selected. It can be replaced by an *infinite* sequence of machine B's with an annual cost $40,855, whereas machine A is replaceable by an *infinite* sequence of Machine A's with an annual cost $50,096.

EXHIBIT 6.14 Cash Outflows and Present Values of Cost for Two Investments with Unequal Life Spans.

| END OF YEAR | SEQUENCE OF TWO MACHINE A'S | | | | ONE MACHINE B | |
| | CASH OUTFLOWS | | | PRESENT VALUE | CASH OUTFLOWS | PRESENT VALUE |
	MACHINE 1	MACHINE 2	TOTAL	COST OF CAPITAL = 10%		COST OF CAPITAL = 10%
Now	−$80,000		−$80,000	−$80,000	−$120,000	−$120,000
1	−4,000		−4,000	−3,636	−3,000	−2,727
2	−4,000	−$80,000	−84,000	−69,422	−3,000	−2,479
3	−4,000		−4,000	−3,005	−3,000	−2,254
4	−4,000		−4,000	−2,732	−3,000	−2,049
			Present value of costs	−$158,795	Present value of costs	−$129,509

EXHIBIT 6.15 Original and Annuity-Equivalent Cash Flows for Two Investments with Unequal Life Spans.
Figures from Exhibit 6.14 and Appendix 6.1

| END OF YEAR | MACHINE A | | MACHINE B | |
	ORIGINAL CASH FLOW	ANNUITY-EQUIVALENT CASH FLOW	ORIGINAL CASH FLOW	ANNUITY-EQUIVALENT CASH FLOW
Now	−$80,000		−$120,000	
1	−4,000	−$50,096	−3,000	−$40,855
2	−4,000	−50,096	−3,000	−40,855
3			−3,000	−40,855
4			−3,000	−40,855
Present values (10%)	−$86,942	−$86,942	−$129,509	−$129,509

LIMITATIONS OF THE NET PRESENT VALUE CRITERION

Although the net present value criterion can be adjusted for some situations, such as the comparison of two projects of unequal size or unequal life spans, in other situations the required adjustments to the net present value criterion are far too complex to be easily implemented. In most cases, these situations arise because the net present value criterion is a take-it-or-leave-it rule that is based only on the information available at the time the NPV is estimated. Hence, the net present value criterion ignores the opportunities to make changes to the project as time passes and more information becomes available.

NPV is estimated from the stream of *expected* cash flows generated by the proposal and discounted at the project's cost of capital, which is a function of the project's risk. The estimation of both the cash flows and their corresponding cost of capital depends on information available at the time NPV is calculated. This information involves such factors as the marketability of the product, its selling price, the risk of obsolescence, the technology used in manufacturing, and the economic, regulatory, and tax environments.

A project that can adjust easily and at a low cost to significant changes in these factors will contribute more to the value of the firm than indicated by its NPV. It will also be more valuable than an alternative proposal with the same NPV but which cannot be altered as easily and as cheaply. A project's flexibility, that is, the ability of a project to adjust to changing circumstances, is usually described by **managerial options.** These are options that can be exercised to alter a project during its useful life.

MANAGERIAL OPTIONS EMBEDDED IN INVESTMENT PROJECTS

The following sections discuss two important managerial options—the option to switch technologies and the option to abandon a project. We use the designer desk lamp project of Sunlight Manufacturing Company (SMC) to illustrate the concepts.

The option to switch technologies

Suppose SMC can use two different types of machines to manufacture the designer desk lamp during the five years the project is expected to last. One is a multipurpose standard machine and the other is a single-purpose, untested digitally-driven apparatus, which was developed by SMC's research department specifically for the project. Assume that the machine used does not significantly affect the project's NPV. Although engineers at SMC are confident the newer machine will prove to be reliable, the project's manager believes there is a possibility the newer machine will not be able to meet the stringent volume and quality requirements of mass production and may have to be scrapped and replaced with the standard machine. If the standard machine is selected, it can easily be replaced with the newer one, after the new machine has successfully passed extra reliability tests, with minimal disruption and adjustment to the manufacturing process. However, the reverse is not true because replacing the new machine with the standard one would require a complete revamping of the production line. In other words, although management will have the *option to switch* machines while the project is running, this option has more value if the standard machine is chosen.

The importance and the value of the option to switch not only technologies but also production facilities, have long been recognized by firms in some industries. For example, Japanese auto manufacturers have established manufacturing operations in the United States and Europe so they can switch production from one continent to the other when changes occur in the relative costs of producing a car. If the yen appreciates against the U.S. dollar or against European currencies, cars manufactured in the United States or in Europe can be exported to Japan where they can be sold at a higher margin than the locally made cars.

The option to abandon a project

Suppose SMC's designer desk lamp is a flop and does not sell. Although the decision to go ahead with the project implicitly assumed that it will last five years, SMC's management will always have the *option to abandon* the project at an earlier date. Does this option add value to the project's NPV of $263,293?

To help answer this question, we assume that within a year after the project's launch, SMC knows more about the fate of the designer desk lamps. Depending on whether the lamp is a success or a failure, the expected cash flows for the remaining years (from the second to the fifth year) will change as shown in Exhibit 6.16. If the designer desk lamp project is a success, the present value of the remaining cash flows at the project's cost of capital of 10 percent is $2,271,170. If the project turns out to be a failure, the present value is $1,546,289. Assuming that the project can be abandoned at the end of the first year and that the net proceeds from its liquidation will be $1,600,000, what should SMC do one year after it launches the project?

If the designer desk lamps are a success, SMC should continue with the project because the present value of the remaining cash flows ($2,271,170) exceeds the net proceeds from liquidating the project ($1,600,000). But if the lamp is a failure, the present value of the remaining cash flows ($1,546,289) is less than the net proceeds from liquidation and SMC should abandon the project. Thus, in one year, the investment will be worth either $2,271,170 (with the success scenario) or $1,600,000 (with the failure scenario). If there is a 30 percent chance that the project will fail and a 70 percent chance that it will succeed, the expected value of the project in one year's time will be $2,069,819 (30 percent of $1,600,000 plus 70 percent of $2,271,170).

EXHIBIT 6.16   Expected Cash Flows, Years 2 through 5, and Their Present Values for Success and Failure of SMC Designer Desk Lamp.

	YEAR 2	YEAR 3	YEAR 4	YEAR 5	PRESENT VALUE COST OF CAPITAL = 10%
Expected cash flows according to the initial estimation	$832,000	$692,000	$554,000	$466,000	—
Expected cash flows if the project is successful	$890,000	$783,000	$612,000	$520,000	$2,271,170
Expected cash flows if the project is a failure	$662,000	$480,000	$420,000	$340,000	$1,546,289

We can now recalculate the project's NPV taking into account the possibility that it could be abandoned after a year. The initial cash outlay ($2,360,000) and the first year's expected cash flow ($832,000) have not changed, but the cash flows from the second to the fifth years are now replaced by the project's worth at the end of the first year, or $2,069,819.[8] Both the first year's cash flow and the project's worth at the end of that year need to be discounted at the project cost of capital of 10 percent to obtain the NPV with the abandonment option:

$$\text{NPV}_{\text{with abandonment option}} = -\$2,360,000 + \frac{\$832,000 + \$2,069,819}{1 + 0.10} = \$278,017$$

The project's NPV without accounting for the abandonment option was $263,293. Thus, the option to abandon the project after one year adds $14,724 of value ($278,017 less $263,293). Although $14,724 represents only 5.5 percent of the original NPV of the designer desk lamp project and does not affect the investment decision, this may not always be the case. For example, a proposal that is rejected because its NPV is negative can be turned into a positive NPV project, and consequently accepted, when the abandonment option is considered.

---

[8]The expected cash flows in the original estimation of the project NPV are the same as the average of the expected cash flows under the success and the failure scenarios, weighted by the chances of success (70 percent) and failure (30 percent). For example, the original cash flow in year 3 ($692,000) is equal to 70 percent of $783,000 (cash flow if the lamp is a hit) plus 30 percent of $480,000 (cash flow if the lamp is a flop).

DEALING WITH MANAGERIAL OPTIONS

The option to switch technologies and the option to abandon a project are embedded in most investment projects. However, these are not the only managerial options. Managers have many opportunities to enhance the value of an investment during its lifetime as circumstances change. A counterpoint to the option to abandon a project is the *option to expand* the project. For example, suppose the designer desk lamp is a big winner and the project needs to be expanded to meet increased demand. Regardless of the machine used to manufacture the lamps, SMC's management will have the option to expand the production line. But, contrary to the previous cases, it is not clear that the value of this option will be different for different machines because there is no reason to believe that it will be easier to increase the production of lamps with one of the machines. However, this is not always the case, and a project that can be expanded is worth more than a project that cannot.

An investment can usually be postponed, so another important managerial option is the *option to defer* an investment. This kind of option is particularly valuable in the mining and oil extraction industries where the output (mineral or oil) prices are particularly volatile. For example, the net present value of an oil reserve may be negative, given the current market expectations regarding the future price of oil. However, because the development of the reserve can be postponed, sometimes for many years, the capital expenditures needed to start the extraction of oil can be deferred until the market prices rise. And the more volatile the oil prices, the higher the chance that the NPV of the reserve will become positive, and the higher the value of the option to defer the development of the reserve.

The designer desk lamp example explains how an option to abandon can be estimated. However, our result depended to a large extent on (1) the probability that the project will be either a failure or a success and (2) the date at which this failure or success will be recognized. Unfortunately, it is difficult to make reliable estimates on these uncertain outcomes. An alternative approach is to use the option valuation models that were initially developed to value options on financial securities. But these models require data that are usually difficult to obtain and often unreliable. Furthermore, as mentioned above, investment projects have a large number of embedded options and it would be an almost impossible task to identify and evaluate them all.

In the absence of practical and simple ways to value these options, our advice is to remember that an investment decision should not be based on a single number, that is, its net present value. Before arriving at a decision, managers should conduct a sensitivity analysis to identify the most salient options embedded in the project, attempt to value them as we did for the abandonment option, and exercise sound judgment. Options embedded in a project are either worthless or have a positive value. Thus, the net present value of a project will always *underestimate* the value of an investment project. Note that the larger the number of options embedded in the project and the higher the probability that the value of the project is sensitive to changing circumstances, the greater the value of these options and the higher the value of the investment project.

SUMMARY

An investment proposal can be evaluated by estimating the investment's net present value (NPV) and applying the NPV rule. The NPV rule is a good investment decision rule because it adjusts the investment's expected cash flows for both their timing and risk and has the convenient property of being additive. Most important is the capacity of the NPV method to evaluate the value-creating potential of an investment proposal. In addition, the NPV of an investment proposal is an estimate of the current value the proposal will create or destroy if undertaken.

The steps involved in applying the NPV rule to evaluate an investment proposal are summarized in Exhibit 6.17. Two inputs are required to calculate a project's NPV: (1) the expected cash-flow stream that the project will generate over its useful life and (2) the appropriate cost of capital that reflects the risk of the expected cash flows. The cost of capital is the rate at which the project's future cash flows need to be discounted in order to compare their present value with the investment cost. Chapter 8 shows how to estimate a project's expected cash-flow stream, and Chapter 10 shows how to estimate its appropriate risk-adjusted cost of capital.

After these inputs have been estimated, a financial calculator or any computer equipped with a spreadsheet application can compute the project's NPV. If the NPV is positive, the project creates value and should be undertaken. Its future cash-flow stream is expected to more than compensate for the investment cost. If the project's NPV is negative, the project destroys value and should be rejected. In this case, its future cash-flow stream is not expected to cover the investment cost.

The NPV rule can be used to choose between projects with different initial sizes or different life spans. If a firm has a limit on the amount of funds it can invest in new projects, it may not be able to undertake all available positive NPV projects. If the alternative projects have different initial cash outlays (different sizes), then the project's profitability index can be used to select the combination of projects that would create the most value. However, if the constraint on the availability of funds is imposed every year, rather than just during the initial year, the profitability index may lead to suboptimal investment decisions. If projects have unequal life spans, the comparison should be made between sequences of projects of the same duration. The calculations for this comparison are easier if the projects' annuity-equivalent cash flows are compared. The project with the lowest annuity-equivalent cost or the highest annuity-equivalent benefit should be selected.

Most projects have managerial options, options to change course after the project is launched, which are ignored in standard NPV analysis. The added value provided by these options is difficult to estimate. Although sensitivity analysis is not a perfect substitute, it can help identify the most critical options embedded in a project, thus providing valuable information for the final decision to accept or reject.

EXHIBIT 6.17 Steps Involved in Applying the Net Present Value Rule.

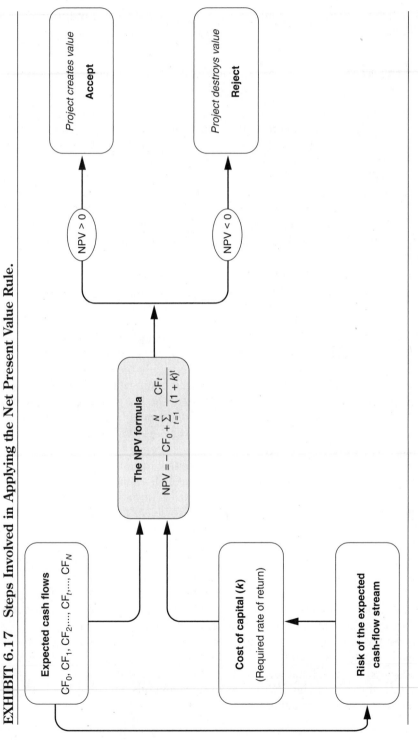

6.1 CALCULATION OF THE PRESENT VALUE OF AN ANNUITY AND THE CONSTANT ANNUAL-EQUIVALENT CASH FLOW OF A PROJECT'S CASH-FLOW STREAM

PRESENT VALUE OF AN *N*-PERIOD ANNUITY

If a cash-flow stream is composed of *equal* and *uninterrupted* periodic cash flows lasting for N periods, then the cash-flow stream is called an N-period **annuity.** Consider a project that is expected to generate the same annual cash flow of $20,000 at the end of each year for the next five years. Its expected cash-flow stream is composed of equal and uninterrupted periodic cash flows, and it is, thus, an annuity. What is the present value of that annuity ($PV_{annuity}$) if the project's cost of capital is 12 percent? It is the sum of the present values of the five $20,000 annual cash flows:

$$PV_{annuity} = \frac{\$20,000}{1 + 0.12} + \frac{\$20,000}{(1 + 0.12)^2} + \frac{\$20,000}{(1 + 0.12)^3} + \frac{\$20,000}{(1 + 0.12)^4} + \frac{\$20,000}{(1 + 0.12)^5}$$

(A6.1)

Performing the calculations on a financial calculator gives $PV_{annuity} = \$72,096$. Thus, a project that generates $20,000 at the end of every year for the next five years is today worth $72,096 at a cost of capital of 12 percent. If the project's initial cash outlay is less than $72,096, the project should be undertaken.

It is not necessary to calculate the present value of each cash flow and add them to determine their present value. There is a simple formula for the present value of an annuity. We begin by multiplying both sides of equation A6.1 by $(1 + 0.12)$:

$$(1 + 0.12) \times PV_{annuity} = \$20,000 + \frac{\$20,000}{1 + 0.12} + \frac{\$20,000}{(1 + 0.12)^2}$$

$$+ \frac{\$20,000}{(1 + 0.12)^3} + \frac{\$20,000}{(1 + 0.12)^4}$$

Subtracting equation A6.1 from this equation gives:

$$(1 + 0.12) \times PV_{annuity} - PV_{annuity} = \$20,000 - \frac{\$20,000}{(1 + 0.12)^5}$$

or:

$$0.12 \times PV_{annuity} = \$20,000 - \frac{\$20,000}{(1 + 0.12)^5}$$

Dividing both sides by 0.12 and factoring out the \$20,000 gives:

$$PV_{annuity} = \$20,000 \times \frac{1 - \dfrac{1}{(1 + 0.12)^5}}{0.12} = \$20,000 \times 3.6048 = \$72,096$$

Generalizing, the present value of any N-period annuity can be computed using the following formula:

$$\textbf{PV}_{\textbf{annuity}} = \textbf{annuity cash flow} \times \frac{1 - \dfrac{1}{(1 + k)^N}}{k} \tag{A6.2}$$

where k is the discount rate.

The term $\dfrac{1 - \dfrac{1}{(1 + k)^N}}{k}$ is referred to as the **annuity discount factor (ADF).** If DF designates the discount factor of the Nth annuity cash flow, we have:

$$\textbf{ADF} = \frac{\textbf{1} - \textbf{DF}}{\textbf{k}} \tag{A6.3}$$

In our example:

$$DF = \frac{1}{(1 + 0.12)^5} = 0.5674$$

and:

$$ADF = \frac{1 - 0.5674}{0.12} = \frac{0.4326}{0.12} = 3.6048$$

If you know the value of the discount factor (DF), you can easily calculate the corresponding value of the annuity discount factor (ADF). However, as you probably guessed, a financial calculator will give the ADF directly if you enter the required inputs for the calculation. Better still, it will generally give the present value of the entire annuity directly if you provide the inputs.

PRESENT VALUE OF AN INFINITE ANNUITY OR PERPETUITY

As a special application of equation A6.2, let's determine the present value a **perpetuity,** that is, an annuity for which N is an infinite number. If N is infinitely large, the term $\dfrac{1}{(1 + k)^N}$ can be considered as equal to zero and equation A6.2 reduces to the annuity cash flow divided by the discount rate:

$$\text{PV}_{\text{perpetuity}} = \frac{\textbf{Annuity cash flow}}{\textbf{Discount rate}} \tag{A6.4}$$

For example, if the $20,000 annuity were a perpetuity and the discount rate is 12 percent, its present value would be $166,667, that is, $20,000 divided by 0.12.

CONSTANT ANNUAL-EQUIVALENT CASH FLOW

The cash-flow stream of machine B and its constant annual-equivalent cash flow are shown as part of Exhibit 6.15 and repeated in Exhibit A6.1. How did we find the $40,855 constant annual-equivalent cash flow? The constant annual-equivalent cash-flow stream must have the same present value as the original cash-flow stream, and the four-year annuity discount factor at a cost of capital of 10 percent is equal to 3.1699. We can now write:

$$\$129,509 = (\text{Constant annual-equivalent cash flow}) \times (3.1699)$$

and thus:

$$\text{Constant annual-equivalent cash flow} = \frac{\$129,509}{3.1699} = \$40,855$$

**EXHIBIT A6.1 Original and Annuity-Equivalent Cash Flows
for Machine B.**

Figures from Exhibit 6.15

END OF YEAR	ORIGINAL CASH OUTFLOW	ANNUITY-EQUIVALENT CASH FLOW
Now	$120,000	
1	3,000	$40,855
2	3,000	40,855
3	3,000	40,855
4	3,000	40,855
Present value at 10%	**$129,509**	**$129,509**

More generally, we have:

$$\text{Constant annual-equivalent cash flow} = \frac{\textbf{Present value of original cash flow}}{\textbf{Annuity discount factor}}$$

(A6.5)

REFERENCES AND FURTHER READING

1. Brealey, Richard, and Stewart Myers. *Principles of Corporate Finance*. 5th ed. McGraw-Hill, 1996. See chapters 2, 3, 10 to 12, and 21.
2. Clark, John, Thomas Hindelang, and Robert Pritchard. *Capital Budgeting: Planning and Control of Capital Expenditures*. 3d ed. Prentice-Hall, 1989. See chapters 1, 3, and 25.
3. Copeland, Tom, Tim Koller, and Jack Murrin. *Valuation*. 2d ed. John Wiley, 1995. See chapter 15.
4. Ross, Stephen, Randolph Westerfield, and Jeffrey Jaffe. *Corporate Finance*. 4th ed. Irwin, 1996. See chapters 4 and 8.
5. Trigeorgis, Lenos. *Real Options: Managerial Flexibility and Strategy in Resource Allocation*. MIT Press, 1996.

REVIEW PROBLEMS

6.1 Present values and the cost of capital.
What is meant by each of the following statements?
a. "The present value of the future cash flows expected from an investment project is $20,000,000."
b. "The net present value (NPV) of an investment project is $10,000,000."
c. "A project's cost of capital is 10 percent."

6.2 Managerial options.
What are managerial options embedded in an investment project? Give some examples.

6.3 Net present value.
The Blaker Company is considering undertaking a project that is expected to generate the following cash-flow stream:

END OF YEAR	EXPECTED CASH FLOW
Now	−$100,000
1	50,000
2	50,000
3	50,000

a. If the project's cost of capital is 12 percent, what is the present value of the project's expected cash-flow stream?
b. What is the net present value of the project?
c. What is the profitability index of the project?
d. Should the project be undertaken? Explain.

6.4 Choosing between two equipments with unequal costs and life spans.
Perfect Color Company (PCC) is in the business of dyeing material. Business is booming and PCC is considering buying a new color printer. There are two printers available in the market: Printer X costs $50,000, requires $5,000 per year to operate, and has a useful life of two years; printer Y costs $60,000, requires $7,000 per year to operate, and will need to be replaced every three years. PCC's cost of capital is 10 percent.
a. What are the present values of the total costs of the two printers over their useful life?
b. Why are the two present values not comparable?
c. What is the annual-equivalent cost for each of the printers?
d. Which printer should PCC purchase?

6.5 Replacing an existing machine with a new one.
Pasta Uno is currently operating an old pasta making machine that is not expected to last more than two years. During that period of time, the machine is expected to generate a cash inflow of $20,000 per year. It could be replaced by a new machine at a cost of $150,000. The new machine is more efficient than the current one and, as a result, is expected to generate a net cash flow of $75,000 per year for three years. The management of Pasta Uno is wondering whether to replace the old machine now or wait another year. Pasta Uno's cost of capital is 10 percent.
a. Assume that the current resale value of the old machine is zero and that the new machine will also have a zero resale value in the future. What is the annual-equivalent cash flow of using the new machine?
b. What should the management of Pasta Uno do?

CHAPTER

7 ALTERNATIVES TO THE NET PRESENT VALUE RULE

The net present value (NPV) rule is not the only criterion available to evaluate a capital investment proposal. You may be familiar with the payback period, the internal rate of return (IRR), or another criterion; your company may be using one or more of these. This chapter examines and explains how to apply the four alternatives to the NPV rule: the *ordinary payback period rule,* the *discounted payback period rule,* the *internal rate of return (IRR) rule,* and the *profitability index rule.* We also analyze whether these four alternatives to the NPV rule satisfy the conditions of a good investment decision rule.

Recall that a good investment decision rule must take into account the timing of a project's expected cash flows and the project's risk. In addition, it should select projects that increase the market value of the firm's equity.

In our analysis of the alternative rules, we identify a number of cases in which these methods lead to a decision that contradicts the NPV rule. We explain why these conflicts occur and why some firms still use some of these techniques to screen investment proposals. We use six projects to illustrate how the four alternatives to the NPV rule are usually applied in making investment decisions and compare their performance with that of the NPV rule. After reading this chapter, you should understand:

- A project's ordinary payback period, discounted payback period, internal rate of return, and profitability index and how to calculate these measures.
- How to apply the four alternative rules to screen investment proposals.
- The major shortcomings of the four alternative rules.
- Why these rules are still used even though they are not as reliable as the NPV rule.

THE PAYBACK PERIOD

A project's **payback period** is the number of periods (usually measured in years) required for the sum of the project's expected cash flows to equal its initial cash outlay. In other words, the payback period is the time it takes for a firm to recover its initial investment. Consider investment A, whose characteristics are reported in Exhibit 7.1 and whose expected and cumulative cash flows are shown in Exhibit 7.2. The investment's payback period is the length of time it takes for the firm to get back its initial cash outlay of $1 million.

As indicated in Exhibit 7.2, we assume that the cash flows occur at the end of each year. Project A has a payback period of three years because it takes exactly three years for the project's *cumulative* cash flows to reach a value equal to the initial cash flow of $1 million. The payback periods for the investment proposals defined in Exhibit 7.1 are shown in Exhibit 7.3.

Sometimes, a project's payback period includes a fraction of a year. For example, investment E requires an initial cash outlay of $1 million and generates a cumulative cash flow of $975,000 after three years and $1,300,000 after four years. The project's payback period is between three and four years. It is equal to three years plus the fraction of year 4 cash flow ($325,000) required to reach the initial cash outlay:

$$\text{Payback period(E)} = 3 + \frac{\text{Initial cash flow} - \text{Cumulative cash flow to year 3}}{\text{Year 4 cash flow}}$$

$$= 3 + \frac{\$1,000,000 - \$975,000}{\$325,000}$$

$$= 3 \text{ years} + 0.08 \text{ year} = 3.08 \text{ years}$$

THE PAYBACK PERIOD RULE

According to the *payback period rule,* a project is acceptable if its payback period is shorter than or equal to a specified number of periods, known as the **cutoff period.** If the choice is between several mutually exclusive projects, the one with the shortest payback period should be selected.

If the firm reviewing projects A–F adopts a cutoff period of four years, then all six projects are acceptable. None of their payback periods exceeds the firm's four-year cutoff period. If the choice is between projects A and B, or C and D, or E and F, then each project within a pair is as good as the other because they have the same payback period. If the choice is between projects A, E, and C, then A should be selected because it has the shortest payback period.

EXHIBIT 7.1   **Expected Cash-Flow Streams and the Cost of Capital in Alternative Investment Proposals.**

All investments are five years long and require an initial cash outlay of $1 million

INVESTMENTS A AND B		
END OF YEAR	INVESTMENT A	INVESTMENT B
1	$600,000	$100,000
2	300,000	300,000
3	100,000	600,000
4	200,000	200,000
5	300,000	300,000
Total cash flows	$1,500,000	$1,500,000
Cost of capital	10%	10%
NPV	$191,399	$112,511

INVESTMENTS C AND D		
END OF YEAR	INVESTMENT C	INVESTMENT D
1	$250,000	$250,000
2	250,000	250,000
3	250,000	250,000
4	250,000	250,000
5	250,000	250,000
Total cash flows	$1,250,000	$1,250,000
Cost of capital	5%	10%
NPV	$82,369	-$52,303

INVESTMENTS E AND F		
END OF YEAR	INVESTMENT E	INVESTMENT F
1	$325,000	$325,000
2	325,000	325,000
3	325,000	325,000
4	325,000	325,000
5	325,000	975,000
Total cash flows	$1,625,000	$2,275,000
Cost of capital	10%	10%
NPV	$232,006	$635,605

EXHIBIT 7.2   Expected and Cumulative Cash Flows for Investment A.

Expected cash flows from Exhibit 7.1

END OF YEAR	EXPECTED CASH FLOWS	CUMULATIVE CASH FLOWS
1	$600,000	$ 600,000
2	300,000	900,000
3	100,000	1,000,000
4	200,000	1,200,000
5	300,000	1,500,000

EXHIBIT 7.3   Payback Periods for Six Investments in Exhibit 7.1.

INVESTMENT	A	B	C	D	E	F
Payback period (in years)	3.00	3.00	4.00	4.00	3.08	3.08

Adjustment for the timing of cash flows?

Consider investments A and B. Both require the same initial cash outlay, have the same useful life, and carry the same risk (they have the same cost of capital). Their payback periods are also the same. But, the timing of their cash flows differs. The largest cash inflow ($600,000) occurs at the end of the *first* year for investment A; it occurs at the end of the *third* year for investment B. Thus, the payback period rule does *not* take into consideration the timing of the cash flows. It simply adds them and ignores the time value of money.

Adjustment for risk?

Now, consider investments C and D. They are both five-year projects and have the same initial cash outlay and expected annual cash flows of $250,000. Even though the expected cash-flow stream of investment D is riskier than that of investment C (the cost of capital for D is higher than the cost of capital for C), their payback periods are identical (four years). Thus, the payback period rule ignores risk.

Maximization of the firm's equity value?

It is unlikely that an investment decision rule that ignores the timing and the risk of a project's expected cash flows would systematically select projects that maximize the market value of the firm's equity. Furthermore, when managers apply the payback period rule they must have the "right" cutoff period. Unfortunately, there is no objective reason to believe that there exists a particular cutoff period that is consistent with the maximization of the market value of the firm's equity. The choice of a cutoff period is always *arbitrary.*

One consequence of this shortcoming is illustrated by comparing investments E and F. The payback period rule does not discriminate between the two projects because they both have the same payback period of 3.08 years. But the firm's managers would certainly prefer to invest in F because, all else being equal, at the end of year 5 that project is expected to generate a cash inflow that is three times larger than the one generated by project E. Clearly, the payback period rule ignores expected cash flows after the cutoff period. As far as the firm is concerned, these cash flows are simply irrelevant. In other words, this decision rule is biased against long-term investments.

WHY DO MANAGERS USE THE PAYBACK PERIOD RULE?

Despite its well-known shortcomings, the payback period rule is still used by many firms. All the studies that survey the techniques employed by managers to make investment decisions reveal a large proportion of payback period users.[1] Which redeeming qualities does the payback period rule offer that can explain its popularity among managers?

The payback period's strongest appeal is its simplicity and ease of application. Managers in large companies make many accept/reject decisions on small and repetitive investments with typical cash-flow patterns. Over time, these managers may develop good intuition regarding the appropriate cutoff periods for which these investments have a positive net present value. Under these circumstances, it is possible that the "cost" of occasionally making wrong decisions with the payback period rule is lower than the "cost" of using more elaborate and time-consuming decision rules.

Another reason firms use the payback period rule is that it favors projects that "pay back quickly" and, thus, contribute to the firm's overall liquidity. This could be an important consideration for small firms that rely primarily on internally generated funds to finance their activities because they do not have easy access to long-term funding through their banks or the financial markets.

Sometimes, two projects have the *same* net present value but have *different* payback periods. In this case, selecting the project with the shortest payback makes sense. To illustrate, we compare investment A in Exhibit 7.1 with investment G, which requires the same initial cash outlay as A ($1 million), has the same cost of capital (10 percent), and is expected to generate the expected cash flows shown in Exhibit 7.4. At a cost of capital of 10 percent, the two investments have the same NPV of $191,399. However, the payback period of investment A is three years while that of G is one year longer. According to the NPV rule, a firm should be indifferent in its choice between the two investments but the payback period rule clearly favors investment A because of its shorter payback period (essentially due to its first-year cash inflow of $600,000).

---

[1] However, most payback period users usually employ this method in addition to other approaches (such as NPV or IRR). The payback period method is rarely used alone to evaluate large projects.

EXHIBIT 7.4   **Comparison of Two Investments with the Same NPV and Different Payback Periods.**

END OF YEAR	INVESTMENT A	INVESTMENT G
Now	−$1,000,000	−$1,000,000
1	600,000	200,000
2	300,000	200,000
3	100,000	300,000
4	200,000	300,000
5	300,000	666,740
NPV (AT 10%)	$191,399	$191,399
PAYBACK PERIOD	3 YEARS	4 YEARS

Finally, because the payback period rule tends to favor short-term projects over long-term ones, it is often employed when future events are difficult to quantify, such as for projects subject to political risk. Suppose a firm has a choice between two investments in a foreign country, one with a three-year payback period and one with a ten-year payback period. An election *may* take place in the foreign country in four years, and there is *some* chance that a new government *may* no longer favor the type of investment the firm intends to undertake. As discussed in Chapter 13, it is very difficult (1) to estimate the probability of the occurrence of this type of event and (2) to quantify its implications on the magnitude of the project's expected cash flows and cost of capital. Even if the longer project has a higher positive NPV than the shorter investment, the firm's managers may opt for the project with the three-year payback period. Many risk-averse managers believe that this type of trade-off is relevant.

THE DISCOUNTED PAYBACK PERIOD

A project's **discounted payback period,** also known as the **economic payback period,** is the number of periods—usually measured in years—required for the sum of the *present values* of the project's expected cash flows to equal its initial cash outlay. To illustrate, we calculate the discounted payback period of investment A. The present values of its expected cash flows, at a cost of capital of 10 percent, are shown in Exhibit 7.5. Project A's discounted payback period is slightly shorter than four years. It is equal to exactly 3.96 years. The discounted payback periods of the investment proposals defined in Exhibit 7.1 are shown in Exhibit 7.6.

The discounted payback periods are longer than the ordinary payback periods calculated earlier. This is not surprising because the discounted payback periods are measured with discounted cash flows that are smaller than the undiscounted cash flows used to calculate the ordinary payback periods. Also, the ranking of the investments according to their discounted payback periods is different from the

EXHIBIT 7.5 Discounted Payback Period Calculations for Investment A.
Expected Cash Flows from Exhibit 7.1

END OF YEAR	EXPECTED CASH FLOWS	DISCOUNT FACTOR AT 10%	PRESENT VALUE	CUMULATIVE PRESENT VALUE OF CASH FLOWS
1	$600,000	0.9091	$545,455	$545,455
2	300,000	0.8264	247,934	793,389
3	100,000	0.7513	75,131	868,520
4	200,000	0.6830	136,603	1,005,123
5	300,000	0.6209	186,276	1,191,399

EXHIBIT 7.6 Discounted Payback Periods for Six Investments in Exhibit 7.1.

INVESTMENT	A	B	C	D	E	F
Discounted payback period (in years)	3.96	4.40	4.58	more than 5	3.86	3.86

ranking according to their ordinary payback periods. Furthermore, investments A and B as well as C and D no longer have the same payback periods.

THE DISCOUNTED PAYBACK PERIOD RULE

As for the ordinary payback period rule, the *discounted payback period rule* says that a project is acceptable if its discounted payback period is shorter than or equal to a specified number of periods, called the cutoff period. If the choice is among several projects, the one with the shortest discounted payback period should be selected.

If the cutoff period is maintained at four years, only investments A, E, and F are acceptable; with the ordinary payback period rule, all six investments could be undertaken.

Adjustment for the timing of cash flows?

Consider investments A and B in Exhibit 7.1. They are identical except that the first-year and third-year cash flows have been interchanged. The largest cash flow of $600,000 occurs at the end of the first year for investment A; it occurs at the end of the third year for investment B. The discounted payback period takes this difference into account because the discounted payback period of A (3.96 years) is shorter than that of B (4.40 years). Thus, the discounted payback period rule takes the time value of money into account but *only* for the cash flows occurring up to the discounted payback period. Those following the payback period are still ignored.

Adjustment for risk?

Consider investments C and D. They have an identical cash-flow stream but investment D is riskier than C. The discounted payback period of C (4.58 years) is shorter than that of D (more than 5 years). Thus, the discounted payback period rule takes the risk of a project's expected cash flows into consideration but, as in the previous case, *only* for those cash flows occurring up to the discounted payback period. The cash flows following the discounted payback period, as well as their risk, are ignored.

Maximization of the firm's equity value?

According to the discounted payback period rule, the present value of a project's expected cash flows up to their discounted payback period is equal to the project's initial cash outlay. In other words, if we calculate the project's NPV for the cash flows that occur up to the project's discounted payback period, we will find that it is equal to zero. If we then include cash inflows expected to occur after the discounted payback period, the project's NPV will be positive. Thus, if a project's discounted payback period is shorter than the cutoff period used to screen projects, the project's NPV, estimated with cash flows up to the cutoff period, is always positive.

We cannot, however, conclude that the discounted payback period will systematically select those projects that contribute the most to the wealth of the firm's owners. A "right" cutoff period must be determined and this is an arbitrary decision. Consider investments E and F. Their discounted payback period is the same, 3.86 years. Like the ordinary payback period rule, the discounted payback period rule cannot discriminate between the two investments because it ignores the fifth year's cash flow, which is three times larger for F than for E. Thus, the discounted payback period rule ignores cash flows beyond the cutoff period and is biased against long-term investments.

THE DISCOUNTED PAYBACK PERIOD RULE VERSUS
THE ORDINARY PAYBACK PERIOD RULE

The discounted payback period rule has two major advantages over the ordinary payback period rule: It considers the time value of money and it considers the risk of the investment's expected cash flows. However, it considers these conditions of a good investment rule only for cash flows expected to occur up to the discounted payback period. The discounted payback period is certainly superior to the ordinary payback period as an indicator of the time necessary to recover the project's initial cash outlay because it takes into consideration the opportunity cost of capital. But it is more complicated to estimate than the ordinary payback period. Indeed, it requires the same inputs as the net present value rule—the project's useful life, its expected cash-flow stream, and its cost of capital. This may explain why the discounted payback period rule is less frequently used than the ordinary payback period rule, particularly for managers making frequent accept/reject decisions.

THE INTERNAL RATE OF RETURN (IRR)

A project's **internal rate of return (IRR)** is the discount rate that makes the net present value (NPV) of the project equal to zero. For example, to compute the IRR of investment A, we set NPV(A) equal to zero and find the discount rate that satisfies this condition. That rate is the investment's IRR:

$$\text{NPV(A)} = 0 = -\$1,000,000 + \frac{\$600,000}{(1 + \text{IRR})^1} + \frac{\$300,000}{(1 + \text{IRR})^2} + \frac{\$100,000}{(1 + \text{IRR})^3}$$
$$+ \frac{\$200,000}{(1 + \text{IRR})^4} + \frac{\$300,000}{(1 + \text{IRR})^5}$$

Unfortunately, there is no simple way to compute the IRR of a cash-flow stream except for the trivial case where the project is a one-period investment or an annuity.[2] For example, if a project requires an initial investment of $10,000 and will generate an expected cash flow of $12,000 in one year, then its IRR is simply equal to 20 percent. For investments with longer lives, we can try to find the IRR by trial and error: We first guess a rate, use it to calculate the project's NPV, and then adjust the rate until we find the value that makes the NPV equal to zero. As you can imagine, this is a very tedious and time-consuming exercise, especially if we want a precise number. Fortunately, any financial calculator or computer spreadsheet application will have an IRR function.[3] Both search for the IRR by the trial-and-error method but do so much more quickly and accurately. Exhibit 7.7 shows the IRR for the investment proposals defined in Exhibit 7.1, as computed on a financial calculator.

In general, if $CF_1, CF_2, \ldots, CF_t, \ldots, CF_N$ is the sequence of expected cash flows from an investment of N periods with an initial cash outlay of CF_0, then the investment's IRR is the solution to the following equation:

$$0 = CF_0 + \frac{CF_1}{(1 + \text{IRR})^1} + \frac{CF_2}{(1 + \text{IRR})^2} + \cdots + \frac{CF_t}{(1 + \text{IRR})^t} + \cdots + \frac{CF_N}{(1 + \text{IRR})^N}$$

EXHIBIT 7.7   IRR for Six Investments in Exhibit 7.1.

INVESTMENT	A	B	C	D	E	F
Internal rate of return	19.05%	13.92%	7.93%	7.93%	18.72%	28.52%

---

[2] An annuity is a cash-flow stream with equal annual cash flows. The calculation of the present value of an annuity is presented in Appendix 6.1.
[3] Have you bought a good financial calculator yet? (We promise that this is our last reminder.)

All that is needed to calculate the IRR of an investment is the sequence of cash flows the investment is expected to generate. In effect, an investment's IRR summarizes its expected cash-flow stream with a single rate of return. The rate is called *internal* because it only considers the expected cash flows related to the investment and does not depend on rates that can be earned on alternative investments.

THE IRR RULE

Consider investment A. Its IRR is 19.05 percent and its opportunity cost of capital is 10 percent. Recall that investment A's opportunity cost of capital is the highest return a firm can get on an alternative investment with the same risk as A.[4] Should the firm accept investment A? Yes; the project's IRR (19.05 percent) is greater than the highest return the firm can get on another investment with the same risk (the 10 percent opportunity cost of capital).

According to the **internal rate of return rule,** an investment should be accepted if its IRR is higher than its cost of capital and should be rejected if it is lower. If the investment's IRR is equal to the cost of capital, the firm should be indifferent between accepting and rejecting the project. A project's IRR can be interpreted as a measure of the profitability of its expected cash flows before considering the project's cost of capital. Thus, if a project's IRR is *lower* than its cost of capital, the project does not earn its cost of capital and should be rejected. If it is *higher,* the project earns more than its cost of capital and should be accepted.[5]

When used in comparison with the IRR, the investment's opportunity cost of capital is usually referred to as the **hurdle rate,** the **minimum required rate of return** or, simply, the investment's *required return.* In other words, if a project's IRR is lower than its required return, it should be rejected; if it is higher, it should be accepted.

Adjustment for the timing of cash flows?

Consider investments A and B in Exhibit 7.1. As already pointed out, Investment A is preferable to B because its largest cash flow ($600,000) occurs earlier. The IRR rule indicates the same preference because the IRR of investment A (19.05 percent) is higher than the IRR of investment B (13.92 percent). Thus, the IRR rule takes into account the time value of money.

---

[4] Refer to Chapter 6 where an investment's opportunity cost of capital is defined.

[5] The IRR should not be confused with the average accounting rate of return sometimes used to evaluate investment proposals. *We do not recommend using the average accounting rate of return under any circumstances.* For this reason, we do not include it among the alternatives to the NPV methods examined in this chapter.

Adjustment for risk?

Compare investments C and D shown in Exhibit 7.1. They have the same expected cash-flow stream, but D, with a cost of capital of 10 percent, is riskier than C, whose cost of capital is only 5 percent. The two investments have the same IRR of 7.93 percent. Does the IRR rule take the risk of the two investments into consideration? Yes it does, indirectly, through the comparison of the investment's IRR with its cost of capital. The IRR of investment C (7.93 percent) is greater than the minimum required return of 5 percent for this type of investment, so it should be accepted. Investment D should be rejected because its IRR of 7.93 percent is lower than the hurdle rate of 10 percent the firm wants to earn on riskier investments similar to D.

The risk of an investment does not enter into the *computation* of its IRR, but the IRR *rule* does consider the risk of the investment because it compares the project's IRR with the minimum required rate of return, which is a measure of the risk of the investment.

Maximization of the firm's equity value?

A project's IRR is determined by setting its NPV equal to zero, so we would expect a project's NPV to be related to its IRR. To illustrate, we compute the net present value of investment E for various discount rates, as shown in Exhibit 7.8.

From the figures in Exhibit 7.8, we can derive a graphical representation of the changes in NPV(E) as the discount rate varies. The graph, known as the project's **NPV profile,** is shown in Exhibit 7.9. NPV(E) is on the vertical axis and the discount rate is on the horizontal axis.

The graph shows an *inverse* relationship between NPV(E) and the discount rate. As the discount rate increases, NPV(E) decreases because its expected cash flows are discounted at increasingly higher rates. The NPV curve intersects the horizontal axis at the point where NPV(E) is equal to zero. At this point, the discount rate used to calculate the NPV of investment E must be equal to the IRR of investment E (the IRR is the discount rate at which the NPV is equal to zero). This discount rate is 18.72 percent.

According to the IRR rule, investment E should be accepted if its cost of capital is lower than its IRR of 18.72 percent and should be rejected if its cost of capital is higher. The graph indicates that for discount rates (or costs of capital) lower than 18.72 percent, the project's NPV is positive and for discount rates higher than 18.72

EXHIBIT 7.8   **Net Present Value of Investment E for Various Discount Rates.**

DISCOUNT RATE	0%	5%	10%	15%	20%	25%	30%
NPV(E)	$625,000	$407,080	$232,006	$89,450	−$28,051	−$125,984	−$208,440

EXHIBIT 7.9   The NPV Profile of Investment E.

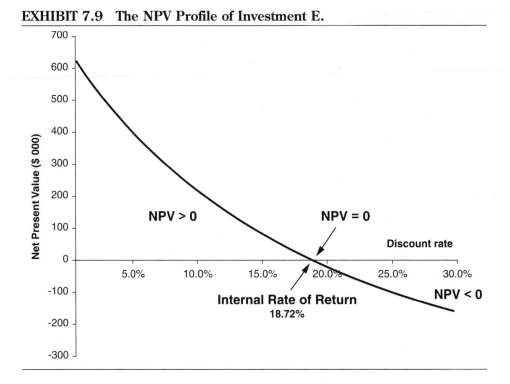

percent, the project's NPV is negative. In other words, the graph indicates that when the NPV is positive, the IRR is higher than the cost of capital and when it is negative, the IRR is lower than the cost of capital. The two rules are thus equivalent. And because the NPV rule is consistent with the maximization of the firm's equity value, so is the IRR rule.

THE IRR RULE MAY BE UNRELIABLE

The IRR rule may sometimes provide the *incorrect* investment decision when (1) the firm is reviewing two mutually exclusive investments (the firm cannot invest in both; if it accepts one, it must reject the other), and (2) the project's cash-flow stream changes sign more than once (the sequence of *future* cash flows contains at least one negative cash flow following a positive one).

Mutually exclusive investments

When two projects are **mutually exclusive,** the IRR rule and the NPV rule may, under certain circumstances, select different investment proposals. Suppose we compare investment E in Exhibit 7.1 with investment H, which has the same useful life (5 years), the same initial cash outlay ($1 million), and the same cost of capital (10 percent) but has the expected cash-flow stream and IRR shown in Exhibit 7.10.

EXHIBIT 7.10   **Comparison of Two Mutually Exclusive Investments with Different Expected Cash Flows and IRR. Useful life = 5 years; $1 million initial cash outlay; $k = 0.10$**

END OF YEAR	INVESTMENT E	INVESTMENT H
1	$325,000	$100,000
2	325,000	100,000
3	325,000	100,000
4	325,000	150,000
5	325,000	1,500,000
IRR	**18.72%**	**16.59%**

EXHIBIT 7.11   **The NPV Profiles of Investments E and H.**

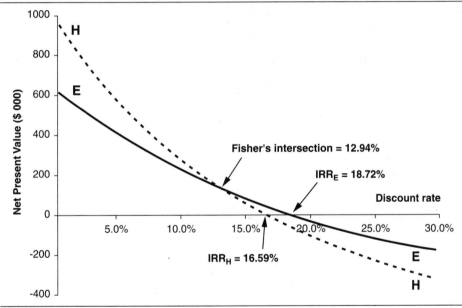

Both investments have an IRR that exceeds the cost of capital of 10 percent, so they should both be accepted according to the IRR rule. However, the investments are mutually exclusive, so the firm can only accept one. Which should it select? Intuition suggests the selection of investment E because it has a higher IRR than H. Unfortunately, intuition does not always lead to the correct decision. According to the NPV rule, investment H is preferable to E: At a cost of capital of 10 percent, the NPV of investment H is $282,519 while that of investment E is only $232,006.

The NPV profiles of investments E and H in Exhibit 7.11 show why the IRR and NPV rules disagree. The graph indicates that both the NPV and IRR rules favor investment E when the discount rate is higher than 12.94 percent (the rate at which the two NPV curves intersect[6]) and lower than 18.72 percent. For rates above 18.72 percent, the two projects should be rejected; both have a negative NPV and a discount rate higher than the IRR. For rates lower than 12.94 percent, the NPV rule favors investment H, but the IRR rule still favors investment E (it has a higher IRR than H).

This situation usually arises when the cash-flow patterns of two mutually exclusive investments differ widely, as is true for investments E and H. Investment E's cash flows are evenly distributed during the project's life while those of H are concentrated in the last year of the project's life. At high discount rates, the discounting effect (the "shrinking" of cash flows resulting from discounting) on distant cash flows is more pronounced than when the rate is low. As a consequence, when the discount rate increases, the NPV of the investment with cash flows concentrated at the end of the project's life (such as investment H) decreases more rapidly than the NPV of the investment whose cash flows arise earlier (such as investment E). The two projects have the same NPV at the point where their NPV curves intersect. After that point, the NPV ranking of the two projects changes.

With a cost of capital of 10 percent, project H is the better investment because its NPV is larger than that of project E, thus creating more value to the firm's shareholders. Because the IRR approach would lead to the opposite choice, it would also have the opposite effect. In general, when a firm wants to rank projects according to their contribution to the value of the firm's equity, it should use the NPV rule rather than the IRR rule.

Investments with some negative future cash flows

The IRR rule may be unreliable when a project's stream of expected cash flows includes negative cash flows. Negative cash flows can occur when an investment requires the construction of several facilities that are built at different times in the future. During the year when a new unit is built, the cash flow generated by the previously installed units might not be large enough to cover the cost of the new one. The result is that the project's total cash flow for that year becomes negative. A project can also have a negative future cash flow if the project's termination requires a major capital expenditure, such as for a strip-mining project. Closing the mine and restoring the area's landscape at the end of the project's useful life may make the project's terminal cash flow negative.

When negative cash flows occur a project may have more than one IRR or none at all. We illustrate this phenomenon with a two-year project that has a cost of capital of 20 percent and the pattern of expected cash flows shown in Exhibit 7.12.

The project has an IRR of 5 percent and an IRR of 40 percent (if you check this, you will find that the project's NPV is zero at both 5 percent and 40 percent). If the

---

[6] The intersection rate is often referred to as **Fisher's intersection,** named after the economist Irving Fisher who was among the first to study this phenomenon.

EXHIBIT 7.12   Expected Cash Flows, IRR, and NPV of a Project with Negative Cash Flows and $k = 0.20$.

END OF YEAR	CASH FLOW
Now	−$1,000,000
1	+$2,450,000
2	−$1,470,000
IRR	**5% and 40%**
NPV(at 20%)	**+$20,833**

project has a cost of capital of 20 percent, it should be rejected if its IRR is 5 percent and accepted if its IRR is 40 percent. There is no obvious choice. What should the firm do in this case? It should ignore the IRR rule and use the NPV rule instead. At a cost of capital of 20 percent, the project has a positive NPV of $20,833 and should be undertaken.

WHY DO MANAGERS USUALLY PREFER THE IRR RULE TO THE NPV RULE?

Despite its shortcomings, the IRR rule is popular among managers. One reason may be that the *calculation* of a project's IRR requires a single input, the cash-flow stream that the project is expected to generate. An estimate of the project's cost of capital is not necessary, whereas the calculation of a project's NPV requires estimates of both the expected cash-flow stream and the cost of capital. However, the application of the IRR *rule* requires both inputs. To decide whether to invest, managers must compare the project's IRR to its cost of capital. Thus, even though the IRR can be computed without knowing the project's cost of capital, the cost of capital is still needed to decide whether to undertake the project. If both methods require the same inputs to select projects, what is the advantage of using the IRR rule?

The advantage may be that it is easier to estimate a project's IRR than its NPV when the project's cost of capital is uncertain (the *computation* of the IRR does not require knowing the cost of capital). Then, others can decide whether to accept or reject the project after an appropriate required return is determined.[7] Our suspicion is that managers favor the IRR rule for a simpler reason. It is easier for them to communicate a project's potential profitability using its IRR rather than its NPV. When "selling" an investment proposal, you will certainly be more convincing if you

---

[7] This would usually happen if the firm adopts a "bottom-up" approach to capital budgeting for some of its difficult-to-assess projects. In this approach, divisions submit projects with their IRR to a committee. The decision to invest is made after collecting all submitted projects and comparing their IRR to risk-adjusted required returns established by the investment committee.

indicate that the proposal has a potential return of 35 percent rather than saying it has an NPV of $4,531,284. Managers usually have a good understanding of what an investment should "return" (partly because they are accustomed to measuring business performance with indicators such as return on sales and return on assets). A comparison of that implicit "return" with the project's IRR is straightforward. A comparison with the project's NPV is not so evident.

Our advice: A project's NPV can be estimated with the same information required to apply the IRR rule, so you should compute both. When both rules lead to the same recommendation, mention the project's IRR instead of its NPV. When the outcome of your analysis indicates a conflict between the two methods, you should trust the NPV rule.

THE PROFITABILITY INDEX (PI)

A project's **profitability index (PI)** is equal to the ratio of the present value of its expected cash-flow stream (CF_1, CF_2, . . ., CF_t, . . ., CF_N) to its initial cash outlay (CF_0):

$$\textbf{PI(investment)} = \frac{\textbf{Present value (CF}_1\textbf{, CF}_2\textbf{, . . . , CF}_t\textbf{, . . . CF}_N\textbf{)}}{\textbf{Initial cash outlay}}$$

or:

$$\text{PI(investment)} =$$

$$\frac{(CF_1 \times DF_1) + (CF_2 \times DF_2) + \cdots + (CF_t \times DF_t) + \cdots + (CF_N \times DF_N)}{CF_0}$$

where $DF_t = \dfrac{1}{(1 + k)^t}$ is the discount factor calculated with the project's cost of capital k.

(Discount factors are explained in Chapter 6 in the computation of present values.) The profitability index is a benefit-to-cost ratio because it is the ratio of the benefit derived from the investment (the present value of its expected cash flows at the cost of capital) to its cost (the initial cash outlay).

Applying the definition to investment A in Exhibit 7.1 (all financial figures in thousands of dollars), we get:

$$\text{PI(A)} =$$

$$\frac{(\$600 \times 0.9091) + (\$300 \times 0.8264) + (\$100 \times 0.7513) + (\$200 \times 0.6830) + (\$300 \times 0.6209)}{\$1,000}$$

$$PI(A) = \frac{\$1,191}{\$1,000} = 1.19$$

The profitability indexes of the investment proposals defined in Exhibit 7.1 are shown in Exhibit 7.13.

THE PROFITABILITY INDEX RULE

According to the *profitability index rule,* a project should be accepted if its profitability index is greater than one and rejected if it is less than one. If the investment's PI is equal to one, the firm should be indifferent between accepting and rejecting the project. According to this rule, all projects except project D should be accepted.

Adjustment for the timing of cash flows?

The PI rule takes into account the time value of money because the projects' expected cash flows are discounted at their cost of capital. Like the NPV and IRR rules, the profitability index rule favors project A over project B (see Exhibit 7.13), and the only difference between these two projects is the timing of their respective expected cash flows.

Adjustment for risk?

The PI rule considers the risk of an investment because it uses the cost of capital (which reflects the risk of the expected cash-flow stream) as the discount rate. Again, like the NPV and IRR rules, the profitability index rule chooses investment C over investment D, and D is the riskier of the two investments.

Maximization of the firm's equity value?

When a project has a profitability index greater than one, the present value of its expected cash flows is greater than the initial cash outlay and the project's NPV is positive. Conversely, if the profitability index is less than one, then the project's NPV is negative. It may seem to follow that the profitability index rule is a substitute

EXHIBIT 7.13   Profitability Indexes for Six Investments in Exhibit 7.1.

INVESTMENT	A	B	C	D	E	F
Profitability index	1.19	1.11	1.08	0.95	1.23	1.64

for the NPV rule and will select projects that contribute the most to enhancing the firm's market value.

Unfortunately, the profitability index rule may lead to an incorrect decision when it is applied to two mutually exclusive investments with different initial cash outlays. To illustrate, we compare investment A in Exhibit 7.1 to investment K, which has the same useful life (5 years) and the same cost of capital (10 percent) but requires an initial cash outlay twice as large as that of investment A and has a different cash-flow stream. The cash-flow streams, net present values, and profitability indexes for the two investments are shown in Exhibit 7.14.

Investment A's profitability index (1.19) is higher than that of investment K (1.12). Before concluding that investment A is superior to K, we should first compare the NPV of the investments. Investment A has a lower NPV than investment K, so the profitability index has chosen the investment that creates the *least* value to the firm's owners. Conclusion: The profitability index rule is not consistent with the maximization of the firm's market value when used to choose between mutually exclusive projects with different initial sizes.

USE OF THE PROFITABILITY INDEX RULE

Despite the problem that occurs when the choice is between mutually exclusive projects of unequal sizes, the profitability index is a useful substitute for the NPV rule. Like the IRR, it is easier to communicate the potential profitability of an investment proposal with the profitability index than with the NPV. The reason is that both the profitability index and the IRR are *relative* measures of an investment's value, whereas the NPV is an *absolute* measure. The index tells how much present

EXHIBIT 7.14   Comparison of Two Mutually Exclusive Investments with Different Initial Cash Outlays and Expected Cash Flows.

END OF YEAR	INVESTMENT A	INVESTMENT K
Now	−$1,000,000	−$2,000,000
1	600,000	100,000
2	300,000	300,000
3	100,000	600,000
4	200,000	200,000
5	300,000	2,100,000
NPV(at 10%)	$191,399	$230,169
Profitability index	1.19	1.12

benefit a project is expected to generate *per dollar* of investment while the NPV provides the present value of the benefits net of the project's initial cost.[8]

SUMMARY

Our analysis of the alternatives to the net present value rule has shown that the net present value rule is the best criterion for selecting desirable investment proposals (projects that are expected to raise the market value of a firm's equity and, thereby, increase the wealth of the firm's owners). This conclusion does not imply that the alternative capital budgeting techniques presented in this chapter should be discarded. A project's profitability index, internal rate of return, and payback period provide useful information to managers and are often easier to interpret and communicate than the NPV.

Recent surveys of capital budgeting techniques employed by firms reveal that companies rarely rely on a single method to screen investment proposals. Those firms using the NPV rule also use alternative decision criteria. But this observation should not distract from the fact that *all* the alternatives to the NPV method have some shortcomings and that some have serious weaknesses in assessing the value-creating capacity of a project.

Exhibit 7.15 summarizes the properties of the five alternative investment evaluation methods. Our final recommendation: When alternative methods provide conflicting signals, the value-creating manager should trust the net present value approach.

REFERENCES AND FURTHER READING

1. Brealey, Richard, and Stewart Myers. *Principles of Corporate Finance.* 5th ed. McGraw-Hill, 1996. See chapter 5.
2. Clark, John, Thomas Hindelang, and Robert Pritchard. *Capital Budgeting: Planning and Control of Capital Expenditures.* 3d ed. Prentice-Hall, 1989. See chapters 5 to 8.
3. Ross, Stephen, Randolph Westerfield, and Jeffrey Jaffe. *Corporate Finance.* 4th ed. Irwin, 1996. See chapter 6.

---

[8] Chapter 6 shows how the profitability index rule can be used to compare investments of unequal sizes (investments with different initial cash outlays).

EXHIBIT 7.15 Properties of Alternative Capital Budgeting Rules.

EVALUATION METHOD	INPUTS REQUIRED		DECISION RULE		DOES THE RULE ADJUST CASH FLOWS FOR		IS THE RULE CONSISTENT WITH THE MAXIMIZATION OF THE FIRM'S EQUITY VALUE?
	FOR CALCULATION	FOR DECISION	ACCEPT	REJECT	TIME?	RISK?	
Net present value (NPV)	• Cash flows • Cost of capital (k)	• NPV	NPV>0	NPV<0	Yes	Yes	Yes, a project's NPV is a measure of the value the project creates or destroys.
Profitability index (PI)	• Cash flows • Cost of capital (k)	• PI	PI>1	PI<1	Yes	Yes	Yes, but *may* fail to select the project with the highest NPV when projects are mutually exclusive.
Internal rate of return (IRR)	• Cash flows	• IRR • Cost of capital (k)	IRR>k	IRR<k	Yes	Yes	Yes, but *may* fail when: • Projects are mutually exclusive. • Cash flows change signs more than once.
Discounted Payback Period (DPP)	• Cash flows • Cost of capital (k)	• DPP • Cutoff period	DPP<Cutoff period	DPP>Cutoff period	Only within DPP	Only within DPP	Only when the project's discounted payback period is *shorter* than its cutoff period
Payback Period (PP)	• Cash flows	• PP • Cutoff period	PP<Cutoff period	PP>Cutoff period	No	No	No

REVIEW PROBLEMS

7.1 Shortcomings of the payback period.
What are the shortcomings of the payback period rule, and why, despite these shortcomings, is the payback period still used by many firms as an important input in the investment decision?

7.2 IRR versus cost of capital.
What is the difference between a project's cost of capital and its internal rate of return?

7.3 IRR versus ROIC.
What is the difference between the internal rate of return and the return on invested capital?

7.4 Shortcomings of the IRR and the profitability index rule.
Under which circumstances may the internal rate of return rule and the profitability index rule lead to the wrong investment decision?

7.5 Evaluating two projects using alternative decision rules.
Two projects have the expected cash flows shown below. The projects have similar risk characteristics and their cost of capital is 10 percent.

EXPECTED CASH FLOWS		
END OF YEAR	PROJECT A	PROJECT B
Now	−$2,000,000	−$2,000,000
1	200,000	1,400,000
2	1,200,000	1,000,000
3	1,700,000	400,000

a. Calculate the net present value of each project. According to the net present value rule, which project should be accepted if they are independent? If they are mutually exclusive?

b. Calculate the payback period and the discounted payback period of each project. If the two projects are mutually exclusive, which project should be accepted?

c. Calculate the internal rate of return of each project. Which project should be accepted if they are independent? If they are mutually exclusive?

d. Calculate the profitability index of each project. Which project should be accepted if they are independent? If they are mutually exclusive?

e. Based on your answers to parts a to d, which criterion leads to the best investment decision if the projects are independent? If they are mutually exclusive?

8 IDENTIFYING AND ESTIMATING A PROJECT'S CASH FLOWS

Chapters 6 and 7 explain rules that can help managers make capital expenditure decisions. All these rules require the estimation of the cash-flow stream the investment is expected to generate in the future. This chapter shows how to identify and estimate the cash flows that are relevant to an investment decision.

There are two fundamental principles that provide some guidance in the determination of a project's cash flows: the *actual cash-flow principle* and the *with/with out principle*. According to the first, cash flows must be measured *at the time they actually occur,* that is, during the period cash is actually received or paid out. According to the second, the cash flows relevant to an investment decision are only those that change the firm's *overall* cash position if the investment is undertaken.

First, we present and explain these principles, and then we show how to apply them. Sunlight Manufacturing Company's designer desk lamp project, whose net present value was first computed in Chapter 6, is used to illustrate our approach. After reading this chapter, you should understand:

- The actual cash-flow principle and the with/without principle and how to apply them to make capital expenditure decisions.
- How to identify a project's relevant and irrelevant cash flows.
- Sunk costs and opportunity costs.
- How to estimate a project's relevant cash flows.

THE ACTUAL CASH-FLOW PRINCIPLE

According to the **actual cash-flow principle,** an investment's cash flows must be measured at the time they actually occur. For example, suppose a proposal is expected to generate a tax expense next year that will be paid the following year. The cash outflow must be taken into account the year the tax is paid, not the year the tax expense is recorded in the firm's income statement.

Investment proposals are often supported with data obtained from projected income statements that show the expected impact of the project on the firm's accounting earnings. But like tax expenses, revenues and expenses reported in the income statement are generally not cash-flow figures. Thus, it is incorrect to use the investment's contribution to the firm's accounting earnings as a proxy for cash flows. This chapter shows how to convert accounting flows into cash flows for the purpose of making investment decisions.

Another implication of the actual cash-flow principle is that the dollar value of a project's future cash flows must be calculated with the prices and costs that are expected to prevail in the future, not with today's prices and costs. In other words, if the prices and costs associated with a project are expected to rise because of inflation, **nominal cash flows,** the cash flows that incorporate anticipated inflation, should be estimated. Further, if the decision to invest is made on the basis of the project's net present value (NPV) or its internal rate of return (IRR), then the cost of capital used to calculate the project's NPV or to compare with the project's IRR must also incorporate the anticipated rate of inflation.

If the impact of future inflation rates on the project's cash flows is too difficult to estimate, such as in countries subject to hyperinflation or a very volatile inflation rate, a project's expected **real cash flows** can be estimated instead of its expected nominal cash flows. Real cash flows are the values of cash flows calculated with the assumption that prices and costs will not be affected by anticipated inflation. However, in this case, the project's cost of capital must also be estimated without the effect of anticipated inflation. Inflation must be treated consistently. If it is excluded from the cash flows, it must also be excluded from the cost of capital. If it is taken into account, it should be incorporated in both the project's expected cash flows and its cost of capital.

Finally, a project's expected cash flows must be measured in the same currency. When an investment decision involves prices or costs that are denominated in a foreign currency, these variables must be converted to their equivalent domestic values at the exchange rates that are expected to prevail in the future. This requirement necessitates forecasting future exchange rates, an issue we address in Chapter 13.

THE WITH/WITHOUT PRINCIPLE

The second guiding principle in estimating an investment's cash flows is the **with/without principle.** According to this principle, the **relevant cash flows** associated with an investment decision are only those cash flows that will *change* the firm's overall future cash position as a result of the decision to invest. In other words, relevant cash flows are **incremental,** or **differential, cash flows.**[1] They are equal to the difference between the firm's expected cash flows if the investment is made (the firm "with" the project) and its expected cash flows if the investment is rejected (the firm "without" the project). If CF_t denotes the cash flows occurring during period t:

Project's CF_t = Firm's incremental CF_t
= Firm's CF_t(with the project) − Firm's CF_t(without the project)

To illustrate, consider trying to decide whether to drive to work or to take public transportation. Suppose you are currently driving to work (this is your situation *without* the project). Last month, you took the train and found it less tiring than driving. The monthly train tickets cost $140. You want to know whether commuting by train on a regular basis (your situation *with* the project) is cheaper than driving. The monthly cash expenses related to your car are:

1. Insurance $120
2. Rent on the garage near your apartment $150
3. Parking fees near your office $90
4. Gas and car service related to commuting $110

If you take the train, your *total* monthly cash expenses will include the cost of the train tickets and the insurance and garage rental costs, which you will still have to pay (we assume you will not sell your car):

$$CF(\text{with the project}) = CF(\text{train}) = -\text{Insurance cost} - \text{Garage rental cost}$$
$$- \text{Train tickets cost}$$
$$= -\$120 - \$150 - 140 = -\$410$$

If you drive your car, your *total* monthly cash expenses will include the office parking fees, gas and car service costs, and the insurance and garage rental costs. Therefore,

$$CF(\text{without the project}) = CF(\text{car}) = - \text{Insurance cost} - \text{Garage rental cost}$$
$$- \text{Office parking fees} - \text{Gas and service cost}$$
$$= - \$120 - \$150 - \$90 - \$110 = -\$470$$

If you take the train, your total monthly cash outflow is $410. If you take the car, it is $470. The project's incremental monthly cash flow is thus $60:

$$\text{Project's CF} = \text{Incremental CF} = CF(\text{train}) - CF(\text{car})$$
$$= [-\$410] - [-\$470] = +\$60$$

---

[1] A similar notion, used in economic analysis, is the concept of marginal cost. The difference between a marginal cost and an incremental cost is that the former usually refers to the additional cost of, say, producing *one* more unit of a product, whereas the latter refers to the *total* extra cost resulting from the acceptance of a project.

The $60 incremental cash flow can be determined more quickly if we begin by identifying which of the four expenses are relevant to commuting by train and which are irrelevant. The **relevant costs** are those cash expenses that will increase your monthly *total* or *overall* expenses; the **irrelevant costs** are those cash expenses that will not affect them. The first two costs (insurance and garage rental) are irrelevant to your decision because they will be incurred regardless of whether you take the train or not. In other words, they are **unavoidable costs.** The third and fourth costs (office parking fees and gas and car service) are relevant costs because they can be saved if you decide to take the train. They are **avoidable costs.** They amount to $200 per month ($90 plus $110). Because the monthly train ticket costs $140, the train is the cheaper commuting alternative. Every month, you would save $60, the difference between $200 and $140, which is exactly the project's monthly incremental cash flow we found above. The difference from the previous approach is that we ignored the common expenses of insurance ($120) and garage rental ($150) because they are irrelevant to the decision.

Note that the $140 you paid *last month* to take the train on a trial basis is irrelevant to your decision. That money has already been spent and will not be recovered whether you decide to go to work by car or by train in the future. These types of costs are called **sunk costs.**

Now, let's add a small complication to the choice between the car and the train. Suppose you drive a colleague to work twice a week with the understanding that he will fill your gas tank once a month at a cost of $35. Is this a relevant cost to your commuting decision? Yes it is because if you take the train, you will no longer receive the $35. In this situation, the advantage of taking the train instead of the car will drop to $25 a month ($60 less $35). The cost we have just described is called an **opportunity cost.** It is relevant because it represents a loss of income if the train alternative is adopted. Sunk costs and opportunity costs are discussed in more detail later in the chapter in the context of Sunlight Manufacturing Company's designer desk lamp project.

The assumption so far is that your car will stay in the garage. But what if your daughter decides to drive to college twice a week now that the car is available? If the monthly cost of these trips (gas and parking) exceeds $25, then commuting to work by train will be more expensive than driving your car. This example illustrates an important point. When estimating a project's incremental cash flows, *all* the side effects must be identified. This can be a challenging task for many investments. But you cannot estimate a project's expected cash flows properly if you have not considered *all* the relevant costs and benefits.

A final comment: The relevant benefits and costs associated with a project cannot all be quantified easily. For example, our analysis indicates that commuting by car is more expensive than taking the train. But you may find that driving is more convenient and less time consuming. While putting a dollar value on these benefits may not be simple, you must do so because they may justify taking the car.

We now turn to the analysis of a complex case—the designer desk lamp project whose net present value is computed in Chapter 6.

THE DESIGNER DESK LAMP PROJECT

Recall that Sunlight Manufacturing Company (SMC) has been successfully producing and selling electrical appliances for the past 20 years and is currently considering a possible extension of its existing product line. The company's general manager has recently proposed that SMC enter the relatively high-margin, high-quality designer desk lamp market. This section describes the project's characteristics, which are summarized in Exhibit 8.1.

A consulting company was hired to do a preliminary study of the potential market for this type of product. Its report indicates that SMC can sell up to 45,000 lamps the first year of the project, 40,000 the second year, 30,000 the third year, 20,000 the fourth year, and 10,000 the fifth year, after which the project will be terminated. The lamps can be sold for $40 each the first year, and that price can be raised annually by no more than 3 percent, a rate of increase equal to the rate of inflation expected to prevail during the project's five-year life. The consulting company billed SMC $30,000 for the study and was paid a month later.

SMC's sales manager is concerned that the new product will likely reduce the sales of standard desk lamps currently produced by SMC. She fears that potential customers will switch from buying standard desk lamps to buying the new designer desk lamps and estimates that SMC's potential losses could reduce the firm's *after-tax* operating cash flows by as much as $80,000 per year.

If SMC decides to produce the designer desk lamp, it will use an already-owned building that is currently unoccupied. Recently, SMC received a letter from the vice-president of a nearby department store who wanted to know whether SMC would be willing to rent the building as a storage area. SMC's accounting department indicates that, given current market rates, the building can be rented for $10,000 a year for five years.

The engineering department has determined that the equipment needed to produce the lamps will cost $2,000,000, shipped and installed. For tax purposes, the equipment can be depreciated using the straight-line method over the next five years, that is, at a rate of $400,000 per year ($2,000,000 divided by 5). The resale value of the equipment is estimated at $100,000 if it is sold at the end of the project's fifth year.

After consulting a few suppliers, the purchasing department indicates that the raw materials required to produce the designer desk lamp will cost $10 per lamp the first year of the project and will most likely rise at the annual expected rate of inflation of 3 percent. To avoid disruption in supply, SMC will need 7 days of raw material inventory. The firm pays its suppliers, on average, 4 weeks (28 days) after raw materials are received and receives payment from its customers, on average, 8 weeks (56 days) after products are sent.

The production department has estimated the project's necessary amount of work in process and finished goods inventories will be worth 16 days of sales. Furthermore, SMC's direct labor costs will rise by $5 per lamp and its energy costs will

EXHIBIT 8.1 Data Summary of the Designer Desk Lamp Project.

ITEM	CORRESPONDING UNITS OR VALUE	TYPE	TIMING
1. Expected annual unit sales	45,000; 40,000; 30,000; 20,000; 10,000	Revenue	End of year 1 to 5
2. Price per unit	$40 the first year, then rising annually at 3%	Revenue	End of year 1 to 5
3. Consulting company's fee	$30,000	Expense	Already incurred
4. Losses on standard lamps	$80,000	Net cash loss	End of year 1 to 5
5. Rental of building to outsiders	$10,000	Revenue	End of year 1 to 5
6. Cost of the equipment	$2,000,000	Asset	Now
7. Straight-line depreciation expenses	$400,000 ($2,000,000 divided by 5 years)	Expense	End of year 1 to 5
8. Resale value of equipment	$100,000	Revenue	End of year 5
9. Raw material cost per unit	$10 the first year, then rising annually at 3%	Expense	End of year 1 to 5
10. Raw material inventory	7 days of sales	Asset	Now
11. Accounts payable	4 weeks (or 28 days) of purchases	Liability	Now
12. Accounts receivable	8 weeks (or 56 days) of sales	Asset	Now
13. Work in process and finished goods inventories	16 days of sales	Asset	Now
14. Direct labor cost per unit	$5 the first year, then rising annually at 3%	Expense	End of year 1 to 5
15. Energy cost per unit	$1 the first year, then rising annually at 3%	Expense	End of year 1 to 5
16. Overhead charge	1% of sales	Expense	End of year 1 to 5
17. Financing charge	12% of the net book value of assets	Expense	End of year 1 to 5
18. Tax expenses on income	40% of pretax profits	Expense	End of year 1 to 5
19. Tax expenses on capital gains	40% of pretax capital gains	Expense	End of year 5
20. Aftertax cost of capital	10% (see Chapter 10)	Not in the cash flows	

234

rise by $1 per lamp the first year of the project. These costs will rise at the expected annual rate of inflation of 3 percent during the project's life. There will not be any significant additional costs to the firm's selling, general, and administrative expenses, because the company's existing personnel and organizational structure are expected to be able to support the sale of the new product.

To cover SMC's overhead costs, the accounting department charges new projects a standard fee equal to 1 percent of the projects' sales revenues. New projects are also charged an additional fee to cover the cost of financing the assets used to support the projects. This financing charge is equal to 12 percent of the book (accounting) value of the assets employed.

Tax laws allow the $2,000,000 worth of equipment to be fully depreciated on a straight-line basis over a five-year period if the equipment has a terminal book value of zero. A terminal book value greater than zero is considered a capital gain. SMC is subject to a 40 percent tax on both earnings and capital gains.

The firm's financial manager must now estimate the project's expected cash flows and find out whether the investment is a value-creating proposal. The aftertax cost of capital that SMC uses for projects similar to the designer desk lamp project is 10 percent.

IDENTIFYING A PROJECT'S RELEVANT CASH FLOWS

In the commuting example earlier in the chapter, the project's relevant cash flows were reasonably easy to determine because the alternative situation was clearly defined; it was to continue driving to work. But, for many investments, the alternative scenario (the firm's *future* situation if the project is *not* undertaken) is not usually clearly defined. This complicates the identification of the project's relevant cash flows, as illustrated below for the designer desk lamp project.

SUNK COSTS

A sunk cost is a cost that has already been paid and for which there is no alternative use at the time when the decision to accept or reject the project is being made. The with/without principle excludes sunk costs from the analysis of an investment because they are irrelevant to the decision to invest or not. The firm has already paid them. For the designer desk lamp project, the $30,000 fee paid to the consulting company (item 3 in Exhibit 8.1) is a sunk cost. It should not affect the decision to produce and launch the new lamp. Most sunk costs are costs related to research and development and to market tests performed prior to the investment decision.

To further clarify the point, assume for a moment that the designer desk lamp project has a net present value of $10,000, *excluding* the aftertax consulting fee of $18,000 ($30,000 × (1 − 40%)). What should SMC's managers do in this case? Should they reject the project because its net present value does not cover the aftertax consulting fee (NPV *with* the fee is a *negative* $8,000) or go ahead with the project? The correct decision is to go ahead with the project because the consulting fee cannot be recovered if the project is *not* undertaken. Taking it into account means that it is counted twice: once when it was paid and again against the project's future cash flows. Accepting the project does not destroy $8,000 of value; it creates $10,000 of value.

OPPORTUNITY COSTS

Based on the discussion about sunk costs, it may seem logical to ignore any costs related to the use of the unoccupied building in which the equipment will be installed because SMC has already paid for the building. However, the building can be rented for $10,000 a year if it is not used for manufacturing the new product (item 5 in Exhibit 8.1). In other words, the decision to undertake the designer desk lamp project means that SMC must forfeit $10,000 annual rental income for the next five years. This "loss" of potential cash is the direct consequence of undertaking the project. According to the with/without principle, it should be considered a $10,000 annual reduction in cash flow.

Costs associated with resources that the firm could use to generate cash if it does not undertake a project are called opportunity costs. These costs do not involve any movement of cash in or out of the firm. But because they are not recorded as a transaction in the firm's books does not mean they should be ignored. The cash revenues a firm can earn if it does not undertake a project are equivalent to a loss of cash if the project is undertaken.

Opportunity costs are not always easy to identify and quantify. In the case of the unused building, SMC has an offer to rent the building and a market price can be established for the rent. But, what if the building cannot be rented because there is no practical way to allow outsiders access to the building without disturbing SMC's normal operations? In this case, there is still an opportunity cost. If the designer desk lamp project occupies the building, then other projects that arise in the future will not be able to use it and new facilities will have to be built. Estimating the dollar value of that potential displacement is not easy but should nevertheless be done. Assigning the currently empty building free of charge to the designer desk lamp project *understates* the real cost of the project.

COSTS IMPLIED BY POTENTIAL SALES EROSION

Recall that SMC's sales manager is concerned about the potential loss of sales for standard desk lamps if the designer desk lamp project is launched (item 4 in Exhibit 8.1). In this case, the cash flows that the new lamps are expected to generate must be reduced by the estimated loss of cash flows due to the sales erosion of standard desk lamps. This appears to be another example of an opportunity cost, similar to the potential loss of rental income if the project is launched.

Sales erosion, however, is more complicated than loss of rental income because sales erosion can be caused by SMC or by a competing firm. Lost sales should be counted as relevant costs *only* if they are directly related to SMC's decision to produce the new lamps. What if SMC will lose sales on its existing standard lamps even if it does *not* launch the new lamps? This situation can occur if competitors decide to launch newly designed desk lamps that compete directly with SMC's standard desk lamps. If the loss of sales is expected to occur *anyway,* then it should not be counted as a relevant cost in the decision to launch the new product. It is an irrelevant cost because it is a part of the "SMC without the project" scenario. If this occurs, sales erosion is no longer similar to an opportunity cost but, rather, is comparable to a sunk cost.

Clearly, the question that SMC's managers must answer is: What will happen to the firm's future cash flows if it does *not* launch the designer desk lamp? In other words, what is the scenario if SMC does *not* undertake the project (the "without" situation)? If SMC's managers believe that some sales erosion will take place, then the corresponding loss of cash flows should be ignored; in this case, they are similar to a sunk cost. Our point is that a firm cannot evaluate an investment properly if it does not know what will happen *if it does not invest.* We return to the issue of sales erosion when we estimate the net present value of the designer desk lamp project.

ALLOCATED COSTS

Like many firms, SMC spreads its overhead costs over a number of projects using standard allocation rules. But according to the with/without principle, these allocated costs are irrelevant because the firm will have to pay them even if the project is not undertaken. *Only increases in overhead cash expenses resulting from the project should be taken into account.* The project should not have to pay a share of the existing overhead expenses. Because no increases in overhead expenses are expected to occur for the designer desk lamp, it would be incorrect to charge this project a fee of 1 percent of sales as required by the accounting department (item 16 in Exhibit 8.1).

DEPRECIATION EXPENSES

If SMC decides to buy the $2 million piece of equipment, it will incur an initial cash outflow of $2 million. The equipment will be listed as a fixed asset on SMC's balance sheet and depreciated at a rate of $400,000 per year (item 7 in Exhibit 8.1). Recall that depreciation expenses do not involve any cash outflows; they are not paid to anyone and are thus irrelevant to the investment decision.

However, firms must pay taxes. Even though depreciation does not affect *pretax* cash flows, it has an impact on *aftertax* cash flows. When the firm pays taxes, depreciation becomes relevant because it reduces the firm's taxable profit. With a lower taxable income, the firm pays less taxes and saves an equivalent amount of cash. With a corporate tax rate of 40 percent (item 18 in Exhibit 8.1), SMC saves 40 cents of taxes for every dollar of depreciation expenses.[2]

TAX EXPENSES

If an investment is profitable, the firm will have to pay more taxes. According to the with/without principle, the *additional* tax the firm must pay as a result of the project's acceptance is a relevant cash outflow. To compute this additional tax payment, we must first estimate the incremental earnings before interest and tax (EBIT) that the project is expected to generate if adopted. The contribution of the project to the firm's total tax bill is then found by multiplying the incremental EBIT by the corporate tax rate applicable to the extra amount of pretax profit. This rate is known as the marginal corporate tax rate. We have:

$$\text{Project tax} = \text{Project EBIT} \times \text{marginal corporate tax rate}$$

where:

$$\text{Project EBIT} = \text{Project Revenues} - \text{Project operating expenses} - \text{Project depreciation}$$

We use the project's EBIT to calculate the project tax so we can account for the tax savings that result from the depreciation of the project's assets. However, the project's EBIT is the incremental profit *before* the deduction of interest expenses. Thus, we seem to have ignored the corporate tax reduction that results from the deduction of interest expenses on the funds borrowed to finance the project. This is not the case. We ignore it in the cash flows but, as shown below, we account for it in the cost of capital, which is measured on an *aftertax* basis. In other words, the tax savings from the deductibility of interest expenses are not taken into account in the project's cash flows but in the project's estimated aftertax cost of capital.

What would happen if SMC had a loss next year and thus had no taxes to pay? Obviously, in this case, the tax savings from the deduction of depreciation and interest expenses will not be available. In order to get the tax savings, SMC must pay some taxes in the first place. If no taxes are paid then none can be saved. Fortunately, the tax authorities in most countries allow companies to carry forward or carry back their tax savings. This means that companies that cannot take advantage of the tax savings during the current tax year (because they made no profit) can do so against profits generated during the previous three to five years (the **carryback** method) or during the forthcoming three to five years (the **carry forward** method).

---

[2] The tax savings from depreciation expenses must be computed from the amount of depreciation expenses allowed by the tax authorities. This is not necessarily the same amount the firm reports in its income statement (see Chapter 2).

FINANCING COSTS

The cost of financing an investment is certainly a relevant cost when deciding whether to invest or not. But financing costs are cash flows *to* the investors who fund the project, not cash flows *from* the project. If a project is analyzed using the net present value rule, the project's expected cash-flow stream is discounted at the project's cost of capital. And, the project's cost of capital is the return required by the investors who will finance the project. Thus, the cost of capital *is* the cost of financing the project. If financing costs are deducted from the project's expected cash-flow stream, the present value calculations will count them twice—once in the expected cash flows and a second time when the cash flows are discounted. Hence, financing costs should be ignored when estimating a project's relevant cash flows. They will be captured in the project's cost of capital.

To illustrate the distinction that must be made between cash flows *from* the project (investment-related cash flows) and cash flows *to* the suppliers of capital (financing-related cash flows), consider the case of a one-year investment that requires an initial cash outlay of $1,000 and will generate a future cash inflow of $1,200. Suppose that the investment is financed with a $1,000 loan at 10 percent. The firm borrows $1,000 from a bank (an initial cash inflow) to finance the project and repays $1,100 at the end of the year (a year-end cash outflow). The cash-flow streams related to the investment and financing decisions, the total cash flows, and the net present values are shown in Exhibit 8.2.

The cash flows related to the financing decision have an NPV of zero. Hence, the project's NPV is the same as the total NPV, which takes into account the cash flows from both the investment decision and the financing decision. Deducting the $100 of financing expenses (10 percent of $1,000) from the project's $1,200 future cash flow, and then discounting the difference at the cost of capital of 10 percent, will introduce the double-counting mentioned earlier.

How can we estimate the appropriate cost of capital for the designer desk lamp project? In the above example, the investment was financed entirely with debt, so the cost of debt is the cost of capital. Chapter 10 explains that 40 percent of the designer desk lamp project will be financed with debt borrowed at 7.25 percent and the remaining 60 percent will be financed with equity capital provided by SMC's shareholders who expect to earn a 13.85 percent return on their equity investment. The 13.85 percent return expected by SMC's shareholders is SMC's cost of equity.

EXHIBIT 8.2   Investment- and Financing-Related Cash-Flow Streams.

TYPE OF CASH-FLOW STREAM	INITIAL CASH FLOW	TERMINAL CASH FLOW	NPV at 10%
Investment-related cash flows	−$1,000	+$1,200	+$91
Financing-related cash flows	+$1,000	−$1,100	Zero
Total cash flows	**Zero**	**+$100**	**+$91**

Given the above financing structure and costs, what is the designer desk lamp project's overall cost of capital? It is the weighted average of the project's *aftertax* cost of debt (interest expenses are tax deductible) and the project's cost of equity. Shareholders receive dividend payments that are *not* tax deductible at the corporate level, so the cost of equity is not measured on an aftertax basis. The weights used in the calculation are the proportions of debt and equity financing. Thus we can estimate the project's weighted average cost of capital, *k,* as follows:

$$\text{Project's cost of capital} = k = [40\% \times 7.25\%(1 - 40\%)] + [60\% \times 13.85\%]$$
$$= [1.7\%] + [8.3\%] = 10\%$$

The project's appropriate cost of capital is 10 percent. It is not the 12 percent rate that SMC's accounting department applies to the book value of the project's assets (item 17 in Exhibit 8.1). The reason is twofold. First, a financing cost should not affect the project's expected cash flows; it affects the project's discount rate or cost of capital. But more to the point, the 12 percent charge is an inappropriate estimate of the project's cost of capital because it is an allocated financial expense that does not reflect the actual opportunity cost of the funds required to finance the project.

INFLATION

The 3 percent annual rate of inflation expected to prevail during the life of the project will affect several of the project's variables. The lamp's price (item 2 in Exhibit 8.1), the cost of raw material (item 9), and the labor and energy costs (items 14 and 15) are all expected to rise at the 3 percent anticipated rate of inflation. SMC's management has little or no control over the expected rise in the costs of raw material, energy, and labor unless SMC can exert pressure on its suppliers and prevent wages from rising, an unlikely outcome given competitive market forces. But management *can* decide not to raise the price of SMC's lamps by the 3 percent annual inflation rate if, for example, competitors keep the price of their products constant.

Inflation is also involved in another cost over which management has no influence. The firm's 10 percent cost of capital, which is entirely determined by the financial markets, is assumed to incorporate the market's 3 percent expected rate of inflation. The suppliers of capital will obviously require compensation to cover the potential erosion of their purchasing power caused by price inflation.

How will the 3 percent expected inflation rate affect the project's evaluation? If the cost of capital already incorporates the market's anticipated rate of inflation, then consistency requires that the inflation rate also be incorporated in the cash-flow stream the project is expected to generate. In other words, the project's cash flows should be measured in nominal terms, inflation included. The only component of cash flows that need not incorporate the 3 percent anticipated inflation rate is the lamp's selling price.[3] For competitive reasons, management can decide to keep that price at a constant $40. In the following analysis of the designer desk lamp project, we first assume that the price of the lamp will rise by the 3 percent expected inflation rate and later examine what would happen to the project's profitability if the price remains constant at $40.

ESTIMATING A PROJECT'S RELEVANT CASH FLOWS

We let CF_t designate the project's relevant cash flow at the *end* of year t.[4] Then, CF_0 denotes the project's initial cash outflow, CF_1 to CF_{N-1} denote the project's intermediate cash flows from year 1 to year N-1, and CF_N denotes the **terminal cash flow,** which is the cash flow at the end of year N, the last year of the project. As shown in Chapter 6, the project's net present value (NPV) can be expressed as:

$$\textbf{NPV (project)} = \textbf{CF}_0 + \frac{\textbf{CF}_1}{(\textbf{1} + \textbf{\textit{k}})^1} + \frac{\textbf{CF}_2}{(\textbf{1} + \textbf{\textit{k}})^2}$$
$$+ \ldots + \frac{\textbf{CF}_t}{(\textbf{1} + \textbf{\textit{k}})^t} + \ldots + \frac{\textbf{CF}_N}{(\textbf{1} + \textbf{\textit{k}})^N} \tag{8.1}$$

where k = the project's cost of capital;

$\dfrac{CF_t}{(1 + k)^t}$ = the present value of CF_t at the project's cost of capital k; and

N = the project's **economic** or **useful life,** that is, the number of years over which the project is expected to provide benefits to the firm's owners.

Recall that if a project has a positive NPV, it is a value-creating proposition and should be undertaken. If it has a negative NPV, it should be rejected. As an illustration, we will estimate the NPV of the designer desk lamp project using an economic life equal to five years ($N = 5$), the same as its **accounting life** or number of years over which the project's fixed assets are depreciated (item 7 in Exhibit 8.1). However, the project may have an economic or useful life that is

---

[3] One other component of a project's cash flows that will *not* be affected by inflation is the tax savings from depreciation expenses. In most countries, accounting conventions do not allow firms to change their depreciation expenses to compensate for the effect of inflation on the value of assets.

[4] This assumption is made for computational convenience because discounting requires that the cash flow occur at a specific point in time. If this assumption is not realistic for the project being analyzed, the length of the cash-flow period should be shortened to six months or less.

longer than five years, meaning that the project may still generate *positive* net cash flows beyond the fifth year. If this occurs, the project will be continued if its NPV at the end of year 5 is higher than the net cash flow resulting from the project's termination at that time.

MEASURING THE CASH FLOWS GENERATED BY A PROJECT

According to the with/without principle, CF_t, the cash flow generated by a project in year t, is equal to the *change* in the firm's *overall* cash flow in year t, if the project is undertaken. It is given by the following general expression (see Chapter 4 for details):

$$\mathbf{CF}_t = \mathbf{EBIT}_t\,(1 - \mathbf{Tax}_t) + \mathbf{Dep}_t - \Delta\mathbf{WCR}_t - \mathbf{Capex}_t \qquad (8.2)$$

where CF_t = the incremental cash flow generated by the project in year t, which is assumed to occur at the end of the year.

$EBIT_t$ = the incremental earnings before interest and tax, or pretax operating profit, generated by the project in year t; it is equal to sales revenues$_t$ − operating expenses$_t$ − depreciation expenses$_t$.

Tax_t = the marginal corporate tax rate applicable to the incremental $EBIT_t$.

Dep_t = the depreciation expenses in year t that are related to the fixed assets used to support the project.

ΔWCR_t = the incremental working capital required in year t to support the sales that the project is expected to generate the *following* year;[5] WCR_t is equal to the project's operating assets (mostly accounts receivable and inventories) less its operating liabilities (mostly accounts payable).

$Capex_t$ = capital expenditures or incremental investment in fixed assets in year t.

CF_t, the cash flow *from* the project, excludes all cash movements related to the financing of the project, such as the cash inflows from borrowing or the cash outflows associated with interest and dividend payments made to lenders and shareholders. These financing costs are captured by the project's weighted average cost of capital.

Because we want to exclude financing costs from the project's cash flows, the first term in equation 8.2 is the aftertax profit generated from the project's *operations*. It is the earnings before interest and taxes (EBIT) adjusted by the

---

[5] WCR builds up throughout the year. Recognizing the change in WCR at the beginning rather than the end of the year will *reduce* the project's NPV because the change in WCR reduces cash flows. This is preferable to recognizing the investment later and *overstating* the project's NPV.

corporate tax rate: $EBIT_t(1 - Tax_t)$.[6] This aftertax operating profit is then converted into an aftertax cash flow by making three adjustments:

1. Depreciation expenses (Dep_t) are added because they are not a cash expense.[7]
2. Any cash used to finance the growth of the working capital required to support the sales generated by the project (ΔWCR_t) is subtracted.
3. The cash used to acquire the fixed assets needed to launch the project and keep it going over its useful life ($Capex_t$) is subtracted.

The following sections examine in detail the estimation of a project's initial, intermediate, and terminal cash flows using the designer desk lamp project as an illustration. A summary of the estimation procedure is presented in Exhibit 8.3.

ESTIMATING THE PROJECT'S INITIAL CASH OUTFLOW

The project's initial cash outflow, CF_0, includes the following items:

1. The cost of the assets acquired to launch the project
2. Any setup costs, including shipping and installation costs
3. Any additional working capital required to support the sales that the project is expected to generate the first year
4. Any tax credits provided by the government to induce firms to invest
5. Any cash inflows resulting from the sale of existing assets when the project involves a decision to replace assets, including any taxes related to that sale

All these costs must be *cash* costs and, as already mentioned, should not include any sunk costs, such as those related to research and development or market research, if these expenses occurred prior to the decision to accept or reject the project.

For the designer desk lamp project, the initial cash outflow is equal to the sum of:

1. The $2,000,000 cost of acquiring and installing the equipment in the existing building (item 6 in Exhibit 8.1)
2. The initial working capital required to support the first year of sales the project is expected to generate

---

[6] The actual tax payment the firm must make is obtained by applying the corporate tax rate to profits *after deducting interest expenses*. However, applying the tax rate to EBIT does not ignore interest expenses and the corresponding reduction in taxes they provide; both are accounted for in the project's cost of capital.

[7] Depreciation expenses are included in EBIT. After we have calculated the tax expenses by applying the tax rate to EBIT, we must add depreciation in order to remove its effect on cash flow. We only need depreciation expenses in the first place in order to calculate the tax liability triggered by the project.

EXHIBIT 8.3 Estimation of the Cash Flows Generated by the Designer Desk Lamp Project.

Figures in thousands of dollars; data from Exhibit 8.1

	Now	End of Year 1	End of Year 2	End of Year 3	End of Year 4	End of Year 5
I. Revenues:						
1. Expected unit sales in thousands		45	40	30	20	10
2. Price per unit, rising at 3% per year		$40.00	$41.20	$42.44	$43.71	$45.02
3. Total sales revenues (line 1 × line 2)	**$0**	**$1,800**	**$1,648**	**$1,273**	**$874**	**$450**
II. Operating expenses						
4. Material cost per unit, rising at 3% per year		10.00	10.30	10.61	10.93	11.26
5. Total material cost (line 1 × line 4)		450	412	318	219	113
6. Labor cost per unit, rising at 3% per year		5.00	5.15	5.30	5.46	5.63
7. Total labor cost (line 1 × line 6)		225	206	159	109	56
8. Energy cost per unit, rising at 3% per year		1.00	1.03	1.06	1.09	1.13
9. Total energy cost (line 1 × line 8)		45	41	32	22	11
10. Loss of rental income (opportunity cost)		10	10	10	10	10
11. Depreciation expenses ($2,000/5)		400	400	400	400	400
12. Total operating expenses (line 5+7+9+10+11)	**$0**	**$1,130**	**$1,069**	**$919**	**$760**	**$590**
III. Operating profit						
13. Pretax operating profit (EBIT) (line 3 − line 12)	0	670	579	354	116	(140)
14. less tax at 40% (when positive, it is a tax credit)	0	(268)	(232)	(142)	(47)	56
15. Aftertax operating profit (line 13 + line 14)	**$0**	**$402**	**$347**	**$212**	**$69**	**($84)**
IV. Cash flow generated by the project						
16. Aftertax operating profit (line 15)	0	402	347	212	69	(84)
17. Depreciation expenses (line 11)	0	400	400	400	400	400
18. Working capital requirement at 20% of next year's sales	360	330	255	175	90	0
19. Change in working capital requirement from previous year	360	(30)	(75)	(80)	(85)	(90)
20. Capital expenditure	2,000	0	0	0	0	0
21. Recovery of the aftertax resale value of equipment						60
22. Cash flow from the project (line 16+17−19−20+21)	**($2,360)**	**$832**	**$822**	**$692**	**$554**	**$466**

We can estimate the project's working capital requirement from the information reported in Exhibit 8.1. Working capital requirement is usually expressed as a percentage of sales. In other words, if we know the expected sales in year t, we can estimate the amount of working capital that is required at the beginning of the year to support these sales. For the designer desk lamp project:

$$\text{Working capital requirement} = \text{Receivables} + \text{Inventories} - \text{Payables}$$

Receivables are equal to 56 days of sales (item 12 in Exhibit 8.1), and inventories are equal to 23 days of sales (items 10 and 13). Payables are equal to 4 weeks of purchases (item 11), which is equivalent to one week (7 days) of sales (the $10 cost for raw material is one fourth of the $40 lamp price, and one fourth of 4 weeks is 1 week). It follows that the project's working capital requirement is equal to 72 days of sales (56 days plus 23 days less 7 days). This is equivalent to 20 percent of annual sales (72 days of sales divided by 360 days of annual sales).

The next step is to estimate sales revenues at the end of the first year. From items 1 and 2 in Exhibit 8.1:

$$\text{Sales revenues at the end of year 1} = 45{,}000 \text{ units} \times \$40 = \$1{,}800{,}000$$

This figure is reported in Exhibit 8.3 in line 3 of the column labeled "End of year 1." Working capital requirement is equal to 20 percent of sales:

$$\text{Initial WCR} = 20\% \times \$1{,}800{,}000 = \$360{,}000$$

Thus, the total initial cash outlay required to launch the project is:

$$CF_0 = \$2{,}000{,}000 + \$360{,}000 = \$2{,}360{,}000$$

The $360,000 initial working capital requirement and the total initial cash flow of $2,360,000 are reported in the "Now" column of Exhibit 8.3, lines 18 and 22, respectively. CF_0 could have been obtained as a special case of equation 8.2, the general cash-flow equation. For CF_0, EBIT and depreciation expenses are zero (there are no initial profit or depreciation expenses), the change in working capital requirement is $360,000 (more precisely, it is $360,000 minus zero because $360,000 is the initial investment in working capital), and capital expenditures are $2,000,000.

ESTIMATING THE PROJECT'S INTERMEDIATE CASH FLOWS

The estimates of the desk lamp project's intermediate cash flows (CF_1 to CF_4) are based on the information in Exhibit 8.1 and are calculated using the project's cash-flow formula given in equation 8.2. Exhibit 8.3 shows the inputs and summarizes the cash-flow estimates.

We illustrate the procedure for CF_1, the cash flow that the project is expected to generate the first year. Sales revenues, as computed earlier, are $1,800,000 (line 3).

Total operating expenses are \$1,130,000 (line 12). They include total material expenses (line 5), total direct labor expenses (line 7), total energy expenses (line 9), the loss of rental income (line 10), and depreciation expenses (line 11). They exclude the \$30,000 fee paid to the consulting company (a sunk cost), the overhead charge of 1 percent of sales (SMC's overhead expenses are not expected to rise if the project is adopted), and the 12 percent financing charge required by the accounting department (financing costs are captured by the project's 10 percent weighted average cost of capital). They also exclude the impact of sales erosion. This item will be examined later.

With \$1,800,000 of sales revenues and \$1,130,000 of total operating expenses, the project's pretax operating profit (EBIT) is \$670,000 (line 13). Deducting 40 percent of tax expenses (line 14), we get an aftertax operating profit of \$402,000 (line 15). In section IV of Exhibit 8.3, this figure is converted into a cash flow by adding back \$400,000 of depreciation expenses (line 17) and deducting -\$30,000 (line 19), the *change* in working capital requirement. (Line 18 indicates that working capital requirement *decreased* from \$360,000 to \$330,000.) Thus, the project's cash flow is \$832,000 at the end of the first year (line 22) because there is no additional capital expenditure in year 1 ($Capex_1 = 0$). Using equation 8.2:

$$CF_1 = (\$1,800,000 - \$1,130,000) \times (1 - 40\%) + \$400,000 - (-\$30,000) - \$0$$

$$CF_1 = \$402,000 + \$400,000 + \$30,000 = \$832,000$$

Working capital requirement declines after the first year because sales decline after the first year and working capital requirement is based on next year's sales. Thus, SMC needs to invest a decreasing amount of cash in its operating cycle to support the project's sales. As a consequence, the changes in working capital requirement from year 1 to year 5 are negative. The sum of all the changes in WCR over a project's life must equal zero because the firm recovers its initial investment in working capital requirement during the project's duration. For the designer desk lamp project, we have:

Sum of the changes in working capital requirement = \$360,000 - \$30,000
    - \$75,000 - \$80,000 - \$85,000 - \$90,000 = 0

ESTIMATING THE PROJECT'S TERMINAL CASH FLOW

The incremental cash flow for the last year of any project, its terminal cash flow, should include the following items:

1. The last incremental net cash flow the project is expected to generate
2. The recovery of the project's incremental working capital requirement, if any
3. The aftertax resale value of any physical assets acquired earlier in relation to the project
4. Any capital expenditure and other costs associated with the termination of the project

At the end of a project, inventories associated with the project are sold, accounts receivable are collected, and accounts payable are paid. In other words, the cash value of the project's contribution to the firm's working capital requirement is recovered. For the designer desk lamp project, working capital requirement at the end of the fourth year, which will be recovered at the end of the fifth year, is worth $90,000.

Some of a project's fixed assets may have a resale value when the project is ended. The sale of these assets will generate a cash inflow that must be counted in the project's terminal cash flow after adjustments for the incidence of any taxes associated with the sale. The resale value of the assets, also known as their **residual value** or **salvage value,** affects the firm's overall tax bill *only if it is different from the assets' book value.* If the resale value is higher than the book value, the project's termination will generate a taxable capital gain (equal to the difference between the resale value and the book value) that will increase the firm's overall tax bill. If they are equal, there are no tax implications. And if the resale value is lower than the book value, then the project's termination will generate a capital loss that will reduce the firm's overall tax bill.

For the designer desk lamp project, the initial equipment has an expected residual value of $100,000 and a book value of zero at the end of year 5. The sale of that asset is thus expected to generate a capital gain of $100,000 that will be taxed at 40 percent. As a result, the project's terminal cash flow, CF_5, should increase by $60,000 ($100,000 less 40 percent of $100,000), the expected *aftertax* resale value of the equipment.

Combining the various items that contribute to the project's terminal cash flow, we have:

$$CF_N = EBIT_N(1 - Tax_N) + Dep_N - \Delta WCR_N + \textbf{Aftertax residual value}_N$$

Applying this formula to the designer desk lamp project, as shown in the last column of Exhibit 8.3, provides a total terminal cash flow, CF_5, of $466,000:

$$CF_5 = -\$84,000 + \$400,000 - (-\$90,000) + \$60,000 = \$466,000$$

The last operating "profit" for the project (line 13 in Exhibit 8.3) is a loss of $140,000. SMC's overall taxable income will be reduced by that amount, providing a tax saving of $56,000 (40 percent of $140,000) and yielding an *aftertax* operating loss of $84,000 for the project. Although the aftertax net income is negative, the net cash flow from the project is positive, and the decision to invest should be based on cash flows not profits.

SHOULD SMC LAUNCH THE NEW PRODUCT?

We have now identified and estimated the entire cash-flow stream the designer desk lamp project is expected to generate during the next five years. It is shown in the last row of Exhibit 8.3. The project's cost of capital is 10 percent (item 20 in

**EXHIBIT 8.4   Calculation of Net Present Value for SMC's Designer
                Desk Lamp Project.**

Figures from Exhibit 8.3

Initial cash outlay $CF_0 =$ ($2,360,000)

$$\text{Present value of } CF_1 \;=\; \$832,000 \times \frac{1}{(1+0.10)^1} \;=\; \$832,000 \times 0.9091 \;=\; \$756,371$$

$$\text{Present value of } CF_2 \;=\; \$822,000 \times \frac{1}{(1+0.10)^2} \;=\; \$82,000 \times 0.8264 \;=\; \$679,301$$

$$\text{Present value of } CF_3 \;=\; \$692,000 \times \frac{1}{(1+0.10)^3} \;=\; \$692,000 \times 0.7513 \;=\; \$519,900$$

$$\text{Present value of } CF_4 \;=\; \$554,000 \times \frac{1}{(1+0.10)^4} \;=\; \$554,000 \times 0.6830 \;=\; \$378,382$$

$$\text{Present value of } CF_5 \;=\; \$466,000 \times \frac{1}{(1+0.10)^5} \;=\; \$466,000 \times 0.6209 \;=\; \$289,339$$

Net present value at 10%	$263,293

Exhibit 8.1). The calculations for the project's net present value according to equation 8.1 are shown in Exhibit 8.4.

The designer desk lamp project has a positive net present value of $263,293,
so SMC should launch the new product.[8] Before concluding, however, we should
perform a sensitivity analysis on the project's NPV because the $263,293 ignores
two important elements: (1) SMC may not be able to raise the price of its new
lamps above $40 and (2) SMC may incur net cash losses of up to $80,000 per year
(item 4 in Exhibit 8.1) as a result of a potential reduction in the sales of SMC's
standard desk lamps. We did not consider the potential sales erosion because we
assumed it would occur whether or not SMC launched the new lamps. However,
if the sales erosion will occur *only as a result of the launch of the new lamps,* then it
must be considered in the calculation of the project's NPV.

SENSITIVITY OF THE PROJECT'S NPV TO CHANGES
IN THE LAMP PRICE

What would happen to the project's net present value if SMC is unable to raise
the price of lamps by the 3 percent expected increase in the annual rate of inflation? If SMC keeps the price constant at $40 while costs are rising by 3 percent,

---

[8] Alternatively, the project's internal rate of return (IRR) is equal to 14.8 percent. Because the project's
IRR exceeds the 10 percent cost of capital, the project is a value-creating proposal.

the project's net present value drops from $263,293 to $161,409, a 39 percent reduction.[9] But the project is still worth undertaking because its net present value remains positive.

SENSITIVITY OF NPV TO SALES EROSION

The present value at 10 percent of the loss of annual net cash flows of $80,000 for five years is equal to $303,280.[10] If we deduct this amount from the project's NPV of $263,293, we have:

$$\text{NPV(project with erosion)} = \text{NPV(project without erosion)} - \text{NPV(erosion)}$$
$$= \$263,293 - \$303,280 = -\$39,987$$

Thus, with $80,000 yearly sales erosion, the designer desk lamp project is no longer a value-creating proposal. However, the project can withstand some sales erosion and still have a positive NPV. The project will break even if the annual reduction in net cash flow is $69,452.[11] In other words, if sales erosion is expected to reduce SMC's net cash flows by more than $69,452 per year for the next five years, then the project will no longer be acceptable. If annual sales erosion is less than $69,452, the project has a positive NPV and may still be acceptable.

The preceding analysis clearly indicates that the size of the possible annual reduction in sales and net cash flows must be determined by SMC's managers before they decide whether to launch the designer desk lamp project. In other words, SMC's managers must have a clear understanding of their firm's competitive position in the standard desk lamp market before they evaluate the value-creating potential of the new product.

Will competitors enter the standard desk lamp market with a competing product that will erode SMC's position in that market? If the answer is yes, then the effect of erosion on the project's cash flows can be ignored. The sales erosion will happen anyway and is, thus, irrelevant to the decision to produce the designer desk lamps. In this case, the project's NPV is positive, and SMC should launch the new product. If the answer is that erosion will take place *only* if SMC launches

---

[9] The estimation procedure is the same as the one shown in Exhibit 8.3, except the price of a lamp remains at $40. Note, however, that in this case WCR will be *less* than 20 percent of sales. Accounts payable are going to be *higher* than one week of sales because the cost of raw material is rising by 3 percent while the price of a lamp remains constant. We kept WCR at 20 percent of sales in our calculation. A lower ratio would have produced larger cash flows and a higher NPV.

[10] This cash-flow stream is an annuity. Appendix 6.1 shows that the present value of an annuity is equal to the constant cash flow multiplied by the annuity discount factor (ADF), where ADF is equal to $(1 - \text{discount factor})$ divided by k. With $k = 10\%$ and $N = 5$, ADF $= (1 - 0.6209)/0.10 = 3.7910$ and the present value of the $80,000 annuity is $80,000 \times 3.7910 = \$303,280$.

[11] The break-even point is obtained when the project's NPV is equal to the present value of the annuity. We have $263,293 = \text{Annuity} \times \text{ADF}$. ADF is equal to 3.7910, so the annuity is equal to $263,293 divided by 3.7910, or, $69,452.

the new lamp, then the effect of erosion on the firm's net cash flows should be carefully estimated and taken into account. If erosion is expected to reduce the firm's annual net cash flows by less than $69,452, the project is still worth undertaking because its NPV is still positive. If management believes that erosion will reduce cash flows by more than $69,452 a year, the project should be rejected.

Sensitivity analysis is a useful tool when dealing with project uncertainty. By showing how sensitive NPV is to changes in underlying assumptions, it helps identify those variables that have the greatest effect on the value of the proposal and shows where more information is needed before a decision can be made.

SUMMARY

Managers can use a number of principles and rules to identify and estimate the cash flows that are relevant to an investment decision. Relevant cash flows are the ones that should be discounted at the project's estimated cost of capital to obtain the project's net present value or used to calculate the project's internal rate of return. The decision of whether to invest or not should be made using only relevant cash flows.

There are two fundamental principles to keep in mind when estimating a project's cash flows. The first is the actual cash-flow principle, according to which a project's relevant cash flows must be measured at the time they occur. Relevant cash flows *exclude* any financing costs associated with the project because these costs are already taken into account in estimating the project's weighted average cost of capital. The weighted average cost of capital is the discount rate that must be used to convert a project's expected future cash-flow stream into its present value equivalent. Deducting the project's initial investment from this present value provides an estimate of the project's net present value. If it is positive the project is a value-creating proposition and should be undertaken.

The second principle is the with/without principle, according to which a project's relevant cash flows are those that are expected to either increase or decrease the firm's *overall* cash position if the project is adopted. Examples of cash outflows that should be ignored are those related to sunk costs. These are costs that are incurred *before* the project's net present value is estimated. These costs cannot be recovered, so they should be ignored. Asking the project to cover them means that the firm pays twice for these costs.

Examples of cash flows indirectly related to a project that should nevertheless be taken into account are those related to opportunity costs. These are usually cash inflows the firm will have to give up if it undertakes the project. Contrary to sunk costs that are relatively easy to determine because they have already been paid, opportunity costs are usually difficult to identify because they involve *potential future* cash flows rather than *actual past* cash flows.

One of the most difficult types of costs to identify is the effect that competitors may have on a firm's existing and potential products or services. For example, a firm's managers considering the launch of a new product must find out whether the new product will cause erosion in the sales of the firm's existing products. In order to make the proper decision to invest or not, managers must first forecast the firm's future development if the firm does not go ahead with the project (the firm without the project). Then, they must compare the firm's future prospect *with* the project to its future outlook *without* the project. If sales erosion is expected to occur even if the firm does not launch the new product, then the sales erosion of existing products is irrelevant to the decision to launch the new product.

REFERENCES AND FURTHER READING

1. Brealey, Richard, and Stewart Myers. *Principles of Corporate Finance.* 5th ed. McGraw-Hill, 1996. See chapter 6.
2. Clark, John, Thomas Hindelang, and Robert Pritchard. *Capital Budgeting: Planning and Control of Capital Expenditures.* 3d ed. Prentice-Hall, 1989. See chapter 4.
3. Ross, Stephen, Randolph Westerfield, and Jeffrey Jaffe. *Corporate Finance.* 4th ed. Irwin, 1996. See chapter 7.

REVIEW PROBLEMS

8.1 Interest payments and project's cash flow.
Why is interest paid on the debt raised to finance an investment project not included in the estimation of the cash flows that are relevant to the evaluation of the project?

8.2 Understanding the structure of the cash-flow formula.
The estimation of a project's cash flows is usually based on the formula Cash flow = EBIT(1 − Tax) + Depreciation − ΔWCR − Capex, where EBIT = earnings before interest and tax, Tax = marginal tax rate, ΔWCR = change in working capital requirement, and Capex = capital expenditures required to support the project. Neither EBIT nor depreciation expenses are cash-flow items. Why do they appear in the cash-flow formula?

8.3 Alternative formula to estimate a project's cash flow.
The cash-flow formula Cash flow = EBIT(1 − Tax) + Depreciation − ΔWCR − Capex is sometimes replaced by the following one: Cash flow = EBITDA(1 − Tax) + (Tax × Depreciation) − ΔWCR − Capex, where EBIT, Tax, ΔWCR, and Capex are defined as in problem 8.2, and EBITDA is earnings before interest and tax, depreciation and amortization. Show that the two formulas are equivalent.

8.4 Identifying a project's relevant cash flows.

Your company, Printers Inc., is considering investing in a new plant to manufacture a new generation of printers developed by the firm's R&D department. Comment on the analysis of the proposal that is summarized below.

1. *Project's useful life:* The plant is expected to operate for five years, from 1998 to 2002.
2. *Capital expenditures:* $6 million which includes the construction costs and the costs of machinery and installation. The plant will be built on a parking lot owned by the company.
3. *Depreciation:* For tax purposes, the building and equipment will be depreciated over 10 years using the straight-line method.
4. *Revenue:* 5,000 printers are expected to be sold in 1998, 10,000 in 1999, and 20,000 thereafter. The printers will be sold at $800 each.
5. *Research and development costs:* $1 million spent in 1996 and 1997.
6. *Overhead costs:* 3.75% of the project revenues, as stipulated by the corporate manual.
7. *Operating costs:* Direct and indirect costs are expected to be $500 per unit produced.
8. *Inventories:* The initial investment in raw material, work in process, and finished goods inventories is estimated at $1,500,000.
9. *Financing costs:* 10% of capital expenditures per year, as stipulated by the corporate manual.
10. *Tax rate:* 40% (includes federal and state taxes).
11. *Discount rate:* 8%. This is Printers Inc.'s current borrowing rate.
12. *Cash-flow stream and net present value (figures are in thousands of dollars):*

	12/31/97	1998	1999	2000	2001	2002
1. Capital expenditures	− $6,000					
2. Inventories	− $1,500					
3. R&D expenses	− $1,000					
4. Revenue		$4,000	$8,000	$16,000	$16,000	$16,000
5. Overhead costs		−150	−300	−600	−600	−600
6. Operating costs		−2,500	−5,000	−10,000	−10,000	−10,000
7. Depreciation		−600	−600	−600	−600	−600
8. EBIT		750	2,100	4,800	4,800	4,800
9. EBIT(1 − Tax rate)		450	1,260	2,880	2,880	2,880
10. Add depreciation		1,050	1,860	3,480	3,480	3,480
11. Net cash flow	**−$8,500**	**$1,050**	**$1,860**	**$3,480**	**$3,480**	**$3,480**
Discount rate	8%					
Net present value	$1,755					

8.5 Estimating a project's relevant cash flows and net present value.
Suppose you are given the following additional information on the investment proposal described in problem 8.4. What is the net present value of the project? Should it be accepted?

1. Salvage value at the end of 2002 is $3 million.
2. Tax rate on capital gains is 20%.
3. Ratio of working capital requirement to sales is 30%.
4. Due to competitive pressure, the printer's sale price is expected to decrease at the following rate: $800 in 1998, $700 in 1999, and $600 thereafter.
5. Fixed operating costs are $800,000 per year.
6. Variable operating costs are $400 per unit produced.
7. Overhead costs will not be significantly affected by the project.
8. Printers Inc. will have to rent parking spaces for its employees at an estimated cost of $50,000 per year.
9. Expected inflation rate is 3%. Inflation is expected to affect only the operating costs that can be assumed to grow at the inflation rate.
10. Cost of capital is 12%.

CHAPTER

9 RAISING CAPITAL AND VALUING SECURITIES

Firms need cash to finance new investments in fixed assets and working capital. For most firms, the major source of funds is the cash they generate from their operations, net of the cash used to service existing debt (pay interest expenses and repay loans), settle taxes, and pay dividends to shareholders. When internally generated cash is not sufficient to maintain existing assets and finance all its new, value-creating investment opportunities, the firm has to raise additional funds from external sources in the form of debt and/or equity capital. Sources of borrowed funds include *bank loans, leases,* and the sale of debt securities to investors; external sources of equity include the sale of *preferred* and *common stocks* to existing and new shareholders. These various sources of capital are surveyed in this chapter. As in previous chapters, the words *funds, financing,* and *capital* are used interchangeably.

Although new funds are usually employed to finance asset growth, a firm may borrow to restructure its capital, that is, to repay part of its existing debt or to buy back some of its outstanding shares. Chapter 11 explains why a firm might want to modify its capital structure. The focus here is on the description of the various forms of debt and equity capital available to firms, the methods employed to raise these funds, and the valuation of the most common types of securities a firm can issue. After reading this chapter, you should understand:

- How to estimate the amount of external funds a firm needs to finance its growth.
- How the financial system works and what functions it performs.
- The differences between the various sources of debt and equity capital.
- How firms raise capital in the financial markets.
- How to value the securities issued by firms.

ESTIMATING THE AMOUNT OF REQUIRED EXTERNAL FUNDS

To determine the amount of external funds it will need, say, next year, a firm must estimate (1) the amount by which its investments are expected to grow during the coming year and (2) the amount of *internal* funds the firm expects to generate next year. If **internally generated funds** are less than the amount by which the firm's assets are expected to grow, the difference is the amount of external funds the firm will need to raise.

Recall from Chapter 3 that a firm's investments include cash and cash-equivalent assets (such as marketable securities), working capital requirement (a measure of the firm's net investment in its operating cycle), and fixed assets. The firm will need to finance any expected growth in these investments. Of course, any reduction in growth would be a source of funds. More precisely, we have:

$$\text{Funding needs} = \Delta\text{Cash} + \Delta\text{WCR} + \Delta\text{Fixed assets}$$

where we define ΔCash as the change in the firm's cash and cash-equivalent holdings; ΔWCR as the change in working capital requirement (any change in inventories, accounts receivable and prepaid expenses less any change in accounts payable and accrued expenses); and ΔFixed assets as *new* capital expenditures and acquisitions less cash raised from the sale of existing fixed assets (disposals and divestitures).

The source of internally generated funds is the firm's retained earnings, that is, the portion of its net profit that is not distributed as dividends. However, depreciation expenses are charged against the firm's net profit but are not cash expenses, so they must be added to retained earnings to obtain the firm's internally generated funds.[1] In general, we have:

$$\text{Internally generated funds} = \text{Retained earnings} + \text{Depreciation expenses}$$

We can now write:

External funds need = [Funding needs] − [Internally generated funds]

(9.1)

or

$$\text{External funds need} = [\Delta\text{Cash} + \Delta\text{WCR} + \Delta\text{Fixed assets}]$$
$$- [\text{Retained earnings} + \text{Depreciation expenses}]$$

---

[1] If there are other noncash expenses charged to the firm's net profit, such as the amortization of goodwill, they should be added back to retained earnings.

EXHIBIT 9.1   OS Distributors' Balance Sheet on December 31, 1996.

Figures in millions of dollars

		DECEMBER 31, 1996
Invested capital or net assets		
• Cash		$12.0
• Working capital requirement (WCR)		63.0
• Net fixed assets		51.0
Gross value	$90.0	
Accumulated depreciation	(39.0)	
Total		**$126.0**
Capital employed (Debt and owners' equity)		
• Short-term debt		$22.0
• Long-term debt[1]		34.0
• Owners' equity		70.0
Total		**$126.0**

Note
[1] Long-term debt is repaid at the rate of $8 million per year.

Any funds needed to pay interest on existing debt and dividends to shareholders are already accounted for in equation 9.1 because retained earnings are calculated after deducting both interest expenses and dividend payments from operating profit.

To illustrate equation 9.1, we revisit OS Distributors, the firm we analyzed in Chapters 2 through 5. We assume it is the end of 1996 and we want to estimate the amount of funds OS Distributors will need to raise externally in 1997. Exhibit 9.1 shows the firm's balance sheet at year-end 1996 in managerial form (see Chapter 3). Exhibit 9.2 shows the asset side of the firm's pro forma (projected) balance sheet at year-end 1997 and its 1997 pro forma income statement. From the pro forma income statement, we see that OS Distributors expects to generate $7 million of retained earnings in 1997. Adding the $8 million of depreciation expenses reported in the income statement, we conclude that OS Distributors expects to generate internally $15 million in 1997.

What are OS Distributors' funding needs for 1997? A comparison of the balance sheets at the end of 1997 and 1996 (see Exhibits 9.1 and 9.2) indicates that OS Distributors' invested capital, or net assets, should grow from $126 million to $138 million: Cash holdings should decrease by $4 million (from $12 million to $8 million), working capital requirement should increase by $14 million (from $63 million to $77 million), and net fixed assets should rise by $2 million (from $51 million to

$53 million). However, the net fixed assets reported in the balance sheets are *net* of depreciation expenses, so the $2 million increase in *net* fixed assets is not the expected increase in fixed assets. The latter figure is $10 million: $12 million for the enlargement of the warehouse less $2 million expected from the sale of existing assets (see the note for the balance sheet in Exhibit 9.2). In total, OS Distributors

EXHIBIT 9.2   OS Distributors' 1997 pro forma Financial Statements.

Figures in millions of dollars

PRO FORMA (PROJECTED) BALANCE SHEET
INVESTED CAPITAL SIDE

		DECEMBER 31, 1997
Invested capital or net assets		
• Cash		$8.0
• Working capital requirement (WCR)		77.0
• Net fixed assets		53.0
Gross value[1]	$93.0	
Accumulated depreciation	(40.0)	
Total		$138.0

PRO FORMA (PROJECTED) INCOME STATEMENT

		1997
• **Net sales**		$480.0
Cost of goods sold	($400.0)	
• **Gross profit**		80.0
Selling, general, and administrative expenses	(48.0)	
Depreciation expenses	(8.0)	
• **Operating profit**		24.0
Extraordinary items	0	
• **Earnings before interest and tax (EBIT)**		24.0
Net interest expenses[2]	(7.0)	
• **Earnings before tax (EBT)**		17.0
Income tax expense	(6.8)	
• **Earnings after tax (EAT)**		$10.2
Dividends	($3.2)	
• **Retained earnings**		$7.0

[1] In 1997, a warehouse will be enlarged at a cost of $12 million and existing assets, bought for $9 million in the past, are expected to be sold at their book value of $2 million.

[2] There is no interest income, so net interest expenses are equal to interest expenses.

funding needs for 1997 can be estimated at $20 million: $14 million to finance the rise in working capital requirement plus $10 million to finance the increase in fixed assets less $4 million of cash reduction.

To summarize, OS Distributors expects to generate internally $15 million in 1997, and its funding needs are expected to amount to $20 million during that period. To bridge the gap, OS Distributors will have to raise $5 million.

If OS Distributors is like most firms, it will raise the $5 million it needs through borrowing. Exhibit 9.3 shows aggregate figures on the funding structures of nonfinancial firms in seven countries. Note that more than half of the funds needed to finance new investments are generated by the firm's own activities with the balance mostly raised through borrowing. Indeed, firms rarely issue new equity. They seem to rely primarily on borrowed funds to cover their cash deficits. Possible reasons for this behavior are examined in Chapter 11. Other statistics show that 60 to 80 percent of total funds available are used to finance capital expenditures with the balance going to finance investment in working capital requirement and cash holdings.

The rest of this chapter explains how firms raise external funds. These funds are raised through the **financial system,** so we begin with a description of the structure of that system and the functions it performs.

EXHIBIT 9.3   Sources of External Financing in Seven Countries (1984-1991).[1]

COUNTRY	INTERNAL FUNDING AS A FRACTION OF TOTAL FUNDING[2]	COMPOSITION OF EXTERNAL FUNDING	
		NET DEBT ISSUANCE[3]	NET EQUITY ISSUANCE[4]
United States	77%	134%	−34%
Germany	67%	87%	13%
Italy	67%	65%	35%
France	65%	39%	61%
Canada	58%	72%	28%
United Kingdom	51%	72%	28%
Japan	44%	85%	15%
Average	61% (All countries)	74% (Excluding the U.S.)	26% (Excluding the U.S.)

[1] Adapted from Ragan and Zingales (*Journal of Finance: December 1995*) based on OECD data for the group of seven (G7) countries, excluding financial companies.

[2] Internal funding as a percentage of total *net* funding (the sum of internal funding, net debt issuance, and net equity issuance).

[3] Net debt issuance is total short-term and long-term debt issuance less debt repayments. The 134 percent figure for the United States indicates that in this country companies issued debt to repurchase equity.

[4] Equity issuance includes the issue of both common and preferred stock and the conversion of debt into equity. Net equity issuance is equal to equity issuance less equity reduction. The negative figure for the United States indicates that in this country companies repurchased more equity than they raised.

THE FINANCIAL SYSTEM: ITS STRUCTURE AND FUNCTIONS

The fundamental role of a financial system is to act as a conduit through which the cash surplus of "savers" is channeled to firms that need cash. A financial system that performs this cash transfer role efficiently, that is, cheaply, rapidly, and safely, is a major driver of sustained corporate growth. Without a financial system, entrepreneurs would have to finance their activities exclusively with their own savings and their firm's internally generated funds. The financial system provides another option by allowing firms with a cash shortage to tap the cash surplus sectors of the economy. Most of that surplus is supplied by the **household sector,** individuals who, on aggregate, save more than they consume. In addition, firms with temporary excess cash may lend it to cash deficit firms for *short* periods of time. All the household sector's savings does not go to cash starved firms, however. Companies usually compete for funds with governments that need to finance budget deficits.

The various components of the financial system and the way they interact are summarized in Exhibit 9.4. The cash deficit firms that want to raise funds are on the right side. (We have excluded the cash deficit governments because our focus is on the fund-raising activities of firms.) The suppliers of capital, mostly the household sector, are on the left side. The institutions and processes that facilitate the transfer of funds between these two groups constitute what we call the financial system. To understand how the financial system operates, we examine the two alternative financing channels, known as **direct** and **indirect financing,** through which the excess funds of the cash surplus sector move to firms with a cash shortage.

DIRECT FINANCING

The most obvious way for firms to raise money is to get it *directly* from savers by selling them securities for cash. A **security** is a certificate issued by a firm that specifies the conditions under which the firm has received the money. For an equity security, called a share of **stock,** the certificate recognizes an *ownership* position in the firm. It provides the holder with a *residual* claim (after all contractual claims have been settled) to the firm's earnings and assets and entitles the holder to vote on matters brought up at shareholder meetings, such as the selection of the firm's board of directors. For a debt security, called a **bond,** the certificate acknowledges a *creditor* relationship with the firm. It provides the holder with a *priority* claim (before shareholders) to the firm's earnings and assets. A bond certificate stipulates the conditions and terms under which the money was borrowed, including the amount borrowed, the duration of the loan, the interest rate the firm must pay, any restrictions on the use of the money, and the rights of the lender if the firm defaults on its obligation. When a security is **negotiable,** it can be traded in the **securities markets,** shown at the center of Exhibit 9.4 and described in the following section. The methods employed by firms to sell securities to potential buyers are examined in a later section.

EXHIBIT 9.4   The Financial System.

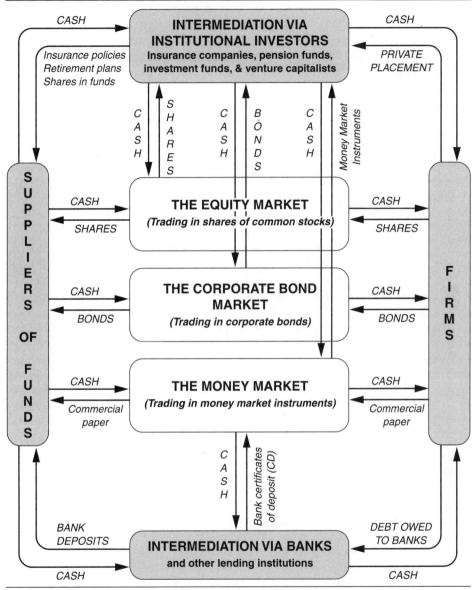

INDIRECT OR INTERMEDIATED FINANCING

Although direct financing may make a lot of sense, many firms are not able to access the financial markets to sell their securities directly to investors. This is the case for many newly established firms and for firms that are too small to issue a sufficiently large amount of securities to appeal to investors. Investors are generally reluctant to buy the securities of little-known firms or firms with relatively small amounts of shares either because it is difficult to assess the risk of the issuer or because the securities do not have much **liquidity,** meaning that they cannot be sold rapidly at a price that is close to their perceived fair value. These firms must rely on *indirect* or *intermediated* financing to raise equity and debt capital. Sometimes, large, well-established firms also rely on indirect financing, particularly to raise short-term funds.

Indirect financing refers to raising capital through **financial intermediaries,** institutions such as commercial banks, insurance companies, pension funds, and venture capital firms that act as agents between the ultimate recipients of capital (the firms with a cash shortage) and the ultimate providers of capital (the cash surplus households). Commercial banks typically offer short- to medium-term loans—terms of one day to ten years. Longer term debt and equity capital can be obtained through **private placement** of securities, usually with insurance companies, pension funds, or venture capital firms, the latter specializing in supplying equity to recently established firms with limited track records.

To see how financial intermediation works, consider a commercial bank. As shown on the bottom of Exhibit 9.4, a bank gets cash from depositors in the form of checking and savings accounts and from investors to whom it sells short-term securities, also called **negotiable certificates of deposit** or **CDs.** The bank then lends these funds to firms by extending short- to medium-term loans.

Note the fundamental difference between direct and indirect financing. In direct financing, ultimate savers hold securities (bonds and stocks) issued by *firms.* In indirect financing, ultimate savers hold securities issued by *banks,* such as checking and savings accounts and CDs. Bank intermediated financing is important because it *facilitates* and *increases* the flow of funds between ultimate savers and cash deficient firms. Individual savers may be reluctant to lend their excess cash directly to firms (will they get their money back?), but find it convenient to deposit their cash in a bank that can then lend it to firms. Banks offer **indirect securities,** such as bank deposits, that are attractive to savers because they can be opened with relatively small amounts of money, they are safe and generally insured by the government, and they can usually be withdrawn on demand. Banks extend loans that are convenient to firms because these loans involve relatively large amounts of money that can be borrowed rapidly for several years and can be renegotiated if the firm encounters some difficulties. Of course, banks must be compensated for performing this intermediation function. Their reward is the difference, or spread, between the interest rate they offer depositors and the higher rate they charge on the loans they extend to firms.

Financing via intermediaries is the dominant channel through which companies raise money. Exhibit 9.5 shows the relative share of assets held by different financial institutions in the United States. Note (1) the rise in the dollar value, though not adjusted for inflation, of financial assets held by financial institutions and (2) the decline in the share of financial assets held by banks and the corresponding rise in the share held by insurance companies, pension funds, and investment funds. Since the early eighties, nonbanking institutions have held the bulk of

EXHIBIT 9.5   **Relative Share of Assets Held by Financial Institutions in the United States from 1860 to 1993.**[1]

TYPE OF FINANCIAL INTERMEDIARY	1860	1900	1939	1970	1980	1993
Banks[2]	89%	81%	65%	58%	56%	35%
Insurance companies[3]	11	14	27	19	16	17
Pension funds	0	0	2	13	17	24
Investment funds	0	0	2	4	4	15
Other	0	5	4	6	7	9
Total (percentage)	100%	100%	100%	100%	100%	100%
Total (billion dollars)	$1	$16	$129	$1,328	$4,025	$13,952

[1] Adapted from Kaufman and Mote, *Economic Perspectives* (pp. 2-21, May/June 1994) Federal Reserve Bank of Chicago.
[2] Includes commercial and savings banks.
[3] Includes life and property and casualty insurance companies.

the securities issued by firms. They purchase them directly from firms or buy them in the securities markets with the cash they receive from ultimate savers.[2] As shown in the upper part of Exhibit 9.4, these savers receive insurance policies, retirement plans, and shares in investment funds in exchange. Nonbanking intermediaries offer insurance and pension products to savers and, in the case of investment funds, convenient and cheap access to the securities markets, risk diversification, and investment management.

Why would a firm borrow from a bank if it can sell debt securities to nonbanking institutions or individual investors? This question brings up a subtle function performed by banks, called *monitoring*. To understand what this function achieves, think of the problem investors face when they consider buying bonds. They wonder whether the issuing firm has told them everything about its ability to service its debt. What if the firm has withheld information that would indicate some potential difficulties in repaying the borrowed funds? Investors try to protect themselves by imposing protective **covenants** in the written contract between the bond issuer and the lenders, known as **indenture.** These covenants would, for example, require the firm to maintain a minimum amount of working capital and restrict its ability to sell assets, pay dividends, or issue new debt. But covenants are not as good as an insider watching over managers' shoulders and preventing them from taking actions that are detrimental to the debtholders. A bank is expected to be this insider. In performing this task, the bank is playing a

[2] With the exception of the United Kingdom, the predominance of banks among financial institutions is generally more pronounced in other countries than in the United States. However, the trends observed in the United States are also at work in other developed countries around the world.

monitoring role that provides bond buyers with additional protection. In other words, although large firms can sell debt securities directly to investors, they are willing to borrow from banks and pay higher rates to reassure the potential buyers of their bonds. In this case, the firm's choice is not between borrowing from a bank or issuing debt securities. Some bank borrowing may be needed to facilitate the firm's access to the debt market.

SECURITIES MARKETS

We now turn to the description of the markets in which debt and equity securities are issued and then traded among investors. Securities markets, shown at the center of Exhibit 9.4, can be classified along several dimensions: whether they are primary or secondary markets, whether they trade equity or debt securities, whether they are organized or over-the-counter markets, and whether they are domestic (within one country) or international (outside the reach of domestic regulators).

Primary versus secondary markets

Primary markets are the markets in which newly issued securities are sold to investors for the first time. When a firm sells equity securities to the general public for the first time, the issue is called an **initial public offering (IPO).** When the firm returns to the market for another public issue of equity, usually a few years later, the process is referred to as a **seasoned issue.** A seasoned issue is not the same as a **secondary public offering,** or a **secondary distribution,** which is the sale to the public of a relatively large block of equity held by an investor who acquired it earlier directly from the firm. An example of a secondary public offering would be the public sale by the Ford Foundation of a block of shares it received initially from the Ford Motor Company.

After they are issued, securities are traded in the **secondary market,** where they are bought and sold by investors. These transactions no longer provide cash to the issuing firm. The securities are exchanged among investors at a price established by the interaction of demand and supply. In the process, the market performs two important functions: It enables the quoted prices to reflect all publicly available information and it provides the liquidity required to facilitate transactions. These functions are performed through the continuous trading of securities among investors on the basis of **fair prices,** prices that can be observed during the time the markets are open and that allow potential buyers and sellers to quickly trade securities and settle their transactions at a relatively low cost.

What exactly are fair prices? The answer to this question can easily fill in an entire chapter. Suffice it to say that there is an extensive body of accumulated empirical evidence indicating that well-developed *market* economies have reasonably **efficient securities markets,** meaning that security prices in these markets reflect all available *public* information regarding the firm that has issued the securities. In other words, they are fair prices in the sense that they provide the best *estimate* of the true, but *unobservable,* value of a firm's securities. The existence of a secondary market is critical for the trading of the securities issued by corporations because investors are more inclined to purchase securities in the primary market when they know that they can sell them later in an active and efficient secondary market.

Equity versus debt markets

Equity securities, or shares in firms' stock, are traded in the equity, or **stock markets.** These markets, shown on the center of Exhibit 9.4, can be either **organized stock exchanges** or **over-the-counter (OTC) markets.** The former are regulated markets and allow firms to list their securities only if the firms meet a number of stringent conditions.[3] In an organized stock exchange, shares are traded by **members of the exchange,** who may act as **dealers** or as **brokers.** Dealers trade shares that they own; brokers trade on behalf of a third party and do not own the traded shares. **Unlisted securities,** usually shares of small companies, trade in over-the-counter markets.[4] These markets do not require companies to meet the listing requirements of organized exchanges. In OTC markets, shares are traded through dealers connected by a telephone and computer network rather than on the floor of an organized exchange.

In most developed countries, the bulk of the trading in the stock markets is done by **institutional investors.** The activities of institutional investors provide an example of another type of financial intermediation, illustrated at the top of Exhibit 9.4: an insurance company or a pension fund issues indirect securities to ultimate savers; insurance policies in the former case and pension contracts in the latter. The funds collected are then invested in securities issued by cash deficit firms. These securities can be purchased either in the financial markets or directly from the issuing firm. The latter channel, private placement, shown on the upper right side of Exhibit 9.4, is discussed in the next section.

Debt securities trade in the debt or **credit markets.** Credit markets are usually identified by the maturity of the debt securities that are traded in them. Debt securities with an **original maturity** not exceeding one year, known as **money market instruments,** are issued and traded in the **money market. Corporate notes** have maturities ranging from one to ten years and **corporate bonds** have maturities exceeding ten years; these securities trade in the **bond market.**[5] Two

---

[3]They must have a minimum acceptable number of publicly held shares, a certain asset size, and a history of dividend payments and must publish financial reports that provide relevant and timely information.

[4]The shares of some large companies are traded in the OTC markets. For example, Microsoft shares were first issued in a OTC market and the firm has chosen to remain there.

[5]The term *financial markets* usually refers to all security markets while the term *capital market* usually refers to the market for long-term securities only, that is, equity and debt securities with a maturity exceeding one year. Thus, financial markets can be divided into capital and money markets and capital markets can be divided into equity and bond markets.

money market instruments are shown in Exhibit 9.4: Certificates of deposit issued by banks, which are mentioned earlier in the discussion of financial intermediation, and **commercial paper (CP),** which is issued by firms with high credit standing to raise short-term debt from the market as an alternative to borrowing short-term from banks. The volume of securities issued in the U.S. financial markets in 1990, 1992, and 1994 is reported in Exhibit 9.6. Note the growth in the volume of securities issued during the early nineties and the dominance of debt instruments over common stocks, preferred stocks, and convertible securities.[6]

Domestic versus international markets

Large and well-established firms can raise funds outside their domestic financial markets by selling their securities in the domestic markets of another country. These foreign securities can be denominated in the currency of the foreign country or in the currency of the issuer's country. For example, a U.S. company can

EXHIBIT 9.6   Securities Issued in the U.S. and the International Markets.
Figures in billions of dollars

TYPE OF SECURITY	1990		1992		1994	
Issued in the U.S. Markets						
1. Debt instruments	$110		$319		$374	
Investment-grade debt		$109		$281		$342
Speculative-grade debt		1		38		32
2. Common stocks	14		57		56	
Seasoned issues		9		33		28
IPOs		5		24		28
3. Preferred stocks (nonconvertible)	4		21		10	
4. Convertible debt and preferred stocks	5		15		11	
Total (1 to 4)	$133		$412		$451	
Issued worldwide (including the U.S.)						
1. Eurobonds	172		269		324	
2. Foreign bonds	26		67		83	
3. Euro common stocks	21		18		32	
4. Other Euro securities	10		4		10	
Total (1 to 4)	$229		$358		$449	

Source: Adapted from issues of *Investment Dealers' Digest.*

[6]These securities and the distinction between investment-grade and speculative-grade debt instruments are examined later in the chapter.

sell **foreign bonds** in the Japanese corporate bond market denominated either in Japanese yen or in U.S. dollars.[7]

Alternatively, a firm can sell bonds in the **Euromarket,** a market that is outside the direct control and jurisdiction of the issuer's country of origin. For example, a U.S. company can sell **Eurobonds** denominated either in U.S. dollars (**Eurodollar bonds**) or Japanese yen (**Euroyen bonds**) to German, French, and Japanese investors simultaneously. In this situation, a group of international banks act as selling agents through, for example, British investment accounts. Eurobonds, which are sold outside the holder's country of residence, are **bearer bonds** and are not subject to the laws, taxes, and regulations that affect domestic issues.[8] As a result, firms can issue Eurobonds at a lower rate than that on an equivalent taxable bond sold in their domestic market or in the domestic market of another country.

If a company issues bonds in a foreign denominated currency, it will be exposed to the risk of unexpected movements in the value of the foreign currency, a risk known as **currency** or **foreign exchange risk.** This risk is examined in detail in Chapter 13.

In addition to foreign bonds and Eurobonds, other securities in international markets include foreign equity (stocks sold in a foreign country), **Euroequity** (stocks sold in the Euromarkets), and **Eurocommercial paper** (EuroCP). The first two are the equity equivalent of foreign and Eurobonds and the third is the Euromarket variation of domestic CP.

The currency in which securities issued outside the jurisdiction of a particular country are denominated is usually referred to as a **eurocurrency.** You have certainly heard of eurodollars, euromarks, or eurofrancs. These are not new currencies and their exchange value is the same as that of their underlying currency. For example, the value of one eurodollar is just the value of one U.S. dollar. However, securities denominated in eurocurrencies are not subject to the regulations and taxes prevailing in the country of origin. The bottom of Exhibit 9.6 reports the volume of securities issued in the international markets. Note that between 1990 and 1994, the dollar value of the securities sold outside the domestic markets of the issuers doubled.

HOW FIRMS ISSUE SECURITIES

Firms can sell their debt and equity securities to the public at large through a **public offering,** or they can sell them to **qualified investors** (individuals and financial institutions that meet some minimum standards set by regulatory authorities) through a private placement. Both distribution channels are usually regulated. In the United States, the regulatory agency is the **Securities and**

---

[7]If the bonds are denominated in yen, they are called **Samurai bonds.** They are called **Shogun bonds** if they are denominated in U.S. dollars. Bonds issued by foreign firms in the United States (denominated in U.S. dollars or other currencies) are called **Yankee bonds.**

[8]The holder's name does not appear on a bearer bond. Domestic bonds are usually **registered bonds** and identify the holder's name.

Exchange Commission (SEC). Most countries with developed securities markets have institutions that perform similar functions. The reasons why some firms choose private placement and the mechanisms through which securities are distributed in a public issue are discussed in this section.

PRIVATE PLACEMENT

A firm that chooses to sell securities privately can have the issue tailored to meet specific needs, such as the option to renegotiate the issue in response to unexpected events. Further, contrary to a public issue, a private placement does not have to be registered with a government agency, which is a costly process. Clearly, private placement provides a firm with a flexible, discreet, and speedy method of raising funds. The drawback is that the absence of organized trading in privately placed securities makes it difficult for the investors who subscribed to the issue to easily resell the securities. As a result, it is generally more expensive for a firm to place its securities privately than to issue them to the public at large. Even so, this may be the only way little-known companies can raise cash.

PUBLIC OFFERINGS

Relatively large firms can offer their securities to the public after they have registered them with a government agency that approves the issuance and distribution of securities and regulates their subsequent trading on public markets. To help with the public offering process, firms use the services of an **investment bank.**[9] At the earliest stage, the bank advises the firm about the type and amount of securities it should be issuing. Then, the bank seeks the approval of all the supervising government agencies, determines an appropriate selling price for the securities (a price that is both acceptable to the firm and attractive to buyers), and determines the best period of time for the offering. Finally, the bank ensures that the securities are purchased by investors by stimulating widespread interest in the offering. The last step, which involves the marketing and distribution of the securities to the public, is the most important function played by the bank in a public offering.

We illustrate this process using a new equity issue, as shown in Exhibit 9.7. Aside from a private placement, a firm can offer its shares to any interested buyer through a **general cash offering** or can offer its shares exclusively to its *existing* stockholders through a **rights offering.**

General cash offerings

In a general cash offering, the investment bank can either do its best to sell the securities on behalf of the firm, or it can buy the securities and then resell them to

---

[9]Firms may also use the services of investment banks to help them place their securities privately.

EXHIBIT 9.7 Alternative Methods Used by Firms and Their Investment Banks to Distribute Equity Securities.

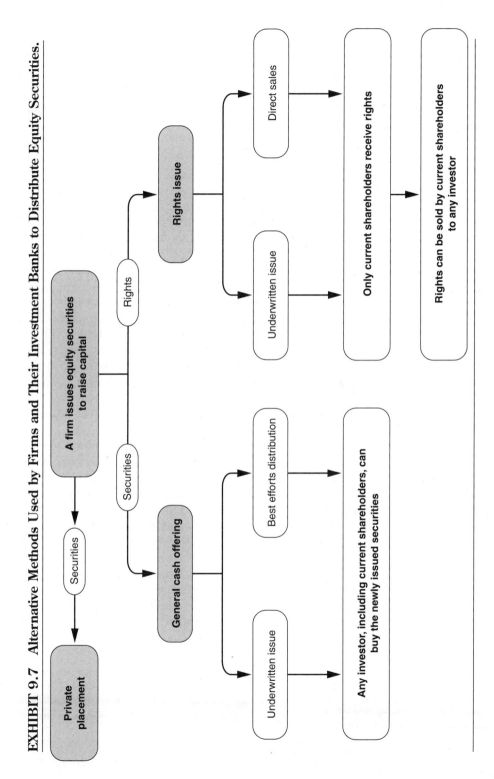

the public *at its own risk.* In the first case, the bank acts as an agent for the firm, distributing securities on a **best efforts basis.** In a best efforts deal, if the bank fails to distribute a predetermined minimum number of shares during a specified period of time, the offering is canceled.

In the second case, the bank is said to act as an **underwriter.** When an issue is underwritten, the bank buys the securities from the firm in order to resell them to the public at a higher price. The **spread** between the price at which the issue is sold to the public and the price paid to the issuing firm is the bank's compensation. Studies of underwritten equity issues in the United States indicate that the spread is between two and eight percent of the value of the issue, depending on its size and quality, and the market conditions. To reduce the risk of being unable to sell the securities at a profit and to reach as many potential buyers as possible, the bank that has initiated the deal, called the **originating house, lead manager** or **bookrunner,** forms an **underwriting syndicate** with other investment banks.[10] The originating house then sells some of the securities to the members of the syndicate, which they in turn sell to the public. To further broaden and speed distribution, a **selling group** is also formed to bring in additional investment banks that agree to sell the securities allocated to them for a fee (members of the selling group do not act as underwriters). If needed, during the distribution period, the members of the underwriting group may buy the security in the open market in order to support its price and ensure the success of the offering. How is the spread shared among the various intermediaries? In a typical transaction in the United States, the originating house receives 15 to 20 percent of the spread, 20 to 30 percent goes to the members of the underwriting syndicate, and the balance is paid to members of the selling group as a **selling concession.**

Although new issues of equity and debt are generally underwritten, there are many cases when securities are distributed on a best efforts basis. Issues sold this way usually fall into two extreme categories. One category includes small and risky firms that are involved in initial public offerings for which investment banks are reluctant to bear the underwriting risk; the other category includes large and well-established companies whose strength and reputation allows them to issue securities that are not underwritten, thus saving the underwriting commission and related expenses.

An investment bank that underwrites a securities issue is providing more than a mechanism to sell securities. The bank is also telling the market that it believes that the securities are of sufficient quality, otherwise it would not have underwritten them. In other words, the bank is playing a **certification role.** Clearly, top quality firms may not need this seal of approval. And, banks may be reluctant to "certify"

---

[10]It is worth pointing out that the underwriting risk in the United States is not very high because the price of the issue is usually set the day before the offering is made. Any price risk prior to that day is actually borne by the issuer, not the investment bank. In the United Kingdom, however, the underwriting risk is higher because the price is announced two to three weeks before the issue is available for trading.

the securities of risky firms fearing that if the issue turns out to be a failure, their reputation may be damaged.

Rights issues

When a firm sells common stocks exclusively to *new* investors, it obviously reduces the fraction of the firm's equity held by its *existing* shareholders. One way to prevent this **dilution** of property rights is to give existing shareholders the right to buy the portion of a new stock issue that will preserve their fractional ownership.[11] The charters of most European companies require them to raise equity capital through rights issues only. This is not the case in the United States, where firms usually issue shares through general cash offers.

We illustrate the mechanics of a rights offering using an example that ignores issuance costs for the sake of simplicity. Suppose Pacific Engines Corporation (PEC) has just announced that it will issue one million new shares of common stock through a rights issue at the **subscription price** of $80. (The subscription price is the selling price of the new shares.) Prior to the announcement, PEC shares were trading at $100 and there were 4 million shares outstanding. Next, PEC will notify its shareholders that they are granted one **right** for every share they hold and that the rights will expire at a specific future date (usually three weeks after the offer date). Before that date, the shares are usually referred to as **rights-on shares;** afterwards, they are called **ex-rights shares.** Shareholders can exercise their rights and subscribe to the issue, they can sell their rights to interested investors if they do not want to buy new shares, or they can do nothing and let the rights expire.

There are several questions to answer at this point: (1) Why is the subscription price ($80) set below the market price prevailing immediately before the announcement of the rights issue ($100)? (2) How many rights are needed to buy one new share? (3) What will happen to the share price when the shares become ex-right shares and what is the value of one right? (4) What impact does the issue have on the wealth of existing shareholders? (5) What is the role played by investment banks in a rights offer?

Setting an Appropriate Subscription Price   The subscription price ($80) is set below the market price ($100) because the rights offer is good for a period of three to four weeks. If the market price falls below the subscription price by the time the offer expires, no rational shareholder will exercise the right to buy a share for more than its prevailing market price. Thus, to ensure the success of the issue, the firm must set the subscription price at a sufficiently large discount to reduce the risk that the market price may drop *below* the subscription price during the period the offer is outstanding.

---

[11]Rights offerings can only be used for seasoned issues and not for IPOs because in the latter case there are no *outside* shareholders to whom the securities can be sold.

Number of Rights Required to Buy One New Share   There were 4 million shares outstanding before the issue was announced, so there will be 4 million rights granted by PEC. This represents 4 rights per new share issued (4 million "old" shares divided by 1 million new shares). In other words, any investor, including the current shareholders, will need to own 4 rights to be able to buy 1 new share. Generalizing, if N_0 is the number of "old" shares and N_n is the number of new shares, the number of rights required to acquire one new share is $N = N_0/N_n$.

The Ex-rights Price of a Share and the Value of a Right   Before the offer was announced, a shareholder who owned four shares had a holding worth $400 (4 times $100). Because she holds four rights, she now has the opportunity to get a fifth share for $80. If she purchases the share, she will have five PEC shares worth $480 ($400 + $80). It follows that the price of a share after the offer will no longer be $100 but $96 ($480 divided by 5). The only difference between the $100 shares and the $96 shares is that the former are rights-on shares (they have a right attached to them) and the latter are ex-rights shares (they no longer carry rights). Consequently, the $4 difference between the two prices represents the price of a right.

To generalize the results, if N is (as above) the number of rights required to buy one new share, the ex-rights price is given by the following formula:

$$\text{Ex-rights price} = \frac{N \times \text{rights-on price} + \text{subscription price}}{N + 1} \qquad (9.2)$$

and the value of a right is the difference between the rights-on price and the ex-rights price:

$$\text{Value of one right}^{12} = \text{Rights-on price} - \text{Ex-rights price} \qquad (9.3)$$

Effect of the Rights Issue on the Wealth of Existing Shareholders   A right is an option issued by the firm to its existing shareholders, giving them the privilege, but *not* the obligation, to buy shares of the firm at a fixed price (the subscription price) over a fixed period of time (the life of the right). This is known as a **call option.** As already mentioned, a shareholder who has received rights can exercise them and buy new shares at the subscription price, or can sell them to other investors, or can let the rights "die."

Whether the shareholder exercises his option by tendering his rights to buy new shares or sells his option, his initial wealth will not change, as shown in Exhibit 9.8. Starting with an initial holding of $480 that includes four PEC shares and $80 in cash, an investor will end up with the same amount of wealth. Only when the shareholder lets his rights expire (usually by ignorance or because the

---

[12]Using the ex-rights price given by equation 9.2, the value of one right is:

$$\text{Value of one right} = \frac{\text{Rights-on price} - \text{Subscription price}}{N + 1} = \frac{\$100 - \$80}{4 + 1} = \frac{\$20}{5} = \$4$$

EXHIBIT 9.8   **Effect of Rights Issue on Wealth of Existing Shareholder.**

INITIAL WEALTH	DECISION	ENDING WEALTH		
	Case 1:	5 shares @ $96	= $480	
	Tender four rights and	Cash	=	0
	buy one new share @ $80	Total	= $480	
Four shares @ $100 = $400				
Cash = 80				
Total = $480	**Case 2:**	4 shares @ $96	= $384	
	Sell 4 rights @ $4 each	Cash ($80 + $16) =	96	
		Total	= $480	

expiration date has passed before he could exercise or sell them), will his wealth be affected by the issue because the rights are then worthless.

The Role of Investment Banks in Rights Offerings   In a rights offering, a firm can sell shares directly to its shareholders (and some firms do) but there is always the possibility that the market price may fall below the subscription price or that some investors may not exercise their rights to buy the new shares. To avoid this situation, the firm can arrange a **standby agreement** with an underwriting syndicate of investment banks. The syndicate agrees to buy any shares that have not been sold during the period the rights offering is outstanding at the subscription price less a **take-up fee.** In this case, investment banks underwrite only the unsold portion of the rights offering for a **standby fee.**

Issuance costs of public offerings

U.S. data indicate that issuance costs of public offerings, measured as a percentage of the gross amount raised, are higher for small issues than for large ones. Furthermore, rights offerings are less expensive than underwritten issues, and a rights offering without standby agreements is the least expensive method for firms to raise new equity capital.

DEBT CAPITAL: CHARACTERISTICS AND VALUATION

We now examine the alternative sources of debt financing available to firms and show how to value the debt securities issued by companies. For most firms, the primary source of borrowed funds is bank loans. These loans can be supplemented by leasing contracts and, for relatively large firms with high credit standing, by the issue of commercial paper and corporate bonds.

BORROWING THROUGH BANK LOANS

Bank loans, particularly short-term loans, are the dominant source of debt. If a firm cannot access the corporate debt markets, then bank loans (short-term, medium-term, and long-term) are the only source of borrowed funds.

Short-term bank loans

Firms that need to finance the seasonal buildup in their working capital requirement usually resort to short-term bank loans. These loans are described as **self-liquidating loans** because banks expect firms to repay the loans with the cash that will be released by the subsequent reduction in working capital requirement. For example, a company selling toys will need to borrow to finance the buildup of its inventory prior to the holiday season. After the goods are sold, some of the collected cash will be used to repay the bank loan. These loans can be extended for several months, after which they must be repaid or renewed for another period. To ensure that the loan is not used to fund long-term investments, banks usually impose a **cleanup clause** that requires the firm to be completely out of debt to the bank for a least one month during the year.

Short-term bank loans are often **unsecured loans,** meaning that the firm does not have to provide any assets as **collateral,** or guarantee, in case of default. When a short-term loan is a secured loan, assets such as accounts receivable and inventories are pledged as collateral. There are three forms of unsecured loans that are commonly used: (1) a **transaction loan** is a one-time loan used to finance a specific, nonrecurrent need; (2) a **line of credit** is a nonbinding arrangement in which the bank lends the firm a stated amount of money over a fixed, but renewable, period of time, usually a year; and (3) a **revolving credit agreement** is the same as a line of credit, except that the bank is *legally committed* to lend the money, a guarantee for which the bank charges a commitment fee on the unused portion of the credit line.

All these loans are extended at the **bank prime rate** (the reference rate for pricing loans to domestic borrowers) plus a spread over prime to reflect the specific credit risk of a particular firm. For example, if the prime rate is 7 percent, a firm that does not have a high credit standing may have to borrow at 9 percent, a 2 percent spread over prime.

Medium- and long-term loans

Medium- to long-term loans are extended by banks and insurance companies and are known as **term loans.** Their duration is between one and ten years and they are usually repaid in equal periodic installments that include the loan reimbursement as well as interest on the loan, a repayment schedule known as an **annuity.** Contrary to most short-term loans, term loans are backed by collateral, that is, the firm must provide the lender with assets in order to secure the loan. For example, a **mortgage loan** is backed by real estate while an **equipment financing loan,** which is often extended by the **captive finance subsidiary** of the equipment manufacturer, is backed by the piece of machinery. These types of loans are also known as **asset-based borrowing.** A popular alternative to term loans is lease financing.

BORROWING THROUGH LEASE AGREEMENTS

Leasing is an alternative source of debt capital that allows firms to finance the *use* of assets—such as computers, copiers, trucks, utility vehicles, or aircraft—without actually owning them. It is estimated that there is as much equipment financed with leasing as through any other source of capital.

A lease is a contractual agreement between the owner of the asset, known as the **lessor,** and the user of the asset, known as the **lessee.** The agreement indicates that the lessee has the right to use the asset in exchange for periodic payments to the lessor. The lessor can be a manufacturer, a financial institution, or an independent leasing company. When the lessor is not the manufacturer, the asset is sold by the manufacturer to the lessor who, in turn, leases it to the lessee. When the contract expires, the asset is returned to the lessor, or, if the contract gives the lessee the option of purchasing the asset, the lessee may decide to buy it.

This section describes two of the most common types of leases: **operating leases** and **financial leases.** Then, after showing that a long-term lease is just another way of borrowing and using the proceeds to purchase the leased asset, we present a procedure for analyzing a leasing-versus-borrowing decision, using a long-term equipment lease as an illustration.

Operating leases

An operating lease is a short-term lease that usually, but not always, has the following characteristics. First, the length of the contract is shorter than the useful life of the asset, which means that the lessor must re-lease the asset or sell it at the expiration of the contract to recover its full cost. Second, the lessor is responsible for the maintenance and insurance costs while the asset is leased. Third, the lessee has the right to cancel the lease contract before it expires. This option is particularly valuable to the lessee when the asset leased is a piece of equipment that can quickly become obsolete due to rapid technological advances. However, to cancel the contract, the lessee may have to pay a cancellation fee.

Financial leases

A financial lease is a long-term lease that differs markedly from an operating lease. It usually extends over most of the useful life of the asset; the lessee, not the lessor, pays the maintenance and the insurance costs; and, generally, it cannot be canceled.

Most financial leases are one of the following: **direct lease, sale and lease-back,** or **leveraged lease.** A direct lease is a contract between the lessee and the owner of the asset. The owner can be the manufacturer of the asset or a leasing company that bought the asset from the manufacturer for the purpose of leasing it. Under a sale and leaseback lease, the firm owning the asset sells it to the leasing company which immediately leases it back to the firm. Finally, in a leveraged lease, the leasing company finances the purchase of the asset with a substantial level of debt, using as collateral the lease contract and the **salvage value** of the asset—its value at the end of the lease contract.

Leasing as an alternative to borrowing

Suppose a firm has decided to change ten forklifts used in its plants and is considering leasing the new ones instead of purchasing them. Because the plants will be in operation for many more years, the lease must necessarily be a long-term, or financial, lease. The decision to lease or buy will not affect the way the vehicles are used, their useful life, or the cost of insuring and maintaining them. Thus, the difference between leasing and purchasing is only financial. If the firm decides to lease, it will not incur any initial large cash outlay to buy the equipment. Instead, it will have to make annual payments to the leasing company. If the firm decides to purchase the forklifts, it will incur a large initial cash outlay equal to the purchase price of the new forklifts. In this case, the firm will also have to pay dividends to its shareholders if the investment is financed with equity or make interest payments to its banks and bondholders if it is financed by debt.

Lease payments, like interest payments, are *fixed* obligations. Thus, the *relevant comparison is between lease financing and debt financing,* not equity financing. In other words, a financial lease is just an alternative to borrowing and using the proceeds of the loan to purchase the (leased) assets. This is why financial analysts count leases as debt in calculating a firm's debt ratios.

Deciding whether to lease or borrow

Chapter 6 explains that the best management decisions are those with the highest net present value (NPV) because these decisions will maximize the firm's equity value. One way to apply the NPV rule to the decision of whether to lease or to borrow and buy is to compute the NPV of the *difference* in cash flows between leasing and buying. This NPV is known as the **net advantage to leasing** or **NAL.** If NAL is positive, the asset should be leased; if it is negative, it should be bought.

To illustrate, we return to the firm that needs to replace 10 forklifts. The replacement decision has a positive NPV. The question is whether the firm should lease the equipment or borrow and buy it. If purchased, the cost is $10,000 per vehicle for a total of $100,000. This expenditure will be financed over the equipment's useful life of five years with a $100,000 loan of the same maturity. The interest rate on the loan is 8 percent. The vehicles will be depreciated for fiscal purposes over five years, according to the straight-line method. In other words, the annual depreciation expenses will be $2,000 per vehicle ($10,000 divided by 5) or $20,000 for the whole fleet (10 times $2,000). The *aftertax* scrap or salvage value of each vehicle is estimated at $1,000, meaning that in five year's time the firm should get $10,000 (10 times $1,000) from the sale of the forklifts. The corporate tax rate is 40 percent.

If the firm leases the forklifts, the terms of the lease call for annual payments of $1,500 per vehicle or $15,000 for all of them. The lease payments are payable at the beginning of the year. The firm is responsible for the maintenance and insurance on the vehicles, regardless of whether it leases or buys.

Exhibit 9.9 summarizes the *difference* between the cash flows from leasing the forklifts and the cash flows from buying them. There are four differences in these cash flows. First, there are the *aftertax* annual lease payments, the first one due *immediately* (the "Now" column in the exhibit). The tax rate is 40 percent, so these annual payments will amount to $9,000 (60 percent of $15,000). Second, because the vehicles will be leased, the firm cannot depreciate them for tax purposes. It will therefore *lose* the tax savings that it would have if it owned the equipment. The annual tax saving resulting from the deductibility of annual depreciation expenses amounts to $8,000 ($20,000 multiplied by a tax rate of 40 percent). Third, the firm will not get the $10,000 aftertax scrap value of the vehicles at the end of the fifth year because it will not own the forklifts. Fourth, if the vehicles are leased, the firm will not have to spend $100,000 to buy them.

The initial differential cash flow is positive while those from year 1 to year 5 are negative. This reflects the fact that by leasing the forklifts the firm trades the purchase price of $100,000 for cash outflows in the following five years. Because leasing is comparable to borrowing, the relevant discount rate is simply the aftertax cost of debt, that is, 4.8 percent [8% × (1 − 0.40)]. Discounting the total differential cash flows at 4.8 percent,[13] we found a positive net present value, or net advantage of leasing, of $16,199. Conclusion: Leasing is "cheaper" than borrowing. The firm should lease the forklifts instead of borrowing to buy them.

EXHIBIT 9.9   Summary of Difference in Cash Flows When Forklifts Are Leased Rather Than Purchased.

LEASE VERSUS BUY	NOW	YEAR 1	YEAR 2	YEAR 3	YEAR 4	YEAR 5
Aftertax lease payments	− $9,000	−$9,000	−$9,000	−$9,000	−$9,000	
Loss of tax savings on depreciation		−8,000	−8,000	−8,000	−8,000	−$8,000
Loss of the aftertax scrap value						−10,000
Cash saved because the forklifts are not bought	+100,000					
Total differential cash flows	+$91,000	−$17,000	−$17,000	−$17,000	−$17,000	−$18,000

[13]If the salvage value is uncertain, it should be discounted at a higher rate to adjust for the additional risk.

BORROWING BY ISSUING SHORT-TERM SECURITIES

As mentioned earlier, large firms with high credit standings can raise short-term funds by issuing commercial paper (CP) in their domestic money markets and EuroCP in the Euromarkets. Commercial paper is usually unsecured, that is, the holder has no claim on the firm's income or assets if the issuing firm defaults. However, a CP issue is almost always backed by bank lines of credit, according to which the bank agrees to lend money to the firm to repay the CP when it is due if, at the CP's maturity date, the firm is unable to issue new securities on preferential terms to repay the maturing paper.

Commercial paper is usually sold in large denominations ($5 million and higher), at a discount from face value, and with a maturity of 2 to 270 days in the U.S. market and up to 360 days in the Euromarkets.[14] The paper can be issued either directly to investors or through brokers specializing in the distribution of commercial paper. In general, firms that are able to access the CP market find this debt instrument slightly cheaper and more flexible than a short-term bank loan.

BORROWING BY ISSUING CORPORATE BONDS

The alternative to borrowing medium and long-term funds through bank loans and lease agreements is to borrow by issuing corporate bonds that can be either sold to the public at large or placed privately. Corporate bonds are long-term securities issued by firms to raise debt capital over periods ranging from 10 years to as many as 100 years, although most corporate bonds are issued with a maturity ranging between 10 and 30 years. As pointed out earlier, issues with a maturity longer than 1 year but shorter than 10 years are usually called corporate notes. For the sake of simplicity in the following discussion, we will not make any distinction between bonds and notes, calling any corporate debt security with a maturity longer than a year a bond.

The issuing firm has a contractual obligation to pay bondholders a fixed annual **coupon payment** over the bond's life and to repay the borrowed funds on the day the bonds have reached their **maturity date.** (Coupon payments are sometimes paid semiannually.) Corporate bonds denominated in U.S. dollars are usually issued at a **par value** or **face value** of $1,000, which is the amount of money that the firm must repay at maturity.[15]

Suppose that Allied Equipment Corporation (AEC) issues 50,000 bonds with a par value of $1,000, a maturity date of five years, and a **coupon rate** of 8 percent. The buyer of one bond will receive a coupon payment of $80 each year (8 percent of $1,000) and will receive $1,000 at the end of the fifth year. If the bond is held to maturity, the holder earns an annual rate of return equal to the 8 percent coupon

---

[14]The terms *price discount, face value,* and *maturity* are explained in the following section on corporate bonds.

[15]The par value is also called the **nominal value** or **principal.**

rate because buying the bond is equivalent to depositing $1,000 in a bank account, receiving an annual interest rate of 8 percent for five years, and withdrawing the $1,000 at the end of the fifth year. AEC will receive $50 million if the bonds are priced at par value; in reality, it will receive a little bit less because of **flotation costs.** AEC will receive less than $50 million if the bonds are offered at a discount. For example, if the **original price discount** is 4.5 percent, the bonds will sell at $955 apiece (4.5 percent less than the par value) and AEC will receive $47.75 million before flotation costs.[16]

Security, seniority, sinking funds, and call provisions

Corporate bonds are usually issued with a number of provisions attached to them that provide specific rights to either the bond buyer or the issuing firm. The buyer is protected by the bond's security, seniority, and sinking funds provisions. The issuing firm is protected against a possible drop in interest rates by a call provision.

Security The issuer of a **secured bond** has provided collateral to the lender. For example, a firm issuing a **mortgage bond** offers as collateral the property it buys with the cash raised from the sale of the bond. If the firm fails to service the bond, the lenders, acting through their **trustee,** can seize and resell the property. **Unsecured bonds,** sometimes called **debentures,** are supported only by the general credit standing of the issuing firm.[17]

Seniority A **senior bond** has a claim on the firm's assets (in the event of liquidation) that precedes the claim of **junior** or **subordinated debt** which, in turn, takes precedence over the claims of the firm's stockholders.

Sinking Fund Provision A **sinking fund provision** requires the bond issuer to set aside cash in a special **trust** account according to a regular schedule. This cash accumulates during the bond's life to allow the firm to either redeem the bonds at maturity or redeem parts of the outstanding bonds before they reach their maturity date. Because the trust is legally separated from the issuer's assets, a sinking fund provision reduces the risk that the issuer will be unable to redeem the bonds at maturity.

Call Provision The issuer of a **callable bond** has the option of redeeming the bond before it reaches its maturity date. For example, suppose AEC issues a five-year, 8.25 percent coupon bond at par ($1,000) that is callable at 2 percent over par ($1,020) any time *after* two years. (In this case, the bond has a **deferred call**

---

[16]Bond prices are usually quoted as a percentage of par value. AEC's bond price will thus be quoted at 95.50 percent of $1,000, which is equivalent to $955 per $1,000 of face value.

[17]This is the terminology used in the United States. In the United Kingdom, debentures refer to secured bonds.

provision.) The call option gives AEC the right to buy the bond from its holder at a **call value** that is 2 percent higher than its par value.

A callable bond is clearly less valuable to its holder than an identical bond that is not callable. The issuer will most likely call the bond when it can issue new ones at a lower coupon rate, thus forcing the holder to replace the original bond with a lower coupon one. This is why the issuer must compensate the holder with a redemption value that exceeds par value and with a higher coupon rate. (AEC's callable bond has a coupon rate of 8.25 percent while the identical noncallable bond has an 8 percent coupon rate.) From the issuer's point of view, the call provision is valuable because it gives the option to retire the bond and refinance at a lower rate if market rates fall. But this option is costly because a callable bond's coupon rate exceeds the rate of an identical, noncallable bond.

Finding the yield of a bond when its price is known

We return to AEC's noncallable bond issue and assume the bonds are sold below par at $955. Although the bond is issued at less than par, it still provides the *buyer* with the same cash-flow stream as if it were issued at par. The bondholder will receive $80 each year for the following four years and will receive $1,080 the fifth year if the bond is kept until maturity (the last $80 coupon plus the $1,000 face value). Thus, the expected return is higher than the 8 percent coupon rate because when the bond is redeemed in five years, the holder will realize a capital gain of $45 ($1,000 less $955). What is this expected return? It is the rate that makes the bond price equal to the *present value* of the bond's future cash-flow stream. This rate is called the bond **market yield, yield to maturity,** or **redemption yield.**[18]

The cash-flow stream expected from the AEC bond is $80 a year for five years plus a principal repayment of $1,000 the fifth year. If y denotes the bond's yield to maturity, the present value of the cash-flow stream as defined in Chapter 6 is:

$$\text{Present value of the cash flows expected from the bond} =$$
$$\frac{\$80}{(1+y)^1} + \frac{\$80}{(1+y)^2} + \frac{\$80}{(1+y)^3} + \frac{\$80}{(1+y)^4} + \frac{\$1,080}{(1+y)^5}$$

Setting the present value of the expected cash flows equal to the bond price of $955, we have:

$$\$955 = \frac{\$80}{(1+y)^1} + \frac{\$80}{(1+y)^2} + \frac{\$80}{(1+y)^3} + \frac{\$80}{(1+y)^4} + \frac{\$1,080}{(1+y)^5}$$

[18]The yield to maturity is the internal rate of return (IRR), as defined in Chapter 7, of the investment in the bond. Thus, a bond's net present value (NPV) calculated at its market yield must be zero because the IRR is the rate that makes the NPV zero. Buying a bond at its market price is thus a zero NPV investment.

This equation could be solved by trial and error to find the yield that makes the present value of the cash-flow stream equal to $955. It is easier to use a financial calculator or a spreadsheet program. Our calculator indicates that the yield is 9.16 percent. This means that investors who buy the bonds at $955 and hold them to maturity can expect to earn a return of 9.16 percent. It also means that AEC is actually borrowing at a cost of 9.16 percent and not at the 8 percent coupon rate or at the bond's **current yield** of 8.38 percent (the $80 coupon payment of the bond divided by its $955 price). The bond market yield (9.16 percent) is higher than its coupon rate (8 percent) because the bond is issued at a price ($955) that is lower than the bond face value ($1,000). The $45 of capital gains at maturity is the reason why the yield exceeds the coupon rate.

Why would AEC issue its bonds at a discount? Why not issue them at par and thus borrow at the 8 percent coupon rate instead of the higher 9.16 percent market yield? AEC cannot issue its bonds at par because firms do not set the yield on their bonds, the market does. The yield of 9.16 percent is the return required by investors to compensate them for the risk of holding a five-year, 8 percent coupon bond issued by Allied Equipment Corporation.

The yield of a bond is determined by its risk

There are two major sources of risk to a bondholder, and the higher these risks, the higher the yield at which the issuing firm will have to sell its bonds. **Market risk,** which reflects the sensitivity of a bond price to changes in market yields, is discussed in a later section. **Credit risk,** or **default risk,** reflects the relative ability of the issuing firm to service its bonds, that is, its perceived capacity to pay the promised coupons on their scheduled dates and to repay the principal on the bond maturity date.

Firms that want to sell their bonds to the public are usually required to first obtain a **credit rating** from a bond rating agency, such as Moody's or Standard and Poor's. That rating provides an overall assessment of the issuer's credit risk. At Standard and Poor's, firms with the highest financial strength are assigned a AAA rating, which is followed by AA, A, and BBB ratings. Bonds that have been assigned one of these four top ratings are known as **investment grade bonds.** They can be purchased by pension funds and other institutional investors without the fear that the issuing firm may run into sudden and unexpected financial trouble. Bonds with lower ratings (BB, B, and CCC) are known as **speculative grade bonds** or **junk bonds.** Their prices are more sensitive to unexpected changes in the firm's financial condition. Thus, they are more risky and investors require higher yields to hold them.

The yield investors require depends on the bond's rating and the rate at which the government is borrowing for the same maturity. The rate for government borrowing is usually the minimum rate for the given maturity because the government cannot *technically* default on debt denominated in its own, domestic, currency (it can always print money to repay investors). An example of the credit risk structure for, say, 10-year bonds is shown in Exhibit 9.10.

EXHIBIT 9.10   Example of Comparison Between Bond Ratings and Market Yields.

BOND RATING	MARKET YIELD	SPREAD OVER GOVERNMENT
Government	7.20%	Zero
AAA	7.45%	0.25% (25 basis points)
A	8.05%	0.85% (85 basis points)
BB	9.25%	2.05% (205 basis points)
CCC	10.70%	3.50% (350 basis points)

The higher the credit risk, the lower the bond rating and the higher the market yield of the bond. Note that the lower the bond rating, the wider its **yield spread** over the government bond with the same maturity (one **basis point** is equal to one hundredth of one percent). The size of the spread is obviously not fixed, it varies over time with changes in market conditions and outlook.

Finding the price of a bond when its yield is known

Suppose that a year has passed since Allied Equipment Corporation issued its five-year, 8 percent coupon bonds. The current maturity of the bonds is four years. Suppose further that you bought a bond for $955 a year ago and that you wish to sell it today. You cannot sell it back to the issuer. You will have to sell it to another investor through the corporate bond market. What price can you expect to receive for your bond? The answer depends on the yield at which *new* corporate bonds, *similar* to yours, are currently being issued. Similar bonds are those with a four-year maturity and with the same risk as the bonds issued by Allied Equipment Corporation. Let's assume that newly issued, four-year corporate bonds with the same credit risk as AEC's bonds are now being issued at par ($1,000) with a 7 percent coupon rate. Thus, investors can earn a 7 percent yield on newly issued, four-year corporate bonds similar to AEC's bonds. But your bond offers a *higher* coupon rate of 8 percent and is, thus, more valuable than the newly issued 7 percent bonds. You should be able to sell it for more than $1,000. The price should be the one at which a buyer will earn a yield of 7 percent on an 8 percent coupon bond. Indeed, by paying *more* than $1,000 for the bond, the buyer will incur a capital *loss* at maturity that will reduce the bond yield to 7 percent.

Earlier, we knew the bond price ($955) and we wanted to find the yield (which we found to be 9.16 percent). Now, we know the yield (7 percent) and we want to find the price. The bond price must be the present value of the remaining four $80 coupons and the $1,000 principal repayment at the end of the fourth year:

$$\text{Bond price} = \frac{\$80}{(1 + 0.07)^1} + \frac{\$80}{(1 + 0.07)^2} + \frac{\$80}{(1 + 0.07)^3} + \frac{\$1,080}{(1 + 0.07)^4} = \$1,033.87$$

Appendix 9.1 shows how to derive the following bond valuation formula, which is much easier to apply than the one above:

$$B = F\left[\frac{c}{y} + \left(1 - \frac{c}{y}\right)\frac{1}{(1 + y)^N}\right]$$ (9.4)

where B is the market price of the bond; F is the face value of the bond; c is the coupon rate; N is the term to maturity; y is the market yield; and $1/(1 + y)^N$ is the present value of one dollar received N years from now and discounted at rate y.

AEC's bond has a face value of $1,000, a coupon rate of 8 percent, a four-year term to maturity and a market yield of 7 percent. According to equation 9.4:

$$B = \$1,000\left[\frac{0.08}{0.07} + \left(1 - \frac{0.08}{0.07}\right)\frac{1}{(1 + 0.07)^4}\right]$$
$$= \$1,000[1.1429 + (1 - 1.1429)0.7629]$$
$$B = \$1,000 \times 1.03387 = \$1,033.87$$

which is the same price found using the original formula.

The bond yield is now *lower* than the coupon rate of the bond, so the bond price is at a $33.87 **premium** over its $1,000 face value. Recall that when the bond price was at a $45 discount from its face value, its 9.16 percent yield was *above* its 7 percent coupon rate. In general, when the yield is *below* the coupon rate the bond price is at a *premium* over face value; when the yield is *above* the coupon rate, the price is at a *discount* from face value.

Zero-coupon bonds

As their name indicates, **zero-coupon bonds** do not pay any coupon payments. Bondholders earn their return on investment entirely through capital gains, that is, the difference between the price at which the bonds are issued and their **redemption value** (their face value or par value). We illustrate with a firm that wishes to issue a 10-year zero-coupon bond.[19] If investors require a 10 percent yield to hold this type of bond, at what price should the bonds be issued if their face value is $1,000?

We can use equation 9.4, the bond valuation formula, to answer the question. Because the coupon rate is zero ($c = 0$), the equation reduces to:

$$B = F\left[\frac{1}{(1 + y)^N}\right] = \$1,000\left[\frac{1}{(1 + 0.10)^{10}}\right] = \$1,000 \times 0.38554 = \$385.54$$ (9.5)

---

[19]The first public issue of a zero-coupon bond in the U.S. market was made in April of 1981 by J.C. Penney (a department store). In June of the same year, Pepsico Overseas issued a three-year zero-coupon Eurobond at 67.25 percent of face value to yield 14.14 percent.

The firm must issue the bonds at an original discount of 61.46 percent of face value ($1,000 less $385.54, divided by $1,000). If it wishes to raise $100 million (before flotation costs), it will have to sell 259,376 bonds ($100 million divided by $385.54).

Perpetual bonds

Perpetual bonds are bonds that never mature; the coupon payments continue forever. This raises the immediate question of whether the issuing entity will be around forever. Because of this uncertainty, *noncallable* perpetual bonds have usually only been issued by governments, such as the British and Canadian governments, although some nongovernment, nonbanking entities have also issued such bonds.[20]

Suppose a firm wishes to raise funds through an issue of perpetual bonds with a 10 percent coupon rate and a $1,000 face value. If investors require a yield of 9.50 percent on this type of corporate bond, what should the issue price be? Again, equation 9.4 provides the answer. In this case, N is infinitely large and the discount factor $\dfrac{1}{(1 + y)^N}$ approaches zero. The formula reduces to the face value multiplied by the ratio of the coupon rate to the market yield:

$$B = F\left[\frac{c}{y}\right] = \$1,000\left[\frac{0.1000}{0.0950}\right] = \$1,000 \times 1.05263 = \$1,052.63 \qquad (9.6)$$

Although perpetual bonds are rarely issued, a number of firms have recently issued bonds with a 100-year maturity.[21] These bonds are, in effect, perpetuals because the present value of their face value is practically worthless today. For example, at the 9.50 percent yield, the $1,000 face value of a 100-year bond is less than 12 cents today.

How changes in market yield affect bond prices

By calculating the price of a bond as a function of its term to maturity, coupon rate, and market yield, we can show how a change in the market yield affects the price of a bond. To illustrate, we examine the price behavior of the three bonds shown in Exhibit 9.11, where the bond prices were calculated according to equations 9.4, 9.5, and 9.6. The first bond is a 10-year, 10 percent coupon bond, the second is a 10-year,

[20]Examples include Canadian railroad companies, and more recently, KLM (the Dutch airline company). In January 1985, KLM offered a first fixed-rate perpetual bond that is repriced every 10 years and callable at any repricing date.
[21]During 1996, more than 40 U.S. companies issued **century bonds,** including IBM.

EXHIBIT 9.11 The Relation Between Market Yields and Bond Prices for Different Types of Bonds.

	COUPON BEARING BOND[1]	ZERO COUPON BOND[2]	PERPETUAL BOND[3]
• **Bond characteristics**			
Coupon rate	10%	0%	10%
Maturity	10 years	10 years	infinite
Face value	$1,000	$1,000	$1,000
• **Bond prices**			
Market yield at:			
9.5%	$1,031.39	$403.51	$1,052.63
10.0%	1,000.00	385.54	1,000.00
10.5%	969.93	368.45	952.38
Sensitivity of the bond prices to changes in the market yield			
$\dfrac{Price_{9.5\%} - Price_{10.5\%}}{Price_{10\%}}$	**6.15%**	**9.09%**	**10.03%**

[1] Bond price calculated according to equation 9.4.
[2] Bond price calculated according to equation 9.5.
[3] Bond price calculated according to equation 9.6.

zero-coupon bond, and the last is a 10 percent perpetual bond. All have a $1,000 face value. Their prices are calculated for three values of the market yield: 9.5 percent, 10 percent, and 10.5 percent. The last row in the exhibit indicates the sensitivity of the price of each of the three bonds to changes in the market yield from 9.5 to 10.5 percent. We can draw several (general) conclusions from the reported price changes resulting from the movement in the market yield:

1. The price of bonds is inversely related to the market yield. (When the yield rises, the prices of *all* bonds fall; when the yield falls, the prices of *all* bonds rise.)
2. The *longer* a bond term to maturity (all else the same), the *higher* the price sensitivity of the bond to a change in market yield. (To see this, compare the 10-year, 10 percent coupon bond to the 10 percent perpetual bond.)
3. The *lower* a bond coupon rate (all else the same), the *higher* the price sensitivity of the bond to a change in market yield. (To see this, compare the 10-year, 10 percent coupon bond to the 10-year, zero-coupon bond.)

Thus, a bond's market risk, which reflects the sensitivity of its price to a change in the market yield, increases when the bond's term to maturity increases or when the bond's coupon rate decreases. If the three bonds shown in Exhibit 9.11 have the same credit risk (assume they are issued by the same firm), then the perpetual bond has more market risk than the zero-coupon bond, which has more market risk than the 10-percent coupon bond.

Floating rate and variable rate bonds

Some corporate bonds are called **floating rate bonds** because they have floating coupon rates; their coupon rates are related to another rate, called the **reference** or **benchmark rate,** that usually changes every six months. The reference rate is often the interest rate at which *international* banks lend U.S. dollars to one another, known as the **London Interbank Offering Rate (LIBOR).** To illustrate, suppose Allied Equipment Company wants to issue five-year bonds but does not wish to pay a fixed coupon rate for the next five years because it expects rates to drop in the future. A **floater** may be the answer. The coupon rate that AEC will pay during the ten consecutive six-month periods in the next five years is the six-month LIBOR prevailing at the beginning of each period, plus a *fixed* spread of, say, 85 basis points (0.85 percent above LIBOR). The five-year floater allows AEC to eliminate its funding risk (the risk of not being able to renew the loan during the five-year period), while still bearing the risk of changing interest rates.

A floating rate bond should not be confused with a **variable rate bond.** The latter is a bond that has a coupon rate set at more than one level; for example, a 15-year bond may have a zero-coupon rate during its first 5 years and have a 10 percent coupon rate during its remaining 10-year life. This pattern of coupon payments is attractive to a firm planning to invest the funds in a long-term project that is not expected to generate positive cash flows before its fifth year.

Convertible bonds

A **convertible bond** can be converted into the firm's common stock at the option of the bondholder. This conversion option, called a **sweetener** or an **equity kicker,** makes these bonds more attractive to investors. At the same time, firms can issue them at a lower rate than bonds without a conversion option. To illustrate, suppose General Metal Corporation (GMC) issues 10-year, 9 percent bonds at $1,000 par value that are convertible into 10 shares of GMC (this is the bond's **conversion ratio**) at a price of $100 per share (this is the **conversion price**). Shares of GMC are currently trading at $80, so the **conversion premium** is 25 percent ($100 less $80, divided by $80) and the bond's **conversion value** is $800 (10 times $80). If GMC issued 10-year straight bonds, it would have to pay a coupon rate of 10 percent. Thus, GMC has reduced its cost of debt by a full percentage point by giving investors the option to convert their bonds into equity.

The value of the conversion option is equal to the difference between the convertible bond value and the value of the bond if it were not convertible, which is called the **bond value** of the convertible. We know the value of the convertible is

$1,000. We can use equation 9.4 to calculate the bond value of the convertible. The bond's face value is $1,000, its coupon rate is 9 percent, its term to maturity is 10, and its yield is 10 percent (the rate it would have had if it were not convertible). Substituting these figures into equation 9.4 provides a bond value of $938.55. Thus, the value of the conversion option is:

$$\text{Option value} = \text{Value of convertible} - \text{Bond value}$$
$$= \$1,000 - \$938.55 = \$61.45$$

The convertible bond that GMC has sold to investors is a 10-year, 9 percent straight bond worth $938.55 plus an option to buy 10 shares of GMC at $100 per share (the option to buy equity) worth $61.45.

Note that the option allows investors to buy shares, currently worth $80, for $100. The option is valuable because there is a chance that GMC's share price will rise above $100 during the next 10 years. If it does, and if it exceeds the convertible bond value, investors will exercise their right to convert and GMC will have to issue equity at $100 in exchange for the bonds. Does the deal make sense for GMC?

If the convertible bond is properly priced, then its option value ($61.45) is the appropriate "payment" that the firm must make in order to lower its cost of debt financing (from 10 percent to 9 percent). The convertible is, in this case, a fair deal that should neither reduce nor enhance the firm's value. Firms do not issue convertibles because the interest cost of a convertible bond is lower than the interest cost of a straight bond. The embedded option gives bondholders the right to convert the bond into the firm's common stock, and we have just shown that this option is valuable to bondholders. As a consequence, they are willing to accept a lower rate of return on the bond portion of the issue. In equilibrium, there should be a perfect trade-off, which explains why the value of the firm should not be affected by a convertible issue.

There are two main reasons why firms may decide to issue convertibles. First, the lower coupon rate of a convertible, as compared to that of a straight bond issue, can be attractive to high growth, high risk, cash starved firms. For these firms, the cash flows from operations may not be high enough to fund their large capital expenditures program. Further, their level of risk may command high interest rates. By issuing convertibles that have lower coupon rates than straight bonds, the pressure on the firm's cash flows can be somewhat relieved and, to some extent, transformed instead into a pressure to generate capital gains for investors.

Second, convertibles may be attractive to bondholders who find it difficult to assess the risk of the firm issuing the securities or who fear that the firm's management may not act in their best interests. The straight bond portion of the convertible package, which obliges the firm to make coupon payments and repay the principal, provides bondholders with some protection if the firm does not do well, and the option to convert the bonds into the firm's stock allows them to share in the increase in the firm's value if the firm does well.

EQUITY CAPITAL: CHARACTERISTICS AND VALUATION

External equity capital comes from two sources: **common stock** and **preferred stock.** Their comparative characteristics are summarized in Exhibit 9.12. Preferred stockholders have priority over common stockholders in the payment of dividends and have a prior claim on the firm's assets in the event of liquidation (if there is anything left after debtholders and creditors have been paid). Preferred stockholders usually have no voting rights, but they may have **contingent voting rights,** such as the right to elect members to the board of directors, *if* the company has skipped dividend payments for a specified number of quarters. Preferred shares, like bonds, may have sinking funds, can be callable, and can be convertible into common equity.

THE VALUATION OF PREFERRED STOCKS

Because straight preferred stocks pay a constant perpetual dividend, they are priced like perpetual bonds. To illustrate, suppose two years ago Allied Equipment Company issued straight preferred stocks that pay a constant dividend of $8. A company in the same sector and with the same risk profile as AEC has just issued straight preferred stocks at $50 that promise to pay a constant dividend of $3.50. What is the current price of one share of AEC preferred stocks (P) given that both AEC and the similar company quote their dividend payment on the basis of a face value of $100? The market yield of the similar preferred stock is 7 percent ($3.50 divided by $50). This is the yield that investors will require to hold AEC's preferred. Applying equation 9.6, the perpetual bond valuation formula, to the preferred share, we get:

$$P = \textbf{Face value of preferred share} \times \left[\frac{\textbf{Dividend rate}}{\textbf{Market yield}} \right] = \$100 \times \frac{0.08}{0.07} = \$114.29$$

$$(9.7)$$

If the preferred shares are both callable and convertible into common stock, the $114.29 price will have to be *reduced* by the estimated value of the call option (which the holder has in effect *sold* to AEC) and *increased* by the estimated value of the option to convert into common stock (which the holder has in effect *purchased* from AEC).

THE VALUATION OF COMMON STOCKS

Suppose Allied Equipment Corporation is expected to pay a $2.00 cash dividend at the end of the year ($DIV_1 = \$2.00$) and that one share of AEC will be worth $30 at

EXHIBIT 9.12   **Comparative Characteristics of Common and Preferred Stocks.**

CHARACTERISTIC	COMMON STOCKS	PREFERRED STOCKS
•*Control and voting rights*	Common stockholders have full control and voting rights.	Preferred stockholders have no control but some voting rights only if the firm skips dividend payments for a specified number of periods.
•*Dividend payments:*		
– Seniority	Can only be paid after payment to preferred stockholders.	Paid before payment to common stockholders but after interest payments to debtholders.
– Are they cumulative?[1]	No.	Most preferred are cumulative.
– Can they vary?	Yes, according to the firm's dividend payment policy.	Yes, with payments often linked to money market rates.
– Is there a maximum payment?	No.	There is usually an upper limit.
– Are they tax deductible for the issuing corporation?	No.	No.
•*Provisions:*		
– Any sinking fund provision?	No.	Some preferred have sinking funds.
– Is it callable by the firm?	Cannot be called.	Some preferred are callable.
– Is it convertible into another type of security?	Cannot be converted.	Some preferred are convertible into common stocks.
•*Why and when are they usually issued?*	To raise permanent equity capital to fund the firm's growth.	Allow owners to raise quasi-equity without losing control. Often used as payment when buying another company.
•*Pricing*	See common stock valuation in Appendix 9.2.	A straight preferred is priced like a perpetual bond (fixed dividend divided by market yield). See equation 9.7.
•*Flexibility to issuing firm*	The most flexible type of security a firm can issue.	More flexible than bonds but less flexible than common stocks.
•*Risk*	Higher than preferred stocks and bonds.	Higher than bonds but lower than common stocks.

[1]Cumulative dividends means that if the firm skips the payment of dividends for a period of time, it will have to pay the missed dividends (called **arrearage**) when it resumes paying dividends.

the same date (S_1 = \$30). What is the estimated value S that one share should have today if investors require a return of 12 percent to hold AEC's common stock (k_E = 0.12, E for equity)? As in the case of a bond, it is the present value of the cash flow expected from holding the security and selling it in one year. At the end of the year, a holder of one share of AEC's common stock is expected to receive DIV_1 plus S_1. At a discount rate of k_E, the present value of this year-end cash flow is:

$$S = \frac{DIV_1 + S_1}{1 + k_E} = \frac{\$2 + \$30}{1.12} = \frac{\$32}{1.12} = \$28.57$$

We can extend this formula to the next period, with a second-year expected cash dividend of DIV_2 and a share valued at S_2 at the end of year 2. We have:

$$S = \frac{DIV_1}{1 + k_E} + \frac{DIV_2 + S_2}{(1 + k_E)^2}$$

If we carry this logic to an infinitely large number of periods we get:

$$S = \frac{DIV_1}{1 + k_E} + \frac{DIV_2}{(1 + k_E)^2} + \dots + \frac{DIV_N}{(1 + k_E)^N} + \dots = \sum_{t=1}^{\text{infinity}} \frac{DIV_t}{(1 + k_E)^t}$$

where $\sum_{t=1}^{\text{infinity}}$ is the sum of the present value of the cash dividends from year one (t = 1) to infinity. This equity valuation formula is known as the **dividend discount model (DDM).**

The constant growth dividend discount model

The find the value of equity using the dividend discount model, we need to know the stream of cash dividends the firm is expected to pay in the future. As you can imagine, a firm's future dividend stream is not easy to predict, making the dividend discount model difficult to apply. As a convenient shortcut, we can assume that cash dividends are expected to grow at a *constant* annual rate g forever. In this case, as shown in Appendix 9.2, the dividend discount model reduces to the ratio of next year's dividend to the difference between the required return k_E and the constant annual growth rate *g:*

$$S = \frac{DIV_1}{k_E - g} \tag{9.8}$$

Equation 9.8 is known as the **constant growth dividend discount model.** Although it is an extreme simplification of reality, it is a convenient formula and we use it in Chapters 10 and 12.

To illustrate equation 9.8, suppose the $2.00 cash dividend that AEC is expected to pay next year is anticipated to grow at a constant annual growth rate of 3 percent forever. The present value of one share of AEC's common stock is:

$$S = \frac{\$2}{0.12 - 0.03} = \frac{\$2}{0.09} = \$22.22$$

There are two points to note about the growth rate used in this valuation formula. The first is related to the theoretical validity of the formula: The growth rate must be lower than the required rate of return, otherwise the formula becomes meaningless. (The growth rate can be negative, however, if dividends are *declining* at a constant rate.) The second is related to the practical application of the formula: The growth rate should not exceed the average expected rate of growth of the economy in which the firm operates, otherwise the firm would one day be as large as the economy. We return to these issues in Chapter 12.

Market efficiency and equity pricing

If investors, on average, have the same required rate of return and make the same forecast of a firm's expected stream of dividend payments, then the observed market price of one share should be the same as the share value inferred from our valuation formula. In this case, the market is efficient in the sense that the share price of the stocks traded in the market reflects investors' consensus forecast regarding the future cash flows they expect to receive from their investment. Thus, in an **efficient market,** the observed share price is the best estimate of the value of a share. In other words, *market efficiency implies that price equals value.* What you pay is what the share is worth. There are neither bargains (undervalued shares) nor shares that must be sold because they are overvalued.

EQUITY WARRANTS

Warrants are options sold by firms that give the holder the right to buy a specific number of shares of common stock at a fixed price (the **exercise price**) during the life of the warrant. In other words, these instruments are **call options** (an option to buy). Warrants are usually issued by firms as a sweetener attached to bonds or preferred shares, although firms have issued "plain" warrants that are not attached to any securities.

An issue of straight bonds sold with warrants is similar to a convertible bond issue. Both combine the features of a straight bond and an option on the firm's common stock and are appropriate financing instruments for high growth, high risk, cash hungry companies. However, there are some differences. A convertible bond does not permit the holder to separate the bond from the option to convert, whereas warrants can be detached and sold separately from the bond. Also, when investors exchange their convertibles into equity, the firm's total capital does not change because the firm issues equity to replace debt. When investors exercise their warrants, equity is also issued (in return for cash), but debt is not retired.

CONTINGENT VALUE RIGHTS (CVR)

Contingent value rights (CVR) are options sold by companies that give the holder the right to *sell* a fixed number of shares to the issuing company at a fixed price during the life of the CVR. These option-type instruments are called **put options.** They are valuable to investors who believe the share price of the issuing firm is currently overvalued and who expect the share price to fall below the exercise price of the CVR before their expiration date.

Why would a firm want to issue this type of financial instrument? One reason is to raise funds, another is to signal to the market that the firm believes that its stock price is *not* overvalued. (If the firm thought its shares were overvalued, it would not issue CVR.) A third reason is that when CVR are sold in conjunction with a stock issue, they are an insurance given to the subscribers. The value of the shares they bought cannot be lower than the exercise price of the CVR because they can sell the shares back to the issuing firm at that price (at least until the CVR expire).

SUMMARY

Most of the funds needed to finance a firm's growth are generated by its internal activities. When firms experience a cash deficit, they must raise external funds. External funds are usually borrowed via bank loans and the issuance of debt securities; however, at times, they are supplemented with new issues of equity.

The source of internally generated funds is retained earnings, adjusted for non-cash expenses such as depreciation. The amount of external financing the firm needs is the difference between these internally generated funds and the expected growth in the firm's investment in cash and marketable securities, working capital requirement, and fixed assets.

External funds are raised through the financial system, which acts as a conduit for savers' excess cash to be channeled to the firms that need it. Funds can be transferred directly from savers to firms or can be transferred indirectly via financial intermediaries. In the first case, the firms sell securities to savers in the form of shares or bonds. In the second case, an intermediary, such as a bank, receives funds from savers, typically in the form of deposits, and lends these funds to firms in the form of loans. Firms can place their debt and equity securities privately with financial institutions, such as insurance companies and pension funds. Alternatively, they can sell them in the securities markets where they can then be traded among investors.

The function of primary markets is to ensure the success of new issues; the function of secondary markets is to ensure that investors can buy and sell existing securities at a fair price, a price that reflects all available public information. In addition to the distinction between primary and secondary markets, securities markets can be classified according to whether they are organized exchanges or over-the-counter markets, equity or debt markets, and domestic or international markets.

Firms issue shares and bonds either through private placement or through public offerings. For an equity issue, firms can raise capital through a general cash offering or via a rights issue. In a rights issue, current shareholders are given subscription rights that allow them to purchase new shares; in a general cash offering, shares are offered to the public at large and no distinction is made between current shareholders and other investors. The various sources of debt financing available to firms include bank loans, lease agreements, and bond issues.

A firm can issue a wide range of securities in addition to common stocks and straight bonds. These include convertibles, perpetual bonds, preferred shares, warrants, and contingent value rights. We explain why these securities are issued by firms and why they appeal to investors. Finally, we discuss various valuation formulas that can be used to price a security traded in an efficient market.

9.1 THE BOND VALUATION FORMULA

The following notations are used in the chapter and this appendix:

B = the bond's price
c = the bond's annual coupon rate
F = the bond's face value
y = the prevailing market yield
N = the bond's term to maturity in years

The bond price is equal to the present value at the market yield y of its promised cash-flow stream:

$$B = \frac{c \times F}{(1 + y)} + \frac{c \times F}{(1 + y)^2} + \frac{c \times F}{(1 + y)^3} + \ldots + \frac{c \times F}{(1 + y)^N} + \frac{F}{(1 + y)^N}$$

Multiplying both sides of the above valuation equation by $(1 + y)$, we get:

$$(1 + y) \times B = C \times F + \frac{c \times F}{(1 + y)} + \frac{c \times F}{(1 + y)^2} + \ldots + \frac{c \times F}{(1 + y)^{N-1}} + \frac{F}{(1 + y)^{N-1}}$$

Subtracting the first equation from the second, we find:

$$(1 + y) \times B - B = c \times F + \frac{F}{(1 + y)^{N-1}} - \frac{c \times F}{(1 + Y)^N} - \frac{F}{(1 + y)^N}$$

which can be written as:

$$y \times B = c \times F - \frac{c \times F}{(1 + y)^N} + \frac{F(1 + y) - F}{(1 + y)^N}$$

Dividing both sides by y and factoring out F, we have:

$$B = F\left[\frac{c}{y} - \frac{c}{y(1+y)^N} + \frac{1}{(1+y)^N}\right]$$

which yields equation 9.4, the bond valuation formula shown in the chapter:

$$B = F\left[\frac{c}{y} + \left(1 - \frac{c}{y}\right)\frac{1}{(1+y)^N}\right]$$

9.2 THE VALUATION FORMULA FOR THE CONSTANT GROWTH DIVIDEND MODEL

A ccording to the constant growth dividend model, the current stock price is equal to the discounted value, at the return required by stockholders, of the expected stream of future dividend payments, which are anticipated to grow at a constant rate forever. The following notations are used in the chapter and this appendix.

S = Stock price

DIV_t = Dividend payment expected in year t

g = Expected *constant* annual growth rate in dividend payments

k_E = Required return by stockholders

We can write:

$$S = \frac{DIV_1}{1 + k_E} + \frac{DIV_2}{(1 + k_E)^2} + \frac{DIV_3}{(1 + k_E)^3} + \cdots$$

and because annual dividend payments are expected to grow at the constant rate g, we have:

$$DIV_2 = DIV_1(1 + g)$$
$$DIV_3 = DIV_2(1 + g) = DIV_1(1 + g)(1 + g) = DIV_1(1 + g)^2$$

and thus:

$$S = \frac{DIV_1}{1 + k_E} + \frac{DIV_1(1 + g)}{(1 + k_E)^2} + \frac{DIV_1(1 + g)^2}{(1 + k_E)^3} + \cdots$$

Multiplying the above equation by $(1 + k_E)$ and dividing it by $(1 + g)$, we obtain:

$$\frac{(1 + k_E)}{(1 + g)} \times S = \frac{DIV_1}{(1 + g)} + \frac{DIV_1}{(1 + k_E)} + \frac{DIV_1(1 + g)}{(1 + k_E)^2} +$$

Subtracting the first equation from the second, we get:

$$\frac{(1 + k_E)}{(1 + g)} \times S - S = \frac{DIV_1}{(1 + g)}$$

Then, multiplying by $(1 + g)$:

$$(1 + k_E)S - (1 + g)S = DIV_1$$

Rearranging the terms yields equation 9.8, the constant growth dividend valuation model shown in the chapter:

$$S = \frac{DIV_1}{k_E - g}$$

REFERENCES AND FURTHER READING

1. Benninga, Simon, and Oded Sarig. *Corporate Finance: A Valuation Approach.* McGraw-Hill, 1997. See chapters 11, 12, and 13 on the valuation of debt and equity securities.
2. Brealey, Richard, and Stewart Myers. *Principles of Corporate Finance.* 5th ed. McGraw-Hill, 1996. See chapters 4, 13 to 15, 20, 22 to 24, 26, and 32.
3. Clark, John, Thomas Hindelang, and Robert Pritchard. *Capital Budgeting: Planning and Control of Capital Expenditures.* 2d ed. Prentice-Hall, 1984. See chapters 23 and 24 on leasing.
4. Kieso, Donald, and Jerry Weygandt. *Intermediate Accounting.* 8th ed. John Wiley, 1995. See chapter 22.
5. Megginson, William. *Corporate Finance Theory.* Addison Wesley Longman, 1997. See chapter 9.
6. Ross, Stephen, Randolph Westerfield, and Jeffrey Jaffe. *Corporate Finance.* 4th ed. Irwin, 1996. See chapters 5, 13, 14, and 19 to 23.
7. Smith, Roy, and Ingo Walter. *Global Banking.* Oxford University Press, 1997. See chapters 1, 8, 9, 10, and 11.

REVIEW PROBLEMS

9.1 Structure and characteristics of financial markets.
Briefly explain the distinction between the two items that make up each of the following pairs:
a. Direct financing versus indirect financing

   b. Primary markets versus secondary markets

   c. Organized exchanges versus over-the-counter markets

   d. Domestic securities versus Eurosecurities

   e. Domestic securities versus foreign securities

   f. Private placement versus public offering

   g. Rights issue versus general cash offering

   h. Underwritten issue versus best-efforts distribution

   i. Originating house versus selling group

   j. Seasoned issue versus secondary distribution

   k. Credit risk versus market risk

   l. Investment grade bonds versus speculative grade bonds

9.2 Estimating external funding needs.

OS Distributors wants to estimate the external funds it will need in 1998 based on the data available in Exhibit 9.2 and the following information and assumptions for 1998.

- Cash need = Same as in 1997
- Working capital requirement = Up 10 percent
- Capital expenditure = $10 million with $1 million annual depreciation
- Depreciation on existing assets = Same as in 1997
- Net profit = Up 10 percent
- Retention rate = Same as in 1997

   a. What are OS Distributors' expected total funding needs for 1998?

   b. What are OS Distributors' expected internally generated funds in 1998?

   c. What are expected external funding needs for 1998?

   d. What should OS Distributors do to cover its external funding needs?

9.3 Leasing versus borrowing.

OS Distributors needs a new truck. It can buy it for $24,000, depreciate it over four years at an annual rate of $6,000, and finance the purchase with a four-year loan at 10 percent. The truck could be sold for $5,000 in four years. Alternatively, it can lease the truck and make four annual lease payments of $6,500 (payments are made at the *beginning* of the year). OS Distributors is subject to a 40 percent corporate tax rate and is responsible for the maintenance and insurance of the truck, regardless of whether it leases or buys.

   a. Should OS Distributors lease or buy the truck?

   b. What resale value of the truck in four years will make OS Distributors indifferent between buying and leasing?

9.4 Rights issue.

MicroElectronics Corporation (MEC) has just announced that it will issue 10 million shares of common stock through a rights issue at a subscription price of $20. Prior to the announcement MEC shares were trading at $26 and there were 50 million shares outstanding.

    a. How many rights will MEC grant to its existing shareholders?

    b. How many rights will an investor need to buy one new share?

    c. What will happen to MEC's share price when the rights issue is announced?

    d. What should be the value of one right?

9.5 Valuation of bonds.

Consider the following four bonds:

	COUPON ISSUE	ZERO COUPON	PERPETUAL	CONVERTIBLE
Maturity	5 years	5 years	infinity	5 years
Coupon rate	6 percent	zero	6 percent	5 percent

    a. If the market yield is 7 percent, what are the values of the three first bonds (assume a face value of $1,000)?

    b. Why are the bond values lower than their face values?

    c. Why is the coupon rate for the convertible bond lower than that for the nonconvertible, coupon issue?

    d. Given that the convertible bond is trading at $1,040, what is the value of the option to convert?

    e. Suppose that the market yield rises to 7.5 percent. What are the bond values at that yield? Explain why the change in the value of the bonds is different.

9.6 Valuation of preferred shares and common stocks.

National Equipment Company (NEC) has both preferred and common stocks outstanding. NEC has just paid a $3 dividend per share of preferred stock and $2 dividend per share of common stock.

    a. Assume the dividend on the preferred is constant and that preferred stocks with similar risk to that of NEC are yielding 8.60 percent. What is its estimated value of NEC's preferred stock?

    b. Suppose NEC's preferred are currently trading at $36.12. How can you interpret the difference between the estimated value and the observed market price?

    c. Assume NEC's dividend per common share is expected to increase by 8 percent per year during the next three years and then rise at a constant rate of 4 percent forever. What is the estimated value of NEC's common stock if the required rate of return for this type of investment is 12 percent?

    d. Suppose NEC's common stocks are currently trading at $31.62. How can you interpret the difference between the estimated value and the observed market price?

10 ESTIMATING THE COST OF CAPITAL

F irms need cash to finance their investment projects. Usually, this cash is generated by the firm's existing assets. If there is a shortage of internally generated
funds, firms will ask investors (lenders and shareholders) to supply them with additional cash. Chapter 9 shows how firms can raise cash from external sources. Whatever its origin, cash is not free; it comes at a price. The price is the cost to the firm
of using investors' money. When this cost is expressed as the return expected by
investors for the capital they supply, it is called the *cost of capital*. Chapter 6 shows
that the cost of capital is the rate at which a project's stream of future cash flows
must be discounted to estimate its net present value (NPV) and to decide whether
the project is worth undertaking, that is, whether it has the potential to create
value. Chapter 7 shows that it is also the rate against which the project's internal
rate of return (IRR) must be compared for the same purpose of deciding whether to
accept or reject the project.

This chapter shows how to estimate the cost of capital to be used in the NPV,
the IRR, or any other discounted cash-flow method applied to the analysis of an
investment project. We call this cost of capital, the *project's* cost of capital, not to be
confused with the *firm's* cost of capital. The latter is the return expected by
investors from *all* the assets acquired and managed by the firm.

As mentioned in Chapter 6, the rate investors require from their investment in a
project is the return they expect to receive from investing their cash in alternative
investments that have the same risk profile as the risk profile of the project. Thus, if
we want to estimate the cost of capital for a particular project, we first need to identify
similar projects available to investors. The problem is that investors usually do not
invest directly in projects; they invest in the firms that undertake projects. The challenge, then, is to identify firms that exhibit the same risk characteristics as the project
under consideration. These comparable firms are called *proxies* or *pure-plays*.

After a proxy company has been identified, we must estimate the returns
expected by the investors who hold the securities (bonds and shares) the proxy

firm has issued. These investors have claims on the cash flows generated by the proxy's assets, which differ depending on the *type* of security held. Bondholders and shareholders of the same company have claims on the same cash flows generated by the firm's assets, but bondholders have a prior and fixed claim on these cash flows and thus bear *less* risk than shareholders. Consequently, the return expected from holding bonds is *lower* than the return expected from holding shares of the same company. This chapter shows how to estimate the expected returns from the two most common financial instruments, straight bonds and common stocks, using financial market data.

The return expected from the assets acquired and managed by a firm belongs to the investors who financed these assets and to no one else. Thus, this return must be the total of the returns expected by bondholders and shareholders, weighted by their respective contribution to the funding of these assets. In other words, a firm's cost of capital must be equal to the weighted average of the costs of each of its financing sources. This cost of capital, which is first mentioned in Chapter 1, is known as the firm's weighted average cost of capital or, simply, the WACC. Although we cannot directly measure the return investors expect from the assets managed by firms, we can use the firm's WACC as a surrogate. We show how to estimate a firm's WACC and how to find a project's cost of capital based on the WACC of proxy firms.

As an illustration, we estimate the cost of capital of Sunlight Manufacturing Company's (SMC) desk lamp project, which is introduced in Chapter 6 and analyzed in detail in Chapter 8. Because this project has the same risk profile as SMC's overall risk, the project's cost of capital is, in this case, the same as the firm's cost of capital. We also discuss another example that illustrates how to estimate the project's cost of capital when the project has a risk that differs from the risk of the firm that would undertake it.

Remember that the terms *cost of capital, investors' required return,* and *investors' expected return* mean the same thing and can thus be used interchangeably. A firm's cost of equity capital is the return expected (required) by investors who hold stock in the firm; a firm's cost of debt capital is the return expected (required) by investors who hold the loans and bonds the firm has issued. After reading this chapter, you should understand:

- How to estimate the cost of debt.
- How to estimate the cost of equity capital.
- How to combine the cost of different sources of financing to obtain a project's weighted average cost of capital.
- The difference between the cost of capital for a firm and the cost of capital for a project.

IDENTIFYING PROXY OR PURE-PLAY FIRMS

Identifying the alternative investments that have risks similar to those of the project is the first and most crucial step in the estimation of a **project's cost of capital.**

Data from these investments are the inputs for the models that are used to estimate the project's cost of capital. Regardless of the degree of sophistication of the models, the reliability of the estimated cost of capital always depends on the quality of the inputs chosen to perform the estimation (remember GIGO: Garbage-in, garbage-out).

When a project is in the same line of business as the firm that would undertake it, in other words, when the project's risk profile is similar to the firm's risk profile, the proxy is the firm itself. This is the case for the designer desk lamp project from Chapter 8 because the firm that wanted to launch the project, Sunlight Manufacturing Company, specializes in the production of small light fixtures.

When the risk of the project is different from the risk of the firm that would undertake it, you need to identify **proxy** or **pure-play firms.** These are firms that have a single line of business, are in the same industry as the project, and compete in the same input and output markets. Pure-plays are usually selected using industry classification codes that identify firms according to their type of business. Unfortunately, these classification systems are far from perfect. The sample of firms must be examined critically and only those firms that replicate as closely as possible the business of the investment project should be selected. Exact duplication is unlikely and often a choice must be made between a small sample of closely comparable companies and a larger sample of firms that are loosely comparable to the project.

In a small sample, the proxies will be more representative of the business to which the project belongs. But if some of the proxies' data have large measurement errors, the sample may be too small for these errors to wash out when the data are averaged across the proxies. In a larger sample, the proxies will be less comparable to the project, but the impact of large measurement errors may be greatly reduced in the averaging process.

Having indicated how to identify pure-plays, we show in the next sections how to estimate the return investors expect from holding debt securities (bonds) and common stocks (shares) issued by firms. These returns are, respectively, estimates of the **cost of debt** and the **cost of equity.**

ESTIMATING THE COST OF DEBT

A firm can borrow from a bank by taking out a loan. In this case, the firm's cost of debt is simply the interest rate the bank charges the firm. Alternatively, if the firm is large enough, it can borrow directly from investors by selling bonds to them. (Bonds are debt securities described in Chapter 9.) This section shows how to use the market price of a firm's bonds to estimate the firm's cost of debt. We use SMC (the company that is considering the investment in the designer desk lamp project) as an illustration.

Assume that *five* years ago SMC publicly issued 90,000 bonds with an original maturity of *ten* years. This means the bonds will be repaid *five* years from now (their current, or remaining, maturity is five years). Each bond has a par value of $1,000 and an annual coupon payment of $100. The bonds' coupon rate is thus 10 percent ($100 divided by $1,000). The current market price of the bonds is $1,112. The bond's expected rate of return, also known as its market yield to maturity, is an estimate of SMC's cost of debt. How can we calculate that rate?

An investor buying an SMC bond now and planning to keep it until maturity can expect to receive from SMC $100 every year for the next five years plus $1,000 at the end of the fifth year. As shown in Chapter 9, in a well-functioning bond market, the $1,112 bond price must be equal to the present, or discounted, value of the future stream of cash payments the bondholder is expected to receive during the next five years. We can write:

$$\$1,112 = \frac{\$100}{1 + k_D} + \frac{\$100}{(1 + k_D)^2} + \frac{\$100}{(1 + k_D)^3} + \frac{\$100}{(1 + k_D)^4} + \frac{\$1,100}{(1 + k_D)^5} \tag{10.1}$$

where k_D, the bondholders' expected return, is the firm's estimated cost of debt. There is no simple way to solve this valuation formula to find the exact value of k_D. One would have to use trial and error until a value of k_D is found that makes the sum of the present values equal to $1,112. However, a financial calculator or a spreadsheet program can provide the answer. Our calculator indicates that k_D is equal to 7.25 percent.

To summarize, if we know the price of the bond, its coupon payments, and its par value, the valuation formula can be solved for the rate of return investors require to hold the security. *This rate is the estimated cost of debt for the issuer.* Why is the bond's 7.25 percent *market yield* (its expected return) the relevant cost of debt instead of the bond's 10 percent *coupon rate,* or its 9 percent *current yield* (the bond's $100 coupon payment divided by its $1,112 price; see Chapter 9)? The reason is simple: SMC's cost of debt is the interest rate it will have to pay if it decided *today* to issue *new* bonds to investors. This rate is the market yield of 7.25 percent. Both the coupon rate and the current yield are based on an interest rate that was set five years ago when the bond was originally issued. If SMC issues new bonds today that have a five-year maturity, it will have to offer investors a yield of 7.25 percent, not 10 percent (the coupon rate on the previously issued bond) or 9 percent (the current yield of the previously issued bond).

If the firm has no bonds outstanding, its cost of debt for a given maturity can be estimated by adding to the market yield on *government* securities (with the *same* maturity) an estimate of the firm's credit risk spread over government securities:

$$\textbf{Cost of debt} = \textbf{Market yield on government security}$$
$$+ \textbf{ Estimated credit risk spread} \tag{10.2}$$

To illustrate, suppose the market yield on government bonds is currently 6.5 percent and the firm has an estimated credit risk spread of 1 percent. (See Chapter 9 for a discussion on how to estimate a firm's credit risk spread.) In this case, the firm's estimated cost of debt is 7.50 percent.

Regardless of the method used to estimate the firm's cost of debt, the cost needs to be adjusted for corporate taxes. Because interest expenses are tax deductible, the **aftertax cost of debt** to the firm is less than its *pretax* cost. For example, if SMC has a marginal tax rate of 40 percent, then every dollar of interest expense reduces the firm's tax bill by 40 cents and the aftertax interest expense is only 60 cents ($1 less 40 cents). With a pretax cost of debt of 7.25 percent and a marginal tax rate of 40 percent, the aftertax cost of debt is 4.35 percent (60 percent of 7.25 percent). In general:

> **Aftertax cost of debt = Pretax cost of debt**
> $$\times\ (1 - \textbf{marginal corporate tax rate})\qquad(10.3)$$

Remember that the above relationship is valid only if (1) the firm is profitable enough to take full advantage of the tax deductibility of interest expenses, or (2) the firm is not profitable enough during the current period but the tax authority allows it to deduct current interest expenses from past or future profits, a rule known as **carryback** or **carry forward.**

ESTIMATING THE COST OF EQUITY: THE DIVIDEND DISCOUNT MODEL

Equity securities are financial instruments that give their holders a proportional right to ownership of the firm's assets. The standard type of equity security is common stock (described in Chapter 9). Owners of common stock have a *residual* claim on any cash left after the firm has paid all its obligations, including interest and principal on debt. Cash dividends are paid by the firm to its shareholders as a return on their investment.

We use DIV_1, DIV_2, DIV_3, . . ., DIV_t, . . . to represent the stream of future annual cash dividends expected from an investment in one share of a company and use k_E to represent the expected return from that share. We know that the expected return k_E is the cost of equity for the firm that issued the share. According to the dividend discount model (see Chapter 9), the price of a share should be equal to the present, or discounted, value of the stream of cash dividends shareholders are expected to receive:

$$P_0 = \frac{DIV_1}{(1 + k_E)^1} + \frac{DIV_2}{(1 + k_E)^2} + \ \dots \ + \frac{DIV_t}{(1 + k_E)^t} + \dots \qquad(10.4)$$

This formula does not explicitly take into account the future prices of the share. As explained in Chapter 9, this does not mean that future share prices are ignored. They are implicitly taken into account by the valuation formula because, for example, the share price in two years can be expressed as a function of the expected cash dividends that will be received after the second year.

We can use equation 10.4 to estimate the firm's cost of equity if we know the firm's share price and the dividends it is expected to pay. The procedure is similar to the one used for estimating the cost of debt. Unfortunately, while we know the expected coupon payments for bonds, we do not know the expected dividend payments for shares. We can circumvent this difficulty if we make some simplifying assumptions regarding the growth of future dividends. The next section examines the particular case where dividends are expected to grow forever at a constant rate.

ESTIMATING THE COST OF EQUITY: DIVIDENDS GROW AT A CONSTANT RATE

Suppose we assume the dividend DIV_1 that a firm is expected to pay next year will grow at a constant rate g forever. Then, the dividend discount model reduces to:

$$P_0 = \frac{DIV_1}{k_E - g}$$

This valuation formula, first presented in Chapter 9, is known as the constant growth dividend discount model. The terms of the formula can be rearranged to define the expected cost of equity k_E as a function of next year's dividend, the current share price, and the expected constant growth rate[1]:

$$k_E = \frac{DIV_1}{P_0} + g \qquad\qquad (10.5)$$

Equation 10.5 indicates that the firm's estimated cost of equity is the sum of two components. The first is the firm's expected **dividend yield,** that is, the firm's expected dividend payment per share divided by its current share price. The second is the expected growth rate in future dividends. Note that a firm whose dividend is expected to stay the same (no growth in dividend payment) has an estimated cost of equity equal to its dividend yield.

To illustrate, we consider the case of Allied Bearing Company (ABC). The company's stock is selling at $50, the company is expected to pay a dividend per share of $3 next year, and the dividend per share is anticipated to grow at 5 percent a year forever. According to equation 10.5, ABC and *all firms that have the same risk profile as that of ABC* have an estimated cost of equity of:

$$k_E = \frac{\$3}{\$50} + 5\% = 6\% + 5\% = 11\%$$

If ABC's dividend payments are expected to remain at $3 *forever,* an unlikely scenario, its estimated cost of equity would drop to 6 percent, which is its dividend yield.

---

[1]Multiply both sides of the price formula by $(k_E - g)$ then divide both sides by P_0 and finally move g from the left to the right side of the equation.

ESTIMATING THE COST OF EQUITY: HOW RELIABLE IS THE DIVIDEND DISCOUNT MODEL?

In its general form, the dividend discount model shown in equation 10.4 is not very useful because it requires forecasting an infinite number of dividends. The model can be reduced to a more manageable form under some simplifying assumptions regarding the future growth of the firm's dividends. Unfortunately, these assumptions are unrealistic.[2] Casual observation of series of dividends paid on common stocks shows that dividends neither stay constant nor grow at a constant rate for very long. Furthermore, a number of firms pay no dividends at all, at least for a certain period of time. For these firms, we would have to estimate the date at which the payment of dividends will resume in addition to estimating the dividend's magnitude and its future rate of growth, quite a challenging task.

The simplified version of the dividend discount model (equation 10.5) can be reliably applied only to the small subset of firms that pay regular dividends with a fairly stable pattern of growth, such as utility companies. For the vast majority of companies, the simplistic and unrealistic assumptions underlying the reduced version of the dividend discount model are not acceptable.

The following section presents an alternative valuation model that directly relates the expected return on any security to its risk. When this model, called the **capital asset pricing model,** or **CAPM,** is applied to common stocks, it provides a better estimate of a firm's cost of equity capital because it does not rely on forecasting future patterns of dividend payments.

ESTIMATING THE COST OF EQUITY: THE CAPITAL ASSET PRICING MODEL

We know that the return required by investors on an investment depends on that investment's risk. The greater the risk, the higher the expected return. But, what is the nature of risk and how is it measured? These topics are considered in this section, along with an examination of the relationship between expected return and risk. This relationship, known as the capital asset pricing model, is used to estimate the cost of equity capital.

DIVERSIFICATION REDUCES RISK

Suppose there exists an island in the Caribbean where the sun shines half of the time and it rains the other half. There are two companies located on the island: One

---

[2]The exception is the dividend from *preferred* stock, which is fixed and does not have a maturity date. In this case, we can apply equation 10.5 with a growth rate equal to zero. For example, if a share of preferred stock sells for $10 and pays a dividend of $1 per share, the expected return from the stock is 10 percent ($1 divided by $10).

company, Sun Cream, Inc., sells suntan lotion; the other, Umbrella & Co., sells umbrellas. The shares of the two firms trade on the local stock exchange. An analysis of their historical monthly returns reveals that they have identical *average* returns of 15 percent. As illustrated on Exhibit 10.1, the actual monthly returns for both stocks vary over time, meaning that investing in either stock is risky. Note that the amplitude and frequency of the returns on both stocks are the same. In other words, their volatility, and thus their risk, is identical.

Suppose you have $1,000 to invest in the two companies' stocks. What investment strategy should you use? Should you invest in only one of the two stocks because they both have the same average return and risk? If you do so, you will become a victim of "weather risk." If you buy shares of Sun Cream, Inc., your investment will perform well when the sun shines but not when it rains. If you buy shares of Umbrella & Co., the opposite will occur; your investment will do well when it rains but not when the sun shines. A smarter strategy, based on the principle of "not putting all your eggs in one basket," would be to buy $500 worth of shares in each of the two firms. Any loss on one share would be offset by a gain on the other, whatever the weather turns out to be. In other words, as shown at the bottom of Exhibit 10.1, regardless of the weather conditions, the strategy locks in a *riskless* return of 15 percent, which is the expected return on an investment in either one of the two stocks.

This example is obviously unrealistic because it is impossible to find two investments whose returns move in exactly opposite directions and in the same proportions. Nevertheless, it does illustrate an important phenomenon: *Diversification helps reduce risk.* When the shares of different firms are held together in a diversified portfolio, variations in their returns tend to average out and the risk of the portfolio goes down rapidly. Studies that have analyzed the effect of diversification on portfolio risk show that portfolios made up of about twenty randomly chosen stocks have a risk that can be as low as 20 percent of the average risk of its component securities. Moreover, investing in twenty stocks is not significantly more costly than investing the same amount of money in a single stock, so portfolio diversification costs almost nothing. As a result, any rational investor who dislikes risk will choose to hold a diversified portfolio of stocks rather than to invest his entire wealth in a single asset.

A major implication of the above analysis is that the risk of holding a single stock can be divided into two risks. One risk can be eliminated through portfolio diversification; the other risk remains despite the risk reduction property of diversification. The first is called **diversifiable,** or **unsystematic, risk.** The second is called **nondiversifiable,** or **systematic, risk.** We can now express the total risk of a stock as:

Total risk = Systematic risk + Unsystematic risk

The origin of unsystematic risk is company-specific events that may have either a positive or a negative effect on share prices. Examples of positive, or favorable, events are the unanticipated win of a liability lawsuit, the discovery of a new product, or the announcement of higher than expected earnings. Examples of negative,

EXHIBIT 10.1   Risk and Return for the Sun Cream and Umbrella Investments.

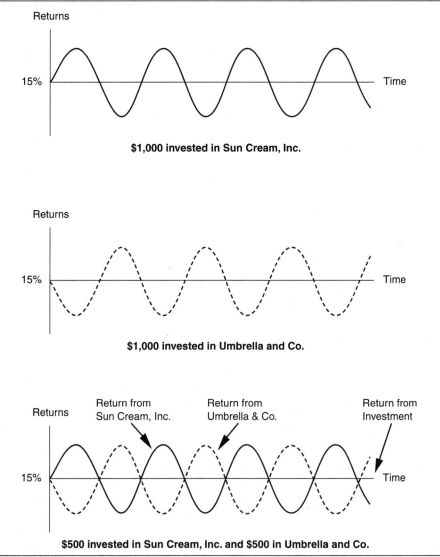

$1,000 invested in Sun Cream, Inc.

$1,000 invested in Umbrella and Co.

Return from Sun Cream, Inc.   Return from Umbrella & Co.   Return from Investment

$500 invested in Sun Cream, Inc. and $500 in Umbrella and Co.

or unfavorable, events are a labor strike, an accident that temporarily shuts down major production facilities, or an unanticipated liability lawsuit. Those events, taken together, are unlikely to have a significant impact on the returns of a well-diversified portfolio because the positive effect of favorable events for some stocks will *cancel* the negative effect of the unfavorable ones for the other stocks. The portfolio's unsystematic risk will approach zero.

The origin of systematic, or undiversifiable, risk is events that affect the entire economy instead of only a single stock. These include changes in the economy's growth rate, inflation rate, and interest rates and changes in the political and social environments. These market-wide events tend to affect all share prices in the *same* fashion. For example, if the market expects the central bank to raise interest rates, an event that is usually interpreted as unfavorable to the stock market, the price of most shares should go down. Because this type of risk affects most shares in a similar fashion, it is called *systematic* risk. And because it cannot be eliminated or reduced through diversified portfolio holdings, it is also called *undiversifiable* risk. Note, however, that some stocks will exhibit more (or less) systematic risk than others because they are more (or less) sensitive to market-wide events.

To summarize, a stock's total risk has two components. One, called *unsystematic risk,* can be eliminated or reduced at very low cost through diversification. The other, called *systematic risk,* cannot be eliminated or reduced through diversified portfolio holdings. This separation of risk between a systematic component and an unsystematic component has an important implication for the determination of the return required by shareholders.

Because unsystematic risk can be eliminated through diversification at practically no significant cost, the financial market will not reward it. Put another way, the financial market will only reward the risk that investors cannot avoid, that is, systematic or undiversifiable risk. We have stated many times that the return required from a financial asset depends on the risk of that asset. We can now state: *The only risk that matters in determining the required return on a financial asset is the asset's systematic risk.* The implication is so important that it is worth repeating: *The required rate of return on a financial asset depends only on the asset's systematic risk.* Which leads to the next question: How is systematic risk measured?

MEASURING SYSTEMATIC RISK WITH THE BETA COEFFICIENT

The systematic risk of an individual stock is usually measured *relative* to a benchmark portfolio called the **market portfolio.** Theoretically, the market portfolio contains all the assets in the world, not just stocks, but also bonds, domestic and foreign assets, currencies, and even real estate. It is the portfolio that ensures maximum diversification and, thus, provides maximum risk reduction. The variations in the returns of this portfolio reflect only the impact of market-wide events, which are the source of systematic risk. In practice, building such a portfolio is a formidable, if not impossible, task. Instead, when estimating an individual stock's systematic risk, analysts use a domestic stock market index that is sufficiently broad, such as the Standard and Poor's Composite Index (S&P 500) in the United States and the Financial Times All Share Index (FT-A) in the United Kingdom.

Measuring the systematic risk of an individual stock relative to the market portfolio boils down to measuring the sensitivity of the stock's returns to changes in the returns of a broad stock market index. This measure of sensitivity is called the stock's **beta coefficient** or simply its **beta.** We show how to estimate a stock's beta using Sunlight Manufacturing Company (SMC) as an illustration.

The graph in Exhibit 10.2 shows the monthly returns of SMC's stocks plotted against the monthly returns of the S&P 500 during the last five years. The 60 monthly returns to SMC stockholders, r_{SMC}, were computed as:

$$r_{SMC} = \frac{\text{End of month stock price} + \text{Dividend (if any)} - \text{Beginning of month stock price}}{\text{Beginning of month stock price}}$$

EXHIBIT 10.2   SMC Stock Monthly Returns versus the S&P 500 Monthly Returns.

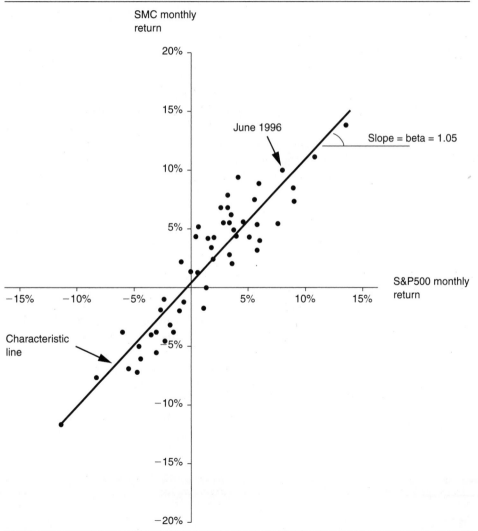

and the monthly returns for the index, $r_{S\&P\ 500}$ were computed as:

$$r_{S\&P\ 500} = \frac{\text{End of month S\&P 500 value} - \text{Beginning of month S\&P 500 value}}{\text{Beginning of monh S\&P 500 value}}$$

Each point on the graph represents a pair of monthly returns (one for SMC's stock and the other for the S&P 500). For example, during the month of June 1996, the price of SMC's shares increased by 10 percent while the S&P 500 rose by 8 percent.

On the graph, we have drawn the line that is closest to *all* the points. This line is called the security's **characteristic line.**[3] Its slope is 1.05, indicating that for each increase (or decrease) of 1 percent in the S&P 500, SMC's stock return increases (or decreases) by 1.05 percent, *on average*. In other words, the slope of the characteristic line measures the sensitivity of SMC's stock returns to changes in the returns of the market index. Therefore, it is an estimate of the beta coefficient of SMC's stock.

As mentioned in the previous section, the return on the market index measures the reaction of the stock market to economy-wide events. For example, in June 1996, these events had a positive impact on the market because the index rose by 8 percent. During the same month, SMC's stock increased by 10 percent. The rise in price of SMC's stock can be divided into two parts. One part reflects the impact of the economy-wide events on SMC's stock, and the other part reflects the impact of events that are specific to SMC, such as the success of a marketing campaign or the successful launch of a new product. What is the contribution of each type of event to the 10 percent return achieved in June 1996? The positive economy-wide events contributed 8.4 percent (a market return of 8 percent multiplied by a beta of 1.05) and favorable SMC-specific events contributed 1.6 percent (the 10 percent total return less the 8.4 percent contributed by the economy-wide events). The volatility of the first part is the systematic risk of SMC's stock while the volatility of the second part is its unsystematic risk, which can be eliminated through diversification.

Each stock has its own beta coefficient. Think of it as an ID number that identifies the stock's systematic risk exposure to economy-wide events. A stock with a beta of one fluctuates, *on average,* the same as the market index against which its volatility is measured because, by definition, the beta of the market index is one. Stocks with a beta higher than one are more sensitive to economy-wide events than the market index is. And stocks with a beta lower than one are less sensitive to economy-wide events than the market index is. Most firms have a beta in the range 0.6 to 1.6. Exhibit 10.3 shows the beta coefficients of the stocks of a sample of U.S. firms. Note that companies with relatively low business risk, such as utilities (Texas Utilities and American Water Works), have significantly lower betas than compa-

---

[3]In statistics, the characteristic line would be called a *regression line*. Its slope can be obtained using a technique called least square regression analysis, which is provided by most computer spreadsheet applications.

EXHIBIT 10.3   Beta Coefficients of a Sample of U.S. Stocks.

Southwest Air	1.60	Anheuser-Busch	1.00
Texas Instrument	1.60	McDonald's	1.00
Compaq Computer	1.40	Walgreen Co.	1.00
Whirlpool Corp.	1.40	Coca-Cola	0.95
AMR Corp.	1.35	Pepsi-Cola	0.95
Motorola, Inc.	1.30	AT&T	0.90
Maytag Corp.	1.30	McGraw-Hill	0.85
BancOne Corp.	1.25	GTE	0.80
Abbott Laboratories	1.20	Bell Atlantic	0.80
Air Gas	1.20	Quaker Oats	0.80
Baxter International	1.15	Ameritech	0.75
General Electric	1.15	Continental Edison	0.75
Viacom, Inc.	1.10	Amoco Corp.	0.75
Turner Broadcasting	1.10	Energy Corp.	0.70
Ford Motor Company	1.05	Texas Utilities	0.65
General Motors	1.05	American Water Works	0.65

Source: Value Line Investment Survey, 1996.

nies with higher business risk, such as airline (Southwest Air) or computer (Compaq Computer) companies.

There is no need for managers to estimate betas. The betas of most listed companies around the world are available from a number of information services. These services estimate betas from market data, updating them regularly and often making them available on-line through a subscription service.

THE IMPACT OF FINANCIAL LEVERAGE ON A STOCK'S BETA

Most firms finance their activities with both debt and equity capital. As mentioned earlier, both bondholders and shareholders have claims on the cash flows generated by the firm's assets and both are affected by the volatility, or risk, generated by these cash flows. This risk, which originates from the firm's assets, is called **business risk.** Bondholders, however, have a priority claim over shareholders on the firm's cash flows (they receive fixed interest payments *before* shareholders receive dividends). As a consequence, shareholders bear *more* risk than bondholders. This additional risk is called **financial risk.** (See Chapters 1 and 5 for details.) As the firm increases its debt relative to its equity capital, financial risk will rise. Conclusion: A firm's beta coefficient will be affected by both business risk and financial risk, and the higher these risks, the higher the firm's beta. How can we measure the respective impact of business risk and financial risk on beta?

We use **asset beta** or **unlevered beta** (designated by β_{asset}) to refer to the beta of a stock *when the firm is all-equity financed.* In this case, the firm's owners face only business risk. There is no financial risk because there is no debt. Hence, the firm's asset or unlevered beta captures the firm's business risk. We use **equity beta, levered beta,** or **market beta** (designated by β_{equity}) to refer to the beta of a stock when the firm has borrowed. In this case, the firm's owners face both business risk and financial risk and the firm's equity, or levered, beta captures both sources of risk. It can be shown that the relationship between a company's unlevered, or asset, beta and its levered, or equity, beta, can be expressed as:

$$\beta_{equity} = \beta_{asset}\left[1 + (1 - \text{tax rate})\frac{\text{Debt}}{\text{Equity}}\right] \qquad (10.6)$$

where debt and equity are measured at their *market* value and not at their book, or accounting, value. Note that as the amount of borrowing increases relative to equity financing, the firm's financial risk increases, the firm's debt-to-equity ratio increases, and the firm's equity, or levered, beta increases.

The terms of equation 10.6 can be rearranged in order to express asset beta as a function of equity beta. We get:

$$\beta_{asset} = \frac{\beta_{equity}}{\left[1 + (1 - \text{tax rate})\dfrac{\text{Debt}}{\text{Equity}}\right]} \qquad (10.7)$$

Consider Sunlight Manufacturing Company. The firm currently has a debt-to-equity ratio of 2-to-3 and is taxed at the marginal rate of 40 percent. Its levered, or equity, beta is estimated earlier at 1.05. Its unlevered, or asset, beta is thus:

$$\beta_{asset,\ SMC} = \frac{1.05}{\left[1 + (1 - 0.40)\dfrac{2}{3}\right]} = 0.75$$

Slightly less than 71 percent of SMC's beta (0.75 divided by 1.05) originates from business risk and the remaining 29 percent comes from financial risk.

THE CAPITAL ASSET PRICING MODEL (CAPM)

Exhibit 10.4 shows the average annual returns for four classes of U.S. securities—common stocks, corporate bonds, government bonds, and Treasury bills—during the period 1926 to 1995. Not surprisingly, common stocks offered the highest returns, followed by corporate bonds, government bonds, and Treasury bills. These four categories of assets have different returns because they have different risks, and the higher the risk, the higher the return.

Common stocks are the riskiest because they do not promise fixed payments; shareholders receive whatever is left after all debtholders are paid. Corporate

EXHIBIT 10.4   **Average Annual Rate of Return on Common Stocks, Corporate Bonds, U.S. Government Bonds, and U.S. Treasury Bills, 1926 to 1995.**

TYPE OF INVESTMENT	AVERAGE ANNUAL RETURN	AVERAGE RISK PREMIUM DIFFERENCE BETWEEN RETURN OF INVESTMENT AND RETURN OF	
		TREASURY BILLS	GOVERNMENT BONDS
Common stocks (S&P 500)	12.2%	**8.5%**	**7.0%**
Corporate bonds	5.7%	**2.0%**	**0.5%**
Government bonds	5.2%	**1.5%**	–
Treasury bills	3.7%	–	–

Source: Ibbotson Associates, Inc., 1996 Yearbook.

bonds are less risky because firms promise bondholders regular coupon payments and the repayment of the amount borrowed when the bonds mature. The U.S. government makes the same promise to the owners of the securities it issues, but its debt is less risky because it has a smaller chance of going bankrupt than a private corporation has. Finally, government bonds offer, on average, a higher return than Treasury bills because bonds, which are long-term securities, are more sensitive to changes in the rate of inflation than short-term bills are. All factors considered, Treasury bills are the safest investment available. This is why their rate of return is usually taken as a surrogate for the riskless, or **risk-free, rate.**

The difference of 8.5 percent between the average return on common stocks (12.2 percent) and the average return on Treasury bills (3.7 percent) represents the *historical* compensation received by investors who have chosen to invest in the riskiest class of assets, that is, stocks, rather than in the safest one, that is, Treasury bills, from 1926 to 1995. In general, the difference between the *expected* return on any security, such as bonds or stock, and the risk-free rate is called the **risk premium** of that security:

Security's risk premium = Security's expected return − Risk-free rate

Rearranging the terms of the above equation, we have:

Security's expected return = Risk-free rate + Security's risk premium   (10.8)

When the risk premium is computed for the portfolio of *all* existing common stocks, it is called the stock market risk premium, or simply the **market risk premium:**

Market risk premium = Market portfolio expected return − Risk-free rate   (10.9)

In Exhibit 10.4, the 8.5 percent risk premium was computed using the S&P 500 index. This index is our proxy for the market portfolio, so we can use 8.5 percent as an estimate of the market risk premium for the 70 years from 1926 to 1995. Furthermore, 70 years is a sufficient length of time to allow the use of historical data as forecasts of expected future data. Thus, we can assume that 8.5 percent is a good estimate of the expected, or *future,* market risk premium.

We know that the beta of a security measures its risk relative to the market portfolio. Thus, the risk premium of a *security* must be equal to the market risk premium multiplied by the security's beta coefficient:

Security's risk premium = Market risk premium × Security's beta

We can now write equation 10.8 as:

Security's expected return = Risk-free rate + Market risk premium
× Security's beta

or

$$R_i = R_F + (R_M - R_F) \times \beta_i \qquad (10.10)$$

where R_i is the expected return on security i, R_F is the risk-free rate, β_i is the security's beta, and R_M less R_F is the market risk premium as expressed in equation 10.9. This formula, which relates a security's expected return to its systematic risk or beta, is the capital asset pricing model or CAPM. Its interpretation is quite straightforward. It says that the expected, or required, return on any security is the sum of two factors: (1) the risk-free rate, which measures the compensation for investing money without taking any risk, and (2) the expected reward for bearing risk, which is equal to the market risk premium multiplied by the security's beta coefficient.

Note that the CAPM is a linear relationship between expected return and risk. This relationship is shown in the graph drawn in Exhibit 10.5. Expected returns are plotted against betas according to the CAPM, where the risk-free rate is set equal to a Treasury bill rate assumed to be 5 percent. The line starts at the point that represents the investment in Treasury bills. That investment bears no risk, so its beta is equal to zero. The line then passes through the point that identifies the market portfolio. By definition, this portfolio has a beta of one. Its expected return is 13.5 percent, the sum of a risk-free rate of 5 percent and a market risk premium of 8.5 percent. The line, called the **security market line,** has a positive slope. This is not surprising because the higher the beta, the higher the systematic risk and the higher the required return.

USING THE CAPM TO ESTIMATE SMC'S COST OF EQUITY

We have identified the relevant risk of a stock, we know how to measure this risk, and we know how to relate the risk to the stock's required return. We are now in a

EXHIBIT 10.5   The Capital Asset Pricing Model.

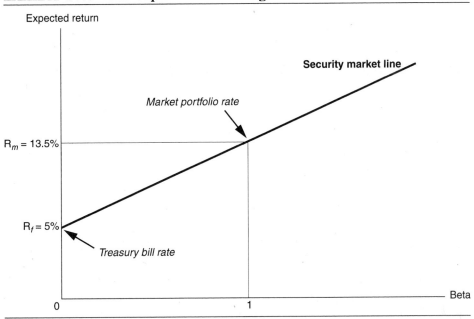

position to estimate the cost of equity for any firm. If $k_{E,i}$ denotes the cost of equity of firm i and $\beta_{equity,i}$ denotes the firm's equity beta, then according to the CAPM:

$$\mathbf{k_{E,\,i} = R_F + (R_M - R_F) \times \beta_{equity,i}} \qquad (10.11)$$

However, the CAPM expressed in equation 10.10 applies to short periods of time because the risk-free rate is measured by the return on Treasury bills, which mature in less than a year. Consequently, a firm's cost of equity derived from equation 10.10 is relevant only for a short period of time, say a year. Because firms' activities continue over many years, we would need, theoretically, to estimate a cost of equity for each coming year, depending on the Treasury bill rate that is expected to prevail that year. In practice, given the difficulties of estimating future Treasury bill rates, only one cost of equity is estimated. This cost of equity, which is an estimate of the average of its expected future values, is obtained from a version of the CAPM in which the Treasury bill rate is replaced by the rate on government bonds. Thus, the relevant market risk premium in equation 10.11 ($R_M - R_F$) is equal to the difference between the return on the market portfolio and the return on government bonds. This average premium, reported in Exhibit 10.4, is equal to 7 percent, the difference between the 12.2 percent average return on the S&P 500 and the 5.2 percent average return on government bonds.

To illustrate, we compute SMC's cost of equity $k_{E,SMC}$. We know that SMC's equity beta is 1.05 and that the market risk premium over the government bond rate is 7 percent. If the market yield on government bonds is *currently* 6.5 percent, SMC's estimated cost of equity is:

$$k_{E,SMC} = 6.5\% + 7.0\% \times 1.05 = 13.85\%$$

Using the same approach, we have estimated the cost of equity in 1996 for a sample of U.K. companies listed on the London Stock Exchange. The results are shown in Exhibit 10.6. Note the wide spread in the estimated cost of equity. It ranges from a high of 18.1 percent for Reuters to a low of 8.8 percent for the Savoy Hotels.

ESTIMATING THE COST OF CAPITAL OF A FIRM

We have defined a project's cost of capital as the return that investors can get from similar investments with the same risk profile. Unfortunately, the proxy firms that have undertaken similar investments do not publish their returns. We are therefore left with the task of estimating the proxy's cost of capital using only information that is publicly available. In this section, we estimate the cost of capital of a *firm*, leaving the estimation of a *project's* cost of capital to the following section.

WHAT IS THE FIRM'S COST OF CAPITAL?

Suppose that a firm is considering a one-year project that requires an initial investment of $3 million to be financed 2/3 with equity ($2 million) and 1/3 with debt ($1 million). If the project and the firm have the same risk profiles, the firm's shareholders will expect a return on the equity portion of the investment that is equal to the firm's cost of equity. And the bondholders will expect a return on the debt portion of the investment that is equal to the firm's cost of debt. If the firm's cost of debt is 6 percent and its cost of equity is 12 percent, the firm is expected, next year, to pay its bondholders $1,060,000 (the initial $1 million plus 6 percent of $1 million) and give its shareholders $2,240,000 (the initial $2 million plus 12 percent of $2 million).

The project will meet bondholders' and shareholders' expectations only if its return on the initial $3 million investment generates a net cash flow of at least $3,300,000 ($1,060,000 plus $2,240,000). This is equivalent to a 10 percent rate of return ($3 million plus 10 percent of $3,000,000). This rate is the project's cost of capital or the project's **weighted average cost of capital (WACC).** It is the *minimum* rate of return the project must generate in order to meet the return expectations of its suppliers of capital. And, because we assumed that the project has the *same risk* as the firm, this rate is also the **firm's cost of capital** or WACC. Generalizing from our example, if a firm finances its activities with E dollars of equity and D dollars of debt, the project's WACC must be such that:

$$(E + D) \times (1 + WACC) = D \times (1 + \text{cost of debt}) + E \times (1 + \text{cost of equity})$$

EXHIBIT 10.6 Estimation of the Cost of Equity Based on the Capital Asset Pricing Model (CAPM) for a Sample of Companies Listed on the London Stock Exchange (1996).

COMPANY	INDUSTRY	GOVERNMENT BOND RATE	MARKET RISK PREMIUM	BETA COEFFICIENT	ESTIMATED COST OF EQUITY WITH THE CAPM
REUTERS	Agency	6%	7%	1.73	6% + (7%) (1.73) = **18.1%**
PEEK	Electronics	6%	7%	1.52	6% + (7%) (1.52) = **16.6%**
BRITISH AEROSPACE	Aerospace	6%	7%	1.34	6% + (7%) (1.34) = **15.4%**
INCHCAPE	Trading	6%	7%	1.30	6% + (7%) (1.30) = **15.1%**
GLAXO HOLDINGS	Health	6%	7%	1.27	6% + (7%) (1.27) = **14.9%**
LUCAS INDUSTRIES	Motor	6%	7%	1.21	6% + (7%) (1.21) = **14.5%**
MARKS & SPENCER	Stores	6%	7%	0.88	6% + (7%) (0.88) = **12.2%**
BRITISH TELECOM	Phone network	6%	7%	0.73	6% + (7%) (0.73) = **11.1%**
SAVOY HOTELS	Hotels	6%	7%	0.40	6% + (7%) (0.40) = **8.8%**

which can be written as:

$$\text{WACC} = \text{cost of debt} \times \frac{D}{E + D} + \text{cost of equity} \times \frac{E}{E + D}$$

To account for the tax deductibility of interest expenses, the cost of debt must be calculated on an aftertax basis. According to equation 10.3, the aftertax cost of debt is $k_D (1 - T_C)$ where k_D is the pretax cost of debt and T_C is the marginal corporate tax rate. If, as before, k_E denotes the firm's cost of equity, then the weighted average cost of capital of any firm that finances its investment projects with debt and equity is:

$$\mathbf{WACC} = \mathbf{\mathit{k}_D} (1 - \mathbf{T_C})\frac{\mathbf{D}}{\mathbf{E + D}} + \mathbf{\mathit{k}_E} \frac{\mathbf{E}}{\mathbf{E + D}} \qquad (10.12)$$

The above formula, which considers a firm financed with only debt and equity, can be easily extended to a firm that also uses other sources of funds such as, for example, P dollars of preferred stocks with a cost equal to k_P. In this case:

$$\text{WACC} = k_D (1 - T_C) \times \frac{D}{E + D + P} + k_E \frac{E}{E + D + P} + k_P \frac{P}{E + D + P} \qquad (10.13)$$

The WACC formula also applies to projects that are financed either exclusively by equity or exclusively by debt. In the former case, the formula reduces to the cost of equity, k_E; in the latter case, it reduces to the aftertax cost of debt, $k_D (1 - T_C)$.

In the following sections, we only consider firms that are financed with a mix of debt and equity. Thus, to estimate a firm's WACC according to equation 10.12, we need four inputs:

1. The debt and equity ratios, $\dfrac{D}{E + D}$ and $\dfrac{E}{E + D}$
2. The cost of debt, k_D
3. The marginal corporate tax rate, T_C
4. The cost of equity, k_E

THE FIRM'S TARGET CAPITAL STRUCTURE

The debt-equity mix to use in the estimation of a firm's WACC must reflect the relative proportions of debt and equity that the firm intends to use in financing its investment projects. We call this mix the firm's **target capital structure.** In this chapter, these proportions are given; Chapter 11 discusses how a firm determines its target capital structure. However, there are two caveats when estimating the relevant proportions of debt and equity in the WACC formula (equation 10.12).

First, the firm's current capital structure may not be its target capital structure. Issuing securities is costly, so firms typically do not issue debt and equity simultaneously when they raise capital. A firm may, for example, issue debt today which will move the firm away from its target capital structure. To restore capital structure to its target values, the firm will have to issue equity at a later date. Because of this process, the firm's capital structure changes over time and the structure we observe at one particular point in time may not be the firm's target capital structure. In computing the WACC, the long-run target capital structure must be used.

Second, the proportions of debt and equity financing in the WACC should be estimated with the *market values* of debt and equity, not with their *accounting* or *book values*. Firms issue stocks and bonds at their market values, not at their book values. Thus, the firm's current book values of debt and equity are irrelevant. To illustrate this point, consider again the case of Sunlight Manufacturing Company (SMC). The firm's managerial balance sheet,[4] shown in Exhibit 10.7, indicates that the firm's book value of equity and debt are both $90 million. Hence, the *book* values of the financing proportions in equation 10.12 are both equal to 50 percent of total financing ($90 million divided by $180 million).

To estimate the *market values* of the debt and equity ratios, we need the market values of the firm's debt and equity. Recall that the market value of SMC's bonds is $1,112. The firm has 90,000 bonds outstanding, so the market value of its long-term debt is $100,080,000 ($1,112 × 90,000). SMC's share price is currently $60. With 2.5 million shares outstanding, the market value of SMC's

EXHIBIT 10.7   SMC's Managerial Balance Sheet.

INVESTED CAPITAL OR NET ASSETS		CAPITAL EMPLOYED	
Cash	$10,000,000	Long-term debt[1]	$90,000,000
		90,000 bonds at par value $1,000	
Working capital requirement	$50,000,000		
		Owners' equity	$90,000,000
		2,500,000 shares at par value $10	$25,000,000
Net fixed assets	$120,000,000	Retained earnings	$65,000,000
Total	$180,000,000	Total	$180,000,000

[1] SMC has no short-term debt.

[4] The managerial balance sheet is a modified version of the standard balance sheet introduced in Chapter 3. On one side it reports the firm's investment in cash, operations (working capital requirement) and fixed assets. On the other side, it shows the amount of capital (borrowed funds and owners' equity) employed to finance these investments.

equity is thus \$150 million (\$60 $\times$ 2.5 million). Based on these market values, the debt and equity ratios are:

$$\text{Debt ratio at market value} = \frac{\$100.080 \text{ million}}{\$100.080 \text{ million} + \$150 \text{ million}}$$

$$= \frac{\$100.080 \text{ million}}{\$250.080 \text{ million}} = 0.40$$

$$\text{Equity ratio at market value} = \frac{\$150 \text{ million}}{\$100.080 \text{ million} + \$150 \text{ million}}$$

$$= \frac{\$150 \text{ million}}{\$250.080 \text{ million}} = 0.60$$

Thus, the 50 percent ratios at *book* value translate to 40 percent and 60 percent at *market* value. In practice, such large differences are not uncommon.

Estimating the market values of the debt and equity ratios requires knowing the market values of the firm's debt and equity. When the firm's shares are publicly traded, the market value of equity is simply the share price multiplied by the number of shares outstanding. The estimation of the market value of debt is more complicated because the bonds of most firms are not publicly traded. One way to circumvent this difficulty is to apply the bond valuation formula (see equation 10.1) to each of the firm's debt issues, and then add these values to obtain the total market value of the firm's debt.[5]

In practice, many analysts would simply use the book value of debt as a surrogate for its unavailable market value. When the firm's shares are not publicly traded, the book value of equity is also used as a substitute for its market value. These approximations are less than satisfactory because ratios based on market values can be quite different from their book values. As an alternative, we suggest using the market value ratios of proxy firms that have publicly traded bonds and stocks.

THE FIRM'S COSTS OF DEBT AND EQUITY

The previous sections present a number of models that can be used to estimate a firm's costs of debt and equity. Let's briefly recapitulate.

The cost of debt k_D can be estimated using the bond valuation formula (equation 10.1) or the credit spread equation (equation 10.2). Recall that if we know the bond price, its promised coupon payments, and its face value, the valuation formula (equation 10.1) can be solved for k_D. When we applied this technique to SMC, we found k_D equal to 7.25 percent.

In practice, firms do not have to perform these calculations. They either use the credit spread approximation (equation 10.2) or simply call their bank. Indeed,

---

[5] If the debt is at a *floating* rate then its book value approximates its market value.

banks and other financial institutions constantly follow changes in bond prices and market interest rates. Thus, a less time-consuming way to estimate k_D is to ask your banker, who will quote you a rate when needed. This alternative is particularly useful for firms that do not have publicly traded bonds from which they can estimate their most recent cost of debt.

The cost of equity k_E can be estimated with the help of the capital asset pricing model using equation 10.11. To estimate k_E, we need the prevailing market yield on government bonds, the firm's equity beta, and the market risk premium. The market yield on government bonds is regularly published in the business pages of major daily newspapers. The historical market risk premium is about 7 percent in the United States and the United Kingdom. Most developed countries with an active equity market have a historical market risk premium in the range of 5 percent to 7 percent. As indicated earlier, the betas of publicly traded stocks can be easily obtained from financial information services.

Using a prevailing government bond yield of 6.50 percent and an equity beta of 1.05, we found SMC's estimated cost of equity equal to 13.85 percent. Recall that we need share prices to estimate betas. However, even when there are no available share prices, which is the case of firms whose shares are not publicly traded, the CAPM can still be applied. In this case, the betas of proxy firms are used. This approach is described later in this chapter.

SUMMARY OF THE FIRM'S WACC CALCULATIONS

Exhibit 10.8 summarizes the four steps required to estimate a firm's weighted average cost of capital. Each of the first three steps corresponds to a particular component of the WACC. For each, the exhibit indicates how to estimate its value and shows the results of the estimation for SMC. The last step is simply the computation of the WACC using equation 10.12. SMC's target financing ratios are 40 percent debt and 60 percent equity. Its pretax cost of debt is 7.25 percent, its cost of equity is 13.85 percent, and the tax rate is 40 percent. Applying equation 10.12, we find:

$$\text{WACC}_{\text{SMC}} = 7.25\% \times (1 - 0.40) \times 0.40 + 13.85\% \times 0.60 = 10\%$$

This is the discount rate SMC should use when making investment decisions involving projects that have the same risk profile as that of the firm. Any proposal that has a risk profile similar to that of SMC but that does not expect to generate a return in excess of 10 percent should be rejected.

ESTIMATING THE COST OF CAPITAL OF A PROJECT

A project's cost of capital is primarily determined by the project's *risk,* which can be classified into one of two categories. The first category includes projects that have

EXHIBIT 10.8 The Estimation of a Firm's Weighted Average Cost of Capital (WACC), Including an Application to Sunlight Manufacturing Company (SMC).

STEPS TO FOLLOW	HOW TO	SMC
Step 1: Estimate the firm's relative proportions of debt (D) and equity (E) financing: $\dfrac{D}{E+D}$ and $\dfrac{E}{E+D}$.	• Use the firm's market values of debt and equity. • The market value of debt is computed from data on outstanding bonds using the bond valuation formula (equation 10.1). • The market value of equity is the share price times the number of shares outstanding. • If the firm's securities are not publicly traded use the market value ratios of proxy firms.	$100,080,000 $150,000,000 $\dfrac{D}{E+D} = 0.40 \quad \dfrac{E}{E+D} = 0.60$
Step 2: Estimate the firm's aftertax cost of debt: $k_D (1 - T_c)$.	• If the firm has outstanding bonds that are publicly traded, use equation 10.1 to estimate k_D. • Otherwise, use the credit spread equation (equation 10.2) or ask the bank. • Use the marginal corporate tax rate for T_c.	$k_D = 7.25\%$ $T_c = 40\%$ $k_D (1 - T_c) = 7.25\% \times (1 - 0.40) = 4.35\%$
Step 3: Estimate the firm's cost of equity: k_E.	• Use the capital asset pricing model (equation 10.11). • The risk-free rate is the rate on government bonds. • The market risk premium is 7% (historical average). • Use the beta of the firm's stock. If the firm's shares are not publicly traded, estimate beta from proxies.	6.5% 7% 1.05 $k_E = 6.5\% + 7\% \times 1.05 = 13.85\%$
Step 4: Calculate the firm's weighted average cost of capital (WACC).	• $\text{WACC} = k_D (1 - T_c)\dfrac{D}{E+D} + k_E\dfrac{E}{E+D}$	$4.35\% \times 0.40 + 13.85\% \times 0.60 = \textbf{10\%}$

risk characteristics *similar* to those of the firm that would undertake them. SMC's designer desk lamp project belongs to this category.

The second category includes projects that have a risk profile *different* from the risk profile of the firm that would undertake them. As an illustration of this type of project, we use a fictitious food processing company called Fine Foods. Managers at Fine Foods, convinced that their company will benefit from vertical integration into fast-food restaurants, are considering opening a chain of restaurants similar to McDonald's under the name Buddy's. The Buddy's restaurants project belongs to the second category because the firm that would undertake the project, Fine Foods, is in the food processing business, not the fast-food restaurant business.

The following sections show how to estimate the cost of capital for these two types of projects.

THE PROJECT'S RISK IS SIMILAR TO THE RISK OF THE FIRM

If the project's risk is the same as the risk of the firm, then the firm is the appropriate proxy for the project and the project's WACC is simply the firm's WACC. The estimation procedure for the firm's WACC is described in the previous section and summarized in Exhibit 10.8. The designer desk lamp project has the same risk as SMC's risk, so the 10 percent WACC of SMC is the appropriate cost of capital for that project. This is the discount rate we used in Chapter 6 to estimate the net present value of the project.

THE PROJECT'S RISK IS DIFFERENT
FROM THE RISK OF THE FIRM

When a project has a different risk profile than the risk profile of the firm that would undertake it, such as in the case of the Buddy's restaurants project, the firm is no longer the right proxy for the project because investors require the project's cost of capital to reflect the risk of the *project,* not the risk of the *firm.* As indicated at the beginning of the chapter, investors expect a return from the project that is at least equal to the return they would get from the proxy firms.

How should the project's cost of capital be estimated in this case? Should it be set equal to the average value of the proxies' WACC, where the WACC of each proxy is estimated as in the previous section? One potential problem with this approach is that the project may have a different target debt and equity ratios than those of the proxy firms. Another problem is that the marginal corporate tax rate of the firm that would undertake the project may differ from the average tax rate of the proxy firms. A solution to these problems is to estimate the cost of capital of the proxy firms *assuming that they have no debt financing and pay no tax.* Then, these estimates are adjusted to reflect the project's target capital structure and tax rate. This procedure is illustrated using the Buddy's restaurants project.

The project's target capital structure

Chapter 11 explains that many factors affect a firm's capital structure, among them the type of assets owned by the firm. Because proxy firms operate in the same line of business as the project and are expected to own assets that are similar to those of the project, it is generally assumed that their capital structure is a good approximation of the degree of financial leverage that investors would require for the project. In other words, the project's financing ratios can be set equal to the *average* of the proxies' financing ratios.

To estimate the proxies' financing ratios, the same approach is used as in the case where the firm itself (SMC) is the proxy. The two caveats mentioned earlier are still valid. First, market values should be used instead of book values. Second, the *observed* capital structure of a particular proxy firm may not be that firm's target structure. However, taking the mean of the proxies' financing ratios should reduce the effect of most measurement errors.

Exhibit 10.9 reports the financing ratios for the Buddy's restaurants proxy firms. The three proxies selected from the restaurant industry are McDonald's, Wendy's International, and CKE Restaurants. Note the wide discrepancies between book value ratios and market value ratios. On average, the proxy firms finance their assets 17 percent with debt and 83 percent with equity.

The project's costs of debt and equity

As mentioned earlier, both the cost of equity and cost of debt depend on the firm's debt ratio. The higher the debt ratio, the higher the financial risk and the greater the returns required by shareholders and bondholders. Therefore, if we want to use the proxies' costs of debt and equity to estimate the project's cost of capital, we must first adjust them for the differences in the financial leverage between the proxies and the project. In practice, however, it is assumed that the cost of debt is less sensitive to changes in financial leverage than is the cost of equity,[6] so only the latter is adjusted for differences in capital structure.

Estimating the cost of debt for the Buddy's Restaurants Project

We can use equation 10.1 to estimate the cost of debt for proxy firms. For proxies that have publicly traded bonds, the required information is generally available in the financial press. For example, the *Wall Street Journal* reports information on various bond issues on a daily basis. In the *Journal* bond table dated June 27, 1996, we found data on a bond issued by McDonald's. Because McDonald's was the only Buddy's proxy firm that was listed in the bond table, we used its market yield as an estimate of Buddy's cost of debt.

---

[6]At least for firms which do not exhibit an extreme degree of financial leverage.

EXHIBIT 10.9   Proxies for Buddy's Restaurants.

	EQUITY BETA[1]	DEBT-TO-EQUITY RATIO[1,2] $\dfrac{D}{E}$ At market value	ASSET BETA[3]
McDonalds	1.01	0.17	0.92
Wendy's International	0.92	0.23	0.81
CKE Restaurants	1.15	0.22	1.02
Average values	**1.03**	**0.21**	**0.92**

	DEBT RATIO[1,2] $\dfrac{D}{E+D}$		EQUITY RATIO[1,2] $\dfrac{E}{E+D}$	
	At market value	At book value	At market value	At book value
McDonalds	0.14	0.41	0.86	0.59
Wendy's International	0.19	0.36	0.81	0.64
CKE Restaurants	0.18	0.47	0.82	0.53
Average values	**0.17**	**0.41**	**0.83**	**0.59**

[1] Data from Alcar, June 1996.
[2] D = debt; E = equity.
[3] Calculated according to equation 10.7 with a corporate tax rate of 40 percent.

The McDonald's bond was identified in the *Journal* bond table as "McDnl $7^{3/8}02$." This means that its coupon rate is $7^{3/8}$ percent (7.375 percent) and that the bond will mature in the year 2002, six years from June 1996. Assuming a par value of $1,000, the annual coupon payment is thus $73.75 (7.375 percent of $1,000). The bond table also reported a closing price of 101 for the McDonald's bond, meaning that bonds were last traded at $1,010 (101 percent of $1,000), again assuming a par value of $1,000. We can use this information to estimate k_D with the bond valuation formula (equation 10.1); we know that the bond's price is $1,010, that its face value is $1,000, and that it will pay annual coupon payments of $73.75 for six years:

$$\$1,010 = \frac{\$73.75}{1+k_D} + \frac{\$73.75}{(1+k_D)^2} + \frac{\$73.75}{(1+k_D)^3} + \frac{\$73.75}{(1+k_D)^4} + \frac{\$73.75}{(1+k_D)^5} + \frac{\$1,073.75}{(1+k_D)^6}$$

Our calculator indicates that k_D is equal to 7.16 percent. We will use this rate as our estimate of the rate of interest required by investors on bonds issued by firms in the fast-food restaurant industry. Consequently, it should also be Buddy's rate of interest. Assuming a marginal tax rate of 40 percent, the project's aftertax cost of debt is thus 4.30 percent $[7.16\% \times (1 - 0.40)]$.

As indicated earlier, in practice, firms do not need to compute the required rates of interest because these rates are readily available from banks and other financial institutions. However, banks will often quote a rate for your company as a whole, not for a specific project. You can use this rate as long as the project's risk is not very different from the risk of your firm. But if this is not the case, you should ask your bank to quote the rates for proxy firms, not the rate for your company.

Estimating the cost of equity for the Buddy's Restaurants Project

Recall that a firm's beta coefficient rises with financial leverage. Thus, if we employ the capital asset pricing model to estimate a project's cost of equity, we want to make sure that the beta coefficient we use reflects the impact of the project's target capital structure. If proxies have different capital structures than the project's target capital structure, their betas need to be adjusted to account for the difference. The adjustment is done in two steps. First, each of the proxies' equity beta is "un-levered," meaning that its corresponding unlevered or asset beta is calculated using equation 10.7. Second, the *mean* of the "un-levered" betas is "re-levered" at the *project's* target capital structure using equation 10.6 in order to obtain the *project's* equity beta. This is the beta coefficient that should be used to estimate the project's cost of equity according to the CAPM.

We illustrate this procedure using the Buddy's restaurants project. The unlevered, or asset, betas of the proxies are shown in Exhibit 10.9. They have a mean value of 0.92. We set the project's target capital structure at the same level as the average of the proxies' capital structures, so we need to re-lever this average asset beta of 0.92 to the proxies' mean debt-to-equity ratio which, as indicated in Exhibit 10.9, is 21 percent. Applying equation 10.6 with a corporate tax rate of 40 percent, we get:

$$\beta_{\text{equity, Buddy's}} = 0.92 \times [1 + (1 - 0.40) \times 0.21] = 1.04$$

Applying the CAPM expressed in equation 10.11 with an equity beta of 1.04, the same risk-free rate of 6.50 percent as in the designer desk lamp project, and a market risk premium of 7 percent, we get the following estimate of the cost of equity for the Buddy's restaurants project:

$$k_{\text{E, Buddy's}} = 6.5\% + 7.0\% \times 1.04 = 13.78\%$$

Estimating the WACC for the Buddy's Restaurants Project

Exhibit 10.10 summarizes the steps required to estimate the cost of capital when the project's risk is different from the risk of the firm. Each step shows the application to the Buddy's restaurants project. Buddy's target financing ratios are 17 percent debt

EXHIBIT 10.10 **The Estimation of a Project's Cost of Capital when the Project Risk Is Different from the Risk of the Firm, Including an Application to the Buddy's Restaurants Project.**

STEPS TO FOLLOW	HOW TO	BUDDY'S RESTAURANTS
Step 1: Estimate the project's relative proportions of debt (D) and equity (E) financing, $\dfrac{D}{E+D}$ and $\dfrac{E}{E+D}$, using proxy firms.	• Use the proxies' market values of debt and equity. • The market value of debt is computed from data on outstanding bonds using the bond valuation formula (equation 10.1). • The market value of equity is the share price times the number of shares outstanding. • Take the mean of the proxies' ratios.	$\dfrac{D}{E+D} = 0.17 \qquad \dfrac{E}{E+D} = 0.83$
Step 2: Estimate the project's after-tax cost of debt: $k_D\,(1 - T_c)$.	• If the proxies have outstanding bonds that are publicly traded, use equation 10.1 to estimate their cost of debt k_D. • Otherwise, use the credit spread equation (equation 10.2) or ask the bank. • Take the mean of the proxies' cost of debt. • Use the marginal corporate tax rate for T_c.	$k_D = 7.16\%$ $T_c = 40\%$ $k_D\,(1 - T_c) = 7.16\% \times (1 - 0.40) = 4.30\%$
Step 3: Estimate the project's cost of equity: k_E.	• Use the capital asset pricing model (equation 10.11). • The risk-free rate is the rate on government bonds. • The market risk premium is 7% (historical average). • Un-lever the proxies' equity betas using equation 10.7 to get their unlevered asset betas. • Re-lever the mean of the proxies' asset betas at the project's target debt-to-equity ratio using equation 10.6 to get the project's equity beta. • Apply the CAPM to the project's equity beta to get the project's cost of equity k_E.	6.5% 7% 1.04 $k_E = 6.5\% + 7\% \times 1.04 = 13.78\%$
Step 4: Calculate the project's weighted average cost of capital (WACC).	• $\text{WACC} = k_D\,(1 - T_c)\dfrac{D}{E+D} + k_E\dfrac{E}{E+D}$	$4.30\% \times 0.17 + 13.78\% \times 0.83 = \mathbf{12.2\%}$

329

and 83 percent equity. Its pretax cost of debt is 7.16 percent, its cost of equity is 13.78 percent, and the tax rate is 40 percent. Applying the WACC formula, we get:

$$\text{WACC}_{\text{Buddy's}} = 7.16\% \times (1 - 0.40) \times 0.17 + 13.78\% \times .83 = 12.2\%$$

This is the appropriate rate managers of Fine Foods should use to decide whether they should open a chain of Buddy's fast-food restaurants.

THREE MISTAKES TO AVOID WHEN ESTIMATING A PROJECT'S COST OF CAPITAL

We close this section by discussing three mistakes that are commonly made when estimating a project's cost of capital. These mistakes reveal some dangerous misconceptions about the precise meaning and the correct estimation of a project's cost of capital.

Mistake #1

"The project is going to be financed entirely with debt, so its relevant cost of capital is the interest rate on the debt." Or, "The project is going to be financed entirely with equity, so its relevant cost of capital is the cost of equity."

Suppose that SMC, being short of funds, decided to borrow $2 million to finance the entire cost of its designer desk lamp project at an interest rate of 7.25 percent (the same rate as the one used earlier). If we mechanically apply the WACC formula (equation 10.12), the project's cost of capital would be 7.25 percent because there is no equity financing in this case. If you think something is wrong with this, you are right. Let's see why.

First, the firm could borrow $2 million at 7.25 percent, not on the merit of the project but because it has enough equity and other valuable assets that serve as guarantees for the lender. While SMC as a whole can borrow $2 million, no bank or any other potential lender would be willing to lend the full cost of the designer desk lamp project with the project's assets as sole guarantee. Second, and more fundamental, the WACC formula was incorrectly used. Remember that the cost of capital of the desk lamp project is the rate of return that the project needs to generate in order to meet investors' return expectations. Because the project has the same risk as SMC's risk, the relevant cost of capital for the project must be the same as SMC's cost of capital. The latter can be estimated using the WACC formula *applied to SMC* which, we know, is *not* 100 percent financed by debt!

Mistake #2

"Although the project does not have the same risk as the firm, its relevant cost of capital should be equal to the firm's WACC because the firm's shareholders and bondholders are paid with cash from the firm's cash flows, not from the project's cash flows."

It is true that dividends and interest expenses are paid out of the firm's cash flows. However, this does not imply that the cost of capital of any project undertaken by the firm must be the same as the firm's cost of capital. The return that investors want to earn on a project is the same as the one they would get from an alternative investment with the same risk characteristics, irrespective of the return they are currently getting from the firm. For example, should the cost of capital of the investments to be made by Buddy's (a chain of fast-food restaurants) be the same as the cost of capital of Fine Foods (a food processing company)? The answer is no, because investors will certainly not view investments made in the fast-food restaurant sector in the same way they view investments in the food processing industry. They would rather compare them to investments made by firms that invest exclusively in fast-food restaurants. Remember: *it is not the firm's cost of capital that determines a project's cost of capital; it is the other way around.* Each project has its own cost of capital and the firm's cost of capital is simply the weighted average of the capital costs of the various projects that the firm has undertaken.

Unfortunately, many firms still use a company-wide cost of capital, often called the **hurdle rate,** cutoff rate, or **benchmark rate,** which they apply indiscriminately to all projects. Unless all these projects have the same risk, this procedure is incorrect.

To illustrate this point, we consider MultiTek, a firm that is using the company's WACC to evaluate all its projects. To simplify, suppose that MultiTek has no debt and that its beta is equal to one. Suppose further that the rate on government bonds is 7 percent and that the market risk premium is also 7 percent. According to the CAPM, expressed in equation 10.11, MultiTek's cost of equity, which is also its WACC because the firm has no debt, is equal to:

$$k_{E, \text{MultiTek}} = \text{WACC}_{\text{MultiTek}} = 7\% + 7\% \times 1.00 = 14\%$$

Note that 14 percent is also the expected return on the market portfolio because MultiTek has a beta coefficient equal to one. Because MultiTek uses its WACC to evaluate its investment proposals, it will accept any project with a return higher than 14 percent and reject any project with a return lower than 14 percent. This decision rule is illustrated in Exhibit 10.11, where the 14 percent line separates the region where projects are accepted from the region where they are rejected.

We have also drawn the security market line (SML), which provides a project's expected return given that project's beta coefficient. It starts at 7 percent, the risk-free rate, and passes through point M, the market expected return of 14 percent. If MultiTek used the projects' betas instead of the firm's beta to evaluate its investment projects, it would reject any project below the SML and accept any project above the SML because the SML represents the relationship between any investment's expected returns and its corresponding beta coefficient. Exhibit 10.11 shows that using a single rate for all types of projects may lead MultiTek to incorrectly accept some high-risk projects and incorrectly reject some low-risk projects.

For example, suppose the firm has two divisions, a low-risk one in the software publishing sector and a high-risk one in the hardware manufacturing sector. Proxy firms for the former have an average asset beta of 0.60; proxies for the latter have an average asset beta of 1.40. Because the firm does not carry any debt, the cost of capital for each of the divisions is its cost of equity. Using the CAPM to estimate each division's cost of capital, we find:

$$k_{E, \text{ Software}} = 7\% + 7\% \times 0.60 = 11.2\%$$

$$k_{E, \text{ Hardware}} = 7\% + 7\% \times 1.40 = 16.8\%$$

If the software publishing division is considering an investment with an internal rate of return (IRR) of 13 percent (see Exhibit 10.11), the project should be accepted because it would provide MultiTek's shareholders with a return that is higher than the required 11.2 percent return. Similarly, if the hardware manufacturing division has a project with an IRR of 15 percent (see Exhibit 10.11), it should be rejected because its IRR is lower than the 16.8 percent return required by Multi-Tek's shareholders. However, under the decision rule applied by MultiTek, the first project is rejected because its expected return is less than the company-wide WACC and the second is accepted because its expected return is higher. If Multi-Tek continues to use its WACC as a cutoff rate for all types of investment, it will, at times, accept unprofitable risky investments and reject profitable and less risky ones. As a result, the risk of the firm will rise over time, its risk adjusted profitability will decline, and its value will go down.

Mistake #3

"When a project's risk is different from the risk of the firm, the project's cost of capital should be lowered to account for the risk reduction that diversification brings to the firm."

It is true that a project whose returns do not vary like those of the firm's existing investments will reduce the firm's overall risk through diversification. For example, you may argue that by diversifying into fast-food restaurants, Fine Foods' total risk will be reduced because earnings in both industries do not move in steps. When the earnings from the food processing industry go up (or down), earnings from the fast-food industry may also go up (or down), but not necessarily in the same proportions. As a result, the volatility of Fine Foods' earnings will be smoother if it decides to invest in fast-food restaurants. You may, therefore, conclude that using fast-food restaurant chains as proxies for Buddy's without accounting for this risk reduction effect is incorrect.

However, although it is true that the total risk of the firm will be reduced if it invests in fast-food restaurants, the effect is irrelevant to its shareholders because they can benefit directly from the same risk reduction by buying shares in McDonald's or Wendy's. Consequently, they would certainly not accept that the return they

EXHIBIT 10.11 Company-Wide Cost of Capital and Projects' Expected Rates of Return.

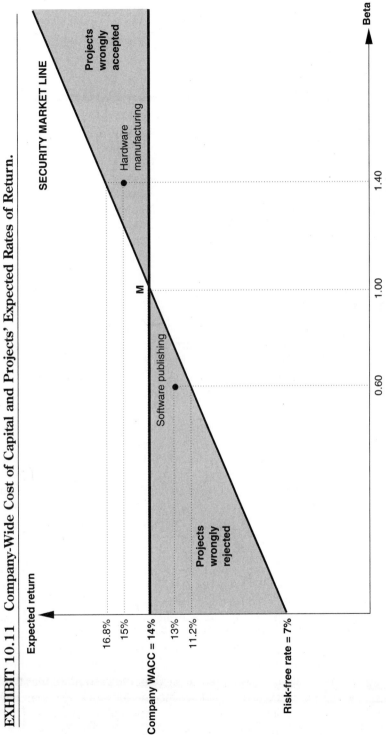

require from the project be reduced because of the risk diversification that they can achieve in their personal portfolio without the help of Fine Foods' managers.

Avoiding mistakes

Mistakes made when estimating a project's cost of capital can lead to a distorted allocation of capital among projects and eventually to value destruction, as in the case of a firm using a company-wide cost of capital irrespective of the systematic risk (beta) of the project it evaluates. Our advice: When in doubt, always remember that *a project's cost of capital is determined by financial markets, not by managers.* What you can do, and must do, is use market data, such as market interest rates, betas, and the capital structure of proxies, to determine the return that the market is expecting from the project being evaluated. What you should *not* do is set values for the weighted average cost of capital that are based on internally generated data, such as accounting data. Doing so could incorrectly influence the outcome of your evaluation.

SUMMARY

The *firm's* cost of capital is simply the return that investors expect to earn on the firm's invested capital. When a project has the *same* risk profile as that of the firm that would undertake it, the *project's* cost of capital is the same as the firm's cost of capital. But when a project's risk is different from the firm's risk, the firm's cost of capital is no longer the appropriate cost of capital for the project. In this case, proxies, or pure-plays, that have the *same* risk as the project's risk must be identified and the proxies' cost of capital must be used to evaluate the project.

Unfortunately, a firm's cost of capital is not directly observable. It must be inferred from the return investors expect to earn on the capital they invest in the firm. This expected return can be estimated using data on the securities issued by the firm to raise capital from investors. These securities include stocks and bonds that represent different claims on the cash flows generated by the firm's invested capital. Consequently, the rate of return expected by investors depends on the type of security they hold. Two fundamental security valuation models can be used to estimate the cost of the most commonly issued securities, namely, bonds and stocks. From bond prices, we can infer the cost of debt. And from common stock prices, we can infer the cost of equity. To determine the overall cost of capital, we simply find the weighted average of the cost of debt and the cost of equity, where the weights are the proportions of debt and equity the firm has raised to finance its assets. This overall cost of capital is called the weighted average cost of capital or WACC.

One valuation model for estimating the cost of capital says that the market value of any security is equal to the present value of the cash flows that the holder of the security expects to receive (dividend income for stocks, coupon payments and face value for bonds), discounted at the rate expected by investors. This model is particularly suitable for the estimation of the cost of debt because a bond's face value and future coupon payments are known. This allows us to calculate the bond's yield to maturity, which is the firm's estimated cost of debt. However, this model is not generally suitable for the estimation of the cost of equity because of the difficulty in forecasting the stream of dividends the firm is expected to pay in the future.

According to the second model, the capital asset pricing model or CAPM, the return expected from a security is the sum of (1) the return that could be expected from a risk-free investment (government securities) and (2) a premium directly related to the risk of the security. The CAPM indicates that the relevant risk of a security is not its total risk but only the portion of its total risk that cannot be eliminated or reduced by diversification, that is, by holding a large portfolio of assets. This nondiversifiable risk, also called systematic risk or beta, is measured relative to a market portfolio, a portfolio that contains all available assets. Because constructing such a portfolio is an almost impossible task, analysts usually measure a security's beta relative to a broad market index, such as the S&P 500 index in the United States and the Financial Times Index in Britain. The risk premium for any security is simply the product of its beta and the expected risk premium for the entire market, which is defined as the difference between the expected return on the market index and the rate on the risk-free investment. We applied the CAPM to estimate a firm's cost of equity using the government bond rate as the risk-free rate and the *historical* average of the market risk premium as an estimate of its expected value.

Having determined a firm's costs of debt and equity, we estimated the return expected from the firm's assets by finding the weighted average of these two costs with weights equal to the relative proportions of debt and equity used in financing the firm's assets. This return is the firm's weighted average cost of capital. It is also the project's cost of capital when the project risk is similar to the risk of the firm that undertakes it. When the project's risk is not identical or similar to that of the firm, the firm's WACC no longer represents the return that investors require from the project. However, we can use the cost of equity and the cost of debt of proxy firms and their capital structure ratios to estimate a WACC that can be used as a substitute for the project's cost of capital.

Finally, the chapter discusses three mistakes that are often made when estimating a project's cost of capital. These mistakes can be traced to some misconceptions regarding a project's cost of capital, and can be easily avoided by remembering that a project's cost of capital is determined by financial markets, not by managers.

REFERENCES AND FURTHER READING

1. Benninga, Simon, and Oded Sarig. *Corporate Finance: A Valuation Approach.* McGraw-Hill, 1997. See chapter 9.
2. Brealey, Richard, and Stewart Myers. *Principles of Corporate Finance.* 5th ed. McGraw-Hill, 1996. See chapters 7 to 9 and 19.

3. Clark, John, Thomas Hindelang, and Robert Pritchard. *Capital Budgeting: Planning and Control of Capital Expenditures.* 3d ed. Prentice-Hall, 1989. See chapters 14 to 17.

4. Copeland, Tom, Tim Koller, and Jack Murrin. *Valuation.* 2d ed. John Wiley, 1995. See chapter 8.

5. Cornell, Bradford. *Corporate Valuation.* Business One Irwin, 1993. See chapter 7.

6. Damoran, Aswath. *Damoran on Valuation.* John Wiley, 1994. See chapter 3.

7. Megginson, William. *Corporate Finance Theory.* Addison Wesley Longman, 1997. See chapter 3.

8. Ross, Stephen, Randolph Westerfield, and Jeffrey Jaffe. *Corporate Finance.* 4th ed. Irwin, 1996. See chapters 9 to 12 and 17.

REVIEW PROBLEMS

10.1 Cost of debt versus cost of equity.

When we say that a firm, a division, or a project has a cost of equity capital of 10 percent and a cost of debt of 8 percent, what do we mean? Why is the cost of debt lower than the cost of equity?

10.2 Cash flows from bonds and stocks.

What are the cash flows associated with a bond? With a share of common stock? How are these cash flows related to the market value of the bond? The market value of the share of common stock?

10.3 The capital asset pricing model.

What does the capital asset pricing model (CAPM) claim?

10.4 Estimation of the cost of capital of a firm.

Royal Corporation has 10 million shares and 250,000 annual-coupon bonds outstanding. It has no financial debt other than the outstanding bonds. The par value of the bonds is $1,000 and the coupon rate is 10 percent. The shares of the company currently trade at $40 and have a beta coefficient of 1.10. The bonds, which have 10 years to maturity, trade at 115 percent of par value. The yield on 10 year government bonds is 6.3 percent and the (equity) market risk premium is 7 percent. The Royal Corporation tax rate is 40 percent. What is the cost of capital for Royal Corporation?

10.5 Estimation of the cost of capital for a division.

Part I: Your company, PacificCom, manufactures telecommunication equipment and communication software. You have just received a copy of a consultant's report that strongly recommends that investment proposals be accepted only if their internal rate of return is higher than 12 percent. The rate of 12 percent is presented as the weighted average cost of capital of PacificCom and was computed as follows:

$$\text{WACC} = k_D \, (1 - T_c) \times \frac{D}{E + D} + k_E \times \frac{E}{E + D}$$

$$\text{WACC} = 8\%(1 - 40\%) \times 30\% + 15.1\% \times 70\% = 12\%$$

where k_D = 8% is the rate at which PacificCom can borrow from its banks; T_c = 40% is the firm's marginal corporate tax rate; [D/(E+D)] = 30% and [E/(E+D)] = 70% are PacificCom financing ratios where D and E are the amount of debt and equity taken from the firm's most recent balance sheet; and k_E = 15.1% is PacificCom's cost of equity. It was calculated using the capital asset pricing model with a risk-free rate equal to the government bond rate of 6.5%, a market risk premium of 7%, and the firm's beta coefficient of 1.23 (k_E = 6.5% + 1.23 × 7% = 15.1%). You are the person in charge of the financial analysis of the equipment division's investment proposals. Do you agree with the consultant's recommendation?

Part 2: Suppose you have identified three single-business companies with activities that are similar to those of the equipment division of PacificCom. You were able to get the following data on these proxy firms from your investment banker:

	PROXY A	PROXY B	PROXY C
Equity beta	0.70	1.00	1.02
Debt-to-equity (D/E) ratio at market values	1.00	0.80	0.70

a. How would you estimate the equipment division's weighted average cost of capital (WACC) if that division's target debt-to-equity ratio has been estimated at 1.20?

b. What would happen if the company-wide WACC of 12% is used by the equipment division to make investment decisions instead of using the division's WACC that has been estimated in the previous question?

11 DESIGNING A CAPITAL STRUCTURE

B roadly speaking, managers need to make two major decisions. They need to decide which investment projects create the most value, and they need to decide which mix of sources of capital is best for financing the firm's investments. Previous chapters show how managers should select value-creating projects. This chapter shows how they should design a value-creating capital structure, keeping in mind that the opportunities to create value through a change in the mix of debt and equity capital are more limited than those available through the selection of superior investment projects.

The decision to finance part of the firm's assets with borrowed funds has important managerial implications. If the firm finds it increasingly difficult to service its debt (paying interest and repaying the borrowed funds) because of excessive borrowing, its management will be under pressure to make decisions that may not be in the best interest of shareholders. For example, management may have to quickly sell *value-creating* assets for less than they are worth to the firm in order to raise the cash needed to make the payments required to service the firm's debt. Conversely, a firm with too little debt may pass up the opportunity to reduce its tax payments and increase its value through tax savings. By replacing equity with debt, the firm can deduct the interest expenses from its taxable income and save the cash that would have been used to pay taxes. If too much debt is damaging and too little debt is fiscally inefficient, what, then, is the right amount of debt? This is the question we want to answer in this chapter.

Managers can choose from a variety of sources of funds to finance their business. Most of these are hybrids of two basic types of capital: debt, such as bank loans and bonds, and equity, which includes retained earnings and common stocks. This chapter examines how managers should combine debt and equity financing to establish a capital structure that *maximizes the value of the firm's assets.* A firm's capital structure is usually identified by its *debt ratios,* either its debt-to-equity ratio (the amount of borrowing divided by the amount of equity) or its debt-to-assets ratio (the portion of the firm's assets financed with borrowed funds). These two debt ratios are often used interchangeably.

The firm's *optimal* or *target capital structure* is the debt ratio that maximizes the market value of the firm's assets (we show that this is generally the same as maximizing the market value of the firm's *equity* and *minimizing* its cost of capital). The optimal debt ratio depends on several factors, some are easily identifiable and measurable and others are not. To find out what these factors are and how they affect the firm's profitability and value, we analyze how a change in the firm's debt ratio affects (1) its profitability, measured with earnings per share (profit after tax divided by the number of shares outstanding), (2) the market value of its assets, (3) its share price, and (4) its cost of capital.

After reading this chapter, you should understand:

- How changes in capital structure affect the firm's earnings per share, market value, share price, and cost of capital.
- The trade-offs that are implied in the capital structure decision.
- How corporate taxes and the costs of financial distress affect the capital structure decision.
- Why firms in different industries and countries can have different capital structures.
- The factors, in addition to taxes and financial distress costs, that must be taken into account when establishing an optimal capital structure, including agency costs and the presence of information asymmetry between managers and outside investors.

THE CAPITAL STRUCTURE DECISION: NO CORPORATE TAXES AND NO FINANCIAL DISTRESS COSTS

This section examines how changes in capital structure affect the firm's profitability, its market value, its share price, and its cost of capital in a world in which firms *do not* pay corporate income taxes (a world in which the tax reduction benefits resulting from interest payments are irrelevant) and *do not* face **financial distress costs** (costs resulting from excessive borrowing that affect the firm's ability to perform efficiently and reduce its value). These two restrictions are lifted in the following sections where financial distress costs are defined and explained. By beginning our analysis without the complications of taxes and financial distress costs, the more general model is easier to understand.

EFFECTS OF CHANGES IN CAPITAL STRUCTURE ON THE FIRM'S PROFITABILITY (NO TAXES AND NO FINANCIAL DISTRESS COSTS)

In physics, leverage refers to the increase in power that comes from using a lever. In finance, **leverage,** or **gearing,** refers to the increase in profitability, usually measured with earnings per share (EPS), that can come from using debt financing.[1] To see why and how financial leverage affects EPS, we examine the Jolly Bear Company (JBC). JBC is currently *all-equity* financed with 2 million shares outstanding that are worth $100 each. The firm's equity value is thus $200 million ($100 × 2 million shares). Because the firm has no debt, the value of its assets is the same as the value of its equity—$200 million. JBC's Chief Financial Officer, Ms. Johnson, is considering borrowing $100 million at 10 percent and using the cash to repurchase one half of the firm's shares. She wants to know how this change in JBC's capital structure—which will increase its financial leverage— might affect the firm's earnings per share.

Exhibit 11.1 illustrates the effect of this **recapitalization** decision on EPS for three possible scenarios for the future performance of the economy—recession, expected performance, and expansion. Note that the firm's profit from operations, or earnings before interest and tax (EBIT),[2] is not affected by the decision to borrow. Operating profit is $10 million under the recession scenario, $30 million under the expected performance scenario, and $40 million under the expansion scenario, irrespective of the amount of debt Ms. Johnson decides to issue.

Consider first the case of the expected scenario. With no debt (upper part of Exhibit 11.1), net earnings are $30 million, the same as EBIT, because there are no interest or tax payments. With 2 million shares outstanding, EPS is equal to $15 ($30 million divided by 2 million shares). With $100 million of debt at an interest rate of 10 percent (lower part of Exhibit 11.1), the interest payment is $10 million and net earnings drop to $20 million. There are only 1 million shares after the share repurchase, so EPS is now $20 ($20 million divided by 1 million shares). Thus, debt financing boosts expected EPS from $15 to $20. Financial leverage seems to have the same effect as leverage has in the world of physics.

Leverage also works to the advantage of shareholders in the expansion scenario, with EPS rising by 50 percent, from $20 to $30. However, under the recession scenario, EPS, which is positive in the no-debt case, is zero in the case of borrowing.

We can see this phenomenon graphically by plotting EPS against EBIT for the current and proposed capital structure, as shown in Exhibit 11.2. The no-debt line

---

[1]The effect of financial leverage on another measure of profitability, the firm's return on equity, is examined in detail in Chapter 5.

[2]Because there is no corporate tax for this situation, operating profit is the same as earnings before interest and tax (EBIT).

EXHIBIT 11.1   **JBC's Earnings Per Share under the Current and Proposed Capital Structures and in the Absence of Taxes.**

CURRENT CAPITAL STRUCTURE: NO DEBT AND TWO MILLION SHARES AT $100 PER SHARE			
	RECESSION	**EXPECTED**	**EXPANSION**
Earnings before interest and tax (EBIT)	$10,000,000	$30,000,000	$40,000,000
Less interest expenses	0	0	0
Less tax	0	0	0
Equals net earnings	$10,000,000	$30,000,000	$40,000,000
Divided by the number of shares	2,000,000	2,000,000	2,000,000
Equals earnings per share (EPS)	**$5**	**$15**	**$20**

PROPOSED CAPITAL STRUCTURE: BORROW $100 MILLION AT 10 PERCENT AND USE THE CASH TO REPURCHASE ONE MILLION SHARES AT $100 PER SHARE			
	RECESSION	**EXPECTED**	**EXPANSION**
Earnings before interest and tax (EBIT)	$10,000,000	$30,000,000	$40,000,000
Less interest expenses	(10,000,000)	(10,000,000)	(10,000,000)
Less tax	0	0	0
Equals net earnings	$0	$20,000,000	$30,000,000
Divided by the number of shares	1,000,000	1,000,000	1,000,000
Equals earnings per share (EPS)	**$0**	**$20**	**$30**

starts at the origin because EPS is zero when EBIT is zero. As EBIT increases, EPS increases one-half dollar for each million dollar rise in EBIT. With $100 million of debt, the line starts with a negative $10 EPS; at this point, EBIT is zero but JBC still has to pay $10 million of interest expenses. The result is a loss of $10 million. Divided by one million shares, this loss produces a $10 loss per share. When EBIT rises, EPS increases twice as fast as when there is no debt, that is, EPS increases one dollar for each million dollar rise in EBIT. The reason should be clear: The number of shares outstanding is reduced by half when the firm borrows $100 million to repurchase equity. Indeed, the higher the amount of debt relative to equity, the lower the number of shares outstanding, the higher the rise in EPS when EBIT increases, and the steeper the EPS line.

Now, consider the point where the two lines intersect. For values of EBIT less than its value at the intersection point, EPS is higher if JBC selects an all-equity capital structure. At the point where the lines intersect, EPS is the same for both financing alternatives. For values of EBIT greater than its value at the intersection point, EPS is higher with debt financing. We determine the values of EBIT and EPS

EXHIBIT 11.2 JBC's Earnings Per Share under Different Capital Structures.

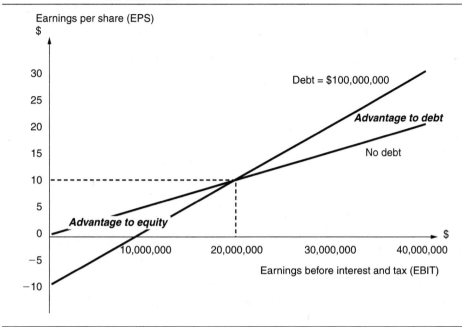

at the intersection point by using the fact that at this point EPS with no debt is equal to EPS with $100 million of debt. For the no-debt line, EPS equals EBIT divided by 2 million shares outstanding, as shown on the left side of the equation below. With $100 million of debt financing, EPS equals EBIT less $10 million of interest expenses divided by 1 million shares, as shown on the right side of the equation. At the intersection point, the two are the same:

$$EPS = \frac{EBIT}{2,000,000} = \frac{EBIT - \$10,000,000}{1,000,000}$$

from which we get:

$$EBIT = \$20,000,000$$

and:

$$EPS = \frac{\$20,000,000}{2,000,000} = \$10$$

Thus, when EBIT equals $20 million, EPS is $10 for both capital structures. Note that when EBIT is $20 million, JBC's return on assets is 10 percent ($20 million of EBIT divided by $200 million of assets), which is the same as the rate of interest on the debt. As long as JBC earns a return on its assets that is higher than its cost of debt, its shareholders are better off with debt financing.[3] From this analysis, Ms. Johnson can draw the following tentative conclusions:

1. The capital structure decision affects the firm's earnings per share.
2. Financial leverage increases earnings per shares as long as EBIT is higher than $20 million, which is the same as saying that return on assets exceeds the 10 percent cost of debt.
3. At the $30 million expected level of EBIT, earnings per share are $15 with no debt financing and $20 with $100 million of debt financing.

Clearly, under the *expected* scenario, financial leverage would benefit JBC's shareholders. However, Ms. Johnson knows that she cannot make a decision on the basis of a single scenario. There is some probability the economy will fall into a recession, in which case financial leverage will hurt rather than benefit shareholders. Before Ms. Johnson makes her decision, she must consider the *risk* that EBIT and return on assets are lower than their threshold values of $20 million and 10 percent, respectively.

THE TRADE-OFF BETWEEN PROFITABILITY AND RISK

The relationship between financial leverage and risk is illustrated in the graph shown in Exhibit 11.3. The lines represent the changes in JBC's earnings per share as a function of time for the two capital structures of the last section: no debt financing and $100 million of debt financing. EPS is calculated for values of EBIT that vary over time between the recession and the expansion scenarios, that is, between $10 million and $40 million. In the absence of debt, EPS varies between $5 and $20, as shown in Exhibit 11.1. The variations in EPS result from changes in general economic conditions and from factors affecting the industry to which JBC belongs. (Examples of such factors include changes in input and output prices, technology, and competition.) The risk generated by these changes, which originates from the business environment in which the firm operates, is rightly called **business risk.** This type of risk is independent of JBC's capital structure. In other words, business risk is the same for any amount of funds that Ms. Johnson decides to borrow.

In the presence of debt, EPS varies between $0 and $30. The graph clearly shows that debt financing amplifies the variability of EPS. The extra risk related to this magnifying effect is called **financial risk.** If Ms. Johnson decides to finance a

---

[3]The same result was obtained in Chapter 5. Remember, however, the two limitations we mention in that chapter. The discussion ignores risk and does not examine whether the higher leverage is accompanied by an increase in the value of the firm. These issues are discussed later in the chapter.

EXHIBIT 11.3   Financial Leverage and Risk.

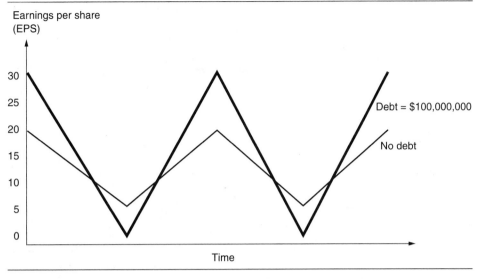

portion of JBC's assets with debt, the risk borne by JBC's shareholders will rise. Ms. Johnson is thus faced with a trade-off between the following:

1. She can issue debt to increase JBC's *expected* earnings per share, but the firm's shareholders will have to take on more risk.
2. She can maintain all-equity financing to reduce risk, but JBC's shareholders will end up with lower *expected* earnings per share.

Unfortunately, the analysis performed so far does not tell us what to do. To find out, we must determine how debt financing affects the firm's *value,* not just EPS. The alternative that produces the highest value for the firm would be preferred. How, then, does debt financing affect the firm's value in the absence of taxes and financial distress costs? The pizza theory of capital structure provides the answer.

EFFECT OF CHANGES IN CAPITAL STRUCTURE ON THE FIRM'S VALUE: THE PIZZA THEORY

In its culinary version, the pizza theory says that no one can increase the size of a pizza by slicing it.[4] In its corporate finance version, the firm's assets are a gigantic

---

[4]We should mention in passing that there is no absolute agreement on this point. When Yogi Berra, a famous baseball player, was asked into how many pieces he wanted his pizza cut, he is said to have replied: "Better make it six, I don't think I can eat eight."

pizza and the firm's shareholders and debtholders are the claimants to the slices, where the slices represent the cash flows generated by the assets. The pizza theory says that the market value of the firm's assets (the pizza) cannot be increased by changing the proportions of the cash flows (the slices) going to the firm's shareholders and debtholders, *provided these cash flows are not taxed.* In other words, the market value of the firm's assets is determined only by the cash flows the assets generate and is not affected by the relative proportions of debt and equity capital used to finance the assets. However, this is true only if the cash flows are *not* taxed.

To illustrate this phenomenon, suppose that Ms. Johnson decides to borrow the $100 million and buys back half of the firm's 2 million shares. Consider the implications of this recapitalization on the wealth of JBC's shareholders. Before the change in capital structure, their claim against JBC's assets amounted to the market value of the entire firm ($200 million) because the firm had no debt. After JBC is levered up, shareholders' claims against the $200 million of assets are reduced by $100 million, which represents the value of the debt now owed by JBC. But this reduction in value is exactly offset by the $100 million shareholders received from the 1 million shares they sold back to the firm. Shareholders will be as well off after the change in capital structure as they were before (their collective and aggregate wealth remains at $200 million). Thus, the change should not have any impact on JBC's share price.

The formal proof of the theory that changes in the firm's capital structure do not affect its total market value or share price was provided by Nobel Prize laureates Merton Miller and Franco Modigliani (MM) in two seminal papers published in 1958 and 1961. The intuition behind the theory is straightforward: The value of a firm's assets is determined only by the ability of its managers to generate as much cash flow as possible from these assets. Simply reshuffling paper claims on these cash flows does not add value to or subtract value from the firm's assets. Furthermore, it does not affect the firm's share price.

Let's follow MM's reasoning as it applies to JBC's capital structure. If JBC borrows $100 million, earnings per share are $0 under the recession scenario, $20 under the expected scenario, and $30 under the expansion scenario. The computations are reproduced on the upper part of Exhibit 11.4, which also shows the corresponding returns on shareholders' equity investment obtained by dividing the EPS by $100, the price of one share. The return is 0 percent under the recession scenario, 20 percent under the expected scenario, and 30 percent under the expansion scenario.

Suppose now that Ms. Johnson decides *not* to change JBC's capital structure (she does not borrow the $100 million and JBC remains with its initial debt-free capital structure). You, a shareholder with one share, would have preferred that the firm borrows the $100 million because you like the higher earnings per share that would result if the economy expands. What can you do? You can try to convince Ms. Johnson to change her mind, but you would probably be wasting your time unless you own a substantial number of shares. Well, you don't need to bother Ms. Johnson. *You can get the capital structure you want even if JBC remains debt-free.*

EXHIBIT 11.4   Corporate Leverage versus Homemade Leverage.

SHAREHOLDER'S RETURN ON A $100 INVESTMENT WHEN JBC BORROWS AT $100 MILLION

	RECESSION	EXPECTED	EXPANSION
JBC's net earnings with debt (from Exhibit 11.1)	$0	$20,000,000	$30,000,000
Divided by the number of shares	1,000,000	1,000,000	1,000,000
Equals earnings per share (EPS)	$0	$20	$30
Return on investment (EPS divided by $100)	**0%**	**20%**	**30%**

SHAREHOLDER'S RETURN ON A $100 NET INVESTMENT WHEN JBC MAINTAINS THE ALL-EQUITY CAPITAL STRUCTURE: THE INVESTOR BUYS TWO SHARES OF JBC, ONE WITH HIS OWN MONEY AND THE OTHER WITH BORROWED MONEY.

	RECESSION	EXPECTED	EXPANSION
JBC's net earnings with no debt (from Exhibit 11.1)	$10,000,000	$30,000,000	$40,000,000
Divided by the number of shares	2,000,000	2,000,000	2,000,000
Equals earnings per share (EPS)	$5	$15	$20
Earnings on two shares	$10	$30	$40
Less interest payment of 10% on $100	($10)	($10)	($10)
Net earnings	$0	$20	$30
Return on investment (net earnings divided by $100)	**0%**	**20%**	**30%**

How is this possible? The trick is to manufacture your own *personal* leverage that will replicate the returns JBC would have delivered if Ms. Johnson had decided to borrow the $100 million.

All you have to do is borrow $100 *at 10 percent* and use the cash to buy another share of JBC. You now own two shares, the one you already had plus the one you just bought. These transactions have created a **homemade leverage,** that is, a personal financial leverage as opposed to a corporate financial leverage. The lower part of Exhibit 11.4 shows how to calculate the returns on your investment under the three scenarios using JBC's earnings per share with all-equity financing (see Exhibit 11.1). Because you own two shares of JBC, you get twice the earnings per share in each of the three scenarios. However, your earnings are reduced in each scenario by the $10 interest payment you have to make on the $100 you borrowed (10 percent of $100). The last row of Exhibit 11.4 shows the net returns on your $100 investment (although you *own* two shares, your *personal* investment, net of borrowing, is only $100). *These returns are exactly the same as those you would have* *achieved if the firm had decided to recapitalize.* In other words, it does not matter whether the firm borrows to leverage its assets or whether investors borrow to leverage their own share holdings. What firms can do to their capital structures, investors can replicate on their own. Therefore, investors would neither reward nor penalize the firm if it decides to change its capital structure. Under those conditions, the firm's share price must remain the same.

You may have noticed the two critical assumptions required to reach this conclusion. The first is that the changes in capital structure must occur in a world without taxes. The second is that investors can borrow at the same rate as the firm (10 percent in the JBC example). Later in this chapter, we examine what happens without the first assumption, that is, when the changes in capital structure occur in a world *with* taxes. You may also think the second assumption is unrealistic because interest rates on personal borrowing are usually higher than the rates at which firms borrow. But investors do not have to borrow directly to build up their home-made leverage. To understand why, recall that investors diversify their investments. They do not buy only the shares of a single firm; they buy shares of other firms as well (see Chapter 10). Consequently, it is the financial leverage of all the firms in the investor's portfolio that is relevant, not just that of a particular firm in the port-folio. Given the large number of publicly traded companies offering a wide range of debt ratios, investors can easily reach any degree of financial leverage *in their port-folio* by constructing it in such a way that its average debt ratio is the one they want. And they do not need to borrow to achieve this, the firms in their portfolio will borrow for them.

The pizza theory of capital structure does not mention risk. But, the previous section shows that any increase in the firm's debt ratio increases the risk borne by its shareholders. How can JBC's share price *not* go down as a result of the increase in risk generated by the firm's decision to borrow $100 million? The answer is straightforward: The increase in risk is exactly offset by the rise in the earnings per share the shareholders can expect from higher financial leverage. In a world without taxes, the trade-off between risk and higher expected EPS that confronts Ms. Johnson does not actually exist. Whichever debt ratio she chooses, JBC's share price will not change because shareholders are exactly compensated for the higher risk with higher expected earnings per share. However, the *return* expected by shareholders from their equity investment in JBC—which is JBC's cost of equity—will rise to reflect the higher risk.

EFFECT OF CHANGES IN CAPITAL STRUCTURE ON THE FIRM'S COST OF CAPITAL (NO TAXES AND NO FINANCIAL DISTRESS COSTS)

If JBC's capital structure remains debt-free, the return expected by its shareholders from their investment in the firm is equal to the return expected from its assets because in this case shareholders are the only claimants to the cash flows generated by the firm's assets. If r_A denotes the expected return from the firm's assets and k_E denotes the firm's cost of equity, then, in the absence of debt and taxes, the two rates are the same ($r_A = k_E$).

If the firm decides to replace some equity with debt, the debtholders will also have claims on the firm's cash flows. In other words, r_A will be split into the return expected by its shareholders (k_E) and the rate required by its debtholders (denoted by k_D). Their claims on the firm's return on assets will be proportional to their respective contributions to the funding of the firm's assets. If E is the amount of equity funding and D is the amount of debt funding, then their relative contributions to the total funding of JBC's assets are $\dfrac{E}{E + D}$ and $\dfrac{D}{E + D}$, respectively. We can write:

$$r_A = k_E \frac{E}{E + D} + k_D \frac{D}{E + D} \qquad (11.1)$$

The right side of the relationship is the firm's weighted average cost of capital, or WACC, which is analyzed in Chapter 10. Assuming a fixed interest rate k_D on the firm's debt, equation 11.1 indicates that any change in the proportions of equity and debt financing must be compensated for by a change in the cost of equity k_E, because the return on assets (r_A) is not affected by the way returns are split between shareholders and debtholders. To show how the cost of equity varies when the debt-to-equity ratio increases, we can rearrange the terms of equation 11.1 to express k_E as a function of r_A, k_D, and the debt ratio. We get:

$$k_E = r_A + (r_A - k_D)\frac{D}{E} \qquad (11.2)$$

To illustrate, we consider JBC under the expected scenario. JBC's expected return on assets, r_A, is 15 percent (EBIT of $30 million divided by $200 million of assets) and its cost of debt, k_D, is 10 percent. Exhibit 11.5 shows JBC's cost of equity and weighted average cost of capital for two alternative debt-to-equity ratios, 0.25 (20 percent debt and 80 percent equity) and 1.00 (50 percent debt and 50 percent equity, the capital structure Ms. Johnson has proposed). With a debt-to-equity

EXHIBIT 11.5   JBC's Cost of Equity and WACC for Two Debt-to-Equity Ratios, $r_A = 15\%$ and $k_D = 10\%$.

DEBT-TO-EQUITY RATIO	$\dfrac{0.20 \text{ DEBT}}{0.80 \text{ EQUITY}} = 0.25$	$\dfrac{0.50 \text{ DEBT}}{0.50 \text{ EQUITY}} = 1.00$
Cost of equity from equation 11.2	15% + (15% − 10%) × 0.25 = **16.25%**	15% + (15% − 10%) × 1.00 = **20%**
Weighted average cost of capital from the right side of equation 11.1	16.25% × 0.80 + 10% × 0.20 = **15%**	20% × 0.50 + 10% × 0.50 = **15%**

ratio of 0.25, JBC's shareholders require a return of 16.25 percent, which is JBC's cost of equity. With a debt-to-equity ratio of 1.00 they require 20 percent to compensate them for the additional financial risk generated by the increase in leverage. However, the firm's weighted average cost of capital, which is the expected return on assets, is a constant 15 percent irrespective of the debt-to-equity ratio.

Exhibit 11.6 shows how the return on assets (r_A), the weighted average cost of capital (WACC), the cost of equity (k_E), and the cost of debt (k_D) vary when the debt-to-equity ratio increases. When the firm carries no debt, its cost of equity and WACC are 15 percent, the same as the expected return on the firm's assets. As the firm replaces equity with debt, shareholders bear increasing levels of financial risk and, therefore, expect higher returns from their investment; but, the firm's WACC remains equal to 15 percent, the return expected from the firm's assets.

An increasing cost of equity is not in contradiction with a constant share price. Shareholders expect a higher return from higher risk and, as shown earlier, they get it through higher expected earnings per share. As a result, the firm's share price does not move. It stays at $100 as shown in Exhibit 11.7. When there is no debt in the capital structure, the firm does not carry any financial risk and the market

EXHIBIT 11.6   **The Cost of Capital as a Function of the Debt-to-Equity Ratio According to the Pizza Theory and in the Absence of Taxes.**

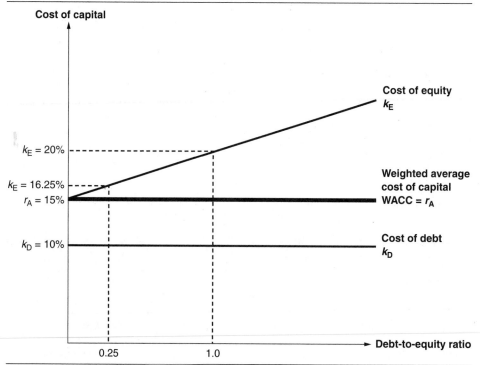

EXHIBIT 11.7   JBC's Share Price for Different Capital Structures.

CAPITAL STRUCTURE	FINANCIAL RISK	MARKET VALUE OF ASSETS (1)	AMOUNT OF DEBT FINANCING (2)	MARKET VALUE OF EQUITY (1) − (2) = (3)	NUMBER OF SHARES (4)	PRICE PER SHARE (3)/(4)
No debt	none	$200 million	none	$200 million	2,000,000	$100
20% debt	low	$200 million	$40 million	$160 million	1,600,000	$100
50% debt	higher	$200 million	$100 million	$100 million	1,000,000	$100

value of its assets ($200 million) is also the market value of its equity. With 2 million shares outstanding, the share price is $100. As the proportion of assets financed by debt rises, financial risk increases. If the firm wants to finance 20 percent of its assets with debt, it must borrow $40 million (20 percent of $200 million) and repurchase 400,000 shares at $100 each. When the recapitalization is over, the firm's equity is $160 million ($200 million minus $40 million worth of repurchased shares) and the number of shares outstanding is 1,600,000 (2 million shares minus 400,000 shares repurchased), yielding a share price of $100 ($160 million divided by 1,600,000 shares). Applying the same reasoning to the case where the firm finances 50 percent of its assets with debt shows that the share price remains at $100.

To summarize, with no taxes or financial distress costs, the pizza theory of capital structure says that a firm's financial structure decision does not affect its market value or its weighted average cost of capital. (This changes in the next section when taxes are included in the analysis.) Note that, so far, we have examined how changes in the firm's capital structure affect the value of the firm's assets and its equity. The distinction between assets and equity is not needed because debtholders' claims on the firm's assets are fixed. Interest and principal payments typically do not vary with the value of the firm's assets, except in the case of extreme leverage where the firm may not be able to service its debt. Thus, any decision that increases (or decreases) the value of the firm's assets will benefit (or hurt) its shareholders.

THE CAPITAL STRUCTURE DECISION: CORPORATE INCOME TAXES AND NO FINANCIAL DISTRESS COSTS

The analysis so far has ignored corporate taxes. What would happen to JBC's profits, share price, and market value if a 50 percent tax is imposed on the firm's earnings? Consider first the case where JBC is all-equity financed. The earnings per share reported in the upper part of Exhibit 11.1 will be reduced by 50 percent, from $5 to $2.5 in the recession scenario, from $15 to $7.5 in the expected scenario, and from $20 to $10 in the expansion scenario. With earnings per share cut in half,

JBC's share price and market value will drop by 50 percent as a result of the tax. Share price will go from $100 to $50 and market value from $200 million to $100 million (the 2 million shares are now worth $50 each).

Exhibit 11.8 summarizes the consequences of a change in capital structure from no debt financing to 50 percent debt financing under two tax regimes—no corporate income tax and a corporate income tax rate of 50 percent. The exhibit shows how the tax change affects the value of the firm's assets and equity, its share price, and its cost of capital when expected earnings before interest and tax are $30 million (the expected scenario). As mentioned earlier, the change in the capital structure will be accomplished by borrowing $100 million and using the cash to buy back 1 million shares at $100 each.

The upper part of the exhibit reproduces the results of our previous analysis (no taxes). The lower left side shows the consequences of the imposition of the 50 percent corporate tax with no debt financing, as described above. Note that the cost of equity and the weighted average cost of capital are still 15 percent, as in the no-tax case. This is why JBC's share price and market value lost half their value. The business risk underlying the firm's assets is not affected by the tax rate, so investors still want to earn 15 percent. With profits and earnings per share at half their original amount, JBC's share price and value must decrease by 50 percent in order for investors to still earn 15 percent on shares purchased after the tax was imposed. Obviously, investors who held JBC's shares *before the tax was imposed* lost 50 percent of the value of their investment.

We now want to find out what will happen to the market value of JBC's assets and its share price if Ms. Johnson decides to change JBC's capital structure by borrowing $50 million (half the value of assets) to repurchase an equal amount of equity. Will the value of JBC's assets and its share price remain the same as in the absence of taxes? The answer is no. In the presence of taxes, both the value of the firm's assets and its share price will *rise* as debt replaces equity in the firm's balance sheet, as shown in the lower right side of Exhibit 11.8.

EFFECT OF CHANGES IN CAPITAL STRUCTURE ON THE VALUE OF A FIRM'S ASSETS AND SHARE PRICE (TAXES AND NO FINANCIAL DISTRESS COSTS)

Corporate tax laws favor debt financing because interest paid by the company to its creditors is a tax-deductible expense while dividends and retained earnings are not. The substitution of debt financing for equity reduces the amount of tax JBC must pay and thus increases the *aftertax* cash flow generated by the firm's assets. A higher cash flow from assets raises the market value of assets and the firm's share price.

To illustrate the tax effect on asset value and share price, we estimate the amount of taxes JBC will save if Ms. Johnson decides to borrow $50 million at 10 percent and use the cash to repurchase one million shares at $50 a share. JBC will

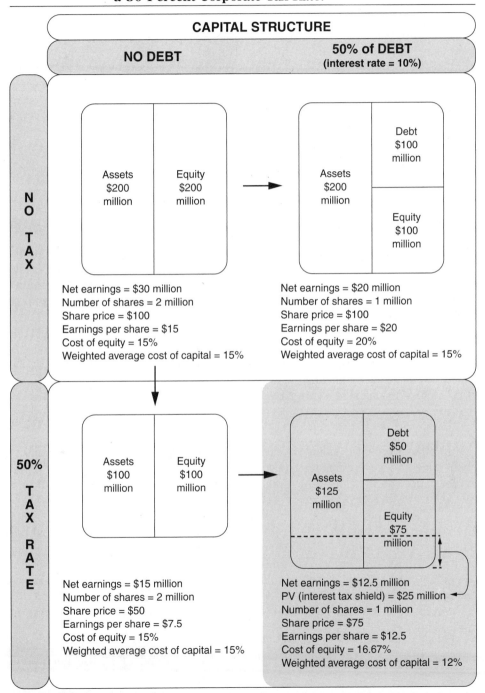

EXHIBIT 11.8 Effects of Changes in Capital Structure on the Firm's Earnings Per Share, Share Price, Market Value, and Cost of Capital Without Corporate Taxes and with a 50 Percent Corporate Tax Rate.

CAPITAL STRUCTURE

NO DEBT

50% of DEBT
(interest rate = 10%)

NO TAX

Assets
$200
million

Equity
$200
million

Assets
$200
million

Debt
$100
million

Equity
$100
million

Net earnings = $30 million
Number of shares = 2 million
Share price = $100
Earnings per share = $15
Cost of equity = 15%
Weighted average cost of capital = 15%

Net earnings = $20 million
Number of shares = 1 million
Share price = $100
Earnings per share = $20
Cost of equity = 20%
Weighted average cost of capital = 15%

50% TAX RATE

Assets
$100
million

Equity
$100
million

Assets
$125
million

Debt
$50
million

Equity
$75
million

Net earnings = $15 million
Number of shares = 2 million
Share price = $50
Earnings per share = $7.5
Cost of equity = 15%
Weighted average cost of capital = 15%

Net earnings = $12.5 million
PV (interest tax shield) = $25 million
Number of shares = 1 million
Share price = $75
Earnings per share = $12.5
Cost of equity = 16.67%
Weighted average cost of capital = 12%

pay $5 million of interest every year, and its taxable income will drop to $25 million ($30 million of earnings before interest and tax less $5 million of interest expenses). Thus, it will pay $12.5 million in taxes (50 percent of $25 million). If the firm does not borrow, its expected annual tax payment will be $15 million (50 percent of an expected EBIT of $30 million). Thus, by borrowing $50 million at 10 percent, JBC can save $2.5 million in taxes every year ($15 million minus $12.5 million), and the annual cash flows generated by its assets will increase by the same amount. Because taxable income is reduced by an amount equal to interest expense, this annual tax saving can be calculated directly by simply multiplying the amount of interest expense by the corporate tax rate. In our case, $5 million multiplied by 50 percent is equal to the $2.5 million of tax saved. More generally, if k_D is the cost of debt and T_c is the corporate tax rate, the annual tax saving from debt financing, which is usually referred to as the annual **interest tax shield,** can be expressed as:

$$\textbf{Annual interest tax shield} = \textbf{T}_c \times \textbf{\textit{k}}_D \times \textbf{Debt} \qquad (11.3)$$

How will this interest tax shield affect the value of the firm's assets and its share price? We know that if the firm borrows, the cash flows generated by its assets will rise every year by an amount equal to the annual interest tax shield. Consequently, when the firm borrows, the value of its assets today is the sum of two components: (1) the value of its assets if the firm does not borrow and (2) the *present value* of the stream of all the *future* interest tax shields its debt will create. If V_L is the market value of the firm's assets when debt is used to finance these assets (the value of the levered firm), V_U is their value without debt (the value of the unlevered or all-equity financed firm), and PV_{ITS} is the present value of the stream of future interest tax shields, we have:

$$\textbf{V}_L = \textbf{V}_U + \textbf{PV}_{ITS} \qquad (11.4)$$

In other words, the value of a firm's assets financed with debt (V_L) is equal to their value if they were financed only with equity (V_U) plus the present value of the interest tax shields that debt financing is expected to generate in the future (PV_{ITS}).[5]

Let's apply this valuation formula to JBC. We know V_U is $100 million when the corporate income tax rate is 50 percent (see the lower left side of Exhibit 11.8); we want to find V_L if JBC borrows $50 million and uses the cash to repurchase $50 million of equity. We know the $50 million will generate a recurrent annual interest tax shield of $2.5 million. If we assume the interest tax shield has the same risk as the debt itself, its present value, PV_{ITS}, is the present value of a perpetual annuity ($2.5 million every year forever) discounted at the rate of interest on debt.

The present value of a perpetual cash flow is simply the recurrent cash flow divided by the rate of interest (see equation A6.4 in Appendix 6.1). JBC borrows at

---

[5]Our result ignores the impact of investors' personal taxes, a point we discuss later in this chapter.

10 percent and its annual interest tax shield is $2.5 million, so the present value of the entire stream of future interest tax shields is:

$$PV_{ITS} = \frac{T_C \times k_D \times \text{Debt}}{k_D} = \frac{0.5 \times 0.10 \times \$50,000,000}{0.10} = \frac{\$2,500,000}{0.10} = \$25,000,000$$

Thus, $2.5 million of interest tax shield every year forever is worth $25 million today.[6] According to equation 11.4:

$$V_L = \$100 \text{ million} + \$25 \text{ million} = \$125 \text{ million}$$

By replacing $50 million worth of equity with debt, Ms. Johnson can increase the value of JBC's assets by $25 million, as shown in the lower right side of Exhibit 11.8. Note that the more JBC borrows, the larger the present value of the interest tax shield and the higher the value of the firm's assets. This phenomenon is illustrated in the graph in Exhibit 11.9. The value of JBC's assets increase as its

EXHIBIT 11.9 The Value of JBC as a Function of Its Debt-to-Assets Ratio in the Presence of Taxes.

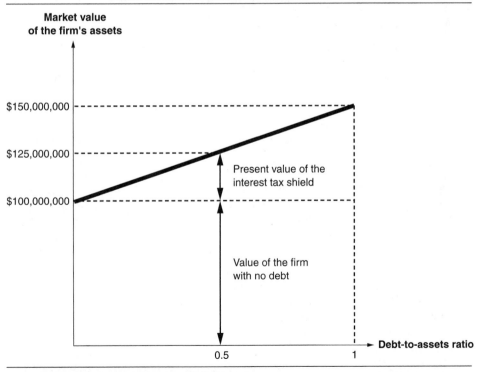

debt-to-assets ratio rises from zero to one. This happens because as the amount of debt financing increases, the firm's interest tax shield increases and its tax bill decreases and, thus, the value of the firm's assets increases.

Consider the result of JBC's proposed recapitalization: By borrowing $50 million to finance the firm's assets, Ms. Johnson can increase the value of the assets by 25 percent, *even though they are exactly the same assets the firm had before borrowing.* They are more valuable not because they generate higher or less risky cash flows *before tax* (the pretax expected cash flow from assets is the same $30 million), but because the recapitalization reduces the portion of these cash flows paid out as corporate tax. By refinancing JBC's assets with debt, Ms. Johnson can make a value-creating *financing* decision. These value-creating opportunities are significantly more limited than those that can be obtained from superior investment decisions because after the firm has reached its **optimal capital structure,** it will obviously no longer be possible to create more value through recapitalization.

There is another way to think about the effect of financial leverage. Suppose another company wants to buy JBC's assets and plans to finance the acquisition with $50 million of debt. This company would be ready to pay up to $125 million to acquire JBC's assets: $100 million for the capacity of these assets to generate operating cash flows (V_U in equation 11.4) and an additional $25 million for the present value of the taxes that will be saved through the $50 million debt financing (PV_{ITS} in equation 11.4).

What will happen to JBC's share price, now at $50, if Ms. Johnson decides to use debt? It will also rise to reflect the tax savings that will go to JBC's shareholders. This phenomenon is illustrated in Exhibit 11.10 for the three capital structures examined earlier: no debt, 20 percent debt financing, and 50 percent debt financing. As JBC's capital structure goes from no debt to 20 percent debt financing, Ms. Johnson increases borrowing from $0 to $20 million (20 percent of $100 million). If we assume the $20 million is used to repurchase 400,000 shares at $50 each, the number of shares outstanding drops from 2 million to 1.6 million. The unlevered value of the firm's assets, obviously not affected by the new capital structure, stays at $100 million. However, these assets become more valuable because the $20 million of debt generates tax savings in the form of a tax shield. The present value of the interest tax shield (which is assumed to last forever) is equal to the corporate tax rate multiplied by the amount of debt (see footnote 6). With a tax rate of 50 percent, the interest tax shield is worth $10 million (50 percent × $20 million). Adding this $10 million to the *unlevered* value of JBC's assets, we obtain a market value of $110 million for the *levered* assets. As a result, the market value of JBC's equity is $90 million ($110 million of assets minus $20 million of debt). Dividing this $90 million by the number of shares outstanding (1,600,000), we get a share price of $56.25. Repeating the same steps with $50 million of debt instead of $20 million, we find a share price of $75.

Note that the share price with leverage rises by an amount equal to the present value of the interest tax shield *per share.* For example, with $50 million of

EXHIBIT 11.10   JBC's Share Price for Different Capital Structures with a 50 Percent Corporate Tax Rate.

CAPITAL STRUCTURE	AMOUNT OF DEBT FINANCING (1)	NUMBER OF SHARES OUTSTANDING (2)	UNLEVERED VALUE OF ASSETS (3)
No debt	No debt	2,000,000	$100 million
20% debt	$20 million	1,600,000	$100 million
50% debt	$50 million	1,000,000	$100 million

PRESENT VALUE OF INTEREST TAX SHIELD (4)	LEVERED VALUE OF ASSETS (3) + (4) = (5)	VALUE OF EQUITY (5) − (1) = (6)	SHARE PRICE (6)/(2)
zero	$100 million	$100 million	$50
$10 million	$110 million	$90 million	$56.25
$25 million	$125 million	$75 million	$75

borrowing, the present value of the interest tax shield is $25 million. Dividing $25 million by 1 million shares, we obtain a present value of interest tax shield of $25 per share, which explains why JBC's share price rises from $50 with no debt to $75 with $50 million of debt. As JBC continues to borrow, the leveraged value of its assets, as well as its share price, keep rising. How long can this process go on?

There is obviously a problem when we carry the logic of debt financing to its extreme. The message seems to be that managers should borrow as much as possible if they wish to maximize the value of the firm's assets and its share price. This advice will have to be re-examined because the excessive use of debt generates a number of problems that we have not yet considered. Before we do so, we examine how the cost of capital is affected by corporate income taxes.

EFFECT OF CHANGES IN CAPITAL STRUCTURE ON THE COST OF CAPITAL (TAXES AND NO FINANCIAL DISTRESS COSTS)

When a firm has no debt and pays taxes, the return expected by its shareholders from their equity investment—the firm's cost of equity (k_E)—is still equal to the return on the firm's assets (r_A). However, when the firm has debt in its capital structure and pays taxes, we must account for the tax reduction resulting from the deductibility of interest expenses. In this case, equation 11.1, which relates r_A to the cost of equity and the cost of debt, is no longer valid. It can be shown that it must be replaced with the following to reflect the tax effect:

$$r_A = k_E \frac{E}{E + D(1 - T_C)} + k_D(1 - T_C)\frac{D}{E + D(1 - T_C)}$$

where T_C is the corporate income tax rate. Rearranging the terms of the above equation in order to express the cost of equity (k_E) as a function of the other variables, we get:

$$k_E = r_A + (r_A - k_D)(1 - T_C)\frac{D}{E} \tag{11.5}$$

Comparing this equation with equation 11.2, we can see that the cost of equity is now *lower* than in the no-tax case because the term $(1 - T_C)$ is less than one. Furthermore, due to the tax deductibility of interest expenses, the relevant cost of debt is now the *aftertax* cost of debt, that is, $k_D (1 - T_C)$, so that the aftertax weighted average cost of capital (WACC) becomes:

$$\textbf{WACC} = k_E \frac{E}{E + D} + k_D(1 - T_C)\frac{D}{E + D} \tag{11.6}$$

This equation for WACC is the same as the one without taxes except that the cost of debt is calculated on an aftertax basis.

Exhibit 11.11 shows how the cost of equity (k_E) in equation 11.5 and the weighted average cost of capital in equation 11.6 vary when the debt-to-equity ratio increases. As in a world without taxes, the cost of equity (k_E) increases with debt because of the financial risk that comes with debt financing. However, it increases at a *lower* rate because shareholders get an extra return in the form of the interest tax shield. The weighted average cost of capital decreases when the firm's borrowing rises because the extra return from the interest tax shield and the lower aftertax cost of debt more than offset the higher financial risk generated by higher levels of debt.

To illustrate, we again consider JBC, where the expected return on assets is 15 percent, the cost of debt is 10 percent, and the corporate tax rate is 50 percent. The previous analysis showed that with $20 million of debt, the market value of JBC's equity is $90 million; with $50 million of debt, it is $75 million. Exhibit 11.12 shows JBC's cost of equity and WACC in this situation. As leverage increases, the cost of equity rises but the weighted average cost of capital declines, as shown in Exhibit 11.11.

In summary, when taxes are taken into account, the type of capital structure affects a firm. The value of the firm increases and its weighted average cost of capital decreases when more and more debt replaces equity in the firm's capital structure. The implication, we know, is embarrassing but clear: When corporate taxes are taken into account, the optimal capital structure is 100 percent debt financing! However, this result is inconsistent with what we observe in practice:

EXHIBIT 11.11   **The Cost of Capital as a Function of the Debt-to-Equity Ratio According to the Pizza Theory and in the Presence of Corporate Taxes.**

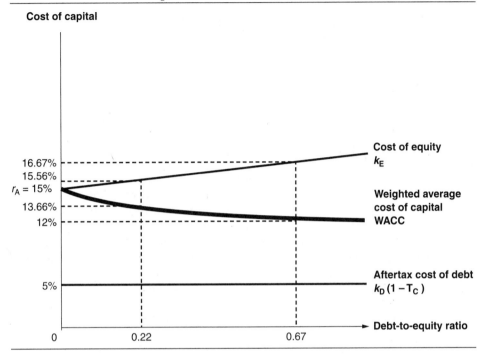

EXHIBIT 11.12   **JBC's Cost of Equity and WACC for Two Debt-to-Equity Ratios, $r_A = 15\%$, $k_D = 10\%$, and $T_C = 50\%$. Value of Equity from Exhibit 11.10.**

AMOUNT BORROWED	$20 MILLION	$50 MILLION
Value of equity	$90 million	$75 million
Debt-to-equity ratio	$\dfrac{\$20\ \text{million}}{\$90\ \text{million}} = 0.22$	$\dfrac{\$50\ \text{million}}{\$75\ \text{million}} = 0.67$
$\dfrac{D}{E + D}$	$\dfrac{\$20\ \text{million}}{\$110\ \text{million}} = 0.18$	$\dfrac{\$50\ \text{million}}{\$125\ \text{million}} = 0.40$
Cost of equity from equation 11.5	15% + (15% − 10%) (1 − 50%) × 0.22 = **15.56%**	15% + (15% − 10%) (1 − 50%) × 0.67 = **16.67%**
Weighted average cost of capital from equation 11.6	15.56% × 0.82 + 5% × 0.18 = **13.66%**	16.67% × 0.60 + 5% × 0.40 = **12.0%**

Most companies do not carry very large amounts of debt. The reasons are discussed in the rest of this chapter.

THE CAPITAL STRUCTURE DECISION WHEN FINANCIAL DISTRESS IS COSTLY

Debt puts pressure on firms because interest and principal payments are contractual obligations firms must meet. If a firm finds it increasingly difficult to service its debt, it will face a situation that is referred to as financial distress and may ultimately go bankrupt. Financial distress generates costs, described below, that reduce the cash flows expected from the firm's assets. In the context of the pizza theory of capital structure, we can say that financial distress costs eat some of the pizza, leaving less of it for investors (both debtholders and shareholders). And as the pizza shrinks, the firm's value and its share price go down. Shareholders bear most of the financial distress costs because debtholders have a prior and fixed claim on the smaller pizza.

The **direct costs of financial distress** are the actual costs the firm incurs if it becomes legally bankrupt. **Bankruptcy** is a legal procedure through which the ownership of the firm's assets is transferred to debtholders. Associated with this transfer are legal and administrative costs and lawyers' and consultants' fees.

However, before a firm legally declares bankruptcy, it may have already incurred significant **indirect costs of financial distress.** The increasing probability that it will have to declare bankruptcy creates a situation that prevents the firm from operating at maximum efficiency. With too much debt outstanding, the firm may have to pass up valuable investment opportunities, cut research and development activities, or reduce marketing expenses in order to conserve cash and avoid bankruptcy. Customers may question the firm's long-term ability to deliver reliable goods and services and decide to switch to other companies. Suppliers may be reluctant to provide trade credit. Valuable employees may leave. Conflicts of interest between managers, shareholders, bondholders, and employees may arise, with each group trying to pursue a different strategy of self-preservation. All these indirect costs, which have a negative impact on the firm's value, become increasingly significant as the firm's indebtedness rises. Note that it is not financial distress *per se* that matters but the fact that, if it occurs, the firm will have to bear new costs that will reduce the cash flows expected from its assets. In other words, if financial distress were *costless,* it would have no effect on the firm's value.

The previous section shows that when the proportion of debt in the firm's capital structure increases, the firm's value rises because of larger interest tax shields. However, these tax-related gains are eventually offset by the expected costs of financial distress. The relationship between the value of the levered firm (V_L), its unlevered value (V_U), and the present value of the interest tax shield (PV_{ITS}) expressed in equation 11.4 must be modified to account for this offsetting effect. If PV_{CFD} is the present value of the expected costs of financial distress, we can adjust the valuation formula to reflect the reduction in value generated by these costs:

$$V_L = V_U + PV_{ITS} - PV_{CFD} \qquad (11.7)$$

How large is the present value of the expected costs of financial distress (PV_{CFD})? The question can only be answered empirically. The evidence indicates that these costs are not insignificant. They can reach 10 to 15 percent of the value of the firm's assets as early as three years prior to filing for bankruptcy.

Exhibit 11.13 shows the graph presented in Exhibit 11.9 (which showed the positive impact of the interest tax shield on the firm's value) with the addition of the negative impact of financial distress costs. At low to moderate levels of debt, the probability of financial distress is negligible and the firm can capture the entire value of the interest tax shield. As more and more debt replaces equity, the probability of financial distress rises and the present value of the associated costs grows at an increasing rate. At some debt level, denoted by the debt-to-assets ratio D/A*, the

EXHIBIT 11.13   **The Value of a Firm in the Presence of Corporate Taxes and Financial Distress Costs as a Function of its Debt-to-Assets Ratio.**

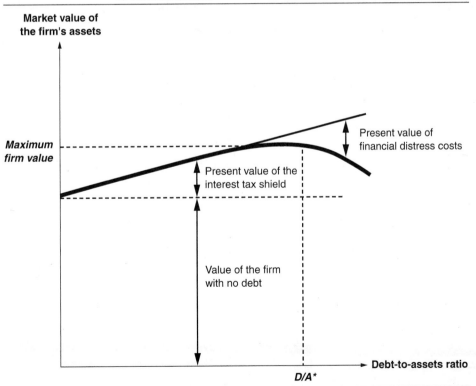

increase in the present value of financial distress costs arising from an extra dollar of borrowing is equal to the increase in the present value of the interest tax shield. At that point, the firm has reached the capital structure that maximizes its value.

Exhibit 11.14 illustrates the impact of changes in capital structure on the firm's cost of capital in the presence of financial distress costs. As shown earlier in Exhibit 11.11, where financial distress costs were nonexistent, the cost of equity increases proportionally with a rise in the debt-to-equity ratio. When the present value of financial distress costs becomes significant, the cost of equity begins to rise at a faster rate. For the same reason, the cost of debt also begins to rise at some point. The weighted average cost of capital declines until the benefit of the interest tax shield is offset by the impact of expected financial distress on the costs of equity and debt. At this point, the firm has reached its optimal capital structure: Its weighted average cost of capital is at its minimum (WACC*), its debt-to-equity ratio is at its optimal value (D/E*), and the value of the firm is maximized. This model of debt financing is known as the **trade-off model of capital structure.**

The conclusion is that there exists, at least conceptually, an optimal capital structure that is the outcome of a trade-off between the benefit of the interest tax shield and the cost of financial distress arising from an increasing use of debt financing. Unfortunately, we cannot tell you how to determine that optimal debt ratio because it is impossible to estimate financial distress costs precisely. However, this does not mean that the information in this chapter is useless. On the contrary,

EXHIBIT 11.14 **The Cost of Capital as a Function of the Debt-to-Equity Ratio in the Presence of Corporate Taxes and Financial Distress Costs.**

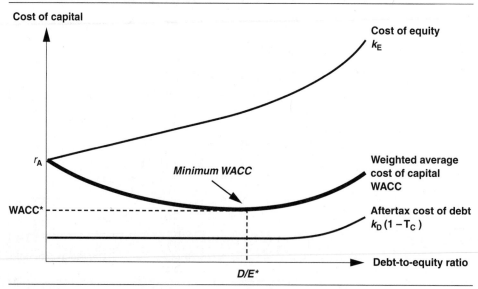

it provides a solid conceptual framework in which to formulate a capital structure policy for your firm.

FORMULATING A CAPITAL STRUCTURE POLICY

The previous analysis of the trade-off model of capital structure looks at the two major determinants of a firm's borrowing decision: the value-creating effect of the tax deductibility of interest expenses and the value-destroying effect of financial distress costs. This section extends the basic trade-off model by examining additional factors that have an impact on the formulation of a capital structure policy. We first examine two questions related to the trade-off model:

1. How do personal taxes, which investors must pay on the income they receive from firms, affect the size of the interest tax shield?
2. Which type of firms are more likely to experience a state of financial distress?

We then look at a number of issues that go beyond the standard trade-off model of capital structure to shed more light on the underlying variables that shape a firm's capital structure:

1. Are there reasons for firms to borrow *even if debt does not provide tax savings?*
2. Are there reasons for firms to abstain from borrowing *even if debt financing generates little or no financial distress costs?*
3. Why do firms prefer to finance their activities with internally generated funds (retained earnings) rather than external funds?

The answers to these questions provide additional insights into the factors that affect a firm's capital structure decision and help both managers and firms' owners establish an appropriate capital structure for their companies.

A CLOSER LOOK AT THE TRADE-OFF MODEL OF CAPITAL STRUCTURE

This section examines two issues that are related to the major determinants of the trade-off model of capital structure. First, we want to determine how personal income taxes influence the value-creating effect of the tax deductibility of interest expenses. Second, we want to find out which types of firms are more likely to be affected by the value-destroying effect of financial distress costs.

The Effect of Personal Taxes

The interest tax shield given in equation 11.3 ignores the tax that debtholders and shareholders must pay on the income they receive from their investments in the firm. Debtholders receive interest payments. Shareholders receive cash dividends and they receive capital gains if they sell shares at a price higher than their purchase price. If the personal tax rate on interest income is T_D and the *average* personal tax rate on equity income (dividends and capital gains) is T_E, it can be shown that the interest tax shield becomes:

$$\textbf{Interest tax shield} = \left[\textbf{1} - (\textbf{1} - \textbf{T}_\textbf{C}) \times \frac{(\textbf{1} - \textbf{T}_\textbf{E})}{(\textbf{1} - \textbf{T}_\textbf{D})} \right] \times \textbf{\textit{k}}_\textbf{D} \times \textbf{Debt} \qquad (11.8)$$

When the personal tax rates on debt and equity income are equal ($T_D = T_E$), equation 11.8 reduces to $T_C \times k_D \times$ Debt, which is the interest tax shield when personal taxes are ignored (equation 11.3). But the personal tax rate on equity income is generally *lower* than that on interest income because capital gains are usually taxed at a lower rate than interest income. In this case, the interest tax shield is lower than the one when personal taxes are not considered.

To illustrate, consider a firm with $50 million of debt, a cost of debt of 10 percent, a corporate tax rate of 50 percent, and personal tax rates of 50 percent on interest income and 25 percent on equity income. The interest tax shield according to equation 11.8 is:

$$\text{Interest tax shield} = \left[1 - (1 - 0.50) \times \frac{(1 - 0.25)}{(1 - 0.50)} \right]$$
$$\times \ 0.10 \times \$50 \text{ million} = \$1.25 \text{ million}$$

This is half the $2.5 million of interest tax shield when the personal tax rates on debt and equity income are equal ($T_C \times k_D \times$ Debt = 50% × 10% × $50 million = $2.5 million). Hence, ignoring the possibility that the personal tax rate on equity income can be lower than the personal tax rate on income from debt is likely to *overestimate* the tax benefit of debt financing.

Factors affecting the risk and cost of financial distress

When a firm increases its borrowing, it also increases the probability (or risk) that it will experience a state of financial distress and incur (financial distress) costs that will reduce its value. But not every firm is exposed to the same risk of financial distress or bears the same costs of financial distress. Some may reach a state of financial distress at lower debt ratios than others. In this section, we identify a number of firm-specific factors that are likely to increase the probability that a firm will experience a state of financial distress. We would expect firms with higher financial distress risk to have relatively lower debt ratios than firms with lower financial distress risk. These factors help explain, for example, why firms in different industries and different countries can have different debt-to-equity ratios.

The Volatility of the Firm's Operating Profits   A firm that has highly volatile and cyclical operating profits and cash flows (that is, a firm with high *business* risk) faces a higher probability of experiencing financial distress than a firm that has steady operating profits and cash flows, even when the firms have the *same debt ratio.* This is why firms with high business risk (such as high technology companies) carry relatively less debt than, say, utility companies, which are usually able to generate a steadier and more predictable stream of operating profits and cash flows. A simple way to find out if a company can take full advantage of the interest tax shield is to draw an aftertax EPS-EBIT graph like the one shown in Exhibit 11.2. Simply check to see if the probability of falling below the break-even point is negligible.

The Type of Assets the Firm Holds   When financial distress occurs, creditors are less likely to extend credit to firms with few tangible assets than to firms with assets that can be valuable in case of liquidation. Thus, firms that have relatively large investments in human capital, research, brands, and other intangible assets face higher costs of financial distress than firms that have the *same debt ratio* but that have large investments in land, buildings, and similar tangible assets that can be sold in case of bankruptcy. Firms with relatively large proportions of intangible assets can reduce the probability of financial distress by borrowing less than firms with relatively large proportions of tangible and liquid assets. This may help explain why software companies, which have comparatively lower amounts of tangible assets, have lower debt ratios than airline or utility companies, which have comparatively higher amounts of tangible assets.

The Type of Products or Services the Firm Sells   When the firm sells a commodity or when the firm's service can be obtained elsewhere, customers do not usually care whether their supplier goes bankrupt because there will always be another firm to fill the void. However, when the product or service is unique, customers are very concerned about the consequences of their supplier experiencing financial distress. Thus, a commodity supplier faces lower costs of financial distress than a supplier of unique goods or services with the *same debt ratio.* The former can afford relatively large levels of debt without making its customers nervous, but the supplier of a unique product or service would rather rely on relatively less debt to reassure its customers that its future viability will not be jeopardized by an excessive debt burden.

Note, however, that even if the product is a commodity, customers may be concerned if the product needs future service or repair. For example, if you believe a car manufacturer will go bankrupt, you will probably not buy one of its cars. But if bankruptcy threatens a food company, you may still buy its products because they do not need to be serviced or repaired.

The Structure of the Country's Financial System   The risk of a firm experiencing financial distress is not related only to factors specific to the firm or its industry. It is also affected by the structure of the financial system in which the firm operates. In countries where banks are owned or controlled by the state or in countries that allow banks to own shares of companies, firms usually have higher debt ratios than in countries where banks are in the private sector and must restrict their activities only to lending.

When banks are state-owned and can be both lenders and shareholders of the same company, they are more likely to help that company avoid bankruptcy, particularly if the company is large. State-owned banks may continue to lend to a company if the state wants to keep the company afloat. Banks that are allowed to own shares in companies may accept converting excessive debt into equity. This may explain why some large companies in countries such as France, Germany, Italy, and Japan usually have higher debt ratios than their counterparts in the United States or the United Kingdom.

FACTORS OTHER THAN TAXES THAT MAY FAVOR BORROWING

The major benefit of debt financing is the tax savings that come from the deductibility of interest expenses. If the tax reductions associated with debt were no longer available (either because the tax authority denies them or because firms cannot take advantage of them), would a firm's owners still have an incentive to borrow? Yes, they would. There are several reasons why a firm's owners may want to borrow that are not based on the tax advantage of debt financing.

Debt is a device that helps reduce the agency costs arising from the separation of ownership from control

Managers may not always act in the best interest of shareholders. They sometimes make decisions that benefit themselves but that reduce the firm's value. Suppose that a firm has generated a large cash surplus because it had an exceptionally good year. Managers may be tempted to spend this cash unwisely, such as on expensive and often useless perquisites that are not really needed or on "empire-building" investments that allow the firm to grow in revenues and size but that do not create value.

This behavior illustrates the **agency problem,** which arises from the separation of ownership and control. When managers run a firm on behalf of shareholders (they act as the agents of shareholders), they may not always make decisions that benefit shareholders. They may make decisions that increase their own level of comfort and satisfaction but that reduce the firm's value. An example is a manager who buys a corporate plane when such an acquisition has no identifiable benefit beyond enhancing the manager's status. This manager reduces the firm's value by an amount equal to the aftertax cost of the plane. This value reduction is referred to as an **agency cost of equity financing.**

Consider another example, directly related to the capital structure decision. The income and wealth of managers are generally not as well diversified as those of shareholders. Managers' income, their job tenure, and most of their wealth depend on the firm that employs them whereas most shareholders only invest a small fraction of their total wealth in a single firm. Because they are poorly diversified, managers are more exposed to risk than their well-diversified shareholders.

Consequently, they may adopt a more conservative debt policy than the one that maximizes the firm's value. The difference between the firm's value under the conservative debt policy and its potential maximum value with more debt financing is another example of an agency cost of equity financing.

One way to reduce agency costs is to turn managers into partial owners by giving them either shares in the firm or options to buy shares at a predetermined fixed price. However, the number of shares or options owned by the managers needs to be substantial to induce them to make the maximization of shareholder value their overriding concern. What if shareholders are reluctant to distribute large amounts of shares or options to managers?

Debt financing can be another solution to the agency problem. Issuing debt and using the cash to buy back shares reduces the agency costs of equity in two ways. First, the portion of the firm's cash flow that goes to shareholders falls because there are fewer shareholders. The portion that goes to debtholders rises because managers must now allocate a larger part of the firm's cash flows to service debt. This means that managers have less of that cash flow to squander on things like airplanes. Second, if managers already have some equity in the firm, their *percentage share* of the firm's ownership rises because, even though they hold the same amount of equity, they now own a bigger portion of the firm's total equity. Both of these debt effects should motivate managers to act in the interest of shareholders. The first acts as the proverbial stick, the second as the carrot. Thus, debt financing becomes a device that helps reduce the agency costs associated with equity financing by aligning managers' interests with those of shareholders.

In this case, borrowing should increase the market value of the firm and its share price through two distinct channels. One is via the tax-induced gains generated by debt financing and the other by the reduction in the agency costs of equity. The latter results from the increased focus and discipline imposed on managers by higher debt levels and the enhanced motivation provided by a higher fractional ownership of the firm for managers who held shares prior to the recapitalization.

Debt is a device that allows current owners to retain control

The choice of debt over new equity may be dictated by the desire of current owners to retain control of their firm. Fresh equity, supplied by new investors, reduces the percentage of the firm's equity capital controlled by the original owners, but debt financing avoids this **dilution** effect. Thus, if the firm needs outside funding and the current owners wish to retain control, they will prefer that the firm borrow rather than issue new shares, regardless of tax considerations.

If the decision to issue debt rather than equity is motivated by control considerations, we can expect the firm's shares to trade at a discount because that will greatly diminish the ability of outsiders to take over the company. If the present value of the tax gains generated by the debt issued to retain control is smaller than the market discount caused by a tight control, the net effect is a *lower* equity value. But this does not mean that shareholders are necessarily worse off. Control may generate nonmonetary benefits that are more valuable to them than the loss of market value.

Debt is a device that helps resolve the problem of information asymmetry between managers and outside investors

There is **asymmetric information** when management knows more about the future prospects of their firm than outside investors (shareholders and creditors) know. This occurs when it is expensive for a company to keep outside investors informed about the firm's current condition and future prospects. It can also arise when management does not want future plans to be public knowledge because such information might be valuable to its competitors. The presence of asymmetric information may create a managerial preference for debt financing.

As an example, suppose JBC has decided to invest in a new project that will require external financing. Ms. Johnson could either issue shares at the current market price of $100 or issue bonds. Suppose Ms. Johnson is convinced the firm's future is rosier than the financial market expects. She believes JBC's equity is underpriced and JBC's shares are worth at least $110. What should she do? If she issues undervalued shares, she penalizes the current shareholders by handing a gift to new shareholders who would pay only $100 for what she values at $110. Ms. Johnson, who cares about the firm's existing shareholders, would rather issue bonds. Now consider the opposite case where Ms. Johnson believes JBC's shares are currently overpriced and a price of $90 would be more in line with her expectation regarding JBC's future prospects. If she issues bonds, the required interest and principal payments may create an added burden when she needs to focus her full attention on improving the firm's prospects. She should issue shares. Note that if she could issue them at a price close to their current price of $100, she would provide a windfall profit to current shareholders at the expense of new shareholders.

There is another point to consider, however. If investors are aware that firms issue shares only when managers think the firm's equity is overvalued, they will revise their expectations downward when a firm announces its intention to issue shares and bid down its share price. The evidence seems to support this view because the price of existing shares usually goes down on the day firms announce their intention to issue new shares. Managers, who typically do not like to see a drop in their firm's share price, are often reluctant to issue shares, whether or not they find their equity underpriced or overpriced. This may explain why, for most corporations, debt is the favored means of external financing, irrespective of the tax benefit it procures.

FACTORS OTHER THAN FINANCIAL DISTRESS COSTS THAT MAY DISCOURAGE BORROWING

Although debt financing provides valuable tax reductions, increasing borrowing eventually generates financial distress costs that rise with higher debt ratios. The question, then, is whether firms would increase borrowing if financial distress costs were not significant. They would not. Some firms may deliberately decide to refrain from borrowing even if financial distress costs are moderate or nonexistent. The debt the firm must issue in order to take advantage of the tax savings may create a number of constraints that owners and/or managers find too costly. If these expected costs are higher than the potential tax benefits of debt financing, the firm may decide not to issue debt.

Excessive debt may prevent firms from taking full advantage of the interest tax shield

To take advantage of the tax savings from interest expenses, a firm needs to generate relatively large operating profits in order to be able to deduct the full amount of interest expenses. Firms that operate in capital-intensive industries can already reduce their tax liability through accelerated depreciation schedules. Consequently, they may not have sufficient pretax operating profits to benefit fully from the additional tax savings offered by the interest expenses generated by high levels of debt. These firms usually have lower debt ratios than those operating in the service industry where the opposite condition occurs. Service-based firms generally do not have significant depreciation expenses on plant and equipment to reduce their tax liability. As a result, they have relatively higher levels of pretax operating profits and can afford higher debt ratios in order to benefit from the interest tax shield.

Excessive debt may create costly conflicts of interest between shareholders and debtholders

Excessive debt may give rise to costly conflicts of interest between shareholders and lenders that can affect the firm's capital structure decision. We use an extreme example to illustrate the point. Suppose that management, acting on the instructions of shareholders, borrows $8 million at 10 percent to invest in a $10 million project that is very risky. Further, assume that the lenders do not have all the details regarding the riskiness of the project. In one year, the project should yield either $30 million or nothing, with an equal probability of occurrence. If the project goes well, the shareholders repay $8.8 million to the lenders (the $8 million loan plus 10 percent interest) and keep the rest ($21.2 million). If the project fails, everyone loses, but the lenders will lose more than the shareholders because they financed 80 percent of the project. This is rightly described as "gambling away" lenders' money. The lenders, of course, anticipate this type of behavior and try to protect their investment by imposing restrictions on the firm's ability to spend the borrowed funds as it wishes. In other words, the lenders make it more expensive for the shareholders to raise debt capital.

The protection the suppliers of debt demand takes the form of **restrictive covenants** in the formal agreement between the borrowing firm and its lenders. For example, these covenants may impose limits on the amount of dividends the firm is allowed to pay, the amount of additional debt it can borrow, or the type of assets it can acquire or sell. The more debt the firm already has, the more restrictive the protective covenants associated with additional borrowing. In other words, additional debt becomes increasingly costly, not only in terms of the higher interest payments lenders may demand but also in the loss of managerial flexibility. The costs eventually reach the point where they offset the benefit of the interest tax shield.

These **bonding** and **monitoring costs** are also referred to as **agency costs of debt financing** because they are the outcome of another type of agency problem. In this case, the shareholders are the agents of the debtholders because they decide how debtholders' funds will be spent. You could argue that agency costs of debt are actually a subset of financial distress costs. Like financial distress costs, they are expected to discourage firms from borrowing too much.

Note that the agency costs of *debt* financing and the agency costs of *equity* financing have *opposite* effects on the firm's value. When a firm increases its borrowing, its agency costs of debt *rise* and the firm's value and share price *fall* (additional debt gets more costly) while, simultaneously, its agency costs of equity *fall* and the firm's value and share price *rise*. The net effect depends on the relative magnitude of the two types of agency costs.

Excessive debt may constrain the firm's ability to pay stable dividends

Managers generally prefer to adopt **stable dividend policies.** They try to distribute dividends regularly and to increase their amount steadily over time to keep pace with the rise in the firm's share price. This maintains a dividend yield (dividend per share divided by share price) acceptable to the market. The objective is usually to attain an unbroken record of dividend payments. When a firm faces a temporary liquidity problem, it will try not to cut its dividend. Cutting or skipping a dividend payment may be interpreted by the market as a signal that the firm is facing a fundamental cash-flow problem that will prevent it from paying dividends for the foreseeable future. The market reaction can be a sharp drop in the firm's share price. To avoid these negative **signaling effects,** firms try to pursue stable dividend policies unless they face a severe cash-flow problem and have no choice but to cut dividends.

The implication for the capital structure decision is clear: Firms with excessive debt may be unable to maintain a stable dividend policy. Consider JBC's alternative capital structures reported in Exhibit 11.1. Suppose the firm pays a $5 dividend per share. With no debt in its capital structure, JBC will be able to pay its dividend even if the worst case scenario occurs. If recession hits, earnings per share will be $5, enough to cover the $5 dividend. But with $100 million of debt, JBC will be unable to pay dividends if recession hits. There will be no cash left after the $10 million of interest on the debt is paid.

If a firm adopts a stable dividend policy and if the market prefers stable dividends, the value of the firm should rise. But this potential increase in value will be offset by the loss of the tax benefits of debt *not* issued. The value of the firm and its share price will rise only if the gains derived from a stable dividend policy exceed the foregone tax benefits of debt financing.

Excessive debt may reduce the firm's financial flexibility and affect its credit rating

Some firms are often tempted to build up cash during good times. This cash buildup, often referred to as **financial slack,** may be valuable because it is immediately available if a value-creating investment opportunity appears. In addition, a cash buildup contributes to increasing the firm's **debt capacity,** that is, its ability to quickly raise debt in the future if a need for funds arises unexpectedly. Clearly, a firm with excessive debt will not be able to enjoy this sort of flexibility. Financial flexibility may be valuable to managers, but does it create value to shareholders? This is a difficult question to answer. Holding cash and reducing debt should have a negative effect on the firm's value because cash does not earn high returns and debt reduction means that valuable tax savings are lost. The net impact on value will be positive only if the expected gains from acting rapidly to take advantage of investment opportunities exceed these negative effects.

Another illustration of how financial flexibility may lead to a capital structure with less than optimal debt, is managers' desire to retain or improve the **credit rating** of their firm's debt. Companies that issue debt securities are required to obtain a rating from a **credit rating agency.** This rating reflects the agency's assessment of the quality of the firm's debt (see Chapter 9 for details). If the agency downgrades the firm's debt, the firm's cost of debt will rise and its ability to raise debt quickly may be impaired, thus reducing the firm's financial flexibility. For this reason, most managers avoid borrowing in excess of the amount that may trigger a credit downgrade, even if more debt makes sense otherwise. Again, the net effect on share price is not obvious.

IS THERE A PREFERENCE FOR RETAINED EARNINGS?

There seems to be a marked preference on the part of managers for retained earnings over external financing, whether in the form of debt or new equity. How can we explain this reticence towards external financing and what are its implications for the capital structure decision?

Contrary to securities, retained earnings do not have issue costs

Contrary to bond and stock issues, retained earnings do not have any **flotation** or **issue costs** and are, thus, less expensive than a stock issue. Flotation costs include administrative costs (such as filing fees, legal fees, and printing fees), taxes, and the costs of using the services of investment banks that sell the firm's securities to the public (see Chapter 9). Most of these costs are fixed, so the total cost of selling bonds and stocks is proportionally lower for large issues than for small ones. This may explain why firms raise large amounts of external funds infrequently rather than small amounts more often. (For issues of the same size, it has been shown that the cost of raising equity is higher than the cost of raising debt.)

Do firms have a preferred order in their choice of financing?

There is evidence that firms usually raise capital according to a **pecking order;** they rely first on retained earnings and then, if external financing is needed, issue debt before raising new equity. Some of the reasons why firms issue bonds rather than stocks are reviewed in the previous section. They include the desire of current owners to retain control, the role of debt as a mechanism to reduce the agency costs of equity, and the negative market reaction to the announcement of a new equity issue, a reaction arising from asymmetric information between managers and outside investors. Firms may prefer to issue bonds rather than stocks, but why would they prefer internal financing (retained earnings) to external financing?

One reason, as mentioned above, is that there are no issue costs associated with retained earnings while there are significant ones for any form of external financing. Another reason is that firms do not have to provide so much information to outsiders to justify a retention of profits as when making a new issue of stocks or bonds. This argument, often defended by the need to prevent competitors from getting valuable information, is generally not well received by shareholders, who interpret it as an excuse for not providing them with valuable information on the use of their funds. This is the dilemma created by shareholders' demand for transparency. Providing it should enhance the firm's value, but it could also harm the firm if competitors use the information to their advantage.

One implication of the pecking order hypothesis is that *firms may not have a particular target debt ratio* or, if they have one, they do not use it consistently. When they have investment opportunities, they retain earnings to fund them. If an investment requires more funds than available internally, the firm will first issue debt and then raise new equity, thus allowing its capital structure to vary over time in response to investment opportunities.

PUTTING IT ALL TOGETHER

We would have liked to provide a formula that ties together all the factors that influence a firm's capital structure and market value and that identifies an optimal debt ratio for a firm. Unfortunately, such a formula does not exist. All we have is a basic framework that tells us an optimal capital structure is reached at the point where the tax benefit of an additional amount of debt is offset by the present value of the expected financial distress costs created by the additional borrowing. From this point, we must make adjustments to reflect the influence of a number of factors that would justify a lower or higher debt-to-equity ratio. These factors are summarized in Exhibit 11.15.

The combined effect of all these factors on the firm's optimal capital structure and market value is practically impossible to estimate with any degree of precision. You will have to exercise a lot of judgment to determine a firm's appropriate capital structure. In making that judgment, the average debt ratio of similar firms in the sector is the best starting point for the analysis. This ratio must then be adjusted upward or downward to reflect the firm's particular conditions and specific situation with respect to the factors surveyed in this section.

After a firm has established a desirable **target capital structure,** it should make financing decisions that are consistent with that target structure. This does not mean that the firm's actual debt ratio must always be equal to its target value. If a firm needs external funds, it does not necessarily need to issue debt and equity in the same proportion as dictated by the target debt ratio. Furthermore, financial market conditions may, at times, favor one type of financing over the other. This means that firms may have to deviate temporarily from their target debt ratio. The objective is to ensure that, *over time,* the firm's average debt ratio is close to its target value. And if the business and financial environments that led to the choice of a particular target debt ratio change, the firm should adjust its target capital structure to reflect the new environment.

SUMMARY

The choice of funds used to finance a firm's investments is important and certain factors need to be taken into account when designing an optimal capital structure, namely, a capital structure that maximizes the firm's value and share price. Our analysis of capital structure begins with how changes in the firm's debt-to-equity ratio affect the firm's profitability, measured by its earnings per share (EPS). By increasing its financial leverage (higher debt ratios), a firm can increase its *expected* EPS but must bear the increasing financial risk (wider swings in EPS) that accompanies higher levels of debt. Unfortunately, the earnings per share approach to capital structure, while providing useful insights about the capital structure

EXHIBIT 11.15 Factors Affecting the Capital Structure Decision

FACTORS THAT FAVOR BORROWING	

- *Primary factor*

Corporate income tax	Debt is a device that allows firms to reduce their corporate income tax because interest expenses are tax deductible whereas dividends and retained earnings are not. However, the interest tax shield at the corporate level may be reduced by the impact of personal income taxes.

- *Important secondary factors*

Agency costs of equity	Debt is a device that helps *reduce* the agency costs of equity arising from the tendency of managers to make decisions that are not always in the best interest of shareholders. Debt increases the firm's value because debt servicing imposes focus and discipline on managers, who will then be less likely to "waste" shareholders' funds.
Retention of control	Debt allows current owners to retain control of the firm. This factor, however, may reduce share price because of the inability of outsiders to take over the company when its ownership is not dispersed.
Information asymmetry	Issuing debt instead of equity allows the firm to avoid the drop in share price that usually accompanies a new equity issue. This drop occurs because outside shareholders think that managers issue shares only when they believe the firm's shares are overvalued.

FACTORS THAT DISCOURAGE (EXCESSIVE) BORROWING	

- *Primary factor*

Costs of financial distress	Excessive debt increases the probability that the firm will experience financial distress. And the higher the probability of financial distress, the larger the present value of the expected costs associated with financial distress and the lower the value of the firm. Firms that face higher probability of financial distress include companies with pretax operating profits that are cyclical and volatile, companies with a relatively large amount of intangible and illiquid assets, and companies with unique products and services or with products that require after-sale service and repair.

EXHIBIT 11.15   (continued)

FACTORS THAT DISCOURAGE (EXCESSIVE) BORROWING	

• *Important secondary factors*

Agency costs of debt	Additional borrowing comes with strings attached. Lenders impose increasingly constraining and costly protective covenants in new debt contracts to protect themselves against the potential misallocation of borrowed funds by managers acting on behalf of shareholders.
Dividend policy	Excessive debt may constrain the firm's ability to adopt a stable dividend policy.
Financial flexibility	Excessive debt may reduce the firm's financial flexibility, that is, its ability to quickly seize a value-creating investment opportunity.

decision, does not identify the ideal trade-off between higher expected EPS and wider fluctuations in EPS. We need to know how debt affects the firm's value.

The pizza theory of capital structure provides a starting point for understanding how debt financing affects the firm's value. The theory says that, like a pizza whose size cannot be increased by slicing it, the value of a firm and its share price cannot be increased by changing the proportions of debt and equity in its capital structure, *provided there are no corporate income taxes.* According to this theory, as the firm increases its financial leverage, the extra benefits accruing to shareholders from higher expected earnings per share is a compensation for the extra risk brought about by that leverage. Although the cost of equity increases with leverage, the firm's weighted average cost of capital, and thus the firm's value, do not change.

When corporate income taxes are considered, debt financing is definitely better than equity financing because the annual interest tax shield resulting from the tax deductibility of interest expenses provides value to shareholders. Similarly, the firm's weighted average cost of capital falls, and the value of the firm rises, as the relative amount of debt financing increases. However, if investors' revenues from equity investment (dividends and capital gains) are taxed at a lower rate than investors' income from holding the firm's debt, then the annual interest tax shield may by lower than predicted. Nevertheless, in a world with corporate income taxes, it appears initially that firms maximize their value by financing 100 percent of their assets with debt.

When financial distress costs are considered, high levels of debt financing become less desirable. Financial distress arises when the firm begins to encounter some difficulties in servicing its debt. When a firm is affected by financial distress, managers' ability to conduct business is impaired, acute conflicts of interest between managers, shareholders, and debtholders emerge, and customers, suppliers, and employees worry about the firm's capacity to meet its contractual obligations. All these factors generate increasing costs that reduce the firm's value as its debt ratio rises.

There is an optimal level of debt financing that is reached when the marginal benefit derived from the interest tax shield is exactly compensated by the additional costs of financial distress. At this level of debt, the firm's weighted average cost of capital is at its lowest and the firm has reached its maximum value. This should be the firm's target debt ratio. This model of optimal financing is called the trade-off model of capital structure.

Finally, a number of additional factors (other than taxes and financial distress costs) need to be examined when formulating a firm's capital structure policy. These factors include the volatility of the firm's operating profits (in other words, its business risk), the type of assets the firm holds, the type of products and services it sells, the presence of agency costs associated with both equity and debt financing, the constraints imposed by dividend policy, the importance of asymmetric information between managers and outside investors, and the existence of a pecking order in the choice of financing sources.

Unfortunately, a formula does not exist that integrates all these factors and tells managers their firm's optimal debt ratio. Designing the right capital structure involves more than applying formulas. It is the art of combining the conceptual framework provided here with judgment, insight, and timing in order to establish a viable debt ratio for the firm.

REFERENCES AND FURTHER READING

1. Benninga, Simon, and Oded Sarig. *Corporate Finance: A Valuation Approach.* McGraw-Hill, 1997. See chapter 8.
2. Brealey, Richard, and Stewart Myers. *Principles of Corporate Finance.* 5th ed. McGraw-Hill, 1996. See chapters 16 to 18.
3. Megginson, William. *Corporate Finance Theory.* Addison Wesley Longman, 1997. See chapter 7.
4. Ross, Stephen, Randolph Westerfield, and Jeffrey Jaffe. *Corporate Finance.* 4th ed. Irwin, 1996. See chapters 15, 16, 18, and 30.

REVIEW PROBLEMS

11.1 Effect of borrowing on share price.

An increase in debt makes equity riskier because the volatility of the earnings per share increases with debt. Suppose there are no taxes and no financial distress costs. Does that necessarily mean that the share price of a firm must decrease when its indebtedness increases? Answer this question if there are taxes and if there are financial distress costs.

11.2 Risk of debt and equity and risk of the firm.
Increasing debt financing makes the firm's equity riskier. It also makes the firm's debt riskier because the probability that the firm will default increases with more debt. Because both equity and debt become riskier, the risk of the firm as a whole should increase. True or false?

11.3 Factors affecting the optimal debt-to-equity ratio.
Assume that the debt-to-equity ratio of Alternative Solutions Inc. is currently optimal. Under which of the following circumstances should the ratio be changed to still be optimal?
a. An increase in the corporate tax rate.
b. An increase in the personal capital gains tax rate.
c. The firm, which specializes in the development of software products, acquires an office building.
d. Management believes strongly that their firm's shares are grossly undervalued.
e. The firm's working capital requirement (the amount it invests in its operating cycle) keeps on decreasing.
f. The firm is taken over by a competitor.

11.4 EBIT–EPS analysis.
Chloroline, Inc., has two million shares outstanding and no debt. Earnings before interest and tax (EBIT) are projected to be $15 million under normal conditions, $5 million for a downturn in the economic environment, and $20 million for an economic expansion. Chloroline considers a debt issue of $50 million with an 8 percent interest rate. The proceeds would be used to buy back one million shares at the current market price of $50 a share. The corporate tax rate is 40 percent.
a. Calculate Chloroline's earnings per share (EPS) and return on investment (EPS divided by share price) under the two scenarios, first before any new debt is issued and then after the recapitalization.
b. From your answers to part a, would you recommend that Chloroline goes ahead with the recapitalization?

11.5 Changes in capital structure and the cost of capital.
Starline & Co. has no debt and its cost of equity is 14 percent. It can borrow at 8 percent. The corporate tax rate is 40 percent.
a. Calculate the cost of equity and the weighted average cost of capital (WACC) of Starline if it decides to borrow up to the equivalent of 25, 50, 75, or 100 percent of its current equity. The proceeds would be used to buy back shares of the firm.

b. Draw a graph showing how Starline's cost of equity, cost of debt, and WACC vary with the debt-to-equity ratio.

c. On the basis of your results, would you recommend that Starline changes its capital structure?

C H A P T E R

12 VALUING AND ACQUIRING A BUSINESS

S hould a manager replace an existing piece of equipment with a newer, more efficient one? Build a plant to launch a new product? Acquire a competitor? Managers should go ahead with these investments only if they are sufficiently confident that undertaking them will raise their firm's market value. This occurs only if the estimated *value* of the assets purchased is higher than the *price* paid to acquire them. This chapter shows how to value a business. The business can be either an entire firm or only part of a firm, such as one of its divisions. In the valuation of an entire firm, we must distinguish between the value of the firm's assets and the value of its equity, where the value of equity represents the claims of shareholders on the firm's assets. Obviously, these values are related because the value of a firm's equity is the difference between the value of its assets and the value of its debts. The value of a division is simply the value of the division's assets.

The most common application of business valuation is the estimation of the price at which the shares of a firm can be acquired. For example, in a takeover, one firm (the bidding company) wants to acquire all or a portion of another firm's shares and needs to determine the price at which the shares of the target firm should be bought. The target firm may be a public firm whose shares are traded and quoted in a stock exchange, or it may be a privately held company with no quoted price. To decide if the acquisition is a value-creating proposal, the bidding firm needs to determine how much the target firm's shares are worth to it (the bidder). If the shares of the target firm are quoted at $20 a share and the bidder estimates their value at $30, buying them for less than $30 is a value-creating decision. In this case, the acquisition is a value-creating investment because the shares are worth more to the bidding firm than the price it has to pay for them. Any acquisition price above an average price of $30 per share is a value-destroying acquisition because the value of the shares the bidding firm acquires are worth less than the price it pays for them.

An initial public offering (IPO) is another typical situation that requires the valuation of a company's equity. In an IPO, a privately held company is considering issuing shares to the public for the first time. An offer price that will ensure the success of the sale to the public must be estimated. A similar situation occurs when state owned firms are privatized, that is, sold to the public.

After a brief introduction to the main valuation methods, this chapter focuses on the methods that are most commonly used. First, we present *valuation by comparables,* which values a firm using stock market data on firms similar to the business or the firm we want to value. As an illustration, we apply the method to the valuation of OS Distributors, a firm we analyze in Chapters 3–5. Then, we present the *discounted cash flow* (DCF) approach, which values a firm's assets by discounting the future cash flows expected from these assets. The estimated value of the firm's equity is the difference between the estimated value of its assets and the value of its debts. We show how the method can be implemented by estimating two different values of OS Distributors' equity — its *"stand-alone"* or *"as-is"* value and its value as an acquisition target (its target value). We examine in detail the sources of value creation in an acquisition and explain how to estimate their impact on the value of the target firm. We also describe why a conglomerate merger, which is the combination of unrelated businesses, is not likely to create value. Finally, we present the *adjusted present value* (APV) method, a variation of the DCF approach. According to the APV method, the value of a firm's assets is equal to their value assuming they are financed only by equity plus the value of the tax savings provided by the portion of the assets financed by debt. OS Distributors is again used as an illustration of this method, this time as a *leveraged buyout* (LBO) target, meaning that the firm's assets will be financed with an unusually high proportion of debt. After reading this chapter, you should understand:

- The alternative methods used to value businesses and how to apply them in practice to estimate the value of a company.
- Why some companies acquire other firms.
- How to value a potential acquisition.
- Why a high proportion of acquisitions usually fail to deliver value to the shareholders of the acquiring firm.
- Leveraged buyout (LBO) deals and how they are put together.

ALTERNATIVE VALUATION METHODS

Suppose the asking price of a 2,000 square foot house you wish to buy is $220,000, and you want to find out whether $220,000 is a fair price for this piece of property. There are two basic ways of estimating the value of the house. First, you can find out the selling price of a *similar* house. A real estate agent tells you that a 1,500 square foot house on the same street sold for $150,000 last week. What can you conclude? The comparable house was sold for $100 per square foot ($150,000 divided by 1,500 square feet). Applying that rate to the house you want to buy gives a value of $200,000 (2,000 square feet times $100 per square foot), $20,000 less than the asking price of $220,000. You have just estimated the value of the house using a method called **valuation by comparables.** By comparing a company to similar firms in its sector, the same procedure can be used to value that company.

The second approach to estimating the value of the house is to determine its rental value. The real estate agent says that you could expect an annual rental income of $21,000 for the house. This amount needs to be compared with what you could earn on your savings if you did not buy the house. An investment in long-term government securities, which you consider as risky as owning this particular house, is currently offering a 10 percent annual return. How much should you pay for the house in order to earn the same 10 percent return based on a $21,000 annual rental income? The answer is $210,000 (an annual rate of 10 percent applied to $210,000 yields an income of $21,000 per year). You have just estimated the value of the house using the **discounted cash flow** or **DCF valuation** method. If rented, the house will generate a constant annual cash flow of $21,000. Discounting this cash-flow stream at a required rate of return of 10 percent provides a DCF value of $210,000. This estimated value is $10,000 less than the asking price of $220,000.

Recall that the comparables approach produced an estimated value of $200,000. Different valuation methods usually lead to different results, but the differences should not be too large. If different methods produce a wide spread in estimated values (say, more than 20 percent), the validity of the assumptions underlying the alternative methods and the reliability of the data used in the valuation process should be checked. For example, the other house on the street should be as similar as possible to the one you want to buy (ideally, it should be identical); and the 10 percent return on long-term government securities should be a good substitute for your required return on the rented house (these two investments should have the same risk characteristics). Poorly estimated input data will lead to unreliable estimated values. (Remember GIGO, "garbage in, garbage out.")

To conclude, what should you offer for the house? An offer between $200,000 and $210,000 would be reasonable based on your estimates. A higher offer would exceed your estimated values and produce an investment with a negative *net present value,* that is, an investment whose price is higher than its estimated value. Of course, it would be best to buy the house at the lowest possible price. But if the real estate market is reasonably efficient, there are few real bargains.

Although valuation by comparables and DCF valuation are the most common approaches to valuing a business, they are not the only methods. Two other measures are the **liquidation value** of a firm's assets and the **replacement value** of a firm's assets. The liquidation value of a firm's assets is the amount of cash you would receive if you sold separately the various items that make up the firm's assets (its trade receivables, inventories, equipment, land, and buildings). The replacement value of a firm's assets is what it would cost today to replace these assets with similar ones in order to start a new business with the same earning power as the one you wish to purchase. Clearly, the liquidation value of a business is the *minimum* price you would expect to pay for its assets. If you could buy the assets for less than their liquidation value and resell them immediately at that value, you would earn a sure profit, a situation unlikely to occur in a properly functioning market. Although the replacement value of a *tangible* asset, such as a building, is the *maximum* price you would pay for it—you would not pay more for a building than what it would cost to build a similar one—you may be ready to offer a higher price for a business if it has some *intangible* assets that are valuable to you and that cannot be replaced, such as patents or trademarks.

VALUING A FIRM'S EQUITY USING COMPARABLES

OS Distributors is an unlisted, privately owned firm whose financial performance is analyzed in Chapters 2–5. The balance sheets of OS Distributors, a nationwide distributor of office equipment and supplies, are reported in Exhibit 12.1 for the years 1995, 1996 and 1997. Its income statements for the years 1995, 1996, and 1997 are presented in Exhibit 12.2. We want to estimate the equity value of OS Distributors in early January 1998.

The 1997 balance sheet indicates that the company's accounting, or book, value of equity at the end of that year is $77 million. This value, recorded as "owners' equity" at the bottom of the balance sheet, measures the *net* cumulative amount of equity capital (cash and retained profits) the firm's shareholders have invested in the company since it was first established. It is a measure of the aggregate amount of net equity capital injected into the firm over time, up to the date of the balance sheet. It is *not* a measure of what shareholders would expect to receive from the sale of their shares. Nor is it a measure of what the firm's equity would be worth if it were listed on a stock market.

The firm has a recent record of steadily increasing profits and dividend payments, and it is likely this trend will continue in the future. Thus, the *market value* of OS Distributors' equity, which is the price it would sell for, should be higher than its book value of $77 million. Because the ownership of a share in a firm's equity entitles the shareholder to receive *future* dividend payments as well as a share of any *future* appreciation in the firm's value, the equity value that matters to investors is the market value, not the book value. The book value of equity, which reflects *past* earnings performance and *past* dividend distributions, is only relevant to the extent that it provides some useful information about the firm's *future* performance.

ESTIMATING THE COMPARABLE VALUE
OF OS DISTRIBUTORS' EQUITY

What would the value of OS Distributors' equity be if the firm were listed in a stock market? One way to estimate this value is to use the valuation by comparables method. First, we need to identify listed companies that are similar to OS Distributors. One of these is General Equipment and Supplies (GES). GES is also a distributor of office equipment and supplies. It is larger than OS Distributors, but is similar in asset and cost structures.

EXHIBIT 12.1 OS Distributors' Balance Sheets.

Fig<None>ures in millions of dollars

	DECEMBER 31, 1995		DECEMBER 31, 1996		DECEMBER 31, 1997	
ASSETS						
• *CURRENT ASSETS*		$104.0		$119.0		$137.0
Cash[1]	$6.0		$12.0		$8.0	
Accounts receivable	44.0		48.0		56.0	
Inventories	52.0		57.0		72.0	
Prepaid expenses[2]	2.0		2.0		1.0	
• *NONCURRENT ASSETS*		56.0		51.0		53.0
Financial assets and intangibles	0.0		0.0		0.0	
Property, plant, and equipment (net)	56.0		51.0		53.0	
Gross value[3]	$90.0		$90.0		$93.0	
Accumulated depreciation	(34.0)		(39.0)		(40.0)	
TOTAL ASSETS		$160.0		$170.0		$190.0
LIABILITIES AND OWNERS' EQUITY						
• *CURRENT LIABILITIES*		$54.0		$66.0		$75.0
Short-term debt	$15.0		$22.0		$23.0	
Owed to banks	$7.0		$14.0		$15.0	
Current portion of long-term debt	8.0		8.0		8.0	
Accounts payable	37.0		40.0		48.0	
Accrued expenses[4]	2.0		4.0		4.0	
• *NONCURRENT LIABILITIES*		42.0		34.0		38.0
Long-term debt[5]	42.0		34.0		38.0	
• *Owners' equity[6]*	64.0	64.0	70.0	70.0	77.0	77.0
TOTAL LIABILITIES AND OWNERS' EQUITY		$160.0		$170.0		$190.0

Notes

1. Consists of cash in hand and checking accounts held to facilitate operating activities.
2. Prepaid expenses is rent paid in advance (when recognized in the income statement, rent is included in selling, general, and administrative expenses).
3. In 1996, there was no disposal of existing fixed assets or acquisition of new fixed assets. However, during 1997, a warehouse was enlarged at a cost of $12 million and existing fixed assets, bought for $9 million in the past, were sold at their net book value of $2 million.
4. Accrued expenses consist of wages and taxes payable.
5. Long-term debt is repaid at the rate of $8 million per year. No new long-term debt was incurred during 1996, but during 1997 a mortgage loan was obtained from the bank to finance the extension of a warehouse (see Note 3).
6. During the three years, no new shares were issued and none were repurchased.

383

EXHIBIT 12.2   OS Distributors' Income Statements.

Figures in millions of dollars

	1995	% of Sales	1996	% of Sales	1997	% of Sales
• Net sales	$390.0		$420.0		$480.0	
Cost of goods sold	($328.0)		($353.0)		($400.0)	
• Gross profit	62.0	15.9%	67.0	15.9%	80.0	16.7%
Selling, general, and administrative expenses	(39.8)		(43.7)		(48.0)	
Depreciation expenses	(5.0)		(5.0)		(8.0)	
• Operating profit	17.2	4.4%	18.3	4.4%	24.0	5.0%
Extraordinary items	0		0		0	
• Earnings before interest and tax (EBIT)	17.2	4.4%	18.3	4.4%	24.0	5.0%
Net interest expenses[1]	(5.5)		(5.0)		(7.0)	
• Earnings before tax (EBT)	11.7	3.0%	13.3	3.2%	17.0	3.5%
Income tax expense	(4.7)		(5.3)		(6.8)	
• Earnings after tax (EAT)	$7.0	1.8%	$8.0	1.9%	$10.2	2.1%
Dividends	$2.0		$2.0		$3.2	
• Retained earnings	$5.0		$6.0		$7.0	

Notes
1. There is no interest income, so net interest expenses are equal to interest expenses.

Exhibit 12.3 shows comparable accounting and financial market data for the two companies.[1] Items 1–3 are from the 1997 income statements and balance sheets of the two companies. Cash flow is reported in quotation marks because, strictly speaking, it is not a measure of cash flow but rather the sum of net profit (EAT) and depreciation expenses, also referred to as bankers' cash flow or **cash earnings** (see Chapter 4). Items 5–7 correspond to items 1–3 restated on a per share basis. Item 8 is the market price of a share in early January 1998, which is only available for GES.

Using the information in items 1–8 in Exhibit 12.3, we can define the following three key ratios for GES (these are items 9–11 in the exhibit):

$$\text{Price-to-earnings ratio} = \frac{\text{Share price}}{\text{Earnings per share}} = \frac{\$20}{\$1.27} = 15.7$$

$$\text{Price-to-cash earnings ratio} = \frac{\text{Share price}}{\text{Cash earnings per share}} = \frac{\$20}{\$2.42} = 8.3$$

$$\text{Price-to-book ratio} = \frac{\text{Share price}}{\text{Book value per share}} = \frac{\$20}{\$10.52} = 1.9$$

These three ratios depend on GES's price per share, which is determined by the market. Thus, the ratios are also referred to as **market multiples.** The price-to-earnings ratio (or **PE ratio**) of 15.7 is GES's **earnings multiple;** it indicates that GES's shares were trading in early January 1998 at a price equal to 15.7 times the firm's most recent earnings per share ($1.27×15.7 = $20). Similarly, the **price-to-cash earnings ratio** is GES's **cash earnings multiple** and indicates that GES's shares were trading in early January 1998 at a price equal to 8.3 times GES's latest cash earnings per share ($2.42×8.3 = $20). The **price-to-book ratio** is GES's **book value multiple** and indicates that GES's shares were trading in early January 1998 at a price equal to 1.9 times GES's most recent book value per share ($10.52×1.9 = $20).

We could easily increase the list of market multiples to include a **sales multiple** (share price divided by sales per share), an **operating profit multiple** (share price divided by earnings before interest and tax or EBIT per share), an **operating cash earnings multiple** (share price divided by the sum of EBIT and depreciation per share), an **asset multiple** (share price divided by assets per share), or any other ratio of share price to a financial account or combination of accounts taken from the firm's income statement and balance sheet.

These market multiples are called **historical,** or **trailing** multiples. They are calculated using *past* earnings, cash earnings, or book values. If we had a forecast of the earnings, cash earnings, or book value for the *next* period we could have calculated **expected,** or **prospective,** multiples.

---

[1] If we could not find a firm similar enough to OS Distributors, we would have compared OS Distributors' performance and characteristics to those of its sector.

EXHIBIT 12.3 Accounting and Financial Market Data for OS Distributors and GES, a Comparable Firm.

	GES	OS DISTRIBUTORS
I. Accounting data (1997)		
1. Earnings after tax (EAT)	$63.5 million	$10.2 million
2. "Cash earnings" = EAT + depreciation expenses	$63.5 + $57.5 = $121 million	$10.2 + $8 = $18.2 million
3. Book value of equity	$526 million	$77 million
4. Number of shares outstanding	50 million shares	10 million shares
5. Earnings per share or EPS [(1)/(4)]	$1.27	$1.02
6. "Cash earnings" per share [(2)/(4)]	$2.42	$1.82
7. Book value per share [(3)/(4)]	$10.52	$7.70
II. Financial Market data (January 1998)		
8. Share price	$20	Not available
III. Multiples		
9. Price-to-earnings ratio [(8)/(5)]	15.7 times	Not available
10. Price-to-cash earnings ratio [(8)/(6)]	8.3 times	Not available
11. Price-to-book value ratio [(8)/(7)]	1.9 times	Not available

We can now estimate the value of OS Distributors based on comparable market multiples. According to this approach, *comparable firms should trade at the same market multiples* (historical or expected). In other words, if OS Distributors is similar to GES, then GES's market multiples can be used to estimate the value that OS Distributors' equity would have if it were listed on the stock market.[2] This is the same procedure we used to estimate the value of the house in the previous section using the price per square foot of the comparable house. For OS Distributors (OSD) we have:

Estimated value of OSD = [Earnings after tax of OSD] × [Earnings multiple of GES]

= [$10.2 million] × [15.7]

= **$160 million**

---

[2]No two firms can be exactly the same. We know that GES is significantly larger than OS Distributors. Furthermore, GES is a listed company known to the market whereas OS Distributors is not. This means that OS Distributors' (unobservable) multiples would most likely not be identical to those of GES. Applying GES multiples to OS Distributors' earnings, cash earnings, and book value figures results in approximate values.

Estimated value of OSD = [Cash earnings of OSD] × [Cash earnings multiple of GES]

= [$18.2 million] × [8.3]

= **$151 million**

Estimated value of OSD = [Book value of OSD] × [Book value multiple of GES]

= [$77 million] × [1.9]

= **$146 million**

We now have three estimated values for OS Distributors' equity based on GES's historical market multiples. These values range from a high of $160 million to a low of $146 million. As pointed out earlier, different valuation approaches usually produce different estimated values. Valuation is not a precise exercise, and as long as the spread is within a reasonable range, you should not be concerned. The highest estimated value for OS Distributors ($160 million) is 10 percent higher than the lowest estimated value ($146 million), not an unusual spread.

Is one multiple more appropriate than the others? Some analysts recommend the use of a particular multiple to value certain types of businesses, suggesting, for example, earnings multiples for industrial companies, cash earnings multiples for real estate firms and hotel companies, and book value multiples for financial service firms, such as banks and insurance companies.

Which value should be used for OS Distributors' equity? We will answer this question after we estimate the discounted cash flow value of OS Distributors' equity. Before we do this, we first examine the factors that explain the magnitude of market multiples. For example, why is the price-to-earnings ratio of GES equal to 15.7 and not a higher or lower number?

FACTORS THAT DETERMINE EARNINGS AND CASH-FLOW MULTIPLES

This section reviews the factors that affect the price-to-earnings ratio and the price-to-cash earnings ratio; Chapter 14 (see Appendix 14.2) looks at the price-to-book value ratio.

Earnings and cash earnings multiples are affected by the general market environment, such as the prevailing level of interest rates, and by factors unique to companies, such as their expected growth and perceived risk. Companies with *high* expected rates of growth and *low* perceived risk usually have *high* multiples. In addition, *low* rates of interest generally boost market multiples. These observations can be explained using the discounted cash flow formula, which is first used in Chapter 9 for estimating the value of a share of common stock. The formula provides the estimated value today (the discounted cash flow or DCF value) of a cash flow that grows *forever* at a constant growth rate g for a given required rate of return (or discount rate) k:

$$\text{DCF value} = \frac{\textbf{Next year's cash flow}}{\textbf{Required return} - \textbf{growth rate}} = \frac{\textbf{Next year's cash flow}}{\textbf{k} - \textbf{g}} \quad (12.1)$$

For example, suppose that next year's cash flow is \$100 and that it is expected to grow forever at the constant annual rate of 5 percent ($g = 0.05$). If *your* required rate of return is 10 percent ($k = 0.10$), the value *to you* of that cash flow is:

$$\text{DCF value} = \frac{\$100}{0.10 - 0.05} = \frac{\$100}{0.05} = \$2,000$$

Note that equation 12.1 is valid only when the rate of growth g is less than the required rate of return k.[3]

Assume now that the price of shares traded in the stock market is related to cash flows according to the equation 12.1, that is, share price is equal to DCF value. Then, the share price of any listed firm can be written as:

$$\text{Share price} = \frac{\text{Next year's cash flow per share}}{k - g}$$

Dividing both sides by next year's cash flow, we get:

$$\frac{\text{Share price}}{\text{Next year's cash flow}} = \frac{1}{k - g}$$

The left side of this equation is the price-to-cash flow ratio (prospective rather than historical and with cash flow defined as cash earnings). The right side of the equation indicates that this ratio rises when the expected growth rate g increases (but remains smaller than k) and/or when the required rate of return k decreases (but remains higher than g). The required rate of return decreases if the market perceives the firm to have low risk or if the level of interest rates declines (when interest rates decline, investors require lower rates of return on *all* assets). The same analysis applies if cash flow is replaced by earnings. Conclusion: *Both earnings multiples and cash earnings multiples are higher when the market expects faster growth in earnings and cash flows, a lower company risk, and an environment of declining interest rates, all else being the same.*

Accounting rules and tax regulations also affect multiples. To illustrate the impact of accounting conventions on earnings multiples, consider the stock market multiples shown in Exhibit 12.4. These are multiples for the entire set of companies that make up the stock market index in each of the three countries' stock

---

[3]If the perpetual growth rate g is greater than k, the company's cash flows are growing into the future at a faster rate than the rate k at which they are discounted back to the present. As a result, the value of the company becomes infinitely large and equation 12.1 is meaningless.

TABLE 12.4   Multiples for Three Markets.

MULTIPLE[1]	UNITED STATES (NEW YORK STOCK EXCHANGE)	UNITED KINGDOM (LONDON STOCK EXCHANGE)	JAPAN (TOKYO STOCK EXCHANGE)
Price-to-earnings	15.8	11.4	35.3
Price-to-cash earnings[2]	7.6	7.3	10.6

[1]Goldman Sachs Equity Research (August 1990)
[2]Cash earnings is defined as the sum of earnings after tax, depreciation expenses, and *all other noncash expenses.*

exchanges. We first compare the earnings multiples. What factors can explain the fact that the Tokyo market has an earnings multiple more than twice the size of the prevailing one in New York or London? A higher expected rate of growth and lower interest rates in Japan than in the United States or the United Kingdom (in 1990) cannot completely explain the difference between these countries' market multiples. The other factors are accounting conventions and tax regulations. The magnitude of aftertax profits reported by companies is affected by accounting and tax rules. In some countries, and Japan is one of them, companies are allowed to depreciate their assets rapidly and make generous provisions against potential losses. The result is *lower* aftertax profits and *higher* earnings multiples (recall that an earnings multiples is share price *divided* by net profit per share) than in countries whose tax laws do not provide similar advantages, such as the United States and the United Kingdom.

One way of eliminating some of the accounting distortions on earnings multiples is to use cash earnings multiples because cash earnings are less affected than accounting earnings by differences in accounting conventions. This explains why the gap between Tokyo's cash earnings multiple and those in New York and London is smaller than the gap between their respective earnings multiples. Conclusion: When comparing values between countries (and even between industries within the same country) cash earnings multiples should be used rather than accounting earnings multiples in order to neutralize some of the distortions introduced by differences in accounting rules across countries (and across industries within a country).

VALUING A FIRM'S ASSETS AND EQUITY USING THE DISCOUNTED CASH FLOW APPROACH

Before we estimate the value of OS Distributors using the discounted cash flow (DCF) approach, we first examine a simpler case to explain the logic behind DCF valuation and to identify the data required to obtain the DCF value of a firm's assets and equity.

ESTIMATING THE DCF VALUE OF A FIRM'S ASSETS

According to the DCF method, the value of an asset is determined by the capacity of that asset to generate future cash flows. When a buyer purchases a company's assets he acquires the entire stream of cash flows these assets are *expected* to produce in the future. How can these cash flows be valued?

Consider the case of No Growth Company (NGC). Each year, its assets generate a cash flow of either $110 or $90 with a 50 percent chance for each of the cash flows. The average, or expected, value of that risky and *perpetual* annual cash flow is $100 (one half of $110 plus one half of $90). Assume you want to earn a return of 10 percent to compensate you for the risk associated with these cash flows and for the time you have to wait to receive them. What value today can you assign to the entire perpetual cash-flow stream that NGC's assets are expected to generate?

Equation 12.1 can be used to answer this question. When the expected growth rate is zero, equation 12.1 reduces to:

$$\textbf{DCF value (no growth)} \;=\; \frac{\textbf{Expected annual cash flow}}{\textbf{Required rate of return}} = \frac{\textbf{CF}}{\textbf{k}} \qquad (12.2)$$

Given an expected cash flow of $100 and a required rate of return of 10 percent:

$$\text{DCF value of NGC's assets} = \frac{\$100}{0.10} = \$1,000$$

The impact of the growth of cash flows on their DCF value

In the discussion of market multiples, our example used a growth rate of 5 percent, the same cash flow of $100, and produced a DCF value of $2,000 (see equation 12.1 and its numerical illustration). Thus, cutting the growth rate from 5 percent to zero has reduced the DCF value by 50 percent. This shows how sensitive the DCF value of a cash-flow stream is to its assumed future rate of growth. In general, the faster the growth rate in cash flows, the higher is their discounted value. We return to this observation when we consider OS Distributors' valuation.

The impact of the risk associated with cash flows on their DCF value

Suppose we now assume that the annual cash flow takes the values of either $120 or $80, again with a 50 percent chance of occurrence for each. The *expected* value of the cash flow is still $100 (one half of $120 plus one half of $80). However, the expected cash flow is now riskier because its two possible outcomes are farther from their average value. In other words, the spread, or volatility in the cash flows is wider. Because the annual cash flow is riskier, you require a higher rate of return to compensate you for the increase in risk.[4] Let's say you now require a return of 12.5 percent. At this rate, the DCF value of the expected annual cash flows of $100 is:

$$\text{DCF value} = \frac{\$100}{0.125} = \$800$$

Thus, the value of the cash-flow stream is 20 percent lower when the cash flows are riskier. In general, the higher the risk of a cash-flow stream, the lower is its discounted value.

A general formula to calculate the DCF value of a firm's assets

We have assumed that NGC generates perpetual and constant annual cash flows. However, the cash flows generated by a firm's assets usually are not constant and do not grow at a constant rate forever. Consequently, the valuation formulas in equations 12.1 and 12.2, which give the DCF value of constant or constant growth cash flows, are not applicable. We need a valuation formula that gives the present value of a stream of future cash flows that is applicable to any growth pattern in cash flows. This valuation formula, which we use in Chapter 6 to compute the present value of an investment, is expressed as follows:

$$\text{DCF}_{\text{value}} = \frac{\textbf{CFA}_1}{\textbf{1 + k}} + \frac{\textbf{CFA}_2}{(\textbf{1 + k})^2} + \ldots + \frac{\textbf{CFA}_t}{(\textbf{1 + k})^t} + \ldots \qquad (12.3)$$

where CFA_1, CFA_2, ..., CFA_t, ... are the cash flows the assets are expected to generate and k is the rate of return required from investing in these assets.

To summarize: *To estimate the DCF value of a company's assets, we must first estimate the expected cash flows these assets will generate in the future and then discount them at a required rate of return that reflects their risk, with riskier expected cash flows discounted at higher rates.*

The estimation of the cash flows generated by a firm's assets is presented in Chapter 4 and the estimation of risk-adjusted discount rates is in Chapter 10. We briefly review these topics in the remainder of this section.

Estimating the cash flows generated by assets

The net cash flow generated by a firm's assets, called **cash flow from assets** or **CFA** (often referred to as **free cash flow**), during a given period is the cash flow

---

[4] The underlying standard assumption is that you, and practically all other investors are **risk-averse,** that is, dislike risk.

generated by its asset-based activities, namely, from the *operating* and *investing* activities during the period. Recall that this cash flow *excludes* any items related to the firm's *financing* activities, such as interest or dividend payments. We show in Chapter 4 that the cash flow generated by operating activities, or net operating cash flow (NOCF), during a given period is:

$$NOCF = EBIT - \text{tax expense} + \text{depreciation expenses} - \Delta WCR$$

where EBIT is earnings before interest and tax and ΔWCR is the *change* in working capital requirement during the period. Working capital requirement, which measures the firm's investment in its operating cycle, is the difference between operating assets (trade receivables, inventories, and prepaid expenses) and operating liabilities (trade payables and accrued expenses). For consistency, the relevant tax expense must be taken *before* interest costs, because the cash flow from assets must exclude any item related to the firm's financing policy. If T_C is the firm's corporate tax rate, the relevant tax expense is T_C multiplied by EBIT because EBIT is earnings *before* interest and taxes. We can write the above equation as:

$$NOCF = EBIT(1 - T_C) + \text{Depreciation expenses} - \Delta WCR$$

Recall that depreciation expenses are added back to earnings because they are not cash expenses. Adding them back to EBIT cancels the depreciation expenses that were deducted from revenues to get EBIT in the first place (see Chapter 4).

If we define net capital expenditures as the amount of cash spent on the acquisition of new assets less any cash raised from the sale of existing assets, the net cash flow from assets is:

$$\text{Cash flow from assets (CFA)} = NOCF - \text{Net capital expenditures}$$

Combining the above two equations yields the following formula for the cash flow generated by a firm's assets:

$$\textbf{CFA} = \textbf{EBIT(1} - \textbf{T}_C\textbf{)} + \textbf{Depreciation expenses} - \Delta\textbf{WCR}$$
$$- \textbf{Net capital expenditures} \qquad (12.4)$$

We can use equation 12.4 to find the cash flow from assets (CFA) for the No Growth Company. The firm does not grow, so its working capital requirement will not change (thus ΔWCR is zero) and its capital expenditures will be equal to its depreciation expenses (the only capital expenditure made by NGC is to *maintain* existing assets). Thus, NGC's expected cash flow from assets reduces to $EBIT(1 - T_C)$. If we assume an expected annual EBIT of \$167 and a tax rate of 40 percent, we get:

$$CFA = EBIT(1 - T_C) = \$167(1 - 40\%) = \$100$$

Note again that the tax rate is applied to EBIT. The tax savings due to the deductibility of interest payments is considered next in the context of the cost of capital.

Estimating the rate of return required to discount the cash flows

The *minimum* required rate of return used to discount the cash flows generated by assets must be at least equal to the cost of financing the assets. For example, if the cost of financing the purchase of an asset is 10 percent, then you will require a return on your investment in this asset of at least 10 percent, otherwise your investment will not cover its financing cost. What, then, is the cost of financing the purchase of an asset? This cost depends on the sources of capital employed (equity capital and borrowed funds), their respective proportions in the total funds raised, and their respective costs. It is the **weighted average cost of capital** or WACC, which is analyzed in detail in Chapter 10. The WACC is defined as:

$$\text{WACC} = \frac{\textbf{equity}}{\textbf{equity} + \textbf{debt}} \times \textbf{k}_\textbf{E} + \frac{\textbf{debt}}{\textbf{equity} + \textbf{debt}} \times \textbf{k}_\textbf{D}(\textbf{1} - \textbf{tax rate}) \qquad (12.5)$$

where k_E is the estimated cost of equity, k_D is the estimated pretax cost of debt, and the weights are the respective proportions of equity and debt used in financing the asset.

Suppose that one half of the funds required to purchase NGC's assets will be in the form of equity capital at an estimated cost of 14 percent and the other half will be borrowed at a cost of 10 percent (the interest rate the bank will charge). We assume a tax rate of 40 percent.[5] Applying equation 12.5 to NGC, we get:

$$\text{WACC} = \frac{1}{2} \times 14\% + \frac{1}{2} \times 10\%(1 - 40\%) = 10\%$$

We estimated NGC's cost of equity capital at 14 percent using the capital asset pricing model (CAPM) discussed in Chapter 10. According to the CAPM, the rate of return required by equity investors, which is the same as the firm's cost of equity, is equal to the rate of return they can get from investing in a *riskless* government bond plus a risk premium that will compensate them for the risk of holding the firm's shares. That risk premium is estimated by multiplying the firm's **beta coefficient** (β) by the risk premium of the entire stock market.[6] We can write:

$$\textbf{k}_\textbf{E} = \textbf{R}_\textbf{F} + \textbf{market risk premium} \times \boldsymbol{\beta} \qquad (12.6)$$

where R_F is the return on the riskless asset.

---

[5] The assumption is that the firm is profitable and pays taxes.

[6] A company's beta coefficient is a measure of the sensitivity of its stock returns to the overall market movements. By definition, the market has a beta of one. Companies whose stock returns fluctuate *more* than the overall market movements are riskier than the market and have betas higher than one. Those with stock returns that fluctuate *less* than the overall market movements are less risky than the market and have betas that are less than one (see Chapter 10). For example, if a company has a beta of 1.50, it means that, on *average,* when the market rises by 1 percent, the company's share price increases by 1.5 percent.

Suppose that the yield on 10-year government bonds is 8.4 percent and the *historical* market risk premium is 7 percent, meaning that in the past, on average, the market returns exceeded the yield on government bonds by 7 percent (different markets and countries can, of course, have different yields on government bonds and different market risk premiums). Let's say that the estimated beta coefficient of NGC is 0.80.[7] Inserting these three figures (R_F = 8.4%, market risk premium = 7%, and β = 0.80) into the CAPM formula (equation 12.6) provides an estimate of NGC's cost of equity. We have:

$$k_E = 8.4\% + 7\% \times 0.80 = 8.4\% + 5.6\% = 14\%$$

Thus, the estimate of the risk-adjusted discount rate for NGC is 10 percent—the combination of an estimated cost of equity of 14 percent and an aftertax cost of debt of 6 percent.

ESTIMATING THE DCF VALUE OF A FIRM'S EQUITY

The preceding analysis produced a value of $1,000 for NGC's *assets* by discounting the $100 perpetual cash flows the assets are expected to generate in the future at a WACC of 10 percent. However, buying a firm's *assets* is not the same as buying that firm's *equity.* Suppose NGC has $400 of debt outstanding (debt it has not yet repaid). If you buy NGC's equity from its existing owners, you will own NGC's assets and you will also assume the firm's existing debt of $400. Because the firm's debt is now yours, the estimated DCF value of the *firm's equity* is only $600, the difference between the estimated value of its assets ($1,000) and the value of its outstanding debt ($400). In general:

DCF value of a firm's equity = DCF value of the firm's assets
− Value of the firm's debt　　　　　(12.7)

ESTIMATING THE DCF VALUE OF OS DISTRIBUTORS' ASSETS AND EQUITY

Now that we have reviewed the various elements required to estimate the discounted cash flow value of a firm's assets and equity, we can turn to the DCF valuation of OS Distributors in early January 1998. In this section, we assume that OS Distributors stays **as is,** meaning that its operating efficiency remains the same as in 1997, the most recent year for which data is available. In other words, we

---

[7] If the No Growth Company is not a listed company, we would take the beta coefficient of a comparable company.

estimate the firm's **stand-alone value.** The four steps required to obtain this value are summarized as follows:

Step 1: Estimate the future stream of expected cash flows that the firm's assets will generate using equation 12.4.

Step 2: Estimate the rate at which the cash flows from assets must be discounted to the present. This rate is the weighted average cost of capital (WACC), which is estimated using equation 12.5, where the cost of equity is estimated with the capital asset pricing model (CAPM) formula (equation 12.6).

Step 3: Calculate the discounted cash flow (DCF) value of the firm's assets by discounting the expected cash-flow stream from assets (CFA) at the WACC.

Step 4: In order to get the estimated DCF value of the firm's *equity,* deduct any *debt outstanding* from the estimated DCF value of assets, as shown in equation 12.7.

STEP 1: ESTIMATION OF OS DISTRIBUTORS' CASH FLOW FROM ASSETS

When estimating the DCF value of a firm's assets, the usual forecasting period is five years. But when a firm is valued as a **going concern** (the assumption is that it will operate forever), we need to estimate the DCF value of the firm's assets *at the end of the forecasting period.* The estimation of this **terminal** (or **residual) value** is based on the cash flows the firm's assets are expected to generate *beyond the forecasting period.* First, we develop a forecast of OS Distributors cash flows during the six-year period from 1998 to 2003. We then estimate the firm's residual value at the end of 2002.

Estimating the cash flows from assets up to year 2003

Our forecast of the cash flows that OS Distributors' assets are expected to generate is shown in Exhibit 12.5. Before we establish these forecasts, we review OS Distributors' *past* performance. The firm's historical efficiency ratios (from 1995 to 1997) are summarized in the first four lines shown in Exhibit 12.5. Sales grew by 7.7 percent during 1996 and 14.3 percent during 1997. Operating expenses, expressed as a percentage of sales, declined during the period, with the cost of goods sold (COGS) decreasing from 84.10 percent of sales in 1995 to 83.33 percent of sales in 1997. Similarly selling, general, and administrative expenses (SG&A) decreased from 10.21 percent of sales to 10 percent of sales during the period. The efficiency with which the firm managed its operating cycle, measured by the ratio of working capital requirement (WCR) to sales, however, deteriorated. In 1995, OS Distributors used $15.13 of working capital to generate $100 of sales. Two years later, that figure rose to $16.04.

EXHIBIT 12.5 Discounted Cash Flow (DCF) Valuation of OS Distributors' Equity at the Beginning of January 1998.

Figures in millions of dollars; historical data from Exhibits 12.1 and 12.2

	Historical Data			Estimated Cash Flows to Year 2003					
	1995	1996	1997	1998	1999	2000	2001	2002	2003
1. Sales growth rate		7.7%	14.3%	10%	8%	7%	5%	4%	3%
2. COGS[1] in percent of sales	84.10%	84.05%	83.33%	83.33%	83.33%	83.33%	83.33%	83.33%	83.33%
3. SG&A[1] in percent of sales	10.21%	10.40%	10.00%	10.00%	10.00%	10.00%	10.00%	10.00%	10.00%
4. WCR[1] in percent of sales	15.13%	15.00%	16.04%	16.04%	16.04%	16.04%	16.04%	16.04%	16.04%
5. Sales	$390.0	$420.0	$480.0	$528.0	$570.2	$610.1	$640.7	$666.3	$686.3
6. *less COGS*	(328.0)	(353.0)	(400.0)	(440.0)	(475.2)	(508.4)	(533.9)	(555.2)	(571.9)
7. *less SG&A*	(39.8)	(43.7)	(48.0)	(52.8)	(57.0)	(61.0)	(64.1)	(66.6)	(68.6)
8. *less depreciation expenses*	(5.0)	(5.0)	(8.0)	(8.0)	(8.0)	(7.0)	(6.0)	(6.0)	(6.0)
9. *equals EBIT[1]*	17.2	18.3	24.0	27.2	30.0	33.7	36.7	38.5	39.8
10. EBIT × (1 – Tax rate of 40%)[1]	$10.3	$11.0	$14.4	$16.3	$18.0	$20.2	$22.0	$23.1	$23.9
11. plus depreciation expenses	5.0	5.0	8.0	8.0	8.0	7.0	6.0	6.0	6.0
12. *WCR at year-end*	59.0	63.0	77.0	84.7	91.5	97.9	102.8	106.9	110.1
13. *less ∆ WCR (change in (12))*		(4.0)	(14.0)	(7.7)	(6.8)	(6.4)	(4.9)	(4.1)	(3.2)
14. *less net capital expenditures*		(0.0)	(10.0)	(8.0)	(8.0)	(7.0)	(6.0)	(6.0)	(6.0)
15. equals cash flow from assets			–$1.6	$8.6	$11.2	$13.8	$17.1	$19.0	$20.7
16. Residual value of assets at the end of year 2002								$250.9	

	Beginning 1998
17. WACC[1]	11.25%
18. DCF[1] value of assets at 11.25%	$196
19. *less book value of debt (short-term and long-term)*	$61
20. equals DCF value of equity	$135

1. COGS = Cost of goods sold, SG&A = Selling, general, and administrative expenses, EBIT = Earnings before interest and tax, WCR = Working capital requirement, WACC = Weighted average cost of capital, DCF = Discounted cash flow.

We now examine the logic behind our forecasting method with particular attention to the forecast for 1998. Line 5 gives the annual sales forecast based on the growth rates assumed in line 1. Note that we assume the growth rate will decline steadily, from its peak value of 14.3 percent achieved in 1997 to a residual rate of 3 percent beyond the fifth year. In other words, *after* year 2002, sales are assumed to grow at a constant rate of 3 percent forever. The high growth rate achieved in 1997 is due to particular circumstances that are not expected to occur again in the future. These assumptions about the sales growth rate are critical because the rest of the forecast is based on the assumed growth rates. If they are unrealistic, the estimated DCF value will not be realistic. (Remember our earlier discussion about the sensitivity of DCF values to the assumed rates at which cash flows grow.)

What is a realistic assumption about growth rates? Unless you have strong evidence and a high level of confidence that the firm's sales will grow at exceptionally high rates for a number of years, you should, without being overly conservative, assume that the growth rate will eventually drop to its residual level of *no more than a few percentage points*. Think of it this way: No company can grow forever at a rate faster than the entire economy. If it did, it would eventually overtake the economy. The *long-term real* growth rate of developed economies is about 2 to 3 percent. Adding a long-term inflation rate of 2 to 3 percent (a reasonable assumption in most well-developed countries[8]) gives a *long-term nominal* growth rate of 4 to 6 percent. Assuming a figure significantly higher than 4 to 6 percent for the residual growth of a company would be clearly unrealistic. Many analysts take the most conservative view and assume a *zero growth rate* beyond the forecasting period. In this case, the cash flows after the forecasting period are assumed to remain the same forever, which, in effect, means that they decline in *real terms* at the expected inflation rate. What if you are dealing with the valuation of a company that is expected to sustain an above average rate of growth beyond 5 years? In this case you should extend the forecasting period to, say, 8 to 10 years, rather than assume a higher residual growth rate.

After the sales growth rates are estimated, expenses are calculated as a percentage of sales as shown in Exhibit 12.5. These percentages depend on the efficiency with which OS Distributors will manage its operations. Because we are valuing the company as is, we assume that the operating efficiency ratios are equal to their latest historical values. (Later in this chapter, we revalue OS Distributors under alternative assumptions regarding its operating efficiency.) Thus, cost of goods sold (COGS) is 83.33 percent of sales, SG&A is 10 percent of sales, and WCR at year end is 16.04 percent of sales.

Based on these assumptions, the expected cash flow from OS Distributors' assets (CFA) in 1998 can be estimated using equation 12.4:

$$CFA = EBIT(1 - T_C) + \text{Depreciation expenses}$$
$$- \triangle WCR - \text{Net capital expenditures}$$

[8]For example, between 1926 and 1996, the Consumer Price Index in the United States rose at an average annual rate of 3.10 percent.

To estimate EBIT in 1998, we start with sales of $528 million (line 5) and deduct the cost of goods sold (line 6), the selling, general, and administrative expenses (line 7), and the depreciation expenses (line 8, assumed to be $8 million, the same as in 1997). Thus, EBIT is equal to $27.2 million (line 9). EBIT adjusted for taxes (line 10) is $16.3 million.[9] We then add back the $8 million of depreciation expenses (line 11) and deduct the *change* in working capital requirement (ΔWCR, line 13). The $7.7 million growth in WCR in 1998 is the difference between WCR at the end of 1998 and WCR at the end of 1997. The $84.7 million of WCR at the end of 1998 is obtained by multiplying the sales figure in line 5 by the ratio of WCR to sales in line 4; the $77 million of WCR at year-end 1997 is computed directly from the balance sheet in Exhibit 12.1. Finally, we deduct the expected net capital expenditures of $8 million for 1998 (line 14) to get an estimated cash flow from assets of $8.6 million in 1998.

We assume the annual net capital expenditures are equal to depreciation expenses (compare line 14 to line 8) because we are valuing OS Distributors as is. Thus, we do not expect any major investment beyond the *maintenance of existing assets,* and we assume that the maintenance costs will be exactly the same as the annual depreciation expenses. Note that although we assume depreciation expenses in 1998 and 1999 are the same as their 1997 historical value of $8 million, we expect them to drop to $7 million in 2000 and $6 million in 2001 and remain at that level thereafter. Depreciation expenses decline in line with the reduction in sales growth and capital expenditure. It is important to be consistent in our assumptions. If the firm's activities slow down, so will its capital expenditure and depreciation expenses.

Applying the same approach for the next five years yields the expected cash-flow stream up to year 2003, as shown on line 15 in Exhibit 12.5. We now need to estimate the residual value of OS Distributors' assets at the end of year 2002.

Estimating the residual value of assets at the end of year 2002

To estimate the residual value of OS Distributors' assets at the end of year 2002, we need two items of information. We need to know the rate at which the cash flows from the firm's assets will grow in perpetuity *after* the year 2002. We argue earlier that we should assume a constant rate of growth that is close to the growth rate of the entire economy. For OS Distributors, we assume a rate of 3 percent, the same as that of sales.[10] We also need to know the weighted average cost of capital

---

[9] The corporate tax rate is assumed to be the same as the historical one. Unless you know that the rate is expected to change, taking the historical corporate tax rate is the standard assumption. As pointed out earlier, the tax is calculated on the basis of EBIT because cash flows from assets ignore interest expenses, which reflect financing activities.

[10] If the growth rate in sales is constant and capital expenditures are equal to depreciation expenses, then the growth of cash flows is equal to the growth in sales.

(WACC) at which these perpetual cash flows will be discounted to the year 2002. We can then use the DCF formula (equation 12.1) to estimate the residual value of assets as follows:

$$\text{Residual value of assets at the end of year 2002} = \frac{\text{Expected cash flow in 2003}}{\text{WACC} - \text{growth rate}}$$

On the basis of a 3 percent growth rate in sales, the expected cash flow in 2003 is $20.7 million (line 15 in Exhibit 12.5). The next section shows that OS Distributors' WACC is 11.25 percent. We insert these estimates into the above valuation formula to find the residual value of assets at the *end of year 2002:*

$$\text{Residual value of assets at the end of year 2002} = \frac{\$20.7 \text{ million}}{0.1125 - 0.03} = \$250.9 \text{ million}$$

Note the sensitivity of the residual value to changes in the growth rate beyond the forecasting period. If this rate is 4 percent instead of 3 percent, the residual value is $285 million. If it is 5 percent, the residual value jumps to $331 million. Thus, great care must be given to the estimation of the perpetual growth rate used in the estimation of the residual value.

STEP 2: ESTIMATION OF OS DISTRIBUTORS' WEIGHTED AVERAGE COST OF CAPITAL

The relevant rate at which to discount the cash flows from assets is the weighted average cost of capital (WACC) in equation 12.5. The WACC reflects the proportion of debt and equity employed to finance the assets and their respective costs. We first estimate the cost of debt and equity funds and then address the issue of the appropriate proportions of debt and equity we should use to get OS Distributors' WACC.

The cost of debt is the aftertax cost of *new* borrowing (short-term and long-term). As mentioned earlier, the relevant cost of debt must be calculated after taxes because interest payments are tax-deductible expenses. OS Distributors can borrow at an average cost of 9 percent (see Chapter 10 for details regarding the estimation of the cost of debt). Given a tax rate of 40 percent, OS Distributors' aftertax cost of debt is 5.4 percent [9 percent $\times$ (1 − 0.40)].

The cost of equity is the cost of raising *new* equity funds. It can be estimated using the CAPM formula (equation 12.6). We need the following data: (1) the yield on long-term government securities (assumed to be 6.06 percent in January 1998), (2) the market risk premium (we use the historical average of 7 percent), and (3) OS Distributors' estimated beta coefficient.

Because OS Distributors is not a listed company, we do not have a beta coefficient for it. However, General Equipment and Supplies (GES), the comparable firm from the section about valuation by comparables, has an estimated beta coefficient of 1.10. We can use this figure for the unobservable beta coefficient of OS Distributors. Applying the CAPM formula:

$$\text{Cost of equity } (k_E) = 6.06\% + 7\% \times 1.10 = 6.06\% + 7.70\% = 13.76\%$$

The appropriate proportions of equity and debt financing must be based on the *market values* of equity and debt, not their accounting or book values (see Chapter 10). Unfortunately, we cannot observe the market values of OS Distributors' equity and debt because neither the firm's equity nor its debt is traded on a stock exchange. We have no choice but to resort to the procedure of using the data from GES, the comparable firm whose equity is listed on a stock exchange.

The market value of GES's equity in early January 1998 was $1,000 million (GES has 50 million shares with an average price of $20, see Exhibit 12.3). Its balance sheet at the end of December 1997 (not provided here) shows $430 million of total debt.[11] We thus have:

$$\text{Proportion of equity} = \frac{\text{Market value of equity}}{\text{Market value of equity } + \text{ Value of debt}} \qquad (12.8)$$

$$= \frac{\$1{,}000 \text{ million}}{\$1{,}000 \text{ million} + \$430 \text{ million}} = \frac{\$1{,}000 \text{ million}}{\$1{,}430 \text{ million}} = 70\%$$

and the proportion of debt is 30 percent.

We now have all the elements we need to estimate OS Distributors' WACC according to equation 12.5:

$$\text{WACC of OS Distributors} = 70\% \times 13.76\% + 30\% \times 5.40\% = 11.25\%$$

This is the WACC shown in line 17 in Exhibit 12.5. It is an estimate of the required rate of return on the cash flows generated by OS Distributors' assets.

STEP 3: ESTIMATION OF THE DCF VALUE OF OS DISTRIBUTORS' ASSETS

We can now estimate the value of OS Distributors' assets using the general valuation formula (equation 12.3). The formula gives the present value of a stream of cash flows expected from a firm's assets. For OS Distributors, the cash flows are our forecasts for 1998 to 2002, including the residual value of assets at year-end

---

[11] We should estimate GES's debt at its market rather than book value. However, if we assume that the average rate of interest OS Distributors is paying on the funds it has borrowed in the past is close to the current market rate of interest, market and book values are not significantly different. The relationship between the market value of debt and interest rates is presented in Chapter 9.

2002 (shown in lines 15 and 16 in Exhibit 12.5). The appropriate discount rate is OS Distributors' WACC of 11.25 percent. We have (dollar figures in millions):

$$\text{DCF value of OS Distributors' assets}$$

$$= \frac{\$8.6}{(1 + .1125)^1} + \frac{\$11.2}{(1 + .1125)^2} + \frac{\$13.8}{(1 + .1125)^3}$$

$$+ \frac{\$17.1}{(1 + .1125)^4} + \frac{\$19.0}{(1 + .1125)^5} + \frac{\$250.9}{(1 + .1125)^5}$$

$$= \$7.73 + \$9.05 + \$10.02 + \$11.16 + \$11.15 + \$147.23 = \mathbf{\$196}$$

which is the value shown in Exhibit 12.5, line 18.

Note the importance of the residual value in comparison to the yearly cash-flow estimates. Its present value of $147.23 million represents 75 percent of the DCF value of OS Distributors' assets. This high percentage is not unusual, particularly in cases where the growth rates during the forecasting period are not exceptionally high and are assumed to decline steadily toward their perpetual level. This is why we insist that great care be given to the estimation of the perpetual growth rate beyond the forecasting period.

STEP 4: ESTIMATION OF THE DCF VALUE OF OS DISTRIBUTORS' EQUITY

The estimated value of OS Distributors' *equity* is found using equation 12.7. It is equal to the estimated value of its assets ($196 million) less the book value of its outstanding debt in 1997. The book value of debt is reported in the balance sheets in Exhibit 12.1. It is equal to $61 million, the sum of $23 million of short-term debt and $38 million of long-term debt:

DCF value of OS Distributors' equity = $196 million − $61 million = **$135 million**

COMPARISON OF DCF VALUATION AND VALUATION BY COMPARABLES

We now have four different estimates for the value of OS Distributors' equity. In increasing order they are: $135 million (DCF value), $146 million (based on a book value multiple of 1.9), $151 million (based on a cash earnings multiple of 8.3), and $160 million (based on an earnings multiple of 15.7). The highest estimate is 19 percent above the lowest, so the estimated values are within an acceptable 20 percent range.

What then is the fair value of OS Distributors? It is probably closer to its DCF value than to any of its comparable values because DCF valuation is based on the projected cash flows from OS Distributors' own assets rather than on a mix of financial market and accounting data from another company (GES), albeit a similar one. We can conclude that a figure in the range of $130 million to $140 million would be a fair estimate of OS Distributors' equity value if the company were listed and traded on a stock exchange. Given that OS Distributors has 10 million shares outstanding, these estimates are equivalent to a share price of $13 to $14.

ESTIMATING THE ACQUISITION VALUE OF OS DISTRIBUTORS

The DCF equity value of $135 million for OS Distributors is an estimated value of the equity of the firm *as is*. It does not take into account any potential improvement in the way the firm is managed. If you acquire OS Distributors and enhance its performance, its value to you is obviously more than $135 million.

Suppose a number of improvements can raise OS Distributors' estimated DCF equity value to $220 million. This represents a *potential* value creation of $85 million ($220 million less $135 million). Acquiring the company for less than $220 is a positive net present value (NPV) investment, an investment whose price is *lower* than its estimated value. Suppose you end up paying $185 million to acquire OS Distributors. This represents a **takeover premium** of $50 million ($185 million less $135 million) over its stand-alone value of $135 million. In this case, the acquisition's net present value is the difference between the potential value creation and the takeover premium:

$$\text{NPV(Acquisition)} = \textbf{Potential value creation} - \textbf{Takeover premium}$$
$$= \$85 \text{ million} - \$50 \text{ million} = \$35 \text{ million}$$

You must be careful not to give OS Distributors' shareholders most of the future value *you* will create *after* you buy the company (the potential value creation) by paying too high a takeover premium. In general, the higher the potential value creation relative to the takeover premium, the larger the acquisition's NPV.

To estimate the acquisition value of OS Distributors, we must first identify the potential sources of value creation in an acquisition. We then show that when these sources are not present, such as when unrelated businesses are combined in a **conglomerate merger,** an acquisition is not likely to create value. After examining a conglomerate merger, we provide a complete analysis of the estimated acquisition value of OS Distributors.

IDENTIFYING THE POTENTIAL SOURCES OF VALUE CREATION IN AN ACQUISITION

The easiest way to identify potential sources of value creation in an acquisition is to look at how the DCF value is determined. In the simple case of a business expected to generate a perpetual cash-flow stream growing at a constant rate, the valuation formula (equation 12.1) shows that the DCF value is equal to the following year's cash flow from assets (CFA) divided by the difference between the weighted average cost of capital (WACC) and the growth rate in the cash flows:

$$\text{DCF value of assets} = \frac{\text{Next year's CFA}}{\text{WACC} - \text{growth rate}}$$

where CFA is given by equation 12.4 and WACC is given by equation 12.5. Thus, in order to create value, that is, to raise the DCF value of the target firm's assets, an acquisition must achieve one of three things, all else being the same:[12]

1. Increase the cash flows generated by the target firm's assets (CFA)
2. Raise the growth rate of the target firm's sales
3. Lower the WACC of the *target* firm

If the acquiring firm is unable to make one or more of the above changes in the target firm, the acquisition should not be carried out. These changes will happen if either or both of the following conditions are met:

1. The target firm is not currently managed at its optimal level of operating efficiency (it has excessive costs and inefficient asset usage), sales growth, or capital structure (it has too little or too much debt financing), *and* the acquiring firm's managers believe they can do a better job of running the target firm. This is usually referred to as the **inefficient management** explanation of why acquisitions occur. Note that in this case, there is no need for an acquisition to actually take place to enhance value. The target's current managers can, in principle, improve their firm's performance if they have the will and the required skills. This is why managers are often advised to run their firm as if it were a potential target.
2. Combining the target firm with the acquiring company creates **economies of scale** that lead to cost and market synergies. This is known as the **synergy** explanation of why acquisitions take place. **Cost synergies** can be achieved, for example, in administration, marketing, and distribution if the target firm's costs and investments can be reduced because these activities can be fully or partly carried out at a *lower* cost with the acquirer's existing resources. **Market synergies** can be achieved, for example, by increasing the target firm's sales by distributing its products and services through the acquiring company's distribution channels.

Together, inefficient management and synergy provide the most powerful reasons to justify an acquisition. Other, less convincing, reasons include the

---

[12] Strictly speaking, an acquisition creates value if the value of the merging firms after the acquisition is higher than the sum of their respective values before the merger. Here, the focus is exclusively on the potential value creation the acquirer can achieve by improving the performance of the target firm.

undervaluation hypothesis, according to which the acquiring company has superior skills in finding undervalued target firms that can be bought cheaply, and the **market power hypothesis,** which claims that after an acquisition the acquiring firm has a larger market share that may enable it to raise the price of its products or services and thus increase its cash flow and value (assuming, of course, that the government does not block the merger for anti-competitive reasons). Although these are plausible hypotheses as to why some acquisitions may take place, there is indirect empirical evidence (from the U.S. and other stock markets) indicating that they are not the major source of value creation behind most acquisitions.[13] We now examine the three specific sources of value creation in an acquisition, which were listed earlier.

Increasing the cash flows generated by the target firm's assets

A reduction in both the cost of goods sold and selling, general, and administrative expenses will widen the target firm's operating margin and, thus, increase its operating profits (EBIT). According to equation 12.4, an increase in EBIT will increase a firm's cash flow. A reduction in tax expenses will have the same effect.

Tax expenses merit a special comment. Suppose the acquiring firm has a pretax profit of $100 million and the target firm has a pretax loss of $40 million. Their combined profits will be $60 million, and the acquirer will pay less tax after the merger than it would have paid on its pre-merger pretax profit of $100 million. However, firms seldom buy one another simply to reduce their tax liabilities because the tax reduction is usually a one time gain whose magnitude rarely justifies an acquisition. Furthermore, in most countries the tax authorities do not allow the reduction in tax liability if the *only* purpose of the acquisition is to reduce taxes; there has to be a "business reason" behind the acquisition.

Another way to increase the cash flows generated by the target firm's assets involves using the assets more efficiently. A more efficient use of assets will result in higher sales and cash flows per dollar of assets employed. A more efficient use of assets can be achieved in several ways. Any over-investment, particularly in cash and in working capital requirement (WCR), should be rapidly reduced to a level that is justified by the firm's current operations and near future developments. Any

---

[13] If the undervaluation hypothesis were valid, then target firms whose share price rises on the announcement of an acquisition (because the market becomes aware of their undervaluation) should *maintain their higher value if the acquisition fails to take place.* The empirical evidence indicates that the share prices of unsuccessful target firms usually drop back to their pre-announcement level, a behavior that is inconsistent with the undervaluation hypothesis. If the market power hypothesis were valid, then the share prices of *all firms* in a sector should rise on the announcement day of a specific acquisition because all firms in the sector should benefit from a potential increase in the price of the product or service, not just the specific target and acquiring firms. The empirical evidence indicates that this is generally not the case.

excess cash that cannot be invested in a value-creating project should be returned to shareholders through a **share repurchase program** or a special dividend payment. If the firm holds excessive working capital requirement that is not justified by the firm's current and expected level of operations, it should be reduced to its optimal level via faster collection of receivables and higher inventory turnover (see Chapter 3). The same logic applies to long-term assets if they are currently under-utilized and have no identifiable use in the near future as support for the firm's value-creating investments.

Raising the sales growth rate

Assuming the target firm is already creating value or will create value under the management of the bidding firm, then, all other things being equal, faster growth in sales will create additional value. This can be achieved by increasing the volume of goods and services sold by the target firm and/or by raising their price (without an offsetting reduction in volume) via superior marketing skills and strategies. A more effective advertising campaign, a better mix of products, a wider and/or different distribution network, a closer relationship with customers, and the development of new markets, both domestically and abroad, are just a few possibilities worth exploring to improve the growth prospects of the target firm.

Lowering the cost of capital

If the target firm's capital structure is currently not close to its optimal level (too little or too much debt financing compared to the optimal debt ratio), then changing the firm's capital structure should lower its weighted average cost of capital (WACC) and raise its value. As shown in Chapter 11, the major advantage of debt financing is that it allows a firm to reduce its taxes (because of the deductibility of interest expenses) and, thus, enhance its aftertax cash flow and value. But the excessive use of debt will expose the firm to financial distress and possibly bankruptcy, which are costly. Hence, the existence of an optimal capital structure at the point where the marginal advantage of debt financing is exactly offset by the marginal costs of financial distress and bankruptcy. It follows that if the target firm has too little or too much debt in its capital structure, a change in the proportion of debt financing relative to equity will lower its WACC and raise its value.

The target firm's WACC, as well as that of the bidder, will also decline if, after the merger, their costs of equity and debt are lower than before the merger. A merger is unlikely to lead to a reduction in the cost of equity (see discussion below), but it is often argued that if the merged firms are perceived by their creditors to be less likely to fail as a combination than as separate entities (this is usually referred to as the **coinsurance effect**), then their post-merger cost of debt should, in principle, be lower. However, a lower cost of debt should be accompanied by an increase in the cost of equity. Equity is now riskier because shareholders have, in effect, given debtholders a superior guarantee against failure. This increase in the cost of equity would balance the decrease in the cost of debt, leaving the firms' WACC unchanged.

WHY CONGLOMERATE MERGERS ARE UNLIKELY TO CREATE LASTING VALUE THROUGH ACQUISITIONS

A **conglomerate merger** is a combination of two or more unrelated (or independent) businesses for which there is no obvious synergy. A firm that grows through conglomerate mergers is unlikely to create lasting value for its shareholders because adding an unrelated business to its existing ones will neither enhance its cash flows by more than the target's cash flows nor reduce its cost of capital. It may, under certain circumstances, increase the conglomerate's earnings per share (EPS), but the growth in EPS is unlikely to be accompanied by a permanent rise in shareholder value.

Acquiring unrelated businesses is unlikely to create lasting value

Suppose a personal computer (PC) firm buys a life insurance company because it believes the merger will provide an opportunity to reduce the business risk of the combined firms via the diversification of their activities. The regular and predictable revenues generated by the life insurance business will smooth out the cyclical revenues from the PC business. The resulting reduction in risk should, in principle, reduce the conglomerate's cost of equity and, thus, raise the market value of its equity beyond the sum of the market values of the two pre-merger firms' equity.

Although this diversification strategy may make sense from the perspective of the PC company's managers, it is unlikely to generate the anticipated increase in market value. The reason is that investors can achieve the same diversification themselves by combining shares of the PC and the insurance companies in their personal portfolios. And, this **homemade diversification** is superior to that of the PC company's diversification strategy because it is cheaper to implement and it allows investors to set their own proportions of holdings. Thus, it is doubtful that investors will be willing to pay a higher price for the diversified firm. As a result, it is unlikely that the financial market will value the combination of the two firms for more than the sum of their pre-merger values.

As pointed out earlier, the only types of business combinations that are likely to create lasting value are those that result in managerial improvements or synergistic gains. An example of such a combination is a **horizontal merger** (two firms in the same sector pooling their resources). Even **vertical mergers** (the integration of, say, a car manufacturer with its major supplier or its major distributor) are not likely to achieve lasting value creation; there is no obvious reason why a vertical merger will result in sales growth or cost reductions in a competitive environment. This explains why some of the most successful value-creating firms focus their efforts on a single activity for which they have developed over time a unique set of skills and competencies that existing and potential competitors cannot easily imitate. It is these "difficult to replicate" skills and competencies that are the sources of a sustained increase in their market value.

Raising earnings per share through conglomerate mergers is unlikely to create lasting value

Some conglomerates grow rapidly by continuously buying firms that have a *lower* price-to-earnings ratios (P/E) than the P/E of the conglomerate firm. The premise is that the market will value the combination for more than the sum of the pre-merger firms. Consider the conglomerate merger described in Exhibit 12.6. The most recent figure for the earnings after tax of the acquiring firm is $300 million while that of the target firm is $200 million (line 1). The acquiring firm has 150 million shares outstanding and the target firm has 100 million (line 2), so their earnings per share (EPS) are the same and are equal to $2 (line 4). The acquirer has a price-to-earnings ratio (P/E ratio) of 20 while the target has a P/E ratio of only 10

EXHIBIT 12.6 Data for a Conglomerate Merger Based on Raising EPS.

	THE ACQUIRING FIRM	THE TARGET FIRM
1. Earnings after tax	$300 million	$200 million
2. Number of shares	150 million	100 million
3. Price-to-earnings ratio (P/E)	20	10
4. Earnings per share (EPS) = (1)/(2)	$2.00	$2.00
5. Share price = (3) × (4)	$40	$20
6. Total value = (2) × (5)	$6,000 million	$2,000 million

	VALUE OF THE MERGED FIRMS IF THE MARKET ASSIGNS THE COMBINATION A P/E THAT	
	IS VALUE NEUTRAL	EXCEEDS VALUE NEUTRALITY
1. Earnings after tax	$500 million	$500 million
2. Number of shares	200 million	200 million
3. Price-to-earnings ratio (P/E)	16	18
4. Earnings per share (EPS) = (1)/(2)	$2.50	$2.50
5. Share price = (3) × (4)	$40	$45
6. Total value = (2) × (5)	$8,000 million	$9,000 million

(line 3), a reflection of the market expectation of a much higher growth rate for the acquirer than for the target. The corresponding share prices and aggregate equity market values are, respectively, $40 and $6,000 million for the acquirer and $20 and $2,000 million for the target firm (lines 5 and 6).

Suppose the acquirer can buy the target firm at its prevailing market value of $2,000 million and pay for the purchase by offering its own shares (worth $40 each) in exchange for those of the target firm (worth $20 each). The acquirer will have to issue 50 million shares ($2,000 million divided by $40) to raise $2,000 million. When the acquisition is complete, the shares of the target firm will no longer exist and the acquirer will have 200 million shares, the original 150 million plus the additional 50 million issued to pay for the acquisition.

If the acquisition is a simple combination that does not create any value, that is, if the merger is "value neutral," then the merged firms must have (1) an aggregate market value of $8,000 million, the sum of the acquiring and target firms' pre-merger values; (2) a total profit of $500 million, the sum of the acquiring and target firms' pre-merger profits; and (3) a price per share of $40, the same price the acquirer had before the merger.

What is the acquirer's earnings per share after the acquisition is completed? With 200 million shares and $500 million of total profit, the resulting EPS is $2.50 ($500 million divided by 200 million shares). The acquirer has increased its EPS from a pre-merger value of $2 to a post-merger value of $2.50, a 25 percent rise. Not bad for a value neutral acquisition, but don't be fooled. This higher EPS does not increase the value of the combined firms to more than $8,000 million because the market assigns an earnings multiple (price-to-earnings ratio) of 16, which leaves the share price unchanged ($2.50 × 16 = $40).

But, what if the market is fooled and assigns an earnings multiple exceeding 16? In this case, the acquirer's share price will rise to more than $40. If, for example, the post-merger market multiple is 18, then the post-merger share price would be $45 ($2.50 multiplied by 18). The acquirer could then use its higher share price to make another acquisition and another and another until the bubble bursts. This phenomenon happened in the U.S. market in the 1960s.

THE ACQUISITION VALUE OF OS DISTRIBUTORS' EQUITY

We now return to DCF valuation. The greatest advantage of this valuation approach over the comparables, or market multiples, method is its ability to provide an estimate of the potential value created by a particular managerial action. The potential value created by increasing OS Distributors' sales, reducing its operating expenses per dollar of sales, managing its WCR tighter, or lowering its average cost of capital, can be determined by modifying the original forecasts in Exhibit 12.5. The forecasts in lines 1 to 4 and line 17 are changed to reflect the managerial action and a computer can be instructed to recalculate the DCF value of OS Distributors' equity. However, first it must be determined that OS Distributors' current performance can be improved. If there is indeed room for improvement, a restructuring plan that can be implemented with a reasonable chance of success should be formulated.

In a horizontal merger, the obvious starting point to determine whether the performance of a target company can be improved is to compare it with that of the acquirer. Clearly, if the target underperforms relative to the acquirer, there are ways to get its performance up to the level of the acquiring firm. In addition, the performance of the target can be improved beyond just better management if there is room for synergistic gains after the acquisition is completed.

Let's assume that your company, which is in the same business as OS Distributors, is considering acquiring it. After a careful analysis of OS Distributors' current performance and its comparison with that of your company, you conclude that a combination of better management and the realization of significant economies of scale in marketing, distribution, and administration can produce the following improvements in the future performance of OS Distributors (without producing any significant changes in the performance of your firm):

1. A reduction of its cost of goods sold by a full percentage point (from 83.33 percent of sales to 82.33 percent of sales)
2. A reduction of its selling, general, and administrative expenses, essentially overhead expenses, by half a percentage point (from 10 percent of sales to 9.5 percent of sales)
3. A decrease of its working capital requirement from its current level of 16.04 percent of sales to 13 percent of sales
4. An increase of its sales growth rates from 1998 to 2002 by 2 percentage points above the figures shown in the first line in Exhibit 12.5 with no increase in the growth rate after 2002

How much are these changes in future performance worth today to your firm? If you can answer this question, you will know how much your company should pay to acquire OS Distributors and still have a positive net present value acquisition. The analysis required to answer this question is shown in Exhibits 12.7 and 12.8. The first exhibit shows the separate effects of a reduction in the cost of goods sold (COGS), selling, general, and administrative expenses (SG&A), and working capital requirement (WCR). The second shows the effect of a higher growth rate in sales and the cumulative impact of improved operational efficiency and faster sales growth. The DCF values are all calculated using a weighted average cost of capital of 11.25 percent, the same as the one used to value OS Distributors' equity as is.

The impact of the improved performance on value creation is summarized in Exhibit 12.9. The reduction in the cost of goods sold and overheads is worth $63 million; the squeeze of working capital requirement, $22 million and the faster growth in sales, $14 million. The four separate improvements add to a potential value creation of $99 million. But taken together they produce a potential aggregate value of $107 million (see the lower section of Exhibit 12.8), which represents an increase of 79 percent over the DCF value of OS Distributors as is.

EXHIBIT 12.7 Impact of Improved Operational Efficiency on the Estimated Value of OS Distributors' Equity at the Beginning of January 1998.

Figures in millions of dollars

	Beginning 1998	1998	1999	2000	2001	2002	2003 and Beyond
Value of OS Distributors' equity as is (see Exhibit 12.5)							
Growth in sales		10%	8%	7%	5%	4%	3%
COGS[1] as % of sales		83.33%	83.33%	83.33%	83.33%	83.33%	
SG&A[1] as % of sales		10.00%	10.00%	10.00%	10.00%	10.00%	
WCR[1] as % of sales		16.04%	16.04%	16.04%	16.04%	16.04%	
Cash flow from assets		$8.6	$11.2	$13.8	$17.1	$19.0	
Residual value of assets at end of year 2002						$250.9	
DCF value of assets at 11.25%	$196						
Less book value of debt	$61						
DCF value of equity	$135						
Impact of a reduction in the cost of goods sold							
COGS[1] as % of sales		82.33%	82.33%	82.33%	82.33%	82.33%	
Cash flow from assets		$11.8	$14.7	$17.5	$21.0	$23.0	
Residual value of assets at end of year 2002						$300.3	
DCF value of assets at 11.25%	$238						
Less book value of debt	$61						
DCF value of equity	$177						
Potential value creation[2]	$42						
Impact of a reduction in selling, general, and administrative expenses							
SG&A[1] as % of sales		9.50%	9.50%	9.50%	9.50%	9.50%	
Cash flow from assets		$10.2	$13.0	$15.7	$19.1	$21.0	
Residual value of assets at end of year 2002						$275.3	
DCF value of assets at 11.25%	$217						
Less book value of debt	$61						
DCF value of equity	$156						
Potential value creation[2]	$21						
Impact of a decrease in the ratio working capital requirement to sales							
WCR[1] as % of sales		13%	13%	13%	13%	13%	
Cash flows from assets		$24.7	$12.5	$15.0	$18.1	$19.7	
Residual value of assets at end of year 2002						$257.8	
DCF value of assets at 11.25%	$218						
Less book value of debt	$61						
DCF value of equity	$157						
Potential value creation[2]	$22						

1. COGS = Cost of goods sold, SG&A = Selling, general, and administrative expenses, WCR = Working capital requirement.
2. Potential value creation = DCF value of equity less $135 million (the value of OS Distributors' equity as is at the top of the exhibit).

EXHIBIT 12.8 Impact of Faster Growth in Sales and Improved Operational Efficiency on the Estimated Value of OS Distributers' Equity at the beginning of January 1998.

Figures in millions of dollars

	BEGINNING 1998	1998	1999	2000	2001	2002	2003 AND BEYOND
Value of OS Distributors' equity as is (see Exhibit 12.5)							
Growth in sales		10%	8%	7%	5%	4%	3%
COGS[1] as % of sales		83.33%	83.33%	83.33%	83.33%	83.33%	
SG&A[1] as % of sales		10.00%	10.00%	10.00%	10.00%	10.00%	
WCR[1] as % of sales		16.04%	16.04%	16.04%	16.04%	16.04%	
Cash flow from assets		$8.6	$11.2	$13.8	$17.1	$19.0	
Residual value of assets at end of year 2002						$250.9	
DCF value of assets at 11.25%	$196						
Less book value of debt	$61						
DCF value of equity	$135						
Impact of faster growth in sales							
Growth in sales		12%	10%	9%	7%	6%	3%
COGS[1] as % of sales		83.33%	83.33%	83.33%	83.33%	83.33%	
SG&A[1] as % of sales		10.00%	10.00%	10.00%	10.00%	10.00%	
WCR[1] as % of sales		16.04%	16.04%	16.04%	16.04%	16.04%	
Cash flow from assets		$7.5	$10.2	$13.1	$16.8	$19.0	
Residual value of assets at end of year 2002						$279.0	
DCF value of assets at 11.25%	$210						
Less book value of debt	$61						
DCF value of equity	$149						
Potential value creation[2]	$14						
Impact of faster growth in sales and improved operational efficiency							
Growth in sales		12%	10%	9%	7%	6%	3%
COGS[1] as % of sales		82.33%	82.33%	82.33%	82.33%	82.33%	
SG&A[1] as % of sales		9.50%	9.50%	9.50%	9.50%	9.50%	
WCR[1] as % of sales		13%	13%	13%	13%	13%	
Cash flow from assets		$28.7	$17.2	$20.5	$24.3	$26.9	
Residual value of assets at end of year 2002						$369.2	
DCF value of assets at 11.25%	$303						
Less book value of debt	$61						
DCF value of equity	$242						
Potential value creation[2]	$107						

1. COGS = Cost of goods sold, SG&A = Selling, general, and administrative expenses, WCR = Working capital requirement.
2. Potential value creation = DCF value of equity less $135 million (the value of OS Distributors' equity as is at the top of the exhibit).

EXHIBIT 12.9   Summary of Data in Exhibits 12.7 and 12.8

SOURCES OF VALUE CREATION	POTENTIAL VALUE CREATION	
1. Reduction in the cost of goods sold to 82.33% of sales	$42 million	(39%)
2. Reduction in overheads to 9.50% of sales	$21 million	(20%)
3. Reduction of working capital requirement to 13% of sales	$22 million	(21%)
4. Faster growth in sales (2 percentage points higher)	$14 million	(13%)
5. Interaction of growth and improved operations	$8 million	(7%)
Total potential value creation	**$107 million**	**(100%)**

The extra $8 million (the difference between $107 million and $99 million) is generated by the interaction of more efficient operating performance on faster growth.

Depending on your confidence in achieving one or more of the changes described above, the target value of OS Distributors' equity could be as high as $242 million ($135 million *as is* plus $107 million of potential value creation). We did not consider the possibility of a reduction in OS Distributors' cost of capital if it is taken over. If its WACC can be lowered below 11.25 percent, then all the potential value creations mentioned above will be higher.

An acquiring firm must not become overconfident about its ability to realize (or even exceed) the full potential value of a target. This overconfidence can lead to paying too much for the target. Unfortunately, the evidence indicates that this often occurs, and the result is an acquisition with a net present value close to zero. This means that most, if not all, of the gains from the acquisition end up in the pockets of the target company's shareholders.

ESTIMATING THE LEVERAGED BUYOUT VALUE OF OS DISTRIBUTORS

In a typical **leveraged buyout (LBO),** a group of investors purchases a presumably underperforming firm by raising an unusually large amount of debt relative to equity capital (up to five dollars of debt for every dollar of equity). The investors often include the firm's managers in association with private equity investors and possibly a **venture capital firm** (an investment firm specializing in the financing of small and new ventures). The strategy is to restructure the firm, rapidly improve its performance, and increase the cash flows generated by the firm's assets in order to repay a large part of the initial debt within a reasonable period of time (three to five years). The new shareholders do not normally receive any cash dividends during the restructuring period. They anticipate cashing in on their investment at the end of that period by selling some (or all) of their shares to the general public. As an alternative to this **exit strategy,** the firm can be sold to another company or to a new group of private investors.

Suppose OS Distributors' current owners wish to retire. In January 1998, four of the firm's most senior managers, in association with a venture capital firm, agree to buy the firm's assets for $200 million. They believe that the current owners have a conservative management policy and that significant value can be unlocked if the firm is managed more aggressively through a combination of tighter control of the firm's expenses, better use of its assets, and faster growth in its sales. The acquisition will be financed with $160 million of debt and $40 million of equity (the management team will invest $10 million and the venture capital firm another $30 million).

To keep the analysis as simple as possible, we assume the $160 million of debt consists of a single loan at a fixed interest rate of 11 percent. The loan must be repaid at the rate of $15 million per year for the next five years, with the first payment due at the end of 1998. After the fifth year, any repayment on the balance of the loan can be refinanced with new borrowing. The cost of debt is two full percentage points higher than the 9 percent rate on new borrowing that OS Distributors' current owners can obtain. The higher borrowing rate simply reflects the higher risk borne by the lenders in a highly leveraged deal such as an LBO.

We can compare the financial structure of OS Distributors before and after the LBO (but before any improvement in the firm's performance) by constructing a balance sheet after the LBO and contrasting it with its actual balance sheet at the end of 1997, as shown in Exhibit 12.10.[14]

EXHIBIT 12.10   Comparison of OS Distributors' Balance Sheet Before and After the LBO.

Figures in millions of dollars; before-LBO figures from Exhibit 12.1

BALANCE SHEET	BEFORE THE LBO		AFTER THE LBO	
Cash	8	(6%)	8	(4%)
Working capital requirement	77	(56%)	77	(39%)
Net fixed assets	53	(38%)	115	(57%)
Net assets	$138		$200	
Total debt	61	(44%)	160	(80%)
Equity	77	(56%)	40	(20%)
Total capital	$138		$200	

[14] The reduced form of the balance sheet is similar to the managerial balance sheet (see Chapter 3). The current liabilities associated with the operating cycle (accounts payable and accrued expenses) are accounted for in the working capital requirement, where they are deducted from the receivables, inventories, and prepaid expenses.

The acquiring team has estimated that OS Distributors' net fixed assets are grossly undervalued and believes they are worth at least $115 million, more than twice the book value of $53 million reported in the firm's balance sheet. Fixed assets are hence recorded in the post-LBO balance sheet at $115 million and will be depreciated on the basis of their higher value. The *additional* yearly depreciation expenses resulting from the revaluation of fixed assets are assumed to equal $10 million for the next 10 years and are fully tax deductible.[15] Cash and working capital requirement are reported in the post-LBO balance sheet at their pre-LBO accounting values. Notice the highly leveraged capital structure in the **pro forma** balance sheet (the *expected* balance sheet after the LBO). The $200 million of assets are financed with $160 million of debt and $40 million of equity, giving the post-LBO firm a debt ratio (debt divided by total capital) of 80 percent, which is significantly higher than the pre-LBO debt ratio of 44 percent.

The structure of debt used to finance a typical LBO is far more complex than that of the single loan we assume for OS Distributors. In practice, a package of different types of loans is put together by the investment bank arranging the deal. At the top of the package is the **senior debt** secured by the firm's assets. (A secured loan is one for which the firm has pledged some of its assets, such as property, trade receivables, or inventories, as **collateral;** the lender can seize and sell these assets if the firm fails to service the loan.) This collateralized debt is also known as **top floor financing.** It is senior to the **subordinated,** or **junior debt,** which is usually **unsecured** (no collateral is offered) and more expensive. This type of debt is often referred to as **mezzanine financing** because it is positioned between top floor financing and equity capital, which is known as **ground floor financing.**

There are two key issues to examine regarding the leveraged buyout of OS Distributors. The first is whether the acquisition of the firm's assets for $200 million is a value-creating investment, that is, an investment with a positive net present value. The second is whether these assets will generate sufficient cash to service the $160 million loan (both interest payments and debt repayment) during the next five years.

ESTIMATING THE LEVERAGED BUYOUT VALUE OF OS DISTRIBUTORS' EQUITY

To find out whether the OS Distributors' LBO is a positive net present value (NPV) acquisition, we must estimate the value of OS Distributors' assets based on the cash flows they are expected to generate under the new and more efficient management. If the estimated asset value exceeds $200 million (the purchase price), the acquisition is a positive NPV investment. In principle, we can estimate the leveraged buyout value of OS Distributors' assets using the discounted cash flow (DCF) approach. However, this approach assumes that the weighted average cost of capital (WACC) remains constant, an assumption that cannot be maintained in the case

---

[15] In some countries, the tax authority may deny the tax reductions resulting from these depreciation expenses.

of an LBO. Remember that the post-LBO debt ratio is 80 percent. The rapid repayment of a large portion of the loan during the next five years will reduce the firm's debt ratio by the end of the year 2002. This means that the firm's WACC will not remain constant during these years. If we want to use the DCF approach to value the LBO, we need to estimate a different WACC for each of the five years, quite a cumbersome task. Fortunately, there is a variant of the DCF valuation approach, called the **adjusted present value (APV)** method, that circumvents this problem.

The adjusted present value method

According to the APV method, the valuation of a firm's assets is done in two separate steps. In the first, the DCF value of the assets is estimated *assuming they are not financed with debt* (in other words, they are entirely financed with equity). This value is called the **unlevered asset value.** If assets are unlevered, then the WACC used in estimating their DCF value must be constant and equal to the cost of equity for an all-equity financed firm (this cost is referred to as the **unlevered cost of equity**). This procedure clearly solves the problem of a WACC changing over time. But ignoring debt means that we fail to take into account the major benefit of debt financing—the reduction in the firm's taxes resulting from the deductibility of the interest expenses related to borrowed funds.[16] The second step in the APV approach corrects for this failure. In this step, the present value of the tax savings the firm will realize in the future if it borrows today to finance its assets is added to the DCF value of the unlevered assets. Thus, according to the APV method, the DCF value of a firm's **levered assets** (the assets financed with debt and equity) can be expressed as follows:

DCF value of *levered* assets =

DCF value of *unlevered* assets + DCF value of future tax savings

The DCF value of unlevered assets is estimated by discounting the cash flows generated by these assets at the unlevered cost of equity. The DCF value of future tax savings from interest expenses is estimated by discounting the future stream of tax savings at the cost of debt.[17]

The leveraged buyout value of OS Distributors' equity

We can now apply the APV approach to estimate the LBO value of OS Distributors' assets. The new management team believes that it can improve operating efficiency by (1) reducing the cost of goods sold to 82.33 percent of sales (from the

---

[16] The impact of debt financing on the value of the firm is examined in detail in Chapter 11.

[17] Each cash-flow stream should be discounted to the present at a rate that reflects its particular risk. We assume here that the tax savings are less risky than the cash flows from assets and should therefore be discounted at a lower rate than the unlevered cost of equity. The standard procedure is to take the cost of debt.

current 83.33 percent level), (2) cutting the selling, general, and administrative expenses to 9.5 percent of sales (from their current 10 percent level), and (3) lowering the working capital requirement to 13 percent of sales (from the current 16.04 percent level). The team also believes it can add 2 percentage points to the growth in sales for the next five years. This, as you may have noticed, is the restructuring plan we analyze earlier in the context of a potential merger. There is, however, a major difference between a potential merger and an LBO. In a merger, some of the performance improvements are expected to come from synergistic gains resulting from combining the two businesses. In an LBO, there is no merger and, thus, there are no opportunities for synergistic gains. All the improved performance must come from better management of the firm.

When OS Distributors is valued as a potential target, the successful implementation of the restructuring plan has a value-creating potential of $107 million (see the bottom of Exhibit 12.8). Unfortunately, we cannot use this figure as a measure of the potential value the LBO deal can create because, as discussed above, the weighted average cost of capital will change over time. We now explain how to use the APV approach to estimate the leveraged value of OS Distributors' assets under the LBO financing plan.

OS Distributors' unlevered cost of equity   According to the capital asset pricing model (see equation 12.6), a firm's cost of equity is equal to the risk-free rate plus the product of the market risk premium and the firm's beta coefficient. The risk-free rate in early 1998 is assumed to be 6.06 percent, and the market risk premium is the historical rate of 7 percent. We want to estimate the *unlevered* cost of equity, so the beta coefficient must be that of an all-equity financed firm. Chapter 10 shows that this beta, called *asset beta,* can be estimated as follows:

$$\textbf{Asset Beta} \ = \ \frac{\textbf{Equity Beta}}{1 \ + \ (1 \ - \ \textbf{tax rate}) \ \times \ \left(\dfrac{\textbf{Debt}}{\textbf{Equity}}\right)}$$

The equity, or levered, beta for OS Distributors is 1.10 (estimated earlier from a comparable firm), the tax rate is 40 percent, and the ratio of debt to equity is 30 percent debt to 70 percent equity (see equation 12.8). Thus:

$$\text{OS Distributors' Asset Beta} \ = \ \frac{1.10}{1 \ + \ (1 \ - \ 40\%) \ \times \ \left(\dfrac{0.30}{0.70}\right)} \ = \ 0.875$$

Equation 12.6 (the capital asset pricing model) provides an estimate of the unlevered cost of equity:

$$\text{OS Distributors' unlevered cost of equity} = 6.06\% + 7\% \times 0.875 = 12.2\%$$

OS Distributors' equity value   The APV valuation steps are described in Exhibit 12.11. We start with the cash flows from assets given at the bottom of Exhibit 12.8

EXHIBIT12.11 Estimated Leveraged Buyout (LBO) Value of OS Distributors' Assets at the Beginning of January 1998.

Figures in millions of dollars

	BEGINNING 1998	1998	1999	2000	2001	2002	2003
Value of unlevered assets							
Unlevered cost of equity = 12.2%							
1. Cash flow from assets (see Exhibit 12.8)		$28.7	$17.2	$20.5	$24.3	$26.9	$30.5
2. Residual value of assets at end of year 2002						$330.7	
3. DCF value of unlevered assets	$270						
Value of tax savings on additional depreciation expenses							
Discount rate = 11%							
4. Additional depreciation expenses for 10 years		$10.0	$10.0	$10.0	$10.0	$10.0	$10.0
5. Tax savings on depreciation (tax rate = 40%)		$4.0	$4.0	$4.0	$4.0	$4.0	$4.0
6. Residual value of tax savings						$14.8	$4.0
7. DCF value of tax savings from depreciation	$23.6						
Value of tax savings on interest expenses							
Cost of debt = 11%							
8. Debt outstanding at the beginning of the year		$160.0	$145.0	$130.0	$115.0	$100.0	$85.0
9. Debt repayment at the end of the year		$15.0	$15.0	$15.0	$15.0	$15.0	
10. Debt outstanding at the end of the year		$145.0	$130.0	$115.0	$100.0	$85.0	$87.6
11. Interest expenses (interest rate = 11%)		$17.6	$16.0	$14.3	$12.7	$11.0	$9.6
12. Tax savings on interest expenses (tax rate = 40%)		$7.0	$6.4	$5.7	$5.1	$4.4	$3.8
13. Residual value of tax savings						$47.5	
14. DCF value of tax savings from interest expenses	$49.4						
15. DCF value of overall tax savings: (7) + (14)	$73						
16. DCF value of levered assets: (3) + (15)	$343						

417

(the cash flow for the year 2003 is not shown in Exhibit 12.8). We can use the cash flows from assets that we estimated in the merger valuation approach because the expected improvements in performance are the same as for the merger. Next, we estimate the assets' residual value at the end of year 2002 (line 2) the same way we estimated the residual value for OS Distributors as a target, but, this time we use the *unlevered* cost of equity of 12.2 percent instead of a WACC of 11.25 percent. Finally, we discount the cash flows from assets and their residual value at the cost of equity of 12.2 percent (line 3), obtaining a DCF value of $270 million for the unlevered assets of OS Distributors. We now determine the tax savings generated by the additional depreciation expenses provided by the revaluation of fixed assets and the interest expenses provided by the $160 million loan. These amounts are then added to the DCF value of the unlevered assets.

Given a corporate tax rate of 40 percent, the additional depreciation expenses will generate annual tax savings of $4 million for 10 years. (This is the amount of tax OS Distributors will *not* pay because its pretax profit is reduced by the $10 million of annual depreciation.) The tax savings from year 1998 to year 2002 are shown in line 5. The residual value of the additional depreciation expenses at the end of year 2002 (line 6) is $14.8 million. (This is the present value of $4.0 million every year for the remaining five years of depreciation discounted at the cost of debt of 11 percent.) The total DCF value of the tax savings from depreciation, using a discount rate of 11 percent, amounts to $23.6 million (line 7).

To estimate the tax savings from interest expenses, we first need to estimate the interest expenses. Line 8 shows the amount of outstanding debt at the end of each year from 1998 to 2003. Due to high annual debt repayments, OS Distributors' debt is expected to decrease very rapidly. Based on the initial borrowing of $160 million and annual repayments of $15 million, the amount of outstanding debt by the end of 2002 will be reduced to $85 million. Assuming that the large debt repayments will stop after 2002, we can expect that the debt and the interest expenses will then increase at the same rate as the growth in sales, which is expected to be 3 percent per year. For example, the amount of debt outstanding at the end of 2003 is expected to be $87.6 million, which represents a 3 percent increase from the debt level of $85 million at the end of 2002. The annual interest expenses in line 11 are obtained by multiplying the amount of debt outstanding at the end of the previous year by the interest rate of 11 percent. Line 12 shows the corresponding tax savings using a tax rate of 40 percent. Line 13 shows the residual value of the tax savings from the expected annual interest after 2002. It is calculated, once again, with equation 12.1, which gives the present value of a constant annuity. In this case, the following year's cash flow is $3.8 million (the tax savings of 2003), the required return is 11 percent (the cost of debt), and the growth term is 3 percent. Adding the present value of the annual tax savings from 1998 to 2002 to that of the residual value of the tax savings estimated at $47.5 million in 2002 gives a total tax savings from interest expenses of $49.4 million (line 14).

Adding the discounted cash flow values of the tax savings from depreciation and interest expenses ($73 million in line 15) to the unlevered asset value of $270 million (line 3) yields an estimated DCF value of $343 million for OS Distributors' assets (line 16). This value is much higher than the $200 million the LBO team will have to pay for the assets. The net present value of the deal is thus positive and equal to $143 million ($343 million less $200 million). Note that the LBO value of the assets ($343 million) is significantly larger than the DCF value of $303 million shown in Exhibit 12.8. Because both valuations assume the same improvements in operational efficiency and sales growth, the difference comes from the tax savings provided by the LBO deal.

With the current debt of OS Distributors at $61 million, the leveraged buyout value of OS Distributor's equity is $282 million ($343 million less $61 million). At the purchase price of $200 million, the LBO has the potential to create $82 million of value.

Will OS Distributors be able to service its debt?

We now consider the issue of whether OS Distributors will be able to service its $160 million loan. Although the LBO deal makes sense from a value-creation perspective (its net present value is positive), OS Distributors' management must still meet the challenge of servicing an inordinate amount of debt, particularly the heavy burden of early and rapid principal repayment. The question is whether the firm's assets under new management will generate enough cash flows to service the firm's debt. If they do not, the financing plan must be revised, that is, borrowing should be reduced and replaced with equity. If additional equity cannot be obtained, the deal may have to be abandoned even though it is a value-creating proposal.

The cash-flow analysis from 1998 to 2003 is summarized in Exhibit 12.12. Part I reports the impact on cash flows of the LBO deal. The total cash flows from assets in line 1.3 are the cash flows from assets estimated in the merger valuation plus the tax savings from the additional depreciation expenses, both taken from Exhibit 12.11. Are these cash flows high enough to service the $160 million loan?

The amount of cash required to service the loan is shown in the exhibit in section 2 of Part I. The amount of debt outstanding at the end of each year, the annual interest expenses and the debt repayments are from Exhibit 12.11. Interest expenses are tax deductible, and they have been adjusted using a tax rate of 40 percent. Every year, except for 1999, there is enough cash to pay the debtholders. The cash flows to equity holders are given in line 3 with their cumulative values in line 4. It appears that the next three to four years will be critical. An unexpected decline in the cash flows from the assets, even if relatively small, may cause a serious liquidity problem.

Part II of the exhibit presents the pro forma, or future, income statements based on current expectations. The earnings before interest and tax (EBIT) are computed as in Exhibit 12.5 but with the operational efficiency ratios and the growth rates in sales expected from the LBO restructuring plan. The earnings after

EXHIBIT 12.12 Financing OS Distributors' Leveraged Buyout.

Figures in millions of dollars

	1997	1998	1999	2000	2001	2002	2003
I. CASH FLOW IMPLICATIONS							
1. Total cash flow from assets							
1.1 Cash flow from assets		$28.7	$17.2	$20.5	$24.3	$26.9	$30.5
1.2 Tax savings on additional depreciation		4.0	4.0	4.0	4.0	4.0	4.0
1.3 Total cash flow from assets		$32.7	$21.2	$24.5	$28.3	$30.9	$34.5
2. Cash flow to debtholders							
2.1 Debt outstanding at the end of the year		$145.0	$130.0	$115.0	$100.0	$85.0	$87.6
2.2 Aftertax interest payment		10.6	9.6	8.6	7.6	6.6	5.8
2.3 Debt repayment		15.0	15.0	15.0	15.0	15.0	Zero
2.4 Total aftertax cash flow to debtholders: (2.2) + (2.3)		$25.6	$24.6	$23.6	$22.6	$21.6	$5.8
3. Cash flow to equity holders: (1.3) – (2.4)		$7.1	($3.4)	$0.9	$5.7	$9.3	$28.7
4. Cumulative cash flow to equity holders		$7.1	$3.7	$4.6	$10.3	$19.6	$48.3
II. PRO FORMA INCOME STATEMENTS							
Earnings before interest and tax (EBIT)	$24.0	$35.9	$40.3	$45.7	$50.4	$53.7	$55.5
Additional depreciation	(0)	(10.0)	(10.0)	(10.0)	(10.0)	(10.0)	(10.0)
Interest expenses	(7.0)	(17.6)	(16.0)	(14.3)	(12.7)	(11.0)	(9.6)
Earnings before tax (EBT)	$17.0	$8.3	$14.3	$21.4	$27.7	$32.7	$35.9
Tax at 40%	(6.8)	(3.3)	(5.8)	(8.6)	(11.1)	(13.1)	(14.5)
Earnings after tax (EAT)	$10.2	$5.0	$8.5	$12.8	$16.6	$19.6	$21.4
III. CAPITAL AND DEBT RATIOS							
Debt outstanding (from above)	$61.0	$145.0	$130.0	$115.0	$100.0	$85.0	$87.6
Equity capital	$77.0	$45.0	$53.5	$66.3	$82.9	$102.5	$123.9
Total capital	$138.0	$190.0	$183.5	$181.3	$182.9	$187.5	$211.5
Ratio of debt to total capital (debt + equity)	44%	76%	71%	63%	55%	45%	41%

tax (EAT), obtained after deducting the additional depreciation expenses and the interest expenses from EBIT, show that the firm should remain profitable in the future, although its net profits are expected to be lower during the next two years in comparison with the 1997 profit figure of $10.2 million. They should recover strongly after 2000.

Assuming that the firm will not pay any dividends until after 2002, the firm's equity will increase each year by the amount of earnings after tax. Starting with a book (accounting) equity value of $40 million at the end of 1997, we can estimate the book values of equity at the end of each year until 2002. These values are shown in Part III of the exhibit, along with the total capital (equity plus debt outstanding) and the debt ratios (debt-to-total capital) at year-end. The figures clearly show the implication of a rapid repayment of the loan on the firm's debt ratio. After five years the debt ratio is back to its original level of 45 percent, which should allow the firm to begin paying a cash dividend if it wishes.

Should the management team go ahead with the deal? Only those directly involved can answer that question. The $200 million price tag is not excessive if the management team is confident that it can rapidly improve the firm's performance according to the restructuring plan. But they will have to keep a close watch on the firm's cash position in order to avoid any major liquidity problems.

The preceding discussion illustrates two important aspects of an LBO deal. First, good candidates for an LBO acquisition are generally underperforming firms in *stable and predictable* industries. An LBO involving a firm with volatile cash flows from assets is not recommended for two reasons. First, the chances of servicing its debt successfully are lower than in the case of a firm with stable cash flows. Second, because venture capitalist firms are often providers of both equity capital and junior debt financing (which are the riskiest forms of financing an LBO), they usually impose a rapid repayment of debt. Imposing a rapid debt repayment schedule is the best guarantee for the venture capitalists that the management team will do its utmost to achieve the restructuring plan and, consequently, get the returns they expect from their contribution to financing the LBO. Indeed, a rapid restructuring of the firm's assets is ultimately the key to a successful LBO.

SUMMARY

One approach to the valuation of a firm's equity is based on the market multiples of firms similar to the one being valued. Although this valuation technique is easy to apply, it does not allow you to test the impact on the firm's value of alternative assumptions about operational efficiency, growth in sales, and different capital structures. Nor can you estimate the potential value that a particular managerial action is expected to create.

The second approach to valuation, the discounted cash-flow method, is more complex. First, the future cash-flow stream expected from the assets of the target firm must be estimated. Then, these cash-flows must be discounted to the present

at an appropriate risk-adjusted discount rate that must also estimated. This discount
rate is the firm's weighted average cost of capital. To estimate the equity value of
the firm, the value of its current debt is deducted from the estimated DCF value of
its assets. The advantage of the DCF approach is that you can find out how a
change in one or more of the valuation parameters will affect the DCF value of the
firm's assets and the value of its equity. The procedure is more than a valuable tool
in assessing the potential value creation of an acquisition; it is also a powerful diagnostic and strategic technique that can be applied to your own firm to examine
whether a change in management strategy and policies could be a source of value
creation.

A variation of the DCF approach, the adjusted present value (APV) method is
also explained. The advantage of the APV method is that you can value a firm
whose capital structure is expected to change over time. Therefore, it is particularly suitable for valuing a leveraged buyout (LBO) deal. We show how to implement these techniques to estimate three values of OS Distributors: its value as is,
its potential acquisition or target value, and its LBO value.

The three techniques presented in the chapter are summarized in Exhibit
12.13. On the upper left side is the market multiples approach (or valuation by comparables). On the lower left side is the DCF approach based on the weighted average cost of capital (WACC), and on the lower right side is the adjusted present
value (APV) approach. For each approach, Exhibit 12.13 shows the steps and the
required inputs needed to obtain an estimated value of equity.

The exhibit shows a fourth valuation approach that is not presented in the
chapter. It is shown on the upper right side of the exhibit. The **dividend discount
model** provides a direct estimate of the firm's equity value by discounting at the
cost of equity the stream of *dividends* the firm is expected to distribute to its shareholders in the future (see Chapter 9). Although this approach is of little practical
use because of the obvious difficulty of forecasting a firm's stream of expected dividend payments, it is described in Appendix 12.1. Conceptually, the three DCF
methods (the WACC, the APV, and the dividend discount model) should provide
the same equity value. In practice, they will not because the assumptions made to
estimate the cash flows and the discount rates used in the DCF formulas are usually not perfectly consistent across the three methods.

Which of the valuation methods described in this chapter do practitioners use
when they value companies? The valuation by market multiples is certainly the
most commonly employed, with DCF valuation a close second. We recommend the
use of both methods. Each has its own merits and they are not mutually exclusive.
The market multiple approach is relatively easy to implement and, because it is
based on comparables, provides a good approximation of the firm value as is. The
DCF approach is more complicated but is superior when the acquisition of a firm is
expected to generate additional value through improved performance or synergistic gains or, in the case of a leveraged buyout, through significant tax savings.

EXHIBIT 12.13 Alternative Equity Valuation Models.

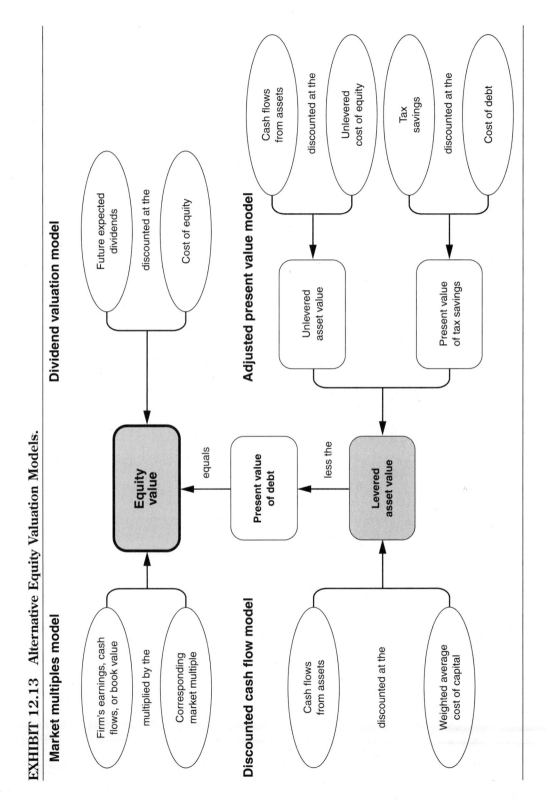

Market multiples model

Dividend valuation model

Discounted cash flow model

Adjusted present value model

Firm's earnings, cash flows, or book value

multiplied by the

Corresponding market multiple

Future expected dividends

discounted at the

Cost of equity

Equity value

equals

Present value of debt

less the

Levered asset value

Cash flows from assets

discounted at the

Weighted average cost of capital

Unlevered asset value

Present value of tax savings

Cash flows from assets

discounted at the

Unlevered cost of equity

Tax savings

discounted at the

Cost of debt

12.1 THE DIVIDEND DISCOUNT MODEL APPROACH TO THE VALUATION OF A FIRM'S EQUITY

The discounted cash-flow method for valuing of a firm's equity begins with the valuation of the firm's assets; then, the firm's outstanding debt is deducted to find the value of the firm's equity. An alternative to this approach, which values a firm's equity directly, is the dividend discount model from Chapter 9. If DIV_1, DIV_2, DIV_3, $\ldots$, DIV_t, $\ldots$, are the dividends expected from a share in year 1, 2, 3, $\ldots$, t, $\ldots$, then, according to the dividend discount model, the share price today is the present value of the expected dividend stream:

$$P_0 \text{ (share today's price)} = \frac{DIV_1}{1 + k_E} + \frac{DIV_2}{(1 + k_E)^2} + \frac{DIV_3}{(1 + k_E)^3}$$
$$+ \ldots + \frac{DIV_t}{(1 + k_E)^t} + \ldots \ldots$$

where k_E is the firm's cost of equity. Multiplying the share price by the number of shares outstanding provides the firm's equity value.

The difficulty in using the dividend discount model is in estimating the entire future stream of expected dividends. As you may recall from Chapter 9, this can be done only if we can make some simplifying assumptions regarding the growth rate of the dividends. For example, if future dividends are expected to stay constant and equal to the current dividend D_0, we get:

$$P_0 = \frac{DIV_0}{k_E}$$

If the dividend expected next year, DIV_1, is anticipated to grow at a constant rate, say g_{div}, forever, then:

$$P_0 = \frac{DIV_1}{k_E - g_{div}}$$

Unfortunately, neither of these assumptions is very realistic. For example, the bottom of Exhibit 12.2 shows OS Distributors' past dividends. In 1995 and 1996, the firm paid $2 million in dividends. In 1997, it paid $3.2 million. If we want to apply the dividend discount model to value OS Distributors' equity on the basis of its recent dividend payments, should we use the 0 percent growth rate in 1996 or the 60 percent growth rate in 1997? The range is so large that our estimates would be meaningless.

As an alternative, we could make yearly estimates of the dividends expected over a forecasting period, say five years, estimate a residual value at the end of the forecasting period based on the assumption that dividends will then grow at a constant rate, and take the present value of these estimates. The approach would be similar to the one we use to estimate the DCF value of OS Distributors based on the future stream of its cash flows from assets. But the estimation of the expected dividend stream would be more difficult than the estimation of the cash flows from assets because we will need to make additional assumptions to estimate expected aftertax earnings and payout ratios (the proportions of earnings distributed as dividends), both of which determine the amount of dividends a firm can distribute. As a result, our estimate of the firm's equity will be much less reliable than the valuation by comparables or the DCF valuation approach. Because of these problems, it is not surprising that, in practice, the dividend discount model is seldom used when valuing a firm's equity.

REFERENCES AND FURTHER READING

1. Benninga, Simon, and Oded Sarig. *Corporate Finance: A Valuation Approach.* McGraw-Hill, 1997. See chapters 1 to 7, 10, and 14.
2. Brealey, Richard, and Stewart Myers. *Principles of Corporate Finance.* 5th ed. McGraw-Hill, 1996. See chapters 25 and 33.
3. Copeland, Tom, Tim Koller, and Jack Murrin. *Valuation.* 2nd ed. John Wiley, 1995.
4. Cornell, Bradford. *Corporate Valuation.* Business One Irwin, 1993.
5. Damoran, Aswath. *Damoran on Valuation.* John Wiley, 1994.
6. Gaughan, Patrick. *Mergers. Acquisitions, and Corporate Restructuring.* John Wiley, 1996.

7. Rappaport, Alfred. *Creating Shareholder Value.* The Free Press, 1998. See chapter 8.
8. Ross, Stephen, Randolph Westerfield, and Jeffrey Jaffe. *Corporate Finance.* 4th ed. Irwin, 1996. See chapter 29.
9. Weston, Fred, Kwang Chung, and Juan Siu. *Takeovers, Restructuring, and Corporate Governance.* Prentice-Hall, 1998.

REVIEW PROBLEMS

12.1. Alternative valuation methods and value-creating acquisitions.
Explain why each of the following statements is generally incorrect:

a. "A company's liquidating value acts as a ceiling on its market value while its replacement value acts as a floor."

b. "Price-earnings ratios should increase when the yield on government securities rises."

c. "Because accounting rules differ across countries, price-earnings ratios are better than price-to-cash flow ratios when making international valuation comparisons."

d. "A company's discounted cash-flow value is usually dominated by the magnitude of its expected cash-flow stream during the future five to ten years while its residual value usually has a negligible effect on its DCF value."

e. "Different valuation methods, if properly applied, will generate estimates of firm values that are practically identical."

f. "Only synergistic mergers have the potential to create value."

g. "If a merger cannot generate synergistic gains through cost reductions, it will not create value."

h. "Conglomerate mergers can create value through superior growth in earnings per share."

i. "There is strong empirical evidence indicating that acquiring firms create value mostly through their superior ability to uncover target companies that are undervalued by the stock market."

j. "The use of high debt ratios to finance leveraged buyouts is essentially a device to capture the tax savings generated by the deductibility of interest expenses."

12.2. Valuation by comparables.
The Light Motors Company (LMC) is privately held. Its owners are thinking of listing at least 45 percent of their company's equity on the local

stock exchange. Thus, they wish to estimate the value of their company using financial data drawn from the National Engine Corporation (NEC), a company listed on the local stock market and comparable to LMC in assets and financial structures. Based on the data given below, provide four estimates of LMC's value. Why do they differ from one another?

	LMC	NEC
1. Sales	$620 million	$1,340 million
2. Earnings after tax (EAT)	$46 million	$90 million
3. Cash earnings = EAT + depreciation expenses	$104 million	$210 million
4. Book value of equity	$270 million	$590 million
5. Number of shares outstanding	Not available	40 million
6. Share price	Unlisted	$30

12.3. Discounted cash-flow valuation.

In problem 12.2, Light Motors Company (LMC), an unlisted company, is valued by comparing it to National Engine Company (NEC), a similar company listed on the local stock exchange.

a. Using the discounted cash-flow method and the following assumptions, provide an estimate of LMC's value.

- Sales, currently at $620 million, will grow by 8 percent for the next 2 years, by 6 percent during the following 2 years, and then by 4 percent in perpetuity.
- Pretax operating margin will remain at 20 percent.
- Capital expenditures will be equal to annual depreciation expenses.
- Working capital requirement will remain at 20 percent of sales.
- LMC has $280 million of debt outstanding, can borrow at 10 percent, and is expected to pay a 40 percent corporate tax rate.
- National Engines Corporation—the comparable firm that is listed in the local stock exchange—has a ratio of equity-to-total capital of 80 percent at *market* value, and a market beta of 1.20.
- Both the risk-free rate and the market risk premium are 7 percent.

b. Assume that LMC's performance can be improved through the following:

(1) A half a percentage point increase in the growth rate in sales every year (for example from 8 percent to 8.5 percent)
(2) An improvement in operating margin from 20 percent to 21 percent
(3) A reduction of the ratio of working capital to sales from 20 percent to 15 percent

(4) A recapitalization that could lower LMC's weighted average cost of capital by 30 basis points

Show how each one of these actions will change the firm's estimated discounted cash-flow value. What will the change in value be if all actions are implemented simultaneously? Why is the sum of the changes in value resulting from each action *smaller* than the change in value resulting from their cumulative effects?

c. Provide an outline of how you would value LMC if the performance improvements listed in the previous question were implemented in the context of a leveraged buyout (LBO).

13 MAKING VALUE-CREATING DECISIONS IN AN INTERNATIONAL ENVIRONMENT

F irms do not operate exclusively in a domestic environment. Many companies have significant foreign operations that provide managers with new opportunities, as well as new constraints, that do not exist in a purely domestic environment. New factors, such as fluctuations in exchange rates, differences in interest rates, accounting rules, tax systems, and the risk of doing business abroad, have to be taken into account. Of course, the fundamental principle of corporate finance still holds: A firm's resources must be managed with the ultimate goal of increasing the firm's market value. Foreign investment projects, like domestic ones, should be undertaken only if they provide a return in excess of that required by investors. The decision criteria in previous chapters, such as the net present value rule, are still valid. But, they are usually more complicated to apply because there is more than one currency involved and because there are some specific risks attached to cross-border investments.

This chapter examines the impact of currency risk (the risk resulting from exchange rate fluctuations) and country risk (the risk resulting from having operations in a politically or regulatory unstable country) on management decisions in an international environment. A firm faces two types of risk exposure when exchange rates fluctuate: (1) accounting or translation exposure, which is the effect of changes in exchange rates on the firm's balance sheet and income statement, and (2) economic exposure, which is the effect of exchange rate fluctuations on the firm's future cash flows. After describing the foreign exchange market, we explain how managers can use financial instruments such as forward, futures, option, and swap contracts to reduce their firm's economic exposure to currency risk. Next, we examine the relationships among exchange rates, inflation rates, and interest rates. We then show how to apply the net present value rule to two cross-border investments, one in a low-risk country and the other in a high-risk country. Finally, we propose a number of techniques and mechanisms to actively manage country risk. After reading this chapter, you should understand:

- The difference between accounting, or translation, exposure and economic exposure to exchange rate fluctuations.
- How the foreign exchange market operates.
- The difference between spot and forward exchange rates.
- How to use financial instruments, such as forward, futures, option, and swap contracts, to hedge exchange rate risk.
- The relationships among spot exchange rates, forward exchange rates, interest rates, and inflation rates.
- How to apply the net present value (NPV) rule to investment projects with cash flows denominated in foreign currencies and to projects in a politically or regulatory unstable environment.
- How to actively manage country risk.

THE FIRM'S RISK EXPOSURE FROM FOREIGN OPERATIONS

When a firm operates in a foreign environment, it is subject to a number of risks. **Foreign exchange risk** is associated with the volatility of exchange rates. If the firm has assets and liabilities, revenues and expenses, and cash flows denominated in a foreign currency, changes in exchange rates will affect their value. **Accounting,** or **translation, exposure** is the effect of changes in exchange rates on the firm's balance sheet and income statement; **economic exposure** is the effect on the value of the firm's future cash flows. There is also the risk of operating in an environment that may not be so politically stable as the domestic one. This risk, called **country risk,** or **political risk,** takes many forms. It extends from the risk of expropriation of the firm's foreign assets without compensation to the relatively milder risk originating from the imposition of exchange controls.

ACCOUNTING, OR TRANSLATION, EXPOSURE

Accounting exposure arises from the need to translate the financial statements of the foreign business unit into the parent company's currency in order to prepare consolidated financial statements. There are a variety of approaches to translating balance sheet and income statement accounts. Most of them are variations of the **monetary/nonmonetary method** and the **current method,** both of which are presented in Appendix 13.1. The objective of these methods is to show how changes in exchange rates affect *reported* earnings and *book* equity values. How important are the translated accounting data to the firm's owners? They provide some useful starting points for a financial analysis of the foreign operations, but they are of limited use for the firm's shareholders because they are not *market* values. Economic exposure is much more relevant to the firm's owners.

ECONOMIC EXPOSURE

Economic exposure focuses on the impact of unexpected changes in exchange rates on the value of the firm's future cash flows. Economic exposure is classified as (1) contractual, or transaction, exposure or (2) operating exposure. **Contractual**, or **transaction**, **exposure** refers to the effect of exchange rate volatility on the expected cash flows from *past* transactions denominated in foreign currencies that are still outstanding. **Operating exposure** is also concerned with future cash flows, but from *future,* not past, transactions. In other words, although both types of exposure examine the impact of exchange rate volatility on future cash flows, contractual exposure focuses on cash flows whose values in foreign currency are *certain,* and operating exposure is concerned with cash flows whose values are *uncertain* even when denominated in a foreign currency. The example in the following sections illustrates the distinction.

Contractual, or transaction, exposure

We assume a U.S. wine distributor just signed a contract with a French company for the delivery of 450 cases of champagne. The contract calls for the payment of 600,000 French francs (FRF) when delivery takes place in three months. As soon as the contract is signed, the distributor is exposed to exchange rate risk because the dollar cost of the champagne will not be known until dollars are exchanged for FRF600,000 at the exchange rate that will prevail in three months. We say that the distributor's contractual, or transaction, exposure is FRF600,000.

In general, contractual exposure arises from the purchase or the sale of goods and services whose prices are denominated in a foreign currency. But, it can also come from financial operations, such as borrowing and lending in a nondomestic currency. For most companies involved in cross-border transactions, the number of outstanding foreign contracts can be very large, with, typically, different maturity dates and different currency denominations. For these firms, the contractual exposure to a particular currency at a particular date is simply the net sum of the contractual (future) cash inflows and cash outflows in that currency measured at that date.

A firm with large and uncovered transaction exposure may find itself in a difficult financial situation arising from adverse exchange rate movements. The situation is similar to a firm borrowing too much debt and experiencing difficulty meeting its repayment schedule. Chapter 11 describes this situation as financial distress and shows that it adversely affects the value of the firm. For example, with too much exposure to exchange rate risk, the firm may have to pass up valuable investment projects, customers may worry about the firm's ability to deliver goods and services and switch to competitors, and suppliers may be reluctant to provide trade credit. All these indirect costs will have a negative impact on the firm's value.

Fortunately, this type of exposure can be controlled using financial instruments such as forward, futures, and option contracts.

Operating Exposure

Each time our U.S. distributor places an order for champagne from France, he enters a contract to deliver French francs to the French champagne exporter and is immediately exposed to foreign exchange risk. If the distributor's business is to sell French champagne, his exposure to foreign exchange risk is not limited to the *outstanding* contracts with his French suppliers. Future purchases of champagne will generate continuous exposure to the volatility of the U.S. dollar-French franc exchange rate. This exposure to future exchange rate changes is an example of an operating exposure.

Importers (or exporters) of goods and services are not the only firms subject to operating exposure. A firm that has only domestic operations can also be exposed to changes in exchange rates. Consider a U.S. distributor of champagne made in the United States. If the value of the French franc decreases relative to the U.S. dollar (you get more francs for a dollar), the U.S. distributor of the French-produced champagne can keep the same margin by selling his champagne at a lower price and, in the process, take market share from the distributor of U.S.-made champagne. A similar situation occurs when domestic firms that buy, produce, and sell domestic goods are faced with competition from abroad. For example, in the early 1980s, U.S. auto manufacturers lost market share to Japanese competitors when the U.S. dollar appreciated against the Japanese Yen.[1]

Operating exposure is more difficult to manage than contractual exposure. It requires a good understanding of the economic and competitive environment in which the firm operates. Although it is nearly impossible to quantify, it needs to be controlled. The firm must anticipate future developments in the foreign exchange market and take measures to reduce the probability of experiencing financial distress from excessive exposure to exchange rate movements. This can be achieved by diversifying operations and financing sources. On the operations side, the firm can diversify its sources of raw materials, the locations of production facilities, and the regions around the world where it conducts sales. On the financing side, diversification can be accomplished by raising funds in more than one currency. The firm can also use instruments available in financial markets to **hedge** against changes in exchange rates. But, the difficulty of forecasting future cash flows, far beyond those arising from outstanding contracts, makes the estimation of operating exposure less precise than the estimation of contractual exposure. As a result, using financial instruments is less efficient in controlling operating exposure than in controlling transaction exposure.

---

[1] The loss in market share by the American automobile makers might also be attributed to quality differences in the cars made in the U.S. and those produced in Japan.

COUNTRY, OR POLITICAL, RISK

A firm is exposed to country, or political, risk when unforeseen political events in a country affect the value of the firm's investments in that country. Changes in the host country political environment may bring changes in government regulations or add new regulations to existing ones, resulting in restrictions or penalties for foreign operations in the country. Examples of regulations that can adversely affect a foreign subsidiary include: (1) imposing ceilings or discriminatory taxation on dividends or royalties paid to the parent company; (2) imposing unfavorable exchange rates for foreign currency transactions; (3) requiring that goods produced contain a certain percentage of local content; (4) requiring that nationals hold top management positions; (5) requiring that a portion of the profits be reinvested locally; (6) allowing only joint ventures with less than 50 percent ownership by the foreign parent; (7) imposing price controls; and, ultimately, (8) expropriating the subsidiary without adequate compensation.

Financial instruments, such as forward, futures, or option contracts, can considerably reduce a firm's exposure to contractual risk but are useless for hedging country risk. However, firms can reduce their exposure to country risk when investing in a politically unstable foreign country by following some simple rules we examine later in this chapter.

THE FOREIGN EXCHANGE MARKET

The **foreign exchange,** or **currency, market** is the world's largest financial market. The Bank for International Settlements (BIS) estimated that the *daily* dollar transactions in the foreign exchange market in 1995 reached $1,300 billion dollars (a fifth of the U.S. gross national product that year) and were growing at an average annual rate of 30 percent. This market exists to handle the buying and selling of currencies. Any firm or individual can buy or sell a currency in the foreign exchange market. **Exchange,** or **currency, rates** are determined by the constant interactions of those who are buying and selling currencies. The quoted exchange rate is the price that has to be paid in one country's currency to buy one unit of another country's currency. For example, if the exchange rate between the U.S. dollar and the British pound is quoted as 1.63 dollars to the pound, then 1.63 U.S. dollars must be paid to buy one British pound.

THE ORGANIZATION OF THE FOREIGN EXCHANGE MARKET

Unlike most stock markets, the foreign exchange market has no central location. It is a network of banks, dealers, brokers, and multinational corporations communicating with each other via computer terminals, telephone lines, and fax machines. Major participants are large commercial banks operating through the **interbank**

market. Operating from rooms especially designed for currency trading, traders are surrounded by telephones and display monitors connected to trading rooms all over the world. If a trader in Chicago wants to exchange U.S. dollars for German marks, high-technology equipment helps her find a trader from another bank in the interbank market who is willing to trade marks for dollars. Over the phone or through computer monitors, the two traders agree on price and quantity. Each trader then enters the transaction in his or her own bank recording system. The entire procedure lasts no more than a few seconds. Later, the two banks send each other written confirmation of the trade, which may take up to two business days to settle. A study conducted by the Federal Reserve Bank of New York reported that the *average* currency transaction soared from $750,000 in 1974 to $10 million in 1994.

A typical interbank foreign exchange quotation mentions two rates. The **bid price** is the price at which a trader in the market is willing to buy, and the **ask,** or **offer, price** is the price at which a trader is willing to sell. The price is given in units of one currency per unit of the other currency with the currencies usually identified by three letters. For example, suppose the French franc is quoted at FRF/USD6.2935-6.3035. This means that some banks are willing to buy U.S. dollars at 6.2935 French francs per dollar (the bid price) and sell them at 6.3035 francs per dollar (the ask price). Note that the exchange rate can be expressed as USD/FRF (the price of one French franc in U.S. dollars) instead of FRF/USD (the price of one U.S. dollar in French francs). However, the convention is to express the exchange rate in units of foreign currency per one U.S. dollar.

The difference between the bid price and the ask price is the banks' compensation for making the transaction, which is the reason why they do not charge commission fees. For widely traded currencies, the size of the **bid-ask spread** is approximately 0.1 to 0.5 percent. Its size varies from one currency to another. For a given currency, the spread depends on the level of competition among traders for that currency, the currency's volatility, and the average volume of daily trade.

It is a common practice among traders to quote all currencies in reference to U.S. dollars. The exchange rate between two currencies when neither is a dollar is calculated from their respective U.S. dollar values. For example, if the French franc is quoted at FRF/USD6.2985 and the Japanese yen at JPY/USD118.42,[2] the JPY/FRF exchange rate is the JPY/USD rate divided by the FRF/USD rate:

$$\frac{\text{JPY/USD118.42}}{\text{FRF/USD6.2985}} = \text{JPY/FRF18.801}$$

Rates between currencies computed as above are called **cross rates.** Quotations of cross rates are provided daily by financial publications. As an example, Exhibit 13.1 shows the quotations published by *The Wall Street Journal* on February 4, 1998.

---

[2]These rates are bid-ask midpoints. For example, FRF/USD6.2985 is at the midpoint between the bid price of FRF/USD6.2935 and the ask price of FRF/USD6.3035.

EXHIBIT 13.1   Currency Cross Rates on February 3, 1998.

Key Currency Cross Rates Late New York Trading Feb 3, 1998

	Dollar	Pound	SFranc	Guilder	Peso	Yen	Lira	D-Mark	FFranc	CdnDlr
Canada	1.4477	2.3839	.98866	.70896	.17235	.01150	.00081	.79939	.23848	....
France	6.0705	9.9963	4.1457	2.9728	.72268	.04822	.00339	3.3520	....	4.1932
Germany	1.8110	2.9822	1.2368	.88688	.21560	.01438	.00101	....	.29833	1.2509
Italy	1788.8	2945.5	1221.6	875.98	212.95	14.208	....	987.71	294.66	1235.6
Japan	125.9	207.32	85.98	61.655	14.988	....	.07038	69.52	20.74	86.966
Mexico	8.4000	13.832	5.7365	4.1136	....	.06672	.00470	4.6383	1.3837	5.8023
Netherlands	2.0420	3.3626	1.3945	....	.24310	.01622	.00114	1.1276	.33638	1.4105
Switzerland	1.4643	2.4113	....	.71709	.17432	.01163	.00082	.80856	.24122	1.0115
U.K.	.60728	....	.41472	.29739	.07229	.00482	.00034	.33533	.10004	.41948
U.S.	....	1.6467	.68292	.48972	.11905	.00794	.00056	.55218	.16473	.69075

Source: Dow Jones

Source: *The Wall Street Journal,* February 4, 1998.

SPOT TRANSACTIONS VERSUS FORWARD CONTRACTS

A **spot transaction** is a trade between two parties in which both agree to a currency exchange at a rate fixed *now* with the delivery of the currencies taking place at a **settlement date,** usually two business days later. Individuals can trade currencies for immediate delivery at the nearest bank. However, the spread is usually quite large.

A **forward contract** is an agreement between two parties, generally a bank and a customer, for the delivery of currencies on a specified date in the *future* but at an exchange rate fixed *today.* The contract specifies the *currencies* to be exchanged, the *fixed date* in the future when the delivery will actually take place, the *amount* of currency to be exchanged, and the fixed *rate* of exchange. Contracts traded in the interbank forward market usually have a maturity of one, three, or six months. However, the delivery date can be tailor-made to accommodate a customer's particular need, usually at a less favorable rate.

Spot rates and **forward rates** are provided daily by major newspapers all over the world. Exhibit 13.2 shows rates for a sample of currencies, reported in the same issue of *The Wall Street Journal* as the cross rates in Exhibit 13.1.

HEDGING CONTRACTUAL EXPOSURE TO CURRENCY RISK

Let's return to our U.S. distributor of French champagne. Recall that he currently has a contractual exposure of FRF600,000, which will remain outstanding for the next three months. As the FRF/USD exchange rate varies during that period of time, the dollar value of the FRF600,000 will change. There are many ways the

EXHIBIT 13.2   Spot Rates and Forward Rates on Feburary 3, 1998.

CURRENCY TRADING

EXCHANGE RATES

Tuesday, February 3, 1998

The New York foreign exchange selling rates below apply to trading among banks in amounts of $1 million and more, as quoted at 4 p.m. Eastern time by Dow Jones and other sources. Retail transactions provide fewer units of foreign currency per dollar.

Country	U.S. $ equiv. Tue	Mon	Currency per U.S. $ Tue	Mon
Argentina (Peso)	1.0001	1.0001	.9999	.9999
Australia (Dollar)	.6806	.6866	1.4693	1.4564
Austria (Schilling)	.07799	.07803	12.822	12.815
Bahrain (Dinar)	2.6525	2.6525	.3770	.3770
Belgium (Franc)	.02670	.02658	37.460	37.625
Brazil (Real)	.8896	.8904	1.1241	1.1231
Britain (Pound)	1.6467	1.6390	.6073	.6101
1-month forward	1.6444	1.6366	.6081	.6110
3-months forward.....	1.6394	1.6316	.6100	.6129
6-months forward.....	1.6322	1.6245	.6127	.6156
Canada (Dollar)	.6908	.6882	1.4477	1.4530
1-month forward	.6912	.6886	1.4468	1.4522
3-months forward.....	.6919	.6893	1.4454	1.4508
6-months forward.....	.6927	.6899	1.4437	1.4494
Chile (Peso)	.002204	.002208	453.65	452.85
China (Renminbi)	.1203	.1208	8.3100	8.2790
Colombia (Peso).........	.0007441	.0007452	1343.90	1342.00
Czech. Rep. (Koruna) ...				
Commercial rate.......	.02876	.02834	34.773	35.291
Denmark (Krone)........	.1450	.1445	6.8960	6.9185
Ecuador (Sucre).........				
Floating rate.............	.0002200	.0002200	4545.00	4545.00
Finland (Markka)	.1818	.1816	5.5001	5.5071
France (Franc)	.1647	.1640	6.0705	6.0965
1-month forward	.1650	.1643	6.0607	6.0867
3-months forward.....	.1656	.1648	6.0403	6.0663
6-months forward.....	.1663	.1656	6.0127	6.0381
Germany (Mark)	.5522	.5503	1.8110	1.8173
1-month forward	.5531	.5512	1.8081	1.8143
3-months forward.....	.5550	.5531	1.8018	1.8081
6-months forward.....	.5576	.5556	1.7935	1.7997
Greece (Drachma)	.003493	.003486	286.30	286.90
Hong Kong (Dollar)	.1293	.1293	7.7360	7.7360
Hungary (Forint)	.004829	.004791	207.08	208.73
India (Rupee)	.02584	.02571	38.700	38.900
Indonesia (Rupiah)	.00009756	.00009709	10250.00	10300.00
Ireland (Punt)..............	1.3854	1.3848	.7218	.7221
Israel (Shekel)	.2791	.2791	3.5827	3.5826
Italy (Lira)	.0005590	.0005571	1788.75	1795.00
Japan (Yen).................	.007943	.007901	125.90	126.56
1-month forward	.007974	.007933	125.41	126.06

Country	U.S. $ equiv. Tue	Mon	Currency per U.S. $ Tue	Mon
3-months forward......	.008042	.008002	124.34	124.97
6-months forward......	.008142	.008099	122.82	123.47
Jordan (Dinar).............	1.4134	1.4134	.7075	.7075
Kuwait (Dinar)	3.2755	3.2733	.3053	.3055
Lebanon (Pound)..........	.0006556	.0006555	1525.25	1525.50
Malaysia (Ringgit).......	.2540	.2442	3.9363	4.0953
Malta (Lira)	2.5253	2.5221	.3960	.3965
Mexico (Peso)				
Floating rate.............	.1190	.1189	8.4000	8.4100
Netherland (Guilder)....	.4897	.4894	2.0420	2.0434
New Zealand (Dollar) ...	.5869	.5914	1.7039	1.6909
Norway (Krone)	.1330	.1331	7.5203	7.5148
Pakistan (Rupee)	.02296	.02296	43.560	43.560
Peru (new Sol)	.3609	.3620	2.7711	2.7621
Philippines (Peso)	.02475	.02433	40.400	41.100
Poland (Zloty)	.2832	.2828	3.5305	3.5360
Portugal (Escudo)........	.005395	.005391	185.34	185.50
Russia (Ruble) (a)	.1658	.1659	6.0310	6.0290
Saudi Arabia (Riyal)	.2666	.2666	3.7505	3.7506
Singapore (Dollar)	.5956	.5860	1.6790	1.7065
Slovak Rep. (Koruna) ...	.02827	.02820	35.375	35.455
South Africa (Rand)	.2027	.2029	4.9345	4.9285
South Korea (Won)	.0006325	.0006431	1581.00	1555.00
Spain (Peseta)	.006518	.006498	153.42	153.90
Sweden (Krona)	.1239	.1241	8.0707	8.0564
Switzerland (Franc)	.6829	.6782	1.4643	1.4745
1-month forward	.6853	.6805	1.4592	1.4695
3-months forward......	.6903	.6854	1.4486	1.4589
6-months forward......	.6975	.6925	1.4337	1.4441
Taiwan (Dollar)	.03022	.02997	33.088	33.370
Thailand (Baht)	.02086	.01967	47.950	50.850
Turkey (Lira)	.00000456	.00000455	219360.00	219690.00
United Arab (Dirham)..	.2723	.2723	3.6730	3.6730
Uruguay (New Peso)				
Financial...................	.1002	.1002	9.9800	9.9800
Venezuela (Bolivar)	.001955	.001955	511.53	511.53
SDR............................	1.3490	1.3437	.7413	.7442
ECU	1.0893	1.0877	---	---

Special Drawing Rights (SDR) are based on exchange rates for the U.S., German, British, French , and Japanese currencies. Source: International Monetary Fund.

European Currency Unit (ECU) is based on a basket of community currencies.

a-fixing, Moscow Interbank Currency Exchange. Ruble newly-denominated Jan. 1998.

The Wall Street Journal daily foreign exchange data for 1996 and 1997 may be purchased through the Readers' Reference Service (413) 592-3600.

Source: *The Wall Street Journal,* February 4, 1998.

distributor can hedge this exchange rate risk, that is, protect himself against currency fluctuations. He can choose among the many hedging techniques commonly used to reduce or eliminate the exchange rate risk associated with the purchase of raw materials, the sale of goods, the purchase of assets, or the issuance of debt when they are denominated in a foreign currency. These techniques use instruments available in the financial markets, such as forward, futures, and option contracts.

HEDGING WITH FORWARD CONTRACTS

The **forward hedge,** which is the hedging technique most widely used by corporations, can completely eliminate the exchange rate risk associated with foreign transactions. The distributor can arrange a forward hedge simply by entering into a forward contract with a bank to buy from that bank FRF600,000 with U.S. dollars in three months. In other words, the distributor can fix *today* the rate at which he will buy FRF600,000 from the bank in three months. The bank will most likely require the importer to establish a **foreign exchange line of credit** to guarantee his ability to deliver U.S. dollars in three months.

What is the *net* result of the two transactions, the purchase of champagne and the purchase of French francs forward? If today's three-month *forward rate* is FRF/USD6.25, the distributor will have to pay the bank $96,000 (FRF600,000 divided by FRF/USD6.25) in three months to get the FRF600,000. Regardless of how the USD/FRF exchange rate changes between the purchase date and the delivery date, the dollar value of the purchase will not change. It will remain equal to $96,000. The exchange rate risk has been eliminated. By entering into a forward contract, the distributor has "locked in" an exchange rate of USD/FRF6.25. Note that this rate is the *forward rate* quoted today and *not* the spot rate, which may be higher or lower than the forward rate.

What would happen if the cases of champagne are not delivered on the agreed upon date and, consequently, the FRF600,000 payment to the French exporter is delayed? The distributor would still have to buy the FRF600,000 from his bank for $96,000 at the date fixed by the forward contract. He would then have the choice of keeping the FRF600,000 until the champagne is delivered or exchanging them for U.S. dollars at the prevailing spot rate.[3] If the distributor exchanges the francs, he will need FRF600,000 to pay the French exporter when the champagne is delivered and will again be exposed to exchange rate risk. However, he can hedge this risk as before by entering into a new FRF600,000 forward contract with the bank. This strategy is known as **rolling over the forward contract.** An alternative to a rollover would be for the distributor to enter a **forward window contract** at the beginning. This contract is the same as a standard forward contract except that the transaction does not have to be settled on a fixed date. It can be settled on any day during an agreed upon period of time known as the *window.* The importer would have to pay an additional fee for this flexibility, but it may be cheaper than rolling over the original contract.

What if the distributor wants to get out of the forward contract before its expiration date? In this situation, he would have to *sell* FRF600,000 forward by entering a forward contract that has the same expiration date as the first contract. The cash settlement for both contracts will take place at their common expiration date. The distributor would gain or lose depending on whether the forward rate on the sec-

---

[3]In this scenario, the money will certainly be kept in a French francs denominated money market account at the bank and will earn some interest.

ond contract is lower or higher than the rate on the first contract (FRF/USD6.25). For example, suppose the forward rate on the second contract is FRF/USD6.10. He will receive $98,361 from this contract (FRF600,000 divided by FRF/USD6.10) and will pay $96,000 on the first contract. His gain will be $2,361 ($98,361 less $96,000). If the forward rate of the second contract is FRF/USD6.40, he will lose $2,250, the difference between the $93,750 from the sale of French francs (FRF600,000 divided by FRF/USD6.40) and the $96,000 on the first contract.

HEDGING WITH FUTURES CONTRACTS

As an alternative to forward contracts, the U.S. distributor of French champagne can use currency futures contracts. **Currency futures contracts,** or simply **currency futures,** are similar to forward contracts, except that they have a standard contract size and a standard delivery date. Currency futures are traded every day on organized **futures markets,** such as the International Monetary Exchange (IMM) in Chicago, the London International Financial Futures Exchange (LIFFE), and the Singapore International Monetary Exchange (SIMEX).

Trading in currency futures contracts

Like currency forward contracts, currency futures contracts are promises to deliver a given number of currency units at a specified price. However, trading in futures contracts differs considerably from trading in forward contracts.

First, the contracts between the purchasers and the sellers of the currency are made through a clearing corporation or clearing house. For example, a contract between seller A and purchaser B is, in fact, a sale by A to the clearing corporation and, simultaneously, a sale by the clearing corporation to B. The clearing corporation provides insurance against default by one of the parties. If A cannot deliver the amount of currency he promised, B will still receive what he purchased, unless, of course, the clearing corporation goes bankrupt. (To cover its losses from default, the clearing corporation charges a small tax on futures transactions.)

Second, currency futures have standard sizes and fixed maturity dates. For example, contracts denominated in Japanese yen have a size of 12.5 million yen, those in pounds sterling have a size of 62,500 pounds, and those in German marks have a size of 125,000 marks. Maturity dates are typically the third Wednesday of March, June, September, and December. The standardization of the contracts' size and delivery date limits the number of contracts traded, thus greatly improving the liquidity of the futures markets compared to what would be the case if any amount and any delivery date were possible.

Third, futures exchanges require traders to deposit collateral to ensure that they can make good on any losses. An **initial margin** must be deposited with the broker who will execute the trade. The size of the initial margin depends on the volatility of the underlying currency.

Fourth, currency futures are **marked-to-market** daily. This means that at the end of each trading day, any profit or loss from the previous trading day is immediately settled by the clearing house at the **settlement price** (the quote of the last trade of the day). For example, suppose you bought a 125,000 German mark (DEM) futures contract at 0.5450 dollars per mark yesterday, and the price is 0.5550 dollars at the close of the market today. You have just made a profit of $1,250 (DEM125,000 multiplied by the difference of 0.01 dollars between the settlement price and the purchase price). The clearing corporation will immediately pay you $1,250, close your previous position, and open a new one at the new futures price of 0.5550 dollars. The system limits the default risk for the clearing corporation to only one day's loss. Further, if a loss causes the margin to fall below a preset level, the trader is asked to post additional margin, known as a **margin call.** The margin deposits and daily settlements considerably reduce the risk borne by the clearing corporation. As a result, no recognized credit standing is required to trade in the futures market.

Finally, the two parties in the futures contract can exit the contract anytime during the life of the contract. The party that *bought* contracts just has to *sell* an offsetting number of the same contract (at the futures price prevailing on the day of the sale); the party that *sold* contracts just has to *buy* an offsetting number of the same contract.

Like forward rates, futures prices are reported in the financial press. Exhibit 13.3 shows the futures prices of major currency trades and is taken from the same issue of *The Wall Street Journal* used in the previous exhibits.

The currency futures hedge

If our champagne distributor wants to use currency futures contracts to hedge his exposure to French francs, he will have to buy three-month futures contracts worth FRF600,000. Because currency futures contracts and forward contracts are similar instruments, the futures hedge should have the same overall effect as the forward hedge. However, there will be some differences.

First, the other party in the futures contract is not a bank, but is instead the clearing corporation. The distributor, through his broker, will have to *buy* French francs futures and then *sell* them later. If, in the meantime, the French franc appreciates (depreciates) relative to the U.S. dollar, the distributor will make a profit (loss) from his futures trade. But, if the franc appreciates (depreciates) relative to the dollar, he will also have to disburse more (fewer) dollars to buy, in the spot market, the FRF600,000 needed to pay his supplier. The profit (loss) made in the futures market will compensate for the increase (decrease) in the amount of dollars needed to buy the FRF600,000 in the spot market.

Second, because the size and the maturity of the futures contracts are standardized, it is not always possible to *perfectly* hedge transaction exposure using a futures contract. For example, if the distributor decides to buy French franc futures contracts at the Chicago Mercantile Exchange (CME), he will have to buy contracts

EXHIBIT 13.3   Currency Futures on Feburary 3, 1998.

First price of the day

Highest price of the day

Lowest price of the day

Settlement price used for marking to market

Change from previous day closing price

FUTURES PRICES

Number of contracts not yet closed by an offsetting trade

Exchange (Chicago Mercantile Exchange)

CURRENCY

Currency

Expiration month

Number of contracts sold

Size of contract

	Open	High	Low	Settle	Change	Lifetime High	Lifetime Low	Open Interest
JAPAN YEN (CME)-12.5 million yen; $ per yen (.00)								
Mar	.7947	.8007	.7947	.7988	+ .0032	.9375	.7512	96,445
June	.8100	.8100	.8072	.8088	+ .0032	.9090	.7637	2,593
Sept	.8185	.8185	.8184	.8187	+ .0032	.8695	.7735	523
Est vol 13,232; vol Mn 18,987; open int 99,565, −343.								
DEUTSCHEMARK (CME)-125,000 marks; $ per mark								
Mar	.5513	.5542	.5494	.5535	+ .0025	.6160	.5383	80,865
June	.5528	.5566	.5522	.5562	+ .0025	.5995	.5470	3,527
Sept	.5566	.5580	.5557	.5586	+ .0025	.5944	.5526	1,626
Est vol 17,820; vol Mn 31,576; open int 86,024, +723.								
CANADIAN DOLLAR (CME)-100,000 dlrs.; $ per Can $								
Mar	.6888	.6923	.6875	.6915	+ .0026	.7670	.6807	56,978
June	.6895	.6942	.6888	.6926	+ .0026	.7470	.6825	5,897
Sept	.6902	.6940	.6895	.6935	+ .0026	.7463	.6845	1,864
Dec	.6917	.6950	.6915	.6943	+ .0026	.7400	.6860	841
Mr99	.6925	.6940	.6915	.6951	+ .0026	.7247	.6875	284
Est vol 9,516; vol Mn 10,591; open int 65,871, +593.								
BRITISH POUND (CME)-62,500 pds.; $ per pound								
Mar	1.6350	1.6456	1.6330	1.6426	+ .0068	1.7020	1.5680	28,920
June	1.6310	1.6368	1.6280	1.6352	+ .0068	1.6940	1.5610	1,333
Est vol 6,923; vol Mn 7,174; open int 30,257, +16.								
SWISS FRANC (CME)-125,000 francs; $ per franc								
Mar	.6820	.6870	.6795	.6863	+ .0051	.7450	.6687	47,665
June	.6882	.6940	.6871	.6934	+ .0052	.7304	.6750	1,283
Sept	.6935	.7003	.6935	.7003	+ .0053	.7310	.6840	1,114
Est vol 13,908; vol Mn 14,852; open int 50,068, −2,469.								
AUSTRALIAN DOLLAR (CME)-100,000 dlrs.; $ per A.$								
Mar	.6855	.6870	.6801	.6805	− .0059	.7590	.6328	16,236
Est vol 1,368; vol Mn 2,661; open int 16,288, −2.								
MEXICAN PESO (CME)-500,000 new Mex. peso, $ per MP								
Mar	.11730	.11740	.11630	.11737	+ 00037	.12340	.09700	20,755
June	.11250	.11342	.11250	.11342	+ 00037	.11985	09200	4,861
Sept	.10915	.10980	.10900	.10977	+ 00037	.11680	.08000	4,949
Dec	....	....	....	.10637	+ 00032	.11440	.08000	7,114
Est vol 5,331; vol Mn 4,859; open int 37,679, −64.								

Source: *The Wall Street Journal,* February 4, 1998.

with a unit size of FRF500,000. If he buys one contract, he will hedge only FRF500,000, leaving FRF100,000 "unhedged." If he buys two contracts for a total of FRF1,000,000, he will "overhedge" his exposure by FRF400,000. Moreover, the distributor will have to decide on the maturity date of the futures contract. The only four expiration dates for a futures contract are the last Wednesday of March, June, September, and December. Suppose the champagne supplier wants to be paid by the end of May? The distributor will buy June futures contracts because their expiration date is closest to the end of May. Then he will *sell* the futures contracts at the end of May. However, he will still be exposed to exchange rate risk because he cannot know at the time the contract is bought what the price of the June futures contracts will be at the end of May. Suppose the supplier agrees to wait until July 1 to be paid and the distributor chooses to hedge with June futures? In this case, the distributor will be exposed to the USD/FRF exchange rate volatility between the last Wednesday of June (when the June futures contracts expire) and July 1.

Finally, the distributor will have to place a margin with a broker. Also, the daily marking to market may trigger margin calls if the USD/FRF futures exchange rate goes down. In this situation, the distributor would have to make additional cash payments until the futures contracts expire.

To summarize, a futures hedge has some disadvantages that are not present in a forward hedge. A futures hedge is more complicated, it does not completely eliminate exchange rate risk, and it requires intermediary cash payments. These drawbacks are particularly significant for our distributor of champagne who may rightly prefer to hedge his contractual exposure with forward contracts. However, there are features of the futures market which, in some circumstances, cause corporations to hedge with futures rather than with forward contracts. For example, a small firm without any established reputation or a firm that does not enjoy a high credit standing may find it convenient to use futures contracts because no credit check is required before trading in the futures market.

HEDGING WITH OPTION CONTRACTS

Suppose our distributor hedges his exposure to the French franc by buying French francs forward at FRF/USD6.25. Regardless of whether the French franc appreciates or depreciates during the hedging period, the U.S. dollar cost of the champagne will be $96,000 (FRF600,000 divided by FRF/USD6.25). If the French franc appreciates, the hedge will have accomplished its purpose, that is, it will have protected the distributor against an increase in the value of the French franc. But if the French franc depreciates, the distributor would have been better off if he had not hedged with forwards because he would then have benefited from the decrease in the value of the French franc. Indeed, it is always the case that a forward hedge protects a firm from unfavorable exchange rate movements but prevents it from benefiting from favorable changes in the exchange rate. Does a hedging technique exist that insulates the distributor from an appreciation of the French franc but allows him to benefit from its depreciation? The answer is yes and the technique is the currency option hedge.

Currency option contracts

A currency option contract is available from either banks or organized exchanges. If you buy a currency **call option,** you have the right to *buy* a stated amount of currency at an agreed upon exchange rate (the **exercise** or the **strike price**) from the seller, or **writer,** of the option. If you buy a currency **put option,** you have the right to *sell* the stated amount of currency at the exercise rate of the option to the writer of the option. The **expiration,** or **maturity, date** of an option is the date after which the option can no longer be exercised. For a **European option,** the exercise of the right can only take place at the maturity date; for an **American option,** the option can be exercised at any time before the maturity date.

Over-the-counter (OTC) options are usually written by banks. As for forward contracts, banks can tailor the currency, size, and expiration date of foreign exchange options to the specific needs of their clients.

Exchange traded options have standard sizes and maturity dates, usually similar to those of futures contracts, with, again, a clearing corporation guaranteeing that the trade will eventually take place.[4] As in the futures market, trades are marked-to-market daily and the clearing corporation imposes stringent margin requirements. However, only the option writer is required to deposit collateral. The owner of the option does not have to deposit collateral because he is not obligated to purchase the underlying currency after the option is purchased.

An option is valuable for its owner because it gives him the right, *but not the obligation,* to buy or sell a currency at a predetermined exchange rate. The price of this right is determined in the option markets. Exhibit 13.4 shows how option prices, also called **option premiums,** are listed in the Philadelphia Options Exchange, as reported in *The Wall Street Journal.*

The currency option hedge

If our distributor of champagne decides to hedge his French franc exposure with options, he will buy a three-month French franc *call* option. This will give him the right to buy French francs at a predetermined exchange rate (the exercise rate). He is not obligated to exercise the option, and he will not do so if the exchange rate is unfavorable. For example, if the spot rate of the French franc in three months is lower than the exercise rate of the option, the distributor will not exercise his option and, instead, will buy the needed francs in the spot market. On the other hand, if the spot rate is higher than the exercise rate, he will exercise his option to get the francs at a lower rate. The option hedge provides a flexibility that is absent in a forward or futures hedge. However, this flexibility comes with a price, which is the price of the option.

To illustrate, suppose the distributor can buy from his bank a three-month French franc European call option at 0.005 dollars per franc, with an exercise rate of

---

[4]Today, only a few exchanges trade in options where the underlying asset is the currency to be bought or sold, the biggest being the Philadelphia Stock Exchange (PHLX) in the United States. Most currency option exchanges now trade in currency futures where the underlying asset is a currency futures contract. When such an option is exercised, one receives a futures contract on the specified currency instead of the currency. The biggest exchanges in which options on currency futures are traded are also the most active currency futures markets (IMM, LIFFE and SIMEX).

EXHIBIT 13.4   Currency Options on Feburary 3, 1998.

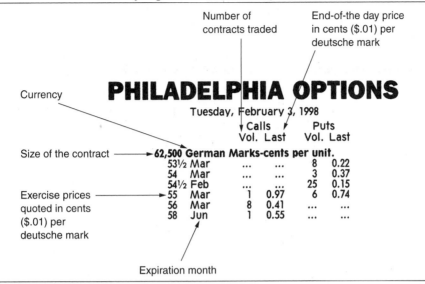

	Number of contracts traded	End-of-the day price in cents ($.01) per deutsche mark

PHILADELPHIA OPTIONS

Tuesday, February 3, 1998

		Calls		Puts	
		Vol.	Last	Vol.	Last
62,500 German Marks-cents per unit.					
53½	Mar	...	...	8	0.22
54	Mar	...	...	3	0.37
54½	Feb	...	...	25	0.15
55	Mar	1	0.97	6	0.74
56	Mar	8	0.41	...	...
58	Jun	1	0.55	...	...

Currency

Size of the contract

Exercise prices quoted in cents ($.01) per deutsche mark

Expiration month

Source: *The Wall Street Journal*, February 4, 1998.

16 cents per franc. This means (1) The distributor must now pay the bank 0.005 dollars per franc, or $3,000 for FRF600,000 ($0.005 multiplied by 600,000 francs) and (2) in three months, the distributor can buy 600,000 French francs from the bank at 16 cents per franc for a total of $96,000 ($0.16 multiplied by 600,000 francs). Whether or not the distributor will exercise the option in three months depends on the USD/FRF exchange rate prevailing at that time. Exhibit 13.5 examines four cases corresponding to the following exchange rates in three months: FRF/USD6.00, FRF/USD6.15, FRF/USD6.25, and FRF/USD6.40.

If the exchange rate is FRF/USD6.00 (USD/FRF0.1667), the distributor will exercise his option because he will be able to buy at 16 cents what is worth 16.67 cents. He will get the FRF600,000 for $96,000 ($0.16 multiplied by FRF600,000) from the bank (the seller of the option) and pay his supplier of champagne. However, the option cost $3,000, so the total cost of the champagne will be $99,000 ($96,000 plus $3,000). If the exchange rate is FRF/USD6.15 (USD/FRF0.1626), he will also exercise his option and the total cost of the champagne will remain at $99,000. If the exchange rate is FRF/USD6.25 (USD/FRF0.16), that is, if it is equal to the exercise rate, there is no longer any incentive for the distributor to exercise the option because he can get the FRF600,000 in the spot market at the same exchange rate. For any USD/FRF exchange rate higher than the exercise rate of 16 cents per franc (or for any FRF/USD exchange rate *lower* than FRF/USD6.25), the distributor will exercise his option and the total cost of the champagne will be $99,000.

If the exchange rate is FRF/USD6.40 (USD/FRF0.1563), the distributor will not exercise his option to buy at 16 cents what is worth only 15.63 cents. He will buy

EXHIBIT 13.5 Comparison of Currency Option Costs for Four Exchange Rates.

Spot rate in three months' time FRF/USD	USD/FRF	Exercise rate USD/FRF	Will the option be exercised?	Dollar amount paid for FRF600,000	Cost of option	Total cost
6.00	0.1667	0.16	Yes	$96,000	$3,000	$99,000
6.15	0.1626	0.16	Yes	$96,000	$3,000	$99,000
6.25	**0.16**	**0.16**	**No**	**$96,000**	**$3,000**	**$99,000**
6.40	0.1563	0.16	No	$93,750	$3,000	$96,750

the FRF600,000 in the spot market at FRF/USD6.40 for a total cost of $93,750 (FRF600,000 divided by FRF/USD6.40) and pay his supplier. However, because he paid $3,000 for the option, the total cost of the champagne will be $96,750 ($93,750 plus $3,000). For any USD/FRF spot rate lower than the exercise rate of 16 cents per franc (or for any FRF/USD exchange rate higher than FRF/USD6.25), the distributor will let the option expire without exercising it and exchange dollars for francs at the spot rate. And the lower the USD/FRF exchange rate, the lower the dollar cost of the champagne.

Exhibit 13.6 shows the net result of the option hedge for the distributor for a wide range of spot rates in three months. The hedge accomplishes the dual goal of (1) protecting the distributor from an appreciation of the French franc by setting an upper limit to the dollar amount he will have to pay for the champagne ($99,000) and (2) allowing him to benefit from a depreciation of the French franc. If the French franc rises above the exercise rate (the FRF/USD rate drops below 6.25), the distributor will exercise his right to buy French francs at that rate; thus, he limits the dollar cost of the FRF600,000 to $99,000, the amount he will pay the bank ($96,000) when exercising the option plus the cost of the option ($3,000). However, if the French franc falls below the exercise rate (the FRF/USD rate rises above 6.25), the distributor will not exercise his option. The dollar cost of the FRF600,000 will be equal to FRF600,000 multiplied by the spot rate in three months plus the $3,000 cost of the option.

WHICH HEDGING TECHNIQUE TO CHOOSE?

Before deciding which technique to use in hedging a currency exposure created by a particular transaction, a manager must first decide if a hedge is needed at all. A hedge is not needed if another business unit belonging to the firm has a currency exposure that is the opposite of the one created by the transaction. However, a business unit manager is not usually informed of the size and timing of the currency

EXHIBIT 13.6   The Option Hedge for the U.S. Champagne Distributor.

Contractual exposure: FRF600,000 to be paid in three months time.

3-month call option price: USD/FRF0.005

Exercise price: $0.16 per franc or FRF/USD6.25

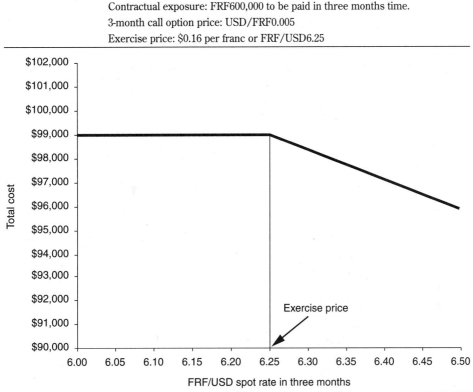

exposure of other business units. This is the reason why large firms engaging in foreign trade have a centralized foreign currency management group that constantly monitors the firm's *net exposure* on a currency-by-currency basis and makes the required hedging decisions. Having all the business units' currency exposures consolidated and managed by a central unit prevents the multiplication of unnecessary and costly hedges.

Currency risk exposure can be further reduced using a procedure known as **leading and lagging.** This process consists of timing the cash inflows and outflows from the different foreign business units to minimize the firm's *overall* exposure to exchange rate risk. For example, if a U.S. company has to make a payment in Japanese yen, it can ask its Japanese subsidiary—assuming it has one—for an early payment of the same amount of yen on any of the subsidiary's outstanding debt to the parent company. This procedure is known as *leading.* If the parent is owed money denominated in yen, it can delay the payment of some of its debt to the subsidiary until that money is received. This procedure is called *lagging.*

What hedging technique should our champagne distributor use? We have shown that a forward hedge is preferable to a futures hedge for eliminating his

EXHIBIT 13.7   The Forward and Option Hedges for the U.S. champagne Distributor.

Contractual exposure: FRF600,000 to be paid in three months' time

3-month forward rate: FRF/USD6.25

3-month call option price: USD/FRF0.005

Option exercise price: $0.16 per franc or FRF/USD6.25

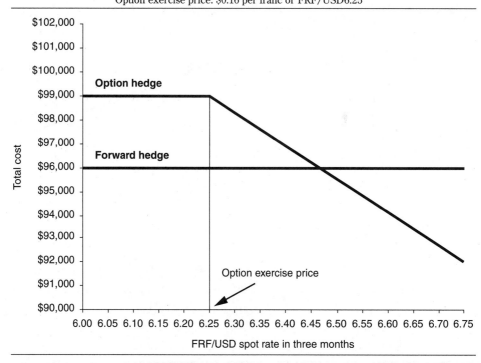

FRF600,000 exposure. What about an option hedge? Exhibit 13.7 shows the net dollar cost of the FRF600,000 when using either the forward hedge or the option hedge for different spot rates in three months. The difference in the outcomes of the two hedging techniques is clear. With a forward hedge, the net cost is $96,000 regardless of the prevailing spot rate in three months. Furthermore, the distributor knows that cost when he enters the contract. With an option hedge, the net cost depends on the spot rate in three months, with the cost limited to $99,000. Thus, the choice depends on the distributor's opinion of future changes in the USD/FRF spot rate. If he strongly believes the French franc will depreciate in the following three months, he may consider that the extra cost of the option hedge—if it turns out the French franc appreciates—is not large enough to dissuade him from taking a chance. However, if he has no strong opinion about future currency movements, he may prefer the certainty of the forward hedge to the uncertain outcome of the costlier option alternative.

EXHIBIT 13.8 **Corporate Use of Currency Forward, Option, and Futures Contracts in Hedging Currency Risk.**

TYPE OF INSTRUMENT	USED OFTEN
Forward contracts	72.3%
Over-the-counter currency options	18.8%
Exchange traded currency options	5.4%
Currency futures contracts	4.1%

Source: Kurt Jesswein, Chuck C.Y. Kwok, and William R. Folks, Jr., "What New Currency Risk Products Are Companies Using and Why?" *Journal of Applied Corporate Finance* 8, Fall 1995, pages 115-124.

Exhibit 13.8 shows the results of a recent survey regarding the use of forward, futures, and option contracts in hedging currency risk by 173 large U.S. corporations. Clearly, the currency forward contract is the favorite hedging tool, followed by the currency option and futures contracts. Note that exchange traded instruments, such as traded options or futures contracts, are not used very often, which may imply that corporations prefer instruments tailored to their particular needs as opposed to those that are more liquid, but standardized.

HEDGING LONG-TERM CONTRACTUAL EXPOSURE TO CURRENCY RISK WITH SWAPS

Although currency forward, futures, and option contracts can be designed for any duration, in practice, they are most often used to hedge short-term exposure to currency risk. A banker may be willing to offer a customized currency forward or option contract for more than a year's maturity, but the risk premium would be high. The longer the contract, the higher the risk that unanticipated events may affect the firm's ability to honor the contract. In addition, the choice for futures or traded options is limited to the contracts available in the market, which, typically, have less than a year's maturity.

To hedge long-term contractual exposure to currency risk, a firm may prefer to enter a **currency swap contract,** or simply a **currency swap,** with its bank. According to the currency swap agreement, the firm will deliver a set of future cash flows denominated in the currency to be hedged in exchange for a set of cash flows denominated in the currency of its choice.

As an illustration, suppose a U.S. company has arranged a five-year, $10 million loan from an American bank to finance its operations in Singapore. The coupon rate, payable annually, is 10 percent or one million dollars. The finance officer of the firm decided against borrowing Singapore dollars (SGD) from a Singapore bank because she could not get the same attractive credit terms as on U.S. dollars borrowed in the

United States. The best quote she could get in Singapore was 9 percent, a 2 percent premium over the prime rate prevailing in Singapore; the rate on the U.S. dollar loan was only 1 percent over the U.S. prime rate. However, the firm is now exposed to exchange rate risk because Singapore dollars (the currency of the firm's income from its operations in Singapore) will need to be exchanged for U.S. dollars to make interest payments and repay the principal on the U.S. dollar loan. But the firm did not need to take this risk. The finance officer could have simply entered a USD/SGD swap agreement with a bank dealing in swaps at the same time she arranged the loan. Under this agreement, the bank would pay the company the U.S. dollars needed to service the $10 million loan, and in exchange, the company would make simultaneous payments in Singapore dollars to the bank. In addition, there would also be an initial and final exchange of the principals. For example, the agreement could result in the cash flows for the company shown in Exhibit 13.9.

From the U.S. dollar loan, the company would receive $10 million in exchange for paying $1 million of interest every year for five years and repaying the $10 million at the end of the fifth year (line 1). From the swap agreement, these U.S. dollar cash flows would be exchanged for Singapore dollars (line 2). The net result would be a series of cash flows, all denominated in Singapore dollars. The initial cash inflow of 15 million Singapore dollars would be followed by five annual payments of 1.2 million and a final payment of 15 million Singapore dollars at the end of the fifth year (line 3). In other words, the swap agreement would transform the U.S.-dollar loan into a Singapore-dollar loan, thus eliminating the currency risk exposure generated by the U.S. dollar debt. Furthermore, the interest rate on the Singapore dollar loan would be 8 percent (1.2 million dollars divided by 15 million dollars), which is lower than the 9 percent rate the company would have paid if it had borrowed the 15 million dollars from a Singapore bank.

This illustration is one of the simplest forms of a currency swap. A more complex one is the swap of a floating coupon rate debt for a fixed coupon rate debt. This type of swap is particularly suited to the needs of most corporate borrowers who prefer fixed financing costs to variable ones but who have better access to the floating-rate bond market than to the fixed-rate bond market. By entering a fixed-for-floating currency swap, they can easily, and cheaply, transform their variable financial obligations into fixed ones and, at the same time, reduce their exposure to exchange rate risk.

EXHIBIT 13.9   Cash Flows for $10 Million Swap Agreement.

Figures in millions

	Initial cash flows		Cash flows: Year 1–4		Cash flows: Year 5	
	USD	SGD	USD	SGD	USD	SGD
1. U.S. dollar loan	+10		−1		−11	
2. Swap agreement	−10	+15	+1	−1.2	+11	−16.2
3. Net cash flow	0	+15	0	−1.2	0	−16.2

THE RELATIONSHIPS AMONG EXCHANGE RATES, INFLATION RATES, AND INTEREST RATES

Which factors determine changes in exchange rates? Intuition tells us that if inflation in country A is expected to be higher than inflation in country B, we can expect country's A currency to weaken relative to country's B currency. At the same time, we would also expect interest rates in country A be higher than interest rates in country B because of country's A higher inflation rate. We would also suspect that forward rates and future spot rates are related. In the following sections, we examine the **parity relations** that link the spot exchange rates, the forward exchange rates, the interest rates, and the inflation rates. Appendix 13.2 provides a detailed analysis of each of these relationships and shows how the rates are linked to one another.

EXCHANGE RATES AND INFLATION RATES: THE PURCHASING POWER PARITY RELATION

The **purchasing power parity (PPP) relation** says that exchange rates should adjust so that the same basket of goods will cost the same in different countries. It is based on the following premise: If the price of goods increases faster in one country than in another because the inflation rate is higher in the first country than in the second, then the exchange rate between the two countries should move to offset the difference in inflation rates and, consequently, the difference in prices. More formally, according to the PPP relation:

Expected future spot rate = current spot rate

$$\times \frac{1 + \text{expected inflation rate in the home country}}{1 + \text{expected inflation rate in the foreign country}}$$

If $S_{h/f}^0$ is the current spot rate and $E(S_{h/f}^1)$ is the expected future spot rate in one year, both expressed in units of the home currency per unit of the foreign currency, and if $E(i_h)$ and $E(i_f)$ are the expected inflation rates for next year at home and in the foreign country, respectively, then:

$$E(S_{h/f}^1) = S_{h/f}^0 \times \frac{1 + E(i_h)}{1 + E(i_f)} \tag{13.1}$$

To illustrate this relationship, suppose that next year's expected inflation rate is 2 percent in the United States and 4 percent in France. Further, suppose that the current spot rate is FRF/USD6.25 or USD/FRF0.16. We have: $E(i_h) = E(i_{US}) = 0.02$, $E(i_f) = E(i_{FR}) = 0.04$, and $S_{h/f}^0 = S_{USD/FRF}^0 = \text{USD/FRF0.16}$. Substituting these values in equation 13.1, we get next year's expected USD/FRF spot rate:

$$E(S_{USD/FRF}^1) = \text{USD/FRF0.16} \times \frac{1 + 0.02}{1 + 0.04} = \text{USD/FRF0.157}$$

The value of one French franc expressed in U.S. dollars is expected to drop from USD/FRF0.16 to USD/FRF0.157. In other words, the U.S. dollar is expected to **appreciate** relative to the French franc. Conversely, the French franc is expected to **depreciate** relative to the U.S. dollar. In our example, the expected appreciation of the U.S. dollar relative to the French franc, expressed as a percent, is:

$$\frac{0.16 - 0.157}{0.16} = 0.019 = 1.9\%$$

Appendix 13.2 shows that when the expected inflation rate of the foreign country is small enough (less than 10 percent), equation 13.1 can be written as:

$$\frac{E(S_{h/f}^1) - S_{h/f}^0}{S_{h/f}^0} = E(i_h) - E(i_f) \tag{13.2}$$

Equation 13.2 is a simpler version of the PPP relation. It says that the expected percentage change in the spot rate, in units of the home currency per unit of the foreign currency, is equal to the expected difference in the inflation rates between the home country and the foreign country. Using the expected inflation rates from the above example, the difference between the expected French and U.S. inflation rates is 2 percent (4 percent in France minus 2 percent in the United States). Thus, according to the simpler version of the PPP relation, the expected appreciation of the U.S. dollar relative to the French franc should be close to 2 percent, which is about a tenth of a percent higher than the 1.9 percent predicted by the PPP relation as given in equation 13.1.

The empirical evidence for the PPP relation is mixed. Many studies show that the relation usually does a poor job of forecasting spot rates in the near future (especially when differences in inflation rates are small). Also, the PPP relation requires a long-term forecast of inflation rates. However, if we need to forecast long-term exchange rates, such as in converting cash flows from a foreign currency to a home currency in the valuation of a cross-border long-term investment project, no other known forecast appears to be superior to the PPP relation.

INFLATION RATES AND INTEREST RATES

Suppose that today you decide to invest $100 in a one-year bank deposit carrying an interest rate of 7.12 percent. This rate, which is the one the bank will *actually* pay you in one year, is called the **nominal interest rate.** Alternatively, with the same amount of money, you could buy 100 bottles of Evian water at your local supermarket. Suppose too, that the inflation rate in the United States is expected to be 4 percent during the coming year and that inflation will affect all goods and services equally. In other words, you expect your local supermarket to charge you $104 for 100 bottles of Evian at the end of the year.

In a year, the bank deposit will be worth $107.12 [$100 times (1 + 7.12 percent)]. With this cash, you can expect to increase the amount of Evian you can buy from 100 bottles to 103 bottles ($107.12 divided by $1.04 per bottle), that is, by 3 percent. In other words, what you expect to *really* earn from your investment is 3 percent, not 7.12 percent. This 3 percent rate is referred to as the **real interest rate.** The difference between the real interest rate and the nominal interest rate reflects, obviously, the expected rate of inflation.

An investor is willing to lend money only if he is compensated for the effect of expected inflation. For example, suppose the real interest rate is 3 percent. If the expected inflation rate is zero, no compensation is needed and the real and nominal interest rates are both equal to 3 percent. However, if the expected inflation rate is 5 percent, the *nominal* rate of interest must be such that one dollar invested now at this rate will grow at the 3 percent *real* rate of interest to become $103 [$100 multiplied by (1+3 percent)] and will also grow at the 5 percent expected inflation rate to become $108.15 [$103 multiplied by (1+5 percent)]. To generalize, we have:

1 + nominal interest rate = (1 + real interest rate) × (1 + expected inflation rate)

If r denotes the *nominal* rate of interest, r_r denotes the real rate of interest, and $E(i)$ denotes the expected inflation rate:

$$1 + r = (1 + r_r) \times (1 + E(i)) \tag{13.3}$$

Solving for r, we get:

$$r = r_r + E(i) + r_r E(i) \tag{13.4}$$

If the expected inflation rate, $E(i)$, is small enough, the term $r_r E(i)$ becomes insignificant and:

$$r = r_r + E(i) \tag{13.5}$$

In this case, the nominal interest rate is simply the sum of the real interest rate and the expected inflation rate. Equations 13.4 and 13.5 indicate that any change in the expected inflation rate is reflected in the nominal interest rate. This effect is known as the **Fisher effect.**

If real interest rates are different between two countries, capital will flow from the country with the lower rate to the country with the higher rate until the rates are equalized. Appendix 13.2 shows that the Fisher effect then implies the following relationship between interest rates and expected inflation rates in the home and foreign country:

$$\frac{1 + r_h}{1 + r_r} = \frac{1 + E(i_h)}{1 + E(i_f)} \tag{13.6}$$

A reasonable approximation of equation 13.6 is:

$$r_h - r_f = E(i_h) - E(i_f) \tag{13.7}$$

Equation 13.7 clearly shows that the difference in interest rates between two countries reflects the difference in their expected inflation rates. This effect is known as the **international Fisher effect.** Most, but not all, of the time, empirical evidence supports the international Fisher effect, especially between countries with open financial markets.

EXCHANGE RATES AND INTEREST RATES: THE INTEREST RATE PARITY RELATION

The **interest rate parity (IRP) relation** describes how the difference in interest rates between two countries is related to the difference between their forward and spot exchange rates. More precisely, if $F_{h/f}^0$ is the forward rate (in units of home currency per unit of foreign currency), $S_{h/f}^0$ is the spot rate, and r_h and r_f are the nominal rates of interest in the home country and the foreign country, we have:

$$\frac{F_{h/f}^0 - S_{h/f}^0}{S_{h/f}^0} = \frac{r_h - r_f}{1 + r_f} \tag{13.8}$$

Appendix 13.2 shows that interest rate parity must hold because of the actions of interbank traders who try to take advantage of any deviation from the parity relation.

The interest rate parity relation is better known under the following simplified version, which assumes that r_f is small compared to one:

$$\frac{F_{h/f}^0 - S_{h/f}^0}{S_{h/f}^0} = r_h - r_f \tag{13.9}$$

Equation 13.9 says that the percentage difference between the forward and the spot rates is equal to the difference in interest rates between the home country and the foreign country.

There is ample evidence that the interest rate parity relation holds in the real world, at least for short-term interest rates. Indeed, when there is no active market for a forward rate, banks often quote their clients a rate computed from the interest rate parity relation.

FORWARD RATES AND FUTURE SPOT RATES

Suppose the one-year forward rate between the U.S. dollar and the French franc is USD/FRF0.18. Would anyone be willing to *buy* francs forward if the *spot rate* in one year is expected to be USD/FRF0.16? No; no one would enter into a contract which states that, at some future date, an asset (French francs in our case) must be bought at a higher price than the market price expected to prevail on that date. Would anyone be willing to *sell* French francs forward if the *spot rate* in one year is expected to be FRF/USD0.2? No again; no one would enter into a contract which states that, at some future date, an asset must be sold at a lower price than the market price expected to prevail on that date. Thus, in equilibrium, the *expected* future spot rate must be equal to USD/FRF0.18. In other words, the forward rate should be equal to the expected future spot rate.

If $E(S^1_{h/f})$ is the expected value of the spot rate one year from now and $F^0_{h/f}$ is the present forward rate (both in units of home currency per unit of foreign currency), the following relation must hold:

$$F^0_{h/f} = E(S^1_{h/f}) \tag{13.10}$$

Dividing both sides of this equation by $S^0_{h/f}$ and then subtracting 1 from both sides, we get:

$$\frac{F^0_{h/f} - S^0_{h/f}}{S^0_{h/f}} = \frac{E(S^1_{h/f}) - S^0_{h/f}}{S^0_{h/f}} \tag{13.11}$$

The empirical evidence for this relation is not clear-cut because risk was not taken into consideration when deriving it. The expected spot rate is only a forecast of what the spot rate will be in the future. The actual rate, which will only be revealed in one year, could be higher or lower. By entering into a forward contract, you fix the price at which you will sell (or purchase) French francs. In effect, you eliminate the currency risk. To eliminate the risk, you are willing to sell (buy) French francs forward at a lower (higher) price than the expected spot price. Despite their failure to properly account for risk, equations 13.10 and 13.11 tend to hold *on average.*

PUTTING IT ALL TOGETHER

Exchange rates fluctuate constantly. The relationships we have presented show how these fluctuations are linked to changes in fundamental economic variables, such as inflation rates and interest rates. These relationships are summarized in Exhibit 13.10. The links among the parity relations are caused by the actions of **arbitrageurs,** the traders in the financial markets who try to make a riskless profit from price discrepancies, mostly in exchange rates (spot and forward) and interest rates across countries. We should expect that the lower the barriers to the free movement of capital flows, the swifter the action of arbitrageurs and the more likely that the parity relations will hold.

When a firm engages in cross-border activities, these relations have some important managerial implications. For example, the purchasing power parity relation can be used to forecast future exchange rates in the analysis of cross-border investment projects. Furthermore, these relations help to avoid classic mistakes, such as trying to increase profit from operations by buying currencies when they go down and selling them when they go up. If you borrow to accomplish these transactions, what you may gain on the foreign exchange transaction you would lose in interest income. The only time you could gain is when the change in the exchange rate is higher than the difference between the interest rates. Another

EXHIBIT 13.10 The Fundamental Relationships Among Spot Exchange Rates, Forward Exchange Rates, Inflation Rates, and Interest Rates.

THE RELATION	WHAT DOES IT SAY?	THE SIMPLIFIED VERSION OF THE RELATION
Purchasing Power Parity (PPP)	Spot exchange rates adjust to keep the cost of living the same across countries. As a consequence, the expected percentage change in the spot rate is equal to the difference in the expected inflation rates between the two countries.	$$\frac{E(S^1_{h/f}) - S^0_{h/f}}{S^0_{h/f}} = E(i_h) - E(i_f)$$ Equation 13.2
International Fisher Effect	The difference in interest rates between two countries is equal to the difference in their expected inflation rates.	$$r_h - r_f = E(i_h) - E(i_f)$$ Equation 13.7
Interest Rate Parity	The percentage difference between the forward and spot exchange rates is equal to the difference in the interest rates between the two countries.	$$\frac{F^0_{h/f} - S^0_{h/f}}{S^0_{h/f}} = r_h - r_f$$ Equation 13.9
Expected Spot Rate and Forward Rate	The percentage difference between the forward rate and the spot rate is equal to the percentage difference between the expected spot rate and the current spot rate.	$$\frac{F^0_{h/f} - S^0_{h/f}}{S^0_{h/f}} = \frac{E(S^1_{h/f}) - S^0_{h/f}}{S^0_{h/f}}$$ Equation 13.11

$E(S^1_{h/f})$ = expected spot rate one year from now expressed in units of home currency per unit of foreign currency.
$S^0_{h/f}$ = current spot rate expressed in units of home currency per unit of foreign currency.
$E(i_h)$ = expected inflation rate in the home country during the next year.
$E(i_f)$ = expected inflation rate in the foreign country during the next year.
r_h = one-year interest rate in the home country.
r_f = one-year interest rate in the foreign country.
$F^0_{h/f}$ = forward rate now in units of home currency per unit of foreign currency.

example is the classic illusion that borrowing at the low Swiss franc rate is cheaper than borrowing at the dollar rate, when indeed they should be the same (on average) after accounting for the expected changes in exchange rates.

ANALYZING AN INTERNATIONAL INVESTMENT PROJECT

Chapter 6 shows how to use the net present value (NPV) rule to select investment projects that create value and reject those that destroy value. The objective of value maximization applies to any management decision, so the NPV rule is also applicable to the decision to invest in a foreign country. However, there are two new factors that must be taken into account. First, the project's future cash flows are usually denominated in a foreign currency with an exchange rate that may fluctuate; second, there is the risk that the cash flows may be affected by changes in local regulations governing foreign investments, a risk we refer to as country risk or political risk. These complications make the NPV rule more difficult to apply.

After a brief review of the NPV rule, we consider Surf'n Zap, a U.S. manufacturer of a small remote control device, called Zap Scan, that can automatically show selected programs on a TV set at regular and brief intervals of time. After a successful entry in the U.S. market, the firm wants to export the device to Europe and has to decide where to locate its regional distribution center. The choice is between Switzerland and Zaragu, two countries with significantly different political risks.

THE NET PRESENT VALUE RULE: A BRIEF REVIEW

The net present value rule is the subject of Chapter 6. Here, we present the rule and review its implications for investment decisions. Let CF_0 be the investment's initial cash outlay, that is, the amount of cash that has to be invested today, and CF_1, CF_2, CF_3, . . . , CF_N, the sequence of future cash flows that the project is *expected* to generate over its useful life. The last cash flow, CF_N, includes the receipts from the liquidation of the investment. Let k be the project's cost of capital, that is, the return that investors *require* from investments that have the same risk characteristics as the project. The net present value (NPV) of the investment is defined as follows:

$$NPV = -CF_0 + \left[\frac{CF_1}{1+k} + \frac{CF_2}{(1+k)^2} + \frac{CF_3}{(1+k)^3} + \ldots + \frac{CF_N}{(1+k)^N} \right]$$

where the sum in brackets is the present value, or the value today, of the expected future cash-flow stream. Notice that the more distant the cash flows, the lower their contribution to the project's present value because the discount factor $1/(1+k)^t$ decreases with time. Note also that the higher the project's risk, the higher the rate of return (k) required by investors and the lower the discount factor, thus, the lower the present value of the expected cash-flow stream. In other words, everything else the same, a riskier project is less desirable because it has a lower NPV.

According to the NPV rule, a project must be accepted when its NPV is positive and rejected when its NPV is negative. The rule simply means that if the present value of the benefits generated by the project (the present value of the future expected cash flows) is larger than the cost of undertaking the investment (the initial cash outlay, CF_0), then the project will create value for the firm's owners and, consequently, must be undertaken. Otherwise, it must be rejected because it will destroy value. The NPV indicates how much richer (or poorer) the firm's investors will be if they put their money in the project rather than in an alternative investment with the same risk characteristics. An NPV equal to zero does not mean that the project has a zero return. It simply means that the project will not change the wealth of investors if undertaken.

SURF'N ZAP CROSS-BORDER ALTERNATIVE INVESTMENT PROJECTS

To export Zap Scan to Europe, Surf'n Zap needs to set up a distribution center there. After an extensive search for the most convenient location, the choice was reduced to two countries, Switzerland and Zaragu. Both countries are located in the center of Europe and from a logistical point of view, neither one appears superior to the other. However, while investing in Switzerland would not carry any country risk, Zaragu has recently been the subject of unfavorable articles in the press. Analysts are concerned that the country's monetary situation may deteriorate in the future and that the earnings from the subsidiaries of foreign companies located in Zaragu may soon be subject to a "foreign" tax in addition to the regular corporate tax. The local currency is the Swiss Franc (CHF) in Switzerland and the zaragupa (ZGU) in Zaragu. Financial data on the alternative projects' cash flows are presented in Exhibit 13.11.

The cost of acquiring and refurbishing a building plus the project's startup costs are estimated at CHF25 million for the Swiss alternative and at ZGU230 million for the Zaragu alternative. It is expected that the investment will last five years, at which time digital TV sets with incorporated zapping devices will make Zap Scan obsolete. The annual cash flows in Exhibit 13.11 are *net of all local and U.S. taxes*. It is estimated that the building can be sold for CHF20 million or ZGU250 million (after taxes) at the end of the fifth year.

The inflation rate in Switzerland has been remarkably stable in the past, at about 2 percent a year, and it is not expected to behave differently during the next few years. In Zaragu, the inflation rate has continuously increased during the recent past. It is now at 10 percent a year and is expected to stay at this level for the foreseeable future. In the United States, the inflation rate is expected to average 3 percent a year for the next five years.

The current spot exchange rates are CHF/USD1.1 and ZGU/USD10. Finally, the rate of return required by Surf'n Zap from its distribution centers in the United

EXHIBIT 13.11 The Zap Scan Project.

Cash flows in millions

	SWITZERLAND ALTERNATIVE IN SWISS FRANCS (CHF)	ZARAGU ALTERNATIVE IN ZARAGUPA (ZGU)
Initial cash outlay	25.0	230
Annual cash flows		
Year 1	4.0	50
Year 2	4.8	60
Year 3	5.0	65
Year 4	5.1	70
Year 5	5.2	75
Liquidation value in year 5	20.0	250
Current annual inflation rate	2%	10%
Current spot exchange rate	CHF/USD1.1	ZGU/USD10

States is 10 percent. Furthermore, Surf'n Zap requires that the NPV for all projects be estimated in U.S. dollars.

The NPV of the Swiss alternative

To compute the NPV of the Swiss alternative of the Zap Scan project, we need to estimate both the project's expected cash flows and its cost of capital in U.S. dollars. The project's cash flows, taken from Exhibit 13.11, are shown in the first row of Exhibit 13.12. To convert these Swiss franc cash flows into their U.S. dollar equivalents, we need to forecast the year-end USD/CHF spot rate for the next five years. We can use the purchasing power parity (PPP) relation to predict these future spot rates.

As indicated in equation 13.1, the PPP relation relates the expected changes in the spot exchange rates to the expected inflation rates in the home country and the foreign country. The inflation rates in the United States and in Switzerland are expected to be 3 percent and 2 percent, respectively, in the near future, so we can use these values for the expected inflation rates $E(i_h)$ and $E(i_f)$ in equation 13.1. To find the expected value of the year-end USD/CHF spot exchange rate for years 1 to 5, we start with the current spot exchange rate of USD/CHF0.9091 (1 divided by CHF/USD1.1). We then solve equation 13.1 successively for each year using the expected spot rate from the previous year. For year 1:

$$E(S^1_{USD/SFR}) = USD/SFR0.9091 \times \frac{1 + 0.03}{1 + 0.02} = SFR/USD0.9180$$

For year 2:

$$E(S^2_{USD/SFR}) = USD/SFR0.9180 \times \frac{1 + 0.03}{1 + 0.02} = SFR/USD0.9270$$

EXHIBIT 13.12 The Zap Scan Project's Expected Cash Flows from the Swiss Alternative.

	INITIAL	END OF YEAR 1	END OF YEAR 2	END OF YEAR 3	END OF YEAR 4	END OF YEAR 5
Expected cash flows in millions of Swiss francs (CHF)						
Annual cash flow	(25.0)	4.0	4.8	5.0	5.1	5.2
Cash flow from liquidation						20.0
Total cash flow	(25.0)	4.0	4.8	5.0	5.1	25.2
Estimation of the USD/CHF spot rate using PPP (Equation 13.1)						
Swiss expected inflation rate		2%	2%	2%	2%	2%
United States expected inflation rate		3%	3%	3%	3%	3%
Current exchange rate: USD/CHF	0.9091					
Expected future spot rate: USD/CHF		0.9180	0.9270	0.9361	0.9453	0.9545
Expected cash flows in millions of U.S. dollars (USD)						
Total cash flow in USD	(22.727)	3.672	4.450	4.681	4.821	24.053
Net Present Value at 10% = USD6.034 million						

458

The result of this calculation for years 1 to 5 is shown in Exhibit 13.12. The expected U.S. dollar value of the project's cash flows is obtained by multiplying the Swiss franc cash flows by the expected exchange rates.

To compute the project's NPV we need to estimate the cost of capital. Surf'n Zap requires a return of 10 percent from its distribution centers in the United States. Should the firm use the same cost of capital for the Swiss alternative or should it use a higher one to account for exchange rate risk, that is, for the probability that the future USD/CHF exchange rate may be different from the expected one? Recall from Chapter 10 that the risk that matters to investors is not the *total* risk of the investment but only the portion of the risk that cannot be reduced or eliminated by diversification. If we assume the portfolios of Surf'n Zap shareholders include either shares of foreign companies or shares of U.S. firms with international business activity, we can assume the shareholders have already eliminated the portion of the Zap Scan project risk associated with USD/CHF exchange rate volatility. In this case, no premium should be added to the domestic (U.S.) cost of capital to account for the exchange rate risk. What if Surf'n Zap shareholders are not diversified internationally? In this case, the Swiss project gives them the opportunity to become diversified, albeit indirectly. As a consequence, the risk of their portfolio of assets would be *reduced,* which would imply a *lower* required rate of return for the project.

Using a cost of capital of 10 percent and the project's expected cash flows in Exhibit 13.12, we can now estimate the project's NPV in millions of U.S. dollars:

$$NPV_{Switzerland} = -USD22.727 + \frac{USD3.672}{1 + 0.1} + \frac{USD4.450}{(1 + 0.1)^2}$$
$$+ \frac{USD4.681}{(1 + 0.1)^3} + \frac{USD4.821}{(1 + 0.1)^4} + \frac{USD24.053}{(1 + 0.1)^5}$$

$$NPV_{Switzerland} = USD6.034 \text{ million}$$

The NPV is positive, so the Swiss project would create value for Surf'n Zap investors. But would the Zaragu project create more value?

The NPV of the Zaragu alternative

The procedure for estimating the expected value of the Zaragu project's cash flows is the same as the one we used for the Swiss alternative. We estimate the U.S. dollar value of the project's expected future cash flows and then discount these cash flows at the project's cost of capital. The PPP relation is again used to estimate the year-end USD/ZGU spot rates for the next five years, using the expected inflation rates in the United States and Zaragu. The cash flows in zaragupas are converted into their U.S. dollar equivalents using the predicted spot rates. The results of our estimation are shown in Exhibit 13.13.

If we assume for a moment that there is no country risk in the Zaragu alternative, there is no need to adjust the project cost of capital for exchange rate risk.

EXHIBIT 13.13 The Zap Scan Project's Expected Cash Flows for the Zaragu Alternative Without Country Risk.

	Initial	End of Year 1	End of Year 2	End of Year 3	End of Year 4	End of Year 5
Expected cash flows in millions of zaragupas (ZGU)						
Annual cash flow in ZGU	(230)	50	60	65	70	75
Cash flow from liquidation in ZGU						250
Total cash flow in ZGU	(230)	50	60	65	70	325
Estimation of the USD/ZGU spot rate using PPP (Equation 13.1)						
Zaragu expected inflation rate		10%	10%	10%	10%	10%
United States expected inflation rate		3%	3%	3%	3%	3%
Current exchange rate USD/ZGU	0.1000					
Expected future spot rate USD/ZGU		0.0936	0.0877	0.0821	0.0769	0.0720
Expected cash flows in millions of U.S. dollars (USD)						
Total cash flow in USD	(23)	4.680	5.262	5.336	5.383	23.400
Net Present Value at 10% = USD7.818 million						

Thus, *in the absence of country risk,* the project cost of capital in the Zaragu alternative is 10 percent, the same as the rate used for similar projects in the United States or Switzerland. Using the U.S. dollar denominated cash flows from Exhibit 13.13, the NPV of the Zaragu alternative is:

$$\text{NPV}_{\text{Zaragu}}^{\text{no country risk}} = -\text{USD}23 + \frac{\text{USD}4.680}{1 + 0.1} + \frac{\text{USD}5.262}{(1 + 0.1)^2} + \frac{\text{USD}5.336}{(1 + 0.1)^3}$$
$$+ \frac{\text{USD}5.383}{(1 + 0.1)^4} + \frac{\text{USD}23.400}{(1 + 0.1)^5}$$

$$\text{NPV}_{\text{Zaragu}}^{\text{no country risk}} = \text{USD}7.818 \text{ million}$$

However, as mentioned earlier, the project will be exposed to country risk because there is some probability that the authorities in Zaragu will impose a "foreign" tax on the project's earnings. To account for this risk, most firms systematically add a risk premium to their domestic cost of capital. We disagree with this procedure for three reasons. First, if we assume that shareholders have already eliminated the country risk by holding a well-diversified portfolio of assets, we do not need to make any adjustment at all. Second, there is no rational way to estimate the size of the risk premium for the particular risk that needs to be taken into account. For example, in the Zaragu alternative, should it be 1, 2, or 10 percent? No one knows. Third, simply adding an arbitrary "fudge" factor to the domestic cost of capital may lead to complacency and prevent managers from thoroughly assessing the impact of country risk on the project.

We suggest that any adjustment for country risk should be made on the project's *expected cash flows* rather than on the cost of capital. An expected cash flow is just a weighted average of the values that the cash flow can take in the future, where the weights are the probability that the cash flow will actually take these values. Thus, we can adjust these cash flows to reflect the likelihood of any form of country risk. If this is done, there is no need to adjust the cost of capital. Furthermore, the estimation of the expected cash flows forces managers to make a thorough analysis of country risk and its impact on the project.

Suppose that after a careful analysis of economic trends in Zaragu, we estimate that there is a 20 percent probability that a monetary crisis will occur at some time during the project's life. Should such a crisis erupt, we can expect the project's earnings to be subjected to a "foreign" tax. When such a tax was imposed in the past, the tax rate was always 25 percent. There is no reason to expect that the rate will be different during the next monetary crisis, so we can apply the same rate to the project. To avoid cumbersome computations, we also assume that the project's *earnings,* which will be subjected to the "foreign" tax, represent, each year, 90 percent of the project's operating cash flows in the absence of "foreign" tax.[5]

---

[5]Recall that taxes are paid on earnings not cash flows. See Chapters 4 and 8 for the conversion of cash flows into earnings for the purpose of estimating the amount of tax payment.

Exhibit 13.14 presents the detailed computation of the project's expected cash flows, taking into account the risk that the "foreign" tax will be imposed on the project. The first section of the exhibit shows the cash flows in the absence of tax taken from Exhibit 13.13. The next section presents the computation of the operating cash flows net of the "foreign" tax if the tax is imposed. The third section shows the computation of the project's expected cash flows, taking into account the probability that the project will be subjected to the tax. If the probability of taxation is 20 percent during the life of the project, the project's *expected* cash flows are the cash flows net of the "foreign" tax multiplied by 20 percent plus the cash flows without the tax multiplied by 80 percent because there is 20 percent chance that the first outcome will occur and 80 percent chance that the second will occur. The last part of the exhibit shows the dollar value of the expected cash flows, using the same expected future exchange rates as in Exhibit 13.13. The NPV of the project, obtained by discounting the cash flows at the 10 percent cost of capital, is:

$$NPV_{\text{Zaragu}}^{\text{with country risk}} = -USD23 + \frac{USD4.471}{1 + 0.1} + \frac{USD5.024}{(1 + 0.1)^2} + \frac{USD5.096}{(1 + 0.1)^3}$$
$$+ \frac{USD5.139}{(1 + 0.1)^4} + \frac{USD23.151}{(1 + 0.1)^5}$$

$$NPV_{\text{Zaragu}}^{\text{with country risk}} = USD6.930 \text{ million}$$

The NPV with country risk is USD888,000 lower than without country risk ($7.818 million less $6.930 million), an 11 percent reduction in value. The difference in NPV between the Zaragu and Swiss alternatives is USD896,000 ($6.930 million less $6.034 million) and is in favor of the Zaragu alternative. Then, should the distribution center be located in Zaragu? The answer depends on how confident we are in the assumptions we used to reach our conclusion.

We made two critical assumptions that could have a significant impact on our result. The first is that the purchasing power parity relation holds between the U.S. dollar and the two foreign currencies. The second is that the probability assessment of the imposition of a "foreign" tax on the project is reliable. More generally, the second assumption refers to the probability that a portion or all of a project's cash flows accruing to the parent will be expropriated and the form this expropriation will take. The only realistic way to improve our confidence in our analysis of the project is to do a *sensitivity analysis* that will show how responsive the project's NPV is to changes in the assumptions. For example, scenarios can be developed using percentage deviations from the purchasing power parity combined with different forms of expropriation that can be expected from the country in which the project would be located. Only then can a decision be made that fully accounts for the project's risk.

In the relatively simple case of the Zap Scan project, the sensitivity analysis can be aimed at the responsiveness of the project's NPV to changes in the probability of having the project subject to a "foreign" tax. Repeating the same computations as in Exhibit 13.14, we estimated the project's NPV with a range of probabilities from

EXHIBIT 13.14 The Zap Scan Project's Expected Cash Flows for the Zaragu Alternative with Country Risk.

	INITIAL	END OF YEAR 1	END OF YEAR 2	END OF YEAR 3	END OF YEAR 4	END OF YEAR 5
Expected cash flows in the absence of a "foreign" tax on the project's earnings, in millions of zaragupas (ZGU)						
Annual cash flow in ZGU	(230)	50	60	65	70	75
Cash flow from liquidation in ZGU						250
Total cash flow in ZGU	(230)	50	60	65	70	325
Expected operating cash flows in the presence of a "foreign" tax on the project's earnings, in millions of zaragupas (ZGU)						
Project's earnings (90% of cash flow) in ZGU		45.000	54.000	58.500	63.000	67.500
"Foreign" Tax (25% of earnings) in ZGU		(11.250)	(13.500)	(14.625)	(15.750)	(16.875)
Annual operating cash flow net of tax in ZGU	(230)	38.750	46.500	50.375	54.250	58.125
Expected cash flows in millions of zaragupas (ZGU)						
Probability that the earnings will be taxed		20%	20%	20%	20%	20%
Annual operating cash flow in ZGU	(230)	$0.2 \times 38.750 + 0.8 \times 50.000 = 47.750$	$0.2 \times 46.500 + 0.8 \times 60.000 = 57.300$	$0.2 \times 50.375 + 0.8 \times 65.000 = 62.075$	$0.2 \times 54.250 + 0.8 \times 70.000 = 66.850$	$0.2 \times 58.125 + 0.8 \times 75.000 = 71.625$
Cash flow from liquidation						250
Total cash flow	(230)	47.750	57.300	62.075	66.850	321.625
Expected cash flows in millions of U.S. dollars (USD)						
Expected spot rate USD/ZGU	0.1	0.0936	0.0877	0.0821	0.0769	0.0720
Total cash flow in USD	(23)	4.471	5.024	5.096	5.139	23.151
Net Present Value at 10% = USD6.930 million						

EXHIBIT 13.15 **The Zap Scan Project's Net Present Value (NPV) for the Zaragu Alternative as a Function of the Probability of the Project being Subjected to the "Foreign" Tax**

Probability that the project will be subjected to the "foreign" tax	0%	10%	20%	30%	40%	50%
Project NPV in USD millions	7.814	7.373	6.930	6.489	6.047	5.605

zero to 50 percent. The results are reported in Exhibit 13.15. The probability for which the NPV of the Zaragu project is the same as the NPV of the Swiss project (USD6.034 million) is approximately 40 percent. This probability is twice the expected probability of 20 percent. The difference is large enough to decide that, despite the presence of some country risk, the Zap's Scan project should be located in Zaragu rather than in Switzerland.

MANAGING COUNTRY RISK

The previous section analyzes the impact on a cross-border investment's NPV if a "foreign tax" is imposed on the cash flows expected from the investment. As indicated earlier in the chapter, the possibility of a special tax being levied on foreign investments is only one aspect of the country, or political, risk that firms confront when investing abroad. The purpose of country risk management is to limit the exposure of the parent company to these direct or indirect impediments to the transfer of funds from its foreign investments. The following sections discuss a few actions that can help a manager design a proactive strategy for managing country risk.

INVEST IN PROJECTS WITH UNIQUE FEATURES

Projects that depend on input or output markets that are controlled by the parent company are less likely to be expropriated by a local government than projects that use raw materials or sell products and services that are readily available worldwide. Projects that require an expertise unique to the parent company are also less likely to be expropriated. For example, if a plant can only be operated by foreign nationals, the local government may not impose discriminatory regulations on the foreign affiliate for fear of having the plant shut down.

USE LOCAL SOURCING

Buying goods and services locally can reduce political risk because it increases local production and local employment. However, the benefits need to be weighed against the risk of having lower quality products or services, unreliable delivery schedules, or high local prices.

CHOOSE A LOW-RISK FINANCIAL STRATEGY

Country risk can be substantially reduced if an agency of the host country government or a powerful international institutional investor is included as a minority shareholder or lender in the cross-border project. The host government is less likely to impose restrictions on dividends or interest payments made by a firm in which either itself or an international investor such as the World Bank or the International Finance Corporation (IFC)[6] is one of the firm's shareholders or bondholders. Furthermore, because dividends to the parent are usually the first remittance from the subsidiary to be limited, blocked, or taxed, it is usually preferable to finance a cross-border investment with as little equity as possible.

DESIGN A REMITTANCE STRATEGY

Dividends or interest payments are not the only way for a parent company to be compensated from its investments in a foreign country. Royalties, management fees, transfer prices, and technical assistance fees are other forms of remittances that can be used to complement financial transfers. Because these transfers of funds are payments for goods and services, they are usually the last on the list of transfer payments to be restricted. However, a manager should not wait for the imposition of controls on dividends or interest payments to set a new funds transfer policy because the move will undoubtedly be seen by the host government as a means of circumventing the new regulation. Any remittance strategy must be implemented long before the imposition of restrictions on transfer payments.

CONSIDER BUYING INSURANCE AGAINST POLITICAL RISK

In many developed countries, government sponsored institutions provide insurance against political risk. Firms should consider buying such insurance for investments made in high-risk countries if alternative measures are difficult or costly to implement. Even if the insurance is not purchased, the insurance premium can be used to estimate the impact of political risk on the NPV of the cross-border investment. If we assume the insurance policy eliminates the impact of any expropriation of the investment's cash flows, the present value of the insurance premium payments during the useful life of the project represents the amount by which the project's NPV should be reduced to account for political risk. This approach, contrary to

---

[6]The International Finance Corporation is a subsidiary of the World Bank, which takes equity positions in privately financed investment projects.

sensitivity analysis, does not rely on the subjective assessment of the consequences of the political risk on the project's expected cash flows.

However, the present value of the insurance premium payments may underestimate the true "cost" of political risk because most insurance policies only cover the accounting value of the cross-border investment, which can be lower than the true value of the damages suffered by the parent company. Also, the insurance is provided by institutions that are generally set up by governments for the purpose of encouraging firms to invest in high-risk countries. Thus, the premium may be somewhat subsidized and be lower than the premium that would have been required by the private insurance market to cover the same level of risk.

SUMMARY

The fundamental principle of financial management still holds in an international environment. Foreign operations must be managed with the objective of creating shareholder value. However, the need to deal with more than one currency raises a number of issues that are specific to the management of foreign operations.

A firm is confronted with several risks when operating in a foreign environment. Changes in exchange rates affect the firm's financial statements. To account for this accounting, or translation, exposure, regulators have established rules that firms may use to translate the financial statements of a foreign business unit into home currency units. The two most commonly used translation methods are the monetary/nonmonetary method and the current rate method. Movements in the exchange rate also affect the value of the cash flows from the foreign business unit, an effect usually called economic exposure. Economic exposure is classified into two types of exposure: (1) contractual, or transaction, exposure, which refers to the impact of exchange rate volatility on the future cash flows from *past* transactions, and (2) operating exposure, which is also concerned with future cash flows, but from *future* transactions. Finally, firms with foreign operations may also be subject to political or country risk arising from an unstable political environment.

The world's largest financial market, the foreign exchange market, is actually a network of banks, dealers, brokers, and multinational corporations communicating with each other by telephone and through computer terminals. Two basic types of transactions take place in the foreign exchange market. A spot transaction is an agreement to exchange currencies at a rate fixed today with the delivery taking place usually within two business days. A forward transaction is also an agreement to exchange currencies at a rate fixed today, with the delivery taking place at some specific date several months in the future.

To hedge economic exposure, firms use a variety of financial instruments, such as forwards, futures, options, and swaps. Firms can use these instruments to reduce and control their contractual exposure to currency risk.

Differences in expected inflation rates and interest rates between countries are the major factors governing the fluctuations in exchange rates. Three fundamental relations, known as the parity relations, link these variables. The purchasing power parity (PPP) relation links exchange rates and inflation rates. The interest rate parity relation relates exchange rates to interest rates. And, the current forward exchange rate is linked to the future spot rate.

The chapter presents a detailed analysis of the decision to invest in a foreign country. A cross-border investment project, like a domestic one, creates value only if its net present value is positive. But it is more complicated to estimate the NPV of a foreign investment than that of a domestic one. First, most of the cash flows from an investment in a foreign country are denominated in the foreign currency and, second, these cash flows may be subject to political or country risk. To convert cash flows denominated in a foreign currency into cash flows denominated in the domestic currency, we recommend using the PPP relation. The converted cash flows will have some exchange rate risk attached to them because there is some probability that future exchange rates may differ from those estimated by the parity relation. In principle, the cost of capital needs to be adjusted in order to account for this extra risk. However, in practice no adjustment is necessary because most shareholders own diversified portfolios in which the exchange rate risk has already been eliminated. To account for the effect of country risk on the NPV of a cross-border investment, we recommend adjusting the expected cash flows for the specific actions that the host government may take to reduce the parent company's claims on the project, rather than adding a "fudge" factor to the project's cost of capital. We also recommend that a sensitivity analysis be performed to show how responsive the project's NPV is to different assumptions regarding the form and the extent of possible expropriation measures.

Finally, country risk can be managed by using techniques and mechanisms that are aimed at reducing the parent's exposure to the expropriation of its foreign investments or to restrictions on the transfer of funds from its foreign subsidiaries.

13.1 TRANSLATING FINANCIAL STATEMENTS WITH THE MONETARY/NONMONETARY METHOD AND THE CURRENT METHOD

THE MONETARY/NONMONETARY METHOD

In the monetary/nonmonetary method, monetary assets, such as cash and accounts receivable, and monetary liabilities, such as accounts payable, accrued expenses, and short-term and long-term debts, are translated at the exchange rate prevailing on the date of the balance sheet. The nonmonetary items, such as inventories and fixed assets, are estimated using the rate prevailing at the date they were entered in the balance sheet—the historical rate. The logic of this approach is that monetary assets and monetary liabilities are contracted amounts that would be redeemed at a rate that is likely to be closer to the rate prevailing on the date of the balance sheet than to the historical rate. The average exchange rate of the reporting period is used to translate the income statement accounts, except for those accounts related to the nonmonetary items, such as depreciation expenses, which are translated at the same rate as the corresponding balance sheet item. Any gain or loss from translating balance sheet accounts is reflected in the income statement and, as a result, affects reported earnings.

The top part of Exhibit A13.1 shows how the balance sheet accounts at year-end 1997 of the French subsidiary of Uncle Sam's Bagel are translated into U.S. dollars according to the monetary/nonmonetary method. Two possible values are shown for the exchange rate, USD/FRF0.15 and USD/FRF0.165, where USD refers to the U.S. dollar and FRF refers to the French franc. The dollar value of cash, trade receivables, trade payables, and financial debt is obtained by multiplying their French franc value by the exchange rate that will prevail on December 31, 1997. The dollar value of inventories and fixed assets is the same regardless of the exchange rate at year-end 1997 because, as nonmonetary assets, their value is determined by the exchange rate on the date when they were recorded in the

EXHIBIT A13.1 Monetary/Nonmonetary Method Applied to the Balance Sheet of the French Subsidiary of Uncle Sam's Bagel on December 31, 1997.

Figures in thousands

	MONETARY/NONMONETARY METHOD			
	VALUE IN FRENCH FRANCS (FRF)	VALUE IN U.S. DOLLARS (USD)		CHANGE IN U.S. DOLLARS
		EXCHANGE RATE ON DECEMBER 31, 1997		
		USD/FRF0.15	USD/FRF0.165	
Assets				
Cash	50,000	50,000 × 0.15 = 7,500	50,000 × 0.165 = 8,250	+750
Accounts receivable	100,000	100,000 × 0.15 = 15,000	100,000 × 0.165 = 16,500	+1,500
Total monetary assets	*150,000*	*22,500*	*24,750*	*+2,250*
Inventories	100,000	16,500	16,500	—
Property, plant and equipment	250,000	46,000	46,000	—
Total nonmonetary assets	*350,000*	*62,500*	*62,500*	*—*
Assets	**500,000**	**85,000**	**87,250**	**+2,250**
Liabilities				
Short-term debt	75,000	75,000 × 0.15 = 11,250	75,000 × 0.165 = 12,375	+1,125
Accounts payable	75,000	75,000 × 0.15 = 11,250	75,000 × 0.165 = 12,375	+1,125
Long-term debt	250,000	250,000 × 0.15 = 37,500	250,000 × 0.165 = 41,250	+3,750
Total monetary liabilities	*400,000*	*60,000*	*66,000*	*+6,000*
Owners' Equity (Assets-Liabilities)	**100,000**	**25,000**	**21,250**	**−3,750**
Liabilities & Owners' Equity	**500,000**	**85,000**	**87,250**	**+2,250**

In the monetary/nonmonetary method, monetary assets and liabilities are translated at the exchange rate on the date of the balance sheet, and nonmonetary assets are valued at the rate when they were entered in the balance sheet.

balance sheet, not on the date of the balance sheet. The dollar value of the subsidiary's owners' equity, which is the difference between the dollar value of its assets and that of its liabilities, depends on the exchange rate at the end of the year. It will be $25 million if the exchange rate is USD/FRF0.15 and $21.250 million if the exchange rate is USD/FRF0.165. The difference, $3.750 million, is equal to the difference between the change in the value of the monetary liabilities and the change in the value of the monetary assets ($6 million less $2.250 million). Note, however, that owners' equity changes in the opposite direction of the change in the exchange rate; it *decreases* when the exchange rate *increases* from USD/FRF0.15 to USD/FRF0.165. This is not surprising because, as long as monetary liabilities are larger than monetary assets, an *appreciation* of the foreign currency (the U.S. dollar cost of one French franc increases) will increase the dollar value of the firm's liabilities relative to that of its assets, thus reducing the dollar value of its owners' equity. For most firms, the value of monetary liabilities is greater than the value of monetary assets, so an *appreciation* of the foreign currency will usually result in a *translation loss* when using the monetary/nonmonetary method. A *depreciation* of the foreign currency will result in a *translation gain.*

THE CURRENT METHOD

In the **current method,** known as FASB (for Financial Accounting Standards Board) 52, *all* the balance sheet assets and liabilities are translated at the exchange rate on the balance sheet date. The income statement accounts can be translated either at the exchange rate at the date when the revenues and expenses are incurred or at the average exchange rate of the period. To avoid large variations in reported earnings, which may be caused by large fluctuations in the exchange rate, translation gains or losses are reported in a separate equity account of the parent balance sheet. The logic behind the current method approach is that it does not distort the structure of the balance sheet as the monetary/nonmonetary method does because all the assets and liabilities are affected proportionally by changes in exchange rates.

Exhibit A13.2 shows how the balance sheet accounts of the French subsidiary of Uncle Sam's Bagel are translated according to the current method, using the same data as in Exhibit A13.1 where the monetary/nonmonetary method is applied to these accounts. When the exchange rate increases from USD/FRF0.15 to USD/FRF0.165, the dollar value of *all* the French subsidiary's assets and liabilities increase by the same proportion as the exchange rate (10 percent). As a result, owners' equity also increases by the same proportion, from $15 million to $16.5 million. Contrary to the previous method, the current method always shows a *translation gain* when the foreign currency *appreciates* and a *translation loss* when the foreign currency *depreciates.*

EXHIBIT A13.2 Current Translation Method Applied to the Balance Sheet of the French Subsidiary of Uncle Sam's Bagel on December 31, 1997.

Figures in thousands

	VALUE IN FRENCH FRANCS (FRF)	VALUE IN U.S. DOLLARS (USD) EXCHANGE RATE ON DECEMBER 31, 1997 USD/FRF0.15	VALUE IN U.S. DOLLARS (USD) EXCHANGE RATE ON DECEMBER 31, 1997 USD/FRF0.165	CHANGE IN U.S. DOLLARS
		CURRENT METHOD		
Assets				
Cash	50,000	$50,000 \times 0.15 = 7,500$	$50,000 \times 0.165 = 8,250$	+1,250
Accounts receivable	100,000	$100,000 \times 0.15 = 15,000$	$100,000 \times 0.165 = 16,500$	+1,500
Inventories	100,000	$100,000 \times 0.15 = 15,000$	$100,000 \times 0.165 = 16,500$	+1,500
Property, plant and equipment	250,000	$250,000 \times 0.15 = 37,500$	$250,000 \times 0.165 = 41,250$	+3,750
Assets	**500,000**	**75,000**	**82,500**	**+7,500**
Liabilities				
Short-term debt	75,000	$75,000 \times 0.15 = 11,250$	$75,000 \times 0.165 = 12,375$	+1,125
Accounts payable	75,000	$75,000 \times 0.15 = 11,250$	$75,000 \times 0.165 = 12,375$	+1,125
Long-term debt	250,000	$250,000 \times 0.15 = 37,500$	$250,000 \times 0.165 = 41,250$	+3,750
Total monetary liabilities	*400,000*	*60,000*	*66,000*	*+6,000*
Owners' Equity (Assets-Liabilities)	*100,000*	*15,000*	*16,500*	*+1,500*
Liabilities & Owners' Equity	**500,000**	**75,000**	**82,500**	**+7,500**

In the current method, all assets and all liabilities are translated at the exchange rate on the date of the balance sheet.

WHICH METHOD IS BETTER?

The difference between the monetary/nonmonetary method and the current method comes from a different valuation of the nonmonetary assets. The first method values them at the historical exchange rate, and the second values them at the current exchange rate. Which is the right approach? Neither approach is right because managing for value creation implies that the relevant value of a firm's assets is their *market* value, not their book value. Whichever method we use to translate the book value of assets from one currency to another, we always get book values, never market values.

Which method do most companies use? Most companies use the current rate method, simply because it is recommended by most accounting regulating bodies worldwide. Why do the regulating bodies favor the current method? Given that neither of the approaches presents a definitive advantage over the other, we believe that their choice is based on practical considerations. The current method is easier to apply and also easier to understand. Another reason why the current method is preferred by most managers may be based on the difference in the treatment of gains or losses from translation adjustments. The monetary/nonmonetary method includes them in the computation of reported income, but the current method does not. Because most managers' performance measures are derived from reported income, it may make sense to account for the impact of changes in exchange rates (over which managers have little control) separately from other sources of gain or loss.

13.2 THE PARITY RELATIONS

THE LAW OF ONE PRICE

Suppose there are no transaction costs (such as transportation costs or taxes) when buying gold in one country, say the United States, and selling it in another, say France. Also, assume the following:

1. The current spot rate is USD/FRF0.18 (18 cents per French franc).
2. Gold can be bought for USD300 an ounce in New York.
3. Gold can be sold at FRF1,750 an ounce in Paris.

Under these conditions, buying gold in New York and selling it in Paris looks like El Dorado. A trader can buy one ounce of gold in New York at USD300, send it to Paris, and sell it there for FRF1,750. The FRF1,750 can be exchanged for USD315 (FRF1,750 multiplied by USD/FRF0.18). The net profit is USD15 (USD315 less USD300). The possibility of making such a riskless arbitrage profit will not remain unnoticed for long. Arbitrageurs will strike and their actions will quickly move prices and exchange rates until the price of gold in New York and Paris is the same whether the currency is denominated in U.S. dollars or French francs. Extending this market mechanism to any traded good, we obtain the **law of one price (LOP),** according to which any traded good will sell for the same price regardless of the country where it is sold.

The law of one price can be written as:

$$\mathbf{P_h} = \mathbf{P_f} \times \mathbf{S_{h/f}^0}$$

where P_h is the price of a good in the home country, P_f is the price of the same good in a foreign country, and $S_{h/f}^0$ is the spot exchange rate today expressed in units of the home currency per unit of the foreign currency.

For the LOP to be true, some assumptions are necessary. For example, transaction costs must be zero, tax systems must be identical all over the world, and regulations (both real and hidden) must not prevent cross-country exchanges. The real world of international trade does not operate in such a frictionless fashion. As an example of the inability of the price of a good to settle at the same level across the countries where it is available, Exhibit A13.3 compares the U.S. dollar price of a "Big Mac" hamburger in different countries in April 1998, where prices are calculated at the spot exchange rate prevailing at the time. If the LOP worked perfectly, the exchange rates would adjust so that the U.S. dollar price of a "Big Mac" would be the same across countries. Note the large spread of values from one country to another, which indicates that the assumptions behind the LOP are far from holding true in the real world.[7]

THE PURCHASING POWER PARITY (PPP) RELATION

The purchasing power parity (PPP) relation is a version of the law of one price with less stringent assumptions. It states that the *general cost of living* should be the same across countries, not the cost of any individual good as the LOP requires. Suppose the USD/FRF exchange rate is 0.18 (18 cents per French franc) and the inflation rate next year is expected to be 2 percent in the United States and 4 percent in France. A basket of goods that currently costs $0.18 will cost $0.1836 in the United States next year [18 cents times (1 + 2 percent)], and will cost 1.04 francs in France next year [one franc times (1 + 4 percent)]. The PPP relation implies that the spot rate must change so that next year one U.S. dollar exchanged into French francs would still buy the same basket of goods. In other words, according to the PPP relation, the spot rate *expected* to prevail next year must be USD/FRF0.1836 divided by FRF1.04 or USD/FRF0.176.

According to the PPP relation, we can write:

$$E(S^1_{h/f}) = S^0_{h/f} \times \frac{1 + E(i_h)}{1 + E(i_f)} \tag{A13.1}$$

where $S^0_{h/f}$ is the current exchange rate, measured in units of the home currency per unit of the foreign currency; $E(S^1_{h/f})$ is the expected exchange rate in one year's time, measured in units of the home currency per unit of the foreign currency; and $E(i_h)$ and $E(i_f)$ are the expected inflation rates for next year at home and in the foreign country, respectively. Equation A13.1 is the same as equation 13.1.

Dividing both sides of equation A13.1 by $S^0_{h/f}$, we get:

$$\frac{E(S^1_{h/f})}{S^0_{h/f}} = \frac{1 + E(i_h)}{1 + E(i_f)}$$

---

[7]If this spread can be partly attributed to differences in taste for food, we should add another assumption for the LOP to hold. Food must taste the same for everybody all over the world.

EXHIBIT A13.3 Big Mac Currencies.

THE HAMBURGER STANDARD

	BIG MAC IN LOCAL CURRENCY	PRICES IN DOLLARS	IMPLIED PPP* OF THE DOLLAR	ACTUAL $ EXCHANGE RATE 6/4/98	UNDER(−)/ OVER(+) VALUATION AGAINST DOLLAR, %
United States[†]	**$2.56**	**2.56**	—	—	—
Argentina	Peso2.50	2.50	0.98	1.00	−2
Australia	A$2.65	1.75	1.04	1.51	−32
Austria	Sch34.0	2.62	13.28	12.96	+2
Belgium	BFr109	2.87	42.58	38.00	+12
Brazil	Real3.10	2.72	1.21	1.14	+6
Britain	£1.84	3.05	1.39[‡]	1.66[‡]	+19
Canada	C$2.79	1.97	1.09	1.42	−23
Chile	Peso1,250	2.75	488	455	+7
China	Yuan9.90	1.20	3.87	8.28	−53
Czech Republic	CKr54.0	1.57	21.1	34.4	−39
Denmark	DKr23.8	3.39	9.28	7.02	+32
France	FFr17.5	2.84	6.84	6.17	+11
Germany	DM4.95	2.69	1.93	1.84	+5
Hong Kong	HK$10.2	1.32	3.98	7.75	−49
Hungary	Forint259	1.22	101	213	−52
Indonesia	Rupiah9,900	1.16	3,867	8,500	−55
Israel	Shekel12.50	3.38	4.88	3.70	+32
Italy	Lire4,500	2.47	1,758	1,818	−3
Japan	¥280	2.08	109	135	−19
Malaysia	M$4.30	1.16	1.68	3.72	−55
Mexico	Peso17.9	2.10	6.99	8.54	−18
Netherlands	Fl5.45	2.63	2.13	2.07	+3
New Zealand	NZ$3.45	1.90	1.35	1.82	−26
Poland	Zloty5.30	1.53	2.07	3.46	−40
Russia	Rouble12,000	2.00	4,688	5,999	−22
Singapore	S$3.00	1.85	1.17	1.62	−28
South Africa	Rand8.00	1.59	3.13	5.04	−38
South Korea	Won2,600	1.76	1,016	1,474	−31
Spain	Pta375	2.40	146	156	−6
Sweden	SKr24.0	3.00	9.38	8.00	+17
Switzerland	SFr5.90	3.87	2.30	1.52	+51
Taiwan	NT$68.0	2.06	26.6	33.0	−20
Thailand	Baht52.0	1.30	20.3	40.0	−49

*Purchasing-power parity: local price divided by price in United States
[†]Against dollar
[‡]Average of New York, Chicago, San Francisco, and Atlanta
[††]Dollars per pound
Source: *The Economist,* April 11, 1998.

Subtracting one from both sides of this equation gives:

$$\frac{E(S^1_{h/f})}{S^0_{h/f}} - 1 = \frac{1 + E(i_h)}{1 + E(i_f)} - 1$$

or:

$$\frac{E(S^1_{h/f}) - S^0_{h/f}}{S^0_{h/f}} = \frac{E(i_h) - E(i_f)}{1 + E(i_f)}$$

When the expected inflation rate in the foreign country is small enough, the term $1 + E(i_f)$ is not significantly different from one, yielding the simpler version of the PPP in equation 13.2:

$$\frac{E(S^1_{h/f}) - S^0_{h/f}}{S^0_{h/f}} = E(i_h) - E(i_f) \tag{A13.2}$$

THE INTERNATIONAL FISHER EFFECT

Real and nominal interest rates are related through equation 13.3, also known as the Fisher effect. This equation is:

$$1 + r = (1 + r_r) \times (1 + E(i)) \tag{A13.3}$$

where r is the nominal interest rate, r_r is the real interest rate, and $E(i)$ is the expected inflation rate. We can rearrange the equation to express the real rate of interest (r_r) as a function of the nominal rate of interest (r) and the expected inflation rate, $E(i)$:

$$1 + r_r = \frac{1 + r}{1 + E(i)}$$

or:

$$r_r = \frac{1 + r}{1 + E(i)} - 1 \tag{A13.4}$$

If *real* interest rates are different from one country to another, capital will flow from the countries with the lowest rate to the countries with the highest rate until rates are equalized. In equilibrium, when the real interest rates are the same in all countries, the right side of equation A13.4 must have the same value in all countries, in particular in the home country and in the foreign country. Thus, if r_h and r_f are the nominal interest rates in the home and foreign countries and $E(i_h)$ and $E(i_f)$ are the expected inflation rates in the home and foreign countries, we must have:

$$\frac{1 + r_h}{1 + E(i_h)} = \frac{1 + r_f}{1 + E(i_f)} \tag{A13.5}$$

or:

$$\frac{1 + r_h}{1 + r_f} = \frac{1 + E(i_h)}{1 + E(i_f)} \qquad \text{(A13.6)}$$

As indicated in the text, a reasonable approximation of equation A13.6 is:

$$r_h - r_f = E(i_h) - E(i_f) \qquad \text{(A13.7)}$$

which is the same as equation 13.7. The relation between interest rates and expected inflation rates as expressed by equation A13.6 or A13.7, is known as the **international Fisher effect.**

THE INTEREST RATE PARITY RELATION (IRP)

Suppose you have USD1 million to invest and you observe the following data for the deutsche mark (DEM) and the U.S. dollar:

- Spot exchange rate: USD/DEM0.58
- 12-month forward rate: USD/DEM0.59
- One-year DEM interest rate: 5 percent
- One-year USD interest rate: 6 percent

It appears you will be better off next year if you invest in U.S. dollars rather than deutsche marks today because 6 percent is higher than 5 percent. But is this assumption warranted? No; you cannot compare two interest rates expressed in different currencies. The correct comparison should be between the two investments *expressed in the same currency.* To invest in marks, you will have to change your dollars into marks and, after you cash in your investment in one year, convert the marks you receive back into dollars. By selling these DEMs forward, you will know precisely the dollar amount you will get in one year. If the forward rate is advantageous, it may compensate for a lower interest rate. The two investment strategies are shown in Exhibit A13.4.

Strategy Two (investment in DEM) produces $8,104 more than Strategy One (investment in USD). The gain from buying spot DEMs at USD/DEM0.58 and selling them forward at USD/DEM0.59 is higher than the 1 percent interest rate foregone from lending at 5 percent instead of 6 percent.

Note that to earn the extra $8,104 you do not need to own $1,000,000. You can just borrow this amount at 6 percent, implement Strategy Two, and repay your debt (interest included) in one year. You will still earn a riskless net profit of $8,104. In the competitive world of the foreign exchange market, such "free lunches" will be short-lived. Interbank traders, acting as arbitrageurs, are quick to identify possible arbitrage transactions and immediately trade to benefit from them. In the above example, their actions will result in a higher interest rate differential and a lower spread between spot and forward exchange rates. The process, which is almost

EXHIBIT A13.4   Investing in USD Versus Investing in DEM.

STRATEGY ONE: INVEST IN USD	STRATEGY TWO: INVEST IN DEM
Now:	*Now:*
Invest USD1,000,000 @ 6 percent	1. Convert USD1,000,000 at the current spot rate: $$\frac{\text{USD}1,000,000}{\text{USD/DEM}0.58} = \text{DEM}1,724,138$$ 2. Invest DEM1,724,138 at 5 percent. 3. Sell forward DEM1,724,138 × (1 + 0.05) = DEM1,810,345 at USD/DEM0.59.
In one year:	*In one year:*
Cash in your U.S. dollar investment. You get:	1. Cash in your DEM investment. You get: DEM1,724,138 × (1 + 0.05) = DEM1,810,345
	2. Settle your forward contract and deliver DEM1,810,345. In exchange you receive: DEM1,810,345 × USD/DEM0.59
USD1,000,000 × (1 + 0.06) = USD1,060,000	**= USD1,068,104**

instantaneous, will end when the outcomes of Strategies One and Two are identical. How do these arbitrage transactions affect the spot exchange rate, the forward exchange rate, and the interest rates?

Looking again at the two investment strategies, let r_h and r_f be the nominal rates of interest in the home country and the foreign country, respectively. In Strategy One, for one unit of home currency invested, you will receive $(1 + r_h)$ in home currency a year later. With Strategy Two, you will first have to exchange one unit of the home currency for $1/S_{h/f}^0$ units of the foreign currency, where $S_{h/f}^0$ is the spot exchange rate (in units of home currency per unit of foreign currency). One year later, you will receive $1/S_{h/f}^0 \times (1 + r_f)$ units of foreign currency that will be converted into $[1/S_{h/f}^0 \times (1 + r_f)] \times F_{h/f}^0$ units of home currency, where $F_{h/f}^0$ is the forward rate (in units of home currency per unit of foreign currency). If the net outcomes of the two strategies are the same, then:

$$1 + r_h = \frac{1 + r_f}{S_{h/f}^0} F_{h/f}^0$$

The terms of this equation can be rearranged to obtain:

$$\frac{F_{h/f}^0}{S_{h/f}^0} = \frac{1 + r_h}{1 + r_f}$$

Subtracting one from both sides of the equation gives:

$$\frac{F^0_{h/f}}{S^0_{h/f}} - 1 = \frac{1 + r_h}{1 + r_f} - 1$$

or:

$$\frac{F^0_{h/f} - S^0_{h/f}}{S^0_{h/f}} = \frac{r_h - r_f}{1 + r_f} \tag{A13.8}$$

Equation A13.8 is called the interest rate parity relation. This relation is better known under its following simplified version, which assumes that r_f is small compared to one:

$$\frac{F^0_{h/f} - S^0_{h/f}}{S^0_{h/f}} = r_h - r_f \tag{A13.9}$$

Equation A13.9 says that the percentage difference between the forward and the spot rates is equal to the difference in interest rates. Equations A13.8 and A13.9 are the same as equations 13.8 and 13.9.

REFERENCES AND FURTHER READING

1. Brealey, Richard, and Stewart Myers. *Principles of Corporate Finance.* 5th ed. McGraw-Hill, 1996. See chapter 34.
2. Clark, John, Thomas Hindelang, and Robert Pritchard. *Capital Budgeting: Planning and Control of Capital Expenditures.* 3d ed. Prentice-Hall, 1989. See chapter 26.
3. Ross, Stephen, Randolph Westerfield, and Jeffrey Jaffe. *Corporate Finance.* 4th ed. Irwin, 1996. See chapters 24 and 31.
4. Giddy, Ian. *Global Financial Markets.* D.C. Heath and Company, 1994.
5. Eiteman, David, Arthur Stonehill, and Michael Moffett. *Multinational Business Finance.* 8th ed. Addison-Wesley, 1998.

REVIEW PROBLEMS

13.1. Accounting versus economic exposure.

What is the difference among accounting, translation, economic, transaction, contractual, and operating exposure? Why is economic exposure more relevant than accounting exposure to shareholders?

13.2. Comparing alternative hedging techniques.

Briefly describe how to hedge contractual exposure with forward, futures, option, and swap contracts. What are the main advantages and disadvantages of these four hedging techniques?

13.3. Parity relations.

Indicate in one sentence what the following parity relations say:

a. Purchasing power parity relation

b. International Fisher effect

c. Interest rate parity relation

d. The relation between forward rates and future spot rates

13.4. Political risk and the cost of capital.

The best way to account for political risk is to add a risk premium to the project cost of capital. True or false?

13.5. Hedging with forwards, futures, and options.

MPC imports computer equipment from Japan for sale in the U.S. market. Monthly imports have averaged JPY250 million to JPY275 million over the past year. A similar volume is expected for the coming year. Because of the volatility of the exchange rate between the Japanese yen (JPY) and the U.S. dollar (USD), MPC's management believes that it must hedge these imports. Using the "typical" exposure of JPY250 million for a 90-day period, how should the company manage its current position? Current market data (June 10), for various instruments appear as follows:

- Spot JPY/USD = 124.09
- 90-day forward JPY/USD = 122.42
- September futures = USD0.8222 per 100 yen (JPY12.5 million per contract); delivery date: 17 September
- 90-day yen call OTC option = USD0.021 per 100 yen (JPY124/USD strike price)

13.6. International capital budgeting.

The Kampton Company, an American firm, considers once again investing in France. The investment will cost FRF100 million and is expected to generate, after taxes, FRF25 million a year during the next five years in real terms, that is, before inflation. The project would be liquidated at the end of the fifth year and its terminal value is estimated at FRF25 million. The annual rate of inflation is expected to be 3 percent in France and 4 percent in the United States. The cost of capital used by Kampton for its investments in the European Union is 5 percent above the yield on government bonds. Currently, the rate on U.S. government bonds is 6 percent and the exchange rate is FRF/USD6.0. Calculate the net present value of the project in U.S. dollars.

14 MANAGING FOR VALUE CREATION

Managing for value creation is more than a business slogan. It is a comprehensive approach to management based on the principle that managers at all levels of the organization must manage their firm's resources with the ultimate objective of increasing the firm's market value. Managing with the goal of creating value provides the basis for a comprehensive and integrated *valued-based management* system that helps managers formulate relevant business plans, make sound business decisions, evaluate actual business performance, and design effective management compensation packages.

This chapter reviews the financial principles underlying a value-based management system, examines the advantages and implications of this approach to management, and explains how the system can be implemented. We first show how to measure the value that a firm has created or destroyed. We then identify the key factors that drive the process of value creation and show how firms can align the interests of managers with those of shareholders by tying managers' performance and reward to these drivers of value creation. Finally, we summarize the value-based management approach using a framework we call the *financial strategy matrix*. This matrix is a convenient business diagnostic tool that can be used as a guide to evaluate and make value-based strategic and financing decisions.

Managing to create value for shareholders is not incompatible with a dedicated work force, a loyal customer base, and a cooperative group of suppliers. Increasing a firm's market value does not mean creating shareholder wealth at the expense of employees, customers, or suppliers. On the contrary, no firm can expect to generate value for its shareholders if it does not also provide value for employees, customers, and suppliers. Motivated employees, delighted customers, and efficient suppliers are an integral part of a successful recipe for enhancing the firm's value. As mentioned in Chapter 1, companies that achieved the largest increase in their stock market value over the ten-year period from 1985 to 1995 were also the most admired for their ability to attract and retain better employees and loyal customers. After reading this chapter you should understand:

- The meaning of managing for value creation.
- How to measure value creation at the firm level using the concept of market value added or MVA.
- Why maximizing market value added is consistent with maximizing shareholder value.
- When and why growth may *not* lead to value creation.
- How to implement a management system based on a value-creation objective.
- How to measure a firm's capacity to create value using the concept of economic value added or EVA.
- How to design management compensation schemes that induce managers to make value-creating decisions.

MEASURING VALUE CREATION

To find out whether management has created or destroyed value as of a particular point in time, we compare the *market value* of the firm's total capital (both equity and debt capital) to the amount of capital that shareholders and debtholders have invested in the firm (the firm's capital employed). The difference between these amounts is called the firm's **market value added** or, simply, **MVA:**

Market value added (MVA) = Market value of capital − Capital employed
$$(14.1)$$

If MVA is positive, value has been created because the market value of the firm's capital (equity and debt) is worth more than the amount of capital that has been invested in the firm (this is the term "capital employed" in equation 14.1). If MVA is negative, value has been destroyed.

Consider InfoSoft, a software company created in 1993. As of December 31, 1997, shareholders had injected $280 million of equity capital into the firm and debtholders had lent the firm $100 million. The total amount of capital available to InfoSoft was thus $380 million. The market value of that capital on that date was $500 million. In other words, at year-end 1997, InfoSoft employed $380 million of capital whose market value was worth $500 million. Deducting the amount of capital employed ($380 million) from InfoSoft's market value ($500 million) provides a measure of the amount of value InfoSoft has created as of December 31, 1997:

$$\text{InfoSoft's MVA}_{12/31/1997} = \$500 \text{ million} - \$380 \text{ million} = \$120 \text{ million}$$

MVA is a positive $120 million, indicating that InfoSoft has created $120 million of value as of December 31, 1997.

Suppose the market value of InfoSoft's equity and debt capital was $300 million instead of $500 million. In this case, InfoSoft would have *destroyed* $80 million of value as of December 31, 1997 because the $380 million of capital would be worth only $300 million on that date.

MVA measures value creation or destruction at a *particular point in time*. To measure the value created or destroyed *during a period of time,* look at the *change* in MVA during that period. For example, if InfoSoft's MVA was $140 million a year earlier (December 31, 1996), the firm's management would have destroyed $20 million of value during 1997 ($120 million less $140 million).

ESTIMATING MARKET VALUE ADDED

To estimate a firm's market value added with equation 14.1, we need to know (1) the market value of the firm's equity and debt capital, and (2) the amount of capital that shareholders and debtholders have invested in the firm. We now examine how these items can be estimated.

Estimating the market value of capital

The market value of capital can be obtained from the financial markets, at least for firms whose equity and debt capital are publicly traded in the form of securities. If the firm is not publicly traded, its market value is unobservable and its MVA cannot be calculated. If someone makes an offer to buy the firm, we could then estimate the firm's MVA based on that offer price.

On December 31, 1997, InfoSoft had debt with a market value of $110 million. The firm had 3.9 million shares outstanding that were trading at $100 a share. The market value of its equity (its **market capitalization**) was thus $390 million ($100 multiplied by 3.9 million shares), and the total market value of its capital was $500 million ($110 million of debt plus $390 million of equity). This is the figure we used to estimate InfoSoft's MVA on December 31, 1997.

Estimating the amount of capital employed

The other value needed to measure a firm's MVA is the estimate of the amount of capital employed by the firm. This figure can be extracted from the firm's balance sheet and associated notes. Debt capital includes short-term and long-term borrowings and sources of capital that are equivalent to debt obligations—items such as lease obligations and provisions for the retirement and pension plans of employees. Estimating the amount of equity capital is more complicated. We must add to the book value of equity reported in the balance sheet a number of items that standard accounting conventions *exclude* from the figure shown in the balance sheet.

Exhibit 14.1 presents two versions of InfoSoft's balance sheets on December 31, 1996 and 1997, reported in their managerial format (see Chapter 3). A managerial

EXHIBIT 14.1 InfoSoft's Managerial Balance Sheets on December 31, 1996 and 1997.

Figures in millions of dollars

UNADJUSTED MANAGERIAL BALANCE SHEETS

Invested capital	12.31.96	12.31.97	Capital employed	12.31.96	12.31.97
Cash	$5	$10	Short-term debt	$40	$20
Working capital requirement¹ (net)	100	100	Long-term debt	40	40
Gross working capital requirement	*$105*	*$110*	Lease obligations	40	40
Accumulated bad debt allowance	*(5)*	*(10)*			
Net fixed assets	185	190	Owners' equity	170	200
Property, plant, & equipment (net)	95	110			
Goodwill (net)	90	80			
Gross goodwill	*$100*	*$100*			
Accumulated amortization	*(10)*	*(20)*			
Total	**$290**	**$300**	**Total**	**$290**	**$300**

ADJUSTED MANAGERIAL BALANCE SHEETS

Invested capital	12.31.96	12.31.97	Capital employed	12.31.96	12.31.97
Cash	$5	$10	Total debt capital	$120	$100
			Short-term debt	$40	$20
Gross working capital requirement	105	110	Long-term debt	40	40
			Lease obligations	40	40
Net fixed assets	235	260	Adjusted equity capital	225	280
Property, plant, & equipment (net)	$95	$110	Book value of equity	170	200
Gross goodwill	100	100	Accumulated bad debt allowance	5	10
Capitalized R&D	40	50	Accumulated goodwill amortization	10	20
			Capitalized R&D	40	50
Total	**$345**	**$380**	**Total**	**$345**	**$380**

1. Working capital requirement = (Accounts receivable + Inventories + Prepaid expenses) − (Accounts payable + Accrued expenses).

balance sheet shows the firm's invested capital (cash, working capital requirement[1], and net fixed assets) and the capital the firm employs (equity plus debt) to fund these investments.

The first balance sheets report invested capital and capital employed according to standard accounting conventions (unadjusted balance sheets); the second ones add to invested capital and the book value of equity a number of items that accounting conventions exclude (adjusted balance sheets). The amount of debt capital at year-end 1997 ($100 million) is the same in both types of balance sheets and is equal to the figure we used to estimate InfoSoft's market value added.

What items are added to the book value of equity to get the $280 million figure in the 1997 adjusted balance sheet? These are items, such as **allowance for bad debt,** the amortization of **goodwill,** and research and development (R&D) expenses, that, according to accounting conventions, are arbitrarily classified as expenses and are deducted from profits. The effect of these deductions is to lower both reported profits and retained earnings. With less earnings retained, the equity account in the balance sheet is *understated.*

Invested capital in the 1997 unadjusted balance sheet in Exhibit 14.1 includes $10 million of accumulated bad debt allowance and $20 million of accumulated goodwill amortization. These two items, as well as $50 million of R&D expenses, are added to the $200 million of reported book value of equity to obtain the $280 million figure reported in the 1997 adjusted balance sheet.

Appendix 14.1 shows why and how these adjustments are made. Notice that their impact on the magnitude of InfoSoft's market value added is not trivial. Ignoring them understates InfoSoft's MVA by $80 million.

INTERPRETING MARKET VALUE ADDED

There are several noteworthy observations to make regarding the definition and interpretation of value creation given by equation 14.1. We examine the most significant ones in this section.

Maximizing MVA is consistent with maximizing shareholder value

Strictly speaking, shareholder value creation should be measured by the difference between the market value of the firm's *equity* and the amount of *equity* capital shareholders have invested in the firm. The former represents the financial market estimation of shareholders' investment in their firm and the latter the actual amount of money they invested in it. But, market value added in equation 14.1 is the difference between the market value of *total* capital (equity and debt) and *total* capital

---

[1]Working capital requirement is the difference between the firm's operating assets (accounts receivable + inventories + prepaid expenses) and operating liabilities (accounts payable + accrued expenses). See Chapter 3 for details.

employed. We can reconcile the two definitions by noting that MVA in equation 14.1 is the sum of (1) an *equity MVA,* defined as the difference between the market value of equity and its adjusted book value, and (2) a *debt MVA,* defined as the difference between the market value of debt and its reported book value. Thus, the definition of MVA in equation 14.1 can be restated as:

$$\text{MVA} = \text{Equity MVA} + \text{Debt MVA} \tag{14.2}$$

For InfoSoft, equity MVA is $110 million (equity market value of $390 million less adjusted equity capital of $280 million) and debt MVA is $10 million (debt market value of $110 million less total debt capital of $100 million). These amounts yield a total market value added of $120 million.

If we assume that debt MVA is different from zero *only because of changes in the level of interest rates*[2], then, *for a given level of interest rates,* maximizing MVA is equivalent to maximizing shareholder value (equity MVA). Because the general level of interest rates is determined by macroeconomic variables over which managers do not have any control, one problem with using MVA as a measure of management performance is that MVA is sensitive to variables that cannot be attributed to the performance of managers. In order to isolate the change in MVA attributable to management decisions, we should first neutralize the part that is due to broader market conditions. One corrective measure would be to deduct an estimate of the change in MVA that arises from those broader market conditions.

Maximizing the market value of the firm's capital does not necessarily imply value creation

Suppose InfoSoft's management retains $15 million of profit and borrows $5 million to invest in a $20 million project. Assume that, as a consequence of the investment decision, InfoSoft's market value increases by $16 million (from $500 million to $516 million). Can we conclude that InfoSoft created $16 million of value? The answer is no. It has actually *destroyed* $4 million of value. To see why, calculate the firm's MVA after the project's announcement. It is $116 million ($516 million of market value less $400 million of capital employed—the original $380 million plus the $20 million investment). MVA is now $4 million *less* than it was before the project was announced ($116 million versus $120 million). This is because the company invested $20 million in a project that led to an increase in its market value of only $16 million.

Consider another example that shows why managers should maximize MVA rather than market value. Suppose we compare InfoSoft's market value to the $1,000 million market value of TransTech. Although TransTech's market value is twice that of InfoSoft's, we cannot infer that TransTech has created twice as much value as InfoSoft. Before we can draw any conclusions, we need to know how much

---

[2]In the case of InfoSoft, interest rates have gone down and the market value of its debt has gone up. See Chapter 9 for an explanation of the inverse relationship between changes in interest rates and market values.

capital TransTech is employing. Its adjusted balance sheet (not provided here) indicates that it employs $940 million of capital. Its MVA is thus $60 million ($1,000 million less $940 million), half of InfoSoft's $120 million MVA. Although the market value of TransTech is twice that of InfoSoft, its management has created half the value created by InfoSoft.

MVA increases when the firm undertakes positive net present value projects

Recall the definition of a project's net present value (NPV) given in Chapter 6. It is the present value of the stream of cash flows the project is expected to generate less the amount of capital spent on it. In the MVA definition given by equation 14.1, capital employed is the same as the total amount of capital the firm has invested in its *past* and *current* investment projects. Thus, the present value of the stream of cash flows these investments are expected to generate in the future is the market value of the firm's capital. In other words, *saying that a firm has raised (or reduced) its MVA is the same as saying that it has invested in positive (or negative) NPV projects.* Later in the chapter, we show that the contribution of an investment project to a firm's MVA is indeed equal to the project's net present value.

A LOOK AT THE EVIDENCE

In the fall, *Fortune* magazine publishes a list of the 1,000 largest U.S. industrial and nonfinancial services companies ranked according to their estimated MVA on December 31 of the previous year.[3] Exhibit 14.2 shows the ten companies that achieved the highest MVA and ten companies that had some of the lowest MVA on December 31, 1996. The first column provides the market value of the companies' total capital (equity and debt), and the second column shows the corresponding amount of capital employed (adjusted for accounting distortions). The difference is the companies' estimated market value added reported in the third column. (The data in the last three columns is explained later in the chapter.) There are several noteworthy observations to make about the companies and their MVA.

First, the top ten companies created over $1,000 billion of value as of December 31, 1996, an amount that exceeds the gross national product (GNP) of most countries.

Second, as pointed out earlier, the firm with the highest market value is not necessarily the one that has created the most value: General Electric has the largest market value but ranks second by MVA.

Third, value creation is measured in *absolute* terms. Compare, for example, the performance of Coca-Cola to that of Microsoft. Coca-Cola was the highest *absolute*

---

[3]The list is compiled by Stern Stewart, a New York consulting firm, that provides similar lists for the largest companies in 11 countries. For British companies, see the London *Sunday Times*. For French companies, see the business magazine *L'Expansion*.

EXHIBIT 14.2 Top Value Creators and Destroyers in the United States.

Ranking by Market Value Added on December 31, 1996 (December 31, 1991 ranking in Parentheses)

THE TOP TEN VALUE CREATORS BY MVA	MARKET VALUE OF CAPITAL ($ BILLION)	CAPITAL EMPLOYED ($ BILLION)	VALUE CREATED (MVA)	RETURN ON INVESTED CAPITAL (ROIC)	COST OF CAPITAL (WACC)	ECONOMIC VALUE ADDED ($ BILLION) (EVA)
1. Coca-Cola (4)	135.7	10.8	+124.9	36.0%	9.7%	+2.4
2. General Electric (6)	175.5	53.6	+121.9	17.7%	12.7%	+2.5
3. Microsoft (14)	95.7	5.7	+90.0	47.1%	11.8%	+1.7
4. Intel (74)	104.0	17.5	+86.5	36.4%	13.6%	+3.6
5. Merck (2)	100.4	22.2	+78.2	23.0%	14.5%	+1.7
6. Philip Morris (3)	109.5	42.9	+66.6	20.1%	12.5%	+3.1
7. Exxon (12)	143.9	88.4	+55.5	12.0%	10.4%	+1.3
8. Procter & Gamble (10)	80.1	25.0	+55.1	14.3%	11.9%	+0.6
9. Johnson & Johnson (7)	69.2	18.1	+51.1	21.8%	13.3%	+1.3
10. Bristol-Myers Squibb (11)	57.0	14.1	+42.9	24.1%	12.8%	+1.5

SOME OF THE LARGEST VALUE DESTROYERS BY MVA	MARKET VALUE OF CAPITAL ($ BILLION)	CAPITAL EMPLOYED ($ BILLION)	VALUE DESTROYED (MVA)	RETURN ON INVESTED CAPITAL (ROIC)	COST OF CAPITAL (WACC)	ECONOMIC VALUE ADDED ($ BILLION) (EVA)
1000. General Motors (1000)	62.2	82.9	-20.7	5.9%	9.7%	-3.5
999. RJR Nabisco (992)	23.0	35.0	-12.0	6.2%	9.8%	-1.2
998. Ford Motor (999)	46.4	58.3	-11.9	12.1%	9.1%	+1.7
997. Digital Equipment (997)	8.1	12.0	-3.9	1.0%	13.1%	-1.4
996. Kmart (153)	12.7	14.9	-2.2	2.1%	8.4%	-1.0
992. Occidental Petroleum (967)	16.0	17.5	-1.5	5.1%	8.9%	-0.7
989. Union Pacific (108)	26.7	28.1	-1.4	7.1%	9.4%	-0.5
984. International Paper (429)	25.7	26.7	-1.0	4.8%	8.2%	-0.8
952. Reynolds Metals (957)	6.5	6.7	-0.2	2.1%	10.7%	-0.6
934. Westinghouse Electric (961)	20.0	20.1	-0.1	2.1%	11.6%	-1.6

Source: Fortune (November 10, 1997).

value creator on December 31, 1996, with an estimated MVA of $124.9 billion; Microsoft was ranked third with a lower estimated MVA of $90 million. But if value created is measured *per dollar of capital employed,* Microsoft outperformed Coca-Cola. It created $15.8 of value per dollar of capital employed ($90 divided by $5.7) compared to $11.6 for Coca-Cola ($124.9 divided by $10.8).

Fourth, value-creating companies are found in a diversity of sectors. The top ten come from eight different sectors: soft drinks (Coca-Cola), diversified industrial and financial holdings (General Electric), software publishing (Microsoft), microprocessors (Intel), pharmaceuticals (Merck, Johnson & Johnson, and Bristol-Myers Squibb), tobacco (Philip Morris), oil (Exxon), and consumer goods (Procter & Gamble).

Fifth, the two car companies, which operate in a cyclical, low-margin and capital-intensive industry, are among the largest value *destroyers.* However, a firm's inability to create value cannot be blamed on industry factors alone. Notice the presence of both value-creating and value-destroying companies in the same or closely related sectors: General Electric and Westinghouse Electric, Philip Morris and RJR Nabisco, Microsoft and Digital Equipment, Exxon and Occidental Petroleum, Wal-Mart Stores (ranked 14 in 1997 and first in 1992) and Kmart.

Sixth, although six of the top ten value creators were also ranked among the top ten five years earlier, the rankings are not immutable: Intel went from number 74 up to number 4, and Union Pacific went from number 157 down to number 989. The next section identifies the factors that drive value creation and helps explain why some companies are value creators while others are value destroyers.

IDENTIFYING THE DRIVERS OF VALUE CREATION

A firm's capacity to create value is essentially driven by a combination of three key factors:

1. The firm's operating profitability, measured by its aftertax return on invested capital (ROIC)
2. The firm's cost of capital, measured by its weighted average cost of capital (WACC)
3. The firm's ability to grow

The aftertax return on invested capital (see Chapters 1 and 5) is defined here as the ratio of the firm's **net operating profit after tax (NOPAT)** over its invested capital measured at the *beginning* of the accounting period:[4]

$$\text{ROIC} = \frac{\text{EBIT} \times (1 - \text{tax rate})}{\text{Invested capital}} = \frac{\text{NOPAT}}{\text{Invested capital}}$$

[4]According to the managerial balance sheet (see Exhibit 14.1), invested capital is the same as capital employed. Thus, return on invested capital (ROIC) is the same as return on capital employed (ROCE). It is also the same as return on net assets (RONA) because net assets are the same as invested capital (see Chapter 5). We can thus use these various terms interchangeably.

where EBIT is earnings before interest and tax, NOPAT is aftertax EBIT (it is equal to EBIT multiplied by $(1 - \text{tax rate})$), and invested capital is the sum of cash, working capital requirement[5], and net fixed assets (see Exhibit 14.1).

The weighted average cost of capital or WACC (see Chapters 1 and 10) is:

$$\text{WACC} = [\text{aftertax cost of debt} \times \text{percentage of debt capital}]$$
$$+ [\text{cost of equity} \times \text{percentage of equity capital}]$$

To illustrate, we again consider InfoSoft, which earned $80 million before interest and tax in 1997 (see Appendix 14.1). Its cost of debt is 10 percent, its estimated cost of equity is 14 percent (see Chapter 10 for how to estimate the cost of equity), and it is subject to a 36 percent corporate tax rate. Its adjusted invested capital at the beginning of 1997 (same as the end of 1996) is $345 million, as shown in the adjusted balance sheet in Exhibit 14.1. Based on these figures, InfoSoft's aftertax return on invested capital is:

$$\text{ROIC} = \frac{\$80 \times (1 - 0.36)}{\$345 \text{ million}} = \frac{\$51.2 \text{ million}}{\$345 \text{ million}} = 14.8\%$$

The weighted average cost of capital should be calculated with *market* value weights (see Chapter 11). Recall that the market value of InfoSoft's equity is $390 million (3.9 million shares worth $100 a share) and that of its debt is $110 million. Thus, WACC is:

$$\text{WACC} = 10\% \times (1 - 0.36) \times \frac{\$110 \text{ million}}{\$500 \text{ million}} + 14\% \times \frac{\$390 \text{ million}}{\$500 \text{ million}}$$

$$\text{WACC} = 6.4\% \times 0.22 + 14\% \times 0.78 = 12.3\%$$

Let's see how we can link a firm's capacity to create value to these two rates (ROIC and WACC) and to the firm's rate of growth.

LINKING VALUE CREATION TO OPERATING PROFITABILITY, THE COST OF CAPITAL AND GROWTH OPPORTUNITIES

To help us understand how return on invested capital (ROIC), the cost of capital (WACC), and the expected rate of growth interact to create value, we examine the particular case—without any loss of generality—of a firm that is expected to grow *forever* at a *constant* annual rate. Appendix 14.2 shows that in this case the firm's market value added (MVA) is given by the following valuation formula:

$$\textbf{Market value added} = \frac{(\textbf{ROIC} - \textbf{WACC}) \times \textbf{Invested capital}}{\textbf{WACC} - \textbf{Constant growth rate}} \qquad (14.3)$$

---

[5]See footnote 1 for a definition of working capital requirement.

Note that WACC must be higher than the constant growth rate (see Chapter 12). The following sections discuss two important and general conclusions that can be drawn from equation 14.3.

To create value, expected ROIC must exceed the firm's WACC

The valuation formula (equation 14.3) indicates that a firm creates value only if the return it *expects* to earn on its invested capital (ROIC) is higher than the cost of financing its investments (WACC). As long as the firm's expected ROIC exceeds its estimated WACC, the numerator of the valuation formula is positive and so is MVA, indicating that the firm creates value. Conversely, if the firm's expected ROIC is lower than its estimated WACC, MVA is negative and the firm destroys value. As an illustration of this point, consider InfoSoft. InfoSoft MVA is $120 million, the difference between its market value of $500 million and its invested capital of $380 million. What is driving InfoSoft's capacity to create value? It is the market expectation that InfoSoft's managers will be able to earn a return on invested capital that exceeds the firm's WACC of 12.3 percent[6].

Let's call the difference between ROIC and WACC the firm's **return spread:**

$$\text{Return spread} = \text{ROIC} - \text{WACC} \qquad (14.4)$$

We can now restate the condition for value creation as: *Positive expected return spreads are the source of value creation and negative expected return spreads are the source of value destruction.* When the return spread is zero, the firm neither creates nor destroys value. This does not mean that the firm is unable to remunerate its suppliers of capital. When the return spread is zero, ROIC is equal to WACC, which means that the firm generates enough profits from operations to provide debtholders and shareholders the exact return they expect and no more. To create value the firm must deliver to its shareholders *more* than what they expect to receive, which is true only when ROIC exceeds WACC. It is important to keep in mind that it is the entire *future* stream of expected return spreads, and not *past* or *historical* return spreads, that drives the process of value creation or destruction.

Thus, the objective of managers should not be the maximization of their firm's operating profitability (ROIC) but the maximization of the firm's *return spread.* This means that rewarding a manager's performance on the basis of ROIC may lead to a behavior that is inconsistent with value creation. For example, suppose one of InfoSoft's divisions has an average ROIC of 17 percent and that its manager must decide whether or not to make a single-year investment whose expected

---

[6]If we assume that InfoSoft's growth rate is constant, perpetual, and equal to 5.1 percent, then, according to equation 14.3, InfoSoft's MVA is equal to:

$$\text{MVA} = \frac{(0.148 - 0.123) \times \$345 \text{ million}}{0.123 - 0.051} = \frac{\$8.63 \text{ million}}{0.072} = \$120 \text{ million}$$

ROIC is 14 percent. The investment's ROIC is expected to exceed the firm's WACC of 12.3 percent, so it should be undertaken. However, the manager whose reward is related to his division's average ROIC may *reject* the investment. Accepting the investment would *lower* the division's *average* performance because the investment has a lower expected ROIC (14 percent) than that of the division (17 percent). Designing a reward linked to the *return spread* avoids this problem.

Do we have any evidence indicating that companies with a ROIC greater than their WACC are value creators, namely, positive MVA firms? This question is difficult to answer because a firm's MVA is related to its *future* stream of *expected* return spreads, not to its *historical* or *past* return spreads. Unfortunately, expected return spreads are not observable. But, we *can* examine the relationship between the MVA of firms and their most recent ROIC and WACC, as reported in Exhibit 14.2. The ten top value creators had a ROIC that exceeded their WACC in 1996. Among the value destroyers, Ford Motor had a *positive* return spread in 1996. Even though the *historical* return spread is positive, the market consensus at the end of 1996 was that the present value of Ford Motor's *future* stream of expected return spreads was negative.

Only value-creating growth matters

Another general implication of the valuation formula (equation 14.3) is that growth alone does not necessarily create value. It is the *sign* of the return spread that drives value creation, *irrespective* of the firm's growth rate. There are high-growth firms that are value destroyers and low-growth firms that are value creators. Only growth that is accompanied by a *positive* return spread can generate value.

As an illustration, we compare the performance of firm A to that of firm B, whose characteristics are given in Exhibit 14.3. Firm A is anticipated to grow at 7 percent, has an expected ROIC of 10 percent, and an estimated WACC of 13 percent. Its return spread is negative (−3 percent). According to equation 14.3, the firm has destroyed $500 million of value. It does not matter if firm A grows faster or slower than 7 percent. It will not create value unless its managers are able to change its negative return spread to positive by raising its expected ROIC above its estimated WACC. Now, consider firm B. It is expected to grow at the slower rate of 4 percent. But its 13 percent anticipated ROIC is higher than its estimated WACC of 10 percent, so firm B has a positive return spread. According to equation 14.3, it is creating $500 million of value even though it is growing at a slower rate than firm A.

LINKING VALUE CREATION TO ITS FUNDAMENTAL DETERMINANTS

We can identify more basic drivers of value creation by separating the firm's expected ROIC into its fundamental components (see Chapter 5). Recall that pretax

EXHIBIT 14.3 **Comparison of Value Creation for Two Firms with Different Growth Rates.**

Dollar figures in millions

FIRM	EXPECTED GROWTH RATE	EXPECTED ROIC	ESTIMATED WACC	EXPECTED RETURN SPREAD	INVESED CAPITAL (MILLIONS)	MARKET VALUE ADDED ACCORDING TO EQUATION 14.3	IS VALUE CREATED?
A	7%	10%	13%	−3%	$100	$\dfrac{-3\% \times \$100}{13\% - 7\%}$ $= \dfrac{-\$30}{0.06} = -\$500$	No
B	4%	13%	10%	+3%	$100	$\dfrac{+3\% \times \$100}{10\% - 4\%}$ $= \dfrac{+\$30}{0.06} = +\$500$	Yes

ROIC can be separated into operating profit margin (defined as the ratio of EBIT to sales) and capital turnover (defined as the ratio of sales to invested capital). Taking the corporate tax into account, we can write *aftertax* ROIC as:

$$\text{ROIC} = \frac{\text{EBIT}}{\text{Sales}} \times \frac{\text{Sales}}{\text{Invested capital}} \times (1 - \text{tax rate})$$

$$= \left[\begin{array}{c} \text{Operating} \\ \text{profit margin} \end{array} \right] \times \left[\begin{array}{c} \text{Capital} \\ \text{turnover} \end{array} \right] \times (1 - \text{tax rate})$$

Thus, management can increase the firm's return on invested capital through a combination of the following actions:

1. *An improvement of operating profit margin,* achieved by generating the largest operating profit per dollar of sales
2. *An increase in capital turnover,* achieved by generating the most sales with the least amount of capital (increasing the efficiency of invested capital can be achieved through faster collection of accounts receivable, speedier inventory turns, and a more efficient use of the firm's fixed assets)
3. *A reduction of the effective tax rate,* achieved, for example, by taking advantage of various tax breaks and subsidies

The various drivers of value creation are summarized in Exhibit 14.4. In addition to the two operating drivers, the exhibit also reports the components of the cost of capital. Together, they determine the sign and the size of the future stream of expected return spreads, which in turn determine the firm's market value added. If MVA is positive, the faster the firm grows, the more value it creates. The ability of managers to grow their business over a sustained period of time is driven by the economic, political, and social environments in which the firm evolves, the struc-

EXHIBIT 14.4 The Drivers of Value Creation.

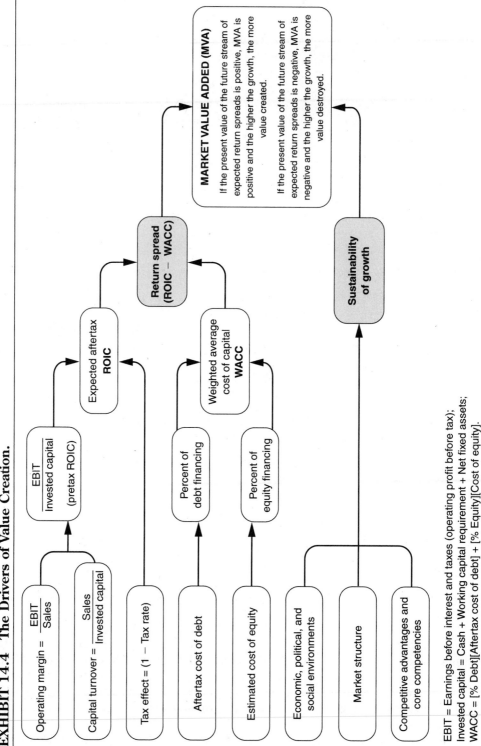

EBIT = Earnings before interest and taxes (operating profit before tax);
Invested capital = Cash + Working capital requirement + Net fixed assets;
WACC = [% Debt][Aftertax cost of debt] + [% Equity][Cost of equity].

ture and dynamics of the particular sector in which it operates, and the competitive advantages and core competencies the firm has developed over time.

LINKING OPERATING PERFORMANCE AND REMUNERATION TO VALUE CREATION

In this section, we use a short case study to explain how a manager's operating performance, his remuneration package, and his ability to create value can be linked.

MR. THOMAS HIRES A GENERAL MANAGER

Mr. Thomas, the sole owner of a toy distribution company called Kiddy Wonder World (KWW), is concerned about his firm's recent lackluster performance. During 1996, sales and profits grew at 5 percent while leading competitors achieved average rates close to 10 percent. The firm's financial statements for the year 1996 are reported in Exhibit 14.5 with the balance sheet on the left side and the income statement on the right side. Both statements have been corrected to adjust for the accounting conventions that could distort the value of invested capital and reported profits.

In early December 1996, when the preliminary results for the year confirmed Mr. Thomas's prediction of poor performance, he decided to step back from day-to-day managerial duties and hired Mr. Bobson as general manager to run the company. Bobson was a successful business manager working for a competitor. The challenge of improving KWW's performance, as well as a higher salary supplemented by a bonus linked to the firm's profits, enticed him to join KWW in early January 1997.

After getting acquainted with the company's operations, Mr. Bobson submitted his business plan for 1997 to Mr. Thomas. The plan was based on two major objectives: (1) increase sales by 10 percent through a more aggressive marketing of existing products and the introduction of a new line of toys and (2) tightly control operating expenses in order to improve operating margin and enhance the firm's profitability. Mr. Thomas approved the plan and gave Mr. Bobson full authority to implement it as he wished.

As the end of 1997 approached, Mr. Thomas received a copy of the company's anticipated financial statements, as reported in Exhibit 14.5. Using these expected figures, Mr. Thomas wants to assess the effectiveness of his general manager and evaluate his firm's expected 1997 performance compared to that of the previous year and to the performance of the leading firms in the sector. He also wonders whether the equity capital he and his family have invested in the company was adequately remunerated for the business and financial risks associated with the toy manufacturing and distribution business. He was recently contacted by a friend with a proposal to invest in an enterprise whose risk profile was similar to that of the toy distribution business and from which he could expect a return of 20 percent.

EXHIBIT 14.5 **Financial Statements for Kiddy Wonder World.**

Figures in thousands of dollars

BALANCE SHEETS ON DECEMBER 31			
		1996	1997
		Actual	Expected
Invested capital			
Cash		$100	$60
Working capital requirement[1]		600	780
Net fixed assets		300	360
	Total	$1,000	$1,200
Capital employed			
Short-term debt		$200	$300
Long-term debt		300	300
Owners' equity		500	600
	Total	$1,000	$1,200

INCOME STATEMENTS FOR THE YEAR		
	1996	1997
	Actual	Expected
Sales	$2,000	$2,200
less operating expenses	(1,780)	(1,920)
less depreciation expenses	(20)	(50)
Earnings before interest and tax (EBIT)	**$200**	**$230**
less interest expenses (10% of debt)	(50)	(60)
Earnings before tax (EBT)	$150	$170
less tax expenses (40% of EBT)	(60)	(68)
Earnings after tax (net profit)	**$90**	**$102**

1. Working capital requirement = (Accounts receivable + Inventories + Prepaid expenses) − (Accounts payable + Accrued expenses).

To carry out his analysis, Mr. Thomas needed financial information about leading firms in the sector. This information, which was provided by a consulting company specializing in the toy manufacturing and distribution business, is reported on the last column of Exhibit 14.6. In addition to information about competitors' performance, Exhibit 14.6 provides figures for KWW's expected 1997 performance (which reflects the outcome of Mr. Bobson's decisions) compared to the 1996 pre-Bobson results. Mr. Thomas must now determine whether Mr. Bobson achieved his dual objectives of faster growth in sales and earnings.

HAS THE GENERAL MANAGER ACHIEVED HIS OBJECTIVES?

Exhibit 14.6 indicates that in 1997 sales grew by 10 percent as expected and earnings grew by 13.3 percent, both exceeding the previous year's results and the corresponding figures for the leading competitors in the sector. Operating expenses grew at a slower rate than sales (7.9 percent versus 10 percent), which explains why net profit grew faster than sales (13.3 percent versus 10 percent). It seems that Mr. Bobson has achieved his two objectives. How did he do it?

A closer look at the figures reported in Exhibit 14.6 reveals another aspect of Mr. Bobson's performance. The company's invested capital grew by 20 percent, much faster than in the previous year (8 percent) and much faster than that of the leading competitors' (10 percent). This growth was mostly due to a relatively high growth in working capital requirement (30 percent). A consequence of the high growth in working capital requirement is the deterioration of the company's liquidity position. This growth, which is largely permanent in nature, was financed through a reduction in cash holding (from $100,000 to $60,000) and a 50 percent increase in short-term borrowings (from $200,000 to $300,000) resulting in a higher percentage of working capital requirement that is financed with short-term debt.[7]

Finally, the firm's operating profitability, measured by return on invested capital, improved slightly from 12.2 percent to 12.5 percent, but is less than the average of 14 percent achieved by leading competitors. However, the reported improvement in ROIC is explained by the fact that invested capital is measured at its average value. If it was measured with year-end values, ROIC would have deteriorated.

Mr. Bobson has increased sales and profits but has he created value? We can find out by looking at the firm's return spread. The firm's latest ROIC is 12.5 percent. To know whether value was created, we compare this return on investment to the average cost of the capital that was required to achieve it. To estimate the firm's WACC, we need to know the proportions of equity and debt financing used to fund the firm's investments, the aftertax cost of debt, and the cost of equity.

The balance sheets in Exhibit 14.5 indicate that KWW's invested capital is financed with an equal amount of equity and debt capital.[8] The income statements in the same exhibit indicate that the company's average *pretax* cost of debt is 10 percent and the tax rate is 40 percent. The average *aftertax* cost of debt is thus 6

---

[7]Chapter 3 shows that reliance on short-term debt to finance a long-term commitment (such as the permanent increase in WCR) is a sign of a deteriorating liquidity position.

[8]Chapter 10 explains that the proportions of equity and debt in the WACC should be estimated from the *market* values of equity and debt. However, KWW is not a traded company, so we used book values as proxies for market values. An alternative would be to use the market value ratios of a similar company.

EXHIBIT 14.6   Comparative Performance of Kiddy Wonder World.

Dollar figures in thousands

PERFORMANCE INDICATOR	KWW PERFORMANCE IN 1996 (BEFORE MR. BOBSON)[1]	KWW PERFORMANCE IN 1997 (WITH MR. BOBSON)[2]	PERFORMANCE OF LEADING COMPETITORS
Growth in sales % change from previous year	5%	10%	9%
Growth in earnings (net profit) % change from previous year	5%	13.3%	10%
Growth in operating expenses % change from previous year	6%	7.9%	8.8%
Growth in invested capital % change from previous year	8%	20%	10%
Growth in WCR % change from previous year	8%	30%	25%
Liquidity position $\dfrac{\text{Short-term debt}}{\text{WCR}}$	$\dfrac{200}{600} = 33.3\%$	$\dfrac{300}{780} = 38.5\%$	25%
Operating profitability $\text{ROIC} = \dfrac{\text{Aftertax EBIT}}{\text{Average invested capital}}$	$\dfrac{200(1-40\%)}{980} = 12.2\%$	$\dfrac{230(1-40\%)}{1,100} = 12.5\%$	14%

1. Previous year's figures are not provided.
2. Percentage changes are calculated with data from the financial statements in Exhibit 14.5.

percent. What is the estimated cost of equity? It is the 20 percent expected return that the firm's owner, Mr. Thomas, could earn if he invested his equity capital in a venture with the same risk profile as KWW.[9] We now have all the required elements we need to estimate KWW's WACC:

$$\text{WACC} = 6\% \times 0.50 + 20\% \times 0.50 = 13\%$$

The firm's WACC of 13 percent is higher than its ROIC of 12.5 percent. The *historical* return spread is thus negative, indicating that the firm is unable to create value at a 13 percent cost of capital even though Mr. Bobson has raised both sales and earnings.[10] Bobson has invested too much capital at a cost (13 percent) that exceeds the return on that capital (12.5 percent). And, as mentioned earlier, the main reason for the growth of the firm's capital is the growth in the firm's working capital requirement (30 percent higher than the previous year).

ECONOMIC PROFITS VERSUS ACCOUNTING PROFITS

The conclusion from our analysis of KWW is that Mr. Bobson was successful in increasing sales and profits but grew the company's working capital requirement much faster than sales and profits. The result was an operating profitability that fell short of the firm's WACC and an inability to create value. In a way, the growth in working capital requirement has provided the general manager with the resources (inventories and receivables) he needed to achieve his sales and profits objectives. One question remains: Why is Mr. Bobson pushing sales and boosting profits but neglecting the management of working capital? Perhaps we should look at the way Mr. Bobson's remuneration package was designed. Recall that Mr. Bobson's compensation includes a bonus related to profits. Not surprisingly, profits are up. Because the growth of working capital does not affect his bonus, he is "rationally" overinvesting in working capital in order to raise profits and increase his bonus.

This behavior could have been prevented if Mr. Bobson had been penalized for his overinvestment in working capital and the increase in the capital required to finance it. One way to achieve this would have been to deduct from Mr. Bobson's net operating profit after tax (NOPAT) a "charge" for the capital he consumed to achieve those profits. This capital charge is determined by multiplying the firm's weighted average cost of capital (WACC) by the amount of invested capital (cash plus working capital requirement plus net fixed assets). We define **economic profit** or **economic value added (EVA)** as NOPAT less this capital charge:

Economic value added (EVA) = NOPAT − WACC × Invested capital   (14.5)

[9]The cost of equity is, in this case, the owner's opportunity cost of capital. For a more specific estimation of the cost of equity, see Chapter 10.
[10]We are using the historical return spread to diagnose Mr. Bobson's ability to create value. We know, however, that value creation is determined by the future expected return spreads. The implicit assumption is that future return spreads are unlikely to become positive with the current growth strategy.

where NOPAT is EBIT $\times$ (1 − tax rate). For KWW, EBIT was $200,000 in 1996 and is expected to reach $230,000 in 1997. The WACC is 13 percent. *Average* invested capital was $962,000 in 1996 and is expected to reach $1,100,000 in 1997 (see Exhibit 14.5). Thus:

$$\text{EVA}_{1996} = \$200,000(1 - 0.40) - 0.13 \times \$962,000 = \$120,000 - \$125,000 = -\$5,000$$

$$\text{EVA}_{1997} = \$230,000(1 - 0.40) - 0.13 \times \$1,100,000 = \$138,000 - \$143,000 = -\$5,000$$

Although KWW is "profitable" when profits are measured according to *accounting* conventions (NOPAT and net profit are positive), it is not profitable when performance is measured with *economic* profits (EVA is negative). Linking Mr. Bobson's performance and bonus to EVA rather than to accounting profits would have induced him to pay more attention to the growth of WCR.

There is another way of expressing the failure of Mr. Bobson's actions to create value. To see this, we factor out the term "invested capital" in the definition of EVA in equation 14.5:

$$\text{EVA} = \left[\frac{\text{NOPAT}}{\text{Invested capital}} - \text{WACC} \right] \times \text{Invested capital}$$

$$\textbf{EVA} = (\textbf{ROIC} - \textbf{WACC}) \times \textbf{Invested capital} \qquad (14.6)$$

Equation 14.6 clearly shows that a positive return spread implies a positive EVA, which, in turn, implies value creation. Again, Mr. Thomas, KWW's owner, should have linked Mr. Bobson's bonus to economic value added rather than to accounting profits. This would have motivated his general manager to pay closer attention to invested capital and to restrict the growth of the firm's assets, particularly the growth of working capital requirement that was used to finance the growth in sales. The next section outlines the key features of an EVA-related compensation plan.

Let's return to Exhibit 14.2. The last column of the exhibit shows the EVA for the top U.S. value creators and destroyers in 1996, estimated according to equation 14.6. Companies with a positive return spread had a positive EVA; companies with a negative return spread had a negative EVA. As discussed earlier, a positive (or negative) *historical* return spread or EVA does not imply that the company is necessarily a value creator (or value destroyer). It is the magnitude and the sign of the firm's *future* stream of *expected* EVA that determine whether a firm is a value creator or destroyer.

DESIGNING COMPENSATION PLANS THAT INDUCE MANAGERS TO BEHAVE LIKE OWNERS

We have argued throughout this book that value creation should be a manager's ultimate objective. But the KWW case study clearly shows that managers do not always behave according to this principle. The challenge, then, is to create a compensation plan that induces them to make value-creating decisions rather than following other objectives. One obvious solution is to turn managers into owners. One way to do this is to remunerate them with equity ownership as opposed to a share of profits. But, owners do not always wish to transfer a portion of their equity investment to managers.

One possible alternative is to partly remunerate managers with a bonus linked to their ability to *increase* economic value added, as mentioned in the previous section. Higher EVAs are the key to value creation. Rewarding managers for their ability to improve EVA should motivate them to take actions consistent with the value-creation objective. But, for this type of compensation system to be effective, a number of conditions must be met.

First, managerial decisions made today (such as capital expenditure decisions) will most likely affect EVA for a number of subsequent years. Thus, the bonus should be related to the manager's ability to generate higher EVA for a period of several years, for example, from three to five years, not just for a single year.

Second, after the compensation plan has been established and accepted, it should not be modified and the reward should not be capped. Exceptional performance should be handsomely rewarded. But, poor performance should be penalized. One way to do this is to allow managers to cash in only a *fraction* of their EVA bonus in a given year, say 25 percent, with the balance remaining on "deposit" with the firm. If EVA declines in subsequent years, the "deposit" will be reduced by an amount that is related to the magnitude of the decline in EVA. After three to five years, managers can withdraw the balance in their EVA deposit.

Third, to have a significant motivational effect on managers' behavior, the reward related to superior EVA performance must represent a relatively large portion of their total remuneration. For example, a remuneration plan in which EVA-related bonuses consist of 5 percent of total compensation, with the remaining 95 percent in the form of a guaranteed salary, is unlikely to be as effective as one in which EVA-related bonuses represent up to 50 percent of the total.

Fourth, as many managers as possible should be on the EVA-related bonus plan. The point is to focus the entire organization on generating economic profits and value. This objective is difficult to achieve if only a few senior managers are on this type of plan, and the rest of the organization is on another type, such as a profit or sales-related bonus plan, or on no bonus plan at all.

Fifth, if an EVA bonus plan is adopted, the book value of capital and the operating profit used to estimate EVA must be restated to correct for the distortions due to accounting conventions, as shown in Appendix 14.1. The adjustments should be limited to a few that are relevant and meaningful to managers. Too many adjustments may unnecessarily complicate a system whose major attraction is its simplicity and ease of understanding.

Finally, an EVA bonus plan must be consistent with the company's capital budgeting process, which is the key to making value-creating investment decisions (see Chapter 6). In other words, inducing managers to maximize EVA over the life of an investment must be consistent with the net present value rule we have advocated when making capital expenditure decisions. We demonstrate in the next section that this is indeed the case.

LINKING THE CAPITAL BUDGETING PROCESS TO VALUE CREATION

Chapter 6 describes how firms should make investment decisions and how they should organize their capital budgeting process. The objective is to make investment decisions that have the potential to increase the firm's market value. In this context, the net present value (NPV) rule or the internal rate of return (IRR) rule plays a key role. A firm should only accept investment proposals that have a positive NPV or, equivalently, have an IRR higher than the project's weighted average cost of capital (WACC). Recall that the NPV of an investment proposal is calculated by discounting to the present the cash flows the investment is expected to generate in the future and then deducting from that present value the initial cash outlay required to launch the project. Chapter 10 shows that the relevant discount rate needed to find the present value of the expected cash-flow stream is the WACC that reflects the risk of the investment. The investment's IRR is simply the discount rate for which the net present value of the investment is equal to zero.

The NPV rule, which is at the heart of the capital budgeting process, is based on cash flows, but the financial management framework described in this chapter is based on market value added (MVA) and economic value added (EVA). Earlier in this chapter, ROIC, WACC, and growth were linked to MVA, and operating performance and remuneration were linked to EVA. We now need to link EVA to MVA and to link the cash-flow based NPV rule to both EVA and MVA. By connecting the measures of performance that are the concerns of the corporate finance function, we can provide a comprehensive financial management system that integrates the value-creation objective with the firm's value, its operating performance, its remuneration and incentive plans, as well as its capital budgeting process.

THE PRESENT VALUE OF AN INVESTMENT'S FUTURE EVAS IS EQUAL TO ITS MVA

We first examine the link between MVA and EVA. The previous section shows that the correct measure of a manager's ability to create value is the economic profit, or EVA, she is able to generate during a period of time, usually a year. Most managerial decisions, however, generate benefits over a number of years, not immediately. Thus, we need to measure the value *today* of the entire stream of future economic profits a business decision is expected to produce in the future, not the economic profit generated during a single year. In other words, we need to measure the present value of the entire stream of future expected EVAs. This present value is the measure of the potential value the business decision will create. The potential value created by a business decision is the MVA of the decision, as shown in equation 14.3. The definition of economic value added is given in equation 14.6. The numerator of equation 14.3 is the same as the EVA defined in equation 14.6. We can thus write equation 14.3 as:

$$\text{MVA} = \frac{\text{EVA}}{\text{WACC} - \text{Constant growth rate}} \qquad (14.7)$$

where the stream of future EVAs is, in this case, expected to grow forever at a constant annual rate. This valuation formula shows that the present value of the future stream of EVAs that a business proposal is expected to generate is the MVA of that proposal. In other words, *management should maximize the entire stream of future EVAs their firm's invested capital is expected to generate in order to maximize their firm's MVA and create shareholder value.*

MAXIMIZING MVA IS THE SAME AS MAXIMIZING NPV

We have just shown that the value-creating manager runs her business with the ultimate goal of maximizing its market value added. In Chapter 6, we show that the value-creating manager makes decisions that maximize net present value. We now want to see if these two decision rules are consistent with one another. We use the example reported in Exhibit 14.7 as an illustration.

The investment   A firm is considering buying a piece of equipment for $1 million as shown in line 1.1 of Exhibit 14.7. The equipment has an expected useful life of two years and a residual value of zero. The equipment will be depreciated over the next two years, providing equal annual depreciation expenses of $500,000 (reported in part 2.1 of the exhibit). The investment is expected to generate sales of $2 million the first year and $4 million the second (line 2.1). At the *beginning* of every year, the firm will have to increase its investment in working capital in order to support the sales that will be generated that year.

Assuming that working capital requirement is equal to 10 percent of expected sales, $200,000 of working capital is required at the *beginning* of the first year (the "now" column) and $400,000 is required at the *beginning* of the second year (the "end-of-year-one" column) (line 1.2). Thus, the firm must make an initial total investment of $1.2 million, followed by another investment of $200,000 at the end of the first year (the increase in WCR needed to support the additional $2 million of year-two sales), and then recover $400,000 of working capital investment at the end of the second year (line 1.3).

The net operating profit after tax (NOPAT) from the investment   Expected profits from operations are shown in part 2 of Exhibit 14.7. Operating expenses other than depreciation are 70 percent of sales and the tax rate is 40 percent. The

EXHIBIT 14.7 Equivalence of Net Present Value Measured with Cash Flows and Net Present Value Measured with Economic Value Added.

Figures in thousands of dollars

	Now	End of Year One	End of Year Two
1. INVESTMENT			
1.1 Equipment	$1,000		
1.2 Working capital requirement (WCR) at 10% of sales	(200)	(400)	$0
1.3 Change in working capital requirement	($200)	($200)	$400
2. NET OPERATING PROFIT AFTER TAX (NOPAT)			
2.1 Sales		2,000	4,000
less operating expenses at 70% of sales		(1,400)	(2,800)
less depreciation expenses		(500)	(500)
2.2 equals pretax operating profits		100	700
less taxes at 40%		(40)	(280)
2.3 equals net operating profit after tax (NOPAT)		60	420
3. CASH FLOWS FROM INVESTMENT AND NET PRESENT VALUE (NPV)			
3.1 Net operating profit after tax (NOPAT in line 2.3)		60	420
depreciation expenses added back		500	500
less change in WCR (line 1.3)	(200)	(200)	400
less capital expenditure (line 1.1)	(1,000)		
3.2 equals **cash flow from investment (CFI)**	**($1,200)**	**$360**	**$1,320**
3.3 **Net present value of CFIs at 10%**	**$218.2**		
3.4 **Internal rate of return of CFI**	**21%**		
4. ECONOMIC VALUE ADDED (EVA) AND MARKET VALUE ADDED (MVA)			
4.1 Net operating profit after tax (NOPAT in line 2.3)		60	420
4.2 Invested capital			
Initial investment in fixed assets (line 1.1)	1,000	1,000	1,000
less accumulated depreciation (line 2.1)		(500)	(1,000)
equals net investment in fixed assets	1,000	500	0
plus working capital requirement	200	400	
equals invested capital	1,200	900	
4.3 Capital charge (10% of beginning invested capital)		(120)	(90)
4.4 equals **economic value added**		**($60)**	**$330**
4.5 **MVA = Present value of EVAs at 10%**	**$218.2**		

result of deducting these expenses from expected sales is a net operating profit after tax (NOPAT) of $60,000 at the end of the first year and $420,000 at the end of the second year (line 2.3).

Cash flows from the investment   Cash flows from the investment are calculated in part 3 of the exhibit. They are equal to the investment's NOPAT plus depreciation expenses less net investments (line 3.1). This calculation produces an initial cash outflow of $1.2 million to launch the project, followed by net cash inflows of $360,000 at the end of the first year and $1,320,000 at the end of the second year (line 3.2).

Net present value and internal rate of return   We assume the investment has an estimated WACC of 10 percent. At that rate, the net present value of the expected cash-flow stream is $218,200 and its internal rate of return is 21 percent. The investment's IRR exceeds its WACC and its NPV is positive. Thus, the investment is a value-creating proposition and should be undertaken.

Economic value added and market value added   The capacity of an investment to create value can also be estimated by calculating its future stream of expected EVAs and discounting them at the WACC to provide the investment's MVA. If MVA is positive, value is created; if it is negative, value is destroyed. The procedure is shown in part 4 of Exhibit 14.7. Expected EVA is computed by deducting from NOPAT a charge for capital equal to 10 percent of the invested capital at the *beginning* of the year. For the first year, NOPAT is $60,000 (line 4.1), invested capital at the beginning of the year is $1.2 million (line 4.2), and the charge for capital is $120,000 (line 4.3). The expected EVA is a negative $60,000 (line 4.4). For the second year, NOPAT is $420,000, the capital charge is $90,000 and EVA is a positive $330,000.

The investment's MVA is equal to the present value of the expected future stream of EVAs discounted at the WACC of 10 percent. This MVA, shown in line 4.5, is equal to $218,200. The MVA is positive, so the investment is a value-creating proposition and should be undertaken even though its first year EVA is *negative*. Note that the investment's MVA in line 4.5 is *exactly the same* as its net present value (NPV) in line 3.3.

Although the two methods are equivalent, management must be careful when using the MVA approach for valuing an investment decision, particularly when estimating the charge for capital consumption (invested capital multiplied by WACC). The relevant figure is the amount of invested capital at the *beginning* of the period, not at the end of the period. The major advantage of the NPV approach is that it takes into account any nonfinancial transactions related to the project that either reduce or add to the firm's cash holding. Thus, when using the NPV method, managers can ignore the amount of invested capital at the beginning of each period and only worry about the cash flows generated by the project. Note that the project in Exhibit 14.7 has a *negative* first-year EVA but a *positive* first-year cash flow, an indication that although there is no value creation the first year, the investment does generate cash. The major advantage of the MVA approach, of course, is its direct relation to economic value added.

PUTTING IT ALL TOGETHER: THE FINANCIAL STRATEGY MATRIX

Exhibit 14.8 summarizes the key elements of a firm's financial management system and shows their managerial implications within a single framework that we call the firm's **financial strategy matrix.** We assume that the firm may have one or several divisions or businesses.

The vertical axis measures the ability of a particular business to create value. This ability is indicated by the sign and magnitude of the firm's return spread (its expected ROIC less its WACC). When the business's return spread is positive (the upper half of the matrix), there is value creation (EVA is positive). When the return spread is negative (the lower half of the matrix), there is value destruction (EVA is negative).

The horizontal axis measures the capacity of a business to finance its growth in sales. This capacity is measured by the difference between the sales growth rate and the self-sustainable growth rate. The self-sustainable growth rate is the maximum rate of growth in sales a business can achieve *without* changing its financing policy (same debt-to-equity ratio, same dividend payout ratio, and no new issue of equity or share repurchase) or modifying its operating policy (same operating profit margin and same capital turnover).[11] The business will experience a cash shortage if the difference between the sales growth rate and the self-sustainable growth rate is positive (the right half of the matrix). In this case, sales are growing faster than the capacity of the business to finance the assets required to support that growth, producing a cash deficit. The business will generate a cash surplus if the difference is negative (the left half of the matrix). In this case, sales are growing at a slower rate than the capacity of the business to finance its growth, producing excess cash.

What are the managerial implications of the matrix in Exhibit 14.8? There are four possible situations a business can face: (1) the business has the capacity to create value but is short of cash (the upper right quadrant); (2) the business has the capacity to create value and generate a surplus of cash (the upper left quadrant); (3) the business is a value destroyer but generates excess cash (the lower left quadrant); and (4) the business is a value destroyer and suffers from a shortage of cash (lower right quadrant).

A firm with a single business will fall into one of these four quadrants. A firm with many different businesses will have to allocate them to their respective quadrant. After this diagnostic stage is completed, management will have to decide what to do with each business according to its position in the financial strategy matrix. We now examine the options available to management in each of the four cases.

---

[11]A business's self-sustainable growth rate is equal to its profit retention rate multiplied by its return on equity (ROE). See Chapter 5 for details.

EXHIBIT 14.8 The Financial Strategy Matrix.

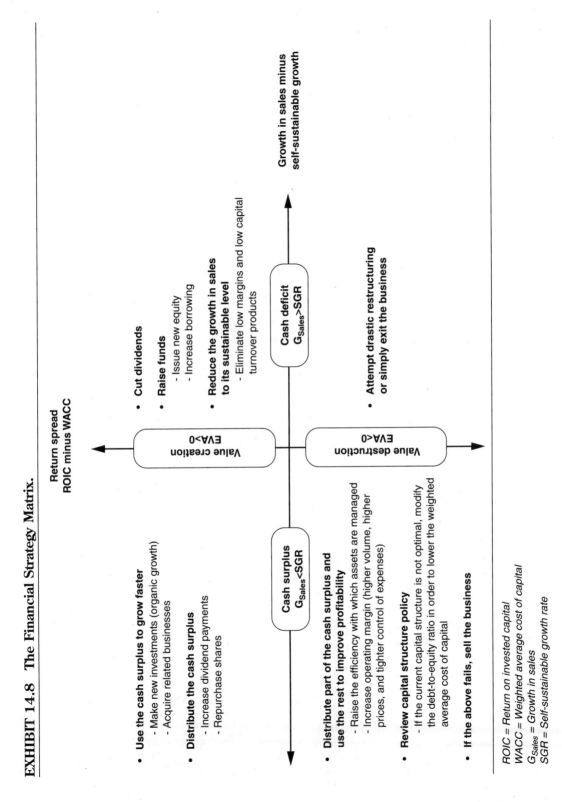

ROIC = Return on invested capital
WACC = Weighted average cost of capital
G_{Sales} = Growth in sales
SGR = Self-sustainable growth rate

THE BUSINESS IS A VALUE CREATOR BUT IS SHORT OF CASH

Management has two obvious options in this case. One is to reduce or eliminate any dividend payments if the business is currently paying a dividend to its parent company and, possibly, to other shareholders. The other option is for the parent company to inject fresh equity capital into the business. If the business is listed on a stock exchange as a separate entity, it can raise equity by issuing new shares to the public. With this additional equity capital, the business can borrow additional funds to maintain its capital structure at its optimal level. (For example, if the optimal structure is a debt-to-equity ratio of one, new equity can be matched with an equal amount of borrowing.)

If additional capital is not available management would be unable to fund a value-creating business. In this case, management may have to scale back some of its operations and reduce the business's overall rate of growth to its sustainable level by eliminating low margin, low capital turnover products and services. This strategy should enhance the value-creating capacity of the remaining activities by allowing the business to compete in a narrower market segment. The danger is that a cash-rich competitor may decide to enter the business and put pressure on margins.

THE BUSINESS IS A VALUE CREATOR WITH A CASH SURPLUS

This is the preferred situation. Management can do one of two things in this case. The first is to use the cash surplus to accelerate the growth of the business. This can be accomplished by increasing internal investment and/or by acquiring similar and related businesses. Suppose organic growth opportunities or related acquisitions are not available. The temptation, of course, would be to use the cash surplus to diversify into *unrelated* businesses that may appear profitable. However, as shown in Chapter 12, this strategy rarely results in success and generally should be avoided.

If the cash surplus cannot be invested at an expected return that exceeds the cost of capital, it should be returned to those who own it—the firm's shareholders. They could then invest it in a value-creating venture of their choice. This cash distribution can be achieved through a special dividend payment and/or a **share buyback,** or repurchase, program.

THE BUSINESS IS A VALUE DESTROYER
WITH A CASH SURPLUS

This type of business should be fixed quickly, before the cash surplus runs out. Part of the excess cash should be returned to shareholders and the rest used to restructure the business as rapidly as possible, with the objective of raising its return on invested capital above its cost of capital.

As shown earlier in this chapter, ROIC can be increased through (1) an improved operating margin via a combination of higher volume, higher prices, and control of operating expenses; and (2) a more efficient management of assets, particularly working capital requirement, that is, with faster collection of trade receivables and higher inventory turns. (See Chapters 3 and 5.)

Management should also review the business's capital structure with the objective of lowering its weighted average cost of capital if it is not currently at its optimal, or minimum level (see Chapters 10 and 11). The danger here is sinking too much cash into a business that has little or no chance of being turned around. The trick is to know when to seriously consider the sale of the business to someone who might manage it better.

THE BUSINESS IS A VALUE DESTROYER THAT IS SHORT OF CASH

This is the worst situation and the one that requires management's immediate attention and swift action. If the business cannot be quickly and drastically restructured, it should be sold as soon as possible. By drastic restructuring, we mean the rapid sale of some of the business's assets to raise cash immediately and the scaling down of remaining activities to allow short-term survival with the ultimate objective of turning these remaining activities into a value-creating business. If there is no hope for a quick and successful turnaround, our advice is to sell the business immediately before it affects the long-term survival of the rest of the company. The temptation to fund the business with the cash surplus generated by other businesses that have excess cash should be resisted at all cost.

SUMMARY

The greatest benefit of a management system that emphasizes value creation as opposed to earnings growth is that it induces managers throughout the organization to pay closer attention to expense control, to make a more effective use of the firm's assets, and to become more aware of the need to earn better returns on the firm's invested capital. Good management can be many things—superior marketing skill, great leadership, a mastery of manufacturing. But good *financial* management is essentially only one thing—good *capital* management, or *the art of deploying scarce capital skillfully.*

How can managers make capital allocation decisions that enhance value? A firm should allocate its existing capital, and, if required, raise new capital, *only* if the return it expects to earn on the capital exceeds its estimated cost. Otherwise, capital should be returned to shareholders through dividend payments and/or a share buyback program. And there is, of course, no point in growing a business that does not earn its cost of capital. If a business cannot be restructured to generate a return in excess of its appropriate risk-adjusted cost of capital, it should be sold. A company creates value only if its market value added (MVA)—defined as the difference between the market value of its capital and the amount of capital invested in it by shareholders and debtholders—is positive. In other words, only when the firm's capital is worth more than its reported (adjusted) book value.

One way to implement a management system that is consistent with and conducive to a value-creation objective is to link the firm's operating performance, investment decisions, and remuneration system to economic profit or economic value added (EVA), defined as the difference between net operating profit after tax and the dollar cost of the capital used to generate that profit. Managers that make decisions that maximize expected future EVAs will increase MVA and create value. Also, this objective is consistent with the net present value rule and the internal rate of return rule used in capital budgeting.

The key drivers of a financial management system can be organized into a financial strategy matrix that can help managers make value-creating strategic decisions. This matrix considers businesses that show positive or negative EVAs and have excess cash or cash shortages.

We conclude this book with one of the clearest and shortest statements a chief executive has made about the nature of his business and the way it is managed. This is how a former chairman of the Coca-Cola Company defined his business and management approach: "We raise capital to make concentrate, and sell it at an operating profit. Then we pay the cost of that capital. Shareholders pocket the difference."[12] If you can think of your own business in those terms, we have achieved our goal of making you a true value manager.

---

[12]Roberto Goizueta in *Fortune* (September 20, 1993), page 24.

14.1 ADJUSTING BOOK VALUES TO ESTIMATE THE AMOUNT OF INVESTED EQUITY CAPITAL AND OPERATING PROFIT

As an illustration of the adjustments needed to correct for the distortions generated by accounting conventions, this appendix shows how we estimated InfoSoft's $380 million of invested equity capital on December 31, 1997, and $80 million of earnings before interest and tax (EBIT) in 1997. These are the figures we used to estimate the firm's MVA, ROIC, and EVA in 1997. Keep in mind, however, that more than 100 accounting adjustments have been identified. Obviously, the secret is to pick those few that make sense for analyzing a company's performance without adding undue complexity.

ADJUSTING THE BOOK VALUE OF EQUITY CAPITAL

On the asset side of InfoSoft's unadjusted 1997 balance sheet in Exhibit 14.1, a $10 million accumulated bad debt allowance was deducted from the gross value of working capital requirement and $20 million of accumulated goodwill amortization was removed from its net fixed assets. Prevailing accounting rules usually require that these **provisions** be charged to (deducted from) both the firm's assets and its profit. In monetary terms, the bad debt allowance represents the percentage of outstanding invoices on December 31, 1997, that InfoSoft did not expect to collect. The amortization of goodwill results from the acquisition of a company two years ago for $100 million *above* its **fair market value** (its value under normal market conditions). The $100 million payment in excess of fair value, or goodwill, is amortized on a straight-line basis over 10 years, that is, $10 million per year.

During the years up to December 31, 1997, the bad debt allowance and the amortization of goodwill have reduced the amount of reported profit by $30 million ($10 million of bad debt allowances and $20 million of amortized goodwill). As a result, the accumulated amount of retained earnings and, consequently, the book value of InfoSoft's equity capital were also reduced by $30 million. Because the capital actually invested by its shareholders was not affected by these accounting adjustments, the book value of InfoSoft's equity capital on December 31, 1997, must be adjusted upward by $30 million, as shown on the right side of the 1997 adjusted balance sheet in Exhibit 14.1.

The next section shows that on December 31, 1997, InfoSoft reported a net profit of $30 million and retained the entire amount (it did not pay any dividends). Thus, the book value of its equity increased by $30 million in 1997. We will see that this profit figure came after the deduction of a $5 million allowance for bad debt, $10 million of goodwill amortization, and $30 million of R&D expenses. We can adjust equity capital to correct for the distortions caused by the way bad debt allowances and goodwill amortization are accounted for in reported profit. Is it necessary to also adjust for the way R&D expenses have been charged to the 1997 profit?

To answer this question, we need to know why $30 million was spent on R&D during 1997. If these expenses were incurred to increase profits only in 1997, it makes sense to account for them fully in that year. But if, as it would certainly be the case in most instances, the $30 million of R&D was disbursed to boost InfoSoft's profits for several years, allocating the full $30 million only to 1997 does not make much sense, although accounting conventions may require doing so.

If we assume that the $30 million spent on R&D will improve profits for a five-year period, each of these five years of profits should account for a portion of the $30 million "consumed" to generate that year's profit and, consequently, that year's increase in invested equity capital. In other words, the R&D expenses, not unlike fixed assets, must be treated as an investment made in 1997 that needs to be amortized over a five-year period rather than fully expensed in 1997. For example, if the $30 million were amortized according to the straight-line method, only $6 million of R&D expenses ($30 million divided by five) should be charged to 1997 profit for the purpose of estimating the invested equity capital at the end of that year. Furthermore, the **capitalization** of the R&D expenses (their conversion to assets) should not be limited to 1997. It should also apply to all the R&D expenses incurred by InfoSoft since its inception in 1993. How can this be done?

First, we add all the R&D annual expenses incurred since 1993, including the $30 million spent in 1997. Then, we apply an amortization schedule to each of these annual expenses, add all the annual amortization expenses up to December 31, 1997, and, finally, subtract the accumulated amortization expenses from the amount actually spent on R&D since 1993. Assuming that the result would be a capitalized value of $50 million on December 31, 1997, we can estimate that the firm's reported pretax profit since 1993 have been underestimated by $50 million. It follows that the firm's equity capital as of December 31, 1997, must be adjusted upward by the same amount, as shown on the right side of the 1997 adjusted balance sheet in Exhibit 14.1.

In total, InfoSoft's book value of equity capital on December 31, 1997, should be increased by $80 million to adjust for the accounting treatment of bad debt allowances ($10 million), goodwill amortization ($20 million), and capitalized R&D costs ($50 million). As a result, InfoSoft's estimated invested capital is $380 million, the sum of its reported book value of $300 million and the $80 million of adjustments.

As it is often the case, InfoSoft's reported invested capital ($300 million) underestimates the actual invested capital ($380 million) and, consequently, the total capital contributed by investors. In general, the extent of the underestimation depends on the number and size of the adjustments that must be made to reported profit. These adjustments, in addition to those related to bad debt allowances, goodwill amortization, and R&D expenses, include the consequences of any accounting convention that would affect reported profit without affecting the capital invested by shareholders and bondholders, such as charges associated with restructuring.

ADJUSTING EARNINGS BEFORE INTEREST AND TAX (EBIT)

Exhibit A14.1 shows both the unadjusted and adjusted 1997 InfoSoft's income statement. InfoSoft reported $55 million of earnings before interest and tax in 1997. This figure must first be adjusted upward by the $5 million increase in bad debt allowance, the $10 million amortization of goodwill, and the $30 million of R&D expenses. It must then be adjusted downward by the amortization of the R&D costs for 1997 that result from the application of the amortization schedule used when estimating the R&D capitalized expenses. If we *assume* an R&D amortization expense of $20 million, InfoSoft's earnings before interest and tax should be increased by a total of $25 million (from $55 million to $80 million)—$5 million for bad debts plus $10 million of goodwill plus $30 million of R&D expenses less $20 million for the amortization of R&D costs. As a final adjustment to InfoSoft's 1997 income statement, we deduct the $8 million of interest expenses (as given in the income statement) and the $17 million of tax expense (36 percent of the $47 million of pretax profit) from the adjusted EBIT to get an adjusted earnings after tax of $55 million. Because we assumed that InfoSoft did not pay any dividend in 1997, this $55 million of adjusted net profit is also the firm's adjusted 1997 retained earnings. Exhibit 14.1 shows that the firm's adjusted owners' equity went up by exactly $55 million, from $225 million at the end of 1996 to $280 million at the end of 1997.

EXHIBIT A14.1 **Infosoft's Income Statement for 1997.**

Figures in millions of dollars

INCOME STATEMENT 1997			
UNADJUSTED		**ADJUSTED**	
Sales	$1,000	Sales	$1,000
Cost of Goods Sold	500	Cost of Goods Sold	500
SG&A expenses	382	SG&A expenses	382
Lease expense	3	Lease expense	3
Depreciation expense	15	Depreciation expense	15
R&D expense	30	Amortization of R&D expense	20
Bad debt provision	5		
Goodwill amortization	10		
Earnings before interest and tax	**$55**	**Earnings before interest and tax**	**$80**
Interest expenses	8	Interest expenses	8
Tax expense (36% of pretax profit)	17	Tax expense	17
Earnings after tax	**$30**	**Earnings after tax**	**$55**

14.2 ESTIMATING MARKET VALUE ADDED (MVA) WHEN FUTURE CASH FLOWS ARE EXPECTED TO GROW AT A CONSTANT RATE IN PERPETUITY

C hapter 12 shows that the discounted cash-flow value of assets—if we assume these assets will generate a cash-flow stream that is expected to grow at a constant annual rate forever—is given by:

$$\text{Value of assets} = \frac{\text{CFA}}{\text{WACC} - \text{Growth rate}} \qquad \text{(A14.1)}$$

where CFA is next year's cash flow from assets and WACC is the weighted average cost of the capital employed to finance the assets. Cash from assets (CFA) is given by:

CFA = EBIT(1 − tax) + Depreciation expenses − ΔWCR − Capital expenditures

where EBIT is earnings before interest and tax, EBIT(1 − tax) is net operating profit after tax or NOPAT, and ΔWCR is the change in working capital requirement. We can rearrange the terms of CFA to:

CFA = NOPAT − [ΔWCR + Capital expenditures − Depreciation expenses]

Capital expenditures less depreciation expenses is equal to the *change* in the firm's *net* fixed assets during the year. When added to the *change* in working capital requirement, the sum represents the *change* in the book value of the firm's invested capital during the year (we assume no change in cash position). Thus:

CFA = NOPAT − ΔInvested capital

Substituting this expression for next year's CFA in the numerator of the valuation formula (equation A14.1) and deducting the term "invested capital" from both sides of the equation, we get:

$$\text{Market value assets} - \text{Invested capital} = \frac{\text{NOPAT} - \Delta\text{Invested capital}}{\text{WACC} - \text{Growth rate}}$$

$$- \text{Invested capital}$$

where the left side of the equation is the market value added or MVA. This equation can be written as:

$$\text{MVA} = \frac{\text{NOPAT} - \Delta\text{Invested capital} - \text{Invested capital} \times (\text{WACC} - \text{Growth rate})}{\text{WACC} - \text{Growth rate}}$$

Factoring out the term "invested capital" in the numerator, we have:

$$\text{MVA} = \frac{\left[\dfrac{\text{NOPAT}}{\text{Invested capital}} - \dfrac{\Delta\text{Invested capital}}{\text{Invested capital}} - \text{WACC} + \text{Growth rate}\right] \times \text{Invested capital}}{\text{WACC} - \text{Growth rate}}$$

The first term in the numerator is the return on invested capital (ROIC) and the second term is the growth rate in invested capital, which is the same as the growth rate in cash flows because the growth rate is constant. Thus,

$$\text{MVA} = \frac{[\text{ROIC} - \text{Growth rate} - \text{WACC} + \text{Growth rate}] \times \text{Invested capital}}{\text{WACC} - \text{Growth rate}}$$

$$\text{MVA} = \frac{[\text{ROIC} - \text{WACC}] \times \text{Invested capital}}{\text{WACC} - \text{Growth rate}}$$

This equation is the valuation formula (equation 14.3).

Note that when MVA is positive, the ratio of market value to adjusted book value is greater than one. The factors that explain the sign of MVA are thus similar to those that explain the magnitude of the ratio of a firm's price per share to its book value per share. The price-to-book value ratio was presented in Chapter 12 where we said that the factors that explain its magnitude would be discussed in Chapter 14. The valuation formula (equation 14.3) indicates that these factors are:

1. Return on equity (the equivalent of ROIC because we now deal with equity rather than total capital)
2. The cost of equity (the equivalent of WACC because we now deal with equity rather than total capital)
3. The firm's growth rate

Thus, when return on equity is higher (lower) than the cost of equity, the price-to-book value ratio will be higher (or lower) than one.

REFERENCES AND FURTHER READING

1. McTaggart, James, Peter Kontes and Michael Mankins. *The Value Imperative.* The Free Press (1994).
2. Rappaport, Alfred. *Creating Shareholder Value.* The Free Press (1986). See chapters 3 to 7 as well as 9 and 10.
3. Stuart, Bennett. *The Quest for Value.* HarperCollins (1991).
4. Weston, Fred, Kwang Chung and Juan Siu. *Takeovers, Restructuring, and Corporate Governance.* Prentice-Hall (1998).

REVIEW PROBLEMS

14.1. Understanding MVA and EVA.

Explain why each of the following statements is generally incorrect:

a. "Management creates value by maximizing the market value of its firm."

b. "The firm with the highest market value is the one that has created the most value for its shareholders."

c. "If a firm's market value added (MVA) is positive, then its current economic value added (EVA) must also be positive."

d. "If a firm's market value added (MVA) is positive, then its current return on invested capital (ROIC) must exceed its weighted average cost of capital (WACC)."

e. "Economic value added (EVA) should be measured on the basis of net profits (the bottom line) and not on the basis of *operating* profit."

f. "One weakness of economic value added (EVA) as a performance measure is that it does not take risk into account."

g. "Growth is the key to increasing a firm's market value added."

h. "This year's economic value added (EVA) is positive, so the firm's market value added must also be positive."

i. "Giving managers a bonus related to their ability to increase the profit of their business unit is one way to enhance shareholder value."

j. "Giving managers a bonus related to their ability to increase the profitability (return on invested capital) of their business unit is one way to enhance shareholder value."

14.2. Adjusting accounting data to estimate economic value added.

The financial statements of the Advance Devices Corporation (ADC) are shown below with balance sheets reported in their managerial form. ADC has an estimated weighted average cost of capital of 11 percent. ADC had an estimated $55 million of R&D expenses that should have been capitalized in 1996 and $70 million that should have been capitalized in 1997. Amortization of R&D expenses in 1997 is $30 million. Using the information given, provide an estimate of ADC's economic value added in 1997 based on initial invested capital and average invested capital.

INCOME STATEMENT FOR 1997 (in millions of dollars)	
Net sales	$1,400
Cost of sales	780
Selling, general, and administrative expenses	330
Depreciation and lease expenses	45
R&D expenses	100
Bad debt provision	6
Goodwill amortization	25
Interest expenses	14
Income tax expenses	40
Net profit	**$60**

MANAGERIAL BALANCE SHEETS
(in millions of dollars)

Invested capital	12.31.96	12.31.97	Capital employed	12.31.96	12.31.97
Cash	$10	$15	Short-term debt	$30	$10
Working capital (net)	140	160			
Gross value	*147*	*173*	Long-term debt	80	80
Accumulated bad debt allowance	*7*	*13*			
Net fixed assets	210	225	Lease obligations	50	50
Tangible (net)	110	150			
Goodwill (net)	100	75	Owners' equity	200	260
Gross value	*120*	*120*			
Accumulated amortization	*20*	*45*			
TOTAL	**$360**	**$400**	**TOTAL**	**$360**	**$400**

14.3. Economic value added analysis.

The Southern Communication Corporation (SCC) currently has $1 billion of capital invested in several telecommunication projects that are expected to generate a *pretax* operating profit of $170 million next year. SCC has an estimated *pretax* cost of capital of 15 percent.

a. What is the *pretax* economic value added (EVA) that SCC is expected to generate next year? Calculate EVA first based on pretax operating profit and then based on expected return on invested capital.

b. SCC is considering five possible actions that should improve its expected pretax EVA.

These are:

1. A $10 million reduction in operating expenses that should not affect revenues

2. A $60 million reduction in invested capital that should not affect operating profit

3. A re-examination of its capital structure (debt-to-equity ratio) that could lower its pretax cost of capital to 14 percent

4. The sale of assets at their book value of $100 million. These assets are expected to generate a pretax operating profit of $10 million next year

5. The acquisition of assets worth $100 million. These assests are expected to generate a pretax operating profit of $20 million next year

Show how each of these decisions would improve SCC's expected pretax economic value added.

14.4. Market value added analysis.

The International Logistics Company (ILC) is considering buying an inventory control software program that will cost $150,000, delivered and installed (including personnel training). The program will allow the company to reduce its inventory by $100,000. The cost of the software will be expensed the year it is bought. ILC is subject to a 40 percent corporate tax rate and its weighted average cost of capital is 10 percent. Should ILC buy the software program? Answer the question using economic value added (EVA) and market value added (MVA) analysis.

14.5. Comparison of investment analysis based on cash flows and EVAs.

The Electronics Machines Corporation (EMC) is considering buying a $300,000 piece of equipment that could raise EMC's sales revenues by $1 million the first year, $2 million the second year, and $1.8 million the third year. The cost of the piece of equipment can be fully depreciated over the three-year investment according to the straight-line method with no residual value. Incremental operating expenses are estimated at 90 percent of sales, excluding depreciation expenses. Working capital required to support the project's sales should be 10 percent of sales with working capital investment (WCR) assumed to occur at the *beginning* of the year. EMC can borrow at 8 percent, is subject to a 30 percent corporate tax rate, and finances 60 percent of its activities with borrowed funds. The firm uses an estimated cost of equity of 14.1 percent.

a. What are the project's net present value and internal rate of return? Should the piece of equipment be purchased?

b. What is the project's market value added? Explain why the piece of equipment should be purchased even though its first-year economic value added (EVA) is negative.

c. What are the key assumptions used in the estimation of the project's cash flows and economic value added that make the project's NPV equal to its MVA?

14.6. MVA analysis of the designer desk lamp project.

Refer to Chapter 8 for a description of the designer desk lamp project. Exhibit 8.3 reports the cash flows the project is expected to generate. Use the information in the exhibit to estimate the project's EVAs and its market value added (MVA). The latter, if measured correctly, must be equal to the project's net present value (NPV) of $263,293. The weighted average cost of capital is 10 percent.

14.7. The financial strategy matrix.

Amalgamated Industries (AI) has four distinct business divisions that are run as separate companies and are listed on a stock market. AI has a majority ownership in the four companies for which the following financial data has been collected:

COMPANY	TRANSPORTATION	RESTAURANTS	BEVERAGES	FOOD
Sales growth rate	8%	15%	7%	4%
ROIC	8%	15%	8%	13%
ROE	12%	20%	12%	15%
WACC	10%	12%	9%	11%
Dividend payout ratio	50%	40%	25%	60%

a. Position the four companies on the financial strategy matrix.

b. What actions should AI take regarding each of these businesses?

GLOSSARY

Terms are followed by the chapter number in which they appear. Bold terms in a definition are defined elsewhere in the glossary.

Accelerated depreciation method (2)   **Depreciation** method according to which annual **depreciation expenses** are higher in the early years of an **asset**'s life and lower in the later years. See **straight-line depreciation method.**

Accounting exposure (13) Effect of changes in **exchange rates** on **balance sheet** and **income statement** accounts. Same as **translation exposure.**

Accounting life (8)   Number of years over which an **asset** is depreciated. See **economic life.**

Accounting period (2)   Time period covered by a **financial statement,** usually one year but sometimes shorter.

Accounting principles (2)   Rules governing the systematic collection, organization, and presentation of financial information. Same as **accounting standards.**

Accounting standards (2)   *See* **accounting principles.**

Accounts payable (1, 2)   Cash owed by a firm to its suppliers for purchases made on credit and not yet paid; reported in the firm's **balance sheet** as a **current liability.** Same as **payables** and **trade creditors.**

Accounts receivable (1, 2)   Cash owed to a firm by its customers for sales made on credit and not yet paid; reported in the firm's **balance sheet** as a **current asset.** Same as **receivables** and **trade debtors.**

Accrual accounting (2)   Accounting system with reporting based on the **realization** and **matching principles.**

Accrued expenses (2)   **Liabilities** other than **accounts payable** that arise from the lag between the date at which these expenses have been incurred and the date at which they are paid.

Accumulated depreciation (2)   The sum of the periodic **depreciation expenses** deducted from the **gross value** of a **fixed asset** in order to obtain its **net book value.** See **acquisition cost principle.**

Accumulated retained earnings (2)   The total amount of retained earnings since the firm was established; reported in the **balance sheet** in the **owners' equity** account.

Acid test (3)   *See* **quick ratio.**

Acquisition cost principle (2) Asset valuation principle according to which the **net book value** of a **fixed asset** is equal to its purchase price less the **accumulated depreciation** since that asset was bought. Same as **historical cost principle.**

Actual cash-flow principle (8) A **capital budgeting** principle according to which the **cash outflows** and **cash inflows** associated with an investment decision must be estimated at the time they actually occur.

Adjusted present value (APV) (12)   A valuation method according to which the value of a firm's **assets** is equal to the sum of (i) their value assuming that they are financed only with **equity capital (unlevered value),** and (ii) the **present value** of the tax savings provided by the portion of the assets financed with debt.

Aftertax cost of debt (1, 10)
(Pretax **cost of debt**) × (1 −
marginal corporate tax rate). See
equation 10.3.

Agency cost of debt financing
(11)   Costs associated with debt
financing (and borne by
shareholders) arising when
lenders impose **restrictive
covenants** that limit the firm's
flexibility (examples: the
dividend the firm can pay or the
assets it can sell). See **bonding
costs** and **monitoring costs.**

Agency cost of equity financing
(11)   Costs associated with
equity capital (and borne by
shareholders) arising when a
firm's managers (acting as
agents of shareholders) make
decisions that benefit them at the
expense of shareholders.

Agency problem (11)   Problem
arising from the separation of
ownership and **control** of a firm.

Aggressive (financing) strategy
(3)   A firm's financing strategy
that uses short-term funds to
finance a portion of the firm's
long-term investments. See
matching strategy and
conservative strategy.

Allowance for bad debts (14)
Provision for the possible
uncollectibility of **accounts
receivable.**

Allowance for doubtful accounts
(2)   *See* **allowance for bad
debts.**

Alternative investment (6)   An
investment used as a benchmark
for evaluating a project. The
alternative investment must have
the same risk, tax, liquidity, and
other characteristics as the project.
See **proxies** and **pure-plays.**

American option (13)   An **option**
that can be exercised at any time

before the option's maturity date.
See **European option.**

Amortization (2)   The process of
converting the cost of an
intangible asset, such as
goodwill, into periodic expenses
reported in the firm's **income
statement.** When the asset is
tangible, the same process is
called **depreciation.**

Annual report (2)   Public report
that is prepared by a firm
annually and that contains the
year's **financial statements.**

Annuity (6)   A cash-flow stream
that is composed of a sequence
of equal and uninterrupted
periodic cash flows.

Annuity discount factor (ADF)
(6)   A **discount factor** that
gives the **present value** of an
annuity. See Appendix 6.1.

Appreciation (currency) (13)
Increase in the value of one
currency expressed in terms of
another currency.

Arbitrage transaction (13)
Transaction that attempts to take
advantage of discrepancies
between asset prices.

Arbitrageurs (13)   Parties
involved in an **arbitrage
transaction.**

Arrearage (9)   Refers to unpaid
dividends for **preferred stock.**

As-is value (12)   *See* **stand-alone
value.**

Asset (2)   An economic resource
that is expected to generate a
profit in the future. See **assets
(of a firm).**

Asset-based borrowing (9)
Loans extended with **tangible
assets** pledged as **collateral** or
guarantee.

Asset beta (10)   The **beta** of a
firm's stock if the firm is all-
equity financed. Same as

unlevered beta. See equation
10.7 and **equity beta.**

Asset multiple (12)   Share price
divided by the **book-value-of-
assets** per share; used to value a
firm. See **valuation by
comparables.**

Asset rotation (1)   *See* **asset
turnover** or **turns.**

Asset turnover or **turns** (1, 5)
Sales divided by **assets.** A
measure of the efficiency of asset
management. See **capital
turnover** and **net asset
turnover.**

Assets (of a firm) (2)   What a
firm's **shareholders** collectively
own on the date of the **balance
sheet.** See **total assets.**

Ask price (13)   The price at
which a trader in the market is
willing to sell. Same as **offer
price.** See **bid price.**

Asymmetric information (11)   A
situation that arises when
managers (as insiders to the
firm) know more about the
firm's current performance and
future prospects than do
outsiders.

**Average age of accounts
receivable** (3)   *See* **average
collection period.**

Average collection period (3)
Accounts receivable at the end
of the period divided by the
average daily sales during that
period. A measure of operating
efficiency. See equation 3.8.

Average cost method (2)
Inventory valuation method that
assigns to all units in inventory
the average cost of the units
purchased. See **first-in, first-out**
and **last-in, first-out methods.**

Average payment period (3)
Accounts payable at the end of
the period divided by the

average daily **purchases** during that period. See equation 3.9.

Avoidable costs (8)   Costs that can be saved if an investment is not undertaken.

Balance sheet (1, 2)   **Financial statement** reporting, at a given date, the total amount of **assets** held by a firm and the **liabilities** and **owners' equity** that finance these assets. See equations 2.1, 2.2, Exhibit 2.1, and the **managerial balance sheet.**

Bank prime rate (9)   The rate **banks** charge their most creditworthy customers.

Bankers' cash flow (4)   **Earnings after tax** plus **depreciation expenses** and other noncash expenses. Same as **cash earnings.**

Bankruptcy (11)   A legal procedure through which the ownership of a firm's **assets** is transferred to **debtholders.**

Banks (1, 9)   *See* **commercial banks** and **investments banks.**

Basis point (9)   One hundredth of one percent. Example: 0.12 percent is equal to 12 basis points.

Bearer bonds/securities (9)   **Bonds/securities** that do not indicate the holder's name. See **registered securities.**

Benchmark rate (9)   Rate to which the **coupon rate** of a **floating rate bond** is linked.

Best efforts basis (9)   A method of distributing **securities** whereby an **investment bank** undertakes to do its best to sell on behalf of the firm the securities the firm has issued.

Beta (coefficient) (10)   A measure of risk based on the sensitivity of an individual stock's returns to changes in the returns of a broad stock market index. Same as **systematic, market, undiversifiable,** and relative **risk.**

Bid-ask spread (13)   The difference between the **bid price** and the **ask price.**

Bid price (13)   Price at which a trader in a market is willing to buy. See **ask price.**

Bidder (12)   In a **takeover,** the firm that wants to acquire all or a portion of another firm's shares.

Bond (9)   A debt **security** acknowledging a creditor relationship with the issuing firm and stipulating the conditions and terms under which the money is borrowed and repaid. See **century, convertible, Eurodollar, floating-rate, foreign, perpetual, Samurai, Shogun, Yankee, zero-coupon bonds** and **Eurobonds.**

Bond market (9)   Market where **bonds** are issued and traded.

Bond rating (9)   Rating assigned by an agency (such as Standard and Poor's or Moody's Investors Service) that provides an assessment of the **bond's credit risk.**

Bond value (9)   **Present value** of a **bond's** expected cash-flow stream discounted at a rate that reflects the risk of that cash-flow stream. See equation 9.4 and Appendix 9.1.

Bond value of a convertible bond (9)   Value of a **convertible bond** if it did not have a **conversion option.**

Bonding costs (11)   Costs (borne by **shareholders**) resulting from lenders placing restrictions on managerial flexibility. See **covenants** and **monitoring costs.**

Book value of asset (2)   Value at which an **asset** is shown in the firm's **balance sheet.**

Book value of equity (1, 2)   *See* **owners' equity.**

Book value multiple (12)   Share price divided by **book-value-of-equity** per share. Same as **price-to-book ratio.** Used to value a firm. See **valuation by comparables.**

Bookrunner (9)   *See* **originating house.**

Bottom line (2)   *See* **earnings after tax.**

Brokers (9)   Individuals or institutions that trade **securities** on behalf of a third party and do not own the securities.

Business assets (5)   **Working capital requirement** plus **net fixed assets.**

Business cycle (of a firm) (1)   Sequence of events starting with the acquisition of **assets** to generate sales, produce profits, pay dividends, retain earnings, build up **equity capital,** raise new debt, and grow the business via asset acquisition, thus, starting the cycle again. See Exhibit 1.6.

Business risk (1, 5, 10, 11)   The cumulative effect of **economic risk** and **operational risk,** stemming from the firm's inability to know for certain the outcome of its current investing and operating activities/decisions. See Exhibit 1.12.

Buy-back program (12, 14)   *See* **share buy-back program.**

Call option (9, 13)   A contract that gives the holder the right (with no obligation) to buy a fixed number of shares or a certain amount of currency at a fixed price during the life of the option (**American option**) or on its **expiration date** (**European option**). See **put option.**

Call provision (9)   **Option** available to a **bond** issuer to repay the bond before it reaches its **maturity date.** This provision can be immediate or **deferred.** See **call value** and **callable bond.**

Call value (9)   The price at which the issuer can buy a **callable bond** from its holder.

Callable bond (9)   A **bond** that gives the issuer the **option** to redeem (repay) the bond before it reaches its **maturity date.**

Capital (1)   The sum of **owners' equity** and all borrowed funds (short- and long-term). Same as **capital employed.**

Capital asset pricing model (**CAPM**) (10)   A formula according to which a **security's** expected return is equal to the **risk-free rate** plus a **risk premium.** It can be used to estimate the **cost of equity** of a firm or a project. See equations 10.10 and 10.11.

Capital assets (2)   *See* **noncurrent assets.**

Capital budgeting decision (6)   *See* capital investment decision.

Capital employed (1, 3, 5, 14)   The sum of **owners' equity** and all borrowed funds (short- and long-term). Equal to **invested capital.** See **managerial balance sheet** and Exhibit 3.2.

Capital expenditure (**capex**) (1, 4)   New investment in **fixed assets.**

Capital expenditure decision (6)   *See* capital investment decision.

Capital investment decision (6)   The decision to spend cash now in order to acquire long-lived **assets** that will be a source of

cash flows in the future. See **diversification, expansion, replacement,** and **required investments.**

Capital rationing (6)   Limit on the amount of capital that can be used to finance investment projects.

Capital structure decision (1, 5, 11)   Deciding on the amount of debt relative to **equity capital** a firm should adopt. Same as **financial structure decision.** See **target capital structure.**

Capital structure ratio (1)   A measure of **financial leverage.** See **debt ratio.**

Capital turnover (5, 14)   Sales divided by **invested capital.** A measure of the efficiency with which invested capital is managed. See equation 5.4.

Capitalization (of R&D) (14)   Conversion of R&D expenses into **assets** reported in the **balance sheet.**

Captive finance subsidiary (9)   A finance subsidiary owned by a firm.

Carry forward (8, 10)   Tax rule that allows a firm to deduct current interest expenses from *future* profits.

Carryback (8, 10)   Tax rule that allows a firm to deduct current interest expenses from *past* profits.

Cash and cash-equivalent (1, 2, 3)   Cash in hand, cash on deposit with banks, and short-term liquid investments with less than a year's maturity (**marketable securities).**

Cash-to-cash period or **cycle** (3)   Period between the date a firm pays its suppliers and the date it collects its invoices from customers. Same as **cash conversion period** or **cycle.**

Cash conversion period or **cycle** (3)   *See* **cash-to-cash period.**

Cash dividend (1, 2)   The portion of a firm's **net profit** distributed to shareholders in cash. See **dividend.**

Cash earnings (4, 12)   **Earnings after tax** plus **depreciation expenses** and other noncash expenses.

Cash-earnings multiple (12)   Share price divided by **cash earnings** per share. Same as **price-to-cash earnings ratio.** Used to value a firm. See **valuation by comparables.**

Cash flow from assets (CFA) (12)   Net cash flow generated by a firm's **assets.** See equation 12.4. Often referred to as **free cash flow.**

Cash flow from project/investment (8, 14)   Net cash flow generated by a project/investment. See equation 8.2.

Cash flow statement (4)   **Financial statement** reporting how a firm's cash position has changed during a particular period of time. See **statement of cash flows.**

Cash inflows (4)   Amount of cash or money that comes into a firm during a given period of time.

Cash outflows (4)   Amount of cash or money that goes out of a firm during a given period of time.

Century bonds (9)   **Bonds** with a 100-year **maturity.**

Certificates of deposit (CDs) (2, 9)   Short-term **securities** sold by banks in the **money markets** in order to raise cash.

Certification role (9)   Role played by **underwriters** with respect to guaranteeing the quality of the underwritten **securities.**

Characteristic line (10) A line whose slope measures the sensitivity of a stock's returns to changes in the returns of a market index. See **beta coefficient.**

Cleanup clause (9) Loan clause that requires the firm to be completely out of debt to the bank for at least one month during the year.

Coinsurance effect (12) Describes a situation in which merged firms are perceived by their creditors to be less likely to fail as a combination than as separate entities.

Collateral (9, 12) Any **assets** pledged as guarantee to a lender in case the borrower defaults.

Commercial banks (1, 9) **Financial intermediaries** that take deposits, make payments, and extend loans.

Commercial paper (CP) (1, 2, 9) **Unsecured security** issued by firms to raise short-term funds in the **money market.**

Common stock (1, 9) Certificate issued by a firm to raise **equity capital** that represents a specified share of total equity funds. See **stock certificate,** Appendix 9.2, and Exhibit 9.12.

Common stock account (2) Balance sheet account indicating the number of shares the firm has issued since its creation multiplied by the **par** or **stated value** of the shares.

Comparables (12) *See* **valuation by comparables.**

Compensating balances (3) Deposits that banks may require their corporate clients to maintain

with them in exchange for services they provide to the firm.

Compound factor (6) **Future value** of one dollar growing at a particular compound (or growth) rate for a given number of years.

Compounded value (6) **Future value** of an amount of money growing at a particular compound (or growth) rate for a given number of years.

Conglomerate merger (12) Combination of unrelated businesses for which there are no obvious **synergies.**

Conservatism principle (2) States that **assets** and **liabilities** should be reported in **financial statements** at a value that would be least likely to overstate assets or to understate liabilities.

Conservative (financing) strategy (3) The use of long-term funds to finance both long-term investments and a portion of short-term investments. See **aggressive strategy** and **matching strategy.**

Constant annual equivalent cash flow (6) An equivalent stream of equal annual cash-flows with the same **present value** as another stream with variable annual cash-flows. See Appendix 6.1 and equation A6.5.

Constant growth dividend discount model (9) Formula that gives the value of a firm's equity as the **present value** of its expected future **dividend** stream discounted at a rate that reflects the risk of that dividend stream, when the dividends are assumed to grow forever at a constant rate. See equation 9.8 and Appendix 9.2. Also known as the Gordon Model.

Contingent value rights (CVR) (9) **Put options** sold by a firm that give the holder the right to sell a fixed number of shares to the issuing firm at a fixed priced during the life of the right.

Contingent voting rights (9) Right given to holders of **preferred stock** to elect members to the board of directors if the company has skipped **dividend** payments for a specified number of quarters.

Contractual exposure (13) Effect of changes in **exchange rates** on the firm's cash flows generated by *past* (contractual) transactions denominated in foreign currency and still outstanding. Same as **transaction exposure.** See **economic exposure.**

Control (retention of) (11) Refers to the policies adopted by current owners or management to prevent any outsiders from sharing or influencing the firm's operation and strategy.

Conversion premium (9) Difference between the **conversion price** of a **convertible bond** and the current price of the **stock,** if the former is higher, divided by the current stock price.

Conversion price (9) Price at which the holder of a **convertible bond** has the right to buy one share of the firm's **common stock.**

Conversion ratio (9) The number of shares into which each **convertible bond** can be converted.

Conversion value (9) The current price of the **stock**

multiplied by the number of shares to which the **convertible bond** can be converted.

Convertible bond (9)   A **bond** that the holder can convert into the firm's **common stock.** See **conversion premium, conversion price, conversion ratio,** and **conversion value.**

Corporate bond market (1, 9) Market in which companies raise long-term funds by issuing corporate **bonds** and **notes** that are then traded in this market. See **primary** and **secondary markets.**

Corporate bonds (9)   Debt **securities** issued by firms that usually have a maturity exceeding ten years.

Corporate notes (9)   Debt **securities** issued by firms that usually have a maturity between one and ten years.

Cost of capital (1, 6, 10)   The return expected by investors for the capital they supply to firms. Also, the highest return on an **alternative investment** with the same risk as the investment under consideration. See **firm's cost of capital** and **project's cost of capital.**

Cost of debt (1, 10)   The cost of borrowing new funds. See equations 10.2 and 10.3.

Cost of equity (1, 10)   Rate of return required by the firm's owners on their **equity capital** used to finance the firm's **assets** or a particular project. Can be estimated with the **constant growth dividend discount model** (equation 10.5) or the **capital asset pricing model** (equation 10.11).

Cost of goods sold (COGS) (2) The cost of the goods the firm has sold during the accounting period; reported in the **income statement** as expenses.

Cost of sales (2)   *See* **cost of goods sold.**

Cost synergies (12)   Cost reductions resulting from combining the operations of two or more firms. See **market synergies.**

Country risk (13)   The risk that the cash flows from a project may be affected by changes in local regulations governing foreign investments. Same as **political risk.**

Counterparty risk (13)   The risk that one party in a **currency swap** does not meet his contractual obligation. See **currency swap contract.**

Coupon payment (9)   The periodic (contractual) interest payment paid to bondholders over the life of a **bond.**

Coupon rate (9)   **Coupon payment** divided by the **face value** of a **bond.**

Covenants (restrictive) (9, 11) Conditions imposed by lenders and stipulated in a bond **indenture** that require managers to achieve certain financial targets or refrain from certain actions that may be detrimental to lenders' interests.

Credit markets (9)   Markets where debt **securities** are issued and traded.

Credit rating agency (9)   An agency, such as Standard and Poor's or Moody's Investment Service, that provides **credit ratings.**

Credit rating (9)   Rating that provides an overall assessment of a borrower's **credit risk.** See **credit rating agency.**

Credit risk (9)   The risk that a borrower will be unable to service its debt. See **debt service.**

Creditors (1)   Parties to whom a firm owes money, including lenders and suppliers.

Cross rates (13)   **Foreign exchange rates** between two currencies computed from their exchange rate with a third currency.

Currency forward contract (13) Agreement between two parties specifying the fixed price at which two currencies will be exchanged at a specified future date (**settlement date**).

Currency futures (contract) (13) A **currency forward contract** that has a standardized contract size and a standardized delivery date; traded on **futures markets.**

Currency market (13)   *See* **foreign exchange market.**

Currency option (contract) (13) A contract that gives the holder the right (with no obligation) to buy (**call option**) or sell (**put option**) a stated amount of currency at a specified exchange rate before (**American option**) or on the **expiration date** (**European option**) of the option.

Currency option hedge (13) Hedging with **currency options.**

Currency rate (13)   *See* **foreign exchange rate.**

Currency risk (1, 9, 13)   Risk arising from unexpected changes in the **exchange rate** between two currencies. Same as **foreign exchange risk.**

Currency swap (contract) (13) Agreement with a bank to exchange a set of future cash flows denominated in one currency for another set denominated in another currency.

Current assets (2)   **Assets** that are expected to be turned into cash within one year. Same as **short-term assets.** Reported in the **balance sheet.**

Current liabilities (2) Obligations of a firm that must be paid within one year. Same as **short-term liabilities.** Reported in the **balance sheet.**

Current maturity (9)   At any point in time, the time remaining until a **bond** is redeemed (repaid).

Current ratio (3)   **Current assets** divided by **current liabilities.** A measure of **liquidity.** See equation 3.13 and **quick ratio.**

Current (translation) method (13)   A method of translating the **financial statements** of a foreign business unit. **Balance sheets** accounts are translated at the **exchange rate** prevailing at the date of the balance sheet. **Revenues** and **expenses** in the **income statement** are translated at the rate when they occur or at the average rate during the period covered by the statement. See Appendix 13.1.

Current yield (9)   A **bond's coupon payment** divided by its price.

Cutoff period (7)   In capital budgeting, the period (usually in years) below which a project's **payback period** must fall in order to accept the project.

Days of sales outstanding (DSO) (3)   *See* **average collection period.**

Dealers (9)   Individuals or institutions that trade securities that they own. See **brokers.**

Debentures (9)   **Bonds** supported by the general credit standing of the issuing firm (U.S. definition).

Debt capital (1)   **Capital** provided by borrowed funds.

Debt capacity (11)   The ability to quickly raise debt in the future if a need for funds arises unexpectedly.

Debt ratio (5, 11)   A measure of **financial leverage.** Usually identified as the **debt-to-invested capital ratio** or the **debt-to-equity ratio.**

Debt service (9, 11)   The timely and full payment of interest on borrowed funds as well as the repayment of the borrowed funds.

Debt-to-equity ratio (5, 11)   Total interest-bearing debt divided by **owners' equity.** A measure of **financial leverage.**

Debt-to-invested capital ratio (5) Debt divided by the sum of debt and equity.

Debtholders (1, 9)   Holders of loans, leasing agreements, **corporate bonds,** and similar **liabilities** issued by firms to raise **debt capital.**

Default risk (9)   *See* **credit risk.**

Deferred call provision (9) Provision that allows the issuer of a **callable bond** to repay (or call) the bond only after a specified date (first date of call).

Deferred tax (liability) (2) Taxes owed to the tax authority originating from the difference between the amount of tax due on the firm's reported pretax profit and the amount of tax claimed by the tax authorities.

Depreciation (accounting) (2) The process of periodic and systematic value-reduction of the **gross value of fixed assets** over their **accounting life.**

Depreciation (currency) (13) Reduction in the value of one currency expressed in terms of another currency.

Depreciation charge (2)   *See* **depreciation expense.**

Depreciation expense (2)   The portion of the cost of a **fixed asset** that is expensed during the accounting period and reported in the **income statement.** Same as **depreciation charge.**

Differential cash flows (8)   *See* **incremental cash flows.**

Dilution (9, 11)   Reduction in the fraction of a firm's equity held by its existing **shareholders** after the firm sells **common stock** to new investors.

Direct costs of financial distress (11)   The actual costs the firm will incur if it becomes legally bankrupt, such as payments to lawyers and other third parties. See **indirect costs of financial distress.**

Direct financing (9)   When firms raise funds by issuing **securities** that are held by ultimate savers **(household sector)** instead of **financial intermediaries.** See **indirect financing.**

Direct lease (9)   A **financial lease** involving a straight contract between the owner of an **asset** (the **lessor**) and the user of that asset (the **lessee**).

Discount factor (DF) (6) **Present value,** at a particular **discount rate,** of one dollar to be received after a specified number of years.

Discount rate (6)   Rate at which future cash flows are discounted to the present. See **discounting.**

Discounted (cash-flow) value (DCF value) (1, 6)   The value today of an expected future cash-flow stream discounted at a rate that reflects its **risk.** The DCF value of a firm's equity equals the DCF value of its **assets**

minus the value of its debt. Same as **present value.** See **discounting.**

Discounted payback period (7) Capital budgeting method that measures a project's **payback period** with cash flows that have been discounted to the present at the project's **cost of capital.** See **discounted payback rule.**

Discounted payback period rule (7) Accept (reject) the project if its discounted payback period is shorter (longer) than a given **cutoff period.** See Exhibit 7.15.

Discounting (1, 6) The mechanism used to convert future cash flows into their equivalent value today.

Discretionary cash flow (4) Cash flow available to the firm for strategic investment and financing decisions after all of the firm's financial obligations are met.

Diversifiable risk (10) Risk that can be eliminated through portfolio diversification. Same as **unsystematic risk** or company-specific risk.

Diversification investments (6) Investments in areas unrelated to the existing activities of the firm.

Dividend (1, 2) The portion of a firm's **net profit** paid out to its owners in cash. Same as **cash dividend.** See **dividend payout ratio, dividend policy,** and **dividend yield.**

Dividend discount model (DDM) (9, 12) A formula that values a firm's equity as the present value of the entire stream of cash dividends the firm is expected to generate in the future. See Appendix 12.1 and **constant growth dividend discount model.**

Dividend payout ratio (1, 5) **Dividends** divided by **net profit.** See **dividend policy.**

Dividend policy (1, 2, 11) The decision regarding the portion of a year's profit that should be paid out in the form of cash dividends to the firm's shareholders. See **stable dividend policy.**

Dividend yield (10) **Dividend** per share divided by share price. See equation 10.5.

Doubtful accounts (2) Accounts arising when it is expected that some customers will not meet their payment obligations towards the firm. See **allowance for bad debts.**

Earnings after tax (EAT) (1, 2) **Revenues** minus all **expenses,** including interest and tax expenses. Same as **net income, net profit** and **bottom line.**

Earnings before depreciation interest and tax (EBDIT) (4) **Revenues** minus all **operating expenses,** excluding **depreciation expenses** and **amortization.** Same as **earnings before interest, tax, depreciation, and amortization (EBITDA).**

Earnings before interest and tax (EBIT) (2) Difference between the firm's **operating profit** and any **extraordinary items** reported in its **income statement.**

Earnings before interest, tax, depreciation and amortization (EBITDA) (4) **Revenues** minus all **operating expenses,** excluding **depreciation** and **amortization.** Same as **earnings before depreciation, interest and tax (EBDIT).**

Earnings before tax (EBT) (1, 2) **Earnings before interest and tax** minus net interest expenses.

Earnings multiple (5, 12) Share price divided by the firm's **earnings per share.** Same as **price-to-earnings ratio.** Used to value a firm. See **valuation by comparables.**

Earnings per share (EPS) (5) **Earnings after tax** divided by the total number of shares **outstanding.** See equation 5.13.

Economic exposure (13) Effect of changes in **exchange rates** on the value of the firm's *future* cash flows generated either by *past* and *known* transactions (**contractual** or **transaction exposure**) or by *future* and *uncertain* transactions (**operating exposure**).

Economic life (8) Number of years over which a project adds value to a firm, as opposed to the number of years over which it is depreciated (**accounting life**).

Economic payback period (7) *See* **discounted payback period.**

Economic profit (1, 14) *See* **economic value added.**

Economic risk (1) Risk arising from unexpected sales fluctuations due to the uncertain economic, political, social, and competitive environment in which firms operate. See **business risk** and Exhibits 1.11 and 1.12.

Economic value added (EVA) (1, 14) **Net operating profit after tax (NOPAT)** minus a charge for the capital consumed to achieve that profit. See equations 14.6 and 14.7. Same as **economic profit.** See **market value added.**

Economies of scale (12) The ability of a firm to reduce its average costs of production and distribution because of size. A motivation to acquire other companies. See **cost** and **market synergies.**

Effective corporate tax rate (5) The tax rate at which a firm actually pays its taxes, which may differ from the **statutory corporate tax rate** if some of the firm's earnings are taxed at a different rate.

Efficient securities markets (1, 9) Markets in which share prices adjust to new and relevant information as soon as it becomes available to market participants.

Entry barriers (1) Barriers that are costly enough to discourage potential competitors from entering a particular market.

Equipment financing loan (9) A medium- to long-term loan backed by a piece of machinery. See **collateral.**

Equity beta (10) The beta of a firm's **common stock.** Same as **levered beta** and **market beta.**

Equity capital (1, 3) Funds contributed by shareholders that are equal to the difference, at a particular date, between what a firm's **shareholders** collectively own, called **assets,** and what they owe, called **liabilities.** Same as **equity funds, owners' equity, shareholders' equity** or **funds,** or **net asset value.**

Equity funds (1) *See* **equity capital.**

Equity kicker (9) The **conversion option** of a **convertible bond.**

Equity multiplier (5) **Invested capital** divided by **owners' equity.** A measure of **financial leverage.**

Eurobonds (9) **Bonds** issued in the **Euromarket.**

Eurocommercial paper (EuroCP) (9) **Commercial paper** issued in the **Euromarket.**

Eurocurrency (9) The currency in which **securities** issued outside the jurisdiction of a particular country are denominated.

Eurodollar bonds (9) **Bonds** denominated in U.S. dollars that are sold simultaneously to investors in several countries via the **Euromarket.**

Euroequity (9) Equity issued in the **Euromarket.**

Euromarket (9) A market that is outside the direct control and jurisdiction of the issuer's country of origin.

European option (13) An **option** that can be only exercised on the maturity date of the option. See **American option.**

Ex-rights shares (9) Shares for which rights were issued but which are no longer traded with their rights attached. See **right, rights-on shares** and equations 9.2 and 9.3.

Exchange rate (13) The price one has to pay in one country's currency to buy one unit of another country's currency. Same as **foreign exchange rate** or **currency rate.**

Exchange rate risk (13) Risk borne by firms with foreign operations that originates from unexpected changes in the exchange rate between two currencies.

Exercise price (currency option) (13) The fixed exchange rate at which a currency can be bought or sold in an **option contract.** Same as **strike price.**

Exercise price (warrant) (9) The fixed price at which the holder of a **warrant** has the right to buy shares. Same as **strike price.**

Exit barriers (5) Barriers, such as high capital investment, that significantly reduce a firm's ability to leave an industry by selling its **assets** rapidly and easily.

Exit strategy (12) The way **leveraged buyout (LBO)** investors cash in on their investment by selling some (or all) of their shares after a period of time (to other investors or through an **initial price offering (IPO)).**

Expansion investments (6) Projects that result in additional sales revenues, margins, and **working capital requirement.**

Expected multiple (12) Multiples calculated using a forecast of future financial data; used to value a firm. See **historical multiples** and **valuation by comparables.**

Expense (2) A firm's activity that results in a decrease in the value of **owners' equity.**

Expiration date (option) (13) The fixed **settlement date** of an **option** contract. Same as **maturity date.**

External funds need (9) **Internally generated funds** less **funding needs.** See equation 9.1

Extraordinary items (2) Nonrecurrent losses or gains.

Face value (9) The fixed amount that has to be paid back to bondholders at the maturity date of a **bond.** Same as **principal, par value,** or **redemption value.**

Fair market value (14) An estimate of the amount that could be received on the sale of an **asset** under normal market conditions (as opposed to an emergency or liquidating sale)

Fair price (9)   Best estimate of the unobservable value of a firm's **assets** and **securities**.

Financial balance (1, 5)   Achieved when the firm can finance its growth without modifying its operating and financing policies and without issuing new equity. See **self-sustainable growth rate**.

Financial cost effect (5)   The negative effect of an increase in debt financing on **return on equity (ROE)**—more debt means larger interest payments, which reduces **earnings after tax** and lowers **ROE**. See **financial structure effect**.

Financial cost ratio (5)   **Earnings before tax** (EBT) divided by **earnings before interest and tax** (EBIT). A measure of **financial leverage** based on **income statement** data. See **financial structure ratio** and **financial leverage multiplier**.

Financial distress (11)   Situation arising when a firm finds it increasingly difficult to service its debt. See **debt service** and **financial distress costs**.

Financial distress costs (1, 11)   Direct and indirect costs borne by a firm with excessive borrowing that has difficulties servicing its debt, and which reduce the firm's value. See **debt service** and **direct** and **indirect costs of financial distress**.

Financial distress risk (11)   The risk that the firm will experience **financial distress costs** as its use of debt financing rises.

Financial flexibility (11)   Having a build up of cash that allows for immediate investment and that increases the firm's **debt capacity**.

Financial gearing (5, 11)   *See* **financial leverage**.

Financial intermediaries (9)   Institutions that act as "middlemen" between the ultimate recipients of capital (firms) and the ultimate suppliers of capital (**household sector**). See Exhibit 9.4.

Financial lease (9)   A long-term lease that extends over most of the **useful life** of the **asset**.

Financial leverage (5, 11)   The use of debt financing to complement equity financing.

Financial leverage multiplier (5)   The **financial cost ratio** multiplied by the **financial structure ratio**. See equation 5.11.

Financial risk (1, 5, 10, 11)   **Business risk** magnified by the presence of borrowing. See Exhibits 1.11, 1.12, **funding risk,** and **interest-rate risk**.

Financial slack (11)   Cash surplus that firms may build up during good times. See **financial flexibility**.

Financial statements (1, 2)   Formal documents issued by firms to provide financial information about their business and financial transactions. See **income statement** and **balance sheet**.

Financial strategy matrix (14)   A diagnostic and managerial tool that compares the capacity of a particular business to create value versus its capacity to finance the growth of its sales. See Exhibit 14.8.

Financial structure decision (5, 11)   *See* **capital structure decision** and **target capital structure**.

Financial structure effect (5)   The positive effect of an increase in debt financing on **return on equity (ROE)**—more debt means less equity capital and thus higher **ROE**. See **financial cost effect**.

Financial structure ratio (5)   **Invested capital** (or **net assets**) divided by **owners' equity**. A measure of **financial leverage** based on **balance sheet** data. See **financial cost ratio** and **financial leverage multiplier**.

Financial system (9)   The institutions and practices that allow the cash surplus of "savers" to be channeled to firms with a cash shortage.

Finished goods inventory (2)   The cost of completed units not yet sold at the date of the **balance sheet**.

Firm's cost of capital (10)   The return expected by investors for the capital they supply to fund *all* the **assets** acquired and managed by the firm.

First-in, first-out (FIFO) method (2)   Inventory valuation method that assigns to all units in inventory the cost of the unit purchased first. See **last-in, first-out method** and **average cost method**.

Fisher effect (13)   States that the **nominal interest rate** is the sum of the **real interest rate** and the expected inflation rate.

Fisher intersection (7)   The point at which the **NPV profiles** of two investments intersect. See Exhibit 7.11.

Fixed asset turnover or turns (5) Sales divided by **fixed assets.** A measure of the efficiency of **fixed assets** management. Same as fixed asset rotation.

Fixed assets (2) *See* **noncurrent asset.**

Flotation costs (9, 11) Costs incurred when issuing **securities.** Same as **issuance** or **issue costs.**

Floating rate bond or floater (9) A **bond** whose rate is linked to another rate which is revised periodically.

Foreign bonds (9) **Bonds** issued in the domestic **bond market** of another country.

Foreign exchange line of credit (13) **Line of credit** demanded by a bank to guarantee a firm's ability to deliver on its **foreign exchange** obligations.

Foreign exchange market (13) Market in which currencies are bought and sold. Same as **currency market.**

Foreign exchange rate (13) *See* **exchange rate.**

Foreign exchange risk (9, 13) Risk arising from unexpected changes in the **exchange rate** between two **currencies.** Same as **exchange risk** and **currency risk.**

Foreign securities (9) **Securities** issued in the domestic market of another country.

Forward contract (currency) (13) *See* **currency forward contract.**

Forward hedge (13) Hedging with **forward contracts.**

Forward rate (13) The fixed rate at which a **forward contract** is settled.

Forward window contract (13) Similar to a standard **forward contract** except that the transaction can be settled over a period of time (the window) instead of on fixed date.

Free cash flow (4) The cash flow generated by a firm's **assets.** See equation 12.4. Same as **cash flow from assets.**

Fundamental finance principle (1) States that a business proposal will raise the firm's value only if the **present value** of the future stream of net cash benefits the proposal is expected to generate exceeds the initial cash outlay required to undertake the proposal. Same as the **net present value rule.**

Funding needs (9) Funds needed to finance the growth of the firm's **invested capital.**

Funding risk (3) Risk arising from the unwillingness of a lender to renew the loans made to finance **assets,** thus forcing the firm to sell part or all of these assets to repay the loan. See **interest-rate risk.**

Future value (6) The value at a future date of an amount deposited today that grows at a given compound, or growth, rate.

Futures contract (13) A **forward contract** that has a standardized contract size and delivery date.

Futures hedge (13) Hedging with a **futures contract.**

Futures markets (13) **Organized exchanges** where **futures contracts** are traded.

Gearing (5, 11) *See* **financial leverage.**

General cash offering (9) The issuance and sale of a firm's **securities** to any investor, including current **shareholders.** Same as **public offering.** See Exhibit 9.7 and **rights offering.**

Going concern (12) An assumption according to which a firm will operate forever.

Goodwill (2) The difference between the (higher) price at which a firm has been acquired and either its reported **net book value** or its estimated **fair value.**

Government bills (2) Short-term **marketable securities** issued by governments.

Gross profit (2) The difference between the firm's net sales and its **cost of goods sold.**

Gross value (of fixed assets) (2) The purchase price of **fixed assets** reported in the **balance sheet.** Same as **historical price.** See **net fixed assets.**

Ground floor financing (12) **Equity capital** financing in a **leveraged buyout (LBO).**

Hedge (currency) (13) The process of protecting the value of an **asset** or a **liability** from currency fluctuations.

High-yield bonds (9) *See* **speculative grade bonds** and **junk bonds.**

Historical cost principle (2) *See* **acquisition cost principle.**

Historical multiples (12) **Multiples** calculated using past financial data. Same as **trailing multiples.** See **expected** or **prospective multiples.** Used to value a firm. See **valuation by comparables.**

Historical price (2) The acquisition price of an **asset.** See **gross value of fixed assets.**

Homemade diversification (12) The **diversification** investors can achieve themselves by combining shares of different companies in their personal portfolios.

Homemade leverage (11) Personal financial leverage as opposed to corporate **financial leverage.**

Horizontal merger (12) Two firms in the same sector pooling their resources.

Household sector (9) The sector of the economy composed of individuals and families.

Hurdle rate (7) An investment's cost of capital (see **weighted average cost of capital**) when used in comparison with the investment's **internal rate of return.** Same as **minimum required rate of return.**

Illiquid firm (3) A firm that is no longer able to pay its creditors.

In the black (2) A firm with positive **earnings after tax.** See **in the red.**

In the red (2) A firm with negative **earnings after tax.** See **in the black.**

Income statement (1, 2) **Financial statement** reporting information about the firm's activities that resulted in changes in the value of **owners' equity** during a period of time, obtained by deducting from **revenues** the corresponding **expenses** incurred during that period of time.

Income tax expense (1, 2) Provision for taxes computed in accordance with **accounting principles.**

Incremental cash flows (8) The difference between the firm's expected cash flows if the investment is made and its expected cash flows if the investment is not undertaken. Same as **differential cash flows.**

Indenture (bonds) (9) Formal contract between a **bond** issuing firm and its lenders.

Indirect costs of financial distress (11) Costs created by the increasing probability that a firm may become bankrupt, thus preventing it from operating at maximum efficiency. Includes loss of customers, departure of key employees, and the inability to obtain credit from suppliers. See **direct costs of financial distress.**

Indirect financing (9) When firms raise funds by issuing **securities** that are held by **financial intermediaries** instead of ultimate "savers." See **direct financing.**

Indirect securities (9) **Securities** issued by banks (checking and savings accounts) and other **financial intermediaries** (such as insurance policies and retirement plans).

Inefficient management hypothesis (12) Refers to a rationale for **takeover** whereby the **target firm** is not currently managed at its optimal level and the **acquiring firm's** managers believe that they can do a better job if they buy the target firm and run it themselves.

Initial margin (13) A requirement to deposit a portion of the initial investment when trading in a **securities** or **futures market.**

Initial public offering (IPO) (9) When a firm sells equity to the public for the first time. See **seasoned new issue.**

Institutional investors (9) Any **financial intermediaries** that invest in the **financial markets.**

Intangible assets (2) **Assets** such as **goodwill,** patents, trademarks, and copyrights.

Interbank (currency) market (13) The **foreign exchange market** whose major participants are large banks.

Interest coverage ratio (5) *See* **times-interest-earned ratio.**

Interest rate parity relation (13) States that the percentage difference between the **forward** and **spot rates** is equal to the difference in interest rates between the home and foreign markets. See equation 13.9, Exhibit 13.10, and Appendix 13.2.

Interest-rate risk (3) Risk arising from unexpected changes in the level of interest rates that affect the firm's future cost of debt financing. See **funding risk.**

Interest tax shield (11) The annual and recurrent tax saving resulting from debt financing. See equations 11.3 and 11.8.

Internal equity financing (1) Refers to **retained earnings,** the part of a firm's profit that the firm's owners decide to invest back into their company.

Internal rate of return (IRR) (1, 7) The discount rate that makes the **net present value** of a project equal to zero.

Internal rate of return rule (1, 7) Accept (reject) a proposal if its **internal rate of return (IRR)** is higher (lower) than its **weighted average cost of capital (WACC).** See Exhibit 7.15.

Internally generated funds (9) The sum of **retained earnings** and **depreciation expenses.** See equation 9.1.

International Fisher effect (13) States that the difference in interest rates between two countries reflects the difference in their expected inflation rates. See equation 13.7, Exhibit 13.10, Appendix 13.2.

Inventories (1, 2) Raw materials, work in process, and finished goods not yet sold, reported in the **balance sheet** as **current assets.** See **first-in, first-out (FIFO), last-in, first-out (LIFO)** and **average cost methods.**

Inventory turn or turnover (3) **Cost of goods sold** divided by ending **inventories.** See equation 3.7 and Exhibit 3.10. A measure of the efficiency of inventory management.

Invested capital (1, 3) The sum of **cash** and **marketable securities, working capital requirement** and **net fixed assets.** Same as **net assets.** Equal to **capital employed.** See equation 3.1 and the **managerial balance sheet.**

Investment banks (1, 9) **Financial intermediaries** that act as "middlemen" between firms wanting to issue **securities** to raise funds and the suppliers of capital. See **bookrunner, lead manager, originating house, merchant bankers,** and **underwriters.**

Investment grade bonds (9) Highly rated **bonds** (BBB and above) that can be purchased by pension funds and other institutional investors. See **speculative grade bonds** and **bond ratings.**

Irrelevant costs (8) Costs (past or future) that the firm must bear even if the investment project is not undertaken. See **unavoidable costs** and **sunk costs.**

Issuance or issue costs (9, 11) Costs incurred when issuing

securities. Same as **flotation costs.**

Junior bond/debt/loan (9) *See* **subordinated bond/debt/loan.**

Junk bond/debt (9) *See* **speculative grade bond/debt.**

Last-in, first-out (LIFO) method (3) Inventory valuation method that assigns to all units in inventory the cost of the unit purchased last. See **first-in, first-out method** and **average cost method.**

Law of one price (LOP) (13) States that any traded good should sell for the same price (when expressed in the same currency) regardless of the country where it is sold. See Appendix 13.2.

Lead manager (9) *See* **originating house.**

Leading and lagging (13) Timing the **cash inflows** and **cash outflows** from different foreign business units to reduce the firm's overall exposure to **exchange rate risk.**

Lease financing (9) *See* **direct lease, financial lease, leveraged lease, operating lease,** and **sale and leaseback lease.**

Lessee (9) The user of the **asset** that is leased.

Lessor (9) The owner of the **asset** that is leased.

Leverage (5, 11) *See* **financial leverage.**

Leveraged buyout (LBO) (12) Transaction in which a group of investors purchase a firm by borrowing an unusually large amount of debt relative to equity capital.

Leveraged lease (12) A **financial lease** in which the leasing company finances the

purchase of the **asset** with a substantial level of debt, using the lease contract as **collateral.**

Levered assets (12) **Assets** financed with some **debt capital.**

Levered beta (10) The beta of a stock when the firm is indebted. Same as **equity** or **market beta.**

Levered firm (12) A firm that finances its **assets** with some borrowed funds.

Liabilities (2) What a firm's shareholders collectively owe on the date of the **balance sheet.**

Line of credit (9) A nonbinding arrangement in which a **bank** lends a firm a stated maximum amount of money over a fixed but renewable period of time, usually one year. In general, no fee is charged but a **compensating balance** is required.

Liquid assets (2) *See* **cash** and **cash equivalents.**

Liquidation value (12) Amount of cash that can be raised if the various items that make up a firm's **assets** are sold separately. Usually the minimum value of assets.

Liquidity (of a firm) (2, 3) The ability of a firm to meet short-term recurrent cash obligations. See **solvency.**

Liquidity (of a security) (9) The speed with which a **security** can be turned into cash without significant loss of value. See **market liquidity.**

Liquidity ratio (3) **Net long-term financing (NLF)** divided by **working capital requirement (WCR).** A measure of a firm's liquidity position. See equation 3.6.

Listed securities (9) **Securities** of firms that meet a number of stringent conditions that allow them to be traded in **organized**

stock exchanges. See **over-the-counter market.**

London interbank offering rate (LIBOR) (9)   The interest rate at which international banks lend U.S. dollars to one another.

Long-term debt/liabilities (2) **Debt/liabilities** due after a period longer than one year.

Long-term financing (3)   **Equity** plus **long-term debt.**

Long-term assets (2)   *See* **noncurrent assets.**

Lower-of-cost-or-market (2) Reporting method according to which **inventories** are shown in the **balance sheet** at their lowest value (their cost or their liquidation value if the latter is the lowest).

Managerial balance sheet (3) Restructured **balance sheet** that shows **invested capital (cash + working capital requirement + net fixed assets)** on one side and capital employed **(debt + equity capital)** on the other side. See Exhibit 3.2.

Managerial options (6)   Options that can be exercised to alter a project during its useful life, including the options to abandon, expand, or defer a project.

Margin call (13)   Call for additional deposit when the margin account has dropped below a preset level. See **initial margin.**

Marked-to-market (13)   **Futures contracts** are marked-to-market when daily profits or losses are settled at the end of each trading day.

Market beta (10)   **Beta** of a **stock** when the firm is indebted. Same as **equity** or **levered beta.**

Market capitalization (1, 14) Market value of a firm's **equity.** Equal to its quoted price per share multiplied by the total

number of shares the company has issued. Also referred to as market cap.

Market liquidity (9) Characterizes a market where buyers and sellers can quickly trade their **securities** at the quoted price and settle their transactions at a relatively low cost.

Market multiples (12)   Ratios used to value a firm. See **valuation by comparables.**

Market portfolio (10)   A benchmark portfolio containing all the assets in a particular market.

Market power hypothesis (12) **Takeover** rationale according to which the acquiring firm has a larger market share after the acquisition that may enable it to raise the price of its products.

Market risk (of a bond) (9) Sensitivity of a **bond price** to changes in interest rates.

Market risk (of common stock) (10)   Sensitivity of a stock price to changes in the general market movements. See **beta coefficient.**

Market risk premium (10)   The difference between the expected return on a portfolio of all existing common stocks and the **risk-free rate.** See **capital asset pricing model.**

Market synergies (12) Increased revenues, beyond pre-merger levels, resulting from combining the operations of two or more firms.

Market-to-book ratio (5, 12) Share price divided by **book-value-of-equity** per share. Used to value firms. See **valuation by comparables.**

Market value added (MVA) of a firm (1, 14)   The difference between the **market value of a**

firm's capital (equity and debt) and the amount of capital that **shareholders** and **debtholders** have invested in the firm.

Market value added (MVA) of a project (14)   The **present value** (at the **project's cost of capital**) of the future stream of annual **economic value added** the project is expected to generate in the future.

Market value of capital (14)   The market value of the firm's total **capital,** that is, the sum of its **market capitalization** and the market value of its **debt capital.**

Market yield (of a bond) (9) The rate that makes the **bond price** equal to the **present value** of the bond's future cash-flow stream.

Marketable securities (2) Short-term, **liquid assets investments** with less than a year's maturity held by a firm as a cash-equivalent asset.

Matching principle (2) Accounting principle according to which **expenses** are recognized in the **income statement** not when they are paid but during the period when they effectively contribute to the firm's revenues. See **accrual accounting.**

Matching strategy (3)   The financing of long-term investments with long-term funds and short-term investments with short-term funds in order to minimize **interest-rate risk** and **funding risk.** See **aggressive strategy** and **conservative strategy.**

Maturity (2,9)   A measure of the time before a **liability** is due.

Maturity date (9, 13)   The date on which the **face value** of a **bond** must be repaid. The date on which an **option contract**

must be settled. For an **option contract,** the maturity date is the same as the **expiration date.**

Members of the exchange (9) **Dealers** and **brokers** who have the right to trade in a **stock exchange.**

Merchant banks (1) *See* **investment banks.**

Mezzanine financing (12) **Junior unsecured** debt in a **leveraged buyout (LBO).**

Minimum required rate of return (7) An investment's cost of capital (see **weighted average cost of capital**) when used in comparison with the investment's **internal rate of return.** Same as **hurdle rate.**

Monetary/nonmonetary (translation) method (13) A method of translating the **financial statements** of a foreign business unit. Monetary **assets** (cash, **receivables**) and monetary **liabilities (payables, short-term** and **long-term debt)** are translated at the **exchange rate** prevailing at the date of the financial statements, and nonmonetary assets **(inventories, fixed assets)** are translated at the rate that prevailed when they were purchased. See Appendix 13.1.

Money market (1, 9) Market in which firms raise short-term funds and **money market instruments** are issued and traded.

Money market funds (2) **Financial intermediaries** that invest in the **money market.**

Money market instruments (9) **Debt securities** with **maturity** not exceeding one year.

Monitoring costs (9, 11) Costs resulting from lenders placing restrictions on the use of the funds they lend to companies. These costs are borne by **shareholders.**

Mortgage bond/loan (9) A medium- to long-term **bond**/loan backed by real estate. See **collateral.**

Multiples (12) Ratios used to value firms. See **historical multiples, expected multiples,** and **valuation by comparables.**

Mutually exclusive investments (7) If one is chosen, the other(s) must be turned down.

Negotiable (security) (9) A **security** that can be traded (exchanged among investors) in the **securities markets.**

Negotiable certificates of deposit (9) Short-term **securities** sold by banks in the **money markets** in order to raise capital.

Net advantage to leasing (NAL) (9) The **net present value** of the difference in cash flows between leasing and buying an asset. If **NAL** is positive, the asset should be leased.

Net asset rotation/turnover or turns (5) Sales divided by **net assets.** A measure of the efficiency of **net asset** management.

Net asset value (2) The difference, at a particular date, between what a firm's **shareholders** collectively own, called **assets,** and what they owe, called **liabilities.** Same as **net worth, owners' equity, shareholders' equity,** and **shareholders' funds.** Not to be confused with **net assets.**

Net assets (2, 3) **Cash** plus **working capital requirement** plus **net fixed assets.** Also, **total assets** less **operating liabilities.** Same as **invested capital.** Not to be confused with **net asset value.**

Net book value (2) The value at which a **fixed asset** is reported in the **balance sheet.**

Net capital expenditures (12) **Capital expenditures** less cash raised from the sales of existing **assets.**

Net cash flow (2) The difference between the firm's **cash inflows** and **outflows** during an **accounting period.**

Net fixed assets (1, 2) Long-term **assets,** such as equipment, machinery, and buildings, from which **accumulated depreciation** expenses have been deducted. See **fixed assets** and **gross value of fixed assets.**

Net income (2) *See* **earnings after tax.**

Net interest expenses (2) The difference between the interest expenses and interest income during an **accounting period.**

Net long-term financing (NLF) (3) **Long-term financing** less **net fixed assets.** See equation 3.4 and **liquidity ratio.**

Net operating cash flow (NOCF) (4) The net cash flow originating from the firm's operating activities during the period under consideration (cash inflows from operations minus cash outflows from operations). See equations 4.1, 4.3, and Appendix 4.1.

Net operating profit after tax (NOPAT) (1, 14) **Earnings before interest and tax** $\times$ $(1 - \text{tax rate})$. See **economic value added.**

Net present value (NPV) (1, 6, 7) The **discounted value** (at the **weighted average cost of capital**) of an investment's future stream of cash flows **(net operating cash flows** less **net**

capital expenditures) less the initial cash outlay required to launch the investment. See **fundamental finance principle** and **net present value rule.**

Net present value (NPV) profile (7) A graphical representation of the changes in the **net present value** of an investment as the discount rate varies.

Net present value (NPV) rule (1, 6) If a business proposal has a positive **net present value (NPV),** it should be carried out because it will increase the firm's value by an amount equal to the proposal's **NPV.** If a proposal's **NPV** is negative, it should be rejected. See Exhibits 6.17 and 7.15.

Net profit (1, 2) *See* **earnings after tax.**

Net profit margin (1) **Net profit** divided by sales. A measure of profitability.

Net sales (2) The **revenues** of the accounting period net of any discounts and allowances for defective merchandise and returned items.

Net short-term financing (NSF) (3) Short-term debt less cash. Equals **working capital requirement** less **net long-term financing.** Same as the portion of WCR financed with **short-term debt.** See equation 3.5.

Net working capital (NWC) (3) **Current assets** less **current liabilities.** See equation 3.12.

Net worth (2) *See* **owners' equity.**

Nominal cash flows (8) Cash flows measured in nominal terms, that is, including inflation.

Nominal interest rate (13) The interest rate that a borrower will actually pay, including a premium for the rate of inflation.

Nominal value (of a bond) (9) *See* **face value.**

Noncurrent assets (2) Long-lived **assets** that are not expected to be turned into cash within a year. Same as **long-term assets, fixed assets,** or **capital assets.** Can be **tangible** or **intangible assets** as well as financial assets.

Noncurrent liabilities (2) Obligations of a firm that are payable after more than one year.

Nondiscretionary cash flows (4) **Cash outflows** that the firm is legally obliged to meet.

Nondiversifiable risk (1, 10) *See* **systematic risk.**

Note (9) A debt **security** acknowledging a creditor relationship with the issuing firm and stipulating the conditions and terms under which the money was borrowed. Same as **promissory notes.**

Notes payable (2) Bank **overdrafts,** drawings on **lines of credit,** short-term **promissory notes,** and the portion of **long-term debt** due within a year.

Offer price (13) *See* **ask price.**

Operating activities (1, 3) The activities related to the management of a firm's existing investments in order to generate sales, profit, and cash.

Operating assets (3) **Assets** related to a firm's **operating cycle,** that is, **trade receivables, inventories,** and the portion of **prepaid expenses** associated with **operating activities.**

Operating cash-earnings multiple (12) Share price divided by **earnings before interest, tax, depreciation, and amortization (EBITDA)**

per share; used to value a firm. See **valuation by comparables.**

Operating cycle (1, 3) The sequence of **operating activities** that begins with the acquisition of raw materials and ends with the collection of cash for the sale of final goods. See Exhibit 3.3.

Operating expenses (2) Expenses related to **operating activities,** that is, **cost of goods sold, selling, general, and administrative expenses,** and **depreciation expenses.** Operating expenses exclude interest expenses, which are related to financing activities.

Operating exposure (13) Effect of changes in **exchange rates** on the firm's cash flows generated by *future* and *uncertain* transactions. See **economic exposure.**

Operating lease (9) A short-term lease for which the length of the contract is shorter than the **useful life** of the **asset** leased.

Operating liabilities (3) **Liabilities** related to a firm's **operating cycle,** that is, **trade payables** and the portion of **accrued expenses** associated with **operating activities.**

Operating profit (2) Net sales less **operating expenses.**

Operating profit margin (5) **Earnings before interest and tax (EBIT)** divided by sales. A measure of profitability.

Operating profit multiple (12) Share price divided by **earnings before interest and tax (EBIT)** per share; used to value a firm. See **valuation by comparables.**

Operational risk (1) The **volatility** of **operating profits** resulting from the presence of fixed **operating expenses** that magnify the volatility of sales. See Exhibits 1.11 and 1.12.

Opportunity cost (8)   Loss of revenues that results from giving up an activity in order to carry out an alternative one.

Optimal capital structure (11) The **debt-to-equity ratio** that maximizes the market value of the firm's **assets.** See **target capital structure.**

Option (contracts) (13)   A contract that gives the holder the right (with no obligation) to buy (**call option**) or sell (**put option**) a fixed number of **securities** or a stated amount of **currency,** at a specified price before (**American option**) or on the **expiration date** (**European option**) of the option.

Option premium (13)   The market price of an **option.**

Organized stock exchanges (9) Regulated markets in which **securities** must meet a number of stringent conditions to be listed and traded. See **over-the-counter markets.**

Original maturity (9)   The time between the day a **bond** is issued and the day it is **redeemed** (repaid).

Original price discount (9)   The difference between the issuing price of a **bond** and its **face value** when the former is lower.

Originating house (9)   The **investment bank** that has initiated and carried out the issuance of **securities** for a firm. Same as **lead manager** or **bookrunner.** See **underwriting syndicate.**

Outstanding securities (1) **Securities** that have been already issued.

Over-the-counter (OTC) markets (9)   Markets that do not require

companies to meet the listing requirements of **organized exchanges.** Stocks are traded through dealers connected by a network of telephones and computers.

Overdraft   A drawing of money against a previously established **line of credit.**

Overhead expenses (2)   *See* **selling, general, and administrative expenses.**

Owners' equity (1, 2)   The difference, at a particular date, between what a firm's **shareholders** collectively own, called **assets,** and what they owe, called **liabilities.** Same as **net asset value, net worth, shareholders' equity** and **shareholders' funds.**

Paid-in capital in excess of par (2)   The difference between the cumulative amount of cash that the firm received from shares issued up to the date of the **balance sheet** and the cash it would have received if those shares had been issued at **par value.**

Par value (2, 9)   For a share of **stock,** an arbitrary fixed value set when shares are issued. For a **bond,** the fixed amount (**face value**) that has to be paid back to bondholders at the maturity date of the bond.

Parity relations (13) Relationships linking the **spot exchange rates,** the **forward exchange rates,** the interest rates, and the inflation rates prevailing in two countries. See Exhibit 13.10 and Appendix 13.2.

Payables (1, 2) *See* **accounts payable.**

Payback period (7)   The number of periods (usually

years) required for the sum of the project's expected cash flows to equal its initial cash outlay. See **payback period rule, cutoff period, discounted payback period.**

Payback period rule (7)   Accept (reject) the project if its **payback period** is shorter (longer) than a given **cutoff period.** See **discounted payback rule** and Exhibit 7.15.

Pecking order (11)   Refers to the order in which firms raise capital, relying first on **retaining earnings** then issuing debt before finally raising new equity.

Pension liabilities (12) **Liabilities** owed to employees and paid to them when they retire.

Perpetual bond (9)A **bond** that never matures. See equation 9.6.

Perpetual cash-flow stream (12) A cash-flow stream with an infinite life.

Perpetuity (9)   An **annuity** with an infinite life. See Appendix 6.1

Political risk (13)   The risk that the cash flows from a project may be affected by changes in local regulations governing foreign investments. Same as **country risk.**

Pretax trading profit (1)   Same as **earnings before interest and tax.**

Preferred stocks (9)   A **security** that has a priority over **common stock** in the payment of **dividends** and a prior claim on the firm's **assets** in the event of liquidation, but has no voting rights. See equation 9.7 and Exhibit 9. 12.

Premium (bond) (9)   The difference between the price of a **bond** and its **face value,** if the former is higher.

Prepaid expenses (2)   Payments made by a firm for goods or services it will receive after the date of the **balance sheet.**

Present value (PV) (6)   The value today of an expected future cash-flow stream discounted at a rate that reflects its **risk.** Same as **discounted value.** See **discounting.**

Price-to-book ratio (P/B) (12)   Share price divided by **book value of equity** per share. Same as **market-to-book ratio** and **book value multiple;** used to value a firm. See **valuation by comparables.**

Price-to-cash earnings ratio (P/CE) (12)   Share price divided by **cash earnings** per share. Same as **cash earnings multiple;** used to value a firm. See **valuation by comparables.**

Price-to-earnings ratio (PER or P/E ratio) (5)   Share price divided by the firm's **earnings per share.** Same as **earnings multiple.** Used to value a firm. See **valuation by comparables**

Primary markets (1, 9)   Financial markets in which newly issued **securities** are sold to the public. See **secondary markets** and **underwriting.**

Principal (9)   *See* **face value.**

Private placement (9)   The issuance and sale of a firm's **securities** directly to financial institutions and **qualified investors,** thus bypassing the financial markets. See **public offering.**

Profit retention rate (1, 5)   **Retained earnings** divided by **net profit.**

Profit and loss statement (P&L) (1, 2) *See* **income statement.**

Profitability index (PI) (6, 7)   The **present value** of an

investment's expected cash-flow stream divided by the investment's initial cash outlay. See **profitability index rule.**

Profitability index rule (Accept (reject) the project if its **profitability index** is higher (lower) than one. See Exhibit 7.15.

Pro forma statements (2, 12)   **Financial statements** based on estimated, or projected, data.

Project's cost of capital (10)   The return expected by investors for the capital they supply to fund a specific project. Same as **project's opportunity cost of capital.**

Project's opportunity cost of capital (6)   The highest return on an **alternative investment** that must be given up in order to undertake another investment with the same risk. See **project's cost of capital.**

Promissory note (9)   A debt **security** acknowledging a **creditor** relationship with the issuing firm and stipulating the conditions and terms under which the money was borrowed.

Property, plant, and equipment (2)   **Tangible assets** such as land, buildings, machines, and furniture reported in the firm's **balance sheet** as **fixed assets.**

Prospective multiples (12)   *See* **expected multiples.**

Provisions (for bad debt) (14)   Provision for possible uncollectibility of **accounts receivable.** Same as **allowance for bad debts.**

Proxies/proxy firms (10)   Firms that exhibit the same risk characteristics as a project and that are used to estimate the **project's cost of capital.** Same as **pure-plays/pure-play firms.**

Public offering (9)   The issuance and sale of a firm's **securities** to the public at large, not only to its existing **shareholders.** Same as **general cash offering.** See Exhibit 9.7 and **rights offering.**

Purchases (3, 4)   **Cost of goods sold** plus change in **inventories** minus production costs. See equations 3.10, 3.11, and Appendix 4.1.

Purchasing power parity (PPP) relation (13)   States that the general cost of living should be the same across countries. See equation 13.2, Exhibit 13.10, and Appendix 13.2.

Pure-plays/pure-play firms (10)   *See* **proxies/proxy firms.**

Put option (9, 13)   A contract that gives the holder the right (with no obligation) to sell a fixed number of shares or a certain amount of currency at a fixed price during the life of the **option (American option)** or at the **expiration date** of the option **(European option).** See **call option.**

Qualified investors (9)   Investors who meet some minimum standards set by regulatory authorities that allows them to buy **securities** directly from firms. See **private placement.**

Quick assets (3)   The sum of cash and **accounts receivable.**

Quick ratio (3)   **Cash** plus **accounts receivable** divided by **current liabilities.** Same as **acid test.** A measure of **liquidity.** See equation 3.14 and **current ratio.**

Raw materials inventory (2)   The cost assigned to materials that have not yet entered the production process at the date of the **balance sheet.**

Real cash flows (8) Cash flows calculated with no adjustment for inflation.

Real interest rate (13) The interest rate adjusted for changes in the cost of living. See **nominal interest rate.**

Realization principle (2) The recognition of a revenue (in an **income statement**) during the period when the transaction generating the revenue has taken place, not when the cash generated by the transaction is received.

Recapitalization (5, 11) The substitution of **debt** for **equity,** leaving **assets** unchanged.

Receivables (1, 2) *See* **accounts receivable.**

Redeeming a bond (9) Repaying a **bond's face value** or **call value.**

Redemption value (of a bond) (9) *See* **face value.**

Redemption yield (of a bond) (9) *See* **yield to maturity.**

Reference rate (9) The rate to which the **coupon rate** of a **floating rate bond** is linked.

Registered bonds/securities (9) **Bonds/securities** that identify the holder's name. See **bearer securities.**

Relevant cash flows (8) Cash flows that are affected by an investment decision.

Relevant costs (8) Costs incurred only if the investment project is undertaken.

Replacement cost (2) The price the firm would have to pay at the date of the **balance sheet** to replace an **asset.**

Replacement cost principle (2) Asset valuation principle according to which the **net book value** of an **asset** is equal to the price the firm would have to pay at the date of the **balance sheet** to replace that asset less the amount of **accumulated depreciation.**

Replacement investments (6) Cost-saving projects that do not generate extra **cash inflows.**

Replacement value (of an asset) (12) What it would cost today to replace a firm's **assets** with similar ones in order to start a new business with the same earning power.

Required investments (6) Investments a firm must make to comply with safety, health, and environmental regulations. See **replacement** and **expansion investments.**

Reserves (2) The accumulation of **retained earnings** since the creation of the firm.

Residual value (of an asset) (8) The resale, or scrap, value of an **asset.** Same as **salvage value.**

Residual value (of a firm) (12) The estimated value that the firm will have at the end of a forecasting period, which is determined by the expected cash flows beyond the forecasting period.

Restrictive covenants (9, 11) *See* **covenants.**

Restructuring plan (12) Changes in a firm's **assets** or financing structures to improve its performance.

Retained earnings (1, 2) The part of a firm's profit that owners decide to invest back into their company. See **retention rate.**

Retention rate (5) **Retained earnings** divided by **earnings after tax (EAT).**

Return on assets (ROA) (5) **Earnings after tax (EAT)** divided by **total assets.** A measure of profitability.

Return on business assets (ROBA) (5) **Earnings before interest and tax (EBIT)** divided by **business assets (working capital requirement** plus **net fixed assets).** A measure of operating profitability.

Return on capital employed (ROCE) (5) **Net operating profit after tax (NOPAT** or **EBIT** $\times$ (1 − tax rate)) divided by **capital employed** (equity plus debt capital). Same as **return on net assets (RONA).** Equal to **return on invested capital (ROIC).** Can also be measured before tax by replacing **EBIT** $\times$ (1 − tax rate) with **EBIT.** A measure of operating profitability.

Return on equity (ROE) (1, 5) **Earnings after tax (EAT)** divided by **owners' equity.** A measure of the firm's profitability to shareholders.

Return on invested capital (ROIC) (1, 5, 14) **Net operating profit after tax (NOPAT** or **EBIT** $\times$ (1 − tax rate)) divided by **invested capital (cash** plus **working capital requirement** plus **net fixed assets).** Same as **return on net assets (RONA).** Equal to **return on capital employed (ROCE).** Can also be measured before tax by replacing **EBIT** $\times$ (1 − tax rate) with **EBIT.** A measure of operating profitability.

Return on investment (ROI) (5) A general measure of profitability that refers to the ratio of a measure of profit to a measure of the investment required to generate that profit.

Return on net assets (RONA) (5) *See* **return on invested capital (ROIC).**

Return on sales (ROS) (5) **Earnings after tax (EAT)** divided by sales. Same as **net profit margin.** A measure of profitability.

Return on total assets (ROTA) (5) **Earnings before interest and tax** divided by **total assets.** A measure of profitability.

Return spread (14) The difference between a firm's, or a project's, aftertax **return on invested capital (ROIC)** and its **weighted average cost of capital (WACC).** See **economic value added.**

Revenues (2) A firm's activities that result in increases in the value of **owners' equity.**

Revolving credit agreement (9) A legal agreement that a bank will lend a stated maximum amount of money over a fixed but renewable period of time. See **line of credit.**

Right (9) The privilege given to existing **shareholders** to buy shares of their firm at a fixed price during a specified period of time. See equation 9.3.

Rights offering (9) Offering of a firm's **common stocks** exclusively to its existing stockholders. See **subscription price, standby agreement, public offering,** and Exhibit 9.7.

Rights-on shares (9) Shares for which **rights** were issued and which are traded with their rights attached. See **ex-rights shares** and equations 9.2 and 9.3.

Risk (1) A term used to describe a situation in which a firm makes an investment that requires a known cash outlay without knowing the exact future cash flow the decision will generate. See **business risk, financial risk,** and Exhibits 1.5 and 1.6.

Risk averse (investors) (6) Investors who would buy shares of firms with riskier projects only if they expect to earn a higher return to compensate them for the higher risk they have to bear.

Risk class (6) A group of investments that exhibit the same risk characteristics.

Risk-free rate (10) The rate of return of a risk-free asset, usually government securities. See **capital asset pricing model.**

Risk premium (10) The difference between the expected return on a **security** and the **risk-free rate.** See **capital asset pricing model.**

Rolling over the forward contract (13) Entering into a new **forward contract** after the first contract expires.

Sale and leaseback lease (9) A **financial lease** under which the **lessee** sells the **asset** to the leasing company which immediately leases it back to the **lessee.**

Sales multiple (12) Share price divided by sales per share; used to value a firm. See **valuation by comparables.**

Sales-to-asset ratio (1, 5) Sales divided by **assets.** A measure of the efficiency of asset management.

Salvage value (8) The resale, or scrap, value of an **asset.** Same as **residual value.**

Samurai bonds (9) **Bonds** issued by non-Japanese firms in the Japanese corporate bond market and denominated in Japanese yen. See **Shogun bonds.**

Seasoned issue (9) When a firm returns to the market after an **initial public offering** for another issue of equity.

Secondary distribution (9) *See* **secondary public offering.**

Secondary market (1,9) Financial market in which **outstanding securities** are traded. See **primary market.**

Secondary public offering (9) The first time sale to the public of a relatively large block of equity held by an outside investor who acquired it earlier directly from the firm. Not to be confused with a **seasoned issue.**

Secured bond (9) A **bond** for which the issuer has provided **collateral** to the lender.

Securities and Exchange Commission (SEC) (9) U.S. government agency that approves the issuance and distribution of **securities** and regulates their subsequent trading on public markets.

Securities markets (9) Markets where **securities** can be traded.

Security (9) Certificate (or a book entry in the securityholder's account) issued by a firm that specifies the conditions under which the firm has received the money. See **bonds** and **preferred** and **common stocks.**

Security market line (SML) (10) A straight line that relates the expected returns on risky investments to their corresponding risk measured by the **beta coefficient.** See Exhibits 10.5 and 10.11 and the **capital asset pricing model.**

Self-liquidating loans (9) Short-term bank loans to firms that need to finance the seasonal buildup in their working capital investment and that bankers expect the firm to repay with the cash that will be released by the subsequent reduction in working capital.

Self-sustainable growth rate (SGR) (1, 5, 14)   The fastest growth rate a firm can achieve by retaining a constant percentage of its profit, keeping both its operating and financing policies unchanged, and not issuing new equity. Equal to the profit **retention rate** multiplied by **return on equity.** Same as **sustainable growth rate.** See equation 5.18.

Selling concession (9)   The fee received by the **selling group** for its efforts to sell the **securities** allocated to them by the **underwriter** of an issue. See **selling group.**

Selling, general, and administrative expenses (SG&A) (2)   Expenses incurred by the firm that relate to the sale of its products and the running of its operations during the **accounting period.**

Selling group (9)   A group of **investment banks** that agree to sell for a fee the **securities** allocated to them by the **underwriter** of an issue. See **selling concession.**

Senior bond/debt/loan (9, 12)   A **bond**/debt/loan that has a claim on the firm's **assets** (in the event of liquidation) that precedes the claim of **junior** or **subordinated debt.**

Settlement date (currency trading) (13)   The date at which the delivery of the currencies takes place.

Settlement price (for currency futures contracts) (13)   The quote of the last trade of the day for a **currency futures** that is **marked-to-market.**

Share buy-back program (14)   The buying by a firm of its own shares for the purpose of reducing the number of shares outstanding. Same as **share repurchase program.** The opposite of a new issue of shares.

Share repurchase program (12, 14)   *See* **share buy-back program.**

Shareholders (1)   Investors who have bought **common stocks** issued by a firm to raise **equity capital.** Shareholders are the owners of the firm.

Shareholders' equity (2)   *See* **owners' equity.**

Shareholders' funds (2)   *See* **owners' equity.**

Shogun bonds (9)   **Bonds** issued by non-Japanese firms in the Japanese corporate bond market and denominated in any currency other than yen. See **Samurai bonds.**

Short-term assets (2)   *See* **current assets.**

Short-term borrowing/debt/financing (2)   Short-term interest-bearing debt that includes bank **overdrafts,** drawings on **lines of credit,** short-term **promissory notes,** and the portion of any long-term debt due within a year.

Short-term liabilities (2)   *See* **current liabilities.**

Signaling effects (11)   Market reactions to a firm's actions, such as a drop in the firm's share price when the firm skips a dividend payment—an action interpreted by the market as a signal of weakening corporate cash flow.

Sinking fund provision (9)   Requires that a **bond** issuing firm set aside cash in a special account according to a regular schedule in order to allow the firm to redeem the bond at **maturity.**

Solvency (3)   A firm's ability to meet its long-term cash obligations.

Speculative grade bonds (9)   Corporate **bonds** with ratings below BBB. Same as **junk bonds** or **high-yield bonds.** See **bond ratings.**

Spot rate (13)   The rate at which a **spot transaction** is executed.

Spot transaction (13)   A trade between two parties in which both agree to a currency exchange at a rate fixed now for immediate delivery. See **currency forward contract.**

Spread (currency) (13)   The difference between the **ask price** and the **bid price** of a currency.

Spread (in floating rate bonds) (9)   The difference between the floating **coupon rate** and the **benchmark rate.**

Spread (in underwriting) (9)   The difference between the price at which an issue is sold to the public and the price paid by the **underwriter** to the issuing firm.

Stable dividend policy (11)   A dividend distribution policy that attempts to maintain a stable **dividend yield** over time.

Stand-alone value (12)   Estimated value of a **takeover target firm** before the acquiring firm factors in any performance improvements. Same as **as-is value.**

Standby agreement (9)   An agreement between a firm and an **underwriting syndicate** of **investment banks** such that the syndicate agrees to buy any shares that have not been sold during the period a **rights offering** is outstanding.

Standby fee (9)   Fee received by **investment banks** for underwriting the unsold portion of a **rights issue.**

Stated value (2)   An arbitrary fixed value attached to each share of **common stock** when it is issued.

Statement of cash flows (2, 4) **Financial statement,** such as FASB Standard 95, that provides information about the cash transactions between the firm and the outside world by separating these transactions into cash flows related to operating, investing, and financing activities. See **cash flow statement.**

Statutory corporate tax rate (5) Tax rate on earnings imposed by the tax authority. See **effective corporate tax rate.**

Stock certificate (9)   An equity **security** that recognizes an ownership position in the issuing firm, that provides holders with a claim on the firm's earnings and **assets,** and that entitles holders to vote at shareholder meetings.

Stock exchange (2, 9)   An **organized market** in which shares of companies are traded.

Stock markets (9)   See **stock exchange.**

Straight-line depreciation method (2)   **Depreciation** method according to which the firm's **tangible fixed assets** are depreciated by an equal amount each year. See **accelerated depreciation method.**

Strike price (13)   See **exercise price.**

Subordinated bond/debt/loan (9)   **Bond**/debt/loan that has a claim on the firm's **assets** (in the event of liquidation) that follows

the claim of **senior debtholders.** Same as **junior bond/debt/loan.**

Subscription price (9)   The price at which shares will be sold to existing shareholders during a **rights issue.**

Sunk costs (8)   Money already spent that cannot be recovered irrespective of future decisions. Same as **irrelevant costs** and **unavoidable costs.**

Sustainable growth rate (1, 5, 14) See **self sustainable growth rate.**

Sweetener (in a convertible bond)   The **conversion option** of a **convertible bond.**

Synergies (12)   See **cost synergies** and **market synergies.**

Systematic risk (10)   Risk that remains despite the risk-reduction property of diversification. Measured with the **beta coefficient.** Same as **market risk, nondiversifiable** or **undiversifiable risk.** See **capital asset pricing model.**

Take-up fee (9)   The discount on the price of the shares offered to the investment bankers engaged in a **standby agreement.**

Takeover (12)   Transaction involving one firm that wants to acquire all or a portion of another firm's shares.

Takeover premium (12)   The difference between the acquisition price paid by the **bidder** and the current market value of the **target firm.**

Tangible assets (2)   **Assets** such as land, buildings, machines, and furniture (collectively called property, plant, and equipment) and long-term financial assets.

Target capital structure (11) The **debt-to-equity** ratio that maximizes the market value of the firm's **assets.**

Target firm (12)   The firm whose shares the bidder is trying to acquire in a **takeover.**

Tax-effect ratio (5)   **Earnings after tax (EAT)** divided by **earnings before tax (EBT).**

Tax shield (11)   See **interest tax shield.**

Taxes payable (2)   The amount of taxes owed on the date of the **balance sheet.**

Technically bankrupt (3)   A firm that is no longer able to pay its creditors.

Term loans (9)   Medium- to long-term loans extended by banks and insurance companies.

Terminal cash flow (8)   Cash flow that occurs in the last year of a project.

Terminal value (of a firm) (12) See **residual value (of a firm).**

Time value of money (6)   Time has value because a dollar received earlier is worth more than a dollar received later.

Times-interest-earned ratio (5) The ratio of **earnings before interest and tax (EBIT)** divided by interest expenses. Same as **interest coverage ratio.** A measure of financial leverage based on **income statement** data.

Top floor financing (12)   **Senior collateralized debt** in a **leverage buyout (LBO).**

Total assets (2, 5)   All the assets listed in firm's **balance sheet.**

Total assets rotation/turnover or turns (5)   **Sales** divided by **total assets.** A measure of the efficiency of total asset use.

Total net cash flow (4) The difference between the total amount of dollars received **(cash inflows)** and the total amount of dollars paid out **(cash outflows)** over a period of time.

Trade creditors (1, 2) *See* **accounts payable.**

Trade debtors (1, 2) *See* **accounts receivable.**

Trade-off model of capital structure (11) **Optimal capital structure** reached by means of a trade-off between the **present value** of the **interest tax shield** and the present value of **financial distress costs.**

Trade payables (1, 2) *See* **accounts payable.**

Trade receivables (1, 2) *See* **accounts receivable.**

Trailing multiples (12) *See* **historical multiples.**

Transaction exposure (13) *See* **contractual exposure.**

Transaction loan (9) A one-time loan used to finance a specific, nonrecurrent need.

Transactions costs (9, 11) Costs incurred when buying or selling an **asset** or a **security.**

Transparency (11) Providing complete information about a firm's operations and future prospects to its (outside) **shareholders.**

Translation exposure (13) *See* **accounting exposure.**

Treasury stock (2) The amount that a firm has spent to repurchase its own shares up to the date of the **balance sheet.**

Trust/Trustee (9) A third party (usually a financial institution) that makes sure the issuer of a **bond** meets all the conditions and provisions reported in the bond's **indenture.**

Unavoidable costs (8) Costs incurred regardless of whether the investment is undertaken. Same as **irrelevant costs** or **sunk costs.**

Undervaluation hypothesis (12) **Takeover** rationale according to which the acquiring company has superior skills in finding undervalued **target firms** that can be bought cheaply.

Underwriter (9) **Investment bank** that buys the **securities** a firm wants to issue and then resells them to the public at a higher price.

Underwriting (an issue) (9) When an **investment bank** buys the **securities** a firm wants to issue.

Underwriting syndicate (9) A group of **investment banks** jointly **underwriting** an issue.

Undiversifiable risk (10) *See* **systematic risk.**

Unlevered asset value (12) The estimated value of **assets** assuming they are financed only with **equity capital.** See **adjusted present value.**

Unlevered beta (10, 12) *See* **asset beta.**

Unlevered cost of equity (10, 12) The **cost of equity** of an all-equity financed firm. Can be estimated with the **capital asset pricing model** using the firm's **asset beta.**

Unlevered firm (5) A firm without borrowed funds, or an all-equity financed firm.

Unlisted securities (9) **Securities** of firms that do not meet the listing requirements of **organized exchanges.**

Unseasoned issue (9) *See* **initial public offering.**

Unsecured bond/debt/loan (9) **Bond**/debt/loan supported only by the general credit standing of the issuing firm.

Unsystematic risk (10) Risk that can be eliminated through portfolio diversification. Same as **diversifiable risk** or company-specific risk.

Useful life (8) *See* **economic life.**

Valuation by comparables (12) A valuation method that uses financial data for firms similar to the business or firm to be valued in order to estimate the market value of its equity. For example, the estimated equity value of a firm is equal to its **earnings after tax (EAT)** multiplied by the **earnings multiple** (or **P/E ratio**) of the comparable firm.

Valued-based management (14) Managing a firm's resources with the goal of increasing the firm's market value.

Variable rate bond (9) A **bond** with a **coupon rate** that takes different (known) values during the bond's life.

Venture capital firm (12) An investment firm specializing in the financing of small and new ventures.

Vertical merger (12) For example, the integration of a car manufacturer with its major supplier or its major distributor.

Volatility (of an asset) (10) Unpredictable fluctuations in the market price of an **asset.**

Wages payable (3) The amount of wages owed and not yet paid at the date of the **balance sheet.**

Warrants (9) Call options sold by a firm that give the holder the right (with no obligation) to buy a specific number of the firm's shares of **common stock** at a fixed price during the life of the warrant. See **contingent value rights.**

Weighted average cost of capital (WACC) (1, 10)　The weighted average of the aftertax **cost debt** and **cost of equity.** The minimum rate of return a project must generate in order to meet the return expectations of its suppliers of capital (lenders and **shareholders**). See equations 10.12 and 10.13, and **hurdle rate.**

With/without principle (8) States that the **cash flows** that are relevant to an investment decision are only those that increase or decrease the firm's overall cash position if the investment is undertaken.

Work-in-process inventory (2) The cost of the raw materials that were used in the production of unfinished units plus labor costs and other costs allocated to these units.

Working capital requirement (WCR) (1, 3)　The difference between **operating assets (trade receivables, inventories,** and **prepaid expenses)** and **operating liabilities (trade payables** and **accrued expenses). WCR** measures the firm's net investment in its **operating cycle.**

Writer (of an option) (13) The party who sells the underlying **asset** in an **option contract.** Same as the seller of an **option.**

Yankee bonds (9)　**Bonds** issued by foreign firms in the United States, denominated in U.S. dollars or other currencies.

Yield spread (9)　The difference between the **market yield** on a nongovernment **bond** and the yield on a government **bond** with the same **maturity** and currency denomination.

Yield to maturity (9)　The rate that makes the **bond** price equal to the **present value** of the bond's future cash-flow stream.

Zero-coupon bond (9)　A **bond** with no **coupon payments** that is sold at an original discount from **face value.** See equation 9.5.

ANSWERS TO REVIEW PROBLEMS

1.1. The fundamental finance principle

a. The cost of equity capital is higher than the cost of debt because equity capital is riskier than debt. As a result, the suppliers of equity capital (the shareholders) expect to receive a higher return (in the form of dividend payments and capital gains) to compensate them for the higher risk they must bear. Equity is riskier than debt because debtholders have a *priority* claim on both the firm's cash flow from operations (in the form of contractual interest payments) and the firm's assets (in case of liquidation), while shareholders have a *residual* claim on these cash flows and assets.

b. A debt-to-equity ratio of 2/3 means that PMC's capital structure is 40% debt and 60% equity. The pretax cost of debt is 10%. With a 25% corporate tax rate, the aftertax cost of debt is 7.5%. Given a cost of equity of 15%, we get a weighted average cost of capital (WACC) of 12%:

$$\text{WACC} = 10\%(1 - 25\%) \times 40\% + 15\% \times 60\% = 3\% + 9\% = 12\%$$

c.
$$\text{NPV (Project A)} = -\$90{,}000 + \text{PV}(\$112{,}000 \text{ at } 12\%)$$
$$\text{NPV (Project B)} = -\$160{,}000 + \text{PV}(\$168{,}000 \text{ at } 12\%)$$
$$\text{NPV (Project C)} = -\$250{,}000 + \text{PV}(\$280{,}000 \text{ at } 12\%)$$

where PV is the present value of the cash flow in parentheses at 12%. To find out what is the present value of, say, $112,000, ask yourself what is the amount of cash you have to invest today, denoted PV, to end up with $112,000 in one year if you could earn 12% on your investment. We have:

$$\text{PV} + \text{PV} \times 12\% = \$112{,}000$$

$$\text{PV}(1 + 12\%) = \$112{,}000$$

$$\text{PV} = \frac{\$112{,}000}{1 + 12\%} = \frac{\$112{,}000}{1.12} = \$100{,}000$$

and thus

$$\text{NPV(Project A)} = -\$90{,}000 + \$100{,}000 = \$10{,}000$$

Because the net present value of project A is positive, the project should be accepted. If undertaken it will create today $10,000 of value.

In the case of project B we have:

$$NPV(B) = -\$160,000 + \frac{\$168,000}{1.12} = -\$160,000 + \$150,000 = -\$10,000$$

Because the net present value of project B is negative, the project should be rejected. If undertaken it will destroy today $10,000 of value.

In the case of project C we have:

$$NPV(C) = -\$250,000 + \frac{\$280,000}{1.12} = -\$250,000 + \$250,000 = 0$$

Because the net present value of project C is zero, the project could be either accepted or rejected. The decision will neither create nor destroy value.

d. The announcement of the decision to undertake Project A should *raise* PMC's share price by 10 cents ($10,000 divided 100,000 shares) or 1%, from $10 to $10.10. The announcement of the decision to undertake Project B should *reduce* PMC's share price by 10 cents (−$10,000 divided 100,000 shares), from $10 to $9.90. The announcement of the decision to undertake Project C should not affect PMC's share price. If the three projects are undertaken, the share price should not change because the sum of the three projects' net present values is zero.

The key assumptions are: (1) the announcements are unanticipated by the market; (2) the market is an efficient "processor" of information regarding firms; and (3) the market agrees with the firm's NPV analysis.

e. A project's internal rate return (IRR) is the rate of return its cash-flow stream is expected to generate. Consider first project A. It requires an initial cash outlay of $90,000 that will produce a net cash benefit of $112,000 in one year. What is the rate of return of that one-period cash-flow stream? We have:

$$IRR\ (Project\ A) = \frac{\$112,000 - \$90,000}{\$90,000} = 24.4\%$$

This IRR is the project's rate of return *before its 12% cost of financing is taken into consideration*. Should PMC undertake that project? Yes, because its internal rate of return is higher than its 12% cost of capital. Undertaking it should create value. Note that finding out project A's IRR is straightforward because it is a one-period project. For projects with a cash-flow stream longer than a year things get significantly more complicated as you will discover in Chapter 7.

For the other two projects we have:

$$IRR\ (Project\ B) = \frac{\$168,000 - \$160,000}{\$160,000} = 5\%$$

Because project B has a return that is lower than the 12% cost of financing it, it should not be undertaken. Undertaking it would destroy value.

$$IRR\ (Project\ C) = \frac{\$280,000 - \$250,000}{\$250,000} = 12\%$$

Because project C has a return that is exactly equal to the cost of financing it, undertaking it will neither create nor destroy value.

f. It would *destroy* value because we were told that PMC's current capital structure is optimal. It is the capital structure for which PMC's value is maximized. Any other capital structure is less desirable. Replacing equity with debt will provide value-enhancing tax savings (due to the tax deductibility of interest expenses). But the additional debt is also expected to generate financial distress costs whose present value will offset the present value of the tax benefits, thus making the suggested new capital structure less desirable.

g. It would *destroy* value because we were told that PMC's current capital structure is optimal. It is the capital structure for which PMC's value is maximized. Replacing debt with equity will reduce the benefit of tax savings from debt financing. Note that it will also reduce the present value of the financial distress costs, but the value-enhancing effect of reduced financial distress costs should be smaller than the loss of the tax benefits, thus making the suggested new capital structure less desirable.

1.2. Cash flow and profitability analysis; capacity to grow and create value

a. The restructured balance sheets in their managerial form, in millions of dollars, are:

	12/31/1996	12/31/1997		12/31/1996	12/31/1997
Invested capital or net assets:			**Capital employed:**		
Cash	$60 (9%)	$75 (10%)	Short-term debt	$70 (10%)	$100 (14%)
WCR	160 (24%)	195 (27%)	Long-term debt	195 (29%)	185 (25%)
Net fixed assets	450 (67%)	460 (63%)	Owners' equity	405 (61%)	445 (61%)
Total	**$670**	**$730**	**Total**	**$670**	**$730**

where working capital requirement (WCR) is trade receivables plus inventories less trade payables. It is a measure of the investment required to support the firm's operating activities. In order to produce and then sell its goods and services GEC will need to extend credit to its customers in the form of receivables as well as hold inventories. These two items will have to be financed, net of any funding provided by suppliers in the form of payables.

b. "Cash Flow Statement" for the year 1997 (in millions of dollars):

Cash flow from operating activities		
Sales[1]	$1,600	
less operating expenses *excluding* depreciation[1]	(1,400)	
less tax expenses[1]	(56)	
less cash used to finance the growth of WCR[2]	(35)	
A. equals net operating cash flow		**$109**
Cash flow from investment activities		
Capital expenditures[3]	(40)	
B. equals net cash flow from investment activities		**($40)**

Cash flow from financing activities

increase in short-term borrowing[2]	30
decrease in long-term borrowing[2]	(10)
less interest payment[1]	(30)
less dividend payment[1]	(44)
C. equals net cash flow from financing activities	**($54)**
D. Total net cash flow = A+B+C	**$15**
E. Cash held at the beginning of the year	**$60**
F. Cash held at the end of the year = E+D	**$75**

Notes:
1. See the income statement.
2. See the change in the managerial balance sheets (part a).
3. See note 1 at the bottom of the balance sheet.

c. Profitability from the perspective of shareholders is measured by return on equity or ROE:

$$\text{ROE (based on 1996 equity)} = \frac{\text{Earnings after tax}}{\text{Beginning owners' equity}} = \frac{\$84}{\$405} = 20.74\%$$

$$\text{ROE (based on average equity)} = \frac{\text{Earnings after tax}}{\text{Average owners' equity}} = \frac{\$84}{(\$445 + \$405)/2} = \frac{\$84}{\$425} = 19.76\%$$

$$\text{ROE (based on 1997 equity)} = \frac{\text{Earnings after tax}}{\text{Ending owners' equity}} = \frac{\$84}{\$445} = 18.88\%$$

Because owners' equity has increased in 1997, ROE based on beginning owners' equity is higher than both ROE based on average owners' equity and ending owners' equity. Most companies would report ROE (in their annual report) based on average owners' equity.

d. Return on invested capital (ROIC) is:

$$\text{ROIC} = \frac{\text{Aftertax operating profit}}{\text{Beginning invested capital}} = \frac{\$170 \times (1 - 40\%)}{\$670} = \frac{\$102}{\$670} = 15.22\%$$

Return on invested capital, which is the same as return on net assets (RONA), is a measure of the firm's profitability resulting from its operating activities, that is, before taking into consideration the way the firm's assets are financed. In other words, if GEC modifies its capital structure, its ROIC will not change.

e. Refer to Exhibit 1.6. We have the following four key ratios driving GEC's business cycle:

1. $$\text{Debt-to-equity ratio (1996)} = \frac{\text{Short- and long-term debt}}{\text{Owners' equity}} = \frac{\$70 + \$195}{\$405} = 65.4\%$$

2. $$\text{Efficiency of asset use (1996)} = \frac{\text{Sales}}{\text{Net assets}} = \frac{\$1,600}{\$670} = 2.39$$

3. $$\text{Net profit margin (return on sales)} = \frac{\text{Net profit}}{\text{Sales}} = \frac{\$84}{\$1,600} = 5.25\%$$

4. Retention rate = $\dfrac{\text{Retained earnings}}{\text{Net profit}} = \dfrac{\$40}{\$84} = 48\%$

f . If GEC does not modify its operating policy (ratios 2 and 3 in part e) or its financing policy (ratios 1 and 4 in part e), and does not issue new equity, its maximum rate of growth is constrained by the growth of its equity capital which is equal to 9.9%:

$$\text{Growth in equity capital} = \frac{\$445 - \$405}{\$405} = 9.9\%$$

g. If it wishes to grow faster than 9.9% via a change in its operating policy, GEC will have to improve the efficiency with which it uses its assets (more sales per dollar of assets) and/or increase its net profit margin (more profit per dollar of sales).

h. If it wishes to grow faster than 9.9% via a change in its financing policy, GEC's will have to raise its debt-to-equity ratio (more debt per dollar of equity) and/or its retention rate (more retained earnings per dollar of profit).

i. GEC's weighted average cost of capital (WACC) using both market and book values of capital in 1997:

SOURCE OF CAPITAL	BOOK VALUE	MARKET VALUE	BOOK VALUE AS PERCENT OF TOTAL	MARKET VALUE AS PERCENT TOTAL
Debt	$285 million	$285 million	39.0%	32.2%
Equity	$445 million	$600 million	61.0%	67.8%
Total capital	$730 million	$885 million	100.0%	100.0%

Given an aftertax cost of debt of 6% (10% pretax with a tax rate of 40%; see income statement) and an estimated cost of equity of 16%, we have:

WACC (Book values) = 6% × 39.0% + 16% × 61.0% = 2.34% + 9.76% = 12.10%

WACC (Market values) = 6% × 32.2% + 16% × 67.8% = 1.93% + 10.85% = 12.78%

The difference between the two estimates is not very large because the market value of equity is close to its book value. The appropriate WACC to perform value analysis is the one based on market values because the fundamental finance principle is driven by market valuation, not book values.

j. To find out whether GEC has created value for its shareholders as of December 31st 1997, we can measure its market value added (MVA) on that date. We have (see the answer to part i):

MVA = Market value of capital − Book value of capital
= $885 million − $730 million = $155 million

Because MVA is positive, we can conclude that value was created. Another evidence of GEC's ability to create value is that:

1. the firm's *return* on equity (20.74%) is *higher* than its estimated *cost* of equity (16%)
2. the firm's *return* on invested capital (15.22%) is *higher* than its average *cost* of capital (WACC = 12.78%)

GEC's economic value added (EVA) is thus:

$$EVA_{1997} = (ROIC - WACC)_{1997} \times \text{Invested capital}_{12/31/96}$$
$$= (15.22\% - 12.78\%) \times \$670 \text{ million} = \$16.3 \text{ million}$$

2.1. Constructing income statements and balance sheets

a. <u>1997 income statement:</u>

IN THOUSANDS OF DOLLARS		1997
Net sales (see items 3,19)		**$320,000**
Cost of goods sold		(260,000)
Material cost[1] (see item 5)	$224,000	
Labor expenses (see item 17)	36,000	
Gross profit		60,000
SG & A expenses (see item 12)	18,000	
Licensing fee (see item 13)	4,000	
Depreciation expenses (see item 9)	9,000	
Operating profit		29,000
Extraordinary loss (see item 27)		(2,000)
Earnings before interest and tax		**$27,000**
Net interest expenses (see items 6, 15, 26)		(3,000)
Earnings before tax		24,000
Income tax expense[2] (see item 2)		(9,600)
Earnings after tax		**$14,400**
Dividends (see item 21)	*$9,360*	
Retained earnings	*$5,040*	

Notes:
[1]You could also infer the cost of material *sold* during the year by noting that:
  Purchases (item 11) = Cost of material sold + change in inventories (item 19), where the change in inventories
    represents the cost of the material purchased but not yet sold.
  We can thus write: Cost of material sold = Purchases − change in inventories = $228,000,000
                              − ($32,000,000 − $28,000,000) = $224,000,000
[2]The tax paid in advance on December 15, 1997 (item 25) was exactly equal to the tax due for 1997.
  The information in item 14 is irrelevant for the construction of 1997 income statement.

b. <u>1996 and 1997 balance sheets:</u>

IN THOUSANDS OF DOLLARS	1996	1997
Cash[1] (see item 24)	$7,500	$3,515
Accounts receivable (see items 7, 1)	32,000	38,400
Inventories (see item 19)	28,000	32,000
Prepaid expenses (see item 28)	1,500	2,085
Net fixed assets (see items 4, 9, 20)	76,000	81,000
Total assets	**$145,000**	**$157,000**

Owed to banks (see item 26)	$3,000	$5,000
Current portion of long-term debt (see item 18)	4,000	4,000
Accounts payable (see items 8, 22, 11)	30,000	35,150
Accrued expenses[2] (see item 10)	4,000	1,810
Long-term debt[3] (see items 15, 18, 20)	23,000	25,000
Owners' equity[4] (see items 23, 16)	81,000	86,040
Total liabilities & owners' equity	**$145,000**	**$157,000**

Notes:

1. You should first identify accounts payable.
2. Wages payable.
3. Net long-term debt (1996) = $27 million (total amount) − $4 million (due this year). See item 15.
Net long-term debt (1997) = Long-term debt (1996) − Debt repayment (item 18) + New debt (item 20)
= $23 million − $4 million + $6 million = $25 million.
4. Owners' equity (1997) = Owners' equity (1996) + Retained earnings ($5,040,000; see income statement).

2.2. Forecasting income statements and balance sheets

a. Pro forma income statement for 1998:

The reference item is for the determination of the 1998 pro forma statement.

IN THOUSANDS OF DOLLARS	*1997 - ACTUAL*		*1998 - PRO FORMA*	
Net sales (see item 1)		*$320,000*		*$352,000*
Cost of goods sold (see item 2)		*(260,000)*		*(286,000)*
Material cost (see item 2)	$224,000		$246,400	
Labor expenses (see item 2)	36,000		39,600	
Gross profit (see item 2)		*60,000*		66,000
SG & A expenses (see item 3)	*18,000*		22,280	
Licensing fee (see item 4)	*4,000*		4,000	
Depreciation expenses (item 4)	*9,000*		9,000	
Operating profit		*29,000*		30,720
Extraordinary item		*(2,000)*		0
Earnings before interest and tax		*27,000*		**30,720**
Net interest expenses (see item 4)		*(3,000)*		(3,000)
Earnings before tax		*24,000*		27,720
Income tax expense (see item 4)		*(9,600)*		*(11,088)*
Earnings after tax		*$14,400*		**$16,632**
Dividends[1] (item 9)	*$9,360*		*$8,922*	
Retained earnings	*$5,040*		*$7,710*	

Notes:

[1] In order to determine the dividend payment, you should first find out how much retained earnings are necessary to "balance" the pro forma 1998 balance sheet. The expected dividend payment will then be the difference between the expected net profit and the anticipated retained earnings (see below).

b. Pro forma balance sheet for 1998:

The reference item is for the determination of the 1998 pro forma statement.

IN THOUSANDS OF DOLLARS	12/31/97 - ACTUAL	12/31/98 - PRO FORMA
Cash (see item 9)	$3,515	$3,515
Accounts receivable (see item 5)	38,400	42,240
Inventories (see item 5)	32,000	35,200
Prepaid expenses (see item 6)	2,085	2,085
Net fixed assets[1] (see items 4, 7)	81,000	81,000
Total assets	**$157,000**	**$164,040**
Owed to banks (see item 8)	$5,000	$5,000
Current portion of long-term debt[2] (see item 8)	4,000	4,000
Accounts payable[3] (see item 5)	35,150	38,480
Accrued expenses (see item 6)	1,810	1,810
Long-term debt[4] (see item 8)	25,000	21,000
Owners' equity[5]	86,040	93,750
Total liabilities & owners' equity	**$157,000**	**$164,040**

Notes:

[1] Net fixed assets (1998) = Net fixed assets (1997) − Depreciation expenses (1998) + New assets (1998)

   = $81 million − $9 million + $9 million.

[2] Long-term debt is repaid at an annual rate of $4 million (item 18 in problem 2.1).

[3] Payables are 1.85 month of purchases with purchases equal to:

   Purchases = Material cost + change in inventories = $246,400,000 + $3,200,000 = $249,600,000.

[4] Long-term debt (1998) = Long-term (1997) − Repayment + New borrowings = $25 million less $4 million.

[5] To "balance" the balance sheet, owners' equity should rise by $7,710,000. Because there is no plan to issue new shares, this is the expected amount of retained earnings.

3.1. Evaluating managerial performance

a. Yes, in 1997 sales grew by 18.5% compared to a growth rate of 12.5% in 1996.

b. The restructured balance sheets in their managerial form, in millions of dollars, are:

	YEAR-END 1995		YEAR-END 1996		YEAR-END 1997	
Cash	$100	14.9%	$90	13.2%	$50	6.5%
Working capital requirement	180	26.9%	205	29.9%	355	46.1%
Net fixed assets	390	58.2%	390	56.9%	365	47.4%
Invested capital	**$670**	**100.0%**	**$685**	**100.0%**	**$770**	**100.0%**
Short-term debt	$80	11.9%	$90	13.2%	$135	17.5%
Long-term debt	140	20.9%	120	17.5%	100	13.0%
Owners' equity	450	67.2%	475	69.3%	535	69.5%
Capital employed	**$670**	**100.0%**	**$685**	**100.0%**	**$770**	**100.0%**

where working capital requirement is equal to trade receivables plus inventories plus prepaid expenses less trade payables less accrued expenses. It is a measure of the investment required to support the firm's operating activities. It is mostly a *long-term* investment because we are told that ACC has little seasonality in its sales, meaning that its working capital requirement is essentially *permanent* in nature.

c. The structure of invested capital has changed between 1995 and 1997: the proportions of cash and net fixed assets have gone down and the proportion of working capital has gone up. The structure of capital employed has also changed, particularly the composition of debt capital: the proportion of short-term debt has risen while that of long-term debt has declined.

d. In 1995, ACC financed its long-term investments (permanent working capital requirement and net fixed assets) with long-term funds, and its short-term investment (cash and cash-equivalents) with short-term debt, indicating a "matched" balance sheet. In 1997, a significant portion of long-term investments were financed with short-term debt, indicating a "mismatched" balance sheet.

e. Operational efficiency ratios:

	YEAR-END 1995	**YEAR-END 1996**	**YEAR-END 1997**
WCR/Sales	15.0%	15.2%	22.2%
Average collection period	61 days	62 days	66 days
Inventory turnover	5.4 times	5.7 times	3.9 times
Average payment period	72 days	68 days	69 days

There is a significant deterioration of the efficiency with which the firm's operating cycle is managed. This is clearly indicated by the rise in the ratio of WCR over sales. It is confirmed by the lengthening of the collection period and the slow down in inventory turnover.

f. Liquidity ratios:

	YEAR-END 1995	**YEAR-END 1996**	**YEAR-END 1997**
NLF/WCR	111%	100%	76%
Current ratio	1.69	1.65	1.67
Quick ratio	1.03	1.02	0.84

where NLF is net long-term financing which is equal to long-term debt plus owners' equity less net fixed assets. The ratio of NLF to WCR, called the liquidity ratio, shows a clear deterioration: the percentage of WCR financed with long-term funds went from 100% in 1995 and 1996 to 76% in 1997. Note that the current ratio does not seem to pick up the deterioration in liquidity, although the quick ratio does.

g. The marketing objective was achieved in terms of growth in sales, but this accomplishment was accompanied by a deterioration in the firm's operational efficiency and the quality of its balance sheet.

3.2. Working capital management for a retailer

a. Operating assets include trade receivables and inventories (other current assets are not related to operations), while operating liabilities include trade payables (other current liabilities are mostly unrelated to operations). Working capital requirement (WCR) is thus (in millions of French Francs):

$$\text{WCR} = \text{Receivables} + \text{Inventories} - \text{Payables}$$
$$\text{WCR}(12/31/95) = 418 + 10{,}860 - 27{,}418 = -\text{FRF}16{,}140$$
$$\text{WCR}(112/31/96) = 540 + 12{,}310 - 29{,}836 = -\text{FRF}16{,}986$$

WCR is negative and thus represents a *source* of capital rather than an *investment* that needs to be financed. Note the magnitude of WCR; it amounts to close to $3 *billion* at the exchange rate prevailing in 1997.

b. Working capital requirement-to-sales ratios (in millions of French Francs):

December 31st, 1995	WCR = −FRF16,140	Sales = FRF144,612	WCR/Sales = −11.2%
December 31st, 1996	WCR = −FRF16,986	Sales = FRF154,905	WCR/Sales = −11.0%

The faster the company grows, the larger its negative WCR because WCR is roughly equal to minus 11% of sales. Carrefour, or any other company with a negative WCR, usually has a relatively stronger liquidity position than firms with positive WCRs.

c. Operational efficiency ratios (data in millions of French Francs):

	YEAR-END 1995	YEAR-END 1996
Average collection period	FRF418/(FRF144,612/365) = 1.1 day	FRF540/(FRF154,905/365) = 1.3 day
Inventory turnover	FRF118,212/FRF10,860 = 10.9 times	FRF125,072/FRF12,310 = 10.2 times
Average payment period	FRF27,418/(FRF118,212/365) = 85 days	FRF29,836/(FRF125,072/365) = 87 days

The negative value of WCR is due to significantly longer payment terms than average, coupled with an extremely short collection period (retailing is essentially a cash business) and a fast inventory turnover.

d. Liquidity ratios (data in millions of French Francs):

	CURRENT RATIO	QUICK RATIO
December 31st, 1995	FRF27,733/FRF37,133 = 0.75	FRF4,486/FRF37,133 = 0.12
December 31st, 1996	FRF30,844/FRF40,561 = 0.76	FRF3,500/FRF40,561 = 0.09

The rule of thumb for the current ratio is that it should be close to two, while for the quick ratio it should be close to one. But these standards apply to firms with positive WCR. Firms with a negative WCR can afford significantly lower ratios without an accompanying deterioration of liquidity.

4.1. Constructing and interpreting cash flow statements

a. Cash flow statement:

IN MILLIONS OF DOLLARS	YEAR 1996	YEAR 1997
Cash flow from operating activities		
Net sales	$1,350	$1,600
less costs of goods sold	(970)	(1,160)
less selling, general, and administrative expenses	(165)	(200)
less change in working capital requirement	(25)	(150)
less tax expenses	(45)	(50)
A. equals net operating cash flow	**$145**	**$40**
Cash flow from investing activities		
Sales of fixed assets	0	0
less capital expenditures[1]	(50)	(30)

B. equals net cash flow from investing activities	*($50)*	*($30)*
Cash flow from financing activities		
Increase in short-term borrowings	10	45
Decrease in long-term borrowings	(20)	(20)
less interest payments	(20)	(25)
less dividend payments	(75)	(50)
C. equals net cash flow from financing activities	*($105)*	*($50)*
Total net cash flow = A+B+C	($10)	($40)
plus opening cash balance	$100	$90
equals closing cash balance	$90	$50

Notes:
1. Capex = Change in net fixed asset + depreciation expenses.
   Capex (1996) = ($390 − $390) + $50 = $50
   Capex (1997) = ($365 − $390) + $55 = $30

In both years cash flow from operations was positive, while cash flows from investment and financing activities were negative. This is the expected pattern for a firm experiencing steady growth. The area of concern is the weakening of the cash flow from operations in 1997 compared to the previous year. This deterioration is essentially due to the growth in working capital requirement, itself the outcome of the deterioration in the firm's operational efficiency, as shown in the answer to problem 3.1(e).

b. Net operating cash flow (NOCF) using earnings before interest and tax (EBIT):

IN MILLIONS OF DOLLARS	**YEAR 1996**	**YEAR 1997**
Earnings before interest and tax (EBIT)	$165	$185
plus depreciation expenses	50	55
less change in working capital requirement (WCR)	(25)	(150)
less tax payments	(45)	(50)
equals net operating cash flow (NOCF)	**$145**	**$40**

The above approach starts with a measure of profit that includes depreciation expenses, a noncash item which must be removed. This is done by adding depreciation expenses to profits. The approach in the previous question starts with sales and simply ignores depreciation expenses.

c. Net operating cash flow (NOCF) using earnings before interest, tax, depreciation and amortization (EBITDA):

IN MILLIONS OF DOLLARS	**YEAR 1996**	**YEAR 1997**
Earnings before interest, tax, depreciation and amortization (EBITDA)	$215	$240
less change in working capital requirement (WCR)	(25)	(150)
less tax payments	(45)	(50)
equals net operating cash flow (NOCF)	**$145**	**$40**

The above approach is essentially the same as the one in the previous question because EBITDA is, by definition, equal to EBIT plus depreciation expenses.

d. Net operating cash flow (NOCF) using cash inflows and cash outflows from operations:

IN MILLIONS OF DOLLARS	YEAR 1996		YEAR 1997	
Cash inflows from operations				
Sales	$1,350		$1,600	
less change in trade receivables	(30)		(60)	
A. equals cash inflows from operations		$1,320		$1,540
Cash outflows from operations				
Cost of goods sold	970		1,160	
plus selling, general, and administrative expenses	165		200	
plus change in inventories	10		130	
plus change in prepaid expenses	0		5	
less change in trade payables	(10)		(40)	
less change in accrued expenses	(5)		(5)	
plus tax expenses	45		50	
B. equals cash outflows from operations		$1,175		$1,500
Net operating cash flow = (A) − (B)		$145		$40

e. **Cash flow from assets:**

IN MILLIONS OF DOLLARS	YEAR 1996	YEAR 1997
Cash flow from operations (NOCF)	$145	$40
plus cash flow from investments	(50)	(30)
equals cash flow from assets	**$95**	**$10**

Cash flow from assets is the sum of the net cash flow generated by *existing* assets—which is net operating cash flow—and the net cash flow generated by net capital expenditures during the year (acquisitions, net of disposals). It is the firm's net cash flow, *excluding* any cash movements related to financing activities.

f. Bankers' cash flow or cash earnings:

IN MILLIONS OF DOLLARS	YEAR 1995	YEAR 1996	YEAR 1997
Earnings after tax (Net profit)	$90	$100	$110
plus depreciation	40	50	55
Cash earnings	**$130**	**$150**	**$165**

Cash earnings in 1997 are significantly lower than net operating cash flow that year because cash earnings ignore the change in working capital (WCR) which was relatively large that year. The major weakness of this cash-flow measure is that it ignores the impact of the change in the size of the balance sheet (the change in WCR). In fact, bankers' cash flow or cash earnings is only based on data from the income statement and, strictly speaking, are not a measure of cash flow.

g. <u>Separation of margin and investment components in NOCF:</u>

IN MILLIONS OF DOLLARS	YEAR 1996		YEAR 1997	
EBITDA	$215		$240	
less tax expenses	(45)		(50)	
A. equals margin component		$170		$190
change in working capital requirement	25		150	
B. equals investment component		$25		$150
Net operating cash flow = (A) − (B)		$145		$40

Clearly, the growth of the investment component in 1997 has dwarfed the improvement in the margin component, resulting in a sharp drop in net operating cash flow.

h. <u>Nondiscretionary versus discretionary cash flow:</u>

IN MILLIONS OF DOLLARS	YEAR 1996		YEAR 1997	
A. Net operating cash flow		$145		$40
B. Nondiscretionary cash flow		(40)		(45)
less long-term debt repaid	$20		$20	
less interest payment	20		25	
Cash flow available for strategic decisions = (A) + (B)		$105		($5)
C. Discretionary cash flow		($115)		($35)
increase in short-term borrowings	10		45	
less capital expenditures	(50)		(30)	
less dividend payment	(75)		(50)	
Total net cash flow = (A) + (B) + (C)		($10)		($40)

The above statement indicates how much cash flow is available to finance activities over which management has some control.

i. <u>"The statement of cash flows" (FASB95):</u>

IN MILLIONS OF DOLLARS	YEAR 1996		YEAR 1997	
A. Cash flow from operating activities		$125		$15
Earnings after tax	$100		$110	
plus depreciation expenses	50		55	
less change in working capital requirement	(25)		(150)	
B. Cash flow from investment activities		($50)		($30)
C. Cash flow from financing activities		($85)		($25)
increase in short-term debt	10		45	
decrease in long-term debt	(20)		(20)	
less dividend payment	(75)		(50)	
Total net cash flow = (A) + (B) + (C)		($10)		($40)

The above statement puts interest expenses into operating cash flow (it is taken into account in earnings after tax). As a consequence, interest expenses are no longer part of cash flow from financing activities.

4.2. Examining the operating cash flow of a retailer

a. Cash flow statement:

IN MILLIONS OF FRENCH FRANCS	YEAR 1996
Cash flow from operating activities	
Income before taxes	FRF5,238
plus depreciation expenses	4,020
less change in working capital requirement	846
less tax expenses	(1,637)
equals net operating cash flow	**FRF8,467**

b. Separation of margin and investment components in NOCF:

IN MILLIONS OF FRENCH FRANCS	YEAR 1996
Income before taxes	FRF5,238
plus depreciation expenses	4,020
less tax expenses	(1,637)
A. equals margin component	**FRF7,621**
change in working capital requirement	(846)
B. equals investment component	**(FRF846)**
Net operating cash flow = (A) − (B)	**FRF8,467**

Because the change in working capital requirement is *negative* (−16,986 less −16,140), the investment component of net operating cash flow is negative and is thus a source of funds that is *added,* rather than deducted, from the margin component. To put it differently, the *faster* Carrefour grows, the *larger* its negative working capital requirement and the *stronger* its cash flow from operations which can then be invested to sustain further growth.

5.1. Profitability analysis

a. The restructured balance sheets in their managerial form are:

IN MILLIONS OF DOLLARS	YEAR-END 1995		YEAR-END 1996		YEAR-END 1997	
Cash	$100	14.9%	$90	13.2%	$50	6.5%
Working capital requirement	180	26.9%	205	29.9%	355	46.1%
Net fixed assets	390	58.2%	390	56.9%	365	47.4%
Total invested capital	**$670**	**100.0%**	**$685**	**100.0%**	**$770**	**100.0%**
Short-term debt	$80	11.9%	$90	13.2%	$135	17.5%
Long-term debt	140	20.9%	120	17.5%	100	13.0%
Owners' equity	450	67.2%	475	69.3%	535	69.5%
Total capital employed	**$670**	**100.0%**	**$685**	**100.0%**	**$770**	**100.0%**

where working capital requirement is trade receivables plus inventories plus prepaid expenses less trade payables less accrued expenses.

b. <u>Return on equity</u> (based on year-end data):

	YEAR-END 1995	YEAR-END 1996	YEAR-END 1997
Pretax ROE	28.89%	30.53%	29.91%
Aftertax ROE	20.00%	21.05%	20.56%

c. <u>Alternative measures of pretax operating profitability</u> (based on year-end data):

	YEAR-END 1995	YEAR-END 1996	YEAR-END 1997
Pretax ROIC = EBIT/Invested capital	22.39%	24.09%	24.03%
Pretax ROTA = EBIT/Total assets	17.05%	18.13%	17.79%
Pretax ROBA = EBIT/Business assets	26.32%	27.73%	25.69%
ROA = EAT/Total assets	*10.23%*	*10.99%*	*10.58%*

where business assets are working capital requirement plus net fixed assets. The first three measures have the same numerator and because total assets are generally larger than invested capital, which is itself usually larger than business assets, it follows that ROBA is higher than ROIC and ROIC is higher than ROTA. ROA is lower than the first three measures of profitability because net profit (EAT) is smaller than pretax operating profit (EBIT).

d. Return on net assets (RONA) is the same as return on invested capital (ROIC) because net assets are defined exactly as invested capital (cash plus working capital requirement plus net fixed assets). Return on capital employed (ROCE) is identical to return on invested capital (ROIC) because, according to the managerial balance sheet, invested capital is identical to capital employed. See the managerial balance sheets in the answer to part a.

e. Return on invested capital (and generally speaking any measure of operating profitability) is driven by operating margin (EBIT/Sales) and capital turnover (Sales/Invested capital). It is equal to the product of these two ratios:

	1995	1996	1997
Operating margin	12.50%	12.22%	11.56%
× Capital turnover	1.79	1.97	2.08
= Return on invested capital	22.39%	24.09%	24.03%

Operating profitability has improved and the improvement is due to a higher capital turnover (more efficient use of capital) while operating margin has actually deteriorated.

f. Pretax ROE is higher than pretax ROIC because the firm finances its investments with borrowed funds (financial debt). This is what we called financial leverage or gearing. If the firm had not used any borrowing, its ROE would have been identical to its ROIC. The relation that links ROE, ROIC and debt financing is given in Appendix 5.2.

g. No. Financial leverage can be unfavorable to shareholders, that is, borrowing may result in an ROE that is lower rather than higher than ROIC. This will happen if ROIC turns out to be lower than the cost of borrowing.

h. Measures of financial leverage:

	1995	1996	1997
Financial cost ratio (EBT/EBIT)	0.87	0.88	0.86
Times interest earned (EBIT/Interest)	7.50	8.25	7.40
Financial structure ratio (Invested capital/Equity)	1.49	1.44	1.44
Debt-to-equity ratio	0.49	0.44	0.44
Debt-to-invested capital ratio	0.33	0.31	0.31

The first two ratios measure the effect of borrowing on the income statement (the impact of *interest* payments on profitability), while the other three ratios measure the effect of borrowing on the balance sheet (the impact of the *amount* borrowed on profitability). All ratios indicate a slight reduction in financial leverage over the three-year period.

i. ROE structure

	1995	1996	1997
Operating margin (EBIT/Sales)	12.50%	12.22%	11.56%
× Capital turnover (Sales/Invested capital)	1.79	1.97	2.08
= ROIC (EBIT/Invested capital)	22.38%	24.08%	24.04%
× Financial structure (Invested capital/Equity)	1.49	1.44	1.44
× Financial cost (EBT/EBIT)	0.87	0.88	0.86
= Pretax ROE	29.00%	30.51%	29.78%
× Tax effect (EAT/EBT)	0.69	0.69	0.69
= Aftertax ROE	20.00%	21.05%	20.54%

Operating profitability improves slightly, mostly due to higher capital turnover (indeed, operating margin declined over the period). ROE, however, did not reflect the slight improvement in operating profitability because of the offsetting effect of a reduction in financial leverage.

j. Valuation ratios

	1995	1996	1997
Earnings per share (EAT/number shares)	$1.80	$2.00	$2.20
Price-earnings ratio (Price/EPS)	11.1	12.0	13.6
Market-to-book ratio (Price/Equity per share)	2.2	2.5	2.8

The price-earnings ratio and the market-to-book ratio indicate a rise in the relative value of ACC over the three-year period, reflecting the growth of its earnings per share.

5.2. ROE structure across industries

Company A is **Boeing:** it has relatively high inventories, high advances from clients (clients make a deposit when they order planes) and high leverage.

Company B is **Singapore Airlines:** it has relatively high fixed assets (the plane fleet), low inventory, good margin.

Company C is **Microsoft**: it has strong profitability, high cash holdings and no financial leverage.

5.3. Sustainable growth analysis

a. Growth in sales in 1997 is 18.5% (($1,600 − $1,350)/$1,350)

$$\text{Sustainable growth rate} = \text{SGR} = (\text{retention rate}) \times (\text{ROE on beginning equity})$$

$$\text{SGR} = (\$60/\$110) \times (\$110/\$475) = 54.5\% \times 23.2\% = 12.6\%$$

ACC has grown faster than its capacity to finance its activities *without* modifying its operating and financing policies. If it continues to grow much faster than 12.6% and does not improve its operating profitability significantly, ACC will most likely experience an increase in financial leverage and a reduction in its capacity to pay dividends, unless it decides to issue new equity.

b.1. If ACC expects to grow its sales by 25% in 1998 and does not modify its financing and operating policies, it will need 25% more equity in 1998 than in 1997, that is, $134 million (25% of its 1997 equity of $535 million). This equity capital can come from two sources: retained earnings or a new issue of equity.

b.2. ACC will have to rely increasingly on debt financing and thus its debt-to-equity ratio would rise.

b.3. ACC will have to rely increasingly on retained profits and thus its retention rate should rise. By how much? ACC's profits in 1998 are expected to be 25% higher than in 1997, that is, $137.5 million ($110 million × 1.25). We know that ACC needs $134 million of new equity. The implication is clear: ACC will have to retain most of its 1998 profits, precisely 97.5% ($134 million/$137.5 million). The question, of course, is whether its shareholders will accept a reduction in dividend of this magnitude.

b.4. The sustainable growth rate will have to rise to 25%, only through an improvement in return on invested capital (ROIC). The retention rate should remain at 54.5% (same as in 1997) and the financial leverage multiplier should remain at 1.24 (refer to the 1997 ROE structure in the answer to problem 5.1 where we found a financial structure ratio of 1.44 and a financial cost ratio of 0.86; multiplying these two ratios we find a financial leverage multiplier of 1.24). Because *aftertax* ROE is equal to *aftertax* ROIC multiplied by the financial leverage multiplier, we can write:

$$\text{SGR} = (54.5\%) \times (\text{aftertax ROIC}) \times (1.24) = 25\%$$

from which we get an expected aftertax ROIC of 37% (25%/(54.5% × 1.24)). With an effective tax rate of 31%, this implies a pretax ROIC of 53.6%, more than double the 1997 figure of 24.04% (see problem 5.1). It is doubtful that ACC could achieve such a dramatic improvement in operating profitability and will have to issue new equity, unless it reduces its rate of growth in sales.

c.1. In this case ACC will grow at a slower rate than its capacity to fund its activities because the sustainable growth rate will exceed the rate of growth in sales. As a consequence, ACC will generate extra cash.

c.2. ACC can use the extra cash to make acquisitions, repay debt, increase dividend payments or repurchase shares. Unless acquisitions are value-creating propositions, they should be avoided. In this case, the extra cash should be returned to shareholders and debtholders through share buy-backs and debt repayment.

6.1. Present values and the cost of capital

a. We mean that if these cash flows could be traded (bought and sold) in a market for investment projects, the estimated *value* at which they would trade is $20 million. This value takes into account the following two factors: (i) the time value of money (the farther into the future the cash flows are, the less value they have); and (ii) the risk attached to these cash flows, that is, the probability that they will actually differ from their expected values (the riskier they are the less value they have). The present value of the cash flows is obtained by discounting them to the present at the project cost of capital.

b. We mean that we expect the market value of the firm's equity to increase by $10 million if the firm decides to go ahead with the project. It is the difference between the present value of the cash flows expected from the project and the initial cash outlay required to launch the project.

c. We mean that investors can get a return of 10% on a comparable or alternative investment. Thus, if they invest in the project under consideration they will have to give up a return of 10%. A comparable investment is one that exhibits the same risk characteristics as the project under consideration.

6.2. Managerial options

Managerial options refer to project-specific features that provide managers with opportunities to make alterations in reaction to changing circumstances regarding the project. Examples include options to switch technologies, options to abandon the project as well as options to expand, retract or defer the project.

6.3. Net present value

a. Present value (PV) of the project's expected cash-flow stream at 12%:

$$PV = \frac{\$50,000}{1 + 0.12} + \frac{\$50,000}{(1 + 0.12)^2} + \frac{\$50,000}{(1 + 0.12)^3}$$

$$= \$50,000 \times 0.8929 + \$50,000 \times 0.7972 + \$50,000 \times 0.7118 = \$120,095$$

Note that if you enter the cash flows in your calculator and discount them at 12% you will find a more accurate present value of $120,091.56.

b. Net present value = $-\$100,000 + \$120,095 = \$20,095$.

c. Profitability index $= \dfrac{\text{Present value of expected cash flows}}{\text{Initial cash outlay}} = \dfrac{\$120,095}{\$100,000} = 1.20$

d. The project should be undertaken because it is expected to increase the value of the firm's equity by $20,095 or, equivalently, because it returns more than one dollar per dollar spent (20% more).

6.4. Choosing between two investments with unequal costs and life spans

a. Present value of printer X costs $= -\$50,000 - \dfrac{\$5,000}{1 + 0.10} - \dfrac{\$5,000}{(1 + 0.10)^2} = -\$58,678.$

Present value of printer Y costs $= -\$60,000 - \dfrac{\$7,000}{1 + 0.10} - \dfrac{\$7,000}{(1 + 0.10)^2} - \dfrac{\$7,000}{(1 + 0.10)^3} = -\$77,408.$

b. The two present values are not comparable because printer X will provide two years of service while printer Y could be used one more year.

c. The annual-equivalent cost of a printer is the cost per year of operating the printer which has the *same* present value as the present value of the total cost. In the case of printer X, we have to find a two-year annuity (that is, two *equal* annual payments) with a present value of $58,678. And in the case of printer Y, we have to find a three-year annuity (that is, three *equal* annual payments) with a present value of $77,408.

To compute these annuities we use formula A6.5 given in Appendix 6.1:

$$\text{Constant annual-equivalent cash flow} = \frac{\text{Present value of original cash flow}}{\text{Annuity discount factor}}$$

For printer X, the two-year discount factor is $\dfrac{1}{(1 + 0.10)^2} = 0.8264$, the annuity discount

factor is $\dfrac{1 - 0.8264}{0.10} = 1.7355$, and the annual-equivalent cost is thus $\dfrac{-\$58,678}{1.7355} = -\$33,810.$

For printer Y, the three-year discount factor is $\dfrac{1}{(1 + 0.10)^3} = 0.7513$, the annuity discount

factor is $\dfrac{1 - 0.7513}{0.10} = 2.4870$, and the annual-equivalent cost is thus $\dfrac{-\$77,408}{2.4870} = -\$31,125.$

d. PCC should purchase printer Y because its effective annual cost of $31,125 is lower than the $33,810 equivalent cost of printer X. Although printer Y is more expensive than printer X to buy and operate, its longer useful life more than offsets the difference in costs.

6.5. Replacing an existing machine with a new one

a. The present value of the expected cash flows from the new machine is:

$$-\$150,000 + \frac{\$75,000}{1 + 0.10} + \frac{\$75,000}{(1 + 0.10)^2} + \frac{\$75,000}{(1 + 0.10)^3} = \$36,514.$$

Use formula A6.5 in Appendix 6.1 to calculate the annual-equivalent cash flow. The three-year discount factor is $\dfrac{1}{(1 + 0.10)^3} = 0.7513$, the annuity discount factor is $\dfrac{1 - 0.7513}{0.10} = 2.4870$, and the annual-equivalent cash flow is thus $\dfrac{\$36,514}{2.4870} = \$14,682.$

b. Why replace a machine that produces an annual cash flow of $20,000 with a new one that will generate only $14,682 a year? The management of Pasta Uno should keep the old machine.

7.1. Shortcomings of the payback period

The payback period rule ignores the time value of money and the risk of the project (unless you use the discounted payback period); it also ignores the cash flows beyond the cutoff period and, more generally, tends to favor short-term investments. Firms still compute the payback period because it is simple to calculate and easy to interpret: it provides an indication of the speed of the recovery of the initial investment.

7.2. IRR versus cost of capital

The cost of capital is the rate of return that investors require from investments with the same risk as the project, while the project's internal rate of return is the discount rate for which the net present value of the project is equal to zero. Put another way, the project's cost of capital is what the firm *should earn* from the project whereas the project's internal rate of return is what the firm *can expect to earn* from it.

7.3. IRR versus ROIC

Both the return on invested capital (ROIC) and the internal rate of return (IRR) are measures of operating profitability but there are several important differences between them:

	RETURN ON INVESTED CAPITAL	**INTERNAL RATE OF RETURN**
Measured with	*Accounting* data	*Cash flow* data
Measurement period	*Single* period	*Multiple* periods
Typically used for analyzing	*Historical* profitability of *firms*	*Expected* profitability of *projects*

7.4. Shortcomings of the IRR and profitability index rules

Internal rate of return: When the choice is between two mutually exclusive investments. In the case where the cash-flow stream of the two investments differ widely, the project with the cash flows concentrated mostly in the earliest years may have a higher internal rate of return than the project with the cash flows concentrated mostly in later years, although the second project may have a higher net present value, meaning that it will contribute the most to the firm's value.

Profitability index: When the size of the two investments are very different. In this case, the profitability index of the smaller project may be higher than that of the *bigger,* although its net present value may be *smaller.*

7.5. Evaluating two projects using alternative decision rules

In what follows, all figures are in thousands of dollars.

a.   Net present value (project A) $= -\$2{,}000 + \$2{,}451 = \$451$

            Net present value (project B) $= -\$2{,}000 + \$2{,}400 = \$400$

If the projects are independent, *both* should be accepted because they both create value ($451 for project A and $400 for project B). If they are mutually exclusive, project A should be preferred because it creates *more* value.

b.   To get the payback periods of the two projects, you need first to compute their cumulative cash flows:

	PROJECT A		**PROJECT B**	
YEAR	**CASH FLOWS**	**CUMULATIVE CASH FLOWS**	**CASH FLOWS**	**CUMULATIVE CASH FLOWS**
Now	−$2,000	−$2,000	−$2,000	−$2,000
1	200	−1,800	1,400	−600
2	1,200	−600	1,000	400
3	1,700	1,100	400	800

The payback period of project A is between 2 and 3 years because the cumulative cash flows become positive between these years. The payback period of project B is between 1 and 2 years. We can write:

$$\text{Payback period project A} = 2 + \frac{\$600}{\$1{,}700} = 2.35 \text{ years.}$$

$$\text{Payback period project B} = 1 + \frac{\$600}{\$1{,}000} = 1.60 \text{ year.}$$

To get the discounted payback period, you need to compute the cumulative *present value* of the two projects' cash-flow streams. Using a discount rate of 10% we have:

| | PROJECT A | | | PROJECT B | | |
YEAR	CASH FLOWS	PRESENT VALUE OF CASH FLOWS	CUMULATIVE PRESENT VALUE OF CASH FLOWS	CASH FLOWS	PRESENT VALUE OF CASH FLOWS	CUMULATIVE PRESENT VALUE OF CASH FLOWS
Now	−$2,000	−$2,000	−$2,000	−$2,000	−$2,000	−$2,000
1	200	181.82	−1,818.18	1,400	1,272.73	−727.27
2	1,200	991.74	−826.44	1,000	826.45	99.18
3	1,700	1,277.23	450.79	400	300.53	399.71

The discounted payback period is between 2 and 3 years for project A and between 1 and 2 years for project B. However, because discounting reduces the value of the cash flows, the discounted payback periods are longer than the straight payback periods. We have:

$$\text{Discounted payback period project A} = 2 + \frac{\$826.44}{\$1,277.23} = 2.65 \text{ years}$$

$$\text{Discounted payback period project B} = 2 + \frac{\$727.27}{\$826.45} = 1.88 \text{ year}$$

If the two projects are mutually exclusive, the initial investment of $2,000 (which is the same for both projects) will be recovered earlier from project B than from project A. However, this does not mean that you should choose project B because the payback period does not tell you which project will create more value. We know from the answer to the previous question that project A creates more value than project B. Thus project A should be chosen over project B.

c. The internal rate of return (IRR) of the projects is the discount rates for which the net present value of the projects is equal to zero:

$$\text{Net present value project A} = 0 = -\$2,000 + \frac{\$200}{1 + IRR} + \frac{\$1,200}{(1 + IRR)^2} + \frac{\$1,700}{(1 + IRR)^3}$$

$$\text{Net present value project B} = 0 = -\$2,000 + \frac{\$1,400}{1 + IRR} + \frac{\$1,000}{(1 + IRR)^2} + \frac{\$400}{(1 + IRR)^3}$$

Using a financial calculator or a spreadsheet IRR function, we found:

$$\text{Internal rate of return of project A} = 19.60\%$$

$$\text{Internal rate of return of project B} = 23.56\%$$

If the projects are independent, both should be accepted because their internal rate of return is higher than the 10% cost of capital. If the projects were mutually exclusive, intuition would suggest that project B, which has the higher internal rate of return, should be preferred to project A. However, this would be true only if project B was creating more value than project A, which we know is not the case. Thus project A should be preferred, although it has a lower internal rate of return. As the graph below shows, this will always be true as long as the projects' cost of capital is lower than the break-even discount rate of 12.9%. It is only when the cost of capital is higher than 12.9% that the ranking of the two projects is the same, using the net present value or the internal rate of return.

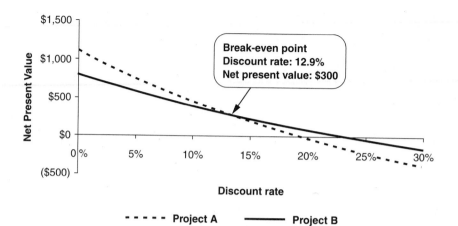

d. Present value of project A future cash flows at 10% = $2,451
Present value of project B future cash flows at 10% = $2,400

$$\text{Profitability index A} = \frac{\text{Present value cash flows (A)}}{\text{Initial cash outlay (A)}} = \frac{\$2,451}{\$2,000} = 1.23$$

$$\text{Profitability index B} = \frac{\text{Present value cash flows (B)}}{\text{Initial cash outlay (B)}} = \frac{\$2,400}{\$2,000} = 1.20$$

Both projects have a profitability index greater than one which means that they both return more than one dollar for one dollar invested ($1.23 for project A and $1.20 for project B). Thus both projects would create value. They should both be accepted if they are independent. If they are mutually exclusive, project A should be accepted because it generates more dollars for each dollar invested. Note that both the net present value rule and the profitability index rule lead to the same decisions: accept both projects if they are independent and choose project A over project B if the two projects are mutually exclusive. As shown in the chapter, this may not always be the case however, especially when both projects differ widely in size.

e. As long as the objective is to accept projects that create value, the only criterion that will always work is the net present value rule. Thus, because both projects have a positive net present value, they should be both accepted if they are independent. If they are mutually exclusive, project A is preferred to project B because it has a higher net present value.

8.1. Interest payments and project's cash flow

Interest payments are cash flows *to* creditors not cash flows *from* the project. They are claims on the cash flows generated by the project and do not affect these cash flows. Interest payments, and, more generally, the costs of financing a project, are taken into account in the project's cost of capital.

8.2. Understanding the structure of the cash flow formula

The term EBIT(1 − Tax) is equal to EBIT − EBIT × Tax, so that the formula can be rewritten as:

Cash flow = EBIT + Depreciation − EBIT × Tax − ΔWCR − Capex.

Note that by adding up depreciation to EBIT, the impact of depreciation on the cash flow is washed out because EBIT includes depreciation as a cost. Furthermore, because EBIT × Tax is the amount of tax to be paid on the operating profit generated by the project, it clearly needs to be accounted for in the cash flow from the project. Finally, by deducting the increase in working capital requirement, the formula takes into account any lead or lag between the accounting revenues and expenses in EBIT and their corresponding cash inflows or cash outflows (see Chapter 4).

8.3. Alternative formula to estimate a project's cash flow

We can write: EBIT = EBITDA − Depreciation

so that the first formula can be rewritten as:

$$\begin{aligned}
\text{Cash flow} &= (\text{EBITDA} - \text{Depreciation})(1 - \text{Tax}) + \text{Depreciation} - \Delta\text{WCR} - \text{Capex}\\
&= \text{EBITDA}(1 - \text{Tax}) - \text{Depreciation} + \text{Tax} \times \text{Depreciation} + \text{Depreciation} - \Delta\text{WCR} - \text{Capex}\\
&= \text{EBITDA}(1 - \text{Tax}) + \text{Tax} \times \text{Depreciation} - \Delta\text{WCR} - \text{Capex}
\end{aligned}$$

which is the second formula. Note that in the second formula the term EBIDT $(1 - \text{Tax})$ overestimates the tax bill because it ignores the deduction of the allowable depreciation expenses. To compensate for this, the tax that would be shielded by the depreciation expense, which is captured by the term Tax × Depreciation, is added back.

8.4. Identifying a project's relevant cash flows

Capital expenditures:
1. Is there any opportunity cost associated with the use of the parking lot? Where will company employees park their cars? Will Printers Inc. need to rent parking spaces? If this is the case, the project should be charged for the rent.
2. A residual value should be included at the end of year 2002.

Revenue: The sale price is assumed to be constant, that is, unaffected by competition, which is unreasonable.

Research and development costs: These are sunk costs (they were spent in 1996 and 1997). They should therefore be ignored.

Overhead costs: The overhead costs charged to the project are not incremental costs, they are accounting allocations. The relevant amount of overhead costs is the increase in the company overhead charges that would result from the adoption of the project, if any.

Operating costs: The direct and indirect costs are assumed to be only variable costs, which is unreasonable.

Inventories:
1. Investment in inventories is supposed to stay constant although sales are multiplied by a factor of 4 between 1998 and 2002. This is also unreasonable.
2. The recovery of the investment in the inventories at the end of the project is ignored.
3. What about receivables? Payables? Working capital requirement?

Financing costs:
1. Financing costs are cash flows to those who invested in the project and not cash flows *from* the project. Therefore, they are irrelevant.
2. Furthermore, they are accounting allocations, not incremental costs, which is incorrect.

Discount rate: The discount rate is the project's cost of capital. It should reflect the risk characteristics of the project as well as the proportion of debt capital and equity capital that are relevant for the project. It is *not* Printers Inc. borrowing rate.

Other: Inflation is ignored.

8.5. Estimating a project's relevant cash flows and net present value (in thousands of dollars)

	31/12/97	1998	1999	2000	2001	2002
I. Revenues:						
1. Expected unit sales in thousands		5,000	10,000	20,000	20,000	20,000
2. Price per unit		$.8	$.7	$.6	$.6	$.6
3. *Sales revenues (line 1 × line 2)*		*$4,000*	*$7,000*	*$12,000*	*$12,000*	*$12,000*
II. Operating expenses						
4. Inflation rate		3%	3%	3%	3%	3%
5. Compounded (1 + inflation rate)		1.030	1.061	1.093	1.126	1.159
6. Fixed costs (1997 value)		$800	$800	$800	$800	$800
7. Fixed costs (line 6 × line 5)		$824	$849	$874	$900	$927
8. Variable costs per unit (1997 value)		$.400	$.400	$.400	$.400	$.400
9. Variable costs per unit (line 8 × line 5)		$.412	$.424	$.437	$.450	$.464
10. Total variable costs (line 9 × line 1)		$2,060	$4,244	$8,742	$9,004	$9,274
11. Depreciation expenses ($6,000,000/10)		$600	$600	$600	$600	$600
12. Rental of parking spaces		$50	· $50	$50	$50	$50
13. *Total operating expenses (lines 7 + 10 + 11 + 12)*		*$3,534*	*$5,743*	*$10,266*	*$10,554*	*$11,850*
III. Operating profit						
13. EBIT (line 3 − line 13)		$466	$1,257	$1,734	$1,446	$150
14. less tax at 40%		($186)	($503)	($694)	($578)	($60)
15. *Aftertax operating profit (line 13 + line 14)*		*$280*	*$754*	*$1,040*	*$868*	*$90*
IV. Cash flow generated by the project						
16. Aftertax operating profit (line 15)		$280	$754	$1,040	$868	$90
17. Depreciation expenses (line 11)		$600	$600	$600	$600	$600
18. Working capital requirement (30% of year-end sales)	$1,200	$2,100	$3,600	$3,600	$3,600	$0
19. Change in working capital requirement	$1,200	$900	$1,500	$0	$0	($3,600)
20. Capital expenditure	$6,000					
21. Recovery of the aftertax resale value of equipment[1]						$3,000
22. Cash flow from the project (lines 16 + 17 − 19 − 20 + 21)	($7,200)	($20)	($146)	$1,640	$1,468	$7,290
24. Cost of capital	12%					
25. Net present value	($1,097)					

[1] Salvage value, year end 2002 = $3 million
Book value, year end 2002   = $6 million − $3 million = $3 million
Capital gain   = $0
Tax on capital gain   = $0
Aftertax cash receipt   = $3 million.

The project's net present value is negative after taking into account the relevant cash flows from the project and discounting them at the cost of capital of 12%. The proposal would destroy value if undertaken and should therefore be rejected.

9.1. Structure and characteristics of financial markets

a. Direct financing refers to raising capital directly from ultimate savers (households with a cash surplus), whereas indirect financing refers to raising capital from financial intermediaries (such as banks and pension funds) in which ultimate savers have invested their savings.

b. Primary markets refer to markets where securities are sold to investors for the first time whereas secondary markets are markets where the securities that have already been issued are bought and sold. Note that the former provide fresh capital to the issuing firm while the latter do not involve the firm.

c. Organized markets are regulated markets where only companies that can meet stringent conditions can list their shares whereas over-the-counter markets have less stringent listing and reporting requirements.

d. Domestic securities are securities issued by firms in their local markets whereas Eurosecurities are issued in the international markets, markets that are outside the direct control and jurisdiction of the issuer's country of origin.

e. Domestic securities are securities issued by firms in their local markets whereas foreign securities are securities issued by firms in the domestic markets of other countries.

f. In a private placement, securities are sold to qualified investors and are not listed or traded in the financial markets, whereas in a public offering, securities are sold to financial markets participants who can trade them without restrictions.

g. In a rights offering, shares are issued exclusively to the firm's existing shareholders, whereas in a general cash offering they are sold to any interested buyer.

h. In an underwritten issue, the investment bank buys the securities from the issuer and then sells them to the public at its own risk (the bank acts as a *dealer* in this case), whereas in a best-efforts distribution, the investment bank does not buy the securities from the issuer; it only sells them on behalf of the issuer (the bank acts as a *broker* in this case).

i. The originating house is the investment bank that has initiated the issue, whereas the selling group consists of a number of banks which are brought in to help distribute portions of the shares that have been allocated to them by the originating house or lead manager.

j. A seasoned issue refers to the issue of securities by a firm that has already issued similar securities in the past, whereas a secondary distribution refers to the sale to the public of a large block of securities held by an investor who acquired them earlier directly from the firm. The former provides fresh capital to the issuing firm while the latter does not involve the firm.

k. Credit risk refers to the ability of a firm to service the bonds it has issued (pay interest and repay the principal) while market risk refers to the unexpected changes in the price of bonds in response to changes in the rates of interest.

l. Investment grade bonds are bonds with a credit rating of AAA, AA, A and BBB (Standard and Poor's classification), whereas speculative grade bonds, also known as junk bonds or high-yield bonds, have credit ratings lower than BBB.

9.2. Estimating external funding needs

a. Total funding needs in 1998 = ΔCash + ΔWCR + Capex = zero + $7.7 million + $10 million = $17.7 million

b. Internally-generated funds = Retained earnings + Depreciation = $7.7 million + $8 million + $1 million = $16.7 million

c. External funding needs = $17.7 million − $16.7 million = $1 million

d. The million dollar gap should be borrowed. It is too small to justify an issue of new equity.

9.3. Leasing versus borrowing

LEASE VERSUS BUY	NOW	YEAR 1	YEAR 2	YEAR 3	YEAR 4
Aftertax lease payments (60% of $6,500)	−$3,900	−$3,900	−$3,900	−$3,900	
Loss of tax savings on depreciation (40% of $6,000)		−2,400	−2,400	−2,400	−$2,400
Loss of the aftertax scrap value (60% of $5,000)					−3,000
Cash saved because the truck is not bought	+24,000				
Total differential cash flow	+$20,100	$6,300	$6,300	$6,300	$5,400

a. Discounting the total differential cash flows at the aftertax cost of debt of 6% (60% of 10%) yields a *negative* net present value, or net advantage of leasing, of −$1,017.

   Conclusion: Leasing is more expensive than borrowing. OS Distributors should buy the truck and borrow to finance the purchase instead of leasing.

b. OS Distributors will be indifferent between buying or leasing if the net advantage of leasing (NAL) in zero, that is, if the present value at 6% of the differential cash flows from year 1 to year 4 is equal to $20,100 (see table above):

$$\$20,100 = \text{Present value } (-\$6,300 \text{ for 3 years}) + \text{Present value (cash flow in year 4)}$$

The first term on the right side of the equation is equal to −$16,840. Thus, the present value of the cash flow in year 4 is $3,260 ($20,100 less $16,840). We have:

$$\$3,260 = \frac{\text{Cash flow in year 4}}{(1 + 0.06)^4} = \frac{\text{Cash flow in year 4}}{1.2625}$$

and the cash flow in year 4 is $4,116 ($3,260 × 1.2625). This figure includes the $2,400 tax savings on depreciation (see year 4 in table above). Deducting $2,400 from $4,116 gives an aftertax scrap value of $1,716. The pretax scrap value is thus $2,860 ($1,716 divided by 60%).

9.4. Rights issue

a. The number of rights MEC will grant must be equal to the number of MEC's shares outstanding, that is, 50 million rights.

b. The number of rights (N) required to buy one new share is five:

$$N = \text{Number of rights} = \frac{\text{Number of outstanding shares}}{\text{Number of new shares}} = \frac{50 \text{ million}}{10 \text{ million}} = 5$$

c. The price will drop to $25 to reflect the fact that the share has gone ex-rights, that is, it entitles the holder to buy new shares at $20. The ex-rights price is (see equation 9.2):

$$\text{Ex-rights price} = \frac{N \times \text{rights-on price} + \text{subscription price}}{N + 1} = \frac{5 \times \$26 + \$20}{6} = \frac{\$150}{6} = \$25$$

where the rights-on price is the share price prior the rights issue announcement ($26).

d. The value of one right is simply $1, the difference between the rights-on price ($26) and the ex-rights price ($25). It can also be calculated directly with the formula in footnote 12:

$$\text{Value of one right} = \frac{\text{Rights-on price} - \text{Subscription price}}{N + 1} = \frac{\$26 - \$20}{6} = \frac{\$6}{6} = \$1$$

9.5. Valuation of bonds

TYPE	COUPON ISSUE	ZERO COUPON	PERPETUAL
Value at 7.0 percent	$959.00	$712.99	$857.14
Value at 7.5 percent	$939.31	$696.56	$800.00
Percentage change	−2.05%	−2.30%	−6.67%

a. The bond values can be calculated with the "cash flow" key of a financial calculator. Alternatively, you can use, respectively, the bond valuation formulas 9.4, 9.5 and 9.6.

b. Bond values are below their face values because the market yield (7%) is above the coupon rate (6%). Rates have gone up (from 6% to 7%) and hence bond values have gone down.

c. Because the convertible provides its holder with a valuable option (the option to convert the bond into common stocks at a fixed price), he/she is willing to accept a coupon that is lower than the one offered by a straight, non-convertible bond.

d. Value of option = Value of convertible − Value if non-convertible = $1,040 − $959 = $81

e. See bond values at 7.5% in the table above. Yield has gone up and thus bond values have gone down. The most sensitive bond to a change in yield is the perpetual because it has the longest maturity. In general, bonds with the *longest* maturity and the *lowest* coupon are the most sensitive to a change in yield.

9.6. Valuation of preferred shares and common stocks

a. Estimated value of the preferred $= \dfrac{\$3}{0.0860} = \$34.88.$

b. The yield of 8.60%, which we took to estimate the value of the preferred, must overestimate the correct yield on NEC's preferred and hence its value is underestimated.

c. To estimate the value of the common stock you must first identify the stream of dividends NEC is expected to pay in the future and then discount it at the required rate of return of 12%. The expected stream of dividend payments is:

	NOW	YEAR 1	YEAR 2	YEAR 3	YEAR 4
Expected growth rate		8%	8%	8%	4% (forever)
Expected dividend	$2.00	$2.16	$2.33	$2.52	$2.62

Year-4 dividend will grow at a constant rate of 4% in perpetuity. The value at the end of *year 3* of that dividend stream is given by the valuation formula 9.8:

$$\text{Value of dividend stream beyond year 3} = \frac{\$2.62 \text{ (Year-4 dividend)}}{0.12 \text{ (Required return)} - 0.04 \text{ (Growth rate)}} = \frac{\$2.62}{0.08} = \$32.75$$

and the estimated share value is thus the present value of the entire dividend stream at 12%:

$$\text{Estimated share value} = \frac{\$2.16}{1 + 0.12} + \frac{\$2.33}{(1 + 0.12)^2} + \frac{\$2.52}{(1 + 0.12)^3} + \frac{\$2.62 + \$32.75}{(1 + 0.12)^4} = \$28.06$$

d. The observed market price of $31.62 is 12.7% higher than the estimated value of $28.06. This can be interpreted as follows. If we assume that the estimated value is "correct" then the shares are overpriced and should be sold. If we assume that the price is "correct" then the model and the assumptions we have used to estimate the value of a share are incorrect and should be revised.

10.1. Cost of debt versus cost of equity

We mean that the amount of equity capital invested in the firm, the division, or the project is *expected* to return 10% to the equityholders, while the amount invested as debt capital is *expected* to return 8% to the debtholders. These returns are those that the investors can get from investing in firms having the same risk as that of the firm, the division, or the project. The cost of debt is lower than the cost of equity because debtholders have a priority claim over the equityholders on the cash flows generated by the firm, the division, or the project. As a consequence, debt is less risky than equity and the cost of debt is thus lower than the cost of equity.

10.2. Cash flows from bonds and stocks

The cash flows associated with a bond are the coupon payments and the principal repayment, while the cash flows associated with a share of stock are the dividends paid to the shareholders. The market value of a bond or a stock is the present value of their respective expected cash-flow streams (see equations 10.1 and 10.4). In the case of a bond, the coupon payments and principal repayment are discounted at the bondholders' expected return, while in the case of a share of stock, the dividends are discounted at the shareholders' expected return. Both returns depend on the risk associated with holding the securities.

10.3. The capital asset pricing model

1. The higher the risk of a security or an asset, the higher its expected return.
2. The only relevant risk of a security is that portion of the security risk that cannot be diversified away. This risk, called systematic, undiversifiable or market risk, is measured by the security beta coefficient. A beta coefficient of one indicates that the security has the same risk as that of a well-diversified portfolio, also called the market portfolio. A beta coefficient higher (lower) than one indicates a higher (lower) risk than that of the market portfolio.
3. The expected return on a security is the sum of the risk-free rate (the rate of return of the safest security, for example the yield on government bonds held to maturity) plus a risk premium. This risk premium is the reward for bearing the systematic risk of the security. It is equal to the security beta coefficient multiplied by the market risk premium (the difference between the return expected from holding the market portfolio and the risk free rate).

10.4. Estimation of the cost of capital of a firm

The relevant cost of capital of Royal Corporation is the weighted average cost of its various sources of capital, that is, the weighted average cost of capital or WACC. To determine that cost according to formula 10.12 reproduced below, apply the following steps.

$$\text{WACC} = k_D(1 - T_C) \times \frac{D}{E + D} + k_E \times \frac{E}{E + D}$$

where k_D = cost of debt capital
T_C = corporate tax rate
$k_D (1 - T_C)$ = aftertax cost of debt
k_E = cost of equity capital
$\dfrac{D}{E + D}$ = proportion of debt financing, measured at market value
$\dfrac{E}{E + D}$ = proportion of equity financing, measured at market value

Step one: *Estimate the aftertax cost debt*

Because Royal Corporation has no debt other than the outstanding bonds, the bonds' yield to maturity is Royal's cost of debt. The current market price of the bonds is $1,150 (115 percent of the $1,000 par value). Coupons are paid annually at a rate of 10 percent, or $100 per year, and the bonds will be repaid 10 years from now. Applying the bond valuation formula (equation 10.1), we have:

$$-\$1,150 = \frac{\$100}{1 + k_D} + \frac{\$100}{(1 + k_D)^2} + \frac{\$100}{(1 + k_D)^3} + \frac{\$100}{(1 + k_D)^4} + \frac{\$100}{(1 + k_D)^5}$$
$$+ \frac{\$100}{(1 + k_D)^6} + \frac{\$100}{(1 + k_D)^7} + \frac{\$100}{(1 + k_D)^8} + \frac{\$100}{(1 + k_D)^9} + \frac{\$1,100}{(1 + k_D)^{10}}$$

Solving for k_D we find k_D = 7.79% (use the IRR key on a financial calculator or spreadsheet). Because the corporate tax rate is 40%, the aftertax cost of debt is:

$$k_D (1 - T_C) = 7.79\%(1 - 0.40) = 4.67\%$$

Step two: *Estimate the proportion of debt and equity financing*

Recall that we have to use market values to compute the relevant financing ratios. Because Royal has 250,000 bonds outstanding selling at $1,150 apiece and 10 million shares selling at $40 each, we have:
D = market value of Royal's debt = 250,000 × $1,150 = $287.5 million
E = market value of Royal's equity = 10 million × $40 = $400 million.

$$\frac{D}{D + E} = \frac{\$287.5 \text{ million}}{\$287.5 \text{ million} + \$400 \text{ million}} = 0.418 \text{ and}$$

$$\frac{E}{D + E} = \frac{\$400 \text{ million}}{\$287.5 \text{ million} + \$400 \text{ million}} = 0.582$$

Step three: *Estimate the cost of equity using the capital asset pricing model*

According to the capital asset pricing model (see equation 10.11) we have:

$$k_E = \text{Risk-free rate} + \text{Market risk premium} \times \text{Beta} = 6.3\% + 7.0\% \times 1.10 = 14.00\%$$

Step four: *Calculate the weighted average cost of capital*

$$\text{WACC} = 4.67\% \times 0.418 + 14.00\% \times 0.582 = 10.10\%$$

10.5. Estimation of the cost of capital of a division

Part 1:

There are two observations to make.

1. The weighted average cost of capital of 12% is the cost of capital of PacificCom, that is, the average of the costs of capital of its two divisions. If the risk, and more precisely the betas, of the two divisions are different, the cost of capital that is needed to evaluate each division's investment proposals cannot be equal to 12%.
2. The amount of debt and equity capital that the consultant has used to compute the financing ratios $D/(E + D)$ and $E/(E + D)$ are taken from PacificCom's balance sheet. In other words, they are accounting values whereas a proper WACC should be calculated with market values.

Part 2:

a. To estimate the equipment division weighted average cost of capital, you need to estimate its aftertax cost of debt, its relevant financing ratios as well as its appropriate cost of equity according to the capital asset pricing model using the data on proxy firms. Apply the following procedure:

Step one: Estimate the division's aftertax cost of debt

We assume that the division's aftertax cost of debt is the same as that of the firm.

$$k_D (1 - T_C) = 8\%(1 - 0.40) = 4.8\%$$

Step two: Estimate the division's cost of equity based on data from proxy firms

According to the capital asset pricing model (see equation 10.11) we have:

$$k_E = \text{Risk-free rate} + \text{Market risk premium} \times \text{Beta}$$

where the risk-free rate is 6.5% and the market risk premium is 7%. The beta coefficient we need is the *equity* beta of the equipment division. This equity beta can be estimated from the data on proxy firms by applying the following three-step procedure:

Step 2.1: Estimate the asset betas of the proxy firms using the equation 10.7

$$\beta_{asset} = \frac{\beta_{equity}}{1 + (1 - \text{Tax rate})\dfrac{\text{Debt}}{\text{Equity}}}$$

For proxy A we have:

$$\beta^A_{asset} = \frac{0.70}{[1 + (1 - 0.40) \times 1.00]} = 0.43$$

For proxy B we get:

$$\beta^B_{asset} = \frac{1.00}{[1 + (1 - 0.40) \times 0.80]} = 0.68$$

For proxy C we find:

$$\beta^C_{asset} = \frac{1.02}{[1 + (1 - 0.40) \times 0.70]} = 0.72$$

Step 2.2: Estimate the equipment division's asset beta as the average of the proxies' asset betas

$$\beta_{asset} = \frac{0.43 + 0.68 + 0.72}{3} = 0.61$$

Step 2.3: Estimate the equipment division's equity beta by re-levering the division's estimated asset beta of 0.61 at the division's target debt-to-equity ratio of 1.20, using equation 10.6

$$\beta_{equity} = \beta_{asset}\left[1 + (1 - \text{Tax rate})\frac{\text{Debt}}{\text{Equity}}\right] = 0.61 \times [1 + (1 - 0.40) \times 1.20] = 1.05$$

Step 2.4: Estimate the division's cost of equity using its estimated equity beta of 1.05 and the capital asset pricing model

$$k_E = 6.5\% + 7.0\% \times 1.05 = 13.85\%$$

Step three: Calculate the division's weighted average cost of capital using the division's target debt-to-equity ratio of 1.20, which is equivalent to a debt-to-total financing ratio of 0.55

$$\text{WACC} = 4.8\% \times 0.55 + 13.85\% \times 0.45 = 8.9\%$$

b. The appropriate hurdle rate for the equipment division is its estimated WACC of 8.9%, not the company-wide WACC of 12%. If a hurdle rate of 12% is used instead of 8.9%, the equipment division will incorrectly reject projects with internal rate of returns that are lower than 12% but higher than 8.9%. For example, a project with an IRR of 10% would be rejected even though it is a value-creating project because its IRR exceeds the correct cost of capital of 8.9%. The opposite will take place in the riskier software division. Its correct hurdle rate should be higher than 12%. If 12% is used as a hurdle rate, the division will incorrectly accept some projects which should be rejected. Over time the riskier software division will grow at the expense of the less risky communication division. As a consequence, PacificCom will become riskier and will most likely destroy value.

11.1. Effect of borrowing on share price

1. In the absence of tax and financial distress costs, the share price should not necessarily decrease because, as the firm's debt goes up, the increase of the *expected* earnings per share will offset the negative impact of the increase in its volatility. Indeed, according to Modigliani and Miller, the compensation will be perfect, and the share price should not be affected at all.
2. In the presence of tax, the firm's tax bill decreases in proportion to its indebtedness because interest payments are tax deductible. The firm's share price will go up to reflect the present value of the tax savings that goes to the shareholders.
3. As the firm borrows more and more to take advantage of the interest tax shield, the probability of financial distress increases. If there are costs associated with financial distress, at some point the present value of these costs will be higher than the present value of the interest tax shield and the firm's share price will begin to decrease.

11.2. Risk of debt and equity and risk of the firm

False. When debt is increased there is more of the cash flows generated by the firm's assets going to the debtholders than to the shareholders, that's all. The volatility of the cash flows from the firm's assets is not affected. Therefore, the risk of the firm as a whole will not increase.

11.3. Factors affecting the optimal debt-to-equity ratio

a. *Increase* the debt-to-equity ratio to take advantage of the increase in the interest tax shield.

b. *Increase* the debt-to-equity ratio because a higher personal capital gain tax will increase the spread between the tax rate on equity income and the tax rate on interest income. See equation 11.8.

c. *Increase* the debt-to-equity ratio because acquiring the building will increase the firm's tangible assets and, as a result, the probability of financial distress will decrease.

d. If the ratio is optimal when measured on the basis of the current market value of the firm's equity, it is too high when measured on the basis of the fair value of its equity because the firm's shares are currently undervalued. The firm should issue debt and buy shares with the proceeds, thus providing a strong signal that its shares are undervalued. The process should last until the share price reaches its fair value and the debt-to-equity ratio reverts to its current value.

e. *Do not change* the debt-to-equity ratio because a decrease in the working capital requirement does not usually affect the probability of financial distress.

f. As long as Alternative Solutions Inc. and the acquirer are publicly held firms with well diversified shareholders, the ratio should not change because, in that case, the optimal debt-to-equity ratio is not determined by the identity of the owners of the firm's assets. Note that if Alternative Solutions Inc. were a private company and its new owners were not well diversified investors, the ratio may have to change to reflect the new owners' optimal debt-to-equity ratio.

11.4. EBIT-EPS analysis

a. The following tables show the calculations of Chloroline's EPS and return on investment as a function of the firm's EBIT, without debt and with debt. The graph shows how return on investment changes when Chloroline's EBIT varies.

CURRENT CAPITAL STRUCTURE: NO DEBT AND TWO MILLION SHARES OUTSTANDING

	RECESSION	EXPECTED	EXPANSION
Earnings before interest and tax (EBIT)	$5.0 million	$15.0 million	$20.0 million
Less interest expenses	$0	$0	$0
Equals earnings before tax	$5.0 million	$15.0 million	$20.0 million
Less tax (40 percent of earnings before tax)	$2.0 million	$6.0 million	$8.0 million
Equals net earnings	$3 million	$9.0 million	$12.0 million
Divided by the number of shares	2 million	2 million	2 million
Equals earnings per share (EPS)	**$1.5**	**$4.5**	**$6**
Divided by share price	$50	$50	$50
Equals return on investment	**3.0%**	**9.0%**	**12.0%**

PROPOSED CAPITAL STRUCTURE: BORROW $50 MILLION AT 8 PERCENT AND USE THE CASH TO REPURCHASE 1 MILLION SHARES AT $50 PER SHARE

	RECESSION	EXPECTED	EXPANSION
Earnings before interest and tax (EBIT)	$5.0 million	$15.0 million	$20.0 million
Less interest expenses on debt	($4.0 million)	($4.0 million)	($4.0 million)
Equals earnings before tax	$1.0 million	$11.0 million	$16.0 million
Less tax (40 percent of earnings before tax)	$.4 million	$4.4 million	$6.4 million
Equals net earnings	$.6 million	$6.6 million	$9.6 million
Divided by the number of shares	1 million	1 million	1 million
Equals earnings per share (EPS)	**$.6**	**$6.6**	**$9.6**
Divided by share price	$50	$50	$50
Equals return on investment	**1.2%**	**13.2%**	**19.2%**

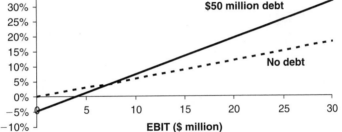

b. The analysis shows that a substitution of debt for equity will increase Chloroline's EPS and return on investment in the expected and expansion scenarios, but will decrease EPS and return on investment in the recession scenario. These results, however, are insufficient to make a recommendation on whether the firm should recapitalize for the following reasons:

1. They do not show the impact of the recapitalization on the market value of Chloroline and its share price.
2. They depend upon the accounting conventions that are used to calculate EBIT.
3. They do not account for the financial distress costs that debt financing generates.

11.5. Changes in capital structure and the cost of capital

a. In the absence of debt, the cost of equity of Starline is equal to the return from its assets because the shareholders are the only claimants to the cash flows generated by these assets. Thus, Starline's return on assets is 14%. This is also Starline's WACC in the absence of debt. As the debt-to-equity ratio goes up from zero to 100%, Starline's shareholders will bear more and more (financial) risk. Equation 11.5 shows how the cost of equity is related to the leverage ratio:

$$k_E = r_A + (r_A - k_D)(1 - T_c)\frac{D}{E}$$

where: k_E = cost of equity
           r_A = return on assets = 14%
           k_D = cost of debt = 8%
           T_c = corporate tax rate = 40%
        D/E = debt-to-equity ratio

$$k_E = 0.14 + (0.14 - 0.08)(1 - 0.40)\frac{D}{E} = 0.14 + 0.036\frac{D}{E}$$

And from equation 11.6, we have:

$$\text{WACC} = k_E\frac{E}{E+D} + k_D(1 - T_c)\frac{D}{E+D} = k_E\frac{1}{1+\dfrac{D}{E}} + k_D(1 - T_c)\frac{\dfrac{D}{E}}{1+\dfrac{D}{E}}$$

D/E	0	25%	50%	75%	100%
k_D	0.08	0.08	0.08	0.08	0.08
k_E	0.14	0.149	0.158	0.167	0.176
WACC	0.14	0.129	0.121	0.116	0.112

b.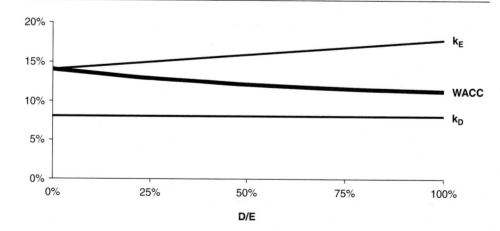

c. According to the above analysis you would be tempted to recommend that Starline increases its indebtedness as much as possible because the higher the level of debt the lower the weighted average cost of capital and the higher the value of the firm. However, the analysis ignores the impact of financial distress costs on the WACC and on the value of the firm when debt is increased. Conclusion: you should not recommend an increase in debt on the basis of this analysis alone.

12.1. Alternative valuation methods and value-creating acquisitions

a. A firm's liquidating value should be its *minimum* value and thus its *floor* (not ceiling) value. And its replacement value should be its *maximum* value and thus its *ceiling* (not floor) value.

b. When the yield on government securities rises, equity investors require a higher return to hold shares. This reduces share prices and *decreases* (not increases) price-earnings ratios.

c. No, price-to-cash flow ratios should be better because firms' cash flows are significantly less sensitive to accounting rules and conventions than are firms' reported earnings (profits).

d. For typical cash-flow streams, it is the present value of the cash flows expected *beyond* the 5- to 10-year forecasting period that dominates: it usually accounts for more than 50% of a company's estimated DCF value.

e. Different valuation methods are expected to generate different estimated values because of conceptual differences among alternative valuation models. Furthermore, different models use different inputs (data) which do not have the same quality or reliability.

f. Value can be created in a merger even in the absence of synergies if the management of the target firm can be improved. This could occur irrespective of synergistic costs reductions or synergistic revenue enhancements.

g. It can create value through synergistic revenue enhancement (post-merger revenues exceeding the sum of the revenues of the pre-merged firms).

h. Growth in earnings per share does not necessarily create value. Value will be created only if the merger has a *positive* net present value.

i. There is no evidence that acquiring firms create value by uncovering undervalued target firms. If they did, the share price of target firms would not drop to their pre-merger level when the mergers are cancelled.

j. In a leveraged buyout, debt financing provides more than valuable tax savings. It is also a device to monitor management (more debt means more pressure on management to generate cash to service debt and thus less wasted cash). And because management usually holds a relatively small *amount* of equity, debt financing is a way to provide them with a higher *percentage* of the firm's total equity (more debt financing means less equity financing and thus a higher fraction of equity in the hand of management).

12.2. Valuation by comparables

Apply the following three-step method.

Step one: *Convert the comparable firm's (NEC) data on a per-share basis*

1. Sales per share ($1,340 million/40 million shares)	$33.50
2. Earnings per share ($90 million/40 million shares)	$2.25
3. Cash earnings per share ($210 million/40 million shares)	$5.25
4. Book value per share ($590 million/40 million shares)	$14.75

Step two: *Calculate the comparable firm's (NEC) corresponding multiples*

1. Price-to-sales ratio ($30/$33.50)	0.90
2. Price-to-earnings ratio ($30/$2.25)	13.33
3. Price-to-cash earnings ratio ($30/$5.25)	5.71
4. Price-to-book value ratio ($30/$14.75)	2.03

<u>Step three:</u> *Estimate LMC's equity value using NEC's multiples*

1. Price-to-sales ratio: $620 million $\times$ 0.90 = $558 million
2. Price-to-earnings ratio: $46 million $\times$ 13.33 = $613 million
3. Price-to-cash earnings ratio: $104 million $\times$ 5.71 = $594 million
4. Price-to-book value ratio: $270 million $\times$ 2.03 = $548 million

These estimated values are not expected to be identical because they are based on different multiples drawn from National Engine Corporation. As long as the highest estimate is about 20 to 25% higher than the smallest, the range of prices is acceptable. In our case the highest estimate ($613 million) is 12% higher than the lowest estimate ($548 million).

12.3. Discounted cash flow valuation

a. Apply the following four-step method.

   <u>Step one:</u> *Estimate the cash flows from assets (CFA) that LMC is expected to generate in the next five years*

$$CFA = EBIT(1 - \text{tax rate}) + \text{Depreciation} - \Delta WCR - \text{Capital expenditures}$$

where EBIT is earnings before interest and tax, or pretax operating profit, and ΔWCR is the change in working capital requirement. But because annual capital expenditures will be equal to annual depreciation expenses, $CFA = EBIT(1 - \text{tax rate}) - \Delta WCR$.

Based on the forecasting assumptions, we can generate the following five-year forecast using a spreadsheet program:

(Data in millions of dollars)		FIVE-YEAR FORECAST				
	CURRENT	YEAR-1	YEAR-2	YEAR-3	YEAR-4	YEAR-5
1. Sales growth		8%	8%	6%	6%	4%
2. Sales in dollars	$620	$669.6	$723.2	$766.6	$812.6	$845.0
3. Operating margin in % of sales		20%	20%	20%	20%	20%
4. EBIT = Line 2 × line 3		133.9	144.6	153.3	162.5	169.0
5. EBIT(1 − tax) = Line 4 × (1 − 40%)		80.3	86.8	92.0	97.5	101.4
6. WCR in % of sales		20%	20%	20%	20%	20%
7. WCR = Line 2 × line 4	124	133.9	144.6	153.3	162.5	169.0
8. ΔWCR		9.9	10.7	8.7	9.2	6.5
9. CFA = Line 5 − Line 8		70.4	76.1	83.3	88.3	94.9
10. Residual value in Year-4[1]					996.8	
11. Total CFA = Line 9 + Line 10		$70.4	$76.1	$83.3	$1,085.1	

[1]The residual value in Year-4 is given by the perpetual, constant-growth, valuation formula (see valuation formula 12.1). In step two we show that LMC's weighted average cost of capital (WACC) is 13.52%. The residual value is thus:

$$\text{Residual value} = \frac{CFA_{\text{Year-5}}}{WACC - \text{Growth rate}} = \frac{\$94.9}{0.1352 - 0.04} = \frac{\$94.9}{0.0952} = \$996.8$$

   <u>Step two:</u> *Estimate LMC's weighted average cost of capital (WACC)*

1. Cost of equity according to the capital asset pricing model (CAPM)
   = 7% + 7% × 1.20 = 15.4%

2. Percentage of equity financing = 80%
3. Aftertax cost of debt = 10% $\times$ (1 − 0.40) = 6%
4. Percentage of debt financing = 100% − 80% = 20%

$$\text{WACC} = 0.80 \times 15.4\% + 0.20 \times 6\% = 13.52\%$$

Step three: *Estimate the discounted cash flow (DCF) value of LMC's assets by discounting the stream of cash flows from assets (CFA) at the WACC*

Estimated DCF value of LMC's assets =

Present value ($70.4; $76.1; $83.3; $1,085.1 @13.52%) = $831 million

Step four: *Estimate the discounted cash flow value of LMC's equity by deducting its debt outstanding ($280 million) from the DCF value of its assets*

Estimated DCF value of LMC's equity = $831 million − $280 million = $551 million.

b. To estimate the changes in equity value resulting from the suggested performance improvements, simply modify the relevant parameter in your spreadsheet. To find the estimated amount of value created, simply deduct $551 million, the DCF value of LMC's equity without improvements, that is, its "as-is value":

ACTION	EXPECTED CASH FLOWS FROM ASSETS	NEW DCF VALUE	VALUE CREATED
None	$70.4; $76.1; $83.3; $1,085.1	$551 million	—
Faster growth	$70.2; $76.2; $83.8; $1,157.6	$595 million	$44 million
Wider operating margin	$74.5; $80.4; $87.9; $1,143.4	$597 million	$46 million
Reduction in WCR-to-sales	$103.9; $78.7; $85.5; $1,104.6	$596 million	$45 million
Lower cost of capital	$70.4; $76.1; $83.3; $1,117.7	$579 million	$28 million
Sum of the four actions			$163 million
Combined actions	$107.9; $83.4; $90.8; $1,282.7	$724 million	$173 million

The sum of the changes in value resulting from each separate action ($163 million) is smaller than their cumulative effects ($173 million) because combining the various actions reinforces their individual impact. For example, a higher cash-flow discounted at a lower cost of capital will generate a higher value than each one of the two changes taken separately.

c. In an LBO, LMC's assets would be purchased with significantly more debt than the firm's current debt ratio. The firm's performance would then be improved and its debt ratio would be lowered gradually over the following, say, five years. Because LMC's capital structure would in this case change over time, its WACC would not be constant and the value of LMC's assets would be more easily estimated using the adjusted present value method. According to that method, the value of LMC's assets is estimated as the sum of two parts. The first is an estimation of the value of the firm's assets assuming they were financed *exclusively* with debt, obtained by discounting the cash-flow stream from assets at the *unlevered* cost of equity (which remains the same over time). The second is the present value of all the tax savings generated by debt financing and the amortization of any revaluation of the firm's assets.

13.1. Accounting versus economic exposure

Accounting and translation exposures are the same thing. Both refer to the effect of exchange-rate changes on the value of the firm's financial statements' accounts. Economic exposure refers to the effect of exchange-rate changes on the value of the firm's *future* cash flows. Transaction, contractual, and operating exposures are subsets of economic exposure. Transaction and contractual exposures are synonymous. Both have to do with the effect of the exchange-rate volatility on the future cash flows expected from past transactions denominated in foreign currencies, while operating exposure is concerned with the effect on future uncertain transactions. In the following table we indicate why economic exposure is more relevant than accounting exposure to shareholders:

Economic exposure	Accounting exposure
1. It is forward looking because it is concerned with *future* cash flows.	It is backward looking because it is concerned with *past* transactions.
2. It focuses on *cash flows* that are directly related to value creation.	It focuses on *accounting values* that are only remotely related to value creation.
3. It affects firms with foreign subsidiaries, export/import firms, as well as those which are subject to foreign competition in the input and output markets.	It only affects a subset of firms that are subject to accounting exposure, that is, those firms which *record* transactions denominated in a foreign currency.
4. Because it focuses on cash flows, it does not depend on the firm's accounting rules	It is affected by the accounting rules chosen by the firm.

13.2. Comparing alternative hedging techniques

	WHAT IS IT?	ADVANTAGES	DISADVANTAGES
Forward hedging	Buying (selling) forward an amount of foreign currency equal to the value of the underlying exposed cash outflow (inflow) denominated in the same currency and for the same delivery date.	It is tailor-made hedge that provides a perfect hedge for transactions of a known amount and known delivery dates.	1. It requires a credit check. 2. It often happens that the effective delivery date is not exactly the anticipated date. 3. The bid-ask spread on forward contracts can be large for infrequently traded currencies. 4. Getting out of a forward contract requires entering into an offsetting forward contract with the same delivery date as the original one.
Futures hedging	Buying (selling) futures contracts in the same currency as the underlying exposed cash outflow (inflow). The number of contracts to buy (sell) and the delivery date should match those of the amount of cash flow exposed and its delivery date.	1. No credit check is needed. 2. Transaction costs are low. 3. Default risk is low due to marking-to-market. 4. It is easy to get out of a position and the cash settlement is immediate.	1. One can only trade standard size contracts with fixed maturity dates. 2. Margin must be deposited. 3. Trades are marked-to-market daily.

| Options hedging | Buying options on the same currency as the underlying exposed cash outflow (inflow). The holder of the option has the right, but not the obligation, to buy (sell) foreign currencies over a specified period. In the case of over-the-counter options, the exercise price and the expiration date are contractually defined. In the case of traded options, the number of contracts to buy (sell) and the delivery date should match those of the amount of cash flow exposed and its delivery date. | 1. It is an insurance against unfavorable exchange rate movements.
2. Contrary to other hedging techniques, there is no obligation to buy (sell) the foreign currency.
3. Transaction costs and default risk of traded options are lower than over-the-counter options.
4. Options can be sold anytime before the expiration date. | 1 The firm has to pay a premium to get an option (the price of the option).

2. In the case of a traded option:
–One can only trade standard size contracts with fixed maturity dates.
–Margin must be deposited. |
| Swap hedging | Exchanging interest and principal payments in one currency for interest and principal payments in another currency. | 1. It is a low-cost exchange of cash flows denominated in different currencies.
2. The swap market is dominated by banks which reduces the counterparty risk. | 1. Its use is most often limited to long-term exposures.
2. There is potentially some counterparty risk. |

13.3. Parity relations

a. Purchasing power parity says that changes in the exchange rate between two countries' currencies are determined by the difference in the expected inflation rates between the two countries.

b. According to the international Fisher effect, the difference in interest rates between two countries is equal to the difference in the expected inflation rates between the two countries.

c. Interest rate parity says that changes in the exchange rate between two countries' currencies are determined by the difference in interest rates between the two countries.

d. Forward rates are good predictors of future spot rates.

13.4. Political risk and the cost of capital

False. Although it is often the case that firms mark up their domestic cost of capital when analyzing a foreign investment, the practice fails to properly account for political risk. A better way is to reduce the *expected* cash flows of the cross-border project according to the expected consequences of the political risk associated with the country in which the investment would be made. An added advantage of adjusting the cash flows instead of the cost of capital is that it forces management to clearly identify the risks taken. It also allows for sensitivity analysis.

13.5. Hedging imports with forwards, futures, and options

MPC can either do nothing or hedge its position using one of the following hedging techniques:
(1) forward contracts; (2) futures contracts; (3) options. Each of these cases is examined below.

1. Hedging with forward contracts

   Buy JPY250 million at the forward rate of JPY/USD122.42 for delivery on September 8 (90 days later). On September 8, the cost of the computer equipment will be:

   $$\frac{JPY250,000,000}{JPY/USD122.42} = USD2,0242,150$$

2. Hedging with currency futures contracts

   Buy 20 September yen futures on June 10 at USD0.008222 per yen; sell 20 September yen futures on September 8. The price at which MPC would sell the futures on September 8 is not known on June 10 because their expiration date is on September 17. Furthermore, MPC would have to buy 250 million yen in the spot market on September 8 in order to pay its supplier. As a result the net dollar cost of the computer equipment would not be known on June 10.

   For illustration purposes, let us assume that on September 8 the spot rate is JPY/USD0.0083 and the September yen futures rate is USD0.0084. The profit on the futures transaction is the sale of 20 futures on September 8 less the purchase of 20 futures on June 10:

   $$JPY12,500,000 \times 20 \times [USD/JPY0.008400 - USD/JPY0.008222] = USD44,500$$

   The cost of buying JPY250 million at the spot rate on September 8 is:

   $$JPY250,000,000 \times USD/JPY0.0083 = USD2,075,000$$

   The net cost of the computer equipment is thus:

   $$USD2,075,000 - USD44,500 = USD2,030,500$$

3. Hedging with options

   Buy JPY250 million OTC call options on June 10 with a strike price of JPY124/USD, at USD0.00021 per yen. The cost of the option is:

   $$JPY250,000,000 \times USD/JPY0.00021 = USD52,500$$

   Case 1: On September 8, the spot exchange rate is higher than the strike price of JPY/USD124. MPC will exercise its right to buy yen at the spot rate and pay:

   $$\frac{JPY250,000,000}{JPY/USD124} = USD2,016,129$$

   The net cost of the computer equipment would thus be:

   $$USD2,016,129 + USD52,500 = USD2,068,629$$

   Case 2: On September 8, the spot exchange rate is lower than the strike price of JPY/USD124. MPC would not exercise its option. The dollar cost of the equipment, although not known on June 10, would be lower than USD2,068,629.

   What should MPC do?

   Unless (1) MPC has another yen exposure that is the opposite of the one created by the purchase of the computer equipment, or (2) the size of the exposure (JPY250 million) is not significant when compared to MPC cash revenues, we would not recommend that it leave its position open (not hedging). Unless MPC creditworthiness is so low that it cannot find another party (bank) to be the counterparty in a forward transaction, we would recommend the forward hedge over the futures hedge. Unless MPC believes strongly that the yen will depreciate between June 10 and September 8, we would recommend the forward hedge over the option hedge.

13.6. International capital budgeting

Using the same approach applied in the chapter to the Swiss alternative of the Zap Scan project, we estimated the French investment cash flows as follows:

<u>Step one:</u> *Change the project's real cash flows into nominal cash flows by compounding the real values at the expected inflation rate of 3 percent (figures in millions)*

	NOW	YEAR-END 1	YEAR-END 2	YEAR-END 3	YEAR-END 4	YEAR-END 5
Real cash flows	(FRF100)	25	25	25	25	50
Expected inflation rate		3%	3%	3%	3%	3%
Compounded inflation rate		$(1 + 0.03)^1 =$ 1.0300	$(1 + 0.03)^2 =$ 1.0609	$(1 + 0.03)^3 =$ 1.0927	$(1 + 0.03)^4 =$ 1.1255	$(1 + 0.03)^5 =$ 1.1593
Nominal cash flows	(FRF100)	FRF25.75	FRF26.52	FRF27.32	FRF28.14	FRF57.96

<u>Step two:</u> *Estimate the future exchange rate (FRF/USD) using purchasing power parity (see equation 13.1)*

	NOW	YEAR-END 1	YEAR-END 2	YEAR-END 3	YEAR-END 4	YEAR-END 5
French inflation rate		3%	3%	3%	3%	3%
U.S. inflation rate		4%	4%	4%	4%	4%
Current exchange rate (FRF/USD)	FRF/USD6.0					
Expected future spot rate		$6.0 \times \dfrac{1.03}{1.04} =$ FRF/USD5.94	$6.0 \times \dfrac{1.03^2}{1.04^2} =$ FRF/USD5.89	$6.0 \times \dfrac{1.03^3}{1.04^3} =$ FRF/USD5.83	$6.0 \times \dfrac{1.03^4}{1.04^4} =$ FRF/USD5.77	$6.0 \times \dfrac{1.03^5}{1.04^5} =$ FRF/USD5.72

<u>Step three:</u> *Estimate the expected future cash flows in U.S. dollars (millions)*

	NOW	YEAR-END 1	YEAR-END 2	YEAR-END 3	YEAR-END 4	YEAR-END 5
FRF nominal cash flows	(FRF100)	FRF25.75	FRF26.52	FRF27.32	FRF28.14	FRF57.96
FRF/USD spot rate	FRF/USD6.0	FRF/USD5.94	FRF/USD5.89	FRF/USD5.83	FRF/USD5.77	FRF/USD5.72
USD nominal cash flows	USD16.67	USD4.34	USD4.50	USD4.69	USD4.88	USD10.13

<u>Step four:</u> *Estimate the project cost of capital in U.S. dollars*

Cost of capital = U.S. government bond rate (6%) + risk premium (5%) = 11%

<u>Step five:</u> *Estimate the project net present value*

$$NPV_{USD} = -USD16.67 + \frac{USD4.34}{1 + 0.11} + \frac{USD4.50}{(1 + 0.11)^2} + \frac{USD4.69}{(1 + 0.11)^3}$$

$$+ \frac{USD4.89}{(1 + 0.11)^4} + \frac{USD10.13}{(1 + 0.11)^5} = USD3.55 \text{ million}$$

14.1. Understanding MVA and EVA

a. Value is created by maximizing the *difference* between the market value of capital and the amount of capital employed to produce that value, that is, the firm's market value added, not its absolute market value.

b. The firm with the highest *market value added,* which is not necessarily the one with the highest market value, is the one that has created the most value for its shareholders.

c. Market value added is determined by the stream of EVAs the firm is expected to generate in the future. If the present value of that future stream is positive so will MVA even though current EVA can be negative.

d. Positive MVA means that the present value of the *future* stream of EVAs is positive. This does not necessarily imply that *current* ROIC exceeds the firm's WACC.

e. Net profit is calculated by deducting interest expenses from operating profit, which means that net profit is adjusted for the cost of debt. If we then deduct a capital charge based on the WACC, we would be counting the cost of debt twice, once in net profit and again in the WACC.

f. EVA takes risk into account via the WACC. The riskier an entity's operating profit, the higher its WACC and the lower its EVA.

g. Growth will increase a firm's MVA only if expected ROICs exceed the firm's WACC. If this is not the case, growth will destroy value.

h. Not necessarily so. See comments to (c).

i. Higher profits are only half of the story. If the charge for capital employed exceeds (operating) profit, value is destroyed.

j. Higher ROIC is only half the story. ROIC must exceed the WACC in order to create value. A business will still create value if its ROIC falls, as long as ROIC remains above the WACC.

14.2. Adjusting accounting data to estimate economic value added

EVA = NOPAT − Charge for capital employed

where: NOPAT = Net operating profit after tax = EBIT × (1 − tax rate)

Charge for capital employed = WACC × capital employed (same as invested capital)

To estimate EVA, apply the following procedure:

Step one: *Estimate earnings before interest and tax (EBIT)*

Sales	$1,400 million
Cost of sales	(780 million)
Selling, general, and administrative expenses	(330 million)
Depreciation and lease expenses	(45 million)
Amortization of R&D expenses	(30 million)
EBIT	$215 million

Step two: *Estimate the tax rate (data in millions of dollars)*

Tax rate = Tax expenses divided by *pretax* profit = $40/($60 + $40) = $40/$100 = 40%

Step three: *Calculate NOPAT*

NOPAT = EBIT × (1 − tax rate) = ($215 million) × (1 − 0.40) = $129 million.

Step four: *Estimate the amount of capital employed (in millions of dollars)*

Capital employed		12.31.96		12.31.97
Total debt capital		$160		$140
Adjusted equity capital		282		388
Book value of equity	$200		$260	
Accumulated bad debt allowance	7		13	
Accumulated goodwill amortization	20		45	
Capitalized R&D	55		70	
Total capital employed		$442		$528

Step five: *Calculate EVA given that ADC has an estimated weighted average cost of capital (WACC) of 11 percent (data in millions of dollars)*

EVA (Beginning capital employed) = $129 − 11%[$442] = $129 − $48.6 = $80.4

EVA (Average capital employed) = $129 − 11%[($442 + $528)/2] = $129 − $53.4 = $75.6

14.3. Economic value added analysis

a. Pretax economic value added (EVA) based on initial invested capital:

EVA = Pretax operating profit − (Pretax cost of capital) × (Invested capital)
EVA = $170 million − 15% × $1,000 million
   = $170 million − $150 million = $20 million

Pretax economic value added (EVA) based on return on invested capital (ROIC):

Pretax ROIC = $170 million divided by $1,000 million = 17%
EVA = (Pretax ROIC − Pretax cost of capital) × Invested capital
EVA = [17% − 15%] × $1,000 million = 2% × $1,000 million = $20 million

b. 1. Reducing operating expenses by $10 million would raise EVA by $10 million:

EVA = [$170 million + $10 million] − $150 million = $30 million

2. Reducing invested capital by $60 million would raise EVA by $9 million:

EVA = $170 million − 15% × ($1,000 million − $60 million)

= $170 million − $141 million = $29 million

3. Lowering pretax cost of capital to 14 percent would raise EVA by $10 million:

EVA = $170 million − 14% × $1,000 million

= $170 million − $140 million = $30 million

4. Selling assets (at book value) for $100 million will reduce capital employed to $900 million and cut pretax operating profit by $10 million thus raising EVA by $5 million (note that these assets have an expected ROIC of 10% which is *lower* than the WACC of 15%):

EVA = $160 million − 15% × $900 million = $160 million − $135 million = $25 million

5. Buying assets for $100 million will raise capital employed to $1,100 million and add $20 million in pretax operating profit thus raising EVA by $5 million (note that these assets have an expected ROIC of 20% which is *higher* than the WACC of 15%):

EVA = $190 million − 15% × $1,100 = $190 million − $165 million = $25 million

14.4. Market value added analysis

Acquiring the inventory-control software program costing $150,000 will immediately cut *aftertax* operating profit by $150,000 × (1 − 40%), that is, $90,000 and reduce EVA by the same amount. But *all* future EVAs will rise by $10,000 because invested capital will decrease permanently by $100,000 × 10%, that is, $10,000, due to the permanent reduction in inventories. To determine the net effect on ILC's value, we must get the present value of the entire stream of EVAs. This present value is a measure of the impact of the decision to buy the software program on ILC's market value. In other words, it is the decision's market value added (MVA). Because that MVA is positive (+$10,000), the software acquisition is a value-creating proposition:

$$\text{MVA(Software)} = -\$90,000 + \frac{\$10,000}{0.10} = -\$90,000 + \$100,000 = +\$10,000$$

Note: Because the future stream of EVAs is a constant perpetuity, its present value is that constant amount divided by the cost of capital (see the valuation formula 14.7; the growth rate in EVAs is zero in our case).

14.5. Comparison of investment analysis based on cash flows and EVAs

The estimated streams of cash flows and EVAs the project is expected to generate are:

ESTIMATED CASH FLOW FROM PROJECT (data in thousands of dollars)

	Now	END OF YEAR 1	END OF YEAR 2	END OF YEAR 3
1. Sales		$1,000	$2,000	$1,800
2. Operating expenses @ 90% sales		(900)	(1,800)	(1,620)
3. Depreciation (1/3 of $300)		(100)	(100)	(100)
4. Earnings before interest & tax		0	100	80
5. Tax @ 30% of line 4		0	30	24
6. Net operating profit after tax		**0**	**$70**	**$56**
7. *WCR @ 10% of next-year sales*	*$100*	*200*	*180*	
8. Change in WCR	(100)	(100)	20	180
9. Capital expenditure	(300)	0	0	0
10. Cash flow from project	**($400)**	**$0**	**$190**	**$336**

ESTIMATED EVA FROM PROJECT (data in thousands of dollars)

	Now	END OF YEAR 1	END OF YEAR 2	END OF YEAR 3
11. NOPAT (line 6)	$0	$0	$70	$56
12. Invested capital:				
WCR (line 7)	100	200	180	
Net fixed asset	300	200	100	
	400	400	280	
13. Previous-year invested capital × 9%		36	36	25.2
14. EVA (line 11 − line 13)	**$0**	**($36)**	**$ 34**	**$30.8**

Notes (corresponding to the line number):
Line 4 = EBIT = Line 1 − line 2 − line 3
Line 6 = NOPAT = Line 4 − line 5
Line 7 = WCR = Working capital requirement
Line 10 = NOPAT (line 6) + Depreciation (line 3) − Change in WCR (line 8) − Capex (line 9)
Line 12 = Net fixed asset = $300 less accumulated depreciation
Line 13 = Weighted average cost of capital = 60% × 8% × (1 − 0.30) + 40% × 14.1% = 9%

a. The net present value of the cash flows from project at a WACC of 9% is equal to $19,370. The project's internal rate of return is equal to 10.99%. Because the project's NPV is positive and its IRR exceeds the WACC, the project is a value-creating proposition and should be undertaken.

b. The project's market value added is equal to the present value of its stream of EVAs at a WACC of 9%. It is equal to $19,370, the same as the project's NPV. Because the project's MVA is positive, the project is a value-creating proposition and should be undertaken even though its first year EVA is negative. What matters is the present value of the entire future stream of expected EVAs, not the sign of a single-year EVA.

c. When estimating EVA, invested capital must be measured at the *beginning* of the period and the stream of EVAs must be discounted at the same cost of capital as the cash flows (that is, at the WACC).

14.6. MVA analysis of the designer desk-lamp project

The estimation of the future stream of economic value added (EVAs) that the designer desk-lamp project is expected to generate is given below. It is based on data taken from Exhibit 8.3 in Chapter 8. The project's market value added (MVA) is found by discounting the stream of EVAs at 10%, the project's WACC.

(IN THOUSANDS OF DOLLARS)	NOW	END OF YEAR 1	END OF YEAR 2	END OF YEAR 3	END OF YEAR 4	END OF YEAR 5
I. <u>Aftertax operating profit</u>						
1 Aftertax operating profit (line 15 in Exhibit 8.3)	$0	$402	$347	$212	$69	($84)
2. Exceptional gain (line 21 in Exhibit 8.3)						$60
3. Net operating profit after tax		**$402**	**$347**	**$212**	**$69**	**($24)**
II. <u>Invested capital at the beginning of the year</u>						
4. Working capital requirement (line 18 in Exhibit 8.3)	360	330	255	175	90	0
5. Net book value of fixed assets[1]	2,000	1,600	1,200	800	400	0
6. Total invested capital (line 4 + line 5)	2,360	1,930	1,455	975	490	0
7. Capital charge (10% of previous year's invested capital)[2]		**$236**	**$193**	**$145.5**	**$97.5**	**$49**
8. Economic value added (EVA = line 3 less line 7)		**$166**	**$154**	**$66.5**	**($28.5)**	**($73)**
9. Market value added[3] (MVA = Present value of EVAs at WACC of 10%)	**$263.293**					

Notes:

1. The initial investment is depreciated at the rate of $400 per year.

2. The project's weighted average cost of capital (WACC) is 10%.

3. This is equal to the project's net present value (NPV) found in Chapter 8. The EVAs have been discounted separately and added up in the same fashion as in Chapter 8. If you use your calculator you will find a slightly different result due to rounding.

14.7. The financial strategy matrix

a. To position the four companies in the financial strategy matrix, apply the following two-step procedure.

<u>Step one:</u> *Estimate each company's return spread to determine its capacity to create value.*

The return spread is the difference between a company's return on invested capital (ROIC) and its weighted average cost of capital (WACC). If the return spread is positive, so is economic value added (EVA) and the company has created value during the period under analysis. If the return spread and EVA are negative, value has been destroyed over the diagnostic period.

<u>Step two:</u> *Estimate each company's self-sustainable growth rate to determine its capacity to finance its growth through earnings retention.*

The self-sustainable growth rate (SGR) is equal to the retention rate (b) multiplied by return on equity (ROE). Compare each company's SGR to its growth in sales. If the growth rate in sales is higher than SGR, the company is experiencing a cash shortage or deficit. If the growth rate in sales is lower than SGR, the company is experiencing a cash surplus.

We have:

Company	ROIC − WACC	b × ROE = SGR	Growth in sales − SGR
A. Transportation	8% − 10% = −2%	0.50 × 12% = 6%	8% − 6% = +2%
B. Restaurants	15% − 12% = +3%	0.60 × 20% = 12%	15% − 12% = +3%
C. Beverages	8% − 9% = −1%	0.75 × 12% = 9%	7% − 9% = −2%
D. Food	13% − 11% = +2%	0.40 × 15% = 6%	4% − 6% = −2%

The transportation company destroys value and is short of cash (point A). The restaurant company creates value and is short of cash (point B). The beverages company is destroying value but generating a cash surplus (point C). The food company is creating value and generating a cash surplus (point D).

b. Refer to Exhibit 14.8 and the corresponding text in the chapter where you will find a summary of the decisions/actions that Amalgamated Industries should take regarding each one of the four companies.

INDEX